# A REVERSAL
# OF
# FORTUNE

## Germantown, Tennessee, during the Civil War Era

George C. Browder

HERITAGE BOOKS
2015

# HERITAGE BOOKS

*AN IMPRINT OF HERITAGE BOOKS, INC.*

**Books, CDs, and more—Worldwide**

For our listing of thousands of titles see our website
at
www.HeritageBooks.com

Published 2015 by
HERITAGE BOOKS, INC.
Publishing Division
5810 Ruatan Street
Berwyn Heights, Md. 20740

International Standard Book Numbers
Paperbound: 978-0-7884-5597-1
Clothbound: 978-0-7884-6079-1

**In Memoriam**

**Lucile Bagby**

To the Staff of the Special Collections
and the Mississippi Valley Collection
with Thanks for your Help,

*[signature]*

# CONTENTS

## Maps, Tables and Images

# Foreword

Among the vast Civil War literature, military and political history has drawn the most attention. Increasingly, however, social and economic aspects have come into the picture, especially the African-American experience, but also the daily life of the civilian population and the war's impact on them. So far, all such work has focused on broad topics or regions. What is offered here is a case study of one community – neither typical nor atypical. It offers both a detailed picture of life and the impact of war on that life. This was a town intermittently, but heavily occupied by Union troops in the midst of a theater of guerrilla warfare that has not yet drawn much attention.

When an historian covers a topic or region that is broad, the available evidence is usually rich enough to paint a solidly based picture. To make that focus as specific as a particular community, however, one needs an unusually rich supply of source material: public records, census and tax data, extensive newspaper coverage of social, political and cultural affairs, personal diaries and correspondence. If one chooses a community regardless of those criteria, one is stuck with what is available.

Germantown's government records for the entire period have been lost. County records at least provide some insights. State records about the town and its civil district are strangely incomplete. Of course, the usual federal census data is available as are the official records of both armies for the war. Memphis-based newspaper coverage was spotty but intriguing. Only one church has an archive of any consequence, while another is rebuilding a better archive from district records. Only three personal diaries survive, one pre-war, and two post-war. Only two Civil War veterans' questionnaires exist. Personal letters and family accounts have surfaced only in two cases plus fragmentary quotations for another. Outsiders' impressions have survived in a few letters and diary references.

Flying in the face of precisely those problems, this book seeks to capture a picture of one town in south-central Shelby County, Tennessee. Why? I began this adventure as a member of the city's Historical Commission. When I argued that the town should do more to advertise its position as an appropriate part of Civil War tourism, I got pressured into doing the research to document historical markers. This drew me into the search for sources, but also into an unfamiliar and vast body of scholarly literature far beyond my former focus. As a retired professor, I had formerly worked entirely on research and writing in modern European history. As I rapidly became aware of the guerrilla warfare environment in which the town had been immersed, I saw the potential for a book to reacquaint people with that aspect of local Civil War history which has not been well covered. Likewise the community needed a broader context in which to place and test its popular and family traditions about both wartime experiences and local life. But mostly, I foresaw a book about people and their lives amidst the turmoil of guerrilla warfare that just might interest anyone. As I fleshed out community life before the war, to set the stage, I found an equally interesting picture. That then led to a search into post-war life to see the consequences of the war, which yielded yet more significant results.

Unfortunately, there is almost no voice from the town's people during the crucial war years. What did they think about what was happening to them? How did it impact them in the long run? Consequently, I have compulsively teased out every available detail about community life before and after. I offer as complete a picture as possible in order to uncover those aspects that were impacted by the war, emancipation, Reconstruction, and the yellow fever epidemics. Sometimes conventional ideas about Southern towns will be confirmed; in others they will be challenged.

While my initial intention had been to focus primarily on civilian life amidst guerrilla warfare, even that required a narrative of other military developments so essential to the context of that life. Especially to uncover their impact, I have recorded details of Union troop presence and activities in and around the town. I soon realized, however, that such a minimal military focus omitted the experiences of the majority of the town's men folk. Consequently, more attention is also given to the military side of their lives to flesh out the picture. That too is inseparable from the town's story. The physical and psychological effects of their war extended well into the peacetime decades that followed.

Perhaps the most striking impression is the strong similarity to America's later involvements in places like Vietnam, Iraq and Afghanistan. The experiences of the occupying Union Army were in so many ways like that of those modern American soldiers, unable to distinguish friends from enemies among the civilians. The civilian experience therefore resembled in some ways that of those countries we have sought to liberate and pacify.

# *Acknowledgments*

Lucile Bagby, late chairperson, Germantown Historical Commission
Katherine Bennett, Librarian, New Bethel Missionary Baptist Church
Darla Brock, Archivist I, Tennessee State Library and Archives
Vincent Clark, Shelby County Archives
Harry Cloyes, late local historian, collector of artifacts and records
Wayne Dowdy and the staff of Memphis and Shelby County Collection,
        Memphis and Shelby County Public Library
Edwin G. Frank, Curator of Special Collections and Mississippi Valley
        Collection, Ned McWherter Library, University of Memphis
Carolyn Gates, chair Germantown History Museum Committee and for
        Kimbrough family traditions
Elisabeth P. Hughes, Shelby County Genealogist
Marilyn Bell Hughes, Archivist, Tennessee State Library and Archives
Howard Johnson, Germantown United Methodist Church History
        Committee
Jennifer Lynch, Senior Research Analyst, Postal History, U.S. Post Office
Joyce McKibben for her invaluable indexes of local, historical
        newspapers
Dan Rambo, for Dr. Martin's family traditions
Jane Sanderson, for Mosby and Sanderson family traditions
Frank Stewart, Shelby County Archives
Susan Thompson for Dr. Martin's family traditions
Walter Wills, preservationist of Kirby Farms and Woodlawn and for
        Kirby-Brooks family traditions
The staff of the Germantown Public Library
The staff of the Germantown Regional History and Genealogy Center

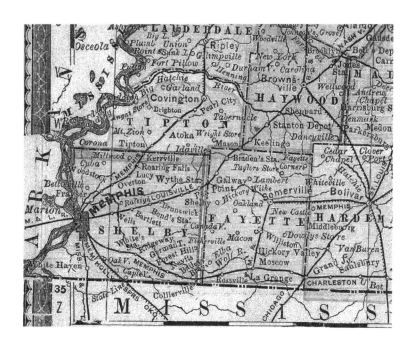

Map 1. Counties of South-West Tennessee

# Introduction

Our subject is the people who inhabited the area around Germantown, Tennessee. That area and the larger context in which it lay provided a somewhat special environment. Although today the present city of Germantown is almost surrounded by Memphis, except for its eastern border with the city of Collierville, in those days it was fifteen miles from Memphis and surrounded by farms, plantations and wild river bottoms.

Although by no means a unique community in the mid-nineteenth century South, its location had produced some promising differences. Unfortunately, however, it would also produce a succession of overwhelming obstacles.

Its location in the south-west corner of the state sets the stage. Tennessee is divided into three distinct "grand divisions," East, Middle and West, and six geological sections. West Tennessee in particular has more in common with its neighboring states than with the rest of its own.

Settled later, even by the 1840s it was just emerging from a frontier environment. Consequently by the middle of the century, much of its adult population had been shaped by frontier mores. Under subsequent war-time conditions, lawless and violent proclivities would reemerge adding to the intensity of guerrilla warfare. Also southwest Tennessee was the most committed to cotton farming and its inherent connection with slavery. Bound by the Tennessee and Mississippi Rivers and penetrated by several significant tributaries, even before the arrival of the railroads, large parts of West Tennessee had been more accessible to outside markets for cash-crop farming such as cotton, tobacco, corn and livestock.

Within this western division, there was also much diversity. The rich Tennessee valley was separated from the rest of the division by the hilly western ridge of the Highland Rim, orienting it eastward. Along the Mississippi, lay the swampy bottomlands of tributaries with their frequent floods and unhealthy conditions, so settlers concentrated along the bluffs and ridges. Even the fertile lands that lay between these river valleys developed differently. The northern counties, the Plateau Slope crossed by small-river floodplains, remained thinly populated and less developed, providing the ideal base for guerrilla raiders during the war. Its population was also more strongly divided over the issue of secession. The southern part of the division, especially its south-west counties, was the cotton belt. It would be caught between the guerrilla bases to the north and the cavalry-raider bases in Mississippi.

Lying in the southwest corner of the state, Shelby County was unique in the division. (Map 1.) The large urban center of Memphis

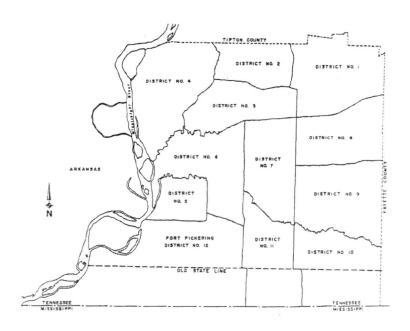

Map 2. Civil Districts, Shelby County

provided the most prominent distinction. By 1850, it had given Shelby the second largest population in the state. Despite this urban center, Shelby was third in the production of cotton, behind only Fayette and Marion. It held the second largest number of slaves after Fayette. Yet north of the Loosahatchie River, it was almost as thinly developed as the northwest quadrant. South of it lay a much more densely settled and developed area with Raleigh on the upper bend of the Wolf River, the second largest community. But specifically the southern highland ridge running between the Wolf and Nonconnah Creek was so well developed that contemporaries described it as "suburban." There lay the towns of Germantown and Collierville.

The area included in this study is more than that of the modern city of Germantown. Specifically, it focuses on the area served then by the Germantown post office. That included almost all of what was then Civil District Eleven (Map. 2), running from the Wolf River on the north to the state line in the south. The western side of the district lay a little west of the present city's border, while the eastern border with Civil District Ten bisected the present city, running a few blocks east of present Germantown Road. Within District Ten, it included about one hundred people in fourteen households living along roads leading into Germantown from as far east as Bray's Station, including the settlement of Forest Hill. North of the Wolf in both Districts Seven and Nine lay a dozen or so households in each, also tied to Germantown as their social and economic center. By 1860, this total area included a population over 900 white people and well over 1300 slaves.

The entire South suffered from the war. Some places recovered and thrived while others did not. After starting to recover, Germantown nevertheless suffered the latter fate. There was a complete shift of the local economic center from Germantown to Collierville.

Before 1860, however, Germantown had been well on its way to being the dominant economic and population center along the transportation lines from Memphis through Shelby and Fayette Counties. Its advantage was its position along those lines into Memphis. In 1850, Germantown, Collierville and LaFayette (present Rossville in Fayette County) were relatively equal in population, and theoretically had the same advantages. Germantown's total population was 245 including slaves; Collierville's was 236, while LaFayette's was 216.[1] But an 1854 gazetteer was soon painting a very unequal picture. While it only gave Collierville and LaFayette simple one-line descriptions as post-villages, it described a more dynamic Germantown. "A thriving post-village of Shelby County, Tennessee, near Wolf River, and on the Memphis and Charleston Railroad, 15 miles E. of Memphis, is situated in a rich cotton growing district, and has an active trade. Population, about 400."[2] This population figure indicated an explosive growth. Another indicator of preeminence – Germantown's post office was the second most heavily used in Shelby County. The town also provided much of the political leadership of county government. It was almost as industrial as agricultural in its economy, with three or four operations that could be termed factories, plus all the usual smithies, gins and mills. Not just a transportation hub, the town was also a cultural center with prestigious private high schools and colleges. It attracted many professionals and merchants.

Despite local traditions, it is impossible to access how extensively both Collierville and Germantown had been destroyed by war's end. Regardless, by 1870, that destruction had already changed their relative positions. While Germantown's population had sunk to 197 white and "colored," and LaFayette's to 161, Collierville had 274.[3] This shift in the balance would increase. Collierville emerged as the major center of economic activity for Shelby and Fayette Counties and De Soto County, Mississippi. According to the Bureau of Agriculture, in 1874 Collierville had a population of 1,000, "quite a pleasant and prosperous village," that had "been built up since the war." About 1,200 bales of cotton shipped out of the town annually, and it had "about twenty-two business houses, mostly supply stores." In contrast, Germantown was simply "a pretty little village ... with a population of 350. It has three general churches, a cotton gin, and two groceries."[4] While Germantown retained its simple prewar row of main street shops, Collierville blossomed with a grand town square of store-fronts, a two-story hotel, public parks and a boulevard lined with fine homes.[5] There had been considerable recovery in both communities before the great Yellow Fever epidemic in 1878, but by 1888 Germantown's population was down to 200.[6] Thereafter there was little growth, and it remained a sleepy little town until the 1970s.

Even so, this relative decline in the population and economic prominence of Germantown is not the most interesting part of the town's experience. The impact of the war and emancipation on the community – on its people psychologically, socially and culturally, on its cohesiveness and the general character of life – though difficult to tease out, offers the best story. The impact of war and natural disaster goes far deeper than economic destruction and loss of life.

*****

This is the story of Germantown, of the community's people and their perseverance. It paints a picture of the town that was mostly lost and the life of its citizens before, during and after that war. Such a perspective is hard to recapture, for such ordinary people rarely recorded their experiences. When they did, those records have rarely survived, or they remain buried in dust covered boxes. Today, even the family traditions that were once recited and elaborated as everyone sat around in the evening are no longer being passed along. Such stories and records are badly needed to give this history more flesh and blood. I hope any readers who have such stories about Germantown and its people or any documents to share will contact me.

George C. Browder
2520 Yester Oaks Drive
Germantown, Tennessee 38139
901-737-4329
gcbrowder@gmail.com

## *A Note on Language*

Because I have to distinguish among those Americans whose ancestors came mostly from Europe and those coming at least partly from Africa, I choose the simplest conventional labels of "white and black." Occasionally I will also have to use the now-unacceptable language of the times, "colored," "negro" (rarely capitalized), "mulatto," and even the pejoratives when they express the meaning they were intended to convey by the people who used them. If one really wants to understand fully our ancestors and the complex historical contexts in which they operated, one has to forgo our contemporary sensitivities and listen to their words.

Finally, to preserve the historical flavor of quotations, I usually ignore the convention of noting misspellings and grammatical errors with the insertion of (sic.). I note only errors in the spelling or accuracy of names.

# Part I

## Antebellum Germantown

As the clouds of war gathered in 1860, Germantown was a growing but small and comfortable town. The state legislature had almost offhandedly incorporated it in 1841, and then fully chartered it in 1850. It and nearby Pea Ridge were already sufficiently significant settlements to appear on maps in the late 1830s. During the 1840s through the 50s, it had emerged as a "place of note."[1] Its position as a major crossroads on the State Line Road into Memphis and on the Memphis-Charleston Railroad made it economically vibrant and gave it a strategic importance during the forthcoming war. The town proper had become more than a typical Southern rural village serving an agricultural countryside. Nevertheless, it and the surrounding agricultural population formed a coherent community that has to be seen as a whole.

These people saw the town as the center of their economic, social and cultural life. The community is best defined as those served by the Germantown post office. They not only came to town for their mail and the news, but also attended its churches and schools, conducted business and legal affairs, used its stores, saloons, and professional services, belonged to its fraternal and political organizations, and attended militia musters and a wide range of social and cultural events.

As a political entity, the incorporated town only covered about one half a square mile. It was governed by a council of mayor and aldermen. Outside town, the majority of the population was served by the elected officials of Civil District Eleven seated at the town, which in turn came under the county governing body of the Quarterly Court. Others, however, lived in adjacent civil districts, so some of their political and legal affairs were managed in those districts. Nevertheless, their social, economic and cultural focus was Germantown.

The town was defined essentially by the State Line Road, along which it ran for a mile. (Map 3) It spread from two-hundred yards north of the road to a half mile south of it.[2] Thus it encompassed less than a square mile straddling the State Line Road, and running predominantly west toward Memphis. Its center was an irregular trapezoidal grid formed by three parallel streets and the intersection of roads connecting with practically every community in the adjacent counties of Tennessee and Mississippi. After its charter in 1851, there seem to be no records of an expansion of the town's limits in either county or state archives, although numerous records of such expansions for other towns exist.

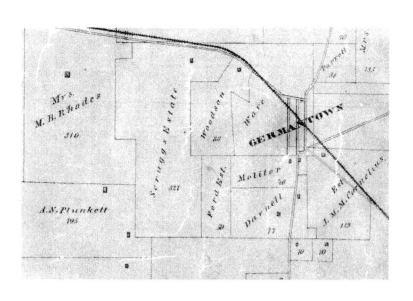

Map 3.  Germantown  (Shelby County Map, 1869, SCA)

Apparently the town's leading citizens saw no advantage in expanding their jurisdiction, despite a burgeoning population.

This prosperous community would soon find itself in the center of a theater of guerrilla warfare. It would undergo all the vicissitudes of war, pillaging, occupation, emancipation and post-war Reconstruction. Many of its men "met the elephant," experiencing combat with all its physical and psychological effects that they would bring back home. The impact of a bitter local partisan and cavalry-raiding warfare on soldier and civilian alike requires a comparison of both antebellum and post-war society to reveal its consequences. Likewise for relations among the black and white citizens, for whom the heritage of slavery birthed some of the most brutal aspects of that war and exaggerated the smoldering racial tensions that followed.

# Chapter 1

## The White People and Their Lives

During the three decades prior to the war, what was a frontier area became fully settled. From the very beginning, some of those settler families would become permanent, leaving descendants who remain today. The vast majority, however, including many of temporary prominence, merely passed through during those decades. Mobility if not instability was a characteristic of the population. Nevertheless, those who moved on were replaced by others who found the area full of opportunity.

There are no census data broken down for the town in 1860, only for civil districts. Even census schedules only indicated the post office that served each schedule sheet. This makes it impossible to know the exact population of the town proper. One can only make reasonable guesses. There were perhaps 85 households with as many as 450 white citizens. In contrast to the surrounding rural district, the town's population had almost tripled during the 1850s; the town had literally burst its seams.

The rural community that focused on the town consisted of all of Civil District Eleven and the western third of District Ten, plus a few families living along the northern bank of the Wolf River above those two districts. (Map 2) From the Wolf, it ran to the Mississippi state line, if not beyond. In all by 1860, the total population exceeded 900 white people and well over 1300 slaves. While the town was growing, the rural population had declined a little.

Life in mid-nineteenth century America was far less stable than our romantic images allow. Only about 16% of the town's 1850 families remained in 1860, but mortality was not a significant cause. What would have seemed to have been stable businesses in a rapidly growing community had been turned over to newcomers. Most all the families of men who had worked for others, journeymen, shop workers, overseers, and laborers had moved on. Their greatest hope for advancement lay in relocation. Even farmsteads turned over surprisingly, for only 22% of the 1850 families in District 11 remained in 1860. Americans in general moved frequently in search of greener fields. Employees, yeomen farmers and small merchants relocated regularly.

To account for all this movement, on the one hand, there was evidently a good deal of upward mobility within western Tennessee, with families buying more lucrative farms and/or business opportunities. On the other, during the 1850s, Tennessee lost many of its native inhabitants. By 1860, one third of those born in the state had gone elsewhere. The opening of Texas was a special draw. The fertile delta lands of Arkansas combined with veterans' bonus-lands offered highly desirable opportunities. Missouri and Illinois also drew many.[3]

The rural population of the district actually declined during the 1850s. Yeomen farmers found it increasingly difficult to compete against the growing plantation slave-labor. This relates to an interesting argument put forth by Steve Baker who contends that the massive influx of black slaves made whites uncomfortable. The almost universally held racist beliefs depicted blacks as inherently and dangerously savage. Fear of bloody slave revolts was widespread. Those not overly dependent on slave labor preferred to go elsewhere.[4] If true, there is nothing new about white flight.

For farmers, another cause was simply the vicissitudes of their life. For instance, in June of 1846, a hail storm totally destroyed the cotton crops of even major planters. Within five miles of Germantown, it dumped a swath of destruction three miles long and a quarter mile wide, covering the ground to a depth of eight inches. Both John D. and Eppy White lost everything in their fields.[5] A yet more common problem – two years in a row, one small farmer lost much of his corn when cattle or hogs got into his fields, and once he lost seven acres of cotton.[6] Any new arrivals, like this man, who had just put in their first crop and needed it to cover their startup expenses would be further in debt or go under. Only a couple of bad crop years in a row could ruin a man trying to get established.

Isham Howse is an example of a farmer who came and went between 1850 and 1860. He was not "typical" in that his major problem was such poor health that he had to inject morphine for the pain and

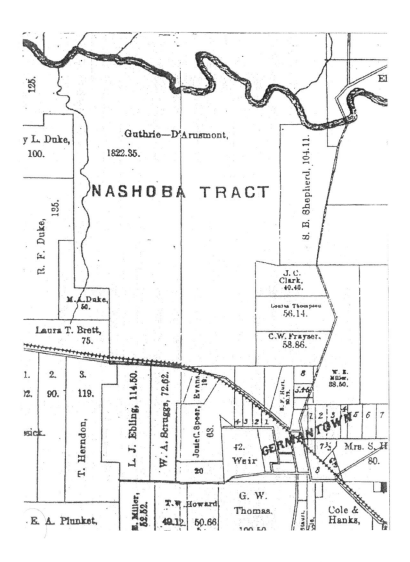

Map 4. Nashoba Tract at Germantown (1880 Plat Map, Shelby County)
The house that Howse occupied was located just across the tracks in the
lower left corner of the tract, barely inside the town's borders.

could do little farm work himself. He relied on his older sons and four slaves, who were also older and infirm. He had given up as a merchant and farmer elsewhere. He owned acreage in several other Tennessee and Mississippi counties as well as town properties, which he rented while trying to sell. He was drawn to the area for its favorable communications with markets, and an arrangement with Fanny Wright to operate her Nashoba lands under very favorable terms. (Map 4) Unfortunately, his health and that of his family and servants suffered from constant bouts of "chills". He was unable to make enough to cover his debts, and left after the 1853 season, after he sold his other properties and could set himself up again as a merchant with two other partners in Mississippi.[7] His land and business ventures, his endless search for a better position, were probably not untypical of the many others on their way through during the decade.

Another major problem was clearing and working enough land – basically a function of affording enough slaves to do the work. Most farmers could improve less than half their acreage. For many years, plowing that land was arduous, for the roots and stumps of trees endured. The Kimbrough's Cotton Plant Plantation, with 66 slaves and 19 mules and 10 oxen, had only 700 improved acres of its 1600 total. Since cotton rapidly exhausted the land, the pressure was on to clear more, leaving the smallholder at a disadvantage.[8]

Finally, no matter how much farmers and planters liked to see themselves as independent and self-reliant, they functioned as dependents of the urban banking and market complex. Despite their status as local elites, even most planters usually had to work through the cotton factors and bankers in Memphis. In a cash poor economy, few were not in need of ready cash. Anyone trying to sell locally lost a considerable percentage of the value of his crop. Rather than sell locally at a discount, you tried for market prices at places like New Orleans. Memphis merchants maintained warehouses to store the cotton and then negotiated the shipping up or down river to market where their contacts sold the cotton. In turn, they or their affiliates imported manufactured goods the country folk needed. They kept open books with their customers who turned their crops over to them when they came in.[9] To gain more economic independence, the more entrepreneurial expanded into cotton trading. Men like Joseph Brooks were able to manage their business directly with New Orleans. The Brooks family had been involved in mercantile activity since its arrival in the 1830s.[10]

Otherwise through this complicated process, a percentage of the ultimate market value of the crop was lost to the planter. To give him money up front, the Memphis merchant went to a local bank to draw a draft or bill of exchange on the firm in some place like New Orleans that would receive the crop. This was in essence a bank loan that carried a fee plus interest until the sale of the crop at its destination, three to four months. Then, the agent also took a percentage, usually 2.5 percent, and sent the proceeds to the Memphis merchant who credited the remainder to the planter's account.[11]

The small farmer simply had to work with local merchants who filled his needs on credit until the crops came in. Unless he could cross the break-even line with the size of a crop, he had to sell locally. Otherwise cotton simply ended in his homespun industry. He lived in a world of semi-subsistence that combined credit and barter.[12]

Part of this complex relationship that plagued the farmers was the instability of paper money, still in its early stages of evolution. By the 1850s, there were a handful of private banks operating in Memphis focused on the cotton and river trade. There was no federal insurance, and these little Memphis operations did not even have the backing of larger institutions elsewhere. To facilitate trade, the federal government allowed such banks to issue their own paper money. Otherwise the gold and silver coinage from the Treasury was insufficient. Such bills could only be used for local business, however, and could only be redeemed for gold or silver at the issuing bank. If so many people sought redemptions that they exceeded the bank's reserves, its bills were useless until the bank could recoup those reserves. Bank failures were a common part of the frequent depressions, threatening local farmers and businessmen who held their valueless notes.[13] One such depression followed the panic of 1857 and lasted to 1860.

With of all these problems facing both agriculturalists and town folk, there was a constant search for better jobs, better positions and better land. The vast majority of incoming residents were either from south-eastern states or immigrants. There were only occasional northerners. All this mobility makes the growth of Germantown proper seem that much more significant. Far more people saw opportunity in town business and life than did those who left.

### Family Life

The 1860 census provides a picture of family life in the 80 odd households in town[14] In addition to two parents, there were typically three children, but the number in a family varied from one to nine. Farm families seemed a little more prolific, but mostly the number of children depended on the length of the marriage. For example, Jobe Lewis, age 38, had his own farm by at least 1850, with a twenty-five year-old wife, Barbara, and four young children. By 1860, Jobe was still on his farm, but his first wife was gone – replaced by thirty-seven year-old Ann.

There were now seven children. Many of the other 1860 families were still young.

It was also common for extended family members to be present in a household, such as one grandparent or one or two siblings or cousins of either the husband or wife. In addition, a household often included one or more boarders who lived and worked in the town. In several cases, they may have been white female servants. For example in 1850, wagon-maker Lewellen (or Lon Allen) Rhodes and his wife Rachel housed his younger brother or cousin as an assistant. By 1860, this family with six children included his older sister and an older gentleman, probably Rachel's father. The boot-maker family of Julius and Mary Resten had only one child, but included (probably) her mother, a carpenter as a boarder, and an eleven year-old girl, who could have been either a family ward or a foundling taken on for service. Real estate broker William and Mary Tate's household included a similarly undefined thirteen year-old girl and boarded a grocer and a clerk. The childless farm family of William and Elizabeth Brooks had three Mosby children living with them. Since the merchant Albert Mosby and his family lived next door with six similarly aged children of their own, one might assume the Brooks and Mosby families were related and the Brooks cared for family orphans.

A few of the juveniles living with families other than their own were in formal indentured service. Parents might apprentice a child to learn a trade, especially if they could not support it. Most were orphans placed by the county. An orphan could be assigned at almost any age "to live after the manner of an apprentice or servant" until age eighteen or twenty-one. The contract for a female provided that "during which time the said orphan girl shall all lawful commands every where obey; and shall not absent herself from her master's service without leave, but in all things behave herself as a faithful servant ought to do." In return the master was required to

> teach and instruct, or cause to be taught and instructed ...
> the amount of English tuition the law requires and also the
> duties of housewifry. And that he will constantly find and
> provide for her ... during the said term, sufficient diet,
> washing, lodging, and apparel fitting for a girl, with every
> necessity both in sickness and in health."[15]

"English tuition" referred to basic literacy. For boys, the contract differed from this formula requiring education in arithmetic and in defining the skill or occupation in which he would be trained. At the end of service, apprentices were guaranteed a severance pay in kind, such as tools or animals, or a suit of clothing at a minimum

Tennessee and, from all appearances, Shelby County were

Illustration 1. Taking the census (Harper's Weekly, January 19, 1870) Idealized illustration of the three-generational household with boarders, employees and servants.

conscientious about protecting apprentices and guaranteeing their rights. They were especially diligent in protecting orphans. There were provisions against "immoderate correction," and apprentices had the right to appeal to the county court against any mistreatment or negligence. Friends and neighbors helped bring the complaints, giving us a further measure of a typical community's sense of collective responsibility. In 1845, Thomas Bleckley, a farmer east of town, had been forced to give up his apprentice, Mary Joyce, on an allegation of mistreatment. Mary took refuge in the home of her older brother William, who had established himself as a framer by that time.[16]

Predictably, there was concern about the moral development of apprentices. Their agreement prohibited gambling, frequenting taverns, fornication or contracting marriage. A female who became pregnant had a full year added to her servitude. If the master was the father, their "collective punishment" was for her to be sold to another person, with an additional year of servitude. All he suffered was the loss of her service. Worse, if she became pregnant by "any negro, mulatto, or Indian," she was sold for a period that included two additional years. As for the poor child, it would be ordered bound by the court for indentured servitude until age thirty-one. This probably tells us as much about the prevalent fears of the times as it does about the behavior of apprentices.[17]

There were no apprentices into skilled labor in the area. They were all for farm work. Isaiah Stout, a farmer east of town, had taken Andrew and Richard Wright into service in 1854. Since their mother got them released five years later, her position must have improved. Obviously feelings about the sanctity of the family prevailed over contract law. Area residents seem to have favored employing free whites over contract servitude. They also had their hands full with the orphans of family and friends. As for the orphans "of color" increasingly indentured by the county during the 1840s-50s, locals preferred the long-range investment in slave children over a contract that terminated at 21.[18]

As another measure of the intimate interrelationships among the town's residents, in 1850 the physician J. M. Cornelius, his wife Eliza and two teenage children also cared for the four-year-old Louisa Ledbetter, either an orphan or the daughter of the Justice of the Peace, who lived alone with his wife. Perhaps, the child needed special medical care. Ten years later, Edward Cornelius had inherited both the practice and Miss Ledbetter. She was attending a local school. The farm family of Julian and Virginia Bedford and their twin daughters hosted a five year-old Edward child, a seventy-one year-old Ms. Lucy Kenney, a fifty year-old Mr. Haskins, and a twenty-eight year-old German immigrant, Mr. Angle, of no given occupation. Mr. Haskins was titled a "gentleman," but was noted as "insane." The nature of his disability was apparently not severe enough to warrant commitment to the state asylum. Germantown's families provided elder care, orphan asylum and job training, assisted living and other social services. In some cases it was remunerated. In others, it grew from a sense of Christian duty.

We traditionally portray early 19th century America, especially the South, as a rigidly patriarchal society in which women had no rights and played no public roles. Of course, educated Southerners rejected the classical model of patriarchy, believing instead that their familial relationships were based on Christian models of love and protection.[19] Studies of the letters and journals of elite and middle class Southern women reveal the female perspective on such relations. Gender differences were absolutely clear and biologically determined, just like "racial" differences. They dictated life choices and aspirations. Women were subordinate, dependent, and not just reliant on their men for protection and security, but expected such as part of the proper order of things. Theirs was the private world of home and family, shunning not only public roles but even public notice. To have one's name in the paper was as bad as being the object of gossip.[20]

No matter how clearly such ideas were expressed by the elite of the antebellum South, such generalizations obscure the subtle realities of both patriarchal and hierarchical societies. On the one hand, the genteel elements of society waxed eloquently about romantic images of the "delicate sex." For instance this passage from the Memphis *Appeal* elaborated on the civilizing effects that the fairer sex had on men.

> Fair woman, in all the characters of life – as mothers, daughters, sweet-hearts and wives – were there, making the scene more joyous, and keeping down, by their refining presence, the grosser qualities of the sterner sex.[21]

It was women who shaped society, its mores and convictions.

> In all the great revolutions which history records, woman has initiated the movement and led the van of public opinion. Her intuitions are more correct, her sympathies more active, and her innate sense of justice more keen than that of hardier man.[22]

In another editorial, it added

> Wherever you find the virtuous woman, you also find pleasant firesides, bouquets, clean clothes, good living, gentle hearts, music, light and model "institutions" generally. She is the flower of humanity, a very Venus in dimity, and her inspiration is the breath of heaven.[23]

This was the more positive feminine stereotype, propagated from the pulpit, in literature, drama, and the popular press. The lady-wife provided the husband-master with a comfortable sanctuary and a safe environment for rearing his children. She made no demands and served faithfully. Real, proper ladies were expected to play these roles, but even in the most respectable area families, the realities of life imposed limits on such stereotypes. There was even an obvious contradiction inherent in the above quotations. Could women really exercise such influence over men in purely passive roles?

Of course, young ladies did not always toe the line of respectability either. We shall hear of their alcohol adventures in the Center Hill Academy, and of men having to defend the honor of their female relatives accused of immoral behavior. This requirement that gentlemen resort to violence to defend the honor of their ladies was a product of the complex of differences between the ideal and reality among the gentlefolk. As for gentility, in 1863, a Federal officer would observe that the young ladies of Germantown "invariably...have some excessively vulgar habit. Yesterday two young misses of sweet 16 or 18 were in to get a pass and they were quite good looking & pleasant. But great scott, how they would spit half way across a good sized room was easily accomplished."[24]    Surely he over generalized from a few cases. Undoubtedly, however, frontier crudeness and proper decorum mixed unevenly in some families.

The older generation of women had all survived a pioneer experience, coming over the mountains in wagons. Although they quickly sought to reestablish some of the status and gentility they had left behind, even the planter ladies were hardly "helpless females." Only their granddaughters and more recent settlers could have been so pampered. The reality of womenfolk in that society was often more like that of the "steel magnolia," with the woman of the household exercising her own influence over family affairs. Most women mastered the art of deferring to conventions while leveraging for their own space or even getting their own way. A few even flaunted conventions in the privacy of the home, and ruled the roost – a "secret" that was often shared throughout the community. Ultimately it was the individual personalities of each partner that determined real power relationships, or shared responsibilities and mutual respect, or something in between. In the "household economy," the management of the house, food and clothing, its processing and production, and in matters of the arts and culture, of child rearing, family health and entertainment, the women ran things. A man might, but usually did not criticize the results.[25]

Although under the man's legal and paternal authority, the "household" was the woman's world. One well established planter remembers that his mother "in addition to usual household duties, did carding, weaving, spinning etc." In this, she was assisted by a cook and a house girl. Another remembers his mother as "looking after her household duties" with four or five household servants.[26]  This speaks of a range of differences even among "elite" planter families.  At one end the ladies were personally productive and self-reliant in many ways. Even at the upper end where their work was primarily managerial, they were hardly helpless and dependent.

On the eve of the war, both rural and town households, regardless of financial level, were still relatively self-sufficient in the production of the food and clothing that the family and slaves needed.  Nevertheless, in direct proportion to the family's market income, they were increasingly purchasing manufactured goods.  Manufactured clothing was for special wear, while the women usually indulged in nice accessories, hoops and such.  Where manufactured cloth replaced homespun, the clothing was still sewn, and scraps of cloth and worn clothing were recycled.  The kitchen garden and orchards, processing food and clothing, all household stores and servants, all of this was the woman's responsibility.  She was the "keeper of the keys" that secured everything that did not go to market.

Among agriculturalists, the man's world was the fields and the hands who worked them, the processing of the produce and their marketing.  In the world of business and industry the same applied.  The lower down the socioeconomic scale, however, the more the wife shared in sales and management, even keeping books when the man was incompetent or dissolute.  The poorer the farmer the more frequently she helped in the fields.

For all the propertied and self-employed classes, aside from the church, anything public was the man's world, business, politics, law, taxes and the defense of home and community.  Defending family honor was also especially the male's responsibility.

Many examples of complex gender relations locally will emerge below.  Nevertheless, in all this men and women generally had separate roles in home and society – men's work and women's work.  In Germantown, the profession of teaching was at least open to women. Otherwise, roles were limited to church work, charity, and cultural affairs, but they were public.  Of course, a woman like Fanny Wright was a scandal.  Although Isham Howse could respect her intellect and public work, he would say, "she did not meet with my approbation.  She stepped out of the sphere of woman into that of man...."[27]

There reached a point, however, when a woman was "emancipated" and had full control over her affairs.  When a widow inherited the estate, legally at least one-third, she might proceed as head of household with only some legal niceties in the hands of a trustee.  Such women in the Germantown area were the planters Sarah Jones, Maria Scruggs and Sarah Walker.  For example, Mrs. Scruggs exercised the responsibility

Illustration 2. The formality of a children's party. (Harper's Weekly, December 24, 1859)

Illustration 3. Christmas presents (Harper's, December 30, 1865)

for providing her "hands" to do road work, and she took it upon herself to advance tuition for the Woodward orphans.[28] The one area in which such a woman usually acknowledged incompetence was the management of recalcitrant slaves. If she did not have an overseer, she called on male relatives or neighbors.[29] More progressive husbands allowed their wives to hold property in their own names, while protective parents tried to insure that the property going to their daughters remained free from the debts or mismanagement of their husbands.[30]

Below the "genteel levels" of society, we have few pictures of the reality of gender relations. There again, however, much had to depend on individual personalities. A hard life made some women as tough as nails and unbending to male dominance. Others were broken into total submission. None, however, conformed to the romantic imagery of the fairer sex. The typical yeoman wife certainly considered herself as much a model of respectability as any other, and was as proud of her family's independence as was her husband. Though not as well educated, the vast majority of those around Germantown were literate, putting them well above southern averages.[31]

Apprenticeship or training by a charitable family was the only hope for girls from below propertied status. At the "poor white" level, "gentlemen" regarded them entirely differently. The above quotation referred to the "virtuous woman" as the source of all those positive qualities and influences. Implicitly, there was the other kind of woman. They could be exploited as labor, even as young girls or they were available for those "entertainments" that proper wives or young ladies should not provide. The wife of an unskilled laborer shared his hopeless poverty with all that implied.

At all levels, women were part of a changing world, and a few were aggressive about making some of those changes. In their capacity as models of morality, the pressure of their Christian consciences drove them out of the private realm. They openly joined their pastors in such righteous crusades as the temperance movement, and this in turn would later lead to feminism and the franchise fight even in the South, or at least in nearby Memphis. Ladies' societies also involved them in other charitable and reform activities, including fund raising, but normally under the supervision of pastors and laymen.

As for generational differences, according to the 1860 census, the population was conventionally divided into age categories according to their economic productivity. Up to age fifteen, one was considered a "dependent." They were supported by means they did not create. This hardly excused them from labor, however, they just were not considered sufficiently productive. Between fifteen and twenty, they were a "forming" or transitional class. Yet from fifteen to seventy one was expected to be "self-sustaining." Within that core labor force, those from twenty to sixty were the "mature – accumulating or contributing class," supporting those under fifteen or over seventy. Locally, more than half the white population was under twenty.[32]

As for those over seventy, the idea of retirement had yet to fully emerge. Negative ideas about the aged as producers were uncommon; instead they were a source of experience, stability or constancy. Yet, in antebellum America, some 30 percent of white males over sixty-five were not gainfully employed. Most of them were probably infirm, or had lost the means of self-support. Accumulating the means to retire was the responsibility of the individual.[33] The few elderly who described their occupations as "gentleman" had done so, but their cushion may have been thin. The elderly heads of household who had mature, live-in sons still thought of themselves as productive and in charge, and many resisted resigning that position until death. The elderly man living in the home of a son or son-in-law was usually infirm. The farmer, mechanic or merchant without an heir to support him, worked until death or until infirmity sent him to the old-folks home. The widows of all these men carried on similarly until their deaths. In the area, less than 3 percent of the white population was over 60.[34]

Although the "dependent" children were expected to work far more than today, even the yeomen and poor farm kids had some time for play and other childhood recreations. Although the only specific childhood memories for Germantown date from the 1870s, things would not have changed much. Especially before school and during recess, the school yard was a loud and boisterous gathering place. Even before the advent of baseball, there were numerous variations of ball and bat games. Marbles, tops and kites also provided entertainment. Less gender specific indoor games were puss in the corner, blind-man's bluff and hide and seek, while outdoors one played base or Fox and Goose. Parties were less fun, "because there was little freedom and much formality."[35]

Of course, Christmas was a special occasion. Although Santa Claus was not yet the phenomenon he would become after the war, Memphis papers specifically advertised toys for him to provide. Santa was already eagerly awaited by some, and children rushed to their stockings first thing in that morning. Special treats awaited, typically fruits, nuts and other goodies of a sort not normally available. Families of means bought manufactured toys advertised in the papers or mail-order catalogs, but more typical was something simple like a pop gun or other handmade toys fashioned by loving parents or relatives. Torpedoes and firecrackers were essential ingredients, even for surprisingly young children.[36]

Girls, even of the planter class, were hardly as restrained as one would suspect, at least not before menarche. Before age four, infants were treated almost equally and girls were not especially sheltered. Thereafter, fathers took girls hunting and fishing. They learned to shoot and had to be able to ride. Aside from playtime, they had to learn all the skills performed by their mothers. This involved girls of the yeomen class in less genteel pursuits. Of course, a respectable young lady of either class had to live with constraints that protected her against all the "threats" to her respectability. Preserving the honor of the family was impressed upon them as strongly as upon boys, but with a significant double standard. By the same token, internal fortitude and toughness were essential qualities to develop. Learning to balance all that against the necessity of showing proper respect to male authority must have generated a great deal of ambivalence about their place in life.[37]

Boys, of course, had more freedom, running through the woods and fields and swimming in the Wolf, where making it across the 40 to 50 yards was a rite of passage. A favorite gathering place in town was the platform of the depot, especially for those intent on mischief. Older boys enjoyed egging the younger into fights. Any boy would have been too embarrassed to refuse a dare that could lead to a fight. He would be "discounted and humiliated." It was rough and tumble with no rules, but few got seriously hurt. Boys of all classes were conditioned from early on for a manly defense of honor. Such fighting was essential to the mutual respect that produced life-long bonds of friendship and trust[38]

### The Social and Cultural Life

Contemporary references do not paint a consistent picture. An 1846 add for a new private school boasted of "the health, intelligence and good morals of the surrounding community." According to an 1858 railroad handbook, "the inhabitants are generally moral, intelligent, and a reading people; supporting three churches...." Yet in 1872, a witty proponent of the town reflected that "Germantown was once famous mainly for drunken brawls. It was filled with whiskey-shops, and there were roaring old debauchees about the village." There were an ample number of saloon/grocery stores, and in 1858, such establishments were castigated for being the source of liquor imported illicitly to corrupt the young ladies of Semple Broaddus College of nearby Center Hill, Mississippi.[39] How does one square such images?

The 1850s farmer, Isham Howse, also painted a mixed picture. He described a community of friendly and supportive people with an active social life, constantly visiting one another and attending church events, yet there were drunkards of whom he sternly disapproved. As for the environment, "It is a beautiful country to the eye, and remarkably convenient to market, etc., but it is sickening to the heart. Labor is not rewarded, and disease lurk about in ambush, ready to seize upon and devour the whole people. ... This is a pleasant place to live, and possesses many rare conveniences; but I feel now that I would not accept the whole estate as a gift...." He and his family suffered bad health on the Nashoba estate. He also said that his planter neighbor, Britten Duke, shared his objections to the country, "its sickness, and its poor, unproductive soil."[40]

Again in contrast, the earlier settler, Wilks Brooks, wrote, "I am indused to beleve from observation that we have the best country taking into consideration all the things that I have seen, we have the health, the climate, soil and near this grate river where we can git any thing from a northern or southern market at fair prices."[41]

Actually the quality of the soil varied greatly. As for sickness, "chills" were not unique to the Germantown area, but were common throughout those parts of the South – probably related to malaria. Given their ignorance of the causes of the various "fevers," people commonly believed that higher elevations were healthier and constantly sought refuge in Germantown from disease ridden Memphis. Amidst all this contradictory imagery, there was one point of agreement; the area was ideally situated for commerce. Unfortunately, Howse's apocalyptic prediction about disease devouring the people would come true after the war. Before that, however, there is plentiful evidence for filling out the picture among these contradictory images.

### *Education:*

For instance, public education in Tennessee was of unequal quality, but generally poor. Despite efforts at reform, state support and guidance were hampered by graft, indifference and opposition to taxes. Shelby County at least sought to provide a modicum of "free" or "common" schooling. Generally, however, private schooling was favored, especially around Germantown, initially retarding free public education, but gradually producing an environment with rich educational opportunities.

Since 1829, the state had authorized local taxes for the support of common schools and began to distribute funds gained from land sales. Yet, "common schools" remained underfunded into the 1850s. In 1854, the Legislature passed an act establishing Tennessee's first state tax for public schools, which seems to have promoted more interest in public education around Germantown.[42]

Meanwhile beginning in 1851, women had been allowed to teach in Tennessee's common schools and to draw pay equal to the male teachers. In 1856, the state finally imposed a requirement on the counties to maintain one or more Common School Commissioners responsible for certifying the competence of teachers hired for the common schools. The subjects of competency included primarily spelling (orthography), reading, writing, arithmetic, geography and English grammar.[43] From all indications, however, such competence requirements were not well enforced, and a lack of reporting for Shelby County as late as 1860 does not bode well for it having been an exception.[44]

Most local historians report that from 1833 Germantown operated a school in a multipurpose log building. Needham Harrison remembered attending a "comfortable log school house," which should have been between 1847 and 1854. He described it as a private school.[45] It was probably a subscription school, whereby the community provided a building, while a teacher earned his living giving instruction for a fee per student. Apparently during the 1840s, county school funds could be used to pay such subscription fees as "tuition from the common school fund." In 1846, for instance, the town's school commissioners dispensed all its allotted funds to seven men and one woman for teaching, in some cases as few as two students.[46]

Surviving records mention only one school building by name, Dukes School House, apparently named after Britton Duke, a prominent community leader and planter living just west of town. Perhaps he had funded it and provided the land, for it was common for public minded citizens to finance school buildings. In the 1850 census, Hartson R. Brown, a teacher who had come from Maine, had been boarding with the Dukes, probably using the building as a subscription school.[47]

Unfortunately, the records of the county and district school commissioners are incomplete, and sometimes grossly contradictory, making it impossible to fully reconstruct the history of the earliest public schooling in the district. By 1850, it seems the district's commissioners had become more parsimonious with school funds, perhaps distributing them only for tuition for poor and orphaned students. For instance, in 1853 when Isham Howse arranged for his three oldest sons to attend the writing school of Samuel Holmes, Sr., Howse, being somewhat strapped for funds, negotiated a fifty percent discount on Holmes' $5 per term fee per student. Howse's sons obviously were not getting county funds. Meanwhile, Howse's wife felt qualified to supplement their income with her own subscription school for younger children, apparently also without funding. Holmes gave up his subscription school at Germantown in the spring of 1853, finding that "his prospects about here are rather unpromising."[48]

By this time, the people of the district had abandoned the idea of supporting any public education. The district commissioners of the common school reported that for the years 1853 and '54 there had been no common school or teachers for the eleventh district. Neither had there been any commissioners in office until their election in September 1854, so the community had acquired no funds.[49] Community leaders were probably satisfied with the growth of private schools in the area, since Needham Harrison, remembered only private schools.

For Germantown, a turnaround in attitudes about common schools probably related to two developments: the arrival in town of John W. A. Pettit in 1852, and the availability of state-tax money after 1854. Pettit quickly became the district's justice of the peace, playing a prominent role in county government. Previously in Memphis, he had been heavily involved in that city's efforts to establish a free public school system in the late 1840s, after which he was elected first superintendent. In district eleven, he would sit on the school commission from September 1854 to June 1856, and his young wife and oldest daughter would soon provide the town with reliable teachers.[50]

Before that, the system of subscription schooling had created an unstable instructional environment. County teacher payment records show that teachers commonly moved about among the districts from session to session, even month to month. The district began operating its first fully free common school perhaps late in 1854. Thereafter, it operated sometimes two common schools, one at the Duke School and another in a rented facility in town. Until 1860, the two Pettit ladies and Achilles N. Plunkett carried most of the teaching load providing consistency. During the 1840s and 50s, Plunkett, a more established professional, had lived in the adjacent 12th district where he taught and boarded a number of students in his house. He and his family had settled in Germantown by 1859, eventually acquiring sizable acreage. During 1860, another two men and a woman filled in for several months each. Miss Florida Pettit had married.[51]

Finally in 1861, Miss Julia Pettit, twenty-year-old daughter of Judge Pettit and newly certified, became the teacher at the common school. In October of that year, she instructed thirty-three "scholars," for which her pay varied from thirty-three to thirty-six dollars a month. It varied monthly depending on the number of students served. The provision of fuel for heat was the collective responsibility of the parents, except those considered indigent.[52]

The significant presence of women among the district's teachers brings us back to gender roles locally. In most parts of the South, women had not been encouraged to teach before the war. Also women's "higher" education did not generally prepare them to pass competency examinations.[53] Yet the town's elite, as well as yeoman's wives and middle class women had taken up the role as early as the 1840s. Another example of how local women seem to have been more progressive.

The quality of instruction was undoubtedly no better or worse than elsewhere at the time. As for student life, one has images from *Little House on the Prairie,* with the students walking or riding mules to school, and playing outside at recess. In school, students worked with the few readers, primers and arithmetic books the commission provided. Large-group, rote recitation of lessons was a common technique, making for a noisy environment. Miscreants got a switching or worse. The current pedagogical theories generally favored corporal punishment even for failure to recite lessons properly as a way of encouraging the desire to learn.

The annual survey of the "scholastic population" counted children of an age to be educated as from six to twenty-one. The state based its funding to the county and district on this "scholastic population." For instance, for distribution in 1861, it allotted district eleven $133.25 for its 1860 scholastic population of 205. Although the education provided by the common school was basic, it is unclear exactly what level was considered finishing and ready to advance to academy. There were no grades by age or level. One teacher's pay record indicated that his students ranged from ages 5 to 14.[54] After they completed the local "field school," tuition could be provided for a few of Germantown's teenagers and young adults at the county academy.[55]

The academy was located at the county seat of Raleigh, which obviously required boarding. There were two academies, one for boys and the other for girls. A typical Tennessee academy had only two teachers and served 58 students.[56] Whatever the quality of education available at these academies, private institutions of higher learning were preferred.

One of those preferred private schools had become available as early as the 1830s when Randolph Webb opened the Webb School for Boys in his house east of town off State Line Road (present Nurnberger House, 2576 Germanwood Lane). From the road it still looks like a typical plantation cottage house, white clapboards, porch across the front, and one full-length window on each side of the door. To each side of the entry hall, two classrooms fully occupied the front wing. One chimney on each side serviced fireplaces, though in later years they probably vented more efficient potbellied stoves. Behind lay the family quarters, forming an L with the classroom wing.[57]

After graduating from the University of North Carolina, Webb had become an English teacher. He came first to Germantown in 1827 to help his friend Nathaniel Thompson bring his family to settle just northeast of what would become the town. According to one family tradition, "it was then and there that Randolph felt a need for an educational facility in the growing community of Germantown." Since there was no such thing in 1827, he may have felt a need for a school on the then

Illustration 4. Classroom discipline (Harper's, March 10, 1866)

Photo 1. Webb schoolhouse and home, front classroom wing facing State Line Road.

frontier. He returned home to Raleigh to settle his affairs. He and his family settled in 1832 on their 36 acre farm.[58]

Webb's school operated throughout the entire period, first as a boys' school and after his death in 1851 under his son Monroe as coeducational. The 1858 railroad handbook described it as "an excellent school for boys and girls." By 1860, his daughter Mary, who also helped maintain the school after Webb's death, was married to the farmer Louis Thompson.[59]

Thomas Pittman, Jr. launched a more ambitious educational project in 1837. For at least a year, he operated the Selma Academy located about a mile and a half east of town on the State Line Road. In Memphis papers, he advertised that his school would go well beyond the basics to include algebra, philosophy, rhetoric, astronomy, Greek and Latin. Tuition would range from $8 to $15 per session, and he would board students for $50. He ceased advertising after 1838, but that may not be an accurate barometer of operations.[60]

In any case, in October 1846 Brooks Trezevant advertised the opening of the English and Classical School in the same location. Trezevant operated through at least 1850, but also had quickly ceased advertising.[61]

The final heir to these ambitious operations opened in August 1854. The Shelby Male High School appeared "a half mile East of Germantown, and facing the road on the north." It was described as being situated "in a beautiful grove fronting the Railroad."[62] Initially the teachers were Reverend Richard R. Evans, A. M. Rafter and L. B. Johnson. A. M. Rafter was Alexander Rafter, the by-then 23 year-old son of farmer James Rafter. Their advertisements read,

> Tuition – one half in advance, and remainder at end of the session – per session of the months in Primary Department $10, $15 and $30 according to the branches taught. In Collegiate Department, $25. Good boarding can be had convenient to the school at from $2 to $2.50 per week.[63]

In addition to tuition, the parents had to buy all the textbooks. The prices ranged from $1.25 for a history textbook to 25 cents for basic arithmetic or speller. For the fifth session 1856-7, it cost John Woodson $16.90 for his son. He paid $7.00 in advance and owed Rafter $9.90. Perhaps the most revealing thing about Woodson's financial dealings with school master Rafter was when in March 1857 Rafter called on Woodson to pay a third party $20, for which he would give Woodson credit.[64] Cash flow in communities like Germantown was still restricted by its limited supply. Commonly, people, even schools, operated on credit, barter and reciprocity.

Reverend Evans was the town's Presbyterian minster. Since he took little or no income from his churches, he must have relied on teaching for a livelihood. Since the Rafters were founders of his Germantown church, that is undoubtedly how he and Alexander became close and hit upon the idea of opening the school when the young man graduated with his academic credentials.[65]

The *Appeal,* so impressed with the new institution, gave considerable coverage to its first public examination and "Exhibition." The school had already attracted forty to fifty students from Arkansas, Mississippi and Tennessee, with many from Memphis. "The young gentlemen generally answered promptly and correctly the various questions propounded, and solved easily the various problems proposed, exhibiting at the same time great politeness and good manners. It seems to be the object of their teachers, not only to make them good scholars, but high toned gentlemen."[66]

For the evening "Exhibition," a large "delegation of ladies and gentlemen from Memphis had come out on an extra train of cars." Reverend Evans' church hosted the assembly which began with a prayer and singing of the national anthem. A quartet entertained with other songs interspersed among eight essays, declamations and orations by students. Three of the town's families proudly listened to the exercises of H. M. Neely, R. F. Duke, and A. T. Cornelius.[67]

Within a year, the school had grown considerably. "A commodious building" had been added for the students' comfort and improved study. The enlarged faculty listed specializations: Mr. Rafter was both Principal and Professor of Natural Science; Reverend Evans Professor of Mental and Moral Philosophy; Johnson was Professor of Mathematics and Principal of a new Commercial Department, plus a new Professor of Ancient Languages and one of Modern Language and Belles-Letters. Evans, a Princeton graduate, brought the school prestige. It now boasted of "a splendid Mathematical, Astronomical, and Geographical Apparatus" and an excellent, growing library. By 1859, it held 1,200 volumes. Membership in the Eromathean Society, "a little association for literary improvement" was available for serious students.[68]  In contrast to Webb's small house, this school required two or more sizable buildings. In addition to a library, several classrooms and other teaching facilities, they apparently had dormitory space and a kitchen with dining hall.

During its first year, the staff had learned some hard lessons about the management of an educational institution in the local environment. For the second year they demanded "tuition positively in advance," and clear rules were laid out prohibiting refunds except "in cases of protracted sickness, or other providential causes."  Room and board could no longer be paid weekly. Students and parents had to understand the need for persistence and consistent attendance in the academic world, and commit themselves to compliance with the schools' rules. They also advertised two "FREE SCHOLARSHIPS" out of a commitment to the advancement of talented but less well financed students.

Rafter's ambitions included the hiring of an additional professor to staff a new Agricultural Chemistry branch. To finance it, he hit on the idea of selling one hundred scholarships for two-year's tuition at $50. These served as bonds, redeemable for the future education of the holder's son. Although the *Appeal* enthusiastically endorsed the idea, it may have caused problems if increased enrollments did not offset the loss of future tuition.[69]

In 1857, Rafter expanded the curriculum to include "military instruction and discipline." Again the *Appeal* waxed eloquent about how they kept the school up to date with the spirit of the age, providing every facility and had "succeeded thus far in securing a patronage of the very best character." The railroad handbook asserted that "This institution – which so advantageously unites a collegiate education with military discipline – enjoys an excellent reputation."[70]

In February 1858, the state assembly followed through by officially authorizing the Shelby Military Institute, with Alexander and his father James appointed to the Board of Trustees. They were empowered to raise funds in order to "erect buildings, purchase grounds, apparatus, books, or any other thing, which may be necessary for the use of the School, for endowing or supporting the same."[71]

Germantown was now poised to acquire a fully collegiate level institution that granted not only degrees but military commissions. It was charged to pursue a level of educational quality comparable to the U.S. Military Academy at West Point. The Board was to elect a President and Commandant qualified to give instruction in such a course of studies. Furthermore

> That the President, Commandant, and Assistants, or Professors, and students, shall constitute a military corps. The Governor shall issue a warrant of appointment to each student who shall be styled a cadet. He also shall issue the commission of Colonel to the President, of Lieutenant Colonel to the Commandant, and such other commissions to the professors and cadets as may be necessary to fill the offices created by the Faculty or Board of Trustees, and is authorized to cause to be issued to the Academy the necessary and suitable arms and equipment....

The Governor also had to appoint an annual Board of Visitors to attend the examination of the cadets and ascertain their proficiency.[72]

Although the 1860 census listed only one military college in

Tennessee, there were at least two other more prominent such schools.[73] Everyone's pretensions to such high academic and military proficiency for the school make one wonder about its actual achievement. Certainly the elevation of young Alexander to the exalted rank of colonel seems specious. At best he must have been the graduate of a suitable military academy. We may never know anything of the military qualifications of his instructors. In contrast, competing institutions at Lagrange and Nashville boasted more specifically of the nature of their training programs including artillery.

Rafter's ambitions had apparently exceeded his reach. Advertisements for the school soon ceased, and Rafter seems to have abandoned his post. In the 1860 census, the only names present associated with the school were Evans and the elder Rafter. By that year, Alexander and his wife Elizabeth were living with their young daughter in Searcy, Arkansas.[74] However, he would be back in town in 1861. The year before the war remains a blank page in the school's history.

Throughout the 50s however, both Rafter and Webb's schools lined up along the State Line Road east of town. Farther out, "on the North side of the road," was the Forest Hill College Institute for Young Ladies, which opened in 1856. It advertised itself as located "in the open country; very beautiful and remote from distracting influences; one hours ride (via Memphis and Charleston Railroad) from Memphis; thus ensuring the real advantages of both city and country." It offered a "corps of accomplished, faithful and experienced Teachers."

> **Expenses** – Boarding, including a furnished room, fuel and lights, (illegible). Tuition in Primary Department, $12; Preparatory $14; Collegiate $20; Music on Piano with use of instrument, Guitar and Violin, each $10; Harp $6. Languages – French, Italian, German, Latin and Greek, each $10; Painting in Water colors, $10; Oil $20; Embroidering $10. Washing per month, $1; Incidental Fee $1.00.

The state legislature granted it status as a collegiate institute with full power to confer degrees in 1858. The proprietor was Barnett Miller, a Baptist minster.[75] It was served by a "Professor of Music," Anton Shide, who also boarded five young ladies as teachers. The Germantown area had become a seat of higher learning for both men and women.

Clearly the town's institutions of higher learning were putting it on the map. Such a reputation attracted others, though less successful. In 1857, James Voorhees tried to open a Male High School "near Forest Hill Seminary," with the support of Reverend Miller and most prominent local residents. He spared no expense advertising from January through March in the papers, but to no avail. He never advertised again.[76]

Then in 1859, a Professor M. Solomon opened an "Academy of Music and Language", which was apparently a mobile operation, for he offered to teach "every language and give instructions upon every musical instrument in Memphis, Germantown and within ten miles of the above places."[77] The "professor" was obviously not only quite mobile, but unbelievably versatile as well. He also made a persistent advertising campaign, but he too does not seem to have been successful.

The educational career of a Germantown lad might involve moving up through at least two of these schools. For instance, Henry Woodson, son of the gin manufacturer, attended the common school for primary education and then the Shelby Military Male High School.[78] The somewhat older Needham Harrison attended the private schools entirely, for seven years and five months to age nineteen. He remembered the schools as operating for ten months per year, and traveled two and half to three miles to get there. He also remembered the boys and girls of the area attending school regularly, although "sometimes during the press of farm work (they) aided in that work as they some do at this time."[79]

Their female counterparts obviously had the advantage of the nearby Forest Hill Academy, where Henry Woodson's sister, Ann, attended.[80] By no means were the local elite limited to opportunities in the county for the refinement of their young ladies. Joseph and Agnes Brooks sent Ann Elizabeth to the Female Institute at Florence, Alabama. In any case, a woman's education was supposed to terminate at the highest at such a "finishing-school" level.

### Other Social and Cultural Institutions:

Among its social institutions, Germantown had an Oddfellows Hall, about which there seems to be no local memory. Nevertheless, the inauguration of this hall in June 1851 was reported in the *Appeal*.

> A procession bearing the banners and insignia of the order, preceded by a fine band, marched in full regalia to the church, where an anniversary address was delivered by Rev. William Hyer of Memphis. A dedicatory oration was ably given by A. J. Maltlock of Germantown. After the conclusion of the ceremonies the members adjourned to a pleasant grove where a sumptious barbecue was prepared under the supervision of J. W. Vaughn. Afterwards the green was cleared, and music and dancing chased the golden hours until time for retiring. A very large number of ladies honored the brethren with their presence.[81]

The town's Masonic Lodge, the Blue Lodge, had formed in 1841 and met in the community's multipurpose log building. One wit claims they were driven out by the nesting wasps. So in 1854, they built an

Photo 2. Old Masonic Hall as it appeared during WWII when it served as a Red Cross office.

Photo 3. Evans Chapel, Germantown Presbyterian Church. Original church building, currently reoriented east-west from its former north-south orientation and set on a basement. The steeple was added in 1867.

impressive two-story lodge south of the Presbyterian Church. The November cornerstone-laying ceremony provided a gala occasion. Masons from the city and area lodges attended in large numbers. "A sumptuous Barbecue" was offered, and Hessing's Brass Band provided entertainment. Perhaps the good Masons of the town attempted to compensate the *Appeal*'s reporter whom they had disappointed by failing to host a gala for the arrival of the rails. He was apparently satisfied, for according to him, "It was gotten up with taste judgement and liberality, and ... went off with great credit to the Masonic fraternity."[82] Once completed, the lodge building provided the town with a venue for public events and services.

The town's social and cultural life was enriched by its educational institutions and their faculty. In addition to the Masonic and Oddfellows halls, the churches also provided venues for cultural events, such as music performances, learned lectures, poetry readings and "appropriate" plays. Less tasteful events had to find other venues. Lucken's Inn was often preferred by politicians for delivering speeches to a lively audience that imbibed his lager.[83] The genteel families would have hosted dance parties and other private entertainments in their homes. Larger public events such as that of the Mason's and Odd Fellows occurred outdoors in good weather, with temporary brush arbors erected and sawdust spread for a ground cover. Spontaneous "fairs" were sponsored by local organizations. Of course, such events included a barbecue, dancing, and fireworks on such as the Fourth of July.

Until the militia companies and their local drills were terminated in 1842,[84] they provided an occasion for some public gathering. The companies for district eleven should have drilled in town or nearby once a year. Things had become rather rag-tag before the end, and drills may have been irregularly held and poorly disciplined events, with some comic relief, especially if the stories about the town drunks are true. Some spectators might have turned out, but especially the children who would have held their own mock ceremonies.

One fair sponsored by the ladies of the Germantown Presbyterian Church to help fund its construction occurred September 22, 1852. The ladies advertised that "they will exhibit for sale many useful and fancy articles at reasonable prices. Also, on the same occasion, a dinner will be provided. The Fair will be continued at night. The public are respectfully invited to attend."[85]

The *Appeal*'s reporter, who traveled to "the neat village of Germantown," described the event.

> On repairing to the church, we found that it had been handsomely decorated
> by fair hands, and that all the taste, tact and skill of the gentler and better

sex had been brought into requisition, to attract the liberal purchaser and exemplify the benevolent feelings of the fair artisans.

(Later, after some political speeches) the company adjourned to discuss the viands which were prepared for the "inner man," and which were disposed of with a heartiness suggestive of the idea of good cheer, and an abundance of it. How could it be otherwise with the hospitable citizens of Germantown?[86]

The Presbyterian Church was one of three in the town. From 1833, the town's multipurpose log building had served the different congregations when they got too big for house church assemblies. By the 1850s, each had its own fine little church building. The Baptists and Methodists had both erected their buildings in the early 1840s. The churches would not acquire full-time pastors for several decades, so each only held full services once or twice a month.[87] Nevertheless, many pastors had taken up residence around Germantown as their home base. In 1860, the Reverends Richard Mills and Richard Evans, resided in town, while Jeremiah Burns (semi-retired) and Joshua Cross, both of the Baptist Church, and Phillip Tuggle, a Methodist circuit rider, farmed outside town with Tuggle operating a sizable plantation. Like many professionals, ministers needed other sources of income than that provided for their services in order to support their families. After receiving his doctorate from Princeton University in 1849, Reverend Evans had become pastor at Germantown in 1850, and was the only minister to remain in residence for the entire period. He acquired prominence in the larger area and served as stated secretary of the Synod of Memphis, always supplementing his income with teaching.[88]

The Presbyterian Church was officially dedicated on Saturday evening, May 15, 1853, with guest sermons and a church dinner in between. The Sunday service included a lecture by the missionary, Mr. Wilson, "on the condition of the heathen in India," followed by an evening service. Actually it seems that when the pastor was in town, he held both a Saturday evening service as well as two on Sunday, at least this was the Presbyterian practice. One farmer in attendance complained about "the perfumed ladies and gentlemen. Sweet scents were too strong for me."[89]

All three churches had similar construction. Set on brick pillars, the exteriors were of white clapboards, and the high windows held only clear glass. Steeples were often later additions, as in the case of the Presbyterian Church. Steps led up to the doors, through which one entered the narthex, a small vestibule, and then the hall with its high ceilings. Heat was provided by a centrally located iron stove. The present Evans Chapel was the original Presbyterian building. The existing old Baptist church is allegedly a close replica of the original. The Methodists apparently had a more modest church, described as a one-room building, perhaps with only four windows per side and a relatively low roof. There was another, more simple, Baptist church or chapel in Forrest Hill to the east.[90]

The Episcopalians had to meet either in their homes or travel a few miles west. There was nothing for any Lutherans, but in both cases the three local churches were always generous with their facilities for other protestant denominations. If any practicing Catholics settled in Germantown, they had to commute to Memphis.[91]

Differences among the congregations were taken seriously, such as the proper form of baptism. The Baptists also segregated the sexes in church. There were separate entrances to the building and seating in the hall. In addition to Sunday school, in all churches children of all ages were expected to sit through the sermons, although mothers brought distractions for the youngest.[92]

The churches were central elements in community life, with people coming from miles around on a Sunday. The better endowed maintained townhouses where they spent the weekend away from their plantations specifically to observe the Sabbath. Despite the great religiosity of the age, the entire population was not so devout. The religiously indifferent and the anti-religious were present, although they have left no records of their attitudes in the town's affairs. Across the South, only forty percent were church members, although many affiliated without such status. Typically the women were the backbones of the churches, with the men often displaying indifference, constituting only a quarter or less of the congregations and attending even less. Salvation and morality were appropriately female concerns. It was religious involvement and a sense of righteous imperative that drove women to be more assertive with their husbands, even at the expense of being accused of "trying to rule." Women might teach Sunday school, but church offices and the exercise of authority and discipline remained the purview of the men.[93] This was an area in which Germantown women played typical roles in the complexity of gender relations.

Attitudes among churchgoers were hardly uniform about strong drink or other "vices." The town produced at least two or three stalwarts in the temperance movement. One local held hard-nosed positions on public impropriety – not just drinking but dancing. He preferred to eschew public festivities although, "Such gatherings sometimes do good; neighbors meet together and form closer attachments." He once consented to take his children to a great barbecue in 1852, commenting, "There may be dancing – I have heard there will be – but I have no love for that exercise, and of course, so far as I am concerned, I had rather

31

there would be none."[94]

Other men were probably as firm in their religious convictions as this Isham Howse, but like him also independently minded about some conventions. Once he asserted,

> Some go to church to see and be seen – for display; some
> to find fault with the preaching, but many I hope go to
> receive instruction, and to worship God in sincerety. When
> I cannot go for this last purpose, I would rather not go at
> all. It is but seldom that I hear a sermon which I approve
> in toto, but I always get some benefit...."[95]

Often Howse found excuses for not attending, instead sending his wife and children.[96]

Poor Howse seems to have had a number of problems with Presbyterians, not to mention those of other faiths. He claimed to have been such a nonconformist on certain points of dogma that they called him "a heretic, and, sometimes, an infidel." They allegedly attributed his poor health and misfortunes to his nonconformity. He saw himself as alienated from the town people. Yet the only point of dissent about which he was specific was, that having been raised a Baptist, he believed strongly in immersion. He accused Reverend Evans and other Presbyterians of being "sectarians," but constantly belied these contentions with frequent, fond references to Evans and many church members regularly visiting and dining with his family and vice versa. It was not they who seem to have been judging. He once lamented, "I dislike intolerance, even in myself; and I often find it lurking in me, ashamed to let itself be known." Yet he admired some "sectarians" for not being "ashamed of religious sentiments."[97]

At one point he contended that at least his wife understood him, but

> I cannot be a member of ... the organized congregation,
> because I cannot unite with any society under its
> organization and its external ceremonies....Baptists were
> once my people, in sentiment, but they have gone aside
> into various bypaths, according to my views. Their
> ceremonies are in accordance with my views, and I could
> live with them if I could esteem them sound in faith. They
> are mixed with Cambellism and Armenianism, and
> membership with them would be anything but true
> fellowship.[98]

Like many religious persons, then and now, he wrestled less with his faith than with points of dogma and the ceremonies of observation. The hypocrisy of others soured him on the allegedly faithful. As he complained, there were those in churches who criticized the pastor and his sermons, and even made life so miserable as to drive him out.

Although a couple of Baptist and Methodist pastors may have had relatively short tenure in their charges, that did not necessarily mean anything negative, and there are no records of problems in pre-war Germantown. However, Reverend A.W. Young of the Edmiston Church was such a victim who took temporary refuge in Germantown with friends and Reverend Evans until he found a new position in Mississippi.[99]

Bible reading was a well-known focus for many of the literate and was part of school curricula. As Howse put it, "I have studied the Bible a great deal, and my writings have been chiefly upon the Scriptures. ... The Bible and my concordance have been my chief books – I might say my only books."[100]

Even for those raised in a church, "becoming a Christian" was not a perfunctory act. Making the public profession of faith was preceded by much soul searching for some. Others became possessed by the spirit in the frequent revival or camp meetings, but even then, actually joining the church was often a serious separate step. It involved prayerful meditation and awaited an epiphany. However, many personalities who were denied such ecstasy eventually made the public commitment anyway.[101]

Howse was undoubtedly not unique in his independent thinking, but most others were simple conformists on such matters. Religion was more a social duty. Locals probably fell along a spectrum ranging from mild to strong sectarian convictions. Although socializing focused mostly on family and fellow church members, it extended to neighbors. Howse to the contrary, the overall impression prevails of a community not overly divided by sectarian differences.

Christian morality, charity and service were certainly central in the community's self-image. It would be wonderful if we had statistics on regular church attendance as a percentage of the local population. Obviously, however, the community supported its churches. The early settler, Wilks Brooks, had donated the land for the Baptist Church in 1841.[102] In a county with only 27 churches, Germantown housed three, with an additional chapel at Forest Hill and another beyond Pea Ridge. There was another Methodist Church, Bethlehem, at Capleville in the south-west corner of the district. A sizable percentage of the rest of the 27 churches were centered on Memphis.[103]

Whatever sectarian divisions there might have been, some social differences also divided the congregations in Germantown. The later arrival of the Presbyterian Church as well as its smaller membership and its highly educated minister marked its more distinct character. Though hardly as elitist as the Episcopalians, they tended to attract a larger proportion of the elite. Their theology was more intellectual than emotional, and they demanded a better educated clergy. The Methodists drew better, building their numbers with their popular camp meetings. Establishing a new church required little more than application to the local conference, which promptly supplied a circuit rider, who also required some theological credentials and endorsement for an appointment. The Baptists beat them both with grassroots evangelism and tub-thumping revivals. With absolutely independent churches and no ecclesiastical organization to get in the way, any group could become a church, and a lack of educational qualifications rarely hindered a would-be preacher. Indeed Jeremiah Burns told how he had veritably taught himself English grammar by Bible study at night after a day's work, but he certainly supported formal education.[104] Although its social base might have been the broadest, it drew its share of the landed elite. Their presence in Germantown's church demanded some intellectual respectability for their pastors also.

### *Health Care, Illness and Death:*

Sixteen men in the Germantown area titled themselves physicians, but the relatively low level of advancement in the science of medicine provided no guarantee of adequate treatment. Earlier efforts to regulate the profession had been repealed. There were two ways by which one could ostensibly qualify as a physician. One could "read" with a practicing doctor, and when he felt that the apprentice had learned all the doctor could teach, the apprentice was considered ready to practice. The other way was to attend one of the numerous schools of medicine and biology, usually for two years. This involved little or no patient interaction or practical experience. The best physicians combined both routes, attending reputable medical schools.[105] Unfortunately during the 1850s the number of private medical schools, focused primarily on profit, had mushroomed, sometimes granting degrees after a few weeks of lectures.[106] For one glaring example, by 1860 William Blair, the son of Germantown's hotel keeper, had achieved the ripe old age of 19. He was not attending any educational institution, so one hopes he was still just working as a physician's assistant. Whatever, he or his proud parents had assigned him the title of "physician" for the census.[107]

A few doctors resided in town, but more lived in the countryside. Dr. Leonidas Richmond, who settled south of the town in 1860, was probably typical for making house calls on horseback – as far north as Cordova and as far south as Olive Branch.[108] As for fees, in 1854 when Britten Duke needed a night-time house call for surgery, he was charged $3.00. The next day for an office visit and prescription - $1.00. For a regular daytime house call - $2.00.[109]

Although fees were posted in terms of cash, the economy was still

Illustration 5. A house call by a country doctor (Harper's March 6, 1869)

heavily involved in barter and reciprocal services. Poorer farmers could pay in produce. Mostly, however, doctors extended credit. One especially unhealthy family ran up $208.44 bill before the farmer could pay it off from the sale of land. The farmer gratefully noted, "Our doctor is a humane man, and will not distress us, but will have patience with us till we can pay him without feeling it badly."[110]

Despite the dismal state of medicine, area residents did have access to the best available without having to travel to Memphis. Even during the 1840s, Dr. R. L. Scruggs was a physician who not only kept on top of the latest medical advances but who contributed regularly to medical journals, sharing his experiences with other professionals. His house calls also took him as far afield as "Upper Mississippi." His published professional reports paint a vivid picture.

In May 1846, he treated a 23 year old man with severe and well-advanced pneumonia. In tune with the age, his first effort was to bleed the patient. Fortunately, Scruggs was astute enough to notice quickly that the treatment weakened the man, so he desisted. Who knows today about the efficacy of all the other treatments that followed, but something may have worked. The man recovered full health, despite that the disease had progressed for four days before Scruggs had been summoned. Scruggs described the physical aspects of the illness and diagnosed accurately.[111]

He was less successful in treating a woman in her fifth or sixth pregnancy suffering from a ruptured uterus. She had already been in labor for three days before he was called, and there he found "an irregular practitioner in attendance, with several old women," undoubtedly the more common child-bearing experience for area women. Their brutal efforts to extract the child had only made matters worse. He could not save either of them.[112]

More impressive were his successful diagnosis and treatment of a rare condition described as "polypus of the uterus." In the spring of 1845, he was called in to treat a slave woman who had been suffering from excessive bleeding during menstruation. Initially, "a skillful physician" had treated the symptoms successfully, but returned episodes had brought her to death's door. Not only was his diagnosis right on, but without surgery and by a process we might call minimally invasive, Scruggs tied off, starved the tumor and removed it. In 1847, he reported, "She recovered rapidly, and has menstruated regularly ever since, not withstanding that she says she is 48 years old and has given birth to twelve healthy children, nine of whom are now living...."[113]

In 1848, he reported on an epidemic of typhoid fever. He noted that he was able to detect the outbreak early because of previous experiences two years before. "Up to this time, I have treated and assisted in the treatment of twenty-two cases: of these, seven occurred at one plantation, eight at another, three at another, and four other places furnished one case each. Out of these, only one case terminated fatally, which result was owing, I think, to the patient's refusing obstinately to submit to treatment." With his readers, he shared his knowledge of early and advanced symptoms. As for its cause, he described it as "extremely obscure." He ruled out contagion, since when it occurred on plantations, all the slaves would visit the sick without any others necessarily catching the disease. For treatment, he bled only when the patient was strong enough, and preferred cupping, blisters, poultices, purgatives, and "stimulants, judiciously administered, tonics, moderate exercise and nutritious food."[114]

For the national population, except during epidemic years the major killers were "consumption" or tuberculosis, pneumonia and other respiratory diseases. Shelby County fared much better than the national average for tuberculosis, but only slightly better for pneumonia. Locally cholera and yellow fever were regular visitors, but the cholera epidemic of 1849-50 was devastating nation-wide. Since 1828, yellow fever epidemics had threatened, the second hitting in 1855. Every summer, local papers reported on the approach of yellow fever coming up river and speculated on the degree of its intensity for the season, which ended with the first hard frost. In 1860, it did not advance much beyond Louisiana. Germantown was always spared its visitations. Although men were more prone to accidental deaths in general, women were 37 percent more susceptible to burns and scalding deaths, because of their work and clothing Death in childbirth was another special threat. During the years of menses, the overall female death rate was slightly higher than for men, but reversed thereafter.[115]

It is no wonder that some women recorded in personal letters and diaries an intense fear of pregnancy. Although they talked about intimacy in ways indicating that they were not otherwise sexually repressed, some became so phobic that they forcefully requested abstinence and often got it.[116] Here again was another measure of the importance of individual personalities in determining the workings of female submissiveness and obedience – even to scriptural admonitions.

For children, the above diseases were especially fatal. Others also reaped a severe toll. In no special order, major child-killers were bronchitis, croup, diphtheria, dysentery, measles, scarlet fever, small-pox, typhus, whooping cough and worms. At least vaccination was beginning to curb small-pox, although immigrants and many country folk had yet to benefit. Scarlet fever hit hard in 1860, especially in the Tennessee area. Death rates were high before age five, decreased over the next five years, but increased again, especially for girls between ages ten and twenty.[117]

Deaths related to childbirth and childhood disease frequently left families in mourning. In Germantown proper, between the 1850 and 1860 censuses, two of the five wives in permanent residence had died in the interim. Several other wives and small children had died in the countryside as well. The farmer family of Benjamin and Sarah Ellis lost two children and replaced them with four others between 1850 and 1860. Sarah had begun the joys and tears of motherhood at age sixteen, birthing a total of eight by age 35 in 1860. The Kimbrough family lost a three-year old daughter in 1859, a two-year old daughter in 1860 and a one-year old daughter and twin fifteen-year old sons in 1861.[118] One other family seems to have met a more terrible fate. In 1850, the family of the blacksmith William Stevenson and his wife Elizabeth, both in their thirties, had three children in ages nine to three. By 1860, only the youngest, little Josephine, remained an apparent orphan. The then thirteen year-old girl resided with the family of carpenter Wiley and Feraby Rochelle and their five children.

Although doctors were generous with credit, a sizable percentage of the population was so pressed for cash that they turned first to alternatives. Folk remedies and midwives were often preferred to professionals, but they could also prove fatal. Isham Howse almost lost his wife when she took a "new remedy." Others like Howse dosed themselves regularly with injections of over-the-counter morphine for pain and quinine for "chills".[119]

Death was certainly a great presence. Based on what we know about common practices, we can surmise something about burial and mourning in the local culture. It was much more highly ritualized and far less commercial than today.[120] Since Victorian rituals had not yet reached their peak, locals were not as immersed in them as in older folk ways. Some of the elite would have been involved with up-to-date practices, but most of the local folk would have inclined toward the simple. The town had no funerary professionals. All arrangements fell to family and friends. Only the most elite might have considered shipping the body to Memphis for expensive mortuary handling and burial. The practice of embalming had come to the U.S. about 1850, but to have your deceased embalmed, you had to ship the body to some place like New York, making arrangements with an agent in Memphis.[121]

The women of the family washed the body. They used folk-remedy recipes for washes and dressed the bodies. The wake or viewing was held as soon as possible. Although elaborate coffins could be brought from Memphis, the men usually made a pine box. Britton Duke's family shelled out $60.75 for his coffin. At least, some of the elite were coming around to buying coffins, and within just a few decades, Germantown would have its own coffin factory.[122]

Families that could not afford a newspaper death notice posted their own around town. The front door was draped in black. All pictures of the deceased and mirrors were either covered or turned to face the wall. Clocks were stopped at the hour of death until after the burial. Whatever flowers the family and friends could gather were there as much to help suppress odors as for other reasons. In warm weather, the box might be closed. As more family and friends arrived, they contributed with food preparation and even dug and filled the grave. Traditionally, the grave had to be dug on the same day as the funeral.[123]

After the viewing, pallbearers carried the coffin to the grave, which was frequently on the family property, even if they lived less than a mile from town. The countryside was dotted with small plots of graves of families and neighbors. In town, the community cemetery was on the Methodist Church property. For burials there, the coffin was loaded on a wagon and a procession followed it to the cemetery. At the grave site, there would be a short service, but for Masons, more elaborate ceremonies. On leaving, mourners usually tossed a handful of dirt on the coffin. There is no record of where pauper burials might have occurred.

After burial, came the period of mourning. A widower was expected to wear black for one month and a black armband for two more. Ideally he waited a year before remarrying, but the realities of life allowed him to find a wife sooner if he had young children. For a widow, however, the conventions were more restrictive, demanding up to two and one half years of formal mourning with a rigorous dress code. For the first four months, "a proper lady" could not even go out in public, except to attend church.[124] Needless to say, only the elite could afford to spare their women for such. Most widows still had to supervise all the work, or do it themselves unless there were mature sons. Even then, these elaborate conventions would not have carried much force below the level of the comfortable classes.

## *Homes and Property*

Rural and town life blended indiscriminately. Homes were widely spaced within the town, and from there they spread out along Germantown's major roads and a network of little lanes radiating out from them. Further east lay the unincorporated hamlet of Forest Hill. Primarily it consisted of a group of two or more buildings of the girls' school, one of which housed the faculty and some employees. The school was the personal property of the rather wealthy minister Barnett Miller. In addition, there was the little Baptist chapel which may also have been part of this establishment, one store and a few houses. Another crossroads settlement at a greater distance was High Hill, where a physician, a blacksmith and a carpenter served local farmers. Someone

Photo 4. The former home of Dr. Cornelius, much expanded from the original log cabin which is now buried inside the rear of the house. The gingerbread decorations and scalloped-shingle siding were undoubtedly a post-war embellishment.

Photo 5. Brooks townhouse adjacent to Baptist Church, used as weekend residence to avoid commuting to church from plantation. More typical of pre-war, unembellished town house.

brought mail out from town for everyone's convenience. It, Forest Hill, and Pea Ridge to the west, were essentially satellites of Germantown, served by its post office.

The oldest homes in Germantown were originally either log cabins or plank-sided, two-room affairs with a separate cook house. Many log cabins were subsequently weather-boarded over, depending on the resources and tastes of the owner. By 1860, however, more commodious, professionally constructed townhouses prevailed. The more typical house resembled the one-story Victorian town house, with surrounding porches, peaked roof, and floor to ceiling windows. They still had plain undecorated exteriors. Gingerbread, which became so popular, was only added to homes later in the century. A few had basements, though most simply sat on brick pillars.

For construction, there was an ample supply of carpenters in the area. There was only one "brick layer," Jackson Lewis. Before the brick factory, any bricks involved in construction had to be fired on site. The lack of any construction artisans in the previous 1850 census probably indicates that most building was do-it-yourself until after mid-century.

The porches, high windows and high ceilings of the homes helped residents cope with summer heat. Two or three brick chimneys served fireplaces or iron stoves for heating. Mantels could be of carved wood or iron, with hearths of stone. Roofs were covered with wooden shingles. There were one-and-a-half and two-story houses for the more well-heeled, and over time a house would grow, acquiring additional wings to accommodate the expanding family. The resultant foot-print could have an L or T or even a C shape with additional porches off one or more of the wings. Two-story town homes looked much like a second story stacked on top of the typical one story house, with a wide variety of gables and porch configurations.[125]

For most town families, outbuildings housed the animals, such as one horse or mule, a milk cow or goats, and chickens. Small, one-room affairs housed the slaves who served the middle and upper-class homes and family businesses. Of course, each house had its own "necessary," one or two holes.

Houses were usually elevated on short piers, screened by laths to allow air circulation. Such foundations were usually not concealed by shrubbery as today, but respectable ladies maintained profuse flower beds, and almost every family had a kitchen garden and fruit trees. The oldest surviving photographs indicate fewer of the lush shade trees so plentiful in modern Germantown. Photographs of the period give the impression that typical townsfolk preferred a more open landscape than today.

Even if there was a private well, many had cisterns to collect

Photo 6. Woodlawn, relocated and restored. The wing on the left is a modern addition.

Photo 7. Davies Plantation, Shelby County. An example of a planter's log house that was not finished over.

rainwater for bathing, watering animals and gardens, and fighting fires. Buried terracotta pipes brought water from collecting roofs, and a hand-cranked bucket chain brought the water up for use.

Some of the residential homes belonged to planters and farmers who commuted to their fields daily if they lived close enough, or they returned to town only for weekends if the fields were too far. On the other hand, farmers who lived outside Germantown would nevertheless have been very much a part of town life. Most of the leadership of the Masonic Lodge lived outside the town, as did many church leaders.[126] Their landholdings marched side-by-side along the roads radiating out from town. Like arteries, with a network of wagon trails leading from more isolated farms, they carried farmers and their crops to the railroad depot, and from there to market. Their families came to town for its shops and stores, its churches, schools, physicians, legal services, and saloons, with all the spiritual, social and cultural stimulation they offered. Unfortunately, this transportation network was navigable only in dry weather. Fortunately, that usually coincided with the harvesting of cotton and other crops.

The survival of "Cotton Plant," the Kimbrough home, until its loss in the 1950s, preserved an image of the grand homes of the wealthier planters. It was a stereotypical southern mansion with Doric columns. The home had been built by James Titus, one of the earliest settlers, in 1820. His slaves had erected the sturdy two-story building from native poplar. After James Kimbrough arrived from South Carolina with his wife Mary Elizabeth, they bought the Titus estate for $22,000 in 1838, to be paid out in installments up to 1843. A long drive, lined with trees and flowering shrubs, led down from the Germantown-Capleville Road (present Cotton Plant Road).[127]

An example of a more typical plantation home is Woodlawn, which still exists, relocated to 2000 Old Oak Drive. (photo 5) When completed, it consisted of only five rooms with a kitchen out back. Its builder, Wilks Brooks arrived in the area from North Carolina in 1834. Like others, it evolved in stages until achieving its classical antebellum form. Brooks and his son had originally built a two-room dogtrot cabin, and then expanded one of the rooms into a two-story, four room building. It took them a year to make the house ready for family habitation. Construction had begun with hand-hewn timbers and round wooden pegs. The planks for the siding were sawed at a water-driven sawmill several miles away on the Wolf River near the location of the present Christian Brothers' High School. Both the bricks for the chimneys and the square nails were manufactured on site. Like all the other finer homes, some interior walls were finished with paneling of mixed woods, others with horsehair plaster over split hickory lathes. Building these homes was a family operation in which father, son and slaves did almost all the work. Despite all this self-sufficiency, it ultimately cost him between two and three thousand dollars.[128]

In 1836, his family arrived to move in. Brooks had originally built the larger home with another dogtrot between the two downstairs rooms, to benefit from the cooling ventilation. This did not suit the refined tastes of his wife, however, so he had to enclose the dogtrot into a proper entry hall. Nevertheless, such typical planter homes had none of the grand sweeping staircases or rooms large enough to accommodate a ball. By sometime around 1840, he had completed the home. The full-bearded Wilks and his beautiful wife became mainstays of the growing community and pillars of the Baptist church. When Wilks died in 1849, he was succeeded by his son Joseph.[129]

A contemporary description of the property of another Germantown area planter emerges from an advertisement and rounds out our image of a typical plantation. He offered 872 acres, 250 of which were cleared, in good cultivation, and mostly bottom-land. Ideally located near the M&C Railroad, it was "in sight of Forest Hill Female Institute." It boasted a neat two-story, eight room, frame house, with all necessary outhouses, a garden, orchard, cotton gin, water well and good negro quarters. Apparently, he was an absentee farmer, living and working in Memphis with an office on Front Row.[130]

Planters ginned their own cotton. One who could not afford such an establishment had to go to a neighbor or an independent gin and pay a percentage of the crop. In addition to buying the machine itself, one had to have a two-story building to house it, the storage bin and lint room. Outside, one needed a giant wooden screw press to compress the cotton into the huge bales in which it was stored and shipped. Usually, both the gin and the press were driven by animal power, but more advanced planters were acquiring steam engines to drive their gins and mills. Farsighted owners built a large cistern nearby to collect water for fire fighting – a common threat around a gin.

As in town, water for a home was provided either by a well or cisterns, or better, a combination of the two. A home like Woodlawn had a pair of cisterns, one at each end. "All the necessary outhouses" included a carriage house, cotton sheds, a smokehouse, chicken coop, pig parlor, stock and feed barn, corn and potato barns, and for the more prosperous and independent, a smithy and a sawmill. In addition to the acreage for cash crops and extensive uncleared land for wood lots, there was a large kitchen garden, orchards of apple, pear, plum, peach and figs, walnut and pecan trees. Together with the slave quarters concentrated along roads leading to the fields, a plantation had the appearance of a little village.[131]

Photo 8. Two-story, dog-trot log cabin (Davies Plantation). Typical of the lesser planters and more wealthy yeoman farmer's home.

Most other farm homes were less pretentious, ranging from one or two room cabins through one story plantation style cottages to two story houses. Needham Harrison's father had built a six-room frame house. They had only 320 acres valued at $5,000, which were originally worked by 25 slaves, just qualifying them as planters as opposed to simple farmers. The father had originally built a "double 2 story hewed log house" which was later weather boarded and sealed. Needham had recently inherited the farm but only had eleven slaves on the eve of the war.[132] Perhaps the others had been divided out in the will or sold to pay debts, which was a common requirement for settling an estate.

Despite the usual descriptions of cotton as the cash crop, most farms and plantations were quite diversified, both for self-sufficiency and the market. Only about sixty percent of farmers produced any cotton for market, some producing fewer than ten bales. Even when cotton was the primary cash crop, corn was secondary, although it also served as feed for livestock which could be marketed. Wheat, a little rye, sweet and Irish potatoes, beans and peas were also cash crops, while everyone produced much of the produce, eggs and dairy products consumed at their tables. Sheep and cattle, but especially swine found their way to markets in the town and Memphis. Butter was marketed, but not milk. A few swineherds were quite sizable, with some small farmers focusing almost entirely on the sale of pork which fed off woodlots. Herds of sheep, sometimes sizable, also provided wool, both for homespun and the market. With the exception of honey which was purely for family consumption, all sweeteners had to be imported.[133]

As an example, we have Isham Howse once again. In mid-January, 1853, his two older sons hauled the last three bales of their cotton crop to Memphis, for which they got about $99. With most of this, they paid off a $75 debt to Street, Daugherty & Co., but ran up a further debt for supplies, since they held on to a precious $20 for some cash on hand. In February, they hauled in a load of wheat and paid another $75 off their debt. In May, they hauled in another wagon of wheat. They were also selling pork and sweet potatoes in Germantown and at White's Station, as well as trading sweet for white potatoes to eat. Meanwhile Howse, his friends, and neighbors were borrowing and repaying small amounts of cash among each other in order to cope with the cash-poor economy. Son Andy was also earning money on the side from local farmers hauling wood for the railroad from their woodlots.[134]

## Some Unusual Disturbances of the Peace.

Life in the town was not always quiet and convivial. There was one recorded homicide, on January 23, 1852. A coroner's inquest was held in town and the jury ruled that William W. Joyce had fatally stabbed William Trammell. The incident occurred in the presence of at least fifteen male and female witnesses. Joyce was a 26 year-old farmer who with his wife cared for three children, probably orphaned. Trammel was a newcomer or visitor to town, but so were many of the witnesses. Being a family man, Joyce did not flee, but remained and surrendered. He was charged with first degree murder, and pleaded not guilty. The charges sounded extreme. The indictment read that Joyce "feloniously willfully premeditatedly deliberately and of his malice of forethought did strike stab and thrust giving the said William Trammel then and there ... one mortal wound." The papers went further, referring to Joyce as repeatedly stabbing Trammel, despite the coroner's report of only one wound. In the face of all this, after posting bail, Joyce fled. By July, when the Sheriff heard that he had returned home, he summoned a posse, arrested and jailed him in Memphis. As late as October 8, the *Appeal* reported a mistrial, the jury being unable to agree "because of the illness of a member."[135]

What a frustrating story! We have no idea of what led to the killing. The killer just seems to have gone home and hung around, with neither the townsfolk, the constable nor the sheriff feeling compelled to do anything until he surrendered. After a hearing and posting bail, he apparently became fearful of his prospects and fled, only to return to his family. Then, either because of a chaotic court or because the cause of the incident was such that a jury could not agree on a verdict, the trial was postponed. Indeed the court records are most puzzling. From September 27 through October 1, the court met repeatedly only to adjourn each day because of jury problems. During that time, thirteen jurors refused to appear, and were fined $2.50 for contempt of court. Then the deputy sheriff was fined $5.00 for "failing to keep order in the court room." After continued jury problems, the case was held over until January. The court considered it necessary to bond the jurors and witnesses heavily.[136] Were Shelby County courts always so chaotic, or was there something special about this case?[137]

What is worse, there is no mention of the subsequent trial in either court records or the newspapers. Meanwhile, if Joyce's problems had not been enough, beginning in November four different creditors brought suit against him. Since they were all petty debts, they were handled by the justices of the peace, holding court in Germantown. Although all four debts together totaled less than three hundred dollars, since he had pledged all his property as credit, Joyce was in danger of losing his 500 acre farm. Both Drs. Morgan and Cornelius tried to come to his assistance with some of the debts.[138] At least all this seems to indicate that he had the sympathy of some of the town's more prominent citizens while his case was pending. Nevertheless, Joyce was apparently convicted, for he was serving a sentence in the Tennessee State Penitentiary in 1853.[139]

Perhaps this was not so atypical a murder trial for those times. "Honor killings" were part of the American culture, especially in the South and close to the frontier. Among "gentlemen," an affront to one's honor often resulted in a formal duel. More ordinary men settled their disagreements with knives, whips, or whatever else was at hand– their affair of honor usually being settled in the heat of the moment. Though officially illegal, prosecuted and punished, a violent defense of honor was still an accepted part of the culture for many, but not all. Howse, for instance, considered it homicide, no matter who or why.[140] Whether a homicide would be seen as justified would have depended heavily on the individual's reputation within his community. Apparently Joyce had a good one. Orphaned as a teenager, while his younger siblings had been apprenticed by the county, he had made the family farm work and established his own family. It was his sister who had been mistreated by Thomas Blakely. This may be why he and his wife had taken in orphans. But none of this was good enough for the county court. This incident tells us something about the culture of which Germantown was a part.

On the one hand, attitudes about formal dueling were complex.[141] Frowned upon by the churches and illegal, duelists were even barred from elected office in Tennessee. Yet the duels of gentlemen and wannabes usually escaped successful prosecution and were the subject of popular interests. Consistently up to 1861, Memphis papers reported local duels several times a year, and frequently from all over the South.[142] They were integral to the southern code of honor required of every man. There were clear double standards, however. While a gentleman planter could be esteemed for his dueling, if he otherwise displayed proper qualities, a yeoman like Joyce ran the risk of local determination to maintain law and order. His punishment may indicate that Shelby County's more "suburban" environment was subject to a greater determination to curb the brawling and mayhem of the lower orders. If true, this would indicate a significant progress toward more "modern" attitudes about law enforcement than normal in much of the South.[143]

With only one of what may have been an honor killing and no other recorded acts of serious violence in antebellum Germantown, one gets the impression of an unbelievably docile and law-abiding population for the age. Nevertheless, there was at least one potentially murderous man living in the area, for in October 1851, a Theophilus Hall from "somewhere near Germantown" reportedly rode all the way to Monroe County, Arkansas, to try to kill one Edward Jackson. Hall and "his friends" seem to have had a serious vendetta against Jackson.[144] At least, local people did not seem to have that much hostility directed toward each other.

The town's previously mentioned reputation for drunken brawling requires further exploration. The pattern of combining grocery stores and drinking establishments created a shopping environment that seems strange today. Each of the two bondings for merchant and tippling was a separate process, so the combination was not assumed. As part of the tipplers license, the proprietor had to promise to keep tax records of his sales in "spiritous and vinous liquors" and decks of playing cards, while maintaining "a peaceable and orderly house," with no gambling allowed. He also had to promise not to sell to any free person of color or to any slave without the written permission of his owner. Although fines for violating this bond were common in the county, no records of any around Germantown have survived.[145] One would suspect that the combination of store, frequented by women and children, with "saloon" curbed excessive drinking and rowdiness, at least during the day. Proper women simply avoided a few notorious grocery-store/saloons. Yet inebriation was a problem at least significant enough to mobilize some of the town's citizens for the temperance movement.

Unlike murders, small town accidents usually did not become news, but one that did tells us something more about town life. On March 25, 1852, P. A. Lewellin accidentally wounded James Kelly, Jr. Lewellin, concerned about his reputation, addressed a letter to the *Appeal* which included a testimony signed by Kelly, his parents and other family members verifying that it was an accident.[146] Obviously Kelly's wound was not serious. It also seems that folks were not as litigious as today, or area lawyers were not as fast on their feet. James Kelly Sr. was a laborer who had actually acquired a home of his own in town for his family of five children. One was James Jr., by then 21. Given the birth-places of his children, previously Kelly had to move about considerably within Tennessee and Mississippi to find enough work to support his growing family. How long he had been settled in Germantown is unclear. The signatures on the testimony reveal that it was family connections that helped Kelly take up roots in town and have a house. His in-laws were William Clark a grocer, and Joseph Clark, a wagon maker. The Clarks probably had helped their sister, Elizabeth, whose marriage had proven less successful. Unfortunately, Lewellin escapes all records, so we can know nothing of him or his relations with the Kelly and Clark families.

More tragic was a fire that had occurred a few weeks earlier. When Dr. Morgan's stable burned, eleven horses died in the conflagration. Morgan was keeping the stage office in conjunction with his hotel. Eight of the horses belonged to the stage contractor, a Mr. Sims. The fire was discovered too late to save the animals. It was blamed on the "carelessness of a negro boy." Despite the blame as reported in one newspaper, the *Appeal* observed that this was "the 3d instant, in the county."[147]

Although Memphis had a firefighting service, it is unlikely that the town had any means for dealing with fires other than a bucket brigade. There was at least one public water pump, with undoubtedly a horse trough, and many private cisterns. At best, the town might have formed a brigade of volunteers for a more organized response to fires. Rescuing people, animals and property was about the best they could do once a fire had established itself.

Fire struck again on July 12, 1860 when the Southern Star Cotton Gin Factory was destroyed. The proprietors suffered a heavy loss, about forty gins amounting to about fifteen to twenty thousand dollars, none of which was insured.[148] They would promptly set about rebuilding.

Undoubtedly the goriest event experienced in the town occurred one month later. The mangled remains of an unknown black man were found on the tracks, run over by the train the previous night. Several local gentlemen had to view the remains and testify as a coroner's jury as to cause of death. For the townsfolk, this was a shocking event, for unlike the people of Memphis, they were unaccustomed to finding bodies of vagrants and wanderers, the victims of homicides, accidents and exposure. Such people occasionally passed through town looking for odd jobs, but they had the decency to expire elsewhere. Fortunately, the county bore the expense of the pauper burial.[149]

In the weeks that followed, Germantown mothers undoubtedly used the occasion to admonish their children about the dangers of playing on the tracks. It was to little avail, however, for hopping a train became a favorite adventure for the boys. When freight trains had to slow to enter a siding outside the town, the boys could catch a ride into the station. Over the years, many took a painful fall, but there are no records of deaths or serious injuries.[150]

# Chapter 2

## Hierarchy and Harmony?

The genteel discreteness that characterized Southern propriety militated against records of disharmony among the town's citizens. To uncover such, one must often read between the lines. For example, after that Southern Star Gin Factory fire in 1860, by May 9, 1861, Joseph Neely and Stephen Trueheart announced that the factory was back in production. The issue of the *Appeal* that advertised the reopening also carried advertisements for a new Hurt Cotton Gin, manufactured by Hurt, Shepherd & Co., Germantown.[1]

This event hints at a rift among the town's entrepreneurs. Barry Hurt was the former foreman of the Southern Star plant, now marketing his own version of a gin. He claimed awards at the Memphis and West Tennessee fairs where it had proven superior to the Steel Comb and Cylinder Gin. What was more, "Capt. John M. Woodson, formerly connected with the above concern," was given as reference for the good performance of Hurt's gin.[2] Woodson was deeply in debt for his involvement in the burned Star Gin factory and must have withdrawn amidst some disagreement. Trueheart, Woodson's former partner, was now Neely's partner. The two companies ran prominent, competing advertisements in the papers for many months. Former partners and employees were now business rivals. To make the story even more intriguing, a Nashville newspaper had reported that the Star Gin fire was "supposed to have been the work of an incendiary."[3] Even if only a rumor, it speaks to what locals were thinking about those involved. This, unfortunately, is the only clue we have of the extent to which this rivalry generated animosities.

Whatever personal tensions this story may reveal, was there any social basis for more widespread disharmony in Germantown? Relations among classes in the antebellum South have been a subject of debate since that time.[4] Some insisted that theirs was a fully egalitarian and meritocratic society. Others argue that the planter class lorded it over small farmers and poor whites. Pursuit of this question leads to many useful insights into life in the Germantown area.

Fred Arthur Bailey gives "some comfort to" the school that insists there were class conflicts. His method involved a highly detailed statistical analysis of a collection of questionnaires completed by Tennessee Civil War veterans.[5] His conclusions are nuanced, but basically he argues that there were pronounced class distinctions and consciousness, if not tension, especially in areas like Shelby County. They make a good starting point for analyzing Germantown's society.

He describes planters, plain folk, and the poor living as neighbors, but their social patterns were vastly different. Wealth, education, and family connections enabled southern elites to move in much wider circles than other whites. Given these advantages, Tennessee's planters, professionals (attorneys, physicians, professors) and prosperous merchants were the important people. Many were vitally concerned with the defense of a southern culture based on the "peculiar institution." They fought the political battles, wrote the proslavery polemics, and defined the popular image of the South. Their community extended far beyond the confines of their rural environment, and their united self-interest caused them to lead their fellow Southerners into war.

Their fellow Southerners were primarily small landholders and tenant farmers. Bailey argues that their worldview was much more restricted. Lacking extensive formal education, relying more on subsistence agriculture and less on a market crop for a living, the plain folk concentrated on the immediate needs of their families and their close friends. The broader worlds of commerce and state or national politics rarely intruded into their daily routines. They were largely undisturbed by the nation-splitting debates over slavery and states' rights, focusing instead upon such community interests as crops, marriages, births, baptisms, and deaths.[6]

Finally, Bailey argues that it was the war and their disproportionately greater suffering that "made the poor and plain folk painfully aware that their needs were in fundamental conflict with those of the planters and professionals. Class resentment resulted."[7] Before the war, however, the classes simply lived in very different worlds, too preoccupied with their own to develop sharp animosities over those differences. Although Bailey's conclusions were based on questionnaires from all over the state, his statistical analyses often broke out the seven counties of Southwe55st Tennessee that clustered around Shelby, constituting a more unique part of the state. Through his work and that of others, we can also see other subtle differences that provide better insight into Germantown's specific society, but all these generalizations have to be tested against the primary evidence about antebellum Germantown.

As elsewhere, the Germantown society manifested socioeconomic distinctions among its citizens. Although everyone knew his "place," it was neither rigidly fixed nor defined. In 1861, an officer stationed in the town observed that one particular, nice lady "was one of the upper ten, rode in a carriage, and two mules to draw it, and a negro to drive."[8] It would be interesting to know if such a phrase as "the upper ten" was actually used in Germantown, and if so, was it just a generic for the upper crust (perhaps ten percent), or a literal list of ten families jockeying to maintain their status against the new families. Given a constant turnover in population, a strong sense of old families versus outsiders could not have been easily maintained. Newcomers would have been quickly assessed and given an "appropriate place" among locals. Initially the reception would have been gracious, as long as the newcomers were equally obliging. Given the closeness in time to the frontier experience, there was undoubtedly a sufficient sense of meritocracy for a newcomer to change the initial evaluation.

Below any such "upper ten" but part of their social circle, were the lesser plantation owners, professionals and successful merchants. Together, these constituted a social "elite." Below them were the yeomen farmers who owned fewer than twenty slaves and less acreage. Included among their rank would be some property-owning "respectable middle-class" merchants and artisans. Part of their identity was possessing at least one household slave or having a live-in white domestic. Renters could be included if of sufficient means otherwise. Only someone acquainted with the community would know how to class the single gentlemen, boarders of professional status or retired men with means among either the elite or the middle. To continue with Bailey's categories, the lower yet still respectable white-strata of society included yeomen farmers and artisans without slaves. Below them were the landless poor, with nothing to sell but their labor and little or no means to improve their lot.

In summary, Bailey tells us that Germantown's social structure should have consisted of four classes: (1) an elite of planters, professionals and merchants; (2) yeomen farmers who owned fewer than 20 slaves, lesser merchants, and well established "mechanics;" (3) yeomen farmers without slaves and small-scale business and craftsmen; and (4) the landless poor – farm, industrial and domestic labor.

Categorizing in this way is essential to the statistical analysis he offers, but such categories have limited value. This society was actually a continuum of families running from the wealthiest and most prestigious to the poorest and most degenerate, with no clear point of delineation between any categories. Nevertheless, we shall follow his reconstruction of this hierarchical society as a model to compare with specific examples.

Part of his analysis focuses on housing. The previous descriptions of houses in Germantown were based primarily on surviving examples, which represent the better constructed and those worthy of preservation. They belonged to the elite or very comfortable middle. The truly poor lived in simple log cabins or shacks, most with two rooms. This class moved about constantly, taking up residence in whatever housing available on the land they farmed. The non-slave-owning yeoman farmer fared better, with more commodious log cabins or frame houses of four or more rooms. A little more than half the small slaveholding farmers also lived in log cabins. Even a sizable minority of planters invested

Photo 9. An example of a substantial log cabin with sleeping loft. Probably typical of families that settled as yeoman farmers. (actual location, Baxter County, Arkansas)

Photo 10. Two-room, weather-boarded house. Most cooking and boiling of water for washing was done out doors. (Davies Plantation)

little in cosmetic improvements of their original log cabin, mostly adding extensions for more rooms and interior refinements. Being a planter was not always synonymous with luxury and gentility. Most of their houses, log or finished, were far more substantial, and comfortable, however. It was also not uncommon for this class to have more than one home. Their multiple landholdings could be widespread, including town or city residences as well.[9]

Given the serious omissions in both the 1860 agricultural and slave schedules for district eleven, only an approximate analysis of the economic status of its agriculturalists can be made. Where the slave count is obviously missing, the non-real property values provide clues. There were at least 23 who technically qualified as planters with over 20 slaves. Nevertheless, this is a misleading qualification, for at least 4 others holding fewer slaves were wealthier than others who qualified.

A breakdown of rural property and/or landed wealth does not reveal so grossly inequitable a distribution as elsewhere in the South. The top ten planters (10%) owned 39 percent of the land. The next eleven operating farms (12%) owned 28 percent. The next ten (10%) owned 14 percent. The next twelve (13%) owned 10 percent. The next twenty-one farmers (23%) owned 7 percent. The remaining twelve landed households (13%) held only 2 percent. The sixteen (17%) other agricultural households rented or leased. Since, however, renters were of wide ranging means, if non-landed resources could be factored in, the distribution would be even less extreme.

A full twenty-two percent would have been seen as reasonably wealthy. Below them the farmers descended smoothly from the comfortably independent yeomen down to the truly poor and landless. Poor is, of course, a relative term, for few of any status had much available cash or many material goods. Even many relatively poor were proud of their self-sufficiency and independence. In any case, there was no large element that would have considered itself hopeless in the context of the times. Of course, there were certainly some who would have felt totally alienated from and hostile toward their "betters," but nothing like a sizable, dangerous underclass. The community lacked the extremes of great wealth and the more gross inequities that create serious social tensions.

As already noted, the wealthiest and probably most prominent planter families were the Kimbroughs and Brooks. The third wealthiest was the widow, Sarah Jones. Since she was working her large estate with only 22 slaves, she must have been renting to tenants or employing white hands to cover the rest of her lands. Though still fourth in order of wealth, the Duke estate seems to have seriously reduced its slave population. Nevertheless, Benjamin Ellis topped them all in slave ownership with 111, one of only five men in the county with more than one hundred.[10]   Among the more prominent of the remaining planters was Phillip Tuggle, a minister.   In the adjacent districts, six more prominent planters oriented toward Germantown, including William Twyford north of the Wolf.  He was the first settler in the area other than Frances (Fanny) Wright, establishing himself in 1825.[11]  Although the largest landowner, Wright was no planter, but a mostly absentee landlord.[12]

In town, the infusion of other forms of wealth and prestige would have complicated perceptions of social rank.  There the major merchants, millers or industrialists and professionals moved in the circles of the elites.   Many owned slaves for business or industrial labor as well as household service.  They were often diversified, also owning plantation land.  Physicians and merchants ranged complexly in status, not just on the basis of wealth, but apparently also their families' roots in the area. The merchants, Samuel Mosby and Albert Wood, were the wealthiest, ranking just below the top ten planters, but unless the slave schedules are in error, they ran their sizable businesses and homes without slaves. Aside from a few, the numerous physicians and their differences in education undoubtedly placed some outside the elite.   The more respectable, Cornelius and Moore, were working 12 and 8 slaves respectively, apparently at farming, although service probably preoccupied some.  Academy teachers and professors were a welcome addition as symbols of the community's cultural quality.   Reverend Evans' academic credentials garnered him highest status, while Pastor Tuggle stood among the second rank of planters, but as a newcomer. Even as teachers, the Pettit sisters shared their father's status among the elite, as women allowed to assume a "position," as opposed to employment.  The family of teachers in the Webb School was equivalent to the yeoman slaveholder category, which is probably why they titled themselves farmers in the censuses rather than teachers.   By 1860, however, Monroe Webb titled himself "gentleman," while his teacher-sister listed no occupation, being a proper farmer's wife.[13]  Below them the other pedagogues descended all the way to the lowest social levels.

The involvement of planters in non-agrarian pursuits casts an interesting light on the argument that elsewhere in the South the conservative, even reactionary, social influence of the planter elite mitigated against modernizing economic trends.  The slave economy, traditional values and family pressures allegedly restricted the occupational horizons of young men to agriculture.   Educational disadvantage made it even more difficult for young men below the planter class.   Northerners and immigrants had the edge in other careers.[14]  Here again, Germantown differed from such a deep-South environment – a town that simply supported an agricultural community. In Germantown's district eleven, of the eighteen craftsmen or mechanics only three were born outside the South. Thirteen who had found careers in white-collar occupations ranging from merchant to clerk were southern born. Of course, among the storekeepers there were the five Germans, plus an Englishman and a northerner. In the book agent consortium, one southerner was outnumbered by four northerners and an Irishman. The professionals, however, including lawyers and ministers were entirely southerners, including all ten physicians. Especially notable were the four or five "industrialists," who were bringing their forms of employment to town. On the other hand, one has to concede that once merchants and professionals established themselves, they frequently invested in plantation farming and slave owning.[15] There, however, they met the planter and more prosperous yeoman who were coming the other way, diversifying not just into real estate speculation and the cotton trade, but also other mercantile and industrial ventures. Among planters, professionals and businessmen alike, the popular speculation in railroad stock was probably also common, but such records simply are not available.

Again because of omissions in the census, the slave owning farmers cannot be numbered precisely, but there were at least 7 of them, probably more. Some among them were active enough in the community for their names to crop up in other records, George Sheppard (or Shepherd), John Gray, several Callises, and Jobe Lewis among them. To draw a clear line between slaveholders and the non-slaveholders is impossible, except for that one difference. The remaining yeomen farmers numbered about 25, but at least 3 renters exceeded the resources of several yeomen owners. At least one farmer who rented his land had two slaves, and our frequently mentioned Isham Howse had four.

Bailey was clear that slave ownership did not constitute a real divide among yeomen farmers. The yeoman farmers, whether slaveholding or not, renters or owners, were independent and proud of their work and what it brought them. A lack of slaves produced little difference in their sense of having had economic opportunity, which was generally quite positive. Blanche Clark's analysis of Tennessee's yeomen farmers presents them as essentially one class, running along a continuum based more on other wealth and resources than on slaveholding.[16] Census statistics bear this out for Germantown.

Unfortunately Clark's statistical analysis did not include Shelby County, but she did cover adjacent Fayette, which closely resembled rural Shelby. Between 1850 and 1860, farmers holding between 35 and 150 acres generally improved their lot, with slaveholding being a variable rather than a constant factor. Slaveholders frequently had more value in livestock and farm implements but not always. "The differences in value were never great enough to set the two groups completely apart. Nor was a man's property due to the fact that he owned a slave; he owned a slave merely because he had a bit of surplus cash to invest. On the whole the non-slaveholder compared favorably to the slaveholder who cultivated a similar acreage." Among the smaller farmers holding fewer than 40 acres, the non-slaveholder often fared better. Perhaps such small farmers had too ambitiously invested in a slave.[17]

As Clark put it, "Unless morally opposed to the institution, many non-slaveholders aspired to slaveholding eventually." A man could "relieve his wife from the necessities of the kitchen and the laundry, and his children from the labors of the field."[18] The motive was no different from today's marginal family aspiring to have cars, many appliances and TVs – as coarse as that may sound.

According to Bailey, the world of the yeoman farmer was distinct from either the class above or below. Highly self-sufficient, they had minimal contact with the commercial world. Their work-a-day life and their ties with family, neighbors and church theoretically consumed all their time, leaving little or none for politics or cultural pursuits. Nevertheless, he reported that in southwest Tennessee, a full third would rise above common school educations to attend academies, and a small percentage would go on to college levels.[19] Of those in district eleven who rented their land, the vast majority sent children to school, but usually not into their teen years.

Clark disagreed with Bailey's description of yeomen as narrowly focused on their local world. "The non-slaveholder took an active interest in politics and was usually better versed than his northern compatriot in political affairs of the day. This was partly due to the stump speakings and political barbecues which were so popular in the South."[20] Indeed Isham Howse, a yeoman farmer, certainly was not apolitical and uninformed. He subscribed to the *Eagle and Enquirer,* monitored international affairs as well as national politics and discussed them, attended and commented on political speeches, voted his Whig convictions, and worried over growing secessionist tendencies.[21]

Since the typical yeoman managed fifty to one-hundred and fifty acres, that certainly tied his life inescapably into the seasonal rhythm of nature. Plowing depended on how late seasonal rains lasted, and when the bottom lands dried. From dawn to dark, he plowed his cleared lands, crisscrossing back and forth. The common simple plow did not break up the soil adequately until after numerous passings. He raced against time to get in the summer crops of cotton, corn and oats. May and June were consumed chopping weeds until the tender crops were established. Then oats and winter wheat had to be harvested. Much of this labor involved the entire family, especially in families without slaves or hired hands. Only when the major crops were laid-by in July was there any free time. The children could get in a couple of months of schooling, while the men could hunt and fish, and everyone visited and attended church socials and revivals. Then from September through autumn they were again fully preoccupied with the harvest, especially cotton. School was hit or miss until winter. It was also time to plow and sow the fields that would host the winter wheat. When cool weather set in, the pigs, a major source of meat and income, were butchered and the meat prepared. Although winter also allowed for some free time, repairs and maintenance of tools, equipment and buildings demanded attention.[22]

Despite this demanding lifestyle, Germantown's yeoman was not the hillbilly who rarely got beyond his mountain valley. Most had moved from other states or counties, and would do so again. Meanwhile, for business and visiting they traveled several times a year as far afield as several counties and frequented Memphis. Likewise they regularly received and hosted visitors – family and friends. They may not get to great cities and resorts, but they were not isolates. Neither were they uncultured or illiterate. Their four-room house might even contain a piano or a real violin; otherwise they manufactured their own instruments. They corresponded almost daily with family and friends.[23]

The world of a wide range of craftsmen, mechanics and petty merchants was not that dissimilar in terms of time-demanding economic pressures. In the jargon of the age, "mechanic" seems to have replaced the older guild-age terms, artisan or craftsman. Although blacksmiths and carpenters were essential to the community and generally respected citizens, some lacked the means to own enough of their own tools, much less to have their own shop. When they were dependent on others to practice their trades, they occupied a less clearly defined social position, "journeyman." In contrast, the independent blacksmith or carpenter provided such a wide range of indispensable tools and services that he acquired some wealth and property.

In 1860, the town's two wagon makers illustrate how widely such a family's economic status could vary. Lon Rhodes could run a business staffed by twelve slaves, adults and children. Well established, he and his business would survive the war, risen to the status of merchant. In contrast, James Helley was on his own and would be gone by 1870. The two blacksmiths also differed in their establishment. John Slough had two male slaves for his work, while the family also maintained three women and a child in service. Telip or Telix Mendenall worked without slaves in his rural location, but was also independently established. Neither would be present by 1870.[24]

The status of such mechanics was apparently more complex than that of yeomen and poor farmers. On the one hand, as a journeyman laborer the average mechanic could earn up to five hundred dollars per year, the equivalent of a plantation overseer or a clerk. Yet mechanic laborers were considered socially lower than the poorest independent farmer. Perhaps that is why the prominent Mr. Molitor labeled himself machinist rather than mechanic. This would seem to be a title falling somewhere between mechanic and engineer, the latter requiring higher-education credentials.[25] Once established, however, artisans or mechanics could range along the social ladder from the equivalent of the small slaveholder to the slaveless farmer. Such status hinged on the ownership of property and equipment as well as slaves.

Given their portrayal in literature and film, overseers constitute an interesting intermediate class, socially well below the planter, and not independent like the yeoman. Most were not "poor," but younger men aspiring to be upwardly mobile. They were usually sons of farmers, for they had to know all the ends and outs of getting their particular crops through the entire process up to market.[26] In district eleven, the planters provided houses for six overseer families who had also accumulated some non-real property. Forty-nine year-old James Watson had $4000 worth, and undoubtedly moved on to better things. Although most generally aspired to becoming planters, the German immigrant William Essmann, who had acquired $2000, established himself in a grocery/saloon and would remain a local citizen. But forty-seven year-old William Wells, with a wife and seven children, who had amassed only $150 in possessions, was clearly stuck, although he may have been happy with his lot. Similarly George Griffin at forty-five had a wife, four children and a mother-in-law to support with no accumulated property.

Like most other local citizens, there was a gap between aspirations and ability or good fortune. Of the remaining six overseers who boarded with the planter, none had acquired any material wealth by 1860. Five of them were young single men just beginning, All were dead or had gone elsewhere by 1870. Since so much depended on the abilities of the overseer, planters were quick to fire, especially if they could not keep the slave operations running smoothly. Their days were sun-up to sun-down, like the slaves whom that had to stay on top of. The hardest part of their job was being what we would call labor relations experts. They had to have control and run an efficient operation, but if they used so much force that slaves complained to master or mistress, they could lose their jobs.[27] They stood between master and slaves with all that implied.

In the seven county block of Southwest Tennessee, 43 percent of the non-slaveholders were landless. In district eleven, however, only 16 seemingly farm families listed no real property. Two others were apparently widows with no recorded resources. The median wealth of 8 such families with less than $1000 in resources was just $290. Three other landless farm families listed absolutely no property of value. Ten other single men were obviously farm hands, boarding with their employer. Several men who may have been laborers, but who listed no occupation were scattered throughout the population. Of seven families with no resources but with children, only three were sending any of them to school (5 out of 17 children).  Such was the self-perpetuating nature of their position.

A simple laborer could earn as little as five dollars a month plus board.  Twenty-five to fifty cents a day was good.  Twelve dollars a month was extraordinary.  Some who rented land had to do extra work to make ends meet.  Such itinerant farmers moved about regularly, owning only a mule and a cow.  With few to no prospects for improving themselves or seeing their children advance, up against the wall of having to compete with slave labor, theirs was seemingly a life of squalor and depression.  Nevertheless, among the state's veterans of this class who completed questionnaires, almost two-thirds felt that economic opportunity had been available to save enough to buy land or set up in business.[28]  Of course, those likely to have been able to respond were probably the exceptionally successful among them.  The almost complete departure of all members of this class from the area between every census seems to belie the idea that there was much opportunity "in the community" for them.  Bailey concludes that they "sank into the social background; they were largely ignored by both the yeomen ... and the planters...."[29]

Ostensibly near the bottom of Germantown's social scale in 1850, was James Kelly.  That 45 year-old, previously-discussed laborer probably had no room to host boarders, no mater how badly his family needed the extra income.  The house they owned, valued at $50, would probably have attracted only the most desperate boarder.  But nothing better indicates the problems of using financial data to assess social status and community relations than Kelly's story.  That shooting accident provided unusual insights into a real case.  Although his pattern of moving constantly to find work fits the poor-laborer model, his ability to own a humble house does not.  He had ties to the Clark families, a grocer and a wagon maker, respectable families of independent means.  Family ties are an element that usually escapes statistical analysis and greatly complicates efforts to define social relationships.

In town, laborers usually boarded.  Many "untitled" boarders were probably unskilled workers in the family home or business.  If they lived in the family's house, their condition and status was far better than if they slept in one of the outbuildings.  This difference brings up the point that not all these propertyless young men appearing as laborers were of propertyless underclass origins.  Many were of respectable yeoman or mechanic origins with no inheritance, beginning to establish themselves through honest labor.

The many young female boarders were either domestics or workers.  Their status would have depended on either having a skill or being placed with family or friends.  Orphans and daughters of the poor would have depended totally on the character of the family that employed them for their future prospects. Those "lucky" enough to be apprenticed had at least some legal protection. Increasingly, however, the county paid families to care for orphans without extended family, and local families contributed to their education. As one sign of *noblesse oblige*, elite ladies might also provide a home for a "respectable" girl, whose family was strapped, providing training to prepare for a better future.[30]

Given the positive self-images and relative wellbeing of such a large part of the population, did social and economic differences generate attitudes that fostered tension and hostility? Although managing ostensibly involved little hard physical labor, most of the elite considered themselves self-made and hard working, especially those who had cleared their lands and built their empires. They often demanded physical labor from their sons to instill a work ethic and a Christian morality. Yet their resources provided enough leisure for some cultural polish. The decade before the war also brought an era of gentility and ease, and perhaps with it an element within this class that disdained manual labor, conspicuously consumed, exhibited pretentious airs, and snubbed the lesser classes – those characteristics traditionally associated with the low country Southern elite planters. We may never know how badly they infected Germantown, if at all.

Otherwise, a few first-hand descriptions of local attitudes about social classes, work ethics, and the community's social relations have survived to enable us to test Bailey's generalizations. Unfortunately, some are the turn-of-the century memories of elderly Confederate veterans, and were undoubtedly subject to nostalgia and romanticizing. One also needs to read them critically for class blindness. They were also probably reacting defensively to the loaded questions designed to "test" negative beliefs about the slaveholding class and about the South in general.

Three such questions were:

18. Was honest toil – as plowing, hauling and other sorts of honest work of this class – regarded in your community? Was such work considered respectable and honorable?

19. Did white men in your community generally engage in such work?

20. To what extent were there white men in your community leading lives of idleness and having others do their work for them?[31]

One local planter insisted that his father "superintended his farm, also assisted in all necessary work." They all asserted that honest physical labor was regarded as respectable and honorable, and that white men generally performed such work. Only a "very few" idlers relied entirely on slaves for the work. John Kirby described his work as a boy as primarily bookkeeping, but "White men did work when necessary."

Needham Harrison remembered that as a boy he "did all that came to hand on farm, could and did do all kinds of farm work."[32]

These two former planters, who represented the full spectrum within their class, denied any form of social discrimination or snobbery relating to differences in slave ownership. Instead social relations were allegedly friendly and owners and non-owners met with equality in public gatherings. John Kirby did not think that slave ownership played a role in politics.[33] The few records of public meetings plus the military elections of officers do indicate a general sense of equality, at least above the level of landless farmers. Nevertheless, everywhere in the state higher political office was often the realm of the elite and comfortable middle.[34] As we shall see in chapter 4, in civil district eleven, the elected offices fell mostly to professionals, mechanics and established yeomen. In the office of constable, the farmer Job Lewis, an example of a modestly well-established farmer, became entrenched in a position that brought him political standing. Needless to say, such offices were never held by the small holder. None would have had the time or the resources to afford it.

Of course, former planters responding to these questions would not have been as sensitive about discrimination as would people below their social level. Finally, the phrasing of the question about "respectable, honorable men" probably precluded from their minds the class of property-less laborers, or certainly that element among them commonly referred to as "poor white trash." Certainly within the full range of Germantown society, they would have made distinctions about whom to invite into one's home. Although the relatively recent ending of the frontier environment mitigated social snobbery among longer-time residents, perhaps the more recent plantation buyers behaved differently.

Certainly the Dukes of the "upper ten" socialized freely with their new neighbors, the marginal farmer-family of the Howses. The wives regularly visited one another, while the children played together and even over-nighted at one or the other house. The husbands had many discussions of current events as well as their work. The Dukes provided neighborly assistance without making it seem like charity, which it probably was not.[35]

As an example of upward mobility with support from social betters, Isham Howse described his future business partner's climb from very poor origins. His success grew from both hard work and the kind support of his "betters."

> Tom Brady ... I have known him intimately for many
> years, from before he was grown. He has had cramped
> opportunities. Of indigent parents, he had to labor as a
> bond servant for his father. ... His educational
> opportunities have been very scanty. Larkin Echoles was

his early friend, and assisted him some, receiving in return, in labor upon his farm, as a common hand, full compensation. ... Tom has lived with me, as a clerk, for a good while, and has boarded with me in my house as one of my family. ... Although uneducated, he is a man of talents and of much promise. He is an honest man ... honest-hearted in every sense of the word. It is therefore needless to add that he is a gentleman in the broadest sense of the word.[36]

This clearly describes a meritocratic society that would accept into "respectability" anyone who pulled himself up to the status of economic self-sufficiency. Although they might judge its "losers" harshly if theirs was not a case of unavoidable misfortune, they assisted any who seemed willing and able.

Yet a majority of the poor of southwest Tennessee, unlike the rest of the state, felt there had been some social conflict. A sizable percentage of them considered that conflict significant. The farther west one went in the state, the greater the sensitivity to such conflict. The greater presence of slavery was not the only factor. The entire western end of the state may have generated higher expectations of opportunity and meritocracy as a result of its more recent frontier status.[37] Between 1850 and 1860, almost the entire non-propertied population had sought their advancement elsewhere and left the Germantown area. Mobility was clearly a factor in having economic opportunity.

Another barometer of social status and tensions was education. There the complex and contradictory nature of Southern elitism is more clearly revealed. Most importantly, the established dominated the school board, controlling the distribution of state funds, and determined what if any local taxes would be levied for additional support. The preferred private schools usually served their own family needs, so their decisions were driven by their perception of how much the "lower" classes desired or appreciated educational opportunity. Clearly the early 1850s hiatus in the common schools of the district indicates a low point in that perception. Perhaps equally important, however, it turned around.

Nevertheless, the elite did devote unremunerated time to the management of the common schools and sometimes built the school buildings at their personal expense. Before the common schools, elite families had guaranteed the educational expenses of orphans and the school board provided tuition for the destitute. Also those who ran the private schools provided scholarships for deserving students with insufficient means. Finally, tuition at local private schools was below the average, lessening the barrier.[38] Certainly the commitments to public education of the prestigious Pettit family are unquestionable, and their arrival in town helped generate the birth of the common schools. The elite seem to have subscribed to the principle of upward mobility through education for all classes, although they were undoubtedly not fully sensitive to the inherent barriers faced by the lower classes. The intrinsic "indifference" to education by the poor based on the necessities of life made it a self-fulfilling prophesy that they would forgo the opportunity more often than not. Despite the genuine *noblesse oblige* of the elite, lower socioeconomic status seriously curtailed opportunity for the majority of the landless poor and some non-slaveholding yeomen. The more unfortunate among them would remain "shiftless and ignorant," as they were often described.

According to Bailey's compilations of Tennessee veterans' questionnaires, in southwest Tennessee the poor received 25% good quality education, the slaveless yeomen 31.2%, while the slaveholding received 37.8% and the elite 73.9%. Generally speaking, these figures were far superior to the rest of the state across all classes and far more equitable.[39] In the counties surrounding Shelby, 68% of the total attended common schools exclusively while 32% went on to academies, as opposed to the rest of the state which averaged 92% and 8% respectively.[40] Memphis undoubtedly skewed these statistics. Across the state, higher or college education with its access to the elite was more grossly unbalanced.[41] The Germantown area undoubtedly shared in a greater level of educational opportunity. Ironically, perhaps the greater educational opportunity in southwest Tennessee helps explain the greater differences in awareness of social conflict than elsewhere in the state.[42] Those who failed to benefit felt it more.

Jennifer Boone, who has also analyzed the veterans' questionnaires, criticizes Bailey for being "most taken...with those (among the respondents) who emphasize distinctions and antagonisms." Emphasizing the strong majority from across the state who were "not aware of differences," she argues that mostly Tennesseans "mingled freely." She notes, "Showing benevolence to neighbors appears as a well-respected tradition.... More than one veteran mentions, for example, the custom of giving away fresh meat to poorer neighbors, a practice confirmed by some former non-slaveholders."[43]

This example of what most contemporaries would have considered to be Christian behavior brings us to her strongest argument. Most respondents "pointed particularly to two institutions, the local church and the community school, that clouded, and sometimes completely obscured, significant economic differences." Indeed in Germantown, the Baptist, Methodist and Cumberland Presbyterian churches "emphasized an individual and personal salvation and had few conventions, like pew rents, that distinguished between richer and poorer church members." All three were grass-roots religions that rejected the aristocratic elements within Anglicanism. Despite their increasing support for slaveholding, "they remained organizations that sustained a feeling of spiritual equality in the face of secular inequality. Some respondents singled out church as the one place where everyone mingled on equal footing, regardless of economic or social standing."[44]

There is no doubt that the services and the social events of these churches as well as their charitable outreach helped homogenize the community and provided moments of true Christian unity. One familiar with all three of these southern protestant churches knows both the strengths and weaknesses of this argument. Finally, none of this takes into consideration the non-churchgoing and even anti-religious elements. Despite their invisibility in the surviving records, they were present. Perhaps they help account for those who felt more hopeless and unaccepted.

Unfortunately, her argument about the leveling influences of the community schools holds less water. "Not only was at least a few months' attendance at one of the old 'field schools' a common experience for many of these veterans, but the values preached through antebellum schoolbooks provided ample encouragement for individualism and equality."[45] The data do indicate that even the education that was available created opportunity for advancement. But the preference for private schooling meant that the common schools that the elite avoided provided less opportunity for social mixing. Finally it is naive to argue that the influence of the ideals propagated in a hit-or-miss schooling was strong enough to undermine the lessons of the harsh reality of a life of poverty and violence.

Adding further to a more nuanced picture of Tennessee's antebellum life, Boone concluded that "Women noticed the differences, and the wealthier ones often made enough of them that more than one veteran pointed out that women did not mingle together as freely as the men did. 'Sometimes I have heard the women folks say of other women,' wrote one veteran, 'Oh, she is stuck up because she has a Negro.'" Others verified that women of slaveholding families discriminated against those without slaves unless they had respectable professional status. When such women extended charity to less fortunate women with an air of condescension, they certainly fueled resentments rather than the gratitude they expected. The working and sporting life of most men was still simple or crude enough that it provided for more bonding and leveling.[46]

Isham Howse spoke constantly of wealthy neighbors like the Dukes and of professionals and businessmen who provided loans and assistance. Neighbors came to nurse them when illness struck especially hard. This sensitive man experienced no social condescension. He himself had helped disadvantaged young men rise above their origins. He spoke admiringly of those who had pulled themselves up to be his social and economic equals. His journal complements those veterans whose memories were of a society of meritocracy and mutual support that transgressed class barriers.

Unfortunately, Howse failed to mention any locals who were truly of the underclass, down and out, embittered or beat down. It was as though none existed, which confirms Bailey's picture of the truly poor. They, sometimes called "poor white trash," were distinct from the yeomen, mechanics, and "honest laborers." As Clark put it, they were "held in contempt by white people and Negroes alike."[47] They cannot be identified with any reliability from among the other "poor" individuals in the census. Their absence from any contemporary descriptions of the area's prewar life implies social invisibility. If they had failed to rise through "honest labor," and were not victims of genuine misfortune, were they considered worthy of charity? Could their children expect anything more than pity? Were they feared as a possible source of crime or vandalism?

Clark's conclusions about social conflict strikes one as more consistent with what one would expect to find in Germantown. "There were, indeed, social distinctions in (such a) society, the same ones which may be found in communities in any period of history. ... It was true that in the South, in particular, a family name often gave a person a place in society which his economic status did not warrant. But ... an accumulated fortune aided in dispensing with the necessity of a family name. ... Of course, there was some antagonism between slaveholders and non-slaveholders." There are always some haughty rich who keep aloof. "More often, however, the feeling of antagonism seemed to come from the poor non-slaveholder."[48] Of course, "antagonism" was felt by the lower class rather than the upper. Clark also had to acknowledge that there was some feeling that slave-owning constituted status.

Boone went beyond Bailey's analysis to cast light on the few who were the true social under-class. She included the data that contrasted the responses of Federal veterans from Tennessee to those of Confederates. Federal veterans showed a far higher belief that they had little chance for economic opportunity (41%) than did Confederates (only 10%). As Boone points out, "These Federal veterans may have perceived themselves as locked in a society that afforded them bleak social and economic futures. Such a society would not be worth fighting for. Confederate veterans, on the other hand, were willing to fight for what they perceived to be a beneficial way of life."[49] This brings us to Bailey's arguments about the war and its effects on social relationships. The wartime experiences, however, must wait until the later chapters to be explored.

Wyett-Brown's analogy of social relations as being more fraternal then patriarchal rings true. If there was no rigid hierarchy, there were clearly significant social differences. With such came an expectation of deference, but not subservience. Deference would be duly given in the same vein as that towards one's elders. In return, as he puts it, "Being affable and condescending was required of the man with rank, but clearly the lower the subject of such attention the less solicitous one had to be." Such interpersonal relations were "bound to be uneasy and, at times, unpredictably violent."[50]

In short, we can assume that before the war Germantown was not without some social tensions and resentments (and some Know-Nothing discrimination as discussed in the next chapter). It probably bubbled mostly below the surface with the more discontented pulling up stakes and going elsewhere. By and large, however, when times were good there was considerable cohesion among the propertied classes, with Christian charity and neighborliness incorporating those below. The test of community cohesion would soon come, however. With politics, there were other sources of tension, but what is more, the above focuses only within white society.

### *Slaveholders and Slave Life*

Although the above account has often mentioned slaves and slavery, it would seem they should have been more central to a picture of white people, whose cohesiveness was reinforced by racial tension and prejudice. Nevertheless, as Bertram Wyatt Brown has argued in his study of Southern life and culture,

> White Southerners seldom forgot the presence of blacks; nevertheless, what mattered most to them was the interchanges of whites among themselves. That is what dominated whites' everyday life, no matter how dependent so many were upon the unceasing toil of the unfree. Had it been otherwise, slavery would have been even more oppressive than it was. Whites' jockeying for positions in their own world gave the underclass some room for fashioning lives apart. Intrusiveness and over concern, sometimes well intentioned, must have been a serious vexation for those in the slave quarters. They preferred to be left alone.[51]

Though undoubtedly accurate and insightful into both black and white lives, this aspect of the Southern mentality has to be squared with their need to worry about the proper management of a frequently troublesome, potentially explosive, but essential energy source. Again, for another crass comparison, few of us worry overly about either the explosive fuel of our automobiles, their safety, or their environmental impact. Instead we have a complex, love-hate relationship with our cars.

In the 1850 census which broke out data on the town itself, there were 31 households with 163 whites and 82 slaves, many undoubtedly serving as domestics, others as workers in town. In the rest of district eleven, there were 1,179 slaves. In 1860 for all of district eleven, the slave schedules listed only 1,168 – not an accurate count.[52] Correlations between the slave schedules and the personal property holdings of the white population, plus other records, make it clear that many slaves are absent from the fifteen pages of forms. The census taker missed entire plantations as well as small holders. The slave population had probably grown by at least two hundred.

In 1860, living in the county outside Memphis there were only 78 "free coloreds," but none were recorded in the districts around Germantown in 1850 or 1860.[53] The absence of freemen in the district resulted primarily from lack of opportunities for freemen, but they were also probably not allowed residence. The reason was white fears, at least according to the well-substantiated argument of Steve Baker. A prime indicator of this was the laws passed in Tennessee at state, county and local levels to control blacks, both free and slave.[54]

During the early decades of settlement, race relations in West Tennessee had been relatively good, given the frontier life style. Many freemen came west for that benefit. In Tennessee, freemen could vote, and in Shelby County the idea of gradual emancipation was popular. The mood gradually shifted, however, as cotton farming became increasingly important, bringing with it a large population of slaves. Then after the Nat Turner slave revolt of 1831, attitudes in Tennessee hardened. The legislature took away voting rights, passed a law forbidding free blacks from immigrating into the state, and required that freemen be sent out of state upon emancipation. Subsequently exceptions were added, but all such waivers required severe restrictions on the freeman's life, and violations resulted in veritable reinslavement. In Memphis in 1850, the city imposed tight restrictions on the movement and assembly of slaves and their association with freedmen.[55] In the county, courts decided on the petitions of freemen and exercised supervision. Even communities like Germantown could add their own constraints. The concern was the fear that they or their simple presence incited revolt and escape.[56]

Although Germantown was hardly a market in the local slave trade, occasional auctions did occur in town, usually at the railroad depot. For instance, to settle an estate, a slave named Sam was auctioned there for the sum of $1,070. The heirs of Sam's owner were apparently opposed to the sale, which had to be forced through court order.[57] One can only guess what kinds of relationships Sam was torn from by this sale.

Aside from acknowledging the inherent evil of the institution, we need to be cautious about oversimplifying the slave experience. The recorded memories of former slaves are replete with examples of life experiences that confound efforts at generalization, without romanticizing them. Not only were owners individuals whose personalities greatly affected the experience of slaves, but the slaves were equally individuals with unique personalities. Although a bold, aggressive, cocky, or ill-tempered personality could prove fatal to a slave under many circumstances, in others they proved advantageous. A few got away with unbelievable acts of defiance or simple self-assertion. Sometimes, they were even protected by their masters from punishment by others zealous to enforce controls.[58]

Southerners like to believe that their ancestors were good to their slaves. Some undoubtedly were. Although no slaves were listed in the schedule for the two Callis households, there were a few. The girl who would become Molly Rankin stayed on with them after emancipation, working as cook while her husband worked the Callis farm. Whatever reasons kept her "home," the Callis' generosity continued in the form of free housing for their growing family.[59] But being "good" to slaves was a relative term. It usually meant employing incentives rather than brutal enforcement and offering rewards or treats beyond just providing the most basic needs. Yet neither paternalism nor Christian kindness compensated for the degradation of enslavement.

During the war and occupation, the many who stayed or returned to work with former owners probably had mixed motives. The slave population responded diversely when the opportunity to escape occurred. Undoubtedly a full spectrum of real-life personalities distinguished those who remained. A few were sufficiently attached to their owner families that they stayed out of concern for the welfare of the white women and children left alone. Some preferred the relative comfort or security of a known working-living relationship, especially if the owner offered incentives. Others were successfully suppressed and unable to visualize opportunities elsewhere.[60]

Since both master and slave were human beings, close relations could develop among them despite the barriers. The number of slaves held was a factor. The owner of a few, in town or country, worked and lived more intimately with his slaves. On large plantations, the field hands were often under an overseer. Even there, many mature household slaves acquired the status of "members-of-the-family," and considerably more freedom than the usual slave. A personal or body servant had often grown up with his or her master/mistress. Compared to the alternatives, someone with little hope might be content with such a status, but not grateful.[61] One extreme example was the relationship between Randolph Webb and his servant Amos. When Webb died, he left Amos his gold watch in appreciation of his service, and when Amos died he insisted on and was buried by his master in the family plot. The inscription of the headstone read, "Well Done. Thy Good Faithful Servant."[62] Although such warm relations undoubtedly did develop, they depended on the continued subordinate status of the slave. A trusted and adept slave could become a driver, in charge of a work gang of other slaves and would receive special treatment. Especially trusted men could assume administrative and even managerial positions.[63]

Slave women or girls frequently bore the offspring of their masters or overseers. Of course, white wives and mothers usually considered this a moral morass for the men folk.[64] In the 1860 slave census in Shelby County, 2,783 of the 16,953 slaves were mulatto, but there were distinct variations in district eleven. In a few cases, high concentrations of mulattoes on a particular plantation may indicate that there had been a "breeding program" or the presence of one or more exploitative white men. When such children were not simply doomed to a life of slave labor, the father provided some education and training, and perhaps a small stake, emancipated them and sent them elsewhere to earn a living. Since the 1860 census reported that 64 percent of the free Black population was mulatto, while only 16 percent of the slaves were, it appears that owners who sired children emancipated them far more frequently than other slaves. Specifically, Shelby County's ratio of freed mulattoes was 178 to 2,783 who were not. This was a far higher ratio than among freed "blacks" at 98 to 14,170.[65]

Slavery is actually a moral and psychological trap for the masters. To exploit slaves and to live with one's conscience, one needed justifications. It is the business of the intellectual leaders of a society to provide such justifications for its institutions. During the 18th and 19th centuries, as products of the psychological needs generated by slavery and imperialism, the emerging natural sciences produced a pseudo-scientific "body of knowledge," a "racial science" that "proved" the inferiority of non-white "races," to reinforce the "common sense" knowledge of white superiority. Of course, lawyers and judges also made their contributions by treating slaves as property and appealing to constitutional and common law guarantees about property rights. Laws written by slave owners made anyone who sought to undermine them in any way a criminal instead of a moral role model.

The Dred Scott decision probably marked the high water mark in legal justification. The decision increased North-South divisions. Yet the language of the majority opinion written by Chief Justice Taney may have been less offensive to most citizens everywhere. Taney probably captured the racial beliefs and attitudes of the majority of white Americans. He attributed to the founding fathers deeply rooted beliefs that denied citizenship to blacks.

> (Negroes) had for more than a century before been regarded as beings of inferior order, and altogether unfit to associate with the white race, either in social or political relations, and so far inferior, that they had no rights which

the white man was bound to respect; and that the negro might justly and lawfully be reduced to slavery for his benefit. ... The opinion was at the time fixed and universal in the civilized portion of the white race. It was regarded as an axiom in morals as well as politics, which no one thought of disputing, or supposed to be open to dispute, and men in every grade and position in society daily and habitually acted upon it in their private pursuits, as well as in matters of public concern, without doubting for a moment the correctness of this opinion.[66]

Although opposition to slavery had grown since the founding father's time, beliefs about the "races" had changed little.

My references to "justifications" should not be taken to mean that slave owners consciously concocted a mythology they did not truly believe. It constituted part of the "consensus reality," that body of self-evident, common sense knowledge that every "reasonably rational" member of any society can plainly see. To question it raises doubts about either one's rationality or motives. In the first place, such thinking was nearly universal in the Western world, even where no longer used to justify slavery. In Christian slaveholding societies, it constituted a world view that one embraced and defended against obviously subversive ideas. Upholding such an order was a Christian duty and a matter of honor.[67]

Theologians reinforced this with biblical proof for both slavery and specifically the place of black Africans as slaves as ordained by God. In the South, the major denominations were all guilty of justifying slavery. Over disagreements about slavery in 1844, the Methodist Episcopal Church congregations split and formed the Methodist Episcopal Church South. Most Baptist churches also separated themselves from the northern churches with their abolitionist tendencies, and formed a separate Southern Baptist Convention in 1845. Shelby County's Big Hatchie Association joined them in 1849. The positions of the Presbyterian and Episcopalian Churches were more complex. As the question of slavery had become increasingly divisive, the general assembly of the majority old school of the Presbyterians interdicted forever agitation on the subject. Only in 1861 did the Presbyterian Church and the Protestant Episcopal Church in the Confederate states secede from their mother churches. Specifically, the Presbytery of Memphis seceded on June 14. In 1862, Lutherans split over the issue of secession rather than slavery which had not been much of an issue for most Lutherans. Despite Pope Gregory XVI's condemnation of slavery, Southern Bishops continued to justify it. Likewise, Southern Jews found ample support for slavery in the Torah.[68]

Reverend Phillip Tuggle, who served the Germantown Methodist Church and its sister churches in the Hernando circuit, must have taught and firmly believed not only in the biblical justifications but also the Christian duties of slaveholders. He began in the Hernando circuit in 1854 and settled near Germantown where he bought and ran a plantation with 52 slaves. To manage them, he relied on a twenty-five year-old overseer, David Dunlap, who lived with the Tuggles.[69] Surely Tuggle preached the proper roles and places of slaveholders and slaves to both his black and white congregations.

Isham Howse, who owned four slaves, subscribed to biblical justifications, but was conflicted about holding slaves.

> But our slaves are well-fed, and clothed, and are happy, in comparison with the poor white slave, either in Europe or in our northern states.... I do not believe that slavery in itself is sinful. God has decreed a difference in mankind, and some men are born inferior to others, some to rule and some to be ruled. Servants need disciplining, and I am incompetent to enforce it. My feelings are too tender.... And, O Lord, if such is thy will, hasten the time when the children of Africa may go home civilized and Christianized! Or if that cannot be done in my day, so order my destiny that I might have nothing to do with slaves as their master. I do not say that the relation of master to slave, even as it exists in these states, is sinful. On the contrary, I believe that God in his providence has sent the black man here for wiser and benevolent purposes – that he may, in the fullness of time, be the means of doing good to the race in their native land. But I am unqualified to discharge a master's duty, and if it would please God, I would rejoice to be so situated as to have nothing to do with slavery. ... I had rather live poor all my natural life than have slaves. ... I must take care of them. It would be a curse to them to free them. How long, Oh, how long will it be before they all will return to their fatherland? [70]

Poor Isham was conflicted about other things as well and long suffering.

The churches certainly felt a responsibility for the spiritual well-being of all blacks. Specifically, all three Germantown churches had both free and slave members. In some churches within services, seating was separated. Others held entirely separate meetings, as did Germantown Presbyterians and Methodists, with the black service either following the white or being held in a nearby brush arbor.

Black membership in the Memphis Presbytery averaged only about 10 or 11 percent of the total congregation during the 1850s, while in 1854 the Methodist circuit that covered Germantown had a ratio of 445 white to 492 "colored."[71] Blacks preferred the Baptists and Methodists to the

Presbyterians as more expressive, and owners generally did not force their own denominations. Although owners could be ambivalent about blacks becoming Christians, increasingly most had decided its effects on their slaves were desirable.[72]

Church leadership was not insensitive to the desires of their "black brethren" for their own instruction in the faith. In 1856, the Baptist Big Hatchie Association acknowledged that it was less successful among blacks than it should have been, because of "a strong prejudice against white teachers." The Association encouraged the white pastors to train blacks to lead blacks, so they could be reached "through their own color." Thereafter the Association reported great success. Of course, white pastors maintained control of that instruction.[73]

For each of their circuits, such as the Hernando circuit that served Germantown, the Methodists maintained a "colored mission," with one pastor serving the circuit apparently supervising black preachers. They held services at the larger plantations or at locations central to several smaller ones. Where a white church served a community like Germantown, a nearby brush arbor served the blacks. There the service met the tastes of their audience. Sometimes white children would sneak out of their service to enjoy the more spirited African-American style. In 1860, Germantown acquired its own separate colored mission, undoubtedly at the instigation of Reverend Tuggle, who held the souls of so many slaves in his hands. This mission apparently never got well established, however, and terminated with the ministerial downsizing and white anxieties about uncontrolled slave assemblies that came with the outbreak of war.[74]

Slave owners were especially concerned about controlling their slaves' access to religious instruction. They feared slaves who were assertive enough to seek their own "liberation theology" in secret services where subversive gospel songs promised liberation - "Tell ol' Pharaoh, Let my people go." Blacks also preferred a service style with more emotional outlets than even the white Baptists provided.[75] That was less a problem for owners who saw it as a useful outlet. The more blacks made Christianity into their own religion, the more complicated its effects on them became. It fortified their spirits and helped them cope, without leading them to accept slavery as proper. It provided them with a personal and communal morality that was not immune to the necessities for dissimulation and the "acquisition" of white property that the realities of their situation required. It also provided a moral scale for judging their masters.[76]

The actual degree of concern that local slaveholders had for the moral development of their "charges" varied greatly, but was clearly circumscribed by practicalities of control and their racial ideology. For instance, although slave holders did not necessarily respect family relations, they had frequently encouraged them, because it made the slaves more likely to accept their lot and it gave the owners leverage. Owners usually did not encourage formal church marriage, but allowed the slaves to devise their own ceremonies and means of communal enforcement. A full Christian wedding was not often desired, because it implied an inviolability that a Christian master should observe. When a pastor did preside, the phrase, "till death do you part," was never included in the ceremony.[77]

During the war, when slaves who had left their owners ended up in the freemen camps, Union authorities, often clergymen, became interested in the morals of their charges. The information they gathered in the camps in which former Germantown slaves would have resided casts light on the consequences of the regimen under which they had lived. These clergymen were especially concerned when they learned that conjugal relations did not exist within proper Christian contexts. Chaplain John Eaton, Jr., the general superintendent of contrabands in Grant's command, circulated a questionnaire to the superintendents of each camp to put to their charges. Eaton compiled the answers on April 29, 1863.

> *Grand Junction.* Most of them have no idea of the sacredness of the marriage tie, declaring that marriage, as it exists among the whites, has been impossible for them. In other cases, the marriage relation exists in all its sacredness without legal sanctions.
>
> *Holly Springs...* [Internees moved to Memphis in the interim]. The greater number have lived together as husband and wife, by mutual consent. In many cases, strongly attached and faithful, though having no legal marriage.
>
> *Memphis.* They know what marriage is among the whites, but have yielded to the sad necessity of their case. Generally, I believe the men to be faithful to the women with whom they live, and the women to reward their faith with like truth. Free and married, they will maintain the marital relations as sacredly as any other race. ...
>
> *La Grange.* Loose & by example.[78]

Among those in the camps at Memphis, none of the 681 men and women was listed as married, which was unusual compared to the other camps. Of course, the local superintendent may have been narrower in his definition. Nevertheless, everywhere the liberated blacks quickly and gladly accepted the legal and religious trappings of a socially approved marriage. It both affirmed their full status as citizens and created a legal basis for property, inheritance, and custody within their families. Whenever such status became available, they sought it without any compulsion.[79]

Differences of opinion among the whites over the proper management and treatment of slaves were a source of tension. When Wilks Brooks left North Carolina to settle at Germantown in 1835, he was allegedly motivated to escape from problems created by such differences. There as a member of the General Assembly, where memories of the Nat Turner Revolt were so vivid, he had argued strongly for the education of slaves to better civilize them. The fear of slave revolts divided owners over whether to employ progressive or repressive methods. After his progressive ideas were voted down, he felt that life there was increasingly unsafe. This allegedly motivated him to move his family.[80] We may never know if the slaveholding society that grew up with him in the Germantown area was more attuned to his views, but Brooks' fear of revolt fueled-by-repression is an interesting variation on Baker's white flight theory. He had apparently brought with him from North Carolina only four of his slaves, but he gradually accumulated several dozen more.[81]

A few slaves who were not deliberately schooled by their masters managed to learn reading and writing through underground means. Most masters made every effort to prevent them from even seeing the written word, and in most places, it was forbidden by law. In the face of such opposition, both the opponents of slavery and compassionate masters made efforts to provide some learning for slaves and freedmen. Predictably, some white children who played regularly with their slave children assumed the role of teacher, even to the point of conspiring against their parents.[82]

In addition to the Sabbath which usually included Saturday afternoon, masters allowed their slaves some respite on occasions such as Christmas or when the whites held special festivities. Some slaves were allowed to attend, but of course, celebrated in segregation when not serving the whites. If the whites had music and danced under the shelter of a brush arbor on a prepared ground covered with sawdust, "the negroes had a dancing place to themselves – in the open air."[83] When the trains were still a new experience at Germantown, young Caroline Burns would bring some slave children to throw cotton bolls and flowers as it passed.[84] In a slave-owning household with white children, their needs for personal servants, playmates or smaller children to serve as play things guaranteed that black children had some playtime up to about age six.

Under even the best conditions, the human spirit rebelled against enslavement with its degradation and humiliation. True, the life of a household slave or one employed in a craft could be reasonably acceptable. On the other hand, the life of the field hand, especially on the larger plantations, was far less so. Research indicates that many planters in the Deep South saw the most profits from literally working slaves to death. More typically, however, expenses for upkeep were simply kept to a minimum, and slaves supplemented their family's diets with fish and game, garden plots, woodland gathering or stealing. Yet, things were not entirely one-sided. Wise masters and overseers realized they could thwart slow-down tactics best by granting some freedoms, privileges and opportunities. The alternative for other masters was brutal punishment. Perhaps the worse fate, however, husbands and wives, mothers and children were torn apart through sales. Threats to do so could be used to control slaves, but ultimately their fate depended on the economic interests of the master. It has been estimated that perhaps one quarter of all slave families in Tennessee were disrupted.[85]

The memories of a young soldier, who had grown up in Mason about twenty-five miles from Germantown, provide some insight into the relative condition of area slaves. When he encountered conditions in southern Alabama, "I left this place with a different view of slavery." The treatment of slaves there contrasted sharply with his view that they were "the most treasured servants and, aside from a human standpoint, a good strong negro was valuable property."[86] Of course, he said this in 1912, by which time such sentiments had become a key point in Old South romanticizing, but it may reflect the nuances of owner-slave relations in the Germantown area. Whatever, personalities determined the slaves' fate. Sadism, cruelty, or simple fits of anger, were the prerogative of master, mistress, sons, daughters, and overseers.

The previously recounted story of Dr. Scruggs treating a slave woman for "polypus of the uterus" also illustrates the complexity of these relations. When she was about age 43, she began severe hemorrhaging. The first doctor was called in promptly, and succeeded in stopping the bleeding. Over the next two years, the mistress had been treating her with remedies that kept the bleeding under control. Ultimately, however, the woman had wasted away so badly she seemed near death. That was when Scruggs was called in and successfully treated the problem. The owners had been generous with the medical expenses for a slave, two doctors and a third as consultant, plus medications.[87] How much more would families have done for their own members? So, one must speculate about motivation.

The doctor's concluding remarks seem pertinent. "She recovered rapidly, and has menstruated regularly ever since, notwithstanding she says she is 48 years old and has given birth to twelve healthy children, nine of whom are now living; she has perfectly recovered her health, and may yet have several children."[88] In one respect, the woman had served successfully as something of a brood mare, producing twelve potential slaves, at least nine of whom were healthy enough to survive to an age of value. Were the owners merely protecting an investment? Considering

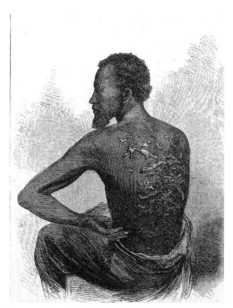

Illustration 6. Scars of brutal lashings

Illustration 7. Slave labor teams under supervision of overseers. (Harper's February 2, 1867)

the woman's age, however, that seems like a long-shot investment. A woman who had survived 48 years of slavery, 12 childbirths and 2 years of debilitating illness must have seemed a poor gamble. Humanitarian or moral concerns, perhaps even affection, must have been among the motives.

Britten Duke is another example of area planters who at least treated their slaves as valuable investments. In 1854, he paid $3.00 to have a physician make an emergency house call and perform a surgery. The next day he paid another $1.00 for a follow-up office visit and prescription.[89] Of course, one cannot deduce the motives that lay behind Duke's behavior. Dr. Scrugg's other observations about treating typhoid fever among the area's slave plantations indicate that many Germantown area plantation owners did not subscribe to the minimum maintenance theory attributed to the deeper South.

Also the common practice of the entire slave population regularly visiting the infected speaks to a strong sense of community among the slaves of a plantation.[90] Even under the worst conditions in West Tennessee, the slave quarters became a community center. Story telling and music lightened the spirits and news of the outside world came in.[91]

There, a wide range of African traditions and cultural colors were preserved among those separated by generations from their origins. Such infectious spores would spread into the white world, enriching Southern culture first.

Regardless of the behavior of Germantown owners, slave life involved enough deprivation to have consequences. In 1860, the average slave's life expectancy was only 33.7 years, a full ten years less than a white person or free blacks who had similar mortality rates. There were also significant differences in the causes of death. Blacks died twice as frequently from violence – executed almost eight times more frequently. Although statistics indicate that only one-third as many blacks committed suicide, one third more black deaths were classed vaguely as "accidental" – perhaps camouflaged suicides. Specifically identified accidents resulted from the slaves' working environment: five times more likely to be struck by lightening, more than three times by burns or scalding. Five times as many died from resultant tetanus. Other mortality statistics reveal a harsh reality. Allegedly far fewer blacks died of exposure, neglect and malnutrition, but specifically identified causes starkly contradict such under-reporting. Far greater percentages died from worms, other parasites, rickets, freezing and eating dirt.[92]

For slave women, death in childbirth was twice as common. Strangely, premature births were more than one third less common, while infant mortality more than made up for it. Deaths among black children were twenty-five percent greater than among whites.[93]

One peculiarity of the slave experience contradicts all expectations, however. If one survived to true old-age, the mortality rates reversed. The census statistics for 1860 recorded far more black deaths from "old age."[94] In the legible portions of the 1860 slave schedule for district eleven, however, there were few slaves over 60. Unfortunately the census taker's flamboyantly swirled numbers make it difficult to distinguish between 2s and 9s, leaving the age of several individuals in doubt. At least one male belonging to the planter William Hamlin and one female belonging to Thomas Goodrich may have been 95 and 90 respectively.

From the above, one can conclude that slaves were inadequately fed generally. Lack of a balanced diet was probably the greatest problem rather than inadequate calorie intake.[95] Clothing could also be problematic, being almost exclusively made by the mistress or under her supervision from homespun materials. Hand-me-downs were highly treasured when given as rewards or favors, and provided the only clothing that could be worn with pride. The housing provided minimal shelter, but not necessarily worse than many of the poorer whites. On the plantations, the houses lined the roads leading from the big house to the fields. On the smaller establishments, two or three slave houses clustered around the owner's. The most common structure was a "single pen," 16 by 18 feet. Sometimes men, women and children not part of family units lived in multi-room barracks.[96] Unfortunately no evidence of Germantown area slave housing survives.

As far as the value of slaves is concerned, it fluctuated over time, rising in Tennessee during the 1850s from $547 to $855 on average.[97] It depended on the careful assessment of the "specimen" at the sale. On the block, they were examined with the same attention as horses. Physical strength and health were the key factors with both sexes. When Britton Duke bought Mariah, age 25, in 1836, he paid the high fee of $1000, undoubtedly because she was both strong and of good breeding stock. When Duke died in 1856, she, now 45, with her three children were valued at $1200. In that same estate, the best man was valued at $1125, but the more typical ones were set at $950 to $750. Younger women ranged from $800 to $600. The older fell to as low as $400.[98] But that was for the purpose of calculating inheritance shares, not sale.

On the plus side, slaves were not without rights and legal protection, especially in Tennessee. Much of Tennessee's slave code and judicial precedent had been set in the earlier years when there was more prejudice against slavery. Such sentiments, if not the letter of the law, were eroded over time, and the slaves' legal recourse depended on many variables. Even so, as late as 1858, a court ruled that slaves were not just simple property, but also persons. "That as persons they are considered by our law, as accountable moral agents, possessed by the power of volition and locomotion. That certain rights have been conferred upon them by positive law and judicial determination, and other privileges and indulgences have been conceded to them by universal consent of their owners."[99]

Although observed more often in the breach, there were legal limits on corporal punishment, such as lashing. Mutilation and torture were illegal, and a slave could not be killed except by proper judicial processes, or extenuating circumstances like self defense, otherwise the killer, even an owner could be charged with murder. In Germantown, when a slave died of any cause, a magistrate serving as coroner conducted an inquest.[100]

There were special courts for trying slaves for criminal offenses, designed as much to protect slave owners' property interests as to guarantee justice. Third parties could be charged for beating another man's slaves. The state Supreme Court was diligent in encouraging humane treatment by masters. It held that families could not be broken up and sold to settle debts against an estate, although this ruling was frequently violated without consequences. Masters were legally required to provide wholesome food, adequate clothing and shelter.[101] Of course, recourse to the law was not easy for an aggrieved slave. Most commonly, masters used the law to protect their slave property from physical damage by third parties intent on punishment.

Probably the most important rights for most slaves were the above mentioned "privileges and indulgences ... conceded to them by universal consent of their owners." Although such rights existed by common law precedent, the slaves simply understood them as traditional rights to be withheld only as punishment. The Sabbath and holy days like Christmas were free days, sometimes Saturday afternoons, and nights were also usually free for family and communal time. They were to be left alone and given freedom of movement within limits, including visitation with family on other plantations. Such travel off the owner's lands required a written pass, but it was a presumed right. Gifts, treats and feasts for special occasions, even small cash payments as rewards could become entrenched traditions. Hunting, fishing and garden rights, even the opportunity to market their own products were incentive strategies employed by owners, rather than rights, but once granted, could become entrenched. Slaves would exercise subtle or even overt forms of protest when they felt such rights were violated.[102]

Petty theft, and sometimes worse, was common, which slaves justified as consuming or employing some of the property of which they were simply a part. Owners usually had to accept it as part of the price of operations. It only became a serious concern when it involved someone else's property. Selling stolen property or produce to white middlemen involved very undesirable contacts.

The dark side of slavery certainly existed around Germantown, for many felt compelled to attempt escape. One of the early attempts from Germantown provides details of how the so-called underground railway worked locally. In 1825 when a slave escaped from John Lewis Phillips, he sought assistance from the freeman, John Bennett in Memphis. To get him up river to freedom, the plan was to seal him up in a wooden box to be shipped by steamboat. Unfortunately the box sat on the wharf in the heat of the summer sun until he had to cry out for help.[103]

In an 1843 newspaper notice, a runaway was described colorfully by his owner William Winfrey.

> RANAWAY from the subscriber, living one mile from Germantown, Shelby county, Tenn., a mulatto man named JOHN, about 25 years of age, six feet high. John is a very sensible negro, and of good manners—is fond of telling extravagant tales for the amusement of those that are present; he professes to be a barber. He has a smooth skin and of good countenance; he took with him a green frock coat of summer cloth; also, a dress coat of light figured stuff, and a pair of blue cloth pants—other clothing not recollected. No doubt but that he will try to get to some one of the free States. John left me on the 10th inst. The above reward will be given for the apprehension of said boy and his confinement, so that I get him.[104]

According to the 1860 census, runaways not only declined in Tennessee during the previous decade, but the escape rate was never very high. In 1850, the reported rate of runaway was 1 in 3,491, and by 1860 1 in 9,509.[105] Yet in the Germantown area during the 1850s, at least six slaves ran away in a five-year period, a much higher rate then this purported average. Considering the total number of slaves in the area, this would have been an extremely high escape rate compared to the reported overall average for the decade.[106] This gives the impression that local slaves were either more desperate than elsewhere or far less well restrained.

In 1856, B. Harrison had to offer a reward of $40 for "two yellow or copper colored boys, names Henry and Mace." In 1857, an anonymous gentleman living near Germantown offered $40 reward for his two runaways, John and Simon. Rather than posting an add in his own name, the owner was using A. R. Cartwright and Goodlet, Nabers & Co. as agents.[107]

Any form of slavery was onerous, and when a slave's conditions improved, he might develop "dangerous" higher expectations. In fact, runaway rates were higher among skilled and educated slaves. Such was the case of one of the two slaves, Henry and Taylor, who ran away from Dr. J. M. M. Cornelius in 1860. How they were employed is unclear, but it should not have been onerous labor for Henry. He was a bearded man of about 30, "intelligent, can read and write, and is very pompous in his language and actions." An educated slave was one groomed for service work of the sort that a doctor might need, even as a butler or gentleman's servant. Perhaps, however, he found himself in the doctor's fields too often. In this case, the slaves' confidence was also high, for each took with him a carpet bag and some changes of clothing.[108] Of course, for some, this was sufficient proof that blacks by nature were an ungrateful sort, and any coddling would backfire.

Another elaborate escape attempt occurred in 1860, revealing more about the local Underground Railroad. An unnamed woman escaped from "a gentleman by the name of Merrick who lived near Germantown." She went to Memphis where she found shelter and support for her flight to freedom. An effort to board a boat north proved futile, so under disguise she boarded a Memphis and Ohio train. A "useful citizen," of Brownsville noticed her as she boarded, because of the thick veil that covered her face. He reported her to the conductor. She confessed her identity and was returned to her owner.[109]

To curb such efforts at escape by boat, stage or train, Tennessee passed laws imposing heavy penalties on ship captains, coach drivers and train conductors. Black passengers had to have passes, so underground railway "conductors" provided a variety of such free services. Since slaves did travel on their owner's business, a black rider with a pass was not necessarily suspected.[110]

Finally, there was one much greater display of resistance. What slaveholders feared most was slaves so badly abused that they would take revenge on their owners. The *Appeal* reported that on October 19, 1858, the Germantown area was in an uproar when a plot "conceived by the slaves" was uncovered to destroy the home of "a planter in that neighborhood." Next to revolt, arson was greatly feared and more common. "Two or three arrests of parties had been made, and the authorities were in pursuit of others connected with the conspiracy."[111] Notably, these were plantation slaves, and the *Appeal* rather thoughtfully failed to report the planter's name, perhaps because most people looked down on anyone abusive enough to precipitate a slave revolt. Of course, more than scruples were involved. Once ignited, slave revolts had the dangerous potential to spread their vengeful destruction against surrounding plantations, and even towns. The *Appeal* unfortunately failed to report any follow-up on the fate of the arrested ring leaders.

Such an event must indeed have generated an uproar around Germantown, for everyone had heard of a far more frightening incident only two years previously in nearby LaFayette (Rossville). A slave girl reported a conspiracy to her mistress. The owners spied on their slaves to determine that such plans were indeed afoot, and then had 32 of them arrested, of whom 23 were considered sufficiently guilty to be jailed at Somerville.

The slaves planned to take advantage of the November election of

1856 when the men would be away from home voting. They allegedly intended to kill all the women and children, seize money and arms, and waylay the men as they returned. They hoped to rally all the slaves in the surrounding counties. Such a story extracted from the culprits was so formulaic that it reminds one of the propensities of the Inquisition to extract confessions that confirmed their most hysterical fears. Vigilant Patrols fanned out to insure all was safe. Rumors spread that the six or eight ringleaders had been lynched by an angry mob at the LaFayette Depot, but in a letter to the Memphis papers one W. E. Eppes protested this slander, insisting, "We are law-abiding citizens about here, and as such, do not like such reports to get about."[112] Death was the punishment for insurrection or conspiracy, but the sentence was supposed to be imposed after a proper trial, not by vigilantes.[113]

During the 1850s, abolitionist agitation had incited fears that they would unleash slave revolts. The incident at LaFayette in 1856 produced a wave of hysteria throughout West and Middle Tennessee with wild rumors of revolt that proved to be nothing more than "loose talk in the slave quarters." Germantown's alarm was part of a second such wave in 1858. As a result, repressive measures were imposed in Memphis and throughout the countryside.[114]

The reference to vigilance patrols called out for the emergency raise the question of whether Germantown and its district felt compelled to maintain regular slave patrols. An act of the legislature in 1806 provided for the appointment of patrolmen by the district militia captain, "for the regulation of the colored population." The number of men and the frequency of their patrols was left up to the local captain. Each town was also to maintain a nightly patrol. Remuneration for service varied over time, and the work was apparently so unpopular that it frequently fell to poorer members of the community. They were to seize weapons, break up unapproved assemblies and arrest slaves loose without passes. They became notorious for exceeding their authority to administer punishment, and owners often had to intervene.[115] Unfortunately local records are mute on the subject of slave patrols before the war.

The 1860 slave schedules for district eleven certainly paint a mixed picture of local slave life. In town, whether the owner was a mechanic, professional or merchant, they might hold either one or two intact families, or their work force was gender biased, probably for specific labor. The wagon maker had 9 males over 10 years of age, and 4 females. The rest were children under 10. Some of the adolescents were probably children of the older slaves. The bootmaker's male and female adults were probably the parents of one child, but another ten year-old mulatto girl is in question. The merchants, Boardman and Massey, hired one slave each in addition to their own. The physician Moore had mostly females indicating domestic work, while Cornelius had 7 adult and adolescent males, many of whom probably worked his land. The farmer John Welson supported children outnumbering his workers 8 to 6. He may literally have been breeding slaves. Two others came close to a 50/50 ratio. Again, presumptions are dangerous. Such people may have simply been supportive of a family life, and children were frequently acquired as investments.

On the plantations, Sarah Walker's 12 working males were outnumbered by the females and their children totaling 28. With 10 under ten years, Sarah was carrying many who did not pay for themselves. Likewise Sarah Jones had 7 out of 22 under ten. Opinions varied widely on the age at which a slave should be put to work. Some believed they should learn early to do their life's work, but most thought it should begin with light chores around age six. Field work could begin at ten or twelve, if not earlier. Of course, women worked as field hands, even house workers shifted back and forth as needed. On the other hand, a large holder like Joseph Brooks had a population skewed toward working males, but still carried 18 under ten. Richard Goodwin carried an even higher percentage of children, but since he had to hire 4 men to cover all his work, he may have been encouraging fruitfulness. Reverend Phillip Tuggle probably had the smallest ratio of children to workers, 10 out of 52.

In addition to field work, women and children did the productive household labor: tending animals, gardening, food processing, cooking, carding, weaving, sewing, washing and cleaning, from sunup to sundown. Nurses for children and personal servants for the women were the only privileged and relatively light labor. Grooming horses and driving were the equivalents for men. The larger the household, the more such employment. In contrast, however, the very first slave a yeoman farmer might purchase would be one girl to relieve his wife from some of her onerous burdens.[116]

Collective and collaborative women's work such as clothing production and washing provided an opportunity to socialize and share information. When the slave woman's work day was over as slave, she returned to her cabin to cook supper and provide what little mothering she could for her children. That is, if she had sufficient energy left and did not simply pass out. Family life in the cabins was certainly problematic. Small children spent most of their time under the supervision of older girls or the aged. Beyond church, what passed for moral or religious education came from a mix of instruction by the mistress, the community life of the slaves, and from a greatly varied parental influence.[117]

One of the more lasting scars of slavery was the frequent severance of family ties. Severance from ones "Roots" is bad enough. Being torn from all loved ones was far worse. The girl who would become Mrs.

Margaret Scales was placed on a stump at the age of 12 and auctioned off. Brought to Germantown, she never saw her mother again.[118]

Although none of these slaves could have known how near emancipation was, the process would bring them great elation, but no great reduction of hardships. For most, the transition would prove even more grueling and dangerous than for their former masters.

# Chapter 3

## A Transportation and Economic Center

Before either the planking of State Line Road or the railroad was available, the only comfortable means of movement to Memphis or the county seat at Raleigh had been the Wolf River. Originally, settlers had hoped it would prove a reliable avenue as far up as La Grange, and indeed keelboats began plying the river from there in 1829, encouraging settlement along the Wolf. Most of the earlier settlements such as Raleigh, Nashoba, La Fayette, Moscow and La Grange located on the river. Traffic was not only limited by periods of low water, but the Wolf could be clogged with ice in winter. Although by the 1840s, it had become problematic, advocates for its navigation persisted. In March 1844, taking advantage of the high water, one "Commodore" Briggs brought down from Moscow 83 bales in his aptly named keelboat *Forlorn Hope*. After demonstrating its continued navigability, he argued that with "a small appropriation by Shelby and Fayette counties" to clear the river of snags, it could be kept navigable to Moscow. Petitions from inhabitants along its course to county and state for clearing apparently ran afoul of other interests, such as using the river for water-driven mills and investment in the new railway craze.[1]

Soon it was so badly snarled with snags and silting that travel beyond Collierville had been abandoned. For a while, a tug hauled barges to Collierville and back, but eventually the river was only navigable below Germantown. To there, a small sternwheeler served passengers, visitors to the resort springs around Germantown. Commercial navigation of the Wolf was slowly abandoned.[2]

It was roads rather than the river that determined the initial significance of Germantown. It was probably the intersection of two or three "highways" that gave the town its place. First of all, the State Line Road ran out from Memphis to the south-east corner of the county and from there into towns across Mississippi and Alabama. By 1841, the town had become the first along that road to be significant enough to be chartered. In 1845, another post road was designated to run from Macon, Tennessee, to Hernando, Mississippi, through what was then the newly chartered town.[3] Although the significance of that intersection was apparently enough to make the town a transportation hub.

Eventually in the system of roads around the town, only the Germantown or State Line Road remained a first class road in terms of construction and maintenance. This meant it had to accommodate stage coaches and was designated a post road. It appeared on maps as early as the 1820s as a county road, but was little improved over the meandering

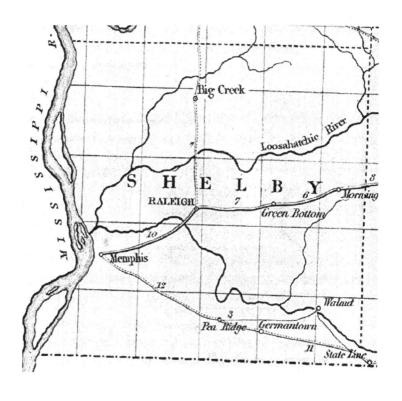

Map 5. Shelby County roads and rivers, 1839. (Map of Kentucky and Tennessee, Library of Congress, Geography and Map Division.)

Indian trail, subject to relocation at the whim of owners over whose property it crossed.[4] Since the county could never finance construction and maintenance at an appropriate level, in 1848 the public highway was turned over to the Memphis and Germantown Turnpike Company. The company was to take over, straighten, improve and maintain the road bed between Memphis and Germantown and then on to Collierville initially. The state act that established several such turnpike companies provided standards for the road beds.

> The said road shall be opened at least thirty feet wide, with sufficient ditches, on each side, at all times to carry off the water, and to drain the same: shall gradually descend from the middle to the side ditches: shall be substantially covered with stone, gravel, sand, wood or charcoal: shall have substantial and sufficient bridges where necessary, and in all respects shall be completed in a faithful and substantial turnpike manner.[5]

Within its corporate limits, Germantown was required to maintain all public roads that passed through it.[6] All roads, no matter how well maintained, were chokingly dusty in dry weather and impassably muddy when wet. For the rest of the road system radiating from the town, the bridges across the Wolf were built in the mid-1840s, followed by a few over the Nonconnah. Before that, one could have forded the Nonconnah much of the year, but the Wolf had to have a ferry. South of town, the Nonconnah remained a barrier on many smaller roads when the water was high.[7]

Even after such improvements, Western Tennessee lacked the better built and maintained roads of the east. Historians contend that this was partly because the area was allegedly deficient in the raw materials for the preferred macadam base (a mix of clay and gravel). This seems strange, since the entire area close around Germantown used to be pockmarked by old gravel pits, not to mention plentiful clay. The presence of these gravel outcroppings around the town was known by at least the late 1850s. Given the abundance of hardwood forests, however, the preferred alternative was to lay planks across the road bed, greatly benefiting the local lumber industry. The thick, twelve-foot planks lay on top of stringers, logs embedded in the mud, and provided a surface that prevented wagons from sinking up to their axles. The required thirty-foot width of the total road allowed adequate shoulders for one wagon to pull off and allow another to pass on the planks. The advocates of planking even argued that theirs was more durable than macadam, lasting eight to twenty years.[8] Regardless, riding on them was something like a trip down a washboard after the boards had aged a little. One could hear the loud rumbling of wagons and stages for some distance as they rolled over the boards. And we think road noise is a modern problem.

In any case, planking was the preferred solution for the turnpike companies, and at least all the problematic stretches of the road were planked. So much so that the section to Germantown was known as the Germantown Plank Road.[9]

Among the gentlemen who organized and subscribed to the Memphis and Germantown Turnpike Company in August 1848 were several residents who saw the need and expected the benefits. In Germantown, the sellers of stock were E. W. Kenny and Britton Duke. They set up shop at the town's post office.[10] By 1849, planking had been completed to Germantown, projected eventually to reach La Grange and Holly Springs, Mississippi. Thereafter, Germantown citizens and area planters got themselves elected as commissioners of the Turnpike to guarantee that their interests were served. For instance in 1859, they entirely dominated the commission with the planters W. C. Harrison and James Kimbrough, and Dr. John Stout. [11]

Initially, not everyone approved of the conversion of the free, county-maintained road to a toll road. Only those living around Germantown and east to Collierville would be paying the bulk of the tolls. The argument that the unimproved road was usable for at least two-thirds of the year did not prevail against those who saw the economic advantages of a plank road.[12]

There was one toll gate, number 4 between Germantown and Collierville, apparently near Forest Hill, and three toll collectors lived in district twelve between Germantown and White's Station. One of their toll gates was at Ridgeway. The first gate was within two miles of Memphis. The tolls that users had to pay varied. For loaded wagons, it ranged from ten to twenty cents, depending on the number of animals drawing. Carriages likewise ranged from ten to twenty cents – something of a luxury tax. Horseback riders and empty wagons paid five cents. Of course, the fee was paid for each gate crossed, and there were stiff fines for trying to sneak around one. At least, farmers hauling their grain to a grist mill were exempt since that was essential to the survival of the poorest family. Also family travel to church and that of militiamen to a muster was free.[13] During the cotton harvest, huge caravans of ox-drawn wagons passed along this road carrying bales for several days' drive, rumbling through town.

In 1860, an act of the legislature required the Germantown Plank Road Company to open its beds to at least twenty feet in width, although it still allowed planking. Consequently in June, plans were announced to regrade the road to Germantown and cover it with gravel to produce what would have been the best road out of Memphis. Completion of the project was expected before winter.[14] Unfortunately, there seems to be no record of how successful this project might have been, but this proposed development clearly shows that the abundant gravel domes of

Illustration 8. Typically crowded stagecoach as it might have appeared stopping at Germantown. Trains would much improve the comfort of travel. (Harper's August 13, 1859)

the area were being exploited. Especially low sections remained planked even after whatever resurfacing.[15]

Before the railroad, several stage lines served the town. The lines through Germantown connected Memphis with all the towns along the southern tier of West Tennessee, but especially major points in northern Mississippi such as Holy Springs, Ripley and Corinth, and Decatur, Alabama. It came twice daily from points east and west along the State Line Road, three times a week on roads from other points.[16] In addition to passengers, it carried the mail that included the newspapers, keeping the town in touch with commercial activities in the city and the world. More than half of each issue carried advertisements for the growing number of products available in Memphis.

On the north side of town lay the Baptist church, Lucken's grocery/saloon and inn, homes and shops, including the blacksmith. In 1860 the blacksmith was John Slough.[17] The depot was located on the south side of the tracks. The middle of the town was the perennial location for several stores, shops and offices alternately containing the itinerant post office in most years. On the south of town lay the Presbyterian Church, and the Masonic Hall as well as other businesses and a grist mill. On the west side sat the Methodist Church and communal cemetery, appropriately located on Church Street. Without any such thing as a commercial district, town houses were interspersed among all this.

Somewhere there was a town commons, referred to also as the green. It is only mentioned in passing in a few surviving documents, and there seems to be no record of its location. Possibly it lay between the Presbyterian Church and the Masonic Hall, for this was always a flat open space and eventually the location for a communal athletic field.[18]

The network of roads in the district was the lifeblood of the business and agricultural community, so they were a focus of attention. Their maintenance was farmed out by the county court to local citizens as overseers who had responsibility for a section of each particular road. For instance, in January of 1861, the section of the Raleigh-Germantown Road from the town to the Wolf River bridge was assigned to William B. Walker, a bachelor or widower farmer who lived in town with his mother. Walker would emerge as a local political leader and public servant. In 1856, James Kimbrough had responsibility for the Germantown-Capleville Road which ran by his lands. For each such section, the overseer and several other local men were responsible for the labor to be provided by their "hands," meaning slaves. Although non-slaveholders shared this legal obligation, none ever appear in the list of "hands" assigned.[19]

The demand for more second and third class roads to serve the local farms was met by the county in response to petitions from persons expecting to benefit. Such undertakings required review as to their benefits and viability by a "jury of view." One would think such a review would involve relatively disinterested parties, but quite often, local politics being what they are, petitioners constituted more than half the jury.[20]

In contrast, bridge maintenance was farmed out to special contractors. In 1860, when major maintenance was performed on the Wolf River bridge, the contractor discovered such an unexpectedly rotten "trussel" that the bridge had been in danger of collapse. Unfortunately, his repair raised one end of the bridge two to three feet higher so that he made the approach steep and abrupt. He earned $300 for the work for which he had contracted, but since he undertook the unexpected repair on his own initiative, it is unclear whether he was rewarded for producing the new obstacle.[21]

Before the arrival of the railroad, for casual and professional passenger travel between Memphis and Germantown, two local gentlemen, George Furber and Samuel W. Ledbetter, had maintained a "hack" service. Ledbetter operated a livery at their station in Memphis, while Furber's house in Germantown served as the town's station. Every day except Sundays, their carriage left the town at 7 A.M. and left the city for the return trip at 3 P.M.[22] For heavy shopping, most families had carriages or wagons to make the trip on their own schedule. Except for the rich with slaves as drivers, shopping trips for women had to correspond with the husband's business in the city.

The arrival of train service changed all this. An enthusiastic crowd turned out for the inaugural event, including slaves allowed to participate in the festivities. People threw cotton bolls and flowers.[23] On September 16, 1852, passengers arrived on the excursion train from Memphis riding on improvised cars. Some 19 people made the trip out, but that hardly compared to the hundreds that had ridden the four special trains to Eppy White's previous grand celebration of the arrival of service at his station.[24]

In fact, the inaugural was probably more anticlimactic than is often described. Train service had approached incrementally every day. By August 2, a daily train was within a mile or two of the town and could be heard from there. Anyone wishing to take it into Memphis simply walked out to the end of the line.[25]

The first engine was the newly built LaGrange, the familiar long-bodied American-type engine with a bell-shaped stack, a front truck of four small wheels behind a cowcatcher and ahead of four large drive wheels (4-4-0), followed by a tender for the fire wood. [26] The engines were bedecked with polished brass, while the cab and wheels usually sported bright colors, mostly shades of red. Despite the high stack, smoke and cinders frequently wafted into the cars. Even after the advent of enclosed cars, tiny cinders in one's eye were a common problem until the end of the era of steam.

For the inaugural ceremony, the town's folk disappointed others by the limits of their enthusiasm, which is probably why only 19 made the trip out. The reporter for the Memphis *Appeal* bemoaned, "It had been expected by many of those who shared in the hospitality of Col. White, at the celebration of the road reaching his house, that the people of Germantown would make a demonstration of their joy by giving a festival. But, as yet, we have heard of no such affair being on the taps."[27] White had thrown a mammoth barbecue.[28] Our disappointed reporter seems to have needed another barbecue fix.

In any case, he went on to express an enthusiasm for the new convenience felt by all except Luddites.

> In a few weeks the road will be opened to Colliersville, and we should not be surprised if the friends of the company should have another grand re-union at that village. We hope that it will be so; for we like to see the people assembling together to view the triumph of industry and enterprise; and to see palpably before them the "iron horse," of whose speed and power they have so frequently heard. Such sights give a new and powerful impetus to the cause of improvement; and it behooves those who feel assured of the great good effect by Railroads, to bring the people together at each pausing place of the "Steam Giant" on his way to the Atlantic.[29]

Two more digs at the parsimony of the people of Germantown?

By September 9, the M&C RR announced that both freight and passenger service would be available, since the passenger cars were arriving soon.[30] On September 18, came the notice, "A daily Passenger Train will leave the temporary Depot, on Beale Street, at 7 A.M. for Germantown; returning, will leave Germantown at 8 A.M." The fare would be 50 cents. Half price for children under twelve and servants. If tickets were not purchased from agents at the stations, there was a 10 cents extra charge. "Negroes must have permit to be delivered to the Conductor, naming the point to which they are to go, and specifying that they are to travel on the Railroad, without which they will not be carried."[31]

Rather than ending all stage service out of Germantown, the arrival of the railroad temporarily stimulated lines running south. The above notice also announced that at Germantown connections could be had with "L. Sims & Brother's daily line of four horse post coaches for Holly Springs, Ripley, Tuscumbia and Decatur." Dr. Morgan ran the stage office in town and maintained its livery stable.[32] By September 1855, however, the extension of the rail network to Saulsbury had quickly

Photo 11. Germantown Depot. Passenger wing on the left; cargo wing on the right had an elevated platform. (GH&GC)

reduced Germantown's increased significance as a passenger hub. The stations at La Grange and Saulsbury became the transfer points for those coach lines into northeastern Mississippi and Alabama.

On September 15, the M&C delivered its first three bales of cotton to the city. It was Collierville rather than Germantown that had the honor of providing the first load. Soon, however, both towns were bustling terminals for the year's new crop. With only the LaGrange making the 24 mile trip to Collierville and back each day, the carrying capacity was still not sufficient, for the *Eagle* reported, "The cotton is piling up on the roadside with a rush and yet there is no perceptible diminution in the number of wagons which pour into the city by the plank roads." In November, the LaGrange, though "in a crippled condition," had generated $4459.20 in freight and passenger service. In December, the line had reached Lafayette, and the arrival of a new engine provided two trains per day.[33] One train served passengers, the other freight. In the month of October alone, the line already carried 5,589 passengers even before this expansion of service

For decades, the railroad ran special trains to Germantown or other places for occasions that attracted significant numbers from the city. When service reached La Grange, the regular plus two special trains carried passengers for that celebration. When they reached Germantown, however, its citizens were disappointed to find the enclosed passenger cars already full and had to ride in the improvised open cars, or stay at home.[34]

The depot was built in 1855, on which the town became centered.[35] As the railroad quickly realized the need for depot buildings, Germantown got one of the first on the west branch. It was wooden, while later towns like Collierville got brick buildings. The facility was larger than the present structure, for it had two wings. One served passengers and their luggage, the other freight with a platform at wagon level for loading and unloading. One observer described it as a "little jewel box," for its ticket office was adorned with a stained glass window. The exterior was a bright yellow with white trim and the roof was green. Under the cover of the broad eaves, passengers mounted the train. From each corner, chains dangled to the ground to carry off rain water deflected from the eves so passengers were not splattered.[36]

During harvest season, Germantown's station turned the surrounding roads into a web focused on the town, carrying heavy traffic from all around and as far south in Mississippi as the Cold Water River. But local farmers had to weigh the relative cost of railroad fees versus their older means of travel on the toll roads. The railroad seems to have been at least as big a boom for passengers and the mail as for commodity shipping.

The cost of shipping determined whether the farmer used the train or continued to rely on his own wagons. With oxen or mules and wagon on hand, the only cost was the tolls. The trip also provided time in town for business and purchases. As one farmer who lived immediately on the line put it, "But what after all is the railroad worth to me? ... I should always do my own hauling.... I am too small...." Nevertheless, he and his family would soon be using it to visit the city and other towns along the line.[37]

The *Appeal* paid special attention to the need for propriety in the new service. It called upon the Company "to appoint careful and gentlemanly Conductors for their passenger train." For "comfort of traveling" passengers need to be "under the direction of polite and gentlemanly officers."[38] After a trip to Germantown on September 24, the reporter was pleased to observe that the new conductor "is obliging, attentive and polite."[39] By 1860, Andrew Allden of Germantown was a conductor operating out of its station. He was only one of several by then. Another resident, William Moore, was clerk and railroad agent, which meant that he managed the station and was also telegrapher.[40]

The railroad generated both business and traffic for the town, which shared in every participant's profits. It announced that for the period March 1853 through February 1856, it hauled 51,340 bales, while over the next twelve months it increased to 61,816.[41] One would love to know the percentage of this traffic that came out of Germantown.[42] Clearly, the available numbers speak of a significant increase in wealth flowing through the area.

By 1855, passengers complained that only one train specifically served them.[43] A second passenger run was needed. How quickly they had become jaded. On the plus side, there was a generous free baggage allowance of 75 pounds per passenger. The railroad even promised to reimburse for lost luggage up to $100. Passenger convenience has clearly eroded in return for today's flying speeds. Finally on October 14, service improved. In addition to the morning mail train which passengers could take, an accommodation train left in the evening. One could now travel both ways along the line twice a day.[44]

The line was finally connected with Atlanta, Charleston and Richmond in 1857 with more direct connections through Chattanooga to Washington and New York. By 1860, the dust was settling on the railroad building frenzy. Germantown was one of a string of way stations feeding passengers and freight into a network connecting all of the eastern United States.[45] The town remained a hub for traffic from as far south as Olive Branch and the Cold Water to as far north the Stage Road to Nashville.

By 1861, the M&C was operating 50 engines, some specialized for either passenger or freight service. The newest first class freight engines boasted ten wheels (4-6-0). The strongest had hauling capacities of 18

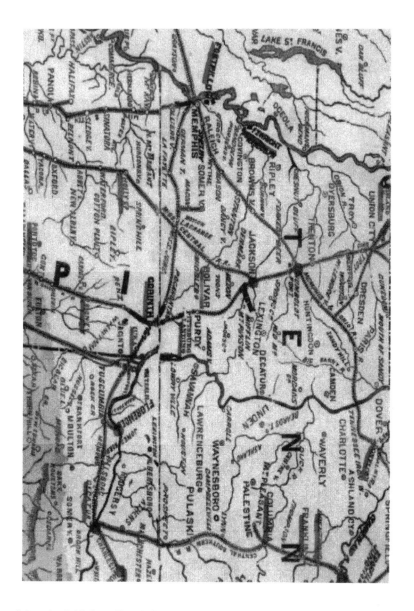

Map 6. M&C Railroad from Memphis to Decatur, Alabama, where it connected with lines to the major cities of the east.

cars, while the older and smaller were limited to 8. There were 30 first-class passenger cars and 9 for second class, plus 2 for branch line service. Unlike today, freight did not constitute the major part of railroad income. In fiscal year 1861, passengers and mail generated over a million dollars, while receipts for freight were only $729,885. By far the largest part of that was local freight.[46]

Along with the new convenience for travel came new dangers. Of course, horseback and wagon travel entailed their fair share of risks, but the greater speed and weight of the trains were new threats. Within the first month of operation, the LaGrange derailed between Collierville and Germantown. Fortunately, only the engine was damaged, and that only slightly. In fact, locomotive speeds were not all that great yet, twelve miles per hour being typical, but soon rising to thirty. In January 1853 after leaving Germantown, an overly adventurous passenger, a Mr. W. B. Nunnemaker, had left the passenger car and was climbing on the tender when he fell. His arm had to be amputated as a price for his daring. The equipment itself was not yet the safest either. Again in September 1854, a couple of miles out of Germantown, three of the wheels of the forward passenger car "gave way." Although the car was badly ripped up – timbers and wheels coming up through the floor – miraculously no one was hurt. The wrecked car was quickly removed, and the passengers had to make the rest of the trip in the baggage and road cars. In January 1857, another break down between Germantown and Collierville forced passengers and mail to come through on the later "accommodation train."[47] Four reported accidents in the Germantown area alone in the first five years of operation was probably a pretty good "track" record in those days. The worst local accident came in 1860, however. Three miles east of town, the night freight derailed killing the fireman and breaking both legs of the conductor.[48]

If passengers had initially felt a spirit of adventure, by 1859 passenger service was already a routine part of local life. Although the M&C was as well built as other southern lines, that did not necessarily make for extraordinary comfort. Ties were two and one-half feet apart and laid almost entirely on a dirt bed. The resultant subsidence in rainy weather made for something of a rolling ride, and increased the chances of derailment. Furthermore, the original ties were of inferior quality and rotted within five years, creating serious safety hazards until extensive replacement during 1860. In the same year, other mechanical improvements created a ride that was "smooth and free from jar and rattle," ending accidents caused by bad rails.[49] Consequently for the next year, the superintendent could boast that only one passenger had been killed during the entire year – one out of 353,646. Two crewmen had been injured.[50] That was probably an enviable safety record for the age.

An early officer of the road described passenger travel rather colorfully.

> The coaches seated 46 passengers, lighted with oil lamps,
> which every now and then made (the railroad) pay for a
> silk dress or fashionable hat. There were open platforms
> and link and pin couplings, and when the engine made an
> unusually quick stop, everyone in every coach
> simultaneously bowed.... Similarly when the engine
> started, unless (the engineer) paid attention to the
> successive slack, the passengers felt that the back of the
> seat was the only thing that kept him from going heels over
> head backward.

***

> There were only the hand breaks with wheels on platforms.
> Each brakeman had charge of two of these breaks, and
> after setting up one, would rush madly through the isle to
> reach the wheel on the next car. Experienced mothers
> learned to know the engineer's whistle to set up the breaks
> and hurriedly gathered their children from the isles to keep
> them from destruction in the wild flight of the brakeman.[51]

The new fifteen-ton, eight-wheeled passenger car was ten feet wide and
forty feet long, and through sleeping-car service to Charleston or
Washington was an heretofore unimagined luxury with upper and lower
berths and dressing rooms.

Of course, for most Germantown folk, the train served primarily as
a local commuter service. Almost 77 percent of passenger traffic was
local or "way" passenger. One paid accordingly for the "flag" stops that
served many locals, retarding the speed of travel. It cost four cents a
mile for "way" travel as opposed to the three and one-quarter for
"through" service between express stations. For instance, between the
regular stations of Germantown and Collierville lay the flag stations at
Forest Hill, Nevil's (Nevelle's), Bailey's and Bray's. Traveling westward
there was Ridgeway before White's Station, then the wood and water
station at Buntyn and another flag station at McGehee's. For better or
worse, the combination of laid-back lifestyle and southern manners
resulted in trains running well behind schedule. As long as passengers
consented, the conductor might hold a train at a station out of
consideration for a lady's tardiness.[52]

Another impact of the railroad was on property values and use
along its tracks. Rather than being shunned as today, the tracks became a
desirable location for homes. As early as 1853, the *Appeal* rightly
predicted that property along almost the entire line as far as LaGrange
would be cut up "into 50 to 100-acre lots by fine family residences."[53]
The process was incremental, but it certainly happened in the
Germantown area with some planters relocating their homes close to the

tracks and new residents buying up subdivided lands. The route was soon being described as having a "suburban" appearance out to Germantown.

Mail was no longer delivered by coach. On the eve of the war, Germantown's post office had become the second busiest in the county. Of course, the gap between the Germantown and Memphis offices was great. Postmasters were paid on a percentage of business basis. While Memphis' postmaster drew around $2,000 per year, Germantown's got a little over $200. Out of this grand sum, he had to pay all expenses for the office and its operations.[54]

The town's post office site was usually the home-office or place of business of the postmaster. The first such was Dr. James M. M. Cornelius. Like almost all towns, there was no designated post office building, rather it moved about as postmasters changed. During much of the 1840s Samuel Ledbetter and Job Lewis alternated the burden between themselves. Thereafter, it seems that the worthies of the town agreed that it was a responsibility to be shared among them with annual appointments. Then in December 1860, William Miller became postmaster and served at least until federal occupation of Memphis.[55] The office was located in his store.

There was no home delivery. People came to the post office for their mail. When it arrived on the morning train, the postmaster sorted and arranged it. No matter how far from town one lived, one had to come to town for the mail, at least until an unofficial substation was finally set up at a place called High Hill, apparently below Nonconnah Creek for those that far south of town.

Train service had greatly improved Germantown's communications with all of the eastern states. After 1855, at the price of one three cent stamp per half-ounce of weight, one could communicate with almost anywhere in the country. In the eastern states delivery took about a week or two. Westward, of course, was more difficult, taking easily up to four weeks to reach the west coast and much longer to get inland from there. Of course, truly urgent communications could go by telegraph throughout the eastern half of the country.[56] People who had settled in Germantown could communicate easily with those left behind. They could receive news of the world, stay professionally and commercially connected, conduct business and legal transactions reasonably and reliably, and order and receive merchandise from far afield.

According to a railroad handbook, in 1858 there were in town two hotels or inns. The German-born merchant, A. H. Lucken was owner of the oldest establishment. His Germantown Tavern sat on Bridge Street across from the Baptist Church and near the State Line Road. Originally a log structure, it had been expanded into a weather-boarded and white-washed hostel. In the 1840s, Carson's Tavern, a two-story building, had

Illustration 9. Picnic grounds. (Harper's June 5, 1858) Undoubtedly there was a greater mix of more rustic costumes at Nashoba Springs.

been another such operation. East of Forest Hill, the Neville home also served as an inn for some years.[57] By 1860, Alexander Blair's family ran Dr. Morgan's hotel, which was undoubtedly also located near both the station and the State Line Road.[58]

Certainly the 1849 advertisement for Ledbetter and Furber's Hack Line implies clearly the presence of professional boarding facilities. In addition to travel between Germantown and Memphis, they offered hack service on demand "from Germantown to the Nashoba Sulphur (sic.) Springs and back – distance two and a half miles." To entice customers, they advertised,

> To those who might wish to leave the city in the afternoon, after the business of day, to return the next morning, this arrangement will prove advantageous. And also for those who, singly, or by families, would like a pleasant day or two in the country in the hot season, with opportunities to visit the Springs as often as wished. The Hacks will be kept running during the season to Germantown.[59]

Before the railroad, Germantown was already something of an area resort town, competing with the more prominent waters at Raleigh.[60] During 1845 through 1846, Madame d'Arusmont, (Frances Wright) had advertised her Nashoba Farm "to rent or lease for a term of years." Consisting of a large tract of land spanning the Wolf, its major attraction was its mineral springs. The *Appeal* saw fit to trumpet their value as a great opportunity for development.

> This land is valuable on many accounts; and especially on account of the medicinal qualities of several springs. Of the curative properties of which we have heard more than one of our physicians speak in the highest terms. If these waters really possess the qualities attributed to them, we should suppose – when the fact of their contiguity to our rapidly improving city is considered – that the leasing the farm for a term of years, with the view of establishing a "*watering place*," would be a profitable investment; especially, as we understand the owner feels more solicitude for its improvement and future value, than for present pecuniary advantage.[61]

This sparked hopes around the town that it could develop a prominent attraction. Farmer and entrepreneur Benjamin Mosby responded and leased the springs with plans for developing a resort with picnic grounds and cabins to rent. Mosby announced its opening for the summer season of 1847 with an "eating house and confectionaries, together with such other refreshments as may contribute to the enjoyment of visitors." Finally, to create a grand attraction, interested parties tried to drum up public enthusiasm for a gala Fourth of July barbecue at the

Photo 12.  Ridgeway Store on Poplar Pike (State line Road).  (courtesy
Walter Wills)

springs to celebrate the veterans from all the surrounding counties of Tennessee and Mississippi. They expected local committees to form spontaneously to approve the project and call for a county meeting "to make suitable arrangements for carrying the proposition into effect." To round out his enterprise, Mosby built a small, flat-bottomed sternwheeler to ferry passengers from the city to his summer resort.[62]

Unfortunately county support never materialized. What was worse, his little sternwheeler and the resort he had so hopefully erected were destroyed by a severe flood or "runout." The boat, tied up at his dock at the resort, and most of the cabins were swept away. According to the *Appeal*, the flood "brought trees, logs and dead cattle down its swirling current and emptied everything into the Mississippi."[63] This disaster apparently discouraged further efforts at developing a serious resort at Nashoba. So many local efforts at enterprise floundered on the vicissitudes of nature and chance.

Nevertheless, Germantown's springs continued to be an attraction for city and area residents, but simply as "watering holes" for bathers, with adjacent picnic grounds. After 1852, Eugene DeLagutery took over the operation of Nashoba from Sylvia d'Arusmont, the heir, in return for paying her an income. Different renters continued to operate the farm south of the river, while its "resort" to the north was apparently just an open attraction. Residents with homes around Germantown remained the focus of visitor-friends from miles around, especially during the hot months of July and August. Some canoed across, while others took carriages around, across the bridge, making an almost steady stream of traffic on some days. Real estate ads in the papers continued to refer to the "celebrated Nashoba Springs."[64]

The 1858 railroad handbook touted the presence of three "favorite resort springs ... delightfully located in groves of evergreens, within a distance of two miles." In addition to Nashoba, it listed "White Sulphur" and "Brunswick." Brunswick Springs lay one mile east of town on higher grounds off the Germantown-Macon Road. There are no local memories of a White Sulphur Springs other than that at Nashoba.

Although a few of the town's business establishments may have been substantial enough to have had brick buildings, most shops were the sort of one-story clapboard affairs one still sees in old towns. Situated directly on the street, they offered a covered porch which, when the buildings formed a tight row, provided a covered sidewalk. The entry sat in the middle of the porch with one or more windows to each side. The building was usually long with a low pitched roof. The facade of store-front rose above the peak of the roof providing above the porch roof a potential signboard. Unless the building included a dwelling or shop in the rear, the only heat source was a centrally located pot belly stove. Wilks Brooks described the interior of his store built in town around

1840. "The store house is 24 by 32, so arranged as to have two rooms besides the store room. 24 by 10 shelves on both sides."[65]

One has to wonder how much business the town's dry goods and grocery stores did, because the records of the farmers and planters indicate that the bulk of their purchases, and subsequent debts were with Memphis merchants. Such firms advertised extensively as providing everything the planter needed, and the credit network among the banks, cotton factors and merchants facilitated bulk purchasing with payment made when crops came in. The town was simply more convenient for small and frequent purchases – an individual item of manufactured clothing, a bolt of cloth, or needles and thread, a comb or brush, some candy, tobacco or a bottle of "spirits." Even then, much of this business was done on credit.

Among the professions in and around Germantown were numerous educators, a lawyer, a dentist, and sixteen who titled themselves physicians. Such professionals typically practiced from offices in their homes. Since the merchant William Miller would describe himself as a druggist in the 1870 census, it is likely his stock already included patent medicines and drugs.

Such a number of physicians suggests the presence of numerous "quacks," but apparently such conditions were hardly unique to Germantown. A surplus of physicians and the presence of "irregular practitioners" were common in rural America. At least Drs. Morgan and Cornelius were considered very distinguished physicians.[66] A later comer, Dr. Richard Martin settled on a large farm just east of town in 1859. He was a graduate of Davidson College and had attended medical school in Philadelphia.[67] In addition to owning the hotel, Dr. Morgan had a sideline managing the stage office and livery stable.[68] Sidelines were common for most "physicians," indicating that the practice itself might have been the sideline. Their glutted ranks kept fees low, so only the most reputable earned enough to live off their practice. For instance, Thomas H. Todd was heavily involved in road construction and overseeing outside the district.[69] Established doctors like Cornelius owned or rented enough farm land to maintain milk and beef cattle and pigs, raising the corn to feed them.

Squire S. W. Ledbetter, in addition to running his stage line and being sometimes postmaster, had been the justice of the peace during the 1840s and early '50s. He was displaced by John W. A. Pettit, who eventually became county judge. The district constable, Jobe Lewis, had a sizable farm outside town. Other services were provided by William Tate, Real Estate Broker, and two speculators, William Warmell and Jonah Deloach, whose new presence spoke of the rapid growth. The two homes of Isaac and Hosea Bliss contained as many as six men listing themselves as "book agents." The term usually applied to men who sold books on commission for a publisher. These men, all from out-of-state, mostly New York, must have been providing books primarily for area schools, but were, however, of some means.[70] This combination of facts seems to imply that they represented something more than a gang of independent salesmen. Their location in Germantown speaks to the cultural prominence the community was acquiring with its private schools. These 6 men constituted 18% of the 33 booksellers in the entire county, most of whom were concentrated in Memphis.[71]

One of the more interesting families was the Molitors. Francis and his wife Cordelia, both born in Westphalia (Prussian Germany), had come to the states by way of Philadelphia where their first son Charles was born around 1833. From there they joined several German settlers seeking their fortunes in the Mississippi Valley and sailed to New Orleans. There are family memories of a storm at sea, undoubtedly in the Gulf, for the ship was forced into Galveston, and some children were lost, perhaps from the Molitor family. They spent some time in Mississippi, where sons Joseph and Francis were born respectively in 1838 and 1848. After moving around a bit, they finally settled in Germantown, sometime between the 1850 and 1860 censuses. Francis owned a grist mill, and titled himself a "machinist," as did his younger son, Joseph. That label apparently applied to anyone who ran "machinery" such as a mill. They also acquired some considerable land holdings, and some slaves. Charles was an engineer.[72] The term, "engineer" was a prestigious title implying formal education, frequently in a military academy. This relatively wealthy family, including Mrs. Cordelia, played a prominent role in town through the 1860s.

Lucken's Inn was famous for the high quality beer he brewed in his basement, one of four "saloons" that Germantown hosted. It was common, however, for them to have been a part of "grocery stores" rather than separate establishments for drinking. Nevertheless, they sold alcohol by the drink as well as by the bottle. For instance when Harrison and Noland opened their Wholesale and Retail Grocery and Produce Business in Germantown, they advertised, "a large and well selected stock of Groceries, fine Wines, Brandies and Whiskey; Hardware, Queensware, Tinware, and a general variety of merchandise."[73] In November 1860, the town gained an additional grocery/saloon when William Essmann acquired merchant and tippler's bonds. A German immigrant, Essmann and his family of five had been in this country for about four years, and by working as an overseer he had managed to save enough to go into business.

By 1860, Barry Hurt, John M. Woodson, William B. Jones, and Stephen D. Trueheart described themselves as "Gin makers." Hurt and Woodson were men of some property, while Jones and Trueheart were boarders, Jones boarding with Hurt.[74] What Trueheart was doing did not keep him from being a sufficiently respected citizen to be an elder of the Presbyterian Church from 1858 to 1904.[75] In fact, one must not be misled by the ambiguous nature of the word "gin." These men were not manufacturers of the "spiritous liquor," but rather of the machinery by that name.

Apparently from 1849, Germantown had something approaching industry to produce just such a machine. A "factory in full operation with steam power, machinery and workmen sufficient to make any number of gins required" was in place. Originally Burdine and Moore were producing their Southwestern Cotton Gins. Who they were is unknown, but apparently they did not last long. By 1854, Neely, Goff & Co., Cotton Gin Manufacturers, were operating the factory which they had named the Star Cotton Gin Manufactory. Their market was the cotton planters of the tri-state area, to whom they offered "Cotton Gins of the best Manufactory, with all of the late improvements. - Our work is propelled by steam, and we are prepared to do all work in our line as well and as cheap as it can be done any where in the United States, not excepting Yankeland." Joseph Neely, oldest son of local planter Moses Neely, was the J. C. Neely of Neely & Goff.[76] Within a year, Neely had a new partner, A. Reid, probably Archibald Reid, local farmer. Their product was now called the Southern Star Cotton Gin, which could turn out one to two bales per day. Most planters operated their own gins. The Star Gin was endorsed as being the "the best Gin in general use" among others by Ja's Kimbrough and Wesley Cole, planters of Germantown. The *Appeal* saw fit to emphasize this venture as "a home manufacturing establishment (that) deserves encouragement." "Their Gins, we believe are equal to any imported...."[77]

John Woodson, who had given up farming in Mississippi and moved to Germantown in 1855, was apparently running the mill by that date. It seems that Woodson and Trueheart had bought out Neely and Reid, and were running the operation by 1857.[78] The factory had at least two white employees, Jones plus Hurt, who was the foreman. The factory was undoubtedly also staffed by slaves. Moses Neely's youngest son, Hugh, had joined the partnership, serving the team as salesman and collector.[79]

According to the 1860 census, there were only 57 gin factories in the entire country. The average gin factory employed eleven people, paying them annually $432 each per year. It generated an average of $20,216 in value less $4,669 in labor costs.[80] Presumably Germantown's operation may have been average or smaller, supplying only a regional market, but clearly it added significantly to the town's economy.

Meanwhile more industry had come to town by 1855. One Henry Rehwoldt chose Germantown as the site for his Tennessee Terra Cotta Works and Pottery despite the fact that Memphis must have been his major market where he had a sales agent. There must have been an ideal clay source nearby, and the railroad eliminated the transportation problem. Rehwoldt offered every imaginable form of pipe and tile for functional and ornamental architectural and water management purposes, plus statues and fountains, which were popular for the lawns and gardens of the planters' homes. He also touted his earthenware cooking pots.[81] Absent from the 1850 census, he was apparently a newcomer to the area, but his equal absence from the 1860 census implies that either his enterprise failed or he sold out to someone else. His works may have been converted into the brick factory that was soon in operation.

There was a commercial cotton gin on the western fringe of town, with a factory for manufacturing cotton scrapers or seed planters, an item patented in 1859 by former town resident Jonathan H. Mitchell. Francis Molitor's grist mill was on the south. It is unclear where W.C. Harrison's steam-driven sawmill was located and if it was a commercial operation or simply a private plantation apparatus. Among the other "mechanical establishments," as they were called, were a cabinet maker, one blacksmith and two wagon manufacturers. By 1860, the other shops included several dry goods and grocery stores, and perhaps a book business. Other crafts practiced that may or may not have had shops were a cobbler, a tailor, several carpenters, and a mason.[82]

Thus by 1861, Germantown had two gin factories, a commercial gin also manufacturing a seed planting device, and some kind of ceramics or brick plant, plus the usual blacksmiths and lumber and grain mills. The city that today eschews industry was by 1861 almost as industrial as it was agricultural.

Finally the economy brought visitors to the area to constantly interact with the population. Real estate investors were undoubtedly the most frequent. Much land was being bought and sold by speculators, while others were absentee landlords. For example, the D'Arusmonts, who held the Nashoba lands, were both renting out and trying to sell their lands. Their agents visited to monitor the holdings. The agents of various other firms with agricultural dealings constituted the upper crust of traveling businessmen, while the drummers who came to town to hawk their wares were the more typical traveling salesman. At the bottom were the peddlers and tinkers who went from house to house. Apparently all were received with hospitality as long as they seemed about honest business. One August evening, Isham Howse, recorded that, "A little German peddler, named Gant, dined with us today. He is from Prussia; and is 17 years old. His whole stock of goods was tied up in a common-sized pocket handkerchief – yet from this small start he may grow rich."[83]

# Chapter 4

## Growing Political Tensions

During the decade before the war, secessionist tensions mounted steadily. Nevertheless, they were hardly the only political issues that concerned area citizens. Locally the political environment evolved around other issues as well.

First, however, local politics must be understood in its larger contexts – national, regional, state, and divisional. From the 1830s, the American two-party system was Democratic Party versus the National-Republican or Whig Party until the Republican Party replaced the Whigs during the decade before the Civil War. During this entire period, the most contentious issue was indeed slavery, or more specifically whether slavery would be allowed to expand into the territories birthing new states. Slave-owning Southerners felt threatened by the abolition movement which ultimately sought to outlaw slavery at the national level. If the slave-holding states became significantly outvoted in Congress, and if legislative and executive power could be combined, slavery could be strangled to death, despite purported constitutional guarantees.[1] Slave-owners would be denied their "property rights" by a "tyrannical majority" imposing its convictions on a helpless minority.

The rhetoric employed by the threatened slaveholders infected even those with little or no human-property rights to defend. It evoked the same sense of oppression as taxation-without-representation had evoked in their ancestors. They frequently compared themselves to those Patriot ancestors, and their opponents to Tory tyrants. Throughout history, the responses of those who have felt threatened with such loss of autonomy have been similar – receptiveness to conspiracy theories, especially focused on their political institutions, and righteous threats of resort to force if necessary to protect their endangered rights.

Furthermore, slaveholders or not, almost all Americans subscribed to contemporary beliefs in the inferiority, even savagery, of "the Negro." In the South, where African-Americans constituted a significant part of the population, there was universal fear that emancipation would result in the liberation of a dangerous horde. In the North, many shared this phobic racism enough to sympathize with the Southerners and have doubts about abolition. Even many abolitionists favored a "return to Africa" as the solution.

The natural response of Southerners to the threat of losing their "rights and freedoms" to a "tyrannical" federal government was resorting to the presumed states' right to secession. Since the formation of the Union, such an untested right had been espoused by states both North and South. By mid-nineteenth century, both the firebrand southern-rights advocates and the radical abolitionists who provoked them were widely perceived as disunionists – threats to the political stability of the nation.

Within Tennessee, the grand geographical divisions differed significantly in their involvement in slavery. In the East there were few slaveholders. Middle and West Tennessee were more heavily involved, with some counties largely committed to tobacco and cotton plantations. Even there, significant parts of the population were yeoman farmers and artisans, disadvantaged by competition with slave labor. The above mentioned racist phobias, however, made them fearful of widespread emancipation. Laborers were even more threatened by the prospect of competing with a mass of freed slaves. Yet among the vast majority of Tennesseans, there was a commitment to a strong national Union as essential to their security and economic well-being. Commitments to the Union and to Southern Rights coexisted in a balanced tension within both political parties throughout Tennessee.

Tennessee's two-party system had emerged during 1837-39 and remained relatively stable until the secession crisis, although Whig dominance gradually declined. At the state level, Whigs increasingly lost control of one or both of the houses to the Democrats after 1847, except for 1851.[2] Whigs and Democrats both appealed consistently to Tennessee's deep (little "r") republican commitments. There was a strong suspicion that centralized presidential power would fall under the control of powerful vested interest groups, undermining government by elected representatives who answered to the wants and interests of the people.[3]

The Democrats accused the Whigs of being elitist Federalists, the party of the rich and powerful who feared the presumed anarchic masses in a true democracy. Democrats insisted that the people should govern themselves and not "be governed by priviliged corporations."[4] Of course, the Whigs rejected such charges and presented themselves as defending the people against a "spoils party" based on demagoguery and greed. They charged that to win votes the Democrats incited a radical, leveling "wild democracy" that would tear down the Constitution's restrictions. Aside from such ideological polemics, a key issue dividing them was the problem of currency in an era when paper money was still in its infancy. This at a time when West Tennessee was still transitioning from a subsistence-barter, frontier economy. Given these socially-loaded appeals with economic undertones, Whigs found more support in areas of stronger urban and commercial development with market crops, while Democrats originally found theirs in more isolated subsistence-farming areas. For instance, in the gubernatorial and presidential elections between 1839 and 1851, Shelby and Fayette counties returned Whig majorities.[5]

Consequently for much of the decade of the forties, the town was the seat of a local party organization and the locus for rallies expected to draw from many miles around. For such a rally in 1840, some 250 people would travel by horse or buggy through heavy rains and over problematic roads to attend. In 1848, after a series of local meetings, persons from the neighboring counties of Tennessee and Mississippi met in Germantown to ratify the nominations of the Whig presidential ticket. Typically on such occasions the local Whigs provided cider and barbecue. Local leaders were William P. Vaden, a farmer from district 10, and James Kimbrough, a major planter of district 11.[6]

Nevertheless, Germantown was gradually becoming a bastion "for the Democracy" as the Memphis *Appeal* put it. In the gubernatorial election of 1843 and again in 1845, the Whigs took Germantown by only seven votes compared to more sizable margins elsewhere in the county. Nevertheless, in the much larger turnout for the 1844 presidential election, the Whig margin was more substantial.[7] In August 1844 for that fight, leading citizens in the vicinity had formed the Democratic Association of Germantown to advance the cause of Democracy, and to promote the election of James K. Polk and the annexation of Texas to the Union. At least 179 local men joined, prompting the *Appeal* to label them "a little band of patriots," and "as examples to most associations in this part of the country." Germantown's Dr. William W. Morgan was elected president, with Dr. John R. Evans and Captain James Boren as vice presidents. H. F. Hammer, Joel H. Hall, farmer, and Henry Jackson, planter, became secretaries, and George C. Furber was standing orator. A list of worthies formed a Committee of Vigilance: Breton (Britton) Duke, local planter, Job A. Lewis, farmer and constable, John Wilson, farmer, John Jackson, planter, Dr. William Evans, Jos Shute, Nathaniel Thompson, planter, Levi McCrosky, and M.G. Deadrick. One citizen of the town boasted to the *Appeal* that he had the names of "*ten whigs* who have been brought to a knowledge of the truth, and to see the utter deformity of Coonery."[8] In the gubernatorial election of 1851, 217 district 11 men voted, but the Whigs still won 116 of them. By the next year's presidential election, however, the tide had turned when 245 men voted, 132 Democratic.[9] Since the 1850 census had recorded just a little over 200 potentially eligible voters, the political involvement of the growing local population was extensive.

The presidential campaign of 1852 reflected the significance of Germantown and Collierville (Civil Districts 11 and 10 respectively) in the process. The active campaign lasted from August 10 to September 18, with the electoral candidates for the 10th Congressional District from both parties going together from community to community, speaking six days a week starting at 11 AM each day. Of course, they started at Memphis, but were promptly at Germantown on August 11 and at Collierville the next day.[10] Candidates stumped routinely at Germantown and Collierville during all subsequent elections.[11]  The two towns were clearly the centers for politicking in the rural southern tier.

Such occasions called for food, drink and a festive atmosphere. Traveling together and speaking in tandem, the candidates normally had to maintain gentlemanly decorum, and an air of good humored confrontation had to prevail over invective. At least the *Appeal* made a point of criticizing disrespectful language, especially attributing it to the opposition. But it seems to have occurred more commonly in partisan assemblies and published formats rather than in the tandem speeches. By modern standards, speeches generally went on interminably with each candidate giving attention to details that would exceed the attention span of modern audiences. They frequently read from newspaper articles and the speeches of other politicians. Surprisingly, their speeches were not always canned repetitions of the previous day, for the journalists traveling with them comparatively evaluated successive speeches.[12]

An account of another political rally in Germantown has also survived.  It was more spontaneous and locally organized than the campaign circuit described above, occurring on the occasion of the Presbyterian Ladies Fair in September.  Nevertheless, it had the same format.  The *Appeal* reporter who attended that event rendered his slightly less than objective observations.  Before dinner, the crowd "proceeded to the ground selected for the political discussion," where Mr. Penn again gave a speech that "seemed to please his (Winfield) Scott friends," although the reporter found it "wide of the mark." After dinner, the real speechifying got under way, with two men addressing the crowd on the part of each party.[13]  Interestingly, the speakers were all county or regional politicians, and no local worthy took advantage of the occasion. Local politicking was undoubtedly reserved for Lucken's tavern, or the porch and cracker-barrel assemblies of the stores/saloons.

Who knows whether it retained its atmosphere of "friendly persuasion" when lubricated by "spiritous liquors?" Perhaps not.  To quote a contemporary referring to Lucken's Inn in particular,

> ...on its piazza the politicians, when they were wont to harangue crowds, used to gather noisy mobs to listen to stale jokes and boisterous eloquence. ...the people ... (amused) themselves by listening to bald polatitudes and bald-eagle oratory....  I have listened to Dave Currin, Walter Coleman, Fred P. Stanton, Governor Jones and many others at different dates, ... while they stood before the Lucken and set the country in an uproar.[14]

With several of Germantown's postmasters being Democratic Committee of Vigilance members, the town's subscribers had been assured of regular delivery of the *Appeal* (a Democratic paper), which came by mail.  From elsewhere, however, during 1849 the *Appeal* got regular complaints that the paper was going lost at their post offices, while "the other papers of our city (Whig rags implied), having the merit of fast and regular travelling." After an investigation showed the papers were leaving the Memphis post office on time and that the problem "lay elsewhere," service suddenly improved. But after things cooled off, papers started going lost again.[15]  Nothing is new in the dirty tricks department.

Aside from stumping by the candidates, locals relied on the Memphis newspapers for their political insights. By the 1850s, there were several with distinct points of view. Among them, the *Appeal* was probably preeminent, challenged after 1855 by the *Bulletin*, and the *Avalanche* after 1858. The *Eagle and Enquirer,* which had fused in 1851, reduced to a weekly after 1858. The *Argus,* after 1859, was the city's official newspaper for publishing public notices. Although it never endorsed any candidates, it ultimately called for unity to defeat Lincoln in 1860. The *Appeal* and the *Avalanche* competed with one another in espousing Democratic Party and Southern-rights perspectives, with the *Avalanche* being outright secessionist. Though allegedly non-partisan, the *Bulletin* put forth a moderate Whig perspective. The more overt *Memphis Daily Whig* ran only from 1852 to 1856. The Whigish *Eagle and Enquirer* endorsed Know-Nothing candidates for a short period. These papers appeared in both daily and weekly formats. The dailies circulated in the city and throughout Shelby County. The weeklies served the tristate area beyond the county.[16]

Regular subscribers got their copies in the mail delivered by the morning train. One could also arrange to pick up copies at the depot when catching a train. Undoubtedly, public houses and hotels provided customers with reading copies. In 1852, as a subscriber to the *Eagle and Enquirer*, Britton Duke regularly shared its news with his neighbors, as did others. By the next year, even some of the more cash-pressed yeomen farmers were shelling out the $2.00 for a subscription.[17]  One had to go well down the economic ladder to find locals who were not politically informed.

If the members of the Democratic Committee favored the *Appeal*, the more Whig inclined had other preferences. In fact, Stephen Toof, a printer for the *Eagle and Enquirer* was the son of a Germantown resident during the 1850s. Locals often gave Toof $2.00 when he was visiting town, and he would negotiate the subscription for them.[18]

The division of Germantowners into Democrats and Whigs, and the gradual shift must have reflected a wide range of attitudes over a variety of hot issues of the time. In the presidential election of 1844, which had prompted the formation of Germantown's Democratic Association, Henry Clay, of the National Republican Party (Whigs) was running against Polk. Clay opposed the annexation of Texas because he feared it would reignite the slavery issue, which he had recently helped to defuse. He also predicted that it would lead to war with Mexico, as it did. Most southerners favored annexation of Texas, a slave state. Other issues, however, complicated things. Polk's hard line stand on the border between Canada and the U.S. was also popular, helping him win.

Two resolutions passed by the Democratic Association on its formation reflect other issues that probably divided the people of Germantown.

> *Resolved,* That in supporting, as we will with all our hearts, the nomination of Polk and Dallas, we believe we are taking the only ground to avert the direst misfortunes to our land: and farther, that *Disunion,* which as Democrats we do condemn and repudiate, can only be produced by foreign influences, at present making most unhappy strides in the present course of the followers of Henry Clay.
>
> *Resolved,* That we will preserve as far as we can the perpetuity of our Union, by opposing all foreign influences showing themselves in the present opposition to the annexation of Texas; and by the election of JAMES K. POLK and GEORGE M. DALLAS.[19]

The peculiar references to "foreign influences" threatening the Union may have been a shot at Northern abolitionists, which seems a strange use of "foreign." More likely it related to a different, growing paranoia. Since the creation of this country, every new wave of immigrants from countries or regions not yet well integrated into American culture has led to concern, often bordering on hysteria. During the 1840s and '50s, the perceived threat was that American society would be overwhelmed by German but especially Irish Catholic immigrants fleeing the inhospitable conditions of their home countries in great numbers. They were perceived as hostile to American values because of their presumed obedience to the Pope in Rome. Pope Pius IX helped put down the recent liberal and nationalist European Revolutions and had emerged as an outspoken advocate of conservative opposition to liberty, democracy and legal equality. This fueled a conspiracy theory that he would subjugate this country through the infiltration of Catholic immigrants controlled by Irish bishops. Immigration exploded during the 1850s, bringing a wave of especially poor, uneducated and unskilled people who crowded into the tenements of the larger cities. The inevitable results were rising crime rates and welfare costs – yet more "proof" of the threats they posed.

Indeed during the '40s and '50s large numbers of poor Irish-Catholics and Germans of Lutheran, Catholic and Jewish persuasions flooded into Memphis. By 1860, over one third of the white population was foreign-born – 4,100 Irish and about 1,500 German. The Pinch district became the equivalent of northern tenements. Locally the "Irish invasion" had been partially attracted by railroad construction. Although the work on the M&C in the Germantown area had initially been done by black labor, all along the line veritable armies of Irishmen appeared as a fascinating spectacle initially. Soon however, the Irish became the primary target of hostility. The Germans of any faith fared better in public opinion, but were occasionally targets of ridicule or hostility.[20]

Memphis' newspapers carried stories of ethnic gangs and crime fueling local nativism. There were also accounts of violence directed at specific ethnic groups. Although rural areas were far less infected, nativist feelings spread out from the city.

All this fear even disrupted the Democratic Party's deepening roots in Tennessee, because the party's leadership included Irish-Americans in many parts of the country, which also "proved" their intents to infiltrate and take-over. These fears split both parties and gave birth to the Native American Party in 1845, which became the American Party in 1855. This movement became know as the Know Nothings, because of their original secrecy about membership. In 1854, the party won major victories in northern cities and states. By that year, the Whig Party, so badly drained of support by the Know Nothings, was nearly defunct nationally. Nevertheless the American Party, like most third parties, failed to achieve successful national party status, and the Republican Party assumed the second place. Thus, in addition to abolition, nativism was part of the confusing mix in national and local politics.

One can only speculate on how this all played out around Germantown. In the early phases, the town was certainly introduced to the potentially violent side of the xenophobic fears generated by the immigration controversy. During the campaign of 1845, the Democrat's candidate for the Tenth District, F. P. Stanton, was accused of being a Roman Catholic.[21] Fierce exchanges ensued in area newspapers, especially between the *Appeal* and the *Eagle* and the *Enquirer*. Between 1844 and 1845, civility evaporated as polarization mounted. Differences of opinion over issues that allegedly threatened the country were no longer respected. Former friends and neighbors, especially prominent members of the opposition, became either fools or villains. Eventually, the radical nativists would go so far as to proclaim, "the time will come when we will have to rise in arms, and massacre the foreigners, or make them our slaves, in order to preserve the free institutions of our country, and transmit them unimpaired to our children."[22]

At least in Germantown, the expectation was that decorum would prevail. When its Democratic Association held a meeting in August 1844, it announced specifically, "Every body – the LADIES *especially* – are invited to attend."[23] Clearly in Germantown, it was assumed that women wanted to be informed about political issues. The Victorian

Photos 13 & 14. Wolf House (Baxter County, Arkansas). Two-story public building with dog trot. The sort of structure that Carson's Tavern might have been.

stereotype of women as too simple for the worldly concerns of men did not prevail. It was indeed common for women to be interested in politics, but they were not to discuss the subject publicly.[24] Since this was a partisan assembly, elsewhere, such as in Memphis, agitators could be expected. But the good people of Germantown considered their community to be immune from the likes of what ensued the very next year.

On July 31, 1845, while in Germantown debating his opponent, Phineas Scruggs, Stanton was shot by Dr. J. R. Christian, one of his more outspoken Whig and nativist critics. The shooting occurred as the speakers were milling about on a property beside Carson's Tavern and his adjacent store. While in Justice Ledbetter's nearby office, Scruggs had told Christian that Stanton had accused him of lying, which upset Christian, who set off to confront Stanton. The conversation that followed between the two men suddenly erupted into violence. Throughout, Christian had his hand in his pocket, from which he drew his pistol. Controversy ensued over whether he deliberately shot Stanton or did so accidentally while attempting to hit him in the face with the gun. Christian then retreated from the scene. He walked calmly back into the tavern, went upstairs to the room where he had boarded overnight and subsequently surrendered his pistol to Constable Lewis. He allegedly appealed to Lewis to protect him from the angry crowd gathered outside. Fortunately, the bullet had struck the side of Stanton's face and was not fatal. He rested in town for several days, attended by numerous physicians including Germantown's Drs. Cornelius and Morgan. Although Stanton could not continue stumping with Scruggs, he went on to win.[25] One wonders what impact this outburst of violence had on the atmosphere in Germantown.

Previously in August 1844, even if the founders of the town's Democratic Association had expressed nativist concerns in their resolutions, the Democratic Party in general and that of Shelby County in particular denounced nativist extremism and the Know-Nothings. Consequently as the Democratic position crystallized during the 1850s, the controversy added further to political divisions around Germantown. After the Shelby County Democrats took a hard line position in December 1855, among the delegates it sent to the state convention was Job Lewis, who must have represented the element that stayed true to the party.[26]

Given the steady influx of immigrants into the town over the years, there was a potential for ethnic-political tensions, but had it manifested itself in any ways that focused on local residents? In the 1850 census in Germantown proper, there were five men of German origin and two from Ireland. Out in the rest of District 11, there were three more German immigrants and two more from Ireland. With the exception of the two

Irishmen living in town and two Germans, they were all men of some means, however. Furthermore, both nationalities had been among the earliest settlers after all.

The Germans were merchants, propertied farmers or mechanics. A. H. Lucken was, of course, the extremely popular innkeeper and entrepreneur. In the 1830s, it had allegedly been proposed that the town be named Luckenville, and his eventual death brought an extremely large funeral procession.[27] Among the town's two Irishmen, one was a shoe and boot-maker boarding in a physician's home, while William White, age 21, was a laborer. Perhaps their lower social status would have made them suspect, especially if these two men were suspected Catholics. Or perhaps they simply fit in with the rest of the areas' old Irish settlers.

Even ten years later by the census of 1860,[28] the threatening flood of foreigners had hardly overwhelmed the Germantown area. Nevertheless, the record speaks of some potential social tensions as well as some interesting complications for the locals to deal with in terms of separating acceptable ethnic sheep from unacceptable religious goats. Among the undoubtedly socially acceptable Germans, there were the very prominent Molitors of considerable means, and Anton Shide, the professor of music at the Forest Hill academy. Even Julius Resten, boot-maker, held $850 in real estate and personal wealth, and William Essmann was worth $2000. Unfortunately, Essmann's original employment as overseer followed by opening a grocery/saloon could give him an ambivalent status. But the laborer John Myers, the French-born tailor, John Harris and his German-born wife, plus the laborer Jacob Modenberger, the gardener William Parringder, and the farm hand Frederick Angle could all have represented a "foreign" presence, if they were Catholic. But then, that was indeed a rare breed in Tennessee, outside Memphis.

Among the more likely Catholic Irish were a peddler, Arthur Carnel, the gardener at the academy, Thomas Magregor, and Patrick Hamilton. Hamilton was not an unskilled poor immigrant, but one of the book agents who boarded with the Blisses. To add to the possibilities, there was even one Italian gardener with the improbable name of James Moss. All this offers the likelihood that if nativism had reared its ugly head in the area, some of its citizens were the source of suspicions.

To add further complexity to the ethnic mix, however, two otherwise respectable "Americans" had married women from Ireland. Joseph Callis, a respected farmer, had married Eliza. James Rafter, another respected farmer, was married to Margaret, whose mother lived with them. If they had originally been Catholic, or if either of these established families had been Catholic, this would have added an interesting social complication. The Rafters, at least, were not, but rather prominent leaders in the Presbyterian Church.

Probably none of the local immigrants, as known entities, generated Americanist suspicions. It is the abstract entity that generates xenophobic fears. Yet, for whatever reasons, it does seems that nativism added another element of local ethnic and political tensions to that already created by slavery. Otherwise the town's political leadership would not have given it lip service.

One area resident during the 1850s demonstrated both strong attitudes about Catholicism and Jews in general, while being open and friendly toward particular individuals of both faiths. He once wrote,

> Catholics, the Pope as their head, say that Peter was the prince of Apostles, and Vicar of Jesus Christ, upon earth, and that the Popes are his regular successors; and they claim for him sovereign and infallible power over the whole church, that in Christ's stead he is as Christ upon earth. This, of course, is all mere assumption. But as successors of St. Peter, they would follow him in one particular, if in no other; they will when they can, use the sword in defense of their rotten system.

A solid Whig, he was among those captured by phobic nativism. On the subject of Jews, he subscribed to the stereotype of Jews exploiting their young gentile serving girls. "Those who will deny and persecute Jesus will misuse and persecute his disciples." Yet this same man spoke of several "Irish friends." There were others he liked whom he feared were "idolaters," probably meaning Catholics. "God preserve them," he noted.[29]

In short, since Irish and Germans had been present from the very beginning, the community probably accepted new immigrants without the tension that occurred elsewhere. The percentage of foreign-born local residents was 50 percent greater than in the state overall and almost four times greater than its comparable rural communities. It was greater than that of any other of the established states in the union. Only the newly opened western farm lands drew more.[30] New immigrants probably encountered little suspicion. More likely, local nativist fears were directed at the abstract "foreign threat," those Irish Catholics or other stereotypes whom one did not know as a neighbor.

Nativist preoccupations have generally been considered insignificant in Southern politics.[31] Such phobias must have been strong enough, however, for during the 1855 elections, Germantown area voters (District 11) swung away from the Democratic Party to vote 58% for the outspoken nativist, American gubernatorial candidate, Meredith Gentry, and similarly for congressmen, senators and representatives. In contrast, however, next-door neighbors in District 10 (including many Germantown area inhabitants and Forest Hill) stood by the Democrats by a margin of about 63%. While the ethnically divided Memphis wards and districts went both ways, only the rural district around Raleigh matched Germantown's defection in favor of the American Party.[32] Of course, with many issues such as slavery and prohibition involved in this election, it would be unwise to assume that nativism was the deciding factor. The very democratic (little d) Democrat, Andrew Johnson, may not have been as appealing to propertied voters.

In contrast to the *Appeal*, the *Whig*, which lamented the Democratic victory elsewhere, warned voters that under Van Buren the Democrats were betraying the South. That true conservatives and "Union-loving men of the country, and particularly of the South," would find the American Party the savior of the South and its interests. Both Democrats and Americans in the South sought to distance their party from the abolitionist voices in their northern branches.[33] As always, the way voters saw how their interests aligned with a particular party would be shaped by how well that party projected its appeals through the psychosocial lenses of the voter. As often as not, that defies rational consistency.

Meanwhile, the stage was being set for the next year's presidential race. One citizen of Collierville specifically claimed that many Whig and Know-Nothings were shifting their votes. Reporting on the debate of July 27 in that town, he quoted Mr. Holmes as holding forth "in the usual strain of Know-Nothing orators, abusing Foreigners, Catholics and the Democratic party." In contrast, Colonel Tilman allegedly "made decidedly the most telling speech of the canvass" in which "he did not indulge in abuse or epithets, but in a quiet, good-natured way, completely dissected (Holmes) *carcass*." In such an atmosphere, Germantown's district eleven votes swung back to the Democratic presidential candidate Buchanan. Its 259 voters supported him by a margin of 13. Yet this was still weaker than Collierville's 96 to 41.[34] All this talk of foreigners and Catholics clearly indicated that nativism had reared its ugly head in at least this part of the South, but its relative significance waned rapidly.

Yet once again in the county elections of 1856, the two neighboring districts split significantly over local candidates. Germantown's 160 odd voters differed widely on every single candidate from district ten's 82 voters. Then as now, local elections generated far less attention and participation, and the mystery of local differences between the districts in politics continued.[35]

The political and social interests of Germantown's Democrats must indeed have been complex. In 1848, several Northern newspapers chose to run a short interest piece on Germantown's political climate. Northern papers always liked to cast a light for their readers on the peculiar behavior of Southerners. In October, the *Boston Investigator* reported, "Madame Darusmont (sic), formerly Fanny Wright, made a speech at a Hunker meeting at Germantown, Tennessee, a short time since. A

Democratic meeting, we presume, is meant by the term 'Hunker' – that being the political nickname of the Democratic party."[36] Like many other tantalizing snippets uncovered about Germantown's early history, this one leaves one wishing for a more detailed report of the subjects addressed and the audience's reactions. At least, she must have been accepted politely, since the papers reported no angry demonstrations of the sort that occurred elsewhere when she spoke.

In addition to being a critic of slavery, Fanny Wright, then a part-time resident of the area, a famous lecturer, author and publisher of a radical journal, espoused feminism, anti-clericalism, interracial marriage and other radical social and religious ideas – scandalous to many minds. Locals viewed her with a combination of awe and disapproval. Her original first neighbor, William Twyford, considered her "a little teched," and "with more money than she knew what to do with."[37] As a boy, Robert Duke, whose lands adjoined her Nashoba tract, remembered her as "the most beautiful woman he'd ever seen. ... He'd never seen anyone that compared with her. She had a magnetism and a charm that was unbelievable. But people were horrified at her modern ideas. ... She was not accepted at all in the community."[38] Nevertheless, locals approved of her charity and good intentions, while fearing "that she accomplished more evil than good" by her irreligion.[39]

It was apparently curiosity that drew large crowds when she spoke, rather than the appeal of her message, a conclusion she herself had drawn much earlier.[40] In Memphis, on an earlier occasion, one listener remarked that she "disbelieved in the othanticity of the Bible, and say it is a Book that will not bear investigation...."[41] It amazes one that such a speaker would have even been invited to speak by a popular political group in mid-nineteenth century rural America. Such a political party event today would produce such loud protests in most parts of America that the party's program organizers would be forced to resign. Yet presumably, she received a polite welcome, if a chilly response. This tells us something about the local curiosity and hunger for intellectual and cultural stimulation.

As always, taxation was a political lightening rod. In July 1852, as the railroad building boom was getting underway in Shelby County, Germantown became the seat of the third in a series of local meetings in opposition to a tax for the construction of the Memphis and Louisville Railroad. They described the $250,000 tax burden as "both inexpedient and impolitic" in light of "the present depressed condition and indebtedness of our county...." The movement had started in Collierville the previous month, with Germantown citizens in attendance, and was followed by a second meeting at nearby Fisherville. Each meeting amended the published responses of the first with increasing intensity.[42] By the time the outraged worthies had gathered in Germantown, their rhetoric foreshadowed the indignity and self-righteousness of the secessionists. They solemnly resolved:

> First, That the operations of this law, if carried into effect, would be oppressive to many, would do them injustice and would be unequal in its benefits.
>
> Second, That this law establishes a dangerous precedence, not sanctioned by the Constitution of the State, in giving to an irresponsible majority the right to dispose of the money of a minority.
>
> Third, That all men are free and equal, and that each should have the right to invest his money in railroad stock or not as he chooses, and that the Constitution of the State teaches us truly, that "the doctrine of non-resistance against arbitrary power and oppression is absurd, slavish and destructive of the good and happiness of mankind."
>
> Fourth, That we are opposed to the enforcement of this tax and will resist it at the ballot box, and by all means within our power.[43]

Among the political movers and shakers of the Germantown area were, as usual the planters James Kimbrough and Britton Duke, joined by Dr. T. H. Todd, uniting both Democrats and Whigs.

Germantown folks exercised yet other concerns. In August 1854, locals incited a meeting at Germantown that drew "more than one hundred citizens of Shelby County, Tennessee, and North Mississippi." They joined popular local efforts to prevent the Memphis Navy Yard from being turned over to the city. They saw it as a premier, "Government-run" facility for the production of rope and naval supplies and the repair of naval vessels, essential to national interests. It "ought not to be allowed to degenerate into a consideration of mere local interest or advantage, but should be determined alone as a national question." Their effort was for naught, because the facility had never been able to develop significantly and was expensive to operate.[44] It is interesting, however, that they opposed the "privatization" of a "big government" operation. Concern about "national defense" apparently prevailed.

Finally, two other issues either interested the local population or infected political discourse. Although neither women's rights nor suffrage had acquired much significance before the war, local women were indeed attentive to political issues. The idea of women voting seemed so outlandish that even some feminists rejected it, or at least considered it premature in their campaign for women's rights. Beyond the suffrage issue, however, women's rights were being discussed. Only after the war would Elizabeth Avery Meriwether begin speaking publicly in Memphis in favor of women's suffrage. The wartime experience of enforced self-sufficiency would embolden many.

The temperance movement, which was giving birth to the feminist movement, was truly vibrant before the war, and an obvious point of strong disagreement in a community with so much interest in the sale and consumption of alcohol. A local temperance society had formed within the Baptist congregation by 1841. By 1853, the Friends of Temperance Reform had become such a forceful movement in Tennessee and Shelby County that it decided to run single-issue candidates for the legislature. The county's candidate was none other than Judge J. W. A. Pettit. Soon, however, they realized the error of trying to compete with one issue in an election involving other important matters. They sought instead to get an advantage by having each candidate print upon his ticket the word "Prohibition." If one would vote for a candidate so marked, but opposed the issue, he had to write "no" in front of "Prohibition."[45] Thus they hoped for a poll that would compel the winner to act accordingly.

Having thus removed the temperance issue from partisan divisions, they expected all the "ministers of the Gospel" to hold forth from their pulpits. They also expected the press to jump on the bandwagon, despite the well-known habits of many journalists. Predictably, although the *Appeal* encouraged a well-informed vote on the issue, it avoided taking a position. Among the speakers officially chosen to stump for the cause was Germantown's Reverend Evans. All ministers in the county were called upon to preach one or more sermons for the cause,[46] and one also must wonder how mixed the reception must have been. Alcohol, tobacco, gambling and dancing had always been important parts of popular Southern culture, and even the major denominations had been slow and uneven coming down against them.[47]

In any case, the cause failed, and over the next two years, the Friends began a campaign to get the state's legislators to impose prohibition despite the apparent lack of enthusiasm among voters. In Shelby County once again, Reverend Evans participated in the temperance convention that ardently pressured the state Democratic convention to select temperance candidates.[48] Needless to say, that was an even more forlorn hope. Since Reverend Evans and Judge Pettit were the only prominent Germantown folk whose names appear as actively involved in the cause, one suspects it was taken seriously around the town by only an impassioned minority.

Isham Howse spoke strongly against drink, but would he impose his convictions on others? At least he approved when his son went with William Duke to a temperance meeting a few miles north of the Wolf. Since this political assembly typically involved barbecue and probably attracted young women, it is hard to be sure what really drew the two young men on a Saturday afternoon.[49]

Around town, the temperance movement appears to have been merely a great frustration for a few ardent crusaders, a nagging nuisance for those who could not dismiss it with a sly wink, and the object of ridicule for the more boisterous imbibers. The cause seems to have lost its edge thereafter and limited itself to educational pamphlets and speakers. Although it had become an issue in the 1855 gubernatorial campaign, it almost disappears from the pages of the papers until the eve of the war when a local Temperance Society reformed itself in Memphis.[50]

One can be certain that many local women were among the supporters of the ministers who led the cause. Even if their names never appeared in the papers, their physical presence would have been prominent. The respectable sphere of religious conviction spilled into the public and political sphere. In private, the men undoubtedly got an ear full, and the limits of deference and subordination were being tested. Well before the war, the temperance movement was drawing women out and providing a unique experience in active public involvement and in testing gender relations.

### Local Government and Politics

As for local government, Shelby County was governed by its Quarterly Sessions Court, composed of each district's justices of the peace and presided over by a judge. To it fell responsibility for law enforcement, legislation, taxation, the certification of voters, teachers, and lawyers, and judicial and other legal matters such as apprenticeships, estates and wills, slave emancipation, and freeman petitions and their bonding. In addition, the county also provided or supervised most of the public services, such as bridges and roads, river maintenance, public buildings, public education, pauper burial, and the bonding of a variety of public officers and private businesses. It operated on taxes which it levied on property, plus fines and fees. With an annual budget of less than $5,000 on average, a county maintained its roads, bridges and public buildings, cared for the poor, and paid salaries and fees for services to the county.[51]

Throughout most of the period, Germantown citizens figured prominently in the quarterly court government. Each district elected two justices of the peace or magistrates. After 1857, a judge was elected county-wide to chair the quarterly court and run the monthly court that handled the county's judicial business. For example, in 1849 before there was an elected judge one of the district's long-standing justices of the peace, Samuel W. Ledbetter presided as the court's chairman for a twenty-one day session. As a member, he drew three dollars per day, and as chairman another two dollars. As justice of the peace, Ledbetter had to post a $500 bond to insure that he forwarded to the county all the fines that he collected for the punishment of petty offenses. In 1850, he was also elected county coroner. In 1854, he was succeeded as magistrate by

John W. A. Pettit, who assumed his role in the court. When Pettit rose to the status of county court judge in January 1860, he presided over the court until its dissolution during the war.[52]

Occasionally townsmen would run for and hold other county offices such as sheriff, or coroner.[53] The most important of these was sheriff, who enforced state and county laws, made arrests, managed the jail, supervised elections (along with the coroner), and collected state and county taxes. As the most lucrative office in terms of commissions for services, its seat could be bitterly contested and a source of corrupt politics.[54]

The civil districts that divided the county had grown out of the original militia organization of frontier times. They constituted an area that was expected to mobilize a company for its defense and the maintenance of law and order. This military responsibility would resume with the reestablishment of an organized militia in 1861. When an act of 1836 regulated the districts, they were to form the lowest level of rural government. Each elected its own justices of the peace and a constable, all of whom were responsible for prosecuting petty offenses too low for the court's attention.[55] Germantown had been designated Civil District Eleven's seat for holding elections since 1837.[56] To carry out functions within the district, such as tax assessment, supervising elections, and managing the district's public school, citizens from the district were appointed or elected according to the nature of the job.

Despite the allegation that the planters controlled politics, even local politics appears to have been a complex interaction among them, professionals like Ledbetter and Pettit, and the smaller planters and established yeomen farmers. Prominent among the planters involved from 1841 through 1860 were Britton Duke, James Kimbrough, and John Gray. They served consistently as judges for state and national elections, as district tax assessors, and as grand and petty jurors for the court, but rarely in elected office.[57] The planters and farmers shared appointed responsibilities for overseeing maintenance of the roads outside the town, just as the professionals and merchants of the town rotated the office of post master, and undoubtedly also those of town aldermen. While the preeminent justice or magistrate was always a professional, the secondary seat went to small planters and farmers. In 1860, William Walker won a position as justice and a role in political leadership that would continue after the war. Likewise for adjacent district 10, T. C. Bleckley, with lands in both districts assumed the same positions of prominence.[58] Both men were substantial farmers and small-holders of slaves. They represented the lowest level of economic achievement that could afford to hold office, and probably also that would be trusted by the land-owning voters who formed the majority of the electorate. Increasingly it was men of Walker's rank, plus professionals, who held most elected offices at district, county, and even state levels, with planters rarely entering the lists.[59]

Law enforcement in the district became a sinecure for an established farmer. Below the level of the county's sheriff, law enforcement was the responsibility of the district constable. Elections occurred every two years. To hold the office, a constable, usually with the help of several other citizens, had to put up a bond of $6,000 to guarantee his propriety. Duties included enforcing the law, executing legal actions, and collecting fines for small offenses.[60] Jobe Lewis, another respected farmer, held that office from at least March of 1842. By January 1845, Lewis had resigned temporarily, to be replaced by Jeremiah Shetter. Shetter, age 23, however, lived in Lewis' home.[61] In other words, he was Lewis' factotum. Lewis probably resigned because he had been holding the office of deputy sheriff under Sheriff Samuel P. Harduway since March 1844.[62] That position must have terminated, however, for in August 1848, Shetter resigned and Lewis resumed the post of constable. Lewis was regularly reelected to his sinecure thereafter.[63]

Education was a significant focus of local politics. Although the state financed an elementary education, such schooling was managed by a district board of common school commissioners under the authority of the county. The few surviving election results for commissioners provide our only glimpse into political tensions inside the district. Conflicting attitudes about public education were exaggerated by the limited state funds available and the need for local taxes to finance anything significant. A few planters like Britten Duke felt the patrician obligation to contribute a building and land for the purpose. Most who could afford it preferred the expense of private schooling to taxes that supported an untrustworthy, plebeian, common school. Those below them financially who preferred the shared costs of a publicly financed education confronted peers who doubted the value of more than the most minimal formal schooling that they could afford.

Initially, the election of commissioners generated limited interest, probably because financing public schools seemed so improbable. For instance, in 1848, there were only twenty-four who voted. In contrast, a much larger turnout in Collierville's district ten elected their school commissioners. By 1856, district eleven's involved voters had risen to fifty-three, still less than a quarter of the electorate.[64] Nevertheless, this represented an increase of interest in the issue .

Since they served without compensation, commissioners had to be citizens of means with some commitment to education and/or concern about the taxes to support it. They conducted the annual scholastic census that justified the state and county funds for common schooling that they dispensed. They certified the pay of the teachers, and decided on the employment of those teachers. How else they intervened in the instructional process is unknown, but since textbooks and classroom supplies were provided, they certified such payment and probably had a voice in selection.[65]

Although available funds from 1846 into 1852 had been expended for tuition at subscription schools, it is impossible to determine if it went for more than the support of destitute children and orphans. There were also suspicious peculiarities in accounting. In September 1849, the clerk of the county commission reported to the county treasurer that no funds had been distributed to district eleven, which would have resulted from the district failing to conduct or report a scholastic census. [66] Nevertheless, the district had continued to dispense funds throughout 1848 and 1849, so this must have been settled retroactively. Then in 1852, the commission stopped dispensing funds, no elections were held to replace them, no scholastic censuses were conducted or reported, so the district received no funding for 1853, nor initially for 1854. Yet in stark contrast, the state school fund trustee in Nashville reported that district eleven had received for 1854 $148 for 370 students, a grossly inflated number. When in September 1854, the newly elected district commission actually reported its census, there were only 216 students reported for which it actually received $207 belatedly. One has to suspect corruption at the state or county level, an added complication for education politics.

This peculiar period terminated with the institution of the free common schools in district eleven. That transition from "private" subscription schools, at least partially supported by commission funding, to fully funded common schools generated local political controversy. The final settlement was heavily influenced by the advent of regular state funding in 1854. It was also reflected in the previously mentioned heavier participation in the election of commissioners.

In the poorly attended election of 1848, the farmers, A. L. Yancey, J. P. Winford and Elijah Brooks overwhelmingly trounced T. M. More, Dr. Cornelius and Britten Duke, the planter with patrician dedication to education. Voters dumped More from his previous position on the commission, to be replaced by Winford. Squire Yancey, a prominent citizen and local politician, served as justice from 1848 through 1854, and as tax successor. John S. Dennis and A. J. Mattlock would later serve as commissioners.[67] From all appearances, district yeomen, possibly concerned over taxes and corruption, prevailed over those more interested in public education. They managed expenses tightly until a complete popular break with public support for schooling had occurred by 1852.

In the summer of 1854, following the hiatus in commission membership and common instruction, Lewallen (Lonallen) Rhodes, wagon maker, J. Cole and Moses Neeley, planter, had been elected commissioners to get things going again with the advent of state funding. In July, Neeley resigned, and was replaced by John Pettit, who also assumed the office of commission clerk for the district.[68] Whether Neely was deferring to Pettit or resigning out of protest, is indeterminable. Pettit was, of course, the county's leading exponent of free public schools. Strangely, Cole seems to have been a short-term resident with no children for his name does not appear as parent in the scholastic census. Rhodes, now dabbling in local politics, represented something of the town's middle-class faction. After the war, he would become a merchant and local Democratic Party leader.

Throughout 1855, Pettit pushed through the reform, perhaps against opposition. Both Rhodes and Cole resigned to be replaced by Pettit's appointees, John Dennis and Matthew Brown.[69] Pettit did not stand for reelection in the following year, but the primary reason was probably his involvement as newly elected magistrate for the district and heavy involvement in county court business. Regardless, the commission and its management of the new common schools seem to have run relatively smoothly with its heavy reliance on the Pettit sisters as teachers.

Commission elections became more hotly contested, with a larger number of voters, indicating increased community interest. In 1856, James Kimbrough began his running tenure on the commission with the largest number of votes. William Harrison and Henry Jones, small planters or established farmers joined him. Thereafter, Joseph Clark and John Winford, farmers, served as commissioners.[70] Whatever the local elite thought most appropriate for their own children's education, by 1857 majority attitudes about the need to finance free public education were strongly in favor. Locals voted almost unanimously (82 to 4) in favor of an additional tax for school purposes.[71] The agrarian alliance of planter and established yeoman would manage the funds and supervise the schooling.

Finally, one has to wonder about the consequences of having the taxable property assessed by a local resident. For this purpose, the court appointed a citizen of each civil district, and paid him one hundred dollars. For instance in 1860 and 1861, that person was the planter John Gray.[72] Was the listing so transparent that everyone knew so well how everyone else was taxed that no accusations of preference would result? Previously in 1853, the assessor, Esqr. Yancey, had not even called upon the people in their houses, but relied upon them to report their own tax list. He was so lax that it was apparently not unusual for one to fall a year in areas without being harassed. How was the assessor protected from the pressures of friends and neighbors? Yancey, at least, had simply relied on their honesty and good citizenship.[73]

As for the town's government, the loss of its archives makes it impossible to reconstruct. Since the town had been first incorporated in 1841, the standard state requirements for the structure and authority of a town government applied. There were seven aldermen, elected by the eligible voters living within the town. They held office for one-year terms, so town elections were annual. They, in turn, chose from among their number, one to serve as mayor. A town constable was to be appointed by the council, to perform the relevant duties within the town itself. An appointed recorder and a treasurer rounded out the town's officialdom.[74]   Unfortunately, I have not been able to uncover any records concerning officeholders. They had to have existed, however, for as long as a town remained chartered, the maintenance of a Board of Mayor and Aldermen was required by law so the town would fulfill its legal obligations to the county and state. The penalties for failure were sufficient to guarantee compliance.[75]

The authority of a town government was extensive, but confined to its borders. The obvious value of having an incorporated town was the services it could provide beyond the limited services of the county. This authority and its services were defined as:

> The several corporations ... shall have full power and authority to enact such by-laws and ordinances as may be necessary and proper to preserve the health, quiet, and good order of their several towns; to prevent or remove nuisances, to establish night watches or patrols; to punish breaches of good order...; to ascertain and declare, when necessary, the boundary of streets and alleys ...; to provide for licensing, regulating and taxing auctions, theatrical and other shows and exhibitions; to restrain and prohibit gambling; to prohibit the exhibition of stallions and jacks...; to pass by-laws and ordinances for the paving of streets, alleys and side walks; to establish and regulate markets and inspection; to provide for the establishment and regulation of fire companies, and the sweeping of chimneys; to dig wells and to erect cisterns; to erect pumps on the streets and public grounds; to impose and collect fines and forfeitures for breaches and violations of the by-laws or ordinances...; to collect taxes upon all property and privileges within their several corporations, which are taxable by the laws of the state... to tax ball, nine pin and ten pin alleys; to pass all by-laws and ordinances, necessary and proper to enforce the powers granted.[76]

This not only reveals what the town's citizens wanted to control and maintain in their community, but also something of popular and sometimes problematic pastimes.   There is, however, one strange omission when compared with the powers originally granted town governments in 1841. There was no mention of restraining tippling houses, which had been specifically included in 1841.[77] Was this an oversight or the result of some successful lobbying in Nashville?

The right to vote in the town's elections fell to any male over age twenty-one owning property in the town, or who had resided there at least six months prior to the election, and to anyone otherwise entitled to vote for members of the state's general assembly..[78]

Based on the above, we have some basis for examining the contention that the planter aristocracy not only shaped the culture but controlled politics, which was becoming less democratic as the war approached.[79] First of all, one must note regional differences – not only those of the more western border states like Tennessee, but also in specific communities like Germantown. Tennessee had gone further with Jacksonian democratic reforms than the older states in terms of voter qualification, office holding requirements and the relative spread of elected versus appointed offices. At the state level, although real property holding among legislators had shifted upward between 1850 and 1860, the vast majority remained in the middle range. The same can be said of personal property holdings. Although slave-owners had taken the majority of seats by 1860, planters remained a distinct minority and there were no large planters at all in the legislature.80 One should not be surprised to see that in any modernizing democracy, the socioeconomic middle would form the political majority, even in the Old South, but especially Tennessee given its diverse demographics. Of course, one would also expect wealthy and influential interest groups like planters to be able to exercise disproportionate political influence. Nomination processes can be manipulated, and both elected officials and voters can be bribed, cajoled or intimidated. The "free press," in addition to partisan divisions, can be ideologically constrained by what its subscribers and advertisers will tolerate. No democratic constitutional process can be immune to such, but it is tricky to assert that one particular class "controlled" such a system.

The relatively few insights we have into county and Germantown's district politics leave us guessing about the question of possible "control," much less by whom. Voting rights and the resultant pollings were certainly democratic among males. Any man in residence for six months and over the age of twenty-one could vote, and they certainly exercised that franchise enthusiastically in federal and state elections. The turnout for district offices, especially the more seemingly petty school board, were more ephemeral. In all cases, the vote was clearly dominated by a majority of the upper to lower middle property holders and men of other means. They and their sons outnumbered both the great landed and the landless.

As the early alignment of the propertied with the Whig party shifted, the planters who stayed true to their party lost control outside their party. Those who joined the Democrats allied themselves with the more (little-d) democratic elements of society, who were by no means always easy to manipulate.

Party positions were more a matter of a community of consensus than of influence – a consensus that could be marshaled to make persuasive political arguments. To argue that the Southern values and interests that this community shared was shaped mostly from above by its elite requires a vulgar Marxist set of assumptions. To argue that the economic system of slavery generated a common set of interests is easier, especially when one adds the racial fears and prejudices that it entailed inherently. Finally regional pride, suspicions and prejudices were deeply entrenched in that culture. They bound together those who benefited from slavery with those who did not.

Both Germantown voters in particular and county voters in general displayed the typical Southern distrust of government and resentment of taxes. Nevertheless, it did not result in the blocking of taxes, regulations and legislation that favored modernization, especially railroad building.[81] They were certainly a source of political contention locally, but usually insufficient to thwart development. The same was true for increasing taxes for education, although again not as generously as truly needed. There, privatization usually prevailed over government initiative, as it had in the case of roads. The belief that government existed primarily to protect private property was a cornerstone – that along with protecting national interests and defense. In the later case, however, government could be seen as more reliable than local or private interests in cases like the Memphis Navy Yard.

With the exception of a few professionals, especially lawyers, the social and economic elite avoided the political hassle of running for and holding office. They often served in the kinds of offices that involved community service, which did provide some influence in issues like taxes and expenditures for education and roads, but they shared these offices with the middle strata. An office like post master was passed around as more of a shared burden. On the other hand, the important district offices of magistrate and constable became something approaching sinecures. But one cannot assume that these men were the tools of an elite few. Constable Lewis may have simply had a personality and style with which everyone was comfortable, making him a popular choice for all, but he had undoubtedly built a base of personal power that reached beyond the district. By 1860, the men who were magistrates had become political scrappers. It seems unlikely they were simply the tools of the elite. More likely they built and maintained a majority base that may have run well down the socioeconomic scale, which is not to say that they would be easily indifferent to influential interests.

Issues like temperance, taxation and finance could be contentious but not seriously divisive. Phobias generated by Know-Nothing Americanism could temporarily disrupt voting trends, but not enough to rend a community like Germantown. Likewise, consensus over the necessity of slavery could not easily produce agreement over secession versus union. That was a crack that could only be patched over temporarily by community pressures responding to overwhelming external developments. In that regard as in all others, it seems that politics around Germantown were shaped more by a sense of community and common interests than by control or manipulation.

## *The Clouds of War Gather*

The Kansas-Nebraska Act had further exacerbated divisions within the Whig and Democratic parties. Since this act would settle the decision over slavery in each new state by popular vote, Democrats unanimously endorsed the act as a victory of republican principles over congressional nullification of slave owner property rights. Unfortunately, the consequence of the 1854 act unleashed the bloody confrontation in "bleeding Kansas" that would plague the nation up to the Civil War, doing much to set the tone of that war in West Tennessee.

In the northwest, the demise of the Whig party and the confrontation over the Kansas-Nebraska Act gave birth to the Republican Party. Southerners saw that party with its opposition to the expansion of slavery as a purely regional party threatening national unity. For its support of the act, in the North the Democratic Party also suffered severe losses in its congressional seats, thus making southerners feel doubly threatened.[82] Meanwhile, however, the emergence of the "Know-Nothing" movement had temporarily curbed the threat of the new Republican Party.

In Tennessee, the American movement divided the Democratic Party and essentially absorbed the Whigs. Put on the defensive during the presidential election of 1856, the Americans ended their organizational secrecy, tried to link opposition to immigrants and Catholics to the defense of southern rights, and pledged to oppose agitation over the slavery question as a threat to the Union. Likewise the Democrats proclaimed themselves the national party for Union in opposition to the Republican threat. Each party appealed to voters as the true national party for defense of the Union, but the Democrats had a stronger southern-rights position. The shift of old Whig leaders and voters to support Buchanan gave the Democrats victory in Tennessee, but especially in West Tennessee where they triumphed in former Whig territory. Democrats swept the state in the 1857 elections, putting the planter and Southern Rights advocate Isham G. Harris into the governor's seat and sending democratic Unionist Andrew Johnson to the Senate. They were indeed a very temporary set of bedfellows, and a perfect example of the complexity of Tennessee politics and sentiments.[83]

In Tennessee, loyal Whigs discarded the American Party title for that of "Opposition," and continued to campaign against the Democrats by blaming them for the economic panic of 1857. They in turn countered by proclaiming themselves the champions of the people against the banks. The Dred Scott case and the fight over the admission of Kansas had kept the expansion of slavery issue center stage, cementing the Democrats' position as defenders of southern rights and preservers of the Union against "Black Republicanism."[84]

In October 1859, as word of John Brown's Raid spread, tensions mounted. Of course, the idea that he seized the Harper's Ferry Arsenal with plans to arm a slave insurrection fanned the racial phobias of all dwellers among the plantation lands whether slaveholders or not. At first, however, the initial response of cooler heads was to rejoice at the prompt suppression, and the initial renunciation of Brown by Republicans and abolitionists. Quickly, however, even relatively moderate papers like the *Appeal* began to see the renunciations as so many pretenses and to argue that John Brown was merely the cutting edge of an increasingly nasty mood among abolitionists whose teachings would incite further threats against Southern lives and property. The abolitionists were seen as pushing the country toward insurrection and war for which Southerners should be preparing.[85]

As the next presidential election approached, however, Tennessee Democrats became split over the candidacy of Steven Douglas. His role in the defeat of Kansas' admission under the Lecompton Constitution made him suspect in the eyes of many Southern-Righters. More pragmatic Democrats, such as the editors of the *Appeal,* argued he was the best bet to unite the Democrats, defeat Lincoln, and preserve the Union. Isham Harris and his organ, the *Avalanche*, however proposed a different candidate, while staunch Southern-Righters pushed for a hard line on slave owners' rights everywhere in the Union. The upshot was the state convention's nomination of Andrew Johnson as their candidate.[86]

Then at the national Democratic convention in Charleston in April 1860, both the national and state parties split hopelessly. When the Party reconvened in Baltimore, a fight over the seating of deep-South delegates resulted in their secession to a separate convention. The majority of Tennessee's delegates joined the secession, while the Douglas wing of the national Party succeeded in his nomination. Despite their firm commitment to the maintenance of the Union, Tennessee's Democrats supported the southern Democratic candidacy of John C. Breckinridge.

Tennessee's Democratic Party was now split into those who

supported Breckinridge and those who stood by the national party. The Opposition became the Constitutional Union Party, nominated John Bell as its candidate, and once again presented itself as the staunch defender of the Union. Although Bell ultimately carried the state, Douglas drew over 20 percent of the votes in West Tennessee.[87] In Shelby County, Douglas drew almost 44 percent. In Germantown's 11th District, 229 voters divided into 100 for Bell, 94 for Douglas and 35 for Breckinridge. In the 10th District, 148 voters split into 68 for Douglas, 50 for Bell and 30 for Breckinridge.[88] This late in the game, Unionist Democrats still had stronger support around Germantown than the secessionists, and a very sizable percentage voted for the Opposition Unionists. The secessionists were a distinct minority.

The town's Whigs had mostly been staunch Unionists. One once proclaimed, "I have no patience with secessionists. He who would willingly see a separation of the states of this union, is a traitor to his country and an enemy of God and man, and deserved to be hung upon a gallows as high as that of Hamon. ... But I have faith in God, that He will put down all evil plottings, and every unhallowed scheme of Northern abolitionists and Southern states rights hypocrites, who, under false pretenses, would destroy the fairest fabric of human government ever established."[89]

As in most of the Southern states, there were no ballots for Lincoln. The Republican Party was still a regional phenomenon, and without the Electoral College system, he could not have won. As has been the case in all such elections, the losers proclaimed the winner without a popular majority to be illegitimate. Southerners had one more justification for secession and defying the President. Lincoln had won, so South Carolina seceded on December 20.

# Summary

On the brink of the war, Germantown hardly resembled typical stereotypes of the Old South. Images of a community of darkies and rednecks, presided over by WASP ladies and gentlemen distorts a more complex reality. The old town was almost as cosmopolitan as the City of Germantown today, at least relatively speaking. Although the majority of its inhabitants had come in from other parts of the state and adjacent southern states, a sizable minority had arrived from northern climes, while more provided a truly international spectrum. In addition to immigrants from England, Ireland, and Wales, there were Germans, French, and Italians, present in greater proportions than in most of the rest of the country. There is no measure of the number of second generation Americans.

Despite its location in the midst of a plantation agricultural community, that environment had not impeded industrialization and trends toward modernity as it had more generally in the plantation South. The tendency of the majority of the population, smaller planters, comfortable yeomen, professionals, machinists and mechanics to diversify and enter into entrepreneurial and industrial ventures counterbalanced the alleged stifling of planter hegemony. The railroads and the growing proximity of Memphis not only encouraged such enterprise, but had a similar effect on social and gender relations. There is certainly no indication that southern traditionalism was being overthrown, but by the same token, Germantown society was not as far behind the north-eastern bourgeoisie in modernization as in the deeper South. It was probably even more industrialized and commercialized than typical farm towns in the border states.[1]

Germantown certainly had its socioeconomic hierarchy. There was a high elite of wealthy planters, professionals and merchants. But they blended almost imperceptibly with the comfortable elite, who in turn blended with the comfortable yeomen and mechanic, which elements simply flowed down to the lowest level of independence among them. Below them were the poor, propertyless whites, but there was still no absolute social barrier until one reached that underclass of "poor white trash." Of course, even below them were the slaves, whose experiences were also closer to those of the border states than the coastal and deep South.

From all appearances, the entire society above the poor whites and slaves experienced less social tension than often attributed to southern society, though certainly no perfect harmony or egalitarianism. There would have been resentment of arrogant and condescending snobs, but no such individuals have appeared prominently in the surviving evidence.

Nothing indicates any class-based as opposed to individual resentments. As one historian has noted, the agrarian community "fostered communalism." Planter and yeoman, professional, businessman and mechanic were bound together in a tight economic relationship. Although each was proudly independent, they all relied on each other. The agriculturalist needed what the others provided. The others needed the food and raw materials the agriculturalist provided. They helped each other with major building projects such as the proverbial "barn raising." They ministered to each other in illness, communed spiritually, and shared public holiday gatherings. "It was the *community* that was self-sufficient, but that self-sufficiency was a product of mutual assistance." Even the "respectable poor" were included, although they would undoubtedly feel the sting of inequality and badly constrained opportunity.[2]

They and those below them have largely escaped our picture of Germantown life. They were a smaller minority than in many other parts of the South, as were the more marginal yeomen. Although there are a few passing hints that the privileged may have suffered the occasional act of hostile revenge, the proverbial "barn burning," property crime and robbery were not prevalent. Ladies were always accompanied in public by at least a servant, especially young ladies, but mostly to protect their reputations rather than to guard against evil threats. There is no indication that the local elites had to accommodate and coexist with a dangerous underclass as described elsewhere.[3] There were almost no reports of gentlemanly violence in defense of honor. Such violence was reserved for the management of slaves.

The real source of social tension was the presence of the large black slave population. Despite the romantic image of happy and faithful slaves, most blacks resented their status, even if they generally avoided displaying it. The black bogyman, the unrestrained or escaped slave, or worse the threat of revolt hung over everyone's head. Slavery created that which was most unique about the South, and Germantown could not escape that pressure. The combination of community and the ideology of white supremacy were the two pillars of white social harmony.

Although often described as pleasant or lovely, Germantown was no sleepy town, but a bustling transportation hub for business and recreation. It boasted graduates from the nation's prestigious universities, renowned professionals, industrious entrepreneurs and inventors, and enviable institutions of higher learning. It provided political leadership in the county. Local folks had every reason to believe in a positive and progressive future as participants in nearly a decade of uninterrupted advances in their well being.[4] It had taken about twenty-five years for frontier settlers to build this thriving community. More than one hundred years had to elapse for such an environment to reemerge after the war.

# Part II

## The War Years

### 1861, Germantown Goes to War

Secession was a hard decision for the people around Germantown, as it was in the rest of the state. Throughout the winter months, Unionist Democrats and Opposition leaders called for voters to stand behind the Union, as a new Union party formed around them. On the secessionist side, Governor Harris called for a state convention to define the position of Tennessee. Unionists suspected secessionists would use demagogic tactics to stampede voters in their direction, so they engineered a popular referendum to require approval of whatever position the convention took. On February 9, although West Tennesseans and Shelby County approved holding a convention by a strong majority, it was rejected state-wide out of fear that it would force secession. Even in West Tennessee, unionist candidates for delegate prevailed over secessionists by a vast majority. Nevertheless, secessionists persisted in the expectation that Tennesseans would lose confidence in the Union.[1]

They waged a hot campaign of pro-secession propaganda. The evolution was reflected in two of Memphis' major Democratic newspapers. The *Appeal* initially favored moderation and compromise (but always stood for Southern rights) and supported the National Democratic ticket. The *Avalanche* espoused radically the cause of secession supporting the States-Rights wing. The pro-secession elements, fueled by the *Avalanche*, managed to do what often happens when a war approaches. The public mood shifted in favor of a necessary war to defend the South against "Northern invasion." By February, the *Appeal* changed its tune, advising promptly joining secession as the way to avoid war by a show of strength through unity. It was soon unrelentingly secessionist.[2] It had already removed the American flag from its masthead, and within the month replaced it with that of the Confederacy.

As the debate raged, secessionists constantly blurred the language, making "abolitionists" and "Northerners," then "Tories," and finally "enemies" and "aliens" synonymous. The illegitimate and usurpatious "black Republican regime in Washington" sought to coerce and subjugate the South. The language was scripted with an eye toward inciting fear and calling for unity against oppression. Such appeals cut across class lines. Plantation owners, yeomen farmers and tenants, financiers, merchants, artisans, and landless laborers in town and country responded

139

alike.[3]

The people of Germantown divided over developments, but the local press persistently beat the drums of war. The *Appeal* carried calls for action that depicted the South as put upon and threatened with invasion to impose Northern interests.

**Who Won the Battles and Purchased the Territories.**—The abolitionists are endeavoring to deprive the South of all the territory acquired by the Mexican war, yet the records show that this very territory was won by southern blood and treasure. While fourteen slave States furnished 45,630 volunteers, the free States and Territories furnished but 23,654.[4]

**Editors Appeal:** For let them (the ladies of Memphis and the South) know of a certainty that it is only to the courage and efficiency of the men of the South, under the blessing of Providence that their lives, and what is infinitely more, their honor is safe, for the northern hordes would gloat in their ruin and murder, and would not, and could not be restrained by their own people wherever they got possession in any part of the country. The abolition government at Washington have designs on Memphis to seize and make it the base of operations in the South-west, and for them once to obtain it would result in the greatest ruin to the whole South, or the greater part. There should be every precaution taken to guard and defend it at every hazzard. Let the people here be vigilant.[5]

Then came the confrontation at Fort Sumter on April 12. Union efforts to hold and supply the fort followed by Lincoln's call for troops, seen as acts of "Northern aggression," undermined the Unionist Party's support. The tide shifted radically, and martial fervor prevailed. While reading warnings that invasion was coming, the citizens of Germantown learned in the papers of enthusiastic local displays of Southern patriotism.[6] On trips to Memphis, they attended entertainments designed to stir secessionist ardor. There was the great Panopticon of the South, with tableaux such as "the bombardment of Fort Sumter, the vessels sailing, the troops in motion, with the bombshels flying through the air, or [sic] their way of distruction."[7]

Once the war had begun against those states in secession, the die was cast for most Tennesseans. Throughout Shelby County, the civil districts held meetings to appoint delegates to a county convention to nominate candidates for the legislature. Those of Germantown's 11th District met on April 15 at the store of Messrs. Cole and Co.[8] One would certainly like to have a report of those proceedings. Unfortunately, unlike their neighbors, the Germantown meeting published only its nominations. Undoubtedly they expressed the same sentiments as those of district ten, many residents of which were part of "greater Germantown." They accused the "Black Republicans" of inciting the slaves to insurrection and murder and launching a war of aggression against the Southern states already in secession. Although they had formerly respected voters for the Union Party, they would no longer regard anyone as a friend who continued to apologize for the Black Republican Government. They resolved to "resist unto the death the aggressive policy of Lincoln's administration."[9] Coolness toward secession had been completely replaced by intolerance of any pro-Union sentiments.

Dr. Cornelius chaired the Germantown meeting with H. M. Neely as secretary. Its delegates to the convention were Henry and M. L. Massey, J. Stout, Charles Molitor, Samuel Cole, Cary and William Harrison, F. B. Crenshaw, Moses Neely, Samuel McKinney, Jos. Brooks, and Jonathan Mitchell. Others active in the meeting were both George and T. D. (sic, Stephen D.) Trueheart, and Solomon Gullet. These men represented a true cross-section of area society, from planter to mechanic.

As early as April 20, General Gideon Pillow, a secessionist consultant to Harris, called upon Tennesseans to form companies "for the defense of the Southern States against invasion." He called for "official reports from all organized corps of the State" to be sent to him, and concluded with an assertion that "I speak not without authority." Indeed, he had already visited President Davis to promise a division of Tennessee troops.[10] Secessionists were now confident that they controlled events.

Governor Harris proceeded to lead Tennessee into a de facto state of secession. On May 1, the General Assembly agreed to a military alliance with the Confederacy. On May 6, they passed a "Declaration of Independence" and submitted it to the voters for approval on June 8. The vote would also decide whether to adopt the constitution of the Confederacy and to send delegates to the provisional Confederate Congress. Also on May 6, the Assembly passed the Military Bill of the State of Tennessee, empowering the governor to create a state army of 55,000 volunteers "for the safety of the State."[11]

While the state, its cities and counties were spontaneously organizing a provisional army for its defense, the secessionists of Memphis organized a county meeting to mobilize voter turnout for secession. Germantown's district representatives included its political leadership, Judge Pettit and Constable Job Lewis, William H. Walker, L. A. Rhodes and T. W. Trueheart, who were to call meetings of the district voters, organize political clubs, and provide liaison with the county organization.[12]

Not only had the mood shifted quickly, but it did so with severity. Former moderates became over-zealous patriots and ardent watchdogs against the slightest whiff of defection, not to mention opposition which became totally intolerable. Unionists soon found themselves uncomfortably isolated and the targets of enmity. Most went along, getting caught up in the pro-war mood of self-defense. Others were intimidated into silence, or left if they had roots elsewhere.

Developments in Memphis were more extreme than in the countryside, but folks there certainly followed them in the press attentively. To prepare the city for the anticipated Northern invasion, the mayor and board of aldermen appointed committees of Military Affairs and of Vigilance. The Military Committee sought to coordinate the spontaneous burst of energy by amateur organizers to raise money and form military companies.[13] The Vigilance Committee was responsible for matters pertaining to the police, promptly issuing orders establishing curfews for free blacks and slaves. Simultaneously, the *Avalanche* ran an inflammatory article about agitation among the city's slave population. The contagion was being spread by "the most degraded whites" and freedmen. "Through their agency all mischievous plots are arranged."[14]

From newspaper reports, it appears that two committees, Vigilance and Safety, had separate origins, but were amalgamated, with the names being used interchangeably. In any case on April 19, the Committee of Safety proclaimed that it had assumed supreme executive authority for matters of security for Memphis and its undefined suburbs, if not the entire county.[15] Surely as news of these committees of safety spread, many citizens reflected uneasily on the similarity to the French Revolution on the eve of the Terror. Constant references to "Tories" also established clear parallels with American committees of safety and their dealings with "traitors" during our Revolution.

Anonymous letters began to appear in the papers that hinted at the fate of those who did not toe the line. One Dr. Wm. T. Bailey called upon others to join him in the formation of a volunteer vigilance committee "for the purpose of hanging or otherwise getting rid of all abolitionists in our midst." An *Avalanche* editorial at least distinguished between good and bad Northerners. "While the Northern spies and pimps in our midst should be burnt at the stake, nailed to the street doers and public lamp-posts, we should at the same time be just and magnanimous to those true men of the north who are unquestionably sound." The latter "are now exiled from their native North on account of their devotion to our rights."[16] On the one hand, there were paranoid warnings about northern spies and arsonists; on the other, appeals for discrimination. The ordeals of victims of suspicion made it especially clear that one had to be ardently patriotic and cautious about any utterance or action that might raise suspicions. The papers filled with proclamations of loyalty by organizations representing every ethnicity that had been the target of Know-Nothing suspicions. French, Irish, Germans, Italians, Swiss, Swedes and Jews rushed to form and finance purely ethnic societies and volunteer companies to prove their willingness to serve, which is not to say that most of them were not as devoted to the new cause as their neighbors.

What followed during subsequent months might well be described as a "Terror." Indeed accounts based on Northern newspapers paint such a picture, while the Memphis press handled affairs with much more circumspect reporting. The number of northerners reported to have fled varied wildly in the northern papers, and it does not seem testable against any reliable statistics. Charles Lufkin has estimated, however, that during the months of April, May, and June of 1861, about 3,000 Northern-born residents of Memphis fled the city. Others from surrounding areas also left. Yet he estimates that only about 20% of the northern-born fled.[17] In Germantown's civil district, of the seventeen men and single women of northern birth reported in the 1860 census, seven were still present for the 1870 census. This was actually a much higher retention rate than for southern-born citizens. Aside from Isaac Bliss, however, all the men involved in the Bliss book-agent operation were no longer present for whatever reason. They, after all, were probably a group of men far less well integrated into the community.

Possibly Germantown offered the kind of tight community support that sheltered "suspects" from the pressures that existed closer to the city. When the Confederacy passed a law to expel all "alien enemies" in August, it excluded such persons who were "citizens of the Confederate States" or who signed a statement of intent to become one.[18] Locals who had settled into businesses or farms of their own were immune. Although a few staunch unionists may have fled, those who had opposed secession but joined the cause thereafter preserved a sense of community cohesion that embraced and protected the large number of former unionists. The pressures that converted them to the cause were grown less of fear than of conformity. Soon however, that sense of community would be sorely stressed during the coming war, especially across class lines, but it would help communities like Germantown avoid the strife that occurred elsewhere during occupation, for its unionists had not been terrorized.

One clearly outright act of intimidation by the Committee of Safety was interference with the secret ballot during the county's final vote on secession. They required the election clerks to assign a number to each name on their voters list, with a corresponding number placed on each voter's ballot. No one could cast a secret vote against secession.

After West and Middle Tennessee voted overwhelmingly for secession, East Tennessee almost seceded from the state, claiming the elections were rigged. Indeed, pro-union voters were intimidated at the polls and unprotected by a secret ballot. In Memphis, where 5,613 votes were cast, only five men had the courage to vote for the union and were stigmatized in the press.[19]

In fact, these were the only five such votes in all of Shelby County. The votes from every civil district like Germantown's were unanimously for secession.[20] In Memphis, the joyous announcement of the results was accompanied by further celebrations. Similar demonstrations may have been held in Germantown, while some of its citizens silently harbored doubts. For what it is worth, on May 21, Union General George B. McClellan had reported on the state of affairs in Tennessee based on the intelligence that he had. He identified Memphis as a stronghold of secessionists, but in other West Tennessee counties pro-union feeling was predominant. There were many unionists "who are now outwardly secessionists," but who could be rallied if supported.[21] Whatever committed unionists remained around Germantown, they kept it to themselves.

A mini-civil-war soon erupted within the state when unionists in the east formed partisan units and initiated guerrilla warfare sabotaging railroad bridges. They were in open, armed revolt by November. Fully aware of pro-union sentiments in Tennessee, in June, with Lincoln's approval, Secretary of War, Simon Cameron ordered General Scott to send recruitment officers into Tennessee to raise 10,000 men. Although most were raised in the East, a recruitment officer was specifically dispatched into West Tennessee to raise one regiment.[22] Undoubtedly, he could not penetrate far into the state, and could have achieved little before occupation. Eventually, at least thirty-thousand Tennesseans joined the fight for the union.[23] It is unlikely any Germantown area men were among the early numbers, for family men would not have left their wives and children unsupported among hostile neighbors. Only single men such as those book agents with the Bliss brothers would have gone north in 1861.

Meanwhile, cities like Memphis had always had volunteer military companies with fancy uniforms and colorful flags. As secession approached, new volunteer companies blossomed along with the flowers of April and May. Hardly a day passed without the newspapers proclaiming such a formation, announcing its first mustering, and describing them in romantic martial language. Names like the Independent Southern Guards or the Tennessee Cadets were supplemented by companies for each of the immigrant nationalities, for many Christian denominations such as the Methodist Military Company, and also for the Jewish community.[24]

The infection spread to the countryside prompting the men around Germantown to meet on April 20. The published record of their assembly provides a list of those involved as well as a picture of their mood. Again Dr. Cornelius was chair, with George Shepherd secretary. They immediately formed a committee of Colonel George Trueheart (lawyer), Joseph Brooks (planter), James Kimbrough (planter), Dr. John T. Harris, O. M. Alsup, M. Rogers, Thomas Coles (merchant) and Reverend Joshua L. Cross. Its task was to consider forming two military companies. They promptly reported in the *Appeal*:

> In view of the perilous dangers by which we are surrounded, and being determined to defend our firesides and country to the last extremity; therefore,
> *Resolved*, That a military company of the citizens of Germantown and vicinity be forthwith formed for the protection of our friends, to be called the "Home Guard."

Any member would be free to withdraw in order to serve in another company for active service abroad.[25] Their language demonstrates the level of fear of invasion by Northerners intent upon harm. "Bloody Kansas" had ignited fears of the lawless rape and pillage that would accompany an invasion. Locals read sensational reports of how "jayhawkers" operating in Kansas, Missouri and Arkansas already used the war as a front for acts of outright pillage and robbery.[26] Such fears would prove not entirely unfounded, but dreams of civilian self-defense were naive. The unionist guerrilla activities in the east and the local militia-self-defense mood in the west set the stage for the worst of what West Tennessee would experience. This military committee was the closest Germantown came to the Safety Committee of Memphis.

In fact, Germantown was responding to the state's military board's call for the formation of volunteer companies, one for home protection and one for service in or out of state.[27] A motion of Dr. John M. Gray was approved to form two such companies. When those present were requested to enroll, about one hundred immediately joined the home guard. "The other company with many names" was also reported as "in process of formation."[28] Eventually, the Secession Guards were recruited with Germantown as its base, drawing recruits from as far afield as Mississippi. Only one junior officer was ultimately elected from District 11. To the east, Civil District Ten, centered on Collierville but including the community of Forest Hill, was becoming the nucleus of the Wigfall Grays.[29]

Another committee was formed to solicit subscriptions to purchase arms and equipment for the home company. It consisted of Messrs. Kimbrough, Brooks (both planters), William Walker (farmer), John Woodson (manufacturer), and Richard Brewster (farmer). Dr. Harris proposed a motion that was approved to the effect that those present who wished to subscribe money should do so. William Walker responded that since his broken arm prevented his service, "he would be one of any number to subscribe $20 for active service abroad, or one of ten to subscribe $50." "Mr. Fresstenheim (Furstenheim), grocer, and many others, made liberal contributions."[30]

The meetings ended with expressions of enthusiasm. "Several short and spirited addresses were made, indicating a firm determination to stand by the South. ... Mr. A. M. Rafter (of the boy's military school) read some patriotic lines of poetry...."[31]  One must wonder why "Colonel" Rafter and his staff did not play some more prominent role in Germantown's mobilization.

Newspaper announcements of the formation of volunteer units were usually accompanied by accounts of how local ladies enthusiastically began sewing the uniforms for their heroic young men.[32]  Soon the papers were filed with appeals for the ladies to form auxiliary organizations for the support of the troops.  The women of Germantown announced, April 26, 1861,

> **Editors Appeal:** We, the ladies of Germantown and vicinity, in consideration of the troubles that are brooding over our native land, have resolved to aid to the best of our ability our relatives and friends who shall engage in the approaching conflict. We, therefore, offer to the soldiers of Germantown all the assistance in our power with our needles, and promise also to aid in the care and sustenance of their families during their absence. And should the war approach our own homes, we will watch over the sick and wounded (though strangers) as our own brothers or fathers.
> [Signed] Mrs. Maria L. Pettit, Mrs. E. B. Cornelius, Mrs. Mills, Mrs. Moliter, Mrs. Morgan, Mrs. Rhodes, Mrs. Harris, Mrs. Hicks, Mrs. Boardman, Mrs. Burnley, Mrs. Goode, and many others.[33]

After several months, the good ladies followed their Memphis counterparts in staging fund-raising entertainments.

> **Exhibition at Germantown.**—The ladies of Germantown and vicinity will give a concert with tableaux, at the Presbyterian church, Thursday evening, the 3d inst., for the benefit of our volunteers.
> Miss Adie Plunkett. Sec'y.
> Germantown, Tenn., Oct. 1, 1861.

Instantaneously, the prominent ladies of the town and countryside had exhibited uncharacteristic behavior for Southern ladies.  They created their own organization, elected officers, set about an organized activity and published their names in the papers.  Although Southern

THE WAR—MAKING HAVELOCKS FOR THE VOLUNTEERS.

Illustration 10.    Both North and South, ladies organizations sewed uniforms for their local units. (Harper's June 29.1861)

women elsewhere made this same transition, Germantown's ladies did so with greater promptness than most.[34] Perhaps they were already in the habit of organizing themselves, but without publicity. They had been greatly encouraged to do so by Memphis papers and the example of the city's women. Undoubtedly their close social ties with the city had involved the town's ladies in similar lower-key activities before the war. Their "suburban" environment had exposed them more than typical plantation isolates.

This experience converted what had been their private household activity into a public operation. They coordinated their own talents, employed their slaves, and put any available sewing machines into teams producing the clothing. They purchased the cloth for uniforms and flags, and although working from patterns, added their own unique decorative touches. Their weavers and spinners produced the coarser materials for equipment. Germantown's ladies may have fully dressed the entire Secession Guards Company with help from neighboring towns. After the initial outfitting, knitting and sewing would have continued to supplement official military supplies until the following spring.[35]

The use of concerts and especially tableaux for fund raising was another example of the greater than usual rapidity with which area women transformed their demeanor. Musical performance had been a part of their school lives, but restricted to assembled family audiences. Especially displaying themselves in public tableaux produced criticism from the socially conservative. In wigs, costumes and makeup, they even posed as men in literary and historical scenarios or patriotic scenes. This was a far cry from church and conventional charity work.[36]

Area women responded to mobilization as women always do – with mixed emotions. Not wanting to lose their men, even temporarily, but also wanting to provide them with psychological support in defending their way of life. The elite and middle class ladies uniformed them, cheered them as they departed, and wrote supportive letters while they were gone. The wives and mothers of small farmers and the landless poor had everything to lose and much less to preserve by sending their breadwinner off to war. Their support was more ambivalent and fragile.

Beyond romantic sentimentalizing about "our brave young men" dying heroically on the field of honor, the good ladies had little sense of how much they would soon be sacrificing nor the horrible sights of the wounded they would eventually see. For some, the first sacrifice would be restricted diets for their families, for most however, that would only come with Union occupation. Less onerous, but certainly a sacrifice, would be the abandonment of stylish dress, for the hoop skirts and crinolines had to go to conserve resources and provide more practical attire for doing the men's work.[37]

On May 15, the Shelby Grays and other companies that had initially formed in the city took train for rendezvous at Germantown where they, including the Wigfall Grays, were sworn into the Tennessee Army as the 4th Tennessee Infantry Regiment. Due to high waters, the original encampment site, "the Sulphur Springs" at Nashoba, had to be changed to the Brunswick Springs, one mile east of town.[38] From Germantown and the surrounding area, the 4th drew more recruits. At least five area men served with the 4th, but perhaps as many as fourteen. Among them was William H. Moore, the railroad agent. John A. Kirby, who would later become a prominent Germantown area resident, had recently settled in Memphis in 1860 where he entered the wholesale grocery business. In May 1861, he promptly enlisted in the Shelby Greys and fought with the regiment until Missionary Ridge, where he was wounded in the leg and captured.

At the end of May, the Secession Guards, recruited at Germantown, joined ten others from surrounding counties, rendezvoused on the old fair grounds at Jackson to be formed into the 13th Tennessee Volunteer Infantry Regiment.[39] It's hard to find descriptions of the uniforms of these local volunteer companies, but fortunately, a fragmentary description of the Secession Guards' uniform has survived. It was "made of gray jeans, trimmed with three stripes red, white, red." "Jeans" referred to the cloth for the uniform.[40] The nature and position of the striping remains a mystery, probably on coat cuffs and collar, but perhaps also down the pants legs.

The 13th should be called a Germantown area regiment more than any other, for it may have contained as many as 33 area men. Twenty-six can be absolutely identified with another 4 highly probable. Most of them clustered in companies C and H, indicating a strong preference for a community of friends and family. The Secession Guard's (Company C) captain elected by the men was J. H. Morgan of Horn Lake. William D. Harrison, the 22 year-old son of the plantation owner, Carey Harrison and his wife Elizabeth, was elected lieutenant and later became its captain. Thompson Tuggle, 20 year-old son of plantation owners John and Martha, was elected one of its corporals, and was joined by his 18 year-old brother, George, and cousin, 16 year-old Joseph Tuggle, son of minister and plantation owners Phillip and Mary. Joseph's brother Phillip joined them, probably lying about his age so he could go along. Needham Harrison, heir to a small plantation, would rise to Sergeant-Major and then Lieutenant. With them were at least several other friends or neighbors, the Ellis brothers, Adolphus and William, sons of Benjamin and Sarah, long-time plantation owners, John Buster, owner of the adjacent plantation, Robert Ford, and Sam Winford or Wainford, farmer and son of John and Martha. There was Richard Small, son of the planter, George and his wife Mary. Undoubtedly their parents felt some comfort at the idea that their sons were being watched over by men they knew. There was James Rodgers, a young student living in the home of Lewis More, overseer, and James Slough, an overseer himself. H. F. Douglas, Joe Patterson and William Prest, must have been missed in the 1860 census, as were J. M. and Richard Scott of Company B.[41]

William B. and another brother from the Duke family also served in Company C. Considerable confusion exists in service records, for while a "Robert T. Dukes" shows up in records of Company C, it was actually "Rolfe T. Duke," who later became a lieutenant in the company. Robert had remained at home to manage the affairs of the plantation. It was Boelif (variously written as Roelif and Rolfe) who served and died in the 13th.[42]

Company H, the Yancy Rifles of Fayette County, had at least three "home boys," Cleon or Clem Callis, William Dunlap, Andrew Moore, but perhaps also David Dunlap. Henry Woodson was later transferred in from the 34th Mississippi. James Lamb, Robert Miller and William Small also probably served among them. Waddie Robards, living across the line in District 10, apparently joined Company A, the Fayette Rifle Grays. James 150, of the Duke plantation, served with Company K, the Dyer Greys. The Thirteenth's commander later described these men as "the 'flower of the South' young men, most of whom were fresh from the best institutions of learning – aspiring, hopeful and ambitious – the very best material for volunteer service."[43]

The elite 154th Tennessee (Senior) Regiment had been created as soon as the state government and its citizens became alarmed about developments in March 1860. It had the status of a special militia regiment formed by the volunteer companies of Memphis, and was to be available to the mayor or sheriff for the suppression of "mob, insurrection, riot or invasion." Such regiments were also on call by the governor for first service to the state.[44] On April 16, 1861, its officers sent out a call for volunteers and contributions to fully arm it for "the defense of Memphis". It consisted initially of the five, then six standing elite companies of the city and the Steuben Artillery. Three newly formed volunteer companies for "foreign service" were soon added.[45] Wiley Rochelle and his son William served together in Company F, joining perhaps six other Germantown area men. These three early regiments were among the first to draw the community's men who would soon find themselves well away from family and home for the duration.

The rest of Germantown's early enlistees were scattered among several other volunteer regiments. Specifically Robison's 2nd Tennessee Infantry may have contained as many as 9 Germantown soldiers. Robison's was organized in Nashville, May 1861, but for some reason contained men recruited in Shelby County. It fought initially at First Manassas or Bull Run before being sent west for Shiloh.

Colonel Nathan Bedford Forrest's 3rd Tennessee Cavalry was organized in Memphis between July and October 1861 and may have had as many as 12 area residents in its ranks. Initially, Company C, the Forrest Rangers, from Shelby County formed the nucleus of what was initially a battalion. Then Company K, McDonald's Dragoons, and Company D under Jesse Forrest were also raised in Shelby County as the unit expanded to a regiment.

Another six independent companies of cavalry had also organized in South-West Tennessee, and under the command of Lieutenant Colonel Thomas Logwood were mobilized in April to join the army at Columbus, KY. Among them were three companies, the Memphis Light Dragoons, the Tennessee Mounted Rifles, and the Shelby Light Dragoons, drawing men from Shelby County.[46] They were mustered into Confederate service as Logwood's Battalion in May. Since many had been among the early independent volunteer companies or rangers, some objected to being mustered into state and then Confederate service, because they thought they had enlisted to serve as independent units for local defense.[47] These units eventually became the 7th Tennessee Cavalry Regiment in 1862 which definitely contained Germantown men. Its men, unlike those of the other regiments, would serve relatively close to home for most of the war, playing a direct role in the impact of war on the town itself.

Aside from the volunteers who entered the regiments, several of the town's professionals undertook special service. The physician, Robert H. McKay, apparently served as Assistant Surgeon in the Medical Staff Infantry Regiment, C.S.A. If McKay served in field hospitals, then his service would have been brutally traumatic, for the work would have been more like butchery involving amputations without benefit of anesthesia or sterilization. On the other had, in base hospital service he would have treated more cases of infections and disease. Dr. Leonidus Richmond also served as a surgeon in the Confederate Army for three years.[48] As for Germantown's other doctors, they undoubtedly performed service when Germantown received casualties from the Battle of Shiloh.

Given the state of the profession and the status of medical science, the regimental surgeon was not much help even before the wounds of war struck. On both sides, far more men died of disease, given the often inadequate diets, insufficient clothing, and the harsh conditions under which they lived, but especially the exposure to contagious disease in close quarters and the general lack of sanitation. Accidents took another high toll. Given inadequate medical knowledge and care, the health of a regiment depended more on its commander. If he maintained a strict discipline of exercise, personal hygiene and a reasonably sanitary camp they could avoid disease. Otherwise, when the men turned out for the regimental surgeon's morning sick call, diagnosis was perfunctory and treatment was a dose of one of the few drugs in his kit. If a man succumbed to serious illness or infection, most regimental surgeons were of little use.[49]  Although the men on both sides suffered from exposure and inadequate clothing, the Southerners were usually worse off.

Another Germantown professional who did special service was A. M. Rafter of the military school.  His colonel's commission as head of the school did not result in his being commissioned to raise a regiment or even a company.  Nevertheless, whatever military background he may have had resulted in his being assigned to the General and Staff Regiment.  For the duration of the war, he served with the title of "agent."  Unfortunately such a designation is too vague to define his role.  He remained in some sort of headquarters service and surrendered with a command at Grenada, Mississippi in May 1865.

None of the area's ministers served, even as chaplains, although many ministers were firebrand rebels.  For instance, a camp journal of the 13th Regiment recorded an exhortation from a Rev. Mr. Tuggle while they were still at their initial Jackson camp.  Perhaps this was Germantown's Methodist pastor, on the occasion of a visit with his underage sons.  He expounded on the irreligious North and how God intended "us to punish them for their infidelity."[50]  Similar messages must have been delivered to the townsfolk until occupation.

The war brought a mobilization of the town's industry as well.  In June, the Neely and Trueheart Southern Star Gin Factory converted to the manufacture of ordinance supplies.  It would continue this work until December when it closed operations.

As for other local developments, Goodspeed's history of Shelby County related the following:

> The whole county became a military camp, or at least an organization.  Speakers were sent to every district in the county. ... The men in the various civil districts were organized into (Home Guard) companies over which were chosen captains and lieutenants. ... $30 were allowed for three months' guard service.  Special taxes were levied for military purposes. [51]

The original Germantown Home Guards became part of the county militia.  Its one hundred volunteers would have been greatly augmented, since all white males between the ages of eighteen and forty-five were required to serve, with exemptions for public officials, government agents, ministers of the gospel and a few other essential occupations.  On April 23, in anticipation of the official call for the formation of a home guard, the military board in Memphis called upon all companies being formed to report themselves.  Each was to report "the name of the company, the name of the captain (elected), the number of men enrolled, the arm of the service (whether infantry, cavalry, or artillery), the head-quarters or drill room, what arms it has ...."  They were to be formed into the Memphis Legion, to consist of two regiments, one from the city and one from its suburbs.[52]

The Memphis Legion became part of the 23rd Militia Brigade, comprising the counties of Shelby and Fayette, and J. A. Carnes of Memphis was elected Brigadier General, despite a strong preference for Farabee in district eleven. By July, Memphis was contributing three regiments, while the civil districts of the county formed two. The company of Germantown's District 11 was part of the 2nd Battalion of the 1st County Regiment, while District 10's was in the 1st Battalion of the 2nd County Regiment. Thus the home-guard citizens around Germantown, through which the district borders ran, were divided into two different companies in different regiments.[53] Nevertheless, former resident of Forest Hill, District 10, the music professor Anton Shide served as a private in Company F, 3rd Battalion, but of which regiment is not indicated.

Not all those joining the Home Guards were true supporters of the cause. Many whether unionist, secessionist or indifferent sought to avoid active service. Others sought to avoid any service at all. In December, one Tennessean wrote,

> I had no idea until the militia was called that we had so many afflicted persons in our community. The lame and the blind, the halt and the deaf, and indeed almost every disease the human family is heir to have presented themselves to the surgeons for certificates of exemption. I fear this calling of the militia is a bad move. I think three months' volunteers would have been preferable.[54]

Volunteers or otherwise, men from the Germantown home guard militia were soon transferred into regular units for "foreign service," essentially drafted into the Confederate Army regardless of original understandings. Some joined voluntarily. Specifically Shide joined Memphis' Steuben Artillery, composed heavily of Germans like himself. He continued to serve in other Tennessee artillery units after it was disbanded.

Shide's departure also relates to the fate of Germantown's schools. With the outbreak of war, most of the higher schools were abandoned by male students and teachers like Shide. Mary Thompson would continue on at the old Webb School, and even moved back into the old house after her husband and brother enlisted. The youth too young to enlist legally often lied about their age. The faculty officers and cadets of the military institute do not seem to have formed themselves as a company as one might suppose, but enlisted in other units.[55]

The initial Home Guard units that had formed in April and incorporated eventually into the 23rd Militia Brigade were succeeded by another Home Guard formation as an adjunct of the militia company. As part of the Act to Raise, Organize and Equip a Provisional Force, passed on May 6, the Assembly authorized the County Courts "to raise, semi-annually, a Home Guard or Minute Men." Shelby County met such needs on May 20 by appointing small companies of Minute Men for three-month service, one company per civil district, appointed from the ranks of its militia company. The county supplied them with arms, undoubtedly antiques, and paid them ten dollars per month at the termination of service. Toward that end, the county courts were also authorized to levy additional taxes, and to issue script or bonds until the "military tax" funds became available.[56]

With so many men going into the service, there was concern about security at home. That was the role to be filled by the Minute Men. One concern, given initial unionist sentiments, was spies, subversives, and saboteurs, and even terrorist acts. The company officers were charged with procuring warrants and arresting "all suspected persons," to be brought to trial. The primary concern, however, was maintaining control over the slaves. The officers were responsible "to see that all slaves are disarmed; to prevent the assemblage of slaves in unusual numbers; to keep the slave population in proper subjection...."[57] The war to defend Southern rights against an allegedly abolitionist government heightened the perennial fears of slave revolt.[58]

These "companies" of Minute Men were initially small, fifteen men, and very heavily officered. Each "company" elected one captain, two lieutenants and a secretary. A General Commander was appointed to coordinate and regulate their duty. Judge Pettit and the Commander constituted a committee to provide the arms and munitions, with the judge empowered to issue warrants for payments to the treasury. Vacancies were to be filled by men appointed by the district's justice of the peace. In June, the Court expanded the size of the companies for districts ten and eleven to sixty-four, rank and file. In July, it extended the terms of service for three more months.[59]

District Eleven's Minute Men consisted initially of John J. Tuggle, farmer age 48, elected captain, Benjamin Ellis, farmer age 46, T. J. Stratton, A. C. Stewart, farmer age 27, James Sims, William Myrick, farmer age 35, H. Boardman, merchant age 30, C. F. Molitor, engineer age 27, William Carter, farmer age 40, I. W. Bliss, book agent age 42, S. D. Trueheart, gin maker age 30, S. Thompson, R. W. Turberville, farmer age 38, L. A. Rhodes, wagon maker age 39, James C. Anderson, farmer age 25. Stewart, Myrick, Carter, Truehart, and Anderson went into regular service and had to be replaced.[60] Soon most Germantown men in Minute Man service were older, most age 40 or above. By October, at the end of their second three-month tour, those who had not already enlisted for active military duty, promptly requested release to return to their regular lives. Nevertheless, the court decided to extend their terms another three months.

The presence of the former New Yorker, Isaac Bliss, in Germantown's Minute Men illustrates the allegiance of local northerners to Southern loyalty. Bliss had owned and employed ten slaves in his operations. He was just a little too old for early conscription, but his local identity remained strong. He and his wife would be counted in the 1870 and 1880 censuses, even though he lost everything in the course of the occupation.[61]

Meanwhile, during the August gubernatorial elections the citizens of the area had another chance to demonstrate their commitment to secession. By then, differences between the voters of districts 10 and 11 had evaporated. In District 10, from the greatly reduced list of eligible voters 127 voted for the Confederate Constitution while 140 did so in District 11. There were no votes against. For Governor Harris the votes were 112 and 125 respectively, with only 12 and 20 for Polk respectively. Nevertheless, as in previous elections, in the votes for candidates lower on the list, like congressmen, senator and representatives, the two districts still demonstrated differences in alignment.[62] Political attitudes about more local issues remain an intriguing mystery.

In October as they began to gear up for the election of a president of the Confederacy, the court appointed election judges for the districts. John Winford and Henry Massey, planters, and Lonallen Rhodes, wagon maker, were chosen.[63] All such men had committed themselves publicly to the cause regardless of any original hesitations over secession.

In addition to paying taxes and doing militia service, those still at home experienced regular visits from recruitment teams and war bonds drives. On August 19, S. P. Hollingsworth, Agent of the Treasury Department, C.S.A., delivered an address at the town "on the subject of subscribing to the LOAN of the Confederate States." For some reason he felt compelled to announce, "The Farmers are especially requested to attend."[64]

Germantown's first known casualty came at the same time as the bond drive, dampening the attendance of one farm family. The death was accidental, which was not untypical. While the Secession Guards was steaming up river, Robert L. Ford fell overboard and apparently drowned. In newspaper notices, Mary and M. L. Ford offered a reward to anyone who found the body.[65]

Otherwise, the first enlistees of the 13th Tennessee initially had a typical, boring introduction to military life. After mustering in Jackson, they boarded train to Memphis, and embarked on steamboat to Randolph. There they drilled and trained for several weeks, marching to the music of their small regimental band. On July 26, they shipped to New Madrid, Missouri, where they were mustered into the Confederate Army. While marching back and forth for several weeks in hot, dry weather, they experienced several alarms, but missed out on all the local skirmishes. Always disappointed, they soon responded to such calls to arms in a perfunctory manner. Perpetually exposed to the elements, individuals frequently furloughed home to recover from fevers and diarrhea. Finally they joined General Pillow's occupation of Columbus, Kentucky. From September to November, when they were not digging fortifications, they were relentlessly drilling – bored by monotonous camp life. On top of all that, they were not receiving their pay, since Tennessee had exhausted its funding and the Confederacy was not yet coming forth. Disillusioned, many of the young men became rebellious and had to be disciplined. What was worse, their first enemy was a plague of measles, which along with other illnesses brought the regiment's next casualties who were buried on the bluffs far from home. One victim of disease was apparently Thompson Tuggle, Germantown's second death. Equally frustrating, the state had not been able to supply proper weapons. At best, some of the men were issued antique smooth-bore muskets; the rest had to provide their own rifles and shotguns from home. Finally, its colonel managed to get them properly equipped with the .69 caliber rifled muskets, fired by percussion caps. For this privilege, however, they would have to pay a price.[66]

Meanwhile, Germantown parents, concerned about their boys, were sending regular "care packets." Many regiments with their Germantown contingents were now in the field, specifically concentrated at Columbus, Kentucky. Before real hostilities had begun in the western theater, among the civilians at least something of an air of holiday-parade-soldering still prevailed. Parents regularly hopped the train to Columbus to visit their boys in camp. This created such a severe disruption of control and discipline that the commanding officers had to forbid civilian visitation within the lines. Even this failed to impress the more persistent. Apparently the phenomenon of today's helicopter parent is not all that new. They were incensed at the authoritarian behavior of the officers who failed to perform the same fatigue and night-time guard duties that their sons were forced to endure. Whenever one took ill, even with a severe case of home-sickness, they insisted that they be allowed to come home to recover.[67] Such petty behavior would soon become totally inappropriate, and parents could only hope for a son's return in sound body while on furlough or as an invalid.

On November 7, the men of the 13th were finally called out for action – "all were excited and anxious to meet the enemy." Their brigade was ferried across the Mississippi to block Grant's advance on Belmont, Missouri. Partially because they were so well-armed, they were given a prominent position in the line, which thanks to General Pillow's misjudgment, put them "in an open field without cover," exposed to "a galling fire" for an hour and a half. Before the day was over, they had lost 27 killed, 73 wounded, and 49 missing out of the 400 engaged – twenty-five per cent of the total Confederate casualties. Among them from Germantown, privates William J. Dunlap of Company H and James Rogers (Rodgers) of Company C were killed, and Richard Small was wounded. William was the son of David and Frances Dunlap, a local farm family, and he fell in the very first volley of fire. James could have been one of two area young men. One was a single young clerk who had been boarding with the Buch family. The other was an interesting enigma – an eighteen year-old of some means living with the family of the overseer Lewis More on the Thomas Goodrich plantation. In any case, James was quoted as saying as he lay dying, "Tell my mother I died in discharging my duty; that was all I could do." Despite its initially heavy losses, the regiment rallied and played a prominent role in the final victory.[68]

One wonders how families learned of their losses. Telegrams and or men in uniform bearing sad news were not yet a phenomenon of war. Before the war, neither federal nor state governments had any system for notification or even burial of the dead. Although regimental commanders were expected to tend to such matters, they were soon overwhelmed by the unexpected numbers and the frequent necessity to abandon the dead when the field of action was lost to the enemy. Men frequently wrote their family on the eve of battle, so they knew some time after a battle of his involvement and anxiously awaited another letter, while perusing the casualty lists in the papers which were relatively prompt but often unreliable.[69] In many cases, the bad news arrived in a letter from a fellow soldier. The black wreaths of mourning were beginning to bloom on Germantown doors. The ladies organization turned its attentions to the bereaved.

As for the men themselves, a study of Civil War letters confirms that their first combat experience changed things. Where before they had been anxious for action and honor, after having experienced the reality, they never again looked forward to combat. Nevertheless, the sense of honor and duty expressed by the dying James Rodgers kept most of them going in the face of constant death or disfigurement. They were now veterans – changed men.[70]

As the two armies had begun to mass against each other, in September, General Albert S. Johnston, Confederate commander in the western area, had already called on Governor Harris for an additional 30,000 troops, which he began to assemble. After its setback at Belmont, Federal forces increased their pressure on the Confederates across Kentucky. General Pillow raised the alarm that he was in danger of being cut of at Columbus and that West Tennessee and the Mississippi valley would fall to the enemy. He and General Johnston called on Harris to mobilize Tennessee's militia, which he promptly did. Again,

Memphis was selected as the western assembly point for that part of the state.[71]

These two calls increased recruitment pressures on the population, but especially the militia call-up seriously disrupted the daily lives of those who had not anticipated having to serve. Selected numbers from each company were ordered to assemble under their officers and then sent into the ranks. Thus more Germantown men found themselves "drafted."

From a population unaccustomed to such emergency measures, voices of dissent arose across the state. Many eligible for the call sought exemptions. Most, however, objected to what they perceived as an autocratic tone in the governor's call, even labeling it Czarist in style. Although area papers joined the criticism of the governor's political insensitivity, they impressed upon the public the wisdom of the governor and General Johnston in warning that the state was in imminent danger.[72]

Since we know the most about area individuals who served in the 13th, it would seem appropriate to return to the questions raised about social relations in the first chapter. That will also add much more to our picture of their wartime experiences.

Even when volunteer regiments were raised by officially designated, prominent men assumed to be worthy of their command, all officers and NCOs were actually elected by the men. Consequently all men technically enlisted as privates, and the majority would remain such for the duration. This militia tradition created a uniquely egalitarian situation for regular armies. Among the Tennessee veterans in the previously described surveys, a surprising 66.5% of the socio-economic elite served throughout in the rank of private.[73] As we shall see, however, this did not mean that their social status counted for nothing. As before, social relationships were complex.

Experience, known leadership skills, poise, self-confidence as well as charisma and congeniality would be compelling factors when soldiers chose the men to lead them. The educated and socially prominent had advantages on all these counts. Indeed, only the elite (1%) and some slave owning farmers (1.2%) rose to officer's rank at the regimental level – that is, major through colonel. Only the elite achieved the rank of general (1.1%). On the side of what must have been meritocracy, however, 3.5% of the poor became captains and lieutenants, while 5.3% of nonslaveholding farmers did also. At NCO levels, the range was 11% poor, 14.2% nonslaveholding farmers, 19.1% slave owners and 16.3% of the elite.[74] The rank of sergeant generally required considerable record keeping, which precluded the poor families that did not or could not spare their boys from the fields. At all ranks, however, all the classes had to stand, work, march, eat and sleep side-by-side. They were locked together in the brotherhood of combat soldiers.

In the 13$^{th}$, only three local men rose to officer's rank. William Harrison was elected lieutenant initially, Boelif Duke became a lieutenant, and Needham Harrison rose through the ranks to sergeant-major and then lieutenant. The only other known NCO was Corporal Thompson Tuggle. William Harrison, Duke and Tuggle were sons of families ranking among the very wealthy planter families. Needham was from a more marginal slave owning family. The prestige of the Shelby military college and its graduates seems to have empowered few Germantown men. Nevertheless, at least among these area men, class seems to have influenced rank.

The basic "family" unit in a regiment was the "mess." Beginning at the camp of instruction and thereafter, a small group of men lived and slept together in a tent, usually accommodating six men. Since there were no regimental cooks and chow halls, each mess cooked its own food and did all the chores related to such housekeeping. For officers, there were usually orderlies or servants. Except where a sergeant shared a mess with his men (a matter of personal choice apparently) all the chores were shared equally. If the social classes were mixed randomly in such messes, social equality would have prevailed. Whether messes were assigned or self-selected among friends and relations is unclear. From some correspondence, one gets the impression that the elite privates sometimes messed together, but the evidence is too fragmentary to draw general conclusions.[75]

One thing is clear, among the elite, military rank frequently played little role in personal relations. Privates visited officers who were their old school chums, socialized and dined with them as equals.[76] Such fraternization would not have occurred between officers and men of significantly different status.

One important distinction belonged to slave owners. They had the unique opportunity of having servants to do the menial chores of their mess. One son of Mississippi made a request of his mother.

> You say that if there is anything I want you will send it, there is one thing I want very much, that is somebody to do my cooking. I can stand a soldiers duties very well, but that of a menial does not come so handy, it is pretty much of a bore after standing guard all night to have to cook breakfast, wash up dishes &c. A great many messes have servants and it helps along amazingly. You might very easily send Stephen down..., he would not only be of great service to me, but he could make a good deal for himself, probably more.[77]

In fact, servants could be so common in some messes that this particular soldier's family heard he did not need one, for they were told his fellow mess mates already had servants. After that misperception was corrected, he wrote,

> I do feel very much relieved by Jim's presence.... I don't mind doing a soldiers work, but I do detest cooking and washing. I never expect to make my living or rise in the world by these means.... A man <u>can</u> do everything that a soldier has to do, but it is needlessly making a slave of himself if he can get some one else to do it for him, before I had scarcely time to write a letter or read a line, now I have plenty to do both.[78]

For Germantown's slaves, a record of some of their service as "body servants" to their masters has survived. After the war, as freemen, many bore the family names of their former owners, so we can even surmise whom they served. In Company C, Baltimore and Dick accompanied some of the sons of the two Tuggle households. Mull probably served William Harrison. Alf must have served the Ellis brothers, who probably shared a mess. None others from the area seem to have had servants for their mess. In all, at least thirty-three slaves served the regiment.[79]

Obviously if the messes were socially mixed, nonslaveholders would benefit equally from their messmate's advantages. Members of a less fortunate mess would, however, have developed a strong sense of inequality and unfairness. Also from correspondence, it is obvious that the well-off got a steady supply of food, clothing and other amenities from home, at least until occupation severed their connections. Again, members of a less well-off family would have been more acutely aware of social differences than they had ever been at home before the war. Finally, the departure of a son from a slave owning family had far less effect on the well-being of his family than did that of a slaveless farmer whose family depended entirely on his labor. Such a distinction weighed heavily on the mind's of the poorer family men. Thus Fred Bailey is undoubtedly correct in arguing that the wartime experiences of the lower classes greatly increased their awareness of social differences and injustice than they had before.[80] Undoubtedly the lack of surviving correspondence from the less educated explains why we remain largely unaware of how such great differences in wealth and privilege might have affected the tight bonds usually formed among combat soldiers. All such problems would be heightened by the advent of conscription.

Occasional newspaper articles also reveal in general a public perception that the privileged escaped service and sacrifice. Early in the war, Memphis' mayor uttered a scathing attack on privileged shirkers, at the expense of his position. By August 1861, the commanders of the Memphis Legion, the remaining not-drafted members of the militia, sought to remain in the city "for the defense of Memphis and immediate vicinity (with the understanding that when not on duty our members may be allowed the privilege of attending to their ordinary business)." As "men of prominence and influence, who have large amounts invested in the commercial and manufacturing interests of this place and cannot leave without great pecuniary sacrifice," they had to stay home to continue supplying the area's needs.[81] Neither soldier nor civilian survived this war without some heightened sense of social injustice.

Meanwhile, secession had seriously disrupted business and communications for the Germantown area. At first the major agricultural business, the cotton trade continued to flow south down to New Orleans, and there was much speculation in the cotton market. Business ties with the north were more problematic, with serious questions raised immediately about whether such transactions were treasonous.

Likewise, mail services gradually became more problematic and tenuous. The Confederate government had established its own Post Office Department in February, but even Tennessee's subsequent secession did not immediately sever all ties with the north. It took Confederate Postmaster John Reagan many months to get his new service fully operational. Until then, Reagan had "instructed southern postmasters to continue to render their accounts to the United States as before." Nevertheless, at some undetermined point, Germantown's postmasters, Charles Parrish who had to account for part of fiscal year 1860/61 and William Miller his successor, had either begun forwarding accounts to Reagan's office, or had been withholding them. They were listed in the U.S. Post Office accounts for 1863 as "owing money." When Reagan officially assumed control in May, Federal Postmaster General Blair ordered the cessation of federal mail service throughout the South. Thereafter Confederate mail service would have its ups and downs.[82] For one thing, rates rose steeply. Except for men in the service, it cost five cents for a letter going under 500 miles, and ten cents for anywhere else in the Confederacy,[83] but that would soon be irrelevant to Germantown.

It became quickly obvious that the absence of the men folk brought hardships to their families, but especially to those less well off. At least during the twelve months before occupation, county authorities provided some help. On May 20, the County Court, pursuant to an act of the General Assembly, ordered establishment of a tax to fund the support of indigent families of volunteers. A committee was established to draw up a list of those eligible, and they were to receive $12 for the wife and each child over age twelve and up to $6 for each child under that age.[84]

But problems immediately arose. Funds were not going to many of those most in need, and food was short.[85] But even after the banks promised to come to the aid of the treasury, ever increasing costs brought the system near to collapse, and the destitute families faced great hardship. In July, the papers announced bad news.

**Families of Volunteers.**—It is stated that ten thousand nine hundred and ninety-two dollars out of the twenty thousand levied by the county court in aid of the families of volunteers, has been paid out, and that another levy cannot be made until the October term. This amount will certainly not meet all the claims that will be presented. ... There may, before October, be the widows and fatherless of those who have given their last breath for their country to be cared for. ... Evidently benevolent efforts must be made. Respecting such efforts we venture to suggest that arrangements should be perfected for giving concerts, balls, costumes, amateur dramatic performances, sacred orations at churches, and such other public performances as may be practicable, once a week, the proceeds to be applied to this important object.[86]

The need for special benevolent efforts arose when it became apparent that the wording of the legislation only covered the families of soldiers on active duty. Once they had made the ultimate sacrifice, there was no provision for their widows and orphans.[87] This too had to be corrected.

One wonders, given the urban perspective of the newspaper reports, how much concern extended to the traditionally self-sufficient farm and small town population. How were the poor rural women to make weekly contact with county officials? Could they afford the train trip to Memphis or Raleigh?

By the October session, some of these problems were solved, with an unfortunate reduction of payments. On the plus side, the evaluation of eligibility was brought down to the civil district. For the eleventh district, William Walker was assigned responsibility.[88] Apparently by early 1862, the Court had finally worked out funding for indigent families, for it made several successive appropriations of $12,000 thereafter.[89]

Benevolence organizations were obviously both necessary and possible for a city like Memphis, but in the country and towns like Germantown, other conditions existed. At least the more intimate life of the small town and its church congregations guaranteed that the poor were not invisible and the better-off were pressured to help. The promises made earlier by Germantown's ladies were probably honored, but their ability to provide such help would not last much beyond the summer of 1862.

The autumn mustering of the militia drew even more area men into newly formed regiments, mostly numbered in the thirties. The 32nd, organized October 28, 1861, was primarily a Middle Tennessee regiment, but inexplicably drew some Shelby residents. James Harrison and James Kimbrough were certainly two such. Research has uncovered no record of how the militia inductees were allotted among regiments. Perhaps men like Harrison and Kimbrough were allotted without regard for local sentiments, for as many as eight area men may have served with this regiment.

Others seemed to have been assigned closer to home. The town eventually became the site of a mustering and training camp known as the Camp of Instruction at Germantown or Camp Sam Hays.[90] Although in May, Germantown had already been on the radar of Union intelligence as a "rendezvous ... undoubtedly occupied" by troops, this may have merely referred to the 4th Regiment's rendezvous there.[91] The camp may not have become an official camp of instruction until October when Colonel W. T. Avery announced that he had been authorized to establish "a CAMP as a rendezvous for the new regiment being raised by me at Germantown, Tenn...."[92] The actual location of this camp is unknown. Possibly it was on the east side of town, perhaps at the previous rendezvous site at Brunswick Springs, just inside Collierville's Civil District 10. This also seems indicated by Tennessee's General Order No. 10 of October 25. It referred to Jackson, Trenton, Collierville and Savannah as West Tennessee's rendezvous sites.[93]

Unlike the other camps of instruction, Camp Hays does not seem to have been so heavily used, probably because of its late establishment. Nevertheless, as early as October 19, the newly promoted General William H. Carroll reported that portions of his brigade were assembling at the camp, his former regiment the 37th,, plus the 38th and 39th.[94] Surviving records of few other regiments mention their having trained there. It seems, however, to have operated until at least late in the year. The last reference to a full regiment indicates it apparently left in November. By then the soon-to-be renumbered 37th Tennessee Infantry, with perhaps seven area men, was a severe case of the problems Tennessee regiments had getting proper armament. When ordered on October 26 to join General Zollicoffer in East Tennessee, its commander "was having trouble getting arms of any sort." By the time they had left camp on November 12, he had only managed to scrape together "an assortment of old shotguns, country rifles and muskets ... mostly unfit for use except in emergency." It had sat at Camp Hays since September awaiting arms. It would not be adequately supplied until January.[95]

The 39th had also been idling at Camp Hays for a similar period. So badly handicapped in getting formed, its companies were dispersed – three remaining at Camp Hays until late in the year.[96] The problem of getting weapons was so severe that the State government required all civilians to turn over their guns in return for payment. Such a motley assemblage had to be refurbished and refitted for military use.[97] Since, however, there was no sufficient means for enforcing such a law, it appears that many citizens were reluctant to part with their weapons so essential for hunting and the protection of home and property. Innumerable stories make it clear that the rural population remained well armed.

The 38th, originally the 8th, was formed in September at nearby Camp Abingdon in Fayette County. It was recruited heavily in Shelby County at Camp Sam Hayes. Perhaps because of connections formed when the brigade was at Germantown, Hugh Neely enlisted in early 1862 along with his business partner Steven Trueheart. After his Star Gin Factory ceased military production, Neely enlisted. He would eventually rise to captain and finally assistant brigade adjutant before resigning for chronic rheumatism in 1865.[98] The 38th also drew as many as ten other Germantown men.

For some time, Germantown was surrounded by many freshly minted Confederate soldiers. Business in the shops must have boomed, the good ladies of the town got another chance to provide the support for the boys that they had pledged, and the finer homes provided many an entertainment for regimental officers. One Lieutenant Colonel Barbierre had pleasant memories of his stay in September and of the leading citizens, Judge Pettit and Mrs. Cornelius whose "attentions I will never forget."[99]

Like Miss Scarlet, the young ladies must have been in heaven. Undoubtedly their parents saw all this as a mixed blessing. Although no records survive for Germantown, letters and diaries from other camp towns relate a vibrant social life, marriages, including social misalliances, and unfaithfulness.[100]

There are a few other references to the Camp of Instruction coming from letters. They cast light on the soldier's lot while living among Germantown's citizens. In October 1861 writing to Tullahoma, Captain A. O. Edwards reported,

> Several of the boys is sick with measels (sic.), there is ten of twelve in the hospitle (sic.) that is in the Methodist Church. They gave it to the Regiment for a hospital, and the ladies come every day and bring them something to eat. I believe there is some of the cleverest ladies here I ever saw. The drill field is full (of them) every evening and they bring some of the nicest boq'ts. I ever saw. I got one last evening from a nice lady.[101]

In all the camps of instruction, measles hit hard the boys who had grown up in rural isolation. Other contagious diseases were at work as well – chicken pox, mumps and small pox. Typhoid and dysentery spread through contaminated drinking water and poor sanitation. But measles might have been the worse, for adults often suffered serious aftermath – pneumonia, deafness and various infections, sometimes death or invalidism. One of the purposes of a camp of instruction was to give the new troops time to get through such contagious diseases before going into the field.[102]  At least, the ladies of the town were living up to their promise to aid all soldiers in need.  Of course, their first ventures into "nursing" were visitations and gifting.  The courser side was left to slaves and orderlies.

Perhaps the generous donation of the Methodist church began the ultimate demise of their building.  Commonly the early hospitals set up by the Confederate medical service to handle the overwhelming load of illness among inductees proved unmanageable.  Samuel Stout, regimental surgeon of the 3rd Tennessee, described the conditions he abandoned on leaving Camp Cheatham.  "The very ground has become in spite of the efforts of the officers to prevent it, odorous with effluvia from the secretions and excretions of sick men."[103]  Captain Edwards' description indicates that Camp Hays' little hospital was neither so overwhelmed nor as poorly maintained as Stout's tent hospital, but the little church would soon experience subsequent assaults on its structure.

# Table 1: Civil War Incidents in and around Germantown, 1862

Aside from a few *significant benchmarks*, all these incidents were relatively minor skirmishes. Omitted are all references to incidents described as "near Memphis." Those "near Germantown" took place within the current boundaries of the town. Even those "near Collierville," but especially west of that town, also fell close to, if not inside, Germantown's present boundaries.

6/7 April 1862, *Battle of Shiloh*
30 May 1862, *abandonment of Corinth.*
6 June 1862, *capture of Memphis.*
18 June, **skirmish at Germantown.**
22 June, **attack on train near Germantown.**
> s**poradic Federal occupation of Germantown begins**
> until July 18
17 July, Grant assumes command of the Armies of the Tennessee
> and Mississippi; Sherman of the Department of West
> Tennessee
18-19 July, **Sherman and Hurlbut's divisions pass through**
> **Germantown; much pillaging ensues**
28 July, **skirmish at Germantown**
August, **short occupation of Germantown**
3-4 October, *Battle of Corinth.*
12 October, **raid through Germantown**
22 October, **running battle from Germantown to Collierville.**
November, **small-scale, permanent occupation begins at**
> **Germantown**.
25 November, **Smith's wing of expedition into Mississippi**
> **staged at Germantown.**
20 December, Sherman departs Memphis to begin assault on
> Vicksburg.

# 1862, The War Comes to Germantown

Undoubtedly expressing the sentiment of most locals, the *Appeal* welcomed the new year with a martial ardor and optimism that would soon be dashed.

> And thus we welcome eighteen sixty-two. ... We welcome it with the thunder of victorious guns, the shouts of armed men, the clangor of the battle, and the shrieks of dying and retreating foes. Big with fate, the new year now is with us—powerless itself for good or ill, bears within its womb the coming days which, one by one, our own strong will and firm right hand may crown with fortune. Come on new year! dauntless we meet you, for we do not *wait* but *make* success; we will not feebly wish for triumph, but by bold deeds command it.[104]

By spring, Tennessee was being cut in half. After the fall of Forts Henry and Donelson in February, Nashville fell and Governor Harris moved his government to the safety of Memphis. Federal gun boats mounted the Tennessee River and the Federal army moved to Pittsburgh Landing to threaten Corinth, Mississippi, and its strategic rail junction.

As the northern armies approached the area, Memphis began to anticipate its fate and troops in West Tennessee were repositioned. In March, all the remaining militiamen of the 23rd Brigade were enumerated, including males between the ages of eighteen and forty-five. One quarter of every company had been called into active duty on March 3. The remainder was called up for regular drills. Rural companies like Germantown's were to drill twice a week, with orders for enforcement of attendance and discipline. In addition at least once a week, all such companies assembled for a regimental drill. The men were to appear with whatever arms they had, muskets, rifles or shotguns.[105]

On March 24, Governor Harris ordered all county court judges to appoint a competent person in each civil district to compile the names of every man between the ages of 18 and 55 for the purpose of forming a Reserve Military Corps. Those under 45 not serving were the active militia. Those over 45 would be reserved for so-called invalid service such as guard duty.[106] Unfortunately, no record of the progress of this reorganization within districts ten and eleven has survived.

Martial law was declared in Memphis and measures were taken to tighten security in the area. The railroad was brought under the Quartermaster's Department, and civilian use was restricted to persons with "proper authority." Farmers shipping cotton into the city required permits, and on the M&C in particular, only "a limited amount of family supplies for local stations" were being accommodated, and even that might be terminated on notice. Details of one officer and five men were assigned to each passenger train. The obvious concern was unionist sabotage.[107] Eventually a police force was established to monitor passenger traffic, but they performed poorly according to an inspection conducted in March. Specifically on the M&C, the officers only asked perfunctory questions and never demanded any written authorization for travel. According to an inspector,

> The military posts on the roads over which I traveled are without guards at the depots, hence no examination of persons getting on or off the trains is made. The interest of the service, as well as comfort of the traveling, would be greatly promoted by placing a sentinel at the door of each car, subjecting all persons to a proper surveillance before entering…(and) preserving due decorum among the soldiers *en route*, who frequently, I regret to say, are guilty of the grossest misconduct.[108]

Martial law brought another damper to Germantown business. It stipulated,

> The sale or supplying in any manner of intoxicating liquors within 5 miles of any station occupied by troops or within 1 mile of any public highway used for military purposes … is prohibited. All grog shops and drinking saloons within such limits will be closed and supplies packed, subject to military inspection. Any violation of this order will be followed by prompt arrest of the offender and destruction of all his stores of liquor.[109]

Germantown's position on the State Line Road would have qualified it for this prohibition. Of course, it also suggests that some drunken disorderliness may have been part of the town's experiences, if not with the camp of instruction then with many troops moving through the area, and this order might have come as a relief to some. Others undoubtedly found an opportunity to bootleg.

The state finally stepped in to assume responsibility for the indigent families of soldiers as well as widows and orphans without any other means of support. As before, Boards of Relief were empowered to appoint commissioners for each civil district to ascertain eligibility. Payment was then made to the district commissioners who distributed the aid.[110] Whatever assistance families of the Germantown area received, it would not last for long.

As the Federal army advanced down through Tennessee, the civilian population experienced the depredations always inflicted by an occupying force, but especially like the poorly disciplined, green civilian soldiers who formed both armies. In response, the *Appeal* admonished citizens elsewhere on how to prepare for occupation.

> All other persons, however, especially the aged and infirm, and such as have been prevented ... from engaging actively in the war, should remain at their homes, and continue to pursue the even tenor of their lives. If they have any slaves, they should be sent to a place of safety, and their cotton and such other produce as the enemy may desire, should be destroyed. By remaining at their homes they may manage to support themselves and families, and protect the little property they have....[111]

Locals would soon find themselves considering whether and how to respond to these instructions.

Meanwhile in response to the Federal threat to Corinth, the Tennessee regiments with their Germantown men marched to meet them at Shiloh or Pittsburgh Landing. The 4th Tennessee with the Shelby and Wigfall Grays was in the advance. A description of its experience there adds to the story of what a Germantown man's war was like.

> Such, also, was the charge made by the Fourth Tennessee, Lieutenant-Colonel Strahl. This was against a battery of heavy guns, which was making sad havoc in our ranks, and was well supported by a large infantry force.
>
> In reply to an inquiry by their cool and determined brigade commander, General Stewart, "Can you take that battery," their colonel said, "We will try," and at the order forward they moved at a double-quick to within 30 paces of the enemy's guns, halted, delivered one round, and with a yell charged the battery, and captured several prisoners and every gun. These prisoners reported their battery was supported by four Ohio and three Illinois regiments.
>
> It was a brilliant achievement, but an expensive one. In making the charge the ... [regiment] lost 31 killed on the spot and (over) 150 wounded; yet it illustrated and sustained the reputation for heroism of the gallant State of which it was a representative.[112]

The 13th with its Company C, Secession Guards, was there as well, now a veteran unit, distinguishing itself in an assault on a Federal battery. Their Colonel A. J. Vaughn, described it.

> The next morning I advanced upon the enemy, who was strongly posted with a battery of six guns, commanding every avenue of approach, and supported by strong detachments of infantry. While in this position I was told by General Bragg that this battery ... must be taken at all hazards ... by a right flank movement. I had proceeded but a short distance when I discovered that I could be exposed

to a heavy fire from two of the enemy's camps. I therefore ordered an advance to be made directly forward at this particular crisis. Four companies of the left wing were separated from the command, but with the remainder of the command, under fire of their batteries, I soon engaged a heavy body of infantry, which, after a severe conflict and a desperate charge, I succeeded in putting to flight, and captured their battery. The ammunition being nearly exhausted, I supplied myself with that found in the enemy's encampments.[113]

This time, like the 4th elsewhere on the field, they had to charge through cannister and grape from the cannons. There it lost two officers, one NCO, 20 privates and 114 wounded and a number of prisoners. For Company C specifically, their report stated, "We went into action on the morning of April 6 with only twenty, having one-half of our number killed and wounded, five of whom were killed and fifteen wounded."[114]

Among them, William Duke was the first of that planter family's losses. Also fell William Stokes, a twenty-nine year old landless farmer. He left a twenty-seven year-old widow and a four year-old daughter with only about $300 worth of material possessions. She was lucky if that included a mule and plow, a milk cow and a few chickens and pigs.[115] If death was a great equalizer, its impact on survivors was not. The yeoman and landless classes would increasingly feel the pain far worse.

Although we always want to honor our veterans, the realty is that a significant number of men in even the best regiments always find ways to avoid the dangers of combat. In this war, they were called "skulkers, sneaks, beats, stragglers, of coffee-coolers."[116] Company C's report also included, "In this engagement all did their part nobly, except Sergeant W. H. Bedee, William T. Lewis and W. D. Hawkins. They ingloriously deserted their company in the first engagements and were not seen anymore until we had drawn off the battlefield."[117]

The reports of other regiments gave clues to the same effect. In addition to its 183 killed and wounded, the 154th reported 11 missing, while in addition to its 37 killed and wounded Forest's Cavalry reported 12 missing. Men missing-in-action (MIAs) were as common as all other wars. As opposed to families that knew their son or husband was dead, being told he was missing left them to uncertainty. They might wait indefinitely for a report of his capture or his return to ranks. Neither the modern technology for identifying remains nor the political motivation that exists today to find them were present. What is more, at Shiloh, because of the early heat, the Confederate bodies were simply dumped in trenches for mass burial.[118] There was not even a known grave to visit for the bereaved. Of course, there was always the possibility the missing had simply "gone astray." If the "missing" turned up at home, emotions must have been mixed, at least at this early stage. The wives of the yeoman and poor would increasingly encourage such behavior, however.[119]

Afterward at Corinth, initial enlistments having expired, most of the men dutifully reenlisted for the duration, and the regiment reorganized. When disease once again struck, many had to be furloughed back home to recuperate.[120] Germantown boys who had a short respite at home would have also found Confederate wounded from the battle being treated there.

Corinth was overwhelmed by some 5,000 wounded, who were joined by 18,000 sick. Trains dropped them off along the line in towns like Germantown, while the main hospitals at Memphis filled to overflowing.[121] Towns along the railroads in Tennessee and Mississippi became one widespread hospital. The Presbyterian Church preserves the memory of the wounded being laid out on its pews. Since the Methodist Church had already been a hospital before, it surely resumed that role, and certainly the Baptist Church housed sick and wounded as well. Those of the town's many physicians who had not gone off to war must have found their hands full. The women, who had originally made uniforms and flags, soon saw the very unromantic side of war as they witnessed amputations, suppurating wounds and death. They tore cloth to make bandages and prepared food, while some may have even performed real nursing duties. Of course not all the wounds were terrible. The doctor in charge of Memphis' General Hospital encouraged citizens to take the less severe cases into their homes to convalesce.[122] Undoubtedly the good citizens of Germantown did just that. Until the fall of Corinth, trains would continue to haul the sick and wounded for distribution among the civilian population.[123]

Confederate conscription laws soon added more distress to the lives of soldiers and civilians alike. It became clear to both sides that reliance on volunteers was insufficient. Although the earlier mobilization of the state militia had constituted a veritable draft, Confederate conscription laws, the first in April 1862, completed the draft. Although it initially applied to men between the ages of 18 and 35, in July 1863 the upper limit would rise to 45.[124] By February 1864, the situation would become so desperate that its reach ranged from 17 to 50. During the last twelve months of the war, draftees counted for from one-fourth to one-third of the troops. It also changed the social composition of the ranks. It drew more heavily on the smaller farmer and unskilled laborer who either could not afford to leave their families or felt less incentive to volunteer.[125]

Conscription may have done more than anything else to raise the consciousness of the poorer parts of the population. As soon as Confederate leadership realized the danger inherent in removing all able-bodied males from the plantations, exemptions were added for overseers or one adult male per household holding more than twenty slaves. A massive protest arose from small-holder down to landless poor against what they called the "twenty Nigger rule." Anyone not heavily invested in slavery felt the injustice. The popularity of the system for which they were fighting came into serious question. As such exemptions were eroded. in response women left alone in plantation households experienced the problems of controlling slaves and the inherent danger to themselves.[126]

Initially, most volunteers had enlisted for twelve-month service. The conscription law extended that to three years or the duration.[127] Many now dispirited, considered this a breach of contract, even grounds for desertion, especially for those who thought they had enlisted to defend their homes but found themselves serving ever farther afield. Conscription was not popular with either the general public or the volunteers. Although cheered by the idea that slackers back home would now serve, volunteers looked down on conscripts, while conscripts bore the stigma of being coerced derelicts.[128]

As for the survivors of the early bloody battles, they would soon endure worries about their families and friends under Union occupation. Locally raised infantry regiments fought the rest of the war away from home, some defending Vicksburg and points south, but mostly to the east, never again coming west of Middle Tennessee. The severe defeats of early 1862 also had a crushing effect on civilian moral among West Tennesseans. Many obviously began to have second thoughts, and the citizens of Germantown were surely affected by what they had seen. A full year later, General Chalmers opined that after Shiloh the people of Tennessee "are now much depressed, and it will be some time before much assistance can be received from them...."[129] Some of West Tennessee's soldiers failed to reenlist as their regiments were reorganized in the spring of 1862. However, they soon found themselves back in ranks as disgruntled draftees. Consequently, desertions became an increasing problem. In 1864, after Forrest had made several sweeps back through West Tennessee, he reported that he had rounded up about 1,000 men who had deserted in the spring of 1862.[130]

In the midst of this chaos, the accidental deaths of warfare were again brought home to the town. Men were risking the danger of hoping freights to travel unobserved. On both the third and the tenth of May, the bodies of soldiers were found near the tracks where they had been run over. As before, William Walker conducted townsmen in an inquest at the gruesome site.[131]

Meanwhile Union forces began descending the Mississippi, taking Island No. 10 on April 7. After the Confederates evacuated Corinth on May 30, the Federal Army divided its forces with that portion under

McClernand and Sherman moving west. The Confederates abandoned Fort Pillow on the Mississippi on June 5, opening the way for the Federal fleet to assault Memphis. Federal forces spread out across the western part of the state.[132]

In the subsequent campaigns, most West Tennessee cavalry had a different history from infantry, as many of them saw service frequently close to home. Thus, after the occupation, they still had opportunities for contact with family and friends. This contact with the local, sympathetic population was one of their major sources of intelligence and collaboration in raiding operations.

This occasional proximity to home offered a unique advantage over the other branches. It was not uncommon for them to range freely over the countryside in smaller units. Under those conditions, discipline could become extremely lax. Men would not hesitate to take as much as a few weeks off to visit family and friends when operating less than forty miles from home. Such absence away without leave (AWOL in modern jargon) was risky. Not only did they have to be constantly alert to avoid Federal patrols, but they also had to risk being charged as true deserters.[133] Knowing how to do all this required something like what we call "street smarts" today.

Specifically, the 7th Tennessee Cavalry often frequented the Germantown area. In April, General Polk had consolidated Logwood's independent cavalry companies into Colonel William H. Jackson's 1st Tennessee Cavalry Regiment. The Memphis and Shelby Dragoons would become companies A and C respectively. In the summer of 1862, the regiment would be renumbered as the 7th, because delays during reorganization would cost it its priority. Such regimental renumbering causes much confusion in the records, but perhaps as many as 7 Germantown area men served with this regiment.

Before the regiment could even form, a surprise attack on their base on March 31 cost them all their equipment and began the process of shaping them into a light and flexible raiding unit. Reassembled at Trenton, they had to resort to inventiveness in cold drizzling rain. The response was crude shelters they called "she-bangs" – blankets, and oil cloths draped over frames of fence rails and loose timber – a frequently employed recourse in subsequent years. Although reequipped from Memphis, the regiment had learned how to operate less encumbered.[134]

If their first experience under Jackson's leadership had not shaken their confidence, the conditions under which they were regimented continued to upset those who had enlisted for independent service. Jackson's nomination as commander by Polk also did not go down well. Even a subsequent election left many unsatisfied. Morale and discipline were undermined. By March, General Beauregard had been forced to issue orders threatening such troops with severe discipline for pillaging the property of their fellow citizens. Specifically in April, Jackson had to report two of his company commanders for stealing horses, disobedience and insubordination.[135] The steady chain of setbacks produced serious blows to morale and set an atmosphere of undisciplined behavior that would run rampant when they operated as small units in the countryside.

During the Union invasion, they were withdrawn south to defend West Tennessee along Grant's western flank, covering the Confederate withdrawal from Fort Pillow. After the Shiloh-Corinth phase when the fate of Western Tennessee had become obvious, Jackson's Cavalry began burning cotton in local counties and removing potential military equipment to keep it out of Union hands.[136] Occasionally resistant civilians further compounded moral and discipline problems. During the short Battle of Memphis on June 6, while crossing the M&C between Germantown and Collierville, they could hear the cannons. That night, they camped at Germantown and shared in the bad news from the city. Thereafter, they operated from bases in Mississippi, maintaining contact with area citizens.[137]

That night of June 6 must have been one of great suspense and concern among townsfolk. The withdrawal of all troops, taking with them bank deposits and resources and destroying everything else that the enemy could use, created great unease. Theoretically the militia was to take up local defense against the invader. But if the sight of Union forces was not sufficient to disabuse such ideas, the departure of all necessary leadership deterred all but the more determined would-be guerrillas. County and district officials turned over authority to the conqueror and would try to continue government and maintain order. Apparently many southerners anticipated the worst at the hands of a brutal Yankee horde. They fled if they could afford to. The more level-headed anticipated an uneasy period of accommodating and negotiating with a strange but not inhumane authority.[138]

From this moment, local women had to consider preventive measures in the face of imminent invasion by an anticipated hoard of barbarians. They accurately expected undisciplined looting. They tried to calculate where best to hide valuables. Livestock were moved into the woods or creek bottoms. A part of romantic memories is how trusted slaves helped bury treasures and secret livestock. Some would be quickly disillusioned, however, when vengeful servants betrayed them. As slaves became restive and more opaque in their demeanor, the illusion of how benevolent mistresses had created a loving staff of child-like servants turned to suspicion and even fear of a potential enemy within.[139]

Following the capture of Memphis, some communities came incrementally under Union occupation, but much of the surrounding countryside was contested for the duration. Throughout rural West Tennessee, the Confederates could even enforce conscription laws and punish deserters under the noses of the occupation forces for the entire period. The result was endless skirmishes and several battles. Shelby County was one of the few in Tennessee to experience almost continual action throughout the remainder of the war, though none were truly major battles. It was mostly guerrilla and lightening cavalry warfare. Although its primary railroad supply lines came south from Columbus, Kentucky, through Jackson to both La Grange and Corinth, the Union objective was to open and maintain the M&C with its river connection as another route of supply for their forces.[140] All the rail lines, however, received the constant attention of partisans and raiders, disrupting operations.

Consequently for the remainder of 1862, Germantown would be veritably cut off from outside connections in the midst of a no-man's-land. Although Memphis' telegraph service to the east had been resumed, the line to and through Germantown would be constantly severed over the next few years, though usually restored within a few hours. Even after reestablishment, rail connections would also be disrupted and dangerous to travel.

Of course, Germantown's connection with the newly established Confederate mail service was severed. Memphis' Confederate postmaster had relocated operations to Grenada, Mississippi.[141] Once cut off, Germantown postmaster William Miller remained to tend his store. Mail smuggled through Union lines was delivered directly by its courier to its destination. Copies of the *Appeal*, its press also moved to Mississippi, had to be smuggled in as well. Papers coming out of Memphis would have been entirely subject to army convenience or the occasional citizen traveling from the city.

Commerce with Memphis became extremely difficult. Not only was travel to and from dangerous, one could not go through the picket lines around the city without a pass. Only persons who took the oath of loyalty to the Federal government could receive such a pass. To encourage farmers to bring in their cotton, a modified parole oath as opposed to an oath of loyalty was offered "people of the country," specifically "persons within the Federal lines north and east of the Memphis and Charleston railroad, and inside of the outer line of pickets south." It merely required a promise not to support the Confederate cause in any way. Otherwise people living outside the city "would be endangered by taking the oath." Finally, civilians were forbidden to carry firearms within the city.[142] This was a serious problem, considering the necessity of self protection moving to or from the city. It would be months before Germantown's citizens would be making such efforts.

Aside from the impact of isolation on their life, severance of all connections with their men in service was an emotional blow. Heretofore, those who could afford to do so had been able to send abundant supplies and even servants to their men. They could visit the camps, and the men could return home easily on furlough. Wives could communicate with husbands for advice on how to manage family business. All this ended when Memphis fell. While Confederate authorities helped other families send generous packages to their men, families around Germantown must have suffered even more from being denied that opportunity.[143]

Topography around Germantown played a significant role in what followed. The town was situated on the hilly ridge that ran from the Memphis bluffs eastward. To the north and south lay the densely wooded, seasonally flooded bottom lands of the Wolf River and Nonconnah Creek respectively. The high and dry ridge formed the strategic route along which ran the Memphis-Charleston Railroad and the State Line Road. The thickly grown river bottoms provided excellent cover for partisans and guerrillas to assault this route.

Union forces in Memphis, responsible for the repair and defense of the railroad, would have to operate along four main roads: The Raleigh Road north to the county seat and then across to the east (present US 64); the Hernando Road (present US 51) into Mississippi with Horn Lake Road as a side-route, the Pigeon Roost Road (present US 78) crossing the M&C and running to Byhalia and beyond, and that Germantown or State Line Road, weaving through Germantown, and just north-west of Collierville forking south into Mississippi or running due west as the La Grange-Memphis Road.[144]

Initially only a couple of regiments occupied Memphis. On June 10, McClernand ordered General Lew Wallace, occupying Bolívar, to spread out his command toward Memphis to secure the Memphis and Ohio Railroad. He marched thorough Somerville to Raleigh. His superiors ordered him to halt within eleven miles of Memphis at Union Depot, where he arrived on June 14. From that base, he was supposed to repair and secure the M&O RR.[145] Nevertheless, some of his troops were probably the first Federals to visit Germantown.

On June 16, he sent out cavalry to Germantown, "a village 13 miles distant from that point, negroes (sic.) having informed me that rebel troops had encamped there." Confederate pickets were indeed driven from the town, and Union loyalists in Germantown informed the officer in charge that a large enemy force lay nearby, preparing for an attack on Memphis.[146]

Usually such tantalizingly brief reports are all that tell about conflicts in and around Germantown. For some days, the townsfolk must have gladly fed and supported whatever Confederate troops were in and around, sharing rumors with them. Then one can only imagine what they experienced as they heard the shots, saw the Confederate pickets retreating quickly through town with Union cavalry in pursuit. Everyone must have snatched up the children and ducked for cover amidst the

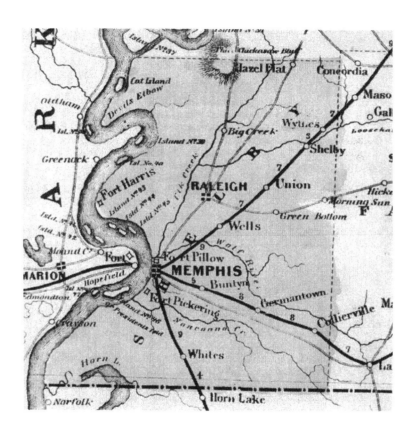

Map 7. Roads and Railroads, Shelby County (Lolyd's Official Map of the State of Tennessee, 1863). There are a few errors.

galloping horses and firing carbines. On this and subsequent occasions, bullets crashed through windows and embedded themselves in walls where they remain to this day. The threat to civilians was like today's drive-by shooting. Obviously the Union troops did not pursue much beyond town, fearing the presence of a large force. Instead they consulted someone they thought trustworthy, who confirmed their fears.

Further reports related that Forrest and Jackson were preparing to raid Memphis on the night of the 18th, so Wallace moved much of his division into Memphis which had been temporarily left poorly defended.[147] Well-intentioned unionists, freemen and slaves, as well as deliberate "dis-informants" frequently plagued Federal officers with distorted images of large and threatening Confederate forces, resulting in erroneous reports going through channels that came to be called "stampedes."[148] Wallace's resultant concentration of his forces in the city left Germantown still outside Federal lines.

Probably the troops reported were little more than Colonel Jackson's 1st (7th) Cavalry, which would hover between Germantown and Lafayette south of the M&C and always within striking distance of any vulnerable target. Jackson had constant intelligence from locals who sought him out anytime they heard of an opportunity. One occurred when General Grant was on his way to his new headquarters in Memphis on June 23, traveling west with "a very insignificant escort" along the State Line Road. Alerted by a Dr. Smith that Grant had stopped at the house of Josiah Deloach at Bray's Station between Germantown and Collierville, Jackson narrowly missed capturing the general by forty-five minutes.[149]

While the Confederates sought to deny the Federals use of the railroad, one event set the stage for unpleasant experiences for Germantown. It has long been reported that on June 22 Jackson's cavalry succeeded in derailing and destroying the first train to be sent out from Memphis, capturing a Colonel Kenney and somewhere between 82 and 56 men, "one mile above Germantown." That would have been a little beyond the crossing of State Line and Holly Ford roads (present Hacks Cross). "In the same vicinity," another detachment killed six and captured eight pickets.[150] Put on the defensive for having allowed the train to run through unsecured territory, Grant argued that cavalry had patrolled through the same area on the same day immediately before and after the incident.[151] The Confederates bragged that the June 22 raid was "well-planned."[152]

In fact, the derailment was undoubtedly the work of locals acting as guerrillas. Before its arrival, the track had been torn up to derail the train and the telegraph wires were cut. Both Colonel Kinney and a Colonel Pride, who had also been on the train, reported that a considerable time elapsed before Jackson's cavalry arrived – up to an hour and a half. The

Union troops even had time to begin eating the supplies broken open.[153] This implies the derailing was the work of local civilian partisans who did not confront the troops but called upon Jackson's men to take advantage of their handiwork. The second in command of the 56th Ohio, whose colonel had been captured in the raid, accused a local plantation owner, a Mr. Davis (perhaps Charles Davis of district ten), of being an informant.[154] Indeed a local later told exaggerated stories of "the band of one Capt. Davis" operating in the neighborhood.[155] Such an early, overt resort to active resistance by the male civilian population was apparently unusual immediately on the arrival of Union forces. Undoubtedly it was encouraged by the spottiness of the occupation, but also implies an initially higher level of local resistance.[156]

Although records are not entirely consistent, there seems to have been another incident at about the same location outside Germantown on June 25 in which nine men of the 56th Ohio were captured escorting the train.[157] Obviously these railroad incidents planted the seeds in Sherman's mind that the citizens of Germantown were especially culpable in supporting the raiders, and that they needed to be taught a lesson. On June 26, he informed Halleck, "that is the place of mischief."[158] On June 28, he wrote, "Had we not better clean Germantown, a dirty hole? There is where was planned the cutting of the wire and destruction of the road. I am told they openly boast the Yankees will never run a train over the road."[159] Such early local resistance was provoking an equally rapid turnaround in the conciliatory Federal occupation policy.

Meanwhile, General Grant sent a cavalry patrol out to Germantown which reported that Jackson's men were hovering along the line in squads burning cotton around the town.[160] Grant stationed the 56th Ohio Infantry Regiment, 429 men, and five companies of cavalry, 382 men, at Germantown to secure the line. From the east, Sherman posted two regiments to guard the line between LaFayette and Germantown, and assigned the Indiana Railroad Regiment to accompany the 56th. The 52nd Indiana and 58th Ohio were apparently these two regiments, describing their camps as being at and near Germantown. This was the first, short occupation of the town, but a sizable force totaling over 800 men and almost 400 horses specifically at the town, plus an equal number of soldiers near the town. The cavalry companies were those of the 6th Illinois, which arrived in Germantown on June 28 and did picket duty and scouting.

Cavalry Colonel B. H. Grierson was in command of these troops, specifically with responsibility for protecting railroad and wagon-trains between Memphis and LaFayette. From his base, he was expected to monitor threatening Confederate cavalry movements. His orders were that citizens in the area "undoubtedly giving information to the enemy" were to be arrested and sent to Grant "with the charges against them stated." Grierson was admonished, however, not to annoy "peaceably disposed citizens," and to take no property from arrested citizens except fire arms.[161] Grierson was left with the problem of deciding who were peaceable and who were collaborators – a perennial problem for local commanders of occupation forces in all wars. Likewise Grant's imposed constraints typically guaranteed little for the actual behavior of troops in direct contact with suspected collaborators. There are no records of which Germantown area citizens came under suspicion.

Grierson's cavalry soon returned to Memphis, since Grant needed them elsewhere, even at the expense of abandoning the railroad. All seem to have been gone by July 18.[162] As soon as they withdrew, the Confederates returned tentatively. On July 28, some of the same companies of the 6th Illinois returned to Germantown on a scout and had a fire-fight with Rebel pickets. Once again the town was terrorized by a running battle. The 6th apparently returned and remained at Germantown for another short period during August.[163] Townsfolk must have felt awash in the tides.

Meanwhile, Grant and Sherman's dispatches reveal considerable alarm over the insecurity of their communications, with much attention focused specifically on the area around Germantown. Grant had to concentrate all his cavalry on the State Line Road. Although on June 29, General McPherson, superintendent of railroads, announced that the line from Memphis to Grand Junction, 49 miles, was fully operational, that did not guarantee its security.[164] The State Line Road was equally vulnerable. On June 30, Grant considered it necessary to have two companies of infantry and one of cavalry simply to escort a wagon train as far as Germantown.[165]

Confederate cavalry raiders ranged freely over the countryside, cutting wires, damaging the rails, burning cotton, and intercepting large Union wagon-trains.[166] Consequently, from June into September, the railroad from Memphis through Germantown to Corinth required extensive pacification and reconstruction. Local planters were required to provide slaves as laborers in railroad repair.[167] No matter how important the railroad was to Union supplies, the line itself was capable of only limited carrying capacity, and it remained always susceptible to temporary disruption. As a result, the State Line Road provided an alternative supply line through Germantown. Even so, that road seemed so insecure that following the incident of June 25 and as late as July 7, Sherman was avoiding it, sending his wagon trains by "back roads," running north of the Wolf. Even then, they were frequently ambushed, and he had to guard them with a full regiment.[168] From its new base in Grenada, the *Appeal* boasted of several successful raids by partisans and raiders.[169]

Illustration 11. Searching a rebel house (Harper's November 16,1861)
Anytime Federal troops moved into an area, they searched homes and
confiscated all weapons to curtail guerrillas.

Illustration 12. Colonel Grierson, a major Federal cavalry commander for

most of the period of occupation around Germantown (Harper's, June 6, 1863)

## *The Partisans and Life in No-Man's Land*

In February, as it had become obvious that the South could loose control of much of Tennessee, the Confederates began authorizing independent partisan units. On April 23, the War Department issued General Order No. 30, an Act to Organize Bands of Partisans. President Davis was "authorized to commission such officers as he may deem proper with authority to form" such bands.[170] The act provided "that for any arms and munitions of war captured from the enemy by any body of partisan rangers and delivered to any quartermaster..., the rangers shall be paid their full value...."[171] Nothing was said about whatever else they might "capture" to support themselves. Thus the opportunity to capture booty provided an additional incentive for partisan as opposed to regular service. Unfortunately this provision to "requisition" legitimately was conducive to outright plundering.

The *Appeal* carried editorials extolling the benefits of guerrilla warfare and recommending it as a service for local young men.

> Hence, in giving commissions to captains to raise companies of this kind, it is expressly stipulated that it shall be an independent command, unattached to any battalion or regiment. Important as is this arm of service, it would not be best to have but few companies independent in their operations. Hence the War Department very judiciously grants but few of these commissions. We have been informed that there are but four or five in the Mississippi valley.
>
> It is complimentary to our city – though but just – that one of these should be held by one of our fellow citizens. Captain E. E. Porter undoubtedly is commissioned to raise and muster into service a company of this kind. ...We submit to our fellow citizens if it is anything but right to share with him the expense of arming and equipping the brave young men who are pecuniarily unable to provide for themselves. Contributions of horses, money or cotton will be judiciously appropriated. Do not wait to be solicited personally.[172]

As invasion threatened, such partisan units became a major alternative to service for Germantown men. There was much dissatisfaction in the ranks of those militia and volunteer independent companies finding themselves incorporated into regular service and marched off to fight far from home. Partisan service offered the opportunity to avoid call-up while feeling that one could still be giving protection to loved ones. Later there was the opportunity to take revenge for losses of home and property. For some personalities, there was also an opportunity for adventurous criminality. The remark at the end of the *Appeal*'s editorial is surprising, coming so early in the history of these operations. "Do not wait to be solicited personally." It was like a veiled warning about how such units might have to "appropriate" their supplies.

Porter was accepting applications in Memphis and in Somerville in Fayette County. He gave the impression that he was recruiting an elite corps of gentlemen representing the most patriotic element.[173]

Among its earliest activities in the face of the Federal advance into West Tennessee:

> *May 18.* -- We were ordered into [service] by General [Pierre Gustave Toutant] Beauregard, since which time we have mostly been engaged in burning cotton in Fayette and Shelby counties of Tennessee and Marshall and De Soto counties of Mississippi.
>
> *May 28.* -- We left Somerville, Tennessee for Holy Springs, Mississippi taking with us a large lot of government harness and also the bank assets of that place.
>
> *June 1.* -- We landed safely at Holy Springs.[174]

By June 6, Porter reported that he had already recruited 150 men, "almost all from large planters." He told General Beauregard that his Partisans had ranged through all the western counties and DeSoto County in Mississippi, burning "upwards to 30,000 bales of cotton," encountering "but little opposition" from the planters. Soon he and others would be burning the bridges and water towers on the Memphis & Charleston and Memphis & Ohio railroads.[175]

> *June 24.* -- Then moved toward Byhalia burning all the cotton in our route. We continued burning cotton until June 24. We learned that by going into the enemy's lines we could inflict great damage upon them. We went as far as the Memphis and Ohio Railroad, capturing a number of drays laden with cotton; destroyed the drays and cotton. Brought the mules. We then attacked a wagon train guarded by the Fifty-ninth Ohio Regiment. Broke up a large number of wagons and took some mules.[176]

Memphis papers reported this ambushed wagon train as near Morning Sun about fifteen miles north of Germantown. The *Appeal* and the *Avalanche* gave contrasting claims about the success of such guerrilla operations against Federal troops, but it is clear they were a nuisance.[177]

The Germantown area saw its share of this partisan action. On July 21, 1862, a "Captain Sherwin" and his "independent scouts," a squad of eight men operating around Germantown, raided as far as White's Station before being stopped by Union forces. They took prisoner a team of men bringing cotton into Memphis, and burned their cargo. They also

Illustration 13. Rebel attack on a supply train (Harper's, May 14, 1864)

Illustration 14. Cotton burners at work.

captured two Federal soldiers, who were soon "shot attempting to escape.[178] As late as November, "Ballentine's guerrillas," including Porter's Rangers, were operating between Germantown and White's Station stopping the delivery of cotton to Memphis.[179]

In response to apparent civilian support for "guerrilla" operations, occupation authorities sought to discourage it by confiscating civilian property as compensation.[180] As raids continued around Germantown, its citizens and area farmers were visited frequently by Federal officers with a legitimate excuse for confiscations.

Caught in the middle, locals had to provide support for their own men both as a matter of patriotism and conscience. If caught doing so, they faced at least confiscation of all movable property. Accusations could come from vengeful slaves or local white informants. The need to obscure any evidence of collaboration became important. When a wounded Confederate was brought to the house of Joseph Brooks, he left tall-tale bloodstains on the floor of the bedroom in which he was placed. After he was gone, the family, unable to remove the stains, used hot coals to singe the floor boards so the stain could not be seen.[181]

With Germantown at the fore in the minds of Union commanders as a center for raiding operations, the town could be targeted for retributive actions. Meanwhile it would suffer from simply being located in a contested no-man's land. Perhaps the first event to occur, according to the *Appeal*, happened early in June near Germantown.

> Two Federal soldiers entered the dwelling of an old citizen, and after being well treated, they demanded the old gentleman's money, and one of the ruffians sought to force a compliance with their demand by leveling his gun at the head of the house. The old lady interposed herself between the gun of the miscreant and her husband, and while the coward hesitated to shoot, a daughter of the aged couple came from an adjoining room, and seeing the situation of efforts, seized a double-barreled shot gun, with which she shot the ruffian through the head, killing him instantly. His companion fled, while the inmates of the house remained uninjured.[182]

Unfortunately, reports of such incidents survive almost exclusively in newspapers, memoirs, and family traditions, all of which glamorized and exaggerated such heroic female resistance. Newspapers were notoriously unreliable and biased. Family traditions and memoirs are problematic. Nevertheless, they bear reporting for the mood they convey and the likelihood of some truth.

A more likely example of stories about Southern ladies involved a daughter of the above mentioned Brooks family. Her family's plantation west of town suffered heavily from Federal pillaging. Of course, she was

Illustration 15. Federal troops foraging (Leslie's Illustrated, January 2, 1864). Official foraging operations could strip a farm of live stock and loose timber for firewood and camp construction. During such operations, some "cramping" could occur, especially if discipline was lax. None of this compared, however, to unregulated pillaging.

unwilling to use inappropriate language for a lady, so she instructed their slaves to curse Sherman "to their hearts' content."[183]

To provide some propriety, Federal authorities established procedures for civilians to make claims for restitution in cases of both official and illegal confiscation of property. A board of claims was established, but even when citizens from around Germantown could make it safely into Memphis, making a properly documented claim would have been most difficult.

From beginning to end, despite Union efforts to prevent soldiers from pillaging, it was inevitable that civilians endured the actions of soldiers taking advantage of an opportunity to suffer from "cramping." This less forceful and perhaps most common practice got its name because witty soldiers explained that when they happened to touch an appealing object, their hands "cramped" and they just could not let go. Sherman observed that "Stealing, robbery and pillage has become so common in this army that it is a disgrace to any civilized people. ... This demoralizing and disgraceful practice of pillage must cease, else the country will rise on us and justly shoot us down like wild beasts."[184] It must be noted that Confederate officers had similar complaints and problems protecting local citizens' property even from their own troops. Such chaos was always worse as long as there were no established occupation headquarters with clearly defined spheres of responsibility. The Germantown area would suffer from such a lack of responsible authority for the bulk of 1862, during which it undoubtedly sustained much of its damages.

Initially, Sherman commanded the area south of the Hatchie from Memphis to the east as far as Bolivar and Grand Junction, with responsibility for repairing and defending the railroad.[185] By June 21, Major General H. W. Halleck, over-all commander, believed that the best line to defend West Tennessee was across north Mississippi.[186] Sherman agreed that it was best to hold the Confederates well back from the line. On July 7, he proposed the Coldwater as their front line, with the divisions operating from bases along the railroads. He suggested that McClernand hold the Junction and La Grange, Hurlbut hold Moscow and Lafayette (Rossville), while he "be in front of Collierville and Germantown. It is there all roads toward Memphis debauch on this line of road."[187]

Rather then being allowed to pursue such a forward position which would have required a constant presence in Germantown, on July 15 Sherman was placed in command of "Memphis and vicinity." On his way from Moscow, Sherman camped his division at Collierville on July 18, and marched the next day through Germantown to White's Station. On the 19[th,] Hurlbut's division camped at Germantown before going on to Memphis to join Sherman.[188]

Shortly thereafter, the *Appeal* got wind of a story from an article in the *Bulletin*, now a Federal-supported newspaper in Memphis. For two days, soldiers in squads of a half-dozen or so encamped a few miles from Germantown, pillaging the town. They broke into stores and homes and carried off or destroyed whatever they could find – furniture, clothing, books, jewelry, silver, and anything else "that suited their fancy." They broke down fences, destroyed gardens, stripped the trees of fruit, green and ripe, "and seemed bent on doing all the malicious mischief in their power." Only one house in the community escaped pillage, but none were burned, contrary to some early reports. The *Appeal* also gleefully reported that, "the traitor, B. D. Nabers, was among the sufferers by the outrages committed by Sherman's soldiery on their march to Memphis." Unaware of his Union sympathies, the vandals did not spare his plantation near Germantown, but completely destroyed everything, taking his slaves and stock.[189]

It was probably during this early period of free-wheeling vandalism that stragglers visited the farm on which Reverend Jeremiah Burns was living – the retired pastor of the Germantown Baptist Church. While they were taking everything, the pastor begged them to leave at least one spoon needed to give his daughter her medicine. They relented, and that spoon remains a family memento to this day, as does this story. Such interactions between the looters and their victims were not unusual. Whenever it was that they burned the pastor's church in town, a neighbor intervened to ask them to save the pulpit Bible. They did and gave it to her.[190]

Such willful destructiveness sounds excessive for the pillaging operations of marauders. It seems extremely focused on Germantown. Indeed, one of the participants reported to his hometown newspaper:

> As we passed through Germantown, which is a perfect hotbed of secession, the soldiers did considerable plundering, and for the first time since leaving Pittsburgh Landing, the officers paid no attention to it. I was glad of it, of all the 'se-e-d' holes, Germantown is the most bitter I have ever seen. This is the place where the train of cars from Memphis was thrown off the tracks and captured. ...I would rejoice at seeing the inhabitants of Germantown stolen poor, and the town burned.[191]

Clearly Sherman's opinions had been passed down to the troops and they had been given tacit permission to teach Germantown a lesson. Fortunately, however, nothing in town was burned despite newspaper exaggerations.[192]

Defense of Memphis now being Sherman's primary responsibility, the closest to Germantown that his troops were to be stationed was for one brigade to guard the State Line Road three miles out from Memphis while the 4th Illinois Cavalry was to picket and patrol as far as White's Station down that road. But when he heard rumors of the arrival of 100 infantry and some cavalry in Germantown, on July 27 he ordered the 6th Illinois Cavalry under Colonel Grierson to scout out along the State Line Road to Germantown and Collierville. No matter what he thought of the strategic importance of Germantown-Collierville, he had to abandon hope of permanently occupying the towns. Instead he periodically sent out expeditions to the north, south and east of Memphis "to clean out the countryside."[193] Among Sherman's command at Memphis, 1,340 cavalry were available for patrolling and raiding.[194] With only 12 such companies, however, he remained mostly in a defensive posture at Memphis.[195] Meanwhile, Grant pressed down from between Jackson and Corinth into Mississippi for an overland assault on Vicksburg.

By August 20, those "guerrillas" operating within Union-held territory in West Tennessee had become such a problem that Grant had to request more cavalry.[196] By their very nature as semi-military formations, partisan officers had to have both the respect and the tolerance of their men. According to one, "There was one thing that could be said of the private Confederate soldiers that could not be said of any other set of soldiers. While they had great respect for the officer they were under and would fight and obey orders when called on, the officer knew, or would soon learn, that he must not get too bossy, for the privates thought they were as good as Mr. Captain or Lieutenant, and if they got too big and bossy they would be thrown up in blankets or something worse."[197]

One problem lay in their need to operate as small units, even after they had been formally organized in partisan battalions under senior officers. Even on the occasions when a command actually operated as a battalion or regiment, it was the rare officer who could control such men. Lack of control combined with a "noble cause" against a venomous enemy and traitorous neighbors provided all the justification they needed to brutalized, kill and confiscate property. They easily crossed the line to bandit behavior. Whatever, their enemies had an excellent opportunity to accuse them of the worst.[198]

No sooner than the Confederacy had commissioned partisan units than it began having second thoughts. Both the government and area commanders issued directives to curb and control them.[199] Consequently as early as August 1862, both the District of Mississippi, which ostensibly commanded West Tennessee, and the Confederate Secretary of War revoked all authority to raise partisan rangers and mustered their conscripts into regular state units, many of which still retained the title partisan rangers.[200] In November, the Secretary of War instructed all district commanders to require the alleged commanders of Partisan Rangers to provide "a copy of their authority for raising their

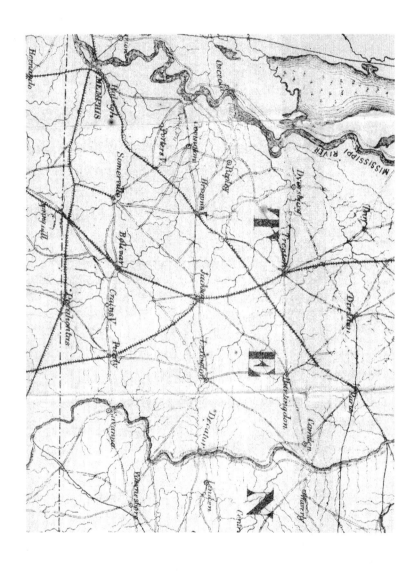

Map 8. Guerrilla Theater north of Germantown (OR *Atlas*)

corps." Those failing to comply would be disbanded.[201]

An article in the *Bulletin* described how they operated so effectively. Most important was the popular support they got for defending locals from alleged "outrages recently committed upon them by bands of men falsely claiming to belong to the Union army. ... It is stated that one advantage which these guerrilla parties possess, is that they wear no uniforms, and, if hotly pursued, they become citizens, and can appear to be about their usual peaceful pursuits, as soon as they can dismount and put away their shot guns and pistols.[202]

Despite Confederate claims that their irregulars were legitimate and to be treated like regular troops, they issued orders that clearly crossed the line. For instance, Captain Porter's Partisan Rangers received orders that instead of destroying railroad bridges that might be later useful to the Confederacy, "the road may be rendered useless to the enemy by frequently firing into trains from places of concealment by small parties of your command or by **citizens**."[203]

A prime example of the problem and the most significant of these West Tennessee Partisan leaders emerged – Colonel Robert Vinkler Richardson, a prominent citizen of Memphis. On September 6, the Confederate Secretary of War authorized Richardson to organize a regiment of Partisan Rangers in Tennessee, vesting him with "large discretion" in his operations. Sometime shortly thereafter, Lieutenant General J. C. Pemberton, commanding the Department of Mississippi and East Louisiana, authorized Colonels Robert F. Looney and Richardson to organize partisan regiments "within enemy lines in Tennessee." Since the approval of Governor Harris was required for them to recruit in Tennessee, they were instructed to apply to him. He, in turn, was to designate their counties of operation. Meanwhile, Richardson rallied two existing bands to his flag, Captain John Green's Company of Tipton County, and Reuben Burrow's from Shelby. Quickly three other companies from Fayette County joined him plus Captain James Hazelwood's from Shelby. He titled his unit the 1st Tennessee Regiment of Partisan Rangers, C.S.A, and began work centered at Galloway Switch in Fayette County. During the four months it took him to recruit and organize, he had to operate constantly around the Union bases at major posts. He claimed that he was "able to hold all of Tipton and Fayette Counties and parts of Haywood, Hardeman, and Shelby Counties."[204]

Typically, Richardson was loose about communicating with his erstwhile superiors. As late as November, Pemberton noted that neither Richardson nor Looney had informed him of having received any authorization by Harris.[205] It is also difficult to evaluate accurately Richardson's achievements, because his reports were boastful and disingenuous. Which is not to say that his bravado was unusual among

Illustration 16. Harper's version of guerrillas murdering Union supporters (November 21, 1863)

the reports of officers on both sides.

By December, according to the Federal commander at Bolívar,
Bands of guerrillas still infest the neighborhood under
Street, Richardson and others, carrying away citizens,
stealing horses, and subsisting by plunder. At present they
harbor in the bends of the river, a few miles above here, in
the neighborhood of Somerville. They watch our forage
trains and assail such of our men as stray beyond our lines,
making occasional captures.[206]

Early on, pro-Union papers were full of accounts of criminal acts by
the partisans, allegedly indifferent to the political sympathies of their
victims. They were described as caring "very little for the success of the
Southern Confederacy, their sole object being to plunder the weak and
helpless." Their unionist victims harbored plans for revenge when the
day of reckoning came. Richardson would become their focus.[207] As an
evil reputation grew around him and his men, and as their victims
mobilized against them, animosity developed among West Tennesseans.

Of course, neither Grant nor Sherman was inclined to tolerate
violation of the rules of war, especially once the Confederates crossed the
line so flagrantly. Initially from headquarters in Corinth, General
Halleck had ordered that every man caught in guerrilla activities be
hung.[208] Apparently, however, Federal commanders began to appreciate
the complexity of the situation and feared retaliations against their men in
Confederate captivity.[209] Typically, on July 13 when General Sherman
reported a guerrilla raid "seven miles south of the Wolf River" against a
forage train, killing one of his men and wounding three, he arbitrarily
selected and arrested twenty-five local men and sent them to La Grange.
In frustration, he knew he could not identify the locals involved, so he
had to take an action that held the entire community responsible.[210] By
August, frustrated over partisan duplicity, he observed, "All the people of
the South are now arming as partisan raiders, daring not to be
guerrillas."[211] Clearly, he had to make a distinction between partisans and
guerrillas. Although partisans almost always lacked uniforms and melted
back into the civilian population, they should have had papers to identify
themselves. By November Grant was refusing to allow partisan POWs to
be exchanged or paroled like regular prisoners.[212] At least they could not
return to their old ways.

Sherman had set a clear pattern for Union retaliation which would
be directed against any community suspected of housing or supporting
guerrillas and saboteurs. On September 8, after an encounter south of
Germantown and west of Olive Branch, Colonel Grierson's' 6th Illinois
cavalry forayed out of Memphis and returned by way of White's Station
where they arrested five prominent citizens.[213] On October 12, a raid
through Germantown surprised and captured a captain with his company

in a camp a few miles beyond the town.[214]   On October 21, a sizable Rebel force had to be driven from Collierville.[215]   After his efforts to placate the population failed, Sherman developed the firm conviction that the war had to be waged against the entire enemy population. After guerrillas fired at Union boats in September, he burned the town of Randolph to the ground. Sherman also ordered that for every boat in the Mississippi fired upon, ten families, identified by lot, would be expelled 25 miles from the city.[216]

Well into autumn, one of Sherman's general patterns was to dispatch his cavalry regiment out State Line Road to Germantown and/or Collierville and from there to sweep either southward into Mississippi or to cross the Wolf River and sweep north, seeking out guerrilla bands. During September 5 through 6, a Captain Christopher Wiboum of Hughes' Mississippi Partisan Regiment combined with some Louisiana Cavalry set out in pursuit of one of Grierson's expeditions that had gone down to Hernando and "had passed on (east) in the direction of Germantown, committing a great many depredations – carrying off Negroes and mules from the citizens." Although Wiboum chased part of the force back up the Germantown and Olive Branch Road and caught them south of Germantown, he found himself badly outnumbered and had to break off.[217]

Even when the town was spared a firefight, the passage of Federal expeditions could be onerous, as one participant described it to his hometown paper:

> Guerrillas seemed to be very scarce, and the people to have a holy horror of National troops. The route of the force can probably be traced for some time. Chickens, turkeys, geese, hogs and sheep, found themselves legitimate objects for capture, and it would be difficult to estimate the number that "fell" to feed the expedition. ... Some of the planters, who admire the work of treason, will look upon farms turned into commons, the fences being used for camp fires. In some instances horses and mules were taken and brought away. Many contrabands came in with the army.... In short the rebels were treated with anything but tenderness.[218]

On August 31, the infamous 7th Kansas Cavalry, the Kansas Jayhawkers, was at Germantown long enough to be mustered and paid.[219] Given their reputation for undisciplined pillaging and expressions of hostility toward secessionists, that must have been a fitful day or two for the townsfolk. The worst of enmity born of the Bloody Kansas years had arrived, but no record of any incident requiring the attention of superior officers has survived.

Then on October 22, according to the official report, Sherman sent

Grierson out again through Collierville, where he disbursed a group of guerrillas, and up the northern route scouring "the country all the way to Randolph, killing 7 guerrillas, wounding 14, and bringing in 17 prisoners." He also destroyed "several buildings used as rendezvous and haunts for guerrillas." Instead of returning by land, he took steamship from Randolph. "The enemy hoping to intercept Grierson on his return, interposed a heavy cavalry force at Germantown, their scouts coming in as far a White's Station...."[220]

It was actually at Germantown that the cavalry first encountered about thirty of Captain O'Neil's cavalry from Outlaw's Alabama Regiment. During the ensuing skirmish, three of O'Neil's men were captured and one wounded, while "two Yankees were made to bite the dust...." Badly outnumbered, O'Neill was forced to retreat through Collierville, after which Grierson made his turn north across the Wolf, "taking with them negroes, horses and mules to any number."[221]

Once again Germantown was the site of a skirmish. A Confederate report stated that some forty cavalrymen had been in the town until a sizable detachment forced them to retire "after a short engagement."[222] The *Bulletin* told another colorful story of town life amidst all this. It reported that O'Neal's men (misidentified as a detachment of Kentucky cavalry) had set up camp east of the town blocking cotton delivery to the city. The townsfolk were preparing them breakfast, and before withdrawing eastward, the captain decided to have his in one of the hospitable homes. While the son of the house was on his way to school, he spotted the approaching Yankees and ran back to give warning. The captain seized his host's horse and barely escaped.[223] Throughout the year, one side would sweep through the town encountering the other, making the town the site of hot little fire fights.

Local farmers trying to bring any surviving cotton crops into Memphis to buy food and supplies were frequently intercepted by the partisans. In October, a detachment of the $2^{nd}$ Mississippi Partisan rangers reported "a considerable amount of cotton en route to Memphis was burned near Germantown."[224] Then after Grierson's October 22 raid, the road was temporarily open long enough for thousands of dollars worth of cotton to get through.[225] Constantly, Germantown experienced the ups and downs of lying in no-man's land. The entire area around the town suffered sizable forces from both sides as well as guerrilla bands coursing through town. By now, the momentary enthusiasm felt over the occasional Rebel success and the temporary presence of Confederate defenders must have worn off. The town periodically experienced the hazards of combat and the depredations of reprisal and scavenging. Their resources were being stolen or destroyed with little opportunity to replace them.

Confronted by the economic realities of survival under an indefinite occupation, area planters sought to sell their cotton in Memphis. If they had willingly let it be burnt before, such patriotic zeal had rapidly abated. Family survival trumped any qualms about disloyalty. For all involved in this dangerous trade, the opportunity for tremendous profits must have made the conflicted feelings less troubling. Where cotton had sold for thirteen cents a pound in 1860, it was at $1.00 a pound by early 1863, and briefly peaked at $1.44 in 1864.[226] Of course, it was not the local farmers who reaped the bulk of this windfall, but the merchants and corrupt officials sitting safely in Memphis. The planters bore the risk of getting the cotton to town, and took what they were offered. By August, Sherman had established payment either in bank notes or Confederate script, or by promissory notes to be paid after the war, or by deposits with trustees that could only be collected in Washington and, therefore, had to be sold locally at significant discount.[227]

Farmers and planters, no longer burning their cotton, were hiding it for some hoped-for future opportunities. The cotton burners had to resort to all sorts of subterfuge to get the hoarders to disclose their hiding places. They even arrested suspects and held them in custody until they revealed their stash.[228] All this within "occupied territory."

Consequently in October, Sherman actually expressed the opinion that the partisans were almost an asset for the occupation. "The band of guerrilla or partisan rangers are doing us much less harm than our enemies, for in their wants and necessities must take meat and corn, and will take it when and where they please, of friend or foe; the consequence is that the farmers and planters begin to realize that they have to submit to be plundered by those bands of marauders, and are getting heartily tired of it." He told of a train of 40 wagons each with a bale of cotton brought in by farmers desperately needing money to buy supplies for their needy families. When guerrillas tried to stop them, the farmers told them that their families

> "were suffering for salt and tea and medicines, shoes, clothing, & c. all of which were abundant in Memphis. When threatened the guerrillas were to destroy this cotton they would have to fight, and they let us pass. ... I think many of the farmers are tired of the war, and especially of guerrillas. I have promised if they will take care of the guerrillas that they may have trade and we will deal only with large armies."[229]

Similar incidents with various outcomes occurred along Germantown Road. Indeed, as late as November, a gentleman coming to Memphis from Germantown reported that guerrillas were hovering in small bands about White's Station waylaying cotton haulers.[230]

Sherman oscillated between seeing the local population as being hopelessly rebel and optimism about turning their attitudes. "We have roused also the Union element, and our enemies, having burned cotton, taken corn, fodder, and supplies from the country people, have shaken their faith in the secession authorities; so that we have really a substantial beginning of the conversion of the people to our cause."[231]   Such sentiments were always in tension in his mind with a "burning" desire to take revenge on the actively disloyal "secesh" population.   The frustration of his hopes that the locals could or would stop the guerrillas led to his ever more severe retaliations against civilians.

By November 7, the *Bulletin* reported that the Confederates had been able to throw up a screen around Memphis from the Nonconnah to White's station "to prevent Federal excursions into their country from Memphis.[232]   This was soon broken by a major expedition through Germantown into Mississippi.   The cycle continued, and despite proclamations of martial law over West Tennessee,[233] Germantown did not benefit from the protection it was supposed to provide.   Rather the town suffered from its negative consequences.   By October, the Nashville *Daily Union* reported that "The people east of Memphis, near Germantown, are said to be suffering for the necessities of life.   Cotton is their only support, and it has been all destroyed by guerrillas."[234]

We may never know how long the town government continued to function during this year providing any the legal authority.   News of the outside world could only be smuggled in.   Letters had to be brought in by persons penetrating the lines.   If and when Memphis newspapers reached town, that news was increasingly shaped by occupation authorities.   All newspaper editors and owners in the District of West Tennessee were required to take the oath of allegiance to continue publication.   Since the *Appeal* had been moved south before the occupation, it continued publication but had to arrive surreptitiously.   Nevertheless, there was still some circulation in the area.   One innovative effort was the production of an enterprising press in Grenada, the *Rebel Picket*.   This tri-weekly seems to have focused on war news from the Confederate perspective.   One late copy survives in the Duke family papers, indicating that it was smuggled into the area.[235]

Finally, the adventures of one young man of the town provide another picture of the trials of life in no-man's-land.   Henry Woodson, the son of the Gin manufacturer, at age sixteen joined a company raised by his uncle in Mississippi in March 1862.   The "Coldwater Rebels" became Company E, 34th Mississippi Infantry.   Like many, he succumbed to disease rather than combat, and was severely ill from June until November.   After recovery, he returned home to Germantown on November 1 for a few day's visit with his parents.   He related what followed.

> But in the midst of my visit the Sixth Illinois Cavalry came
> along and made me a prisoner of war.   To console and

reassure my distressed parents, Captain Starr, the adjutant of the regiment, told them that if I would give my word of honor that I would not make any attempt to escape, I should go with the first batch of prisoners to be exchanged. The solemn promise was given and I was taken on to Memphis, and placed as a prisoner in the old Irving Block on Second Street. My parents and eldest sister [John, Elizabeth and Ann] came several times to visit me in the prison. On one of these occasions, after spending half an hour, they bade me goodbye and left. A few minutes after they had gone, I stepped out into the hallway and to my surprise, the guard was not there. Like Moses of old, I 'looked this way and that way.' The hall seemed deserted and everything was still. I walked lightly to the head of the stairs and looked down on the street. There seemed to be absolutely nothing to prevent an easy escape from that place. At that moment the recollection of my promise came to my mind and I stepped back into the room, closed the door and remained a prisoner a few days longer when I, with a large number of others, was sent by boat to Vicksburg, Mississippi, and exchanged. So the Federal officer, Captain Starr, kept his promise too.[236]

In contrast to the barbarities that were developing around them, such stories paint a much more civil picture. Woodson rejoined his unit at Shelbyville, Tennessee, and was subsequently transferred into the 13th Tennessee.[237]

William Yates, who lived about six or seven miles north of Germantown (in what is now Cordova, a part of Memphis), served in Company H along with Germantown men. He told of more typical furlough experiences during that year.

Was slightly wounded in the breast in Jonesboro. The doctor thought it was a dangerous wound and I was given a 60 day furlough. But it proved slight and I only stayed in the hospital for a few days. Had meazles during war but happened to get home on sick leave before getting down. Lived very well first part of war....[238]

Such furloughs home for recovery were common, even when it involved return into occupied territory like Germantown. The soldier had to carry with him a furlough form that specified where he was to go and how many days he had, "at the expiration of which he will rejoin his command, or be considered a deserter." The Quartermaster's Department provided him transportation within the area still under Confederate control. Beyond that, he was on his own. Upon arrival at home, he was to report to the nearest enrolling officer.[239]   Around occupied

Germantown, the local conscripting officers, such as Richardson, operating behind enemy lines would have gotten a soldier's name sooner or later if he did not return.

For Germantown's men with the Army of Tennessee, the rest of the year's experiences after Shiloh and Corinth were uneven. Effects on morale and motivation were complicated. Smith's August campaign into Kentucky, took them up through the eastern mountains and into the blue grass country. Exhilarated at an opportunity to liberate Kentucky, turn the Union flank and perhaps force them to retreat from their homes, their cause still looked promising. At first, sympathetic citizens provided rich supplies. But then came the retreat. It "was one of greater trial and hardship than any march made during the war. Over a rough and barren country, without shoes and thinly clad, with scarcely anything to eat, the suffering was great, yet it was born with fortitude and without murmur." Or so the commander of the 13th memorialized it. At least no Germantown men of that regiment lay dead in Kentucky this time.[240] The 4th, on the other hand, was so badly reduced that it had to be united with the 5th into the consolidated 4th/5th Regiment.

From Knoxville, they all went by train to Tullahoma where they found badly needed clothing, equipment and supplies. At the end of November, at Murfreesboro the 13th was hit with several cases of small pox. Many of the men promptly experienced their first vaccinations and the potential epidemic was promptly checked. After a short quarantine, however, on December 30, 1862, it suffered its next bleeding. On the first day of the Battle of Murfreesboro, once again its men played an important role in the Confederate advance in the face of heavy resistance. Of its surviving 226 officers and men, it lost 110 killed, wounded and missing. Again, Company C's report elaborated the experience of Germantown's men.

> The company was also in the battle of Stone's River in front of Murfreesborough, Tennessee. In this engagement we lost half killed, wounded and missing. Lieutenant Rolfe T. Duke was killed. Wayne Holman and P. P. Tuggle, Orderly Sergeant P. B. Cash and Private J. W. Wright were missing and supposed to be killed, as they have not been heard from since the battle.[241]

Duke was the second loss for that planter family. Palmer Tuggle died of a sever wound in the left forearm, which probably required amputation. William Ellis was slightly wounded in the foot. From an unknown cause, following the war he became paralyzed for life. In March at Shelbyville, the badly depleted regiment was fused with the 154th as the 13th/154th. The two regiments had fought side-by-side since Belmont.[242] Thereafter, the war took them ever farther from home. At least their sacrifices had kept some of Tennessee still in Confederate hands.

## *The Burning of the Churches*

There is a well established tradition that Germantown was thoroughly burned in July and/or that General Sherman ordered the burning of all the public buildings, including the churches, to prevent assemblies conspiring against the occupation. Also according to this tradition, despite this order the Presbyterian Church was saved when its pastor, Reverend Richard Evans, won over the support of his fellow Mason, Colonel William L. Sanderson, purportedly the local Union commander at the time. As a result, Evan's church was used as a stable, while the Masonic Hall served as a hospital. The Baptist and Methodist churches were burned. Different aspects of this tradition have come down through several channels, but the most intriguing resulted from the coincidental marriage of one couple– a descendant of Moses Neeley, an elder of the church and a participant in the negotiations, and a descendant of Colonel Sanderson. As the two families gathered for the occasion, they shared family stories of the war, including a Sanderson tradition that Colonel William had helped save the church.[243]

According to a different tradition, the Methodist Church, initially survived any burnings. Unfortunately that church was so badly abused that it had to be demolished and rebuilt after the war. Another variant of that tradition is that after its use as a hospital, Federal troops burned it. Either way, the tradition that the Presbyterian Church, of Germantown's three churches, was the only one to survive was technically true.[244] All other aspects of these traditions require careful review.

Testing them and accurately reconstructing these events so important to the Civil War memories of Germantown citizens is not easy. No specific orders about burning Germantown's buildings seem to have survived. No specific orders from Grant or Sherman about retaliations against Germantown. In any case, it was common practice to burn community buildings in retaliation for guerrilla actions, but usually at the initiative of field commanders.

According to the traditions of the Germantown Baptist Church, their old building was burned by Federal troops in 1862. The only surviving eyewitness account was that of Sallie Walker, residing across the street from the church at the time. She described a very methodical process, with the soldiers removing all the furnishings and then thoroughly building fires inside. Through a slave, she intervened with the officer in charge to save the pulpit Bible. Sounds like an official burning, probably precipitated by the community's suspected support of guerrilla activity.[245] Subsequent telling of the story assigned an order by Sherman. That burning occurred probably during one of the raids or temporary occupations and at the orders of the unit commander, at most inspired by Sherman's hostility, but not part of any large scale burning.

To set a precise date for the traditional burning, local historians assert that the *Appeal* of July 23 reported, "The little town of Germantown has been sacked and burned by a band of stragglers from the Federal Army."[246] Unfortunately, no such article exists. There was such an article in the *Bulletin*, copies of which do not seem to have survived. What the *Appeal* actually published on July 25 was the *Bulletin*'s more detailed article retracting some of its previous description by stating that "No houses were burned as was before reported."[247] One more questionable source specifically places burnings in Germantown in late November or very early December, at the hands of the 8th Missouri Infantry Regiment. The 116th Illinois Infantry was also allegedly involved in a house burning about that same time.[248]

The documented presence in the area of the historical personalities and units allegedly involved provides the windows of opportunity for whatever happened. Sherman, who allegedly gave the order, commanded Union forces in the area of western-most Tennessee from July until he departed for Vicksburg, December 20, 1862. The 8th Missouri was with him the entire time. The newly formed 116th Illinois joined him on November 11.[249] On November 25, Sherman made a major foray into Mississippi, ordering Brigadier General M. L. Smith's 1st Brigade, containing the 8th Missouri, to pass through Germantown and then down to Byhalia[250] (the 116th Illinois was listed in a different brigade on a different route).[251] By early December, various northern newspapers were reporting that Germantown had been burned by soldiers of the 8th Missouri, and that the division commander had shot the offenders.[252] War reports in northern newspapers were often notoriously erroneous or greatly exaggerated. So this version cannot be taken too literally.

Nevertheless, if this version of burnings in Germantown grew out of any actual incident, that would place it around the days when the 8th was in Germantown, November 26 and 27. This report clearly contradicts traditions of an officially ordered burning, but would instead have been the act of vandal soldiers. It also would not have included the events told in the traditions of the Presbyterians. Both the 8th and the 116th then campaigned with Sherman into Mississippi, and there was only a small hiatus between their return to Memphis on December 13 and December 20 when they boarded ship.[253]

The diary of Henry C. Bear, private in the 116th Illinois, is the source of the one reference to a possible involvement of the 116th, but unfortunately no indication of when or how. In his entry of December 16 in camp at Memphis, he recorded that their colonel had told them that their regiment had a good reputation, "with the exception of burning a house in Germantown which he said he did not believe we did nor neither do I."[254] This at least implies that the 116th was in or near Germantown at some time, but also clearly indicates vandalism. It certainly reveals that at least one building was burned during this late-November to early-December window by some Union vandals.

As a last complication, there is no evidence that Colonel William L. Sanderson ever commanded in or around Germantown, but he was present for a few days. From June 1862, his 23rd Indiana was part of Major General John A. McClernand's 1st Division headquartered in Jackson, and he was personally in command at Bolivar.[255] His unit remained at Jackson until the end of 1862. On January 10, 1863, he was on the road to Memphis, arriving in Collierville on the eleventh. There his regiment remained until the nineteenth.[256] Thus January 11-19 is the most likely period during which Reverend Evans could have made his acquaintance and established their Masonic bond. This would also have been the time for Sanderson to have intervened with his fellow officers at Germantown to help save the church from whatever fate.

Considering the different official reports and local memories, the burning of buildings in Germantown occurred more than once, and traditions have compounded them into a single event involving General Sherman and Colonel Sanderson. Indeed there are other family traditions of several burning incidents. The burning of the Baptist Church was most likely an early, separate incident.

It might be appropriate to place other burning activities very late in 1862, the time of angry retaliation against guerrilla operations. It is most likely, however, that all the burnings except the Baptist Church were spontaneous vandalism, perhaps inspired by their commanders' hostilities. One likely moment would have been November 27, the day the 8th Missouri left Germantown. After all officers were gone, stragglers would have had the most freedom. That may have been when a few other buildings met their fate. The story of the Methodist church may be entirely different.

Local historian, Elisabeth Hughes, has a different memory source that has been ignored in favor of the popular tradition. She says that because of the severe winter of 1862/63, newly stationed Union troops were dismantling unprotected buildings for firewood.[257] By early January, Colonel Ephraim R. Eckley's 2nd Brigade headquarters, Colonel Samuel A. Holmes' 10th Missouri Infantry, and Lieutenant Colonel Thomas P. Herrick's 7th Kansas Cavalry had settled into occupation of the town proper,[258] so these must have been the commanders in question. According to Hughes, Evans and Neeley persuaded the commanding officers to use the church and Masonic Hall for storage facilities and a hospital so they would be protected. Initially, Evans may have heard rumors of burning orders that mobilized him to seek a meeting with Colonel Eckley. In this more likely version, Colonel Sanderson, visiting fellow officers while staying in Collierville, might have helped to persuade his comrades to arrange this solution. His and Evan's Masonic affiliations may indeed have been the crucial factor, for such Masonic bonds would frequently supersede the hostile emotions generated by the war. Hughes goes on to report that the unprotected Methodist building became a source of firewood for the troops encamped in the adjacent cemetery. This fits with the Methodist tradition that their church was so badly used that after the occupation it had to be demolished.[259] Also a different memory preserved in the Presbyterian Church's historical display case recalls that their church was used as a commissary, not a stable, and the Masonic Hall was the headquarters.[260] This version of the use of that church rings more true than the idea that it was used as a stable. The floors and walls would hardly have survived such abuse.

It is also unlikely that upon taking over the town for his headquarters, Colonel Eckley would have ordered all public buildings burned to prevent conspiratorial assemblies. That would have only been a problem prior to full-time occupation, and public buildings such as schools and the Masonic Hall were useful for the occupiers. For some personal reason, he may have initially avoided occupying churches. Such lack of official use left unoccupied and unguarded buildings subject to vandalism.

Whenever the destruction occurred, by the beginning of 1863, observers would describe Germantown as completely in ruins with all shops and mills and many homes destroyed. Such a statement may have been a bit of hyperbole, but the town was badly damaged.

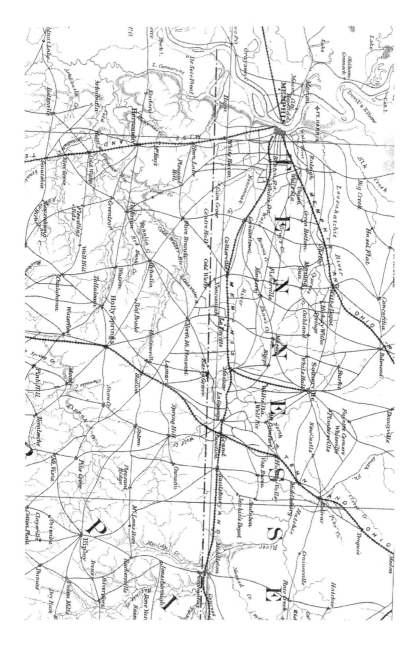

Map 9. Civil War Theater around Germantown (OR *Atlas*, Map Sheet XIX, Plate CLIX.)

# Table 2: Civil War Incidents in and around Germantown, 1863

January, 1863, **regular occupation of Germantown begins**
10 January, Grant moved his headquarters to Memphis; mid-January, Vicksburg campaign.
27 January, **engagement near Germantown.**
28 January, skirmish south of Collierville by 7th Kansas Cavalry out of Germantown.
23 May, **skirmish at Germantown.**
3 July, *fall of Vicksburg.*
8 July, **scout for guerrillas launched from Germantown.**
16-20 July, **scout launched from Germantown.**
18 July, **skirmish at Germantown**.
11 October, Battle of Collierville; **raid at Germantown**.
3 November, Second Battle of Collierville, **Col. Edmund Hatch counterattacks from Germantown**.
November - December, *Forrest's conscription raid into West Tennessee, culminating at Collierville.*

# 1863, Germantown Occupied

### The Impact of Federal and Confederate Forces

After seven months of being caught in a no-man's-land, suffering from the Confederate policy of denying the Federals any resources in the area, from Union reprisals, and from pillaging by Union soldiers, during 1863 Germantown would "benefit" from a year of heavy occupation in and around the town itself. It became again an army camp town, but full of men in blue. This was a mixed blessing.

For one thing, Federal forces felt threatened and suspicious of local collaboration. Pressure on Union forces in West Tennessee was maintained well into 1863 by the cavalry of Major General Earl Van Dorn headquartered at Spring Hill. The object was to preoccupy possible Union reinforcements for the Vicksburg campaign. Even though its major military operations were usually focused on Middle and East Tennessee, that did not reduce the partisan threat in West Tennessee.[1]

Grant proclaimed that he would clean out all guerrillas from the country between Holy Springs and Memphis. "If it cannot be done in any other way I will be compelled to take and destroy the last bushel of grain between the Hatchie and the Tallahatchie, and all the stock. I will make it the interest of the citizens to leave our lines of communication unmolested."[2]  Federal troops had a writ to confiscate and destroy.

In response to the combined threats of partisans and Confederate raiders, Union commanders revised their operations.  What followed was the establishment of regimental and brigade strength bases all along the railroad, such as Germantown, and a constant campaign of large cavalry raids from these bases to repress the partisans and guerrillas.

The forces remaining in West Tennessee were redistributed along more stable defensive lines.  Brigadier General Isaac F. Quinby (7th Division) was sent from Lafayette with orders to temporarily secure the State Line Road westward.  By January 3, his orders had turned into establishing a stationary defense of the railroad.  His 2nd Brigade under Colonel Ephraim R. Eckley guarded the road from Collierville to Germantown; the 3rd Brigade under Colonel George B. Boomer from Germantown to White's Station.[3]  Prior to this, only one company, F of the 59th Indiana Infantry, had been encamped at Germantown since November 1862.[4]

The new disposition put Colonel Eckley headquartered at Germantown with five regiments scattered around the area: the 56th Illinois, the 17th Iowa, the 10th Missouri (specifically in Germantown under Colonel Samuel A. Holmes[5]), and the 80th Ohio east of town at what it called Camp Forest Hill.  One section of the Springfield Light Artillery Battery (Illinois) held a position described as "encamped within the fortifications, commanding Germantown, Tennessee."  Two additional regiments encamped on the east side of town for several weeks each during January and February.  Also from the Cavalry Division under Colonel T. Lyle Dickey, the 7th Kansas Cavalry under Lieutenant Colonel Thomas P. Herrick camped at Germantown between February 28 and April 18.[6]  This placed a brigade headquarters and six full regiments, plus an additional cavalry regiment and artillery in and closely around the town.  Life was drastically changed by an occupation force several times that of the local population.  Although constant rearrangements of the units would reduce this force gradually, for the rest of the year it would remain an overwhelming presence.

Union concern about a hostile population supporting guerrillas and providing the Confederates with intelligence had already resulted in reprisals.  By early January, the mood in the Union Army was clearly revealed in a series of orders that Grant issued to Quinby and Hurlbut.  "Give notice to the citizens on the road to Memphis that if necessary to secure the railroad every family and every vestige of property, except land itself, between the Hatchie and the Coldwater will be removed out of these limits or confiscated.  Arrest and parole all citizens between eighteen and fifty years of age."  Parole would have made them technically ineligible for either conscription or enlistment in the

Confederate army. He ordered Hurlbut that for every raid or attempted raid by guerrillas on the road, he was to arrest ten families of the most prominent secessionists.[7] Tensions between occupation forces and hostile locals could lead to much brutality on both sides. Union troop frustrations at their inability to keep raids from threatening their positions were easily focused on the residents. Under these tense circumstances, patrols occasionally shot suspected civilians, guilty or not, even in front of their families. Such incidents could not have been too common, however, for they were considered significant enough to produce inquiries.[8] They were sufficient enough, however, to deter any man from standing his ground against an abusive soldier.

In April, Colonel W. W. Sanford, in command of the 4th Brigade at Germantown, would be ordered to expel "six rebel families" living near Buntyn Station for an incident.[9] Given the number of incidents near Germantown, one suspects that residents of the immediate area must have also been subjected to expulsions.

On January 6, Hurlbut become commander of the 16th Corps, in command of the entire area. Drunken, venal, and unscrupulous, he became notorious in the eyes of local southerners. His corruption included confiscated property.[10] Over the next few months, he would gradually become the primary authority over the area as Grant began taking McPherson's 17th Corps for the Vicksburg siege, leaving Union defenses further reduced. By January 31, there were only 5,947 cavalry for chasing partisans, but at least that was concentrated along the M&C RR.[11]

Slowly Union occupation and control gradually settled into a territorial division. Specifically for the defense of the M&C Railroad, local Union efforts at "control" ended with their picket lines at Nonconnah Creek. Confederate lines lay along the Coldwater in Mississippi. In between was a no-man's land over which patrols and major raiding forces from both sides operated. But even behind Union lines and all around Union occupied positions, Rebel forces, regular cavalry and partisans, still operated almost with impunity. Nevertheless, direct concentration of large units in occupation of Germantown would at least keep Rebel troops, raiders and resultant firefights out of town.

On January 12, the *Appeal,* quoted the *Bulletin as* boasting that the Federals in Memphis had the M&C repaired once more and were bringing trains safely through from Grand Junction, delivering 399 bales of cotton, confident that the line could be more easily "kept clear of guerrillas and track destroyers." Nevertheless, those repairs were not the best, for one train, coming too rapidly around the infamous curve east of Germantown, derailed when the ties gave way, and two cars went careening off one hundred yards and turned over.[12]

Also, the sounds of action could still be heard all around the area.

From his camp near Germantown, Colonel Eckley reported that on January 27 a forage train from his brigade was unsuccessfully attacked by about seventy-five rebel cavalry. In the same vicinity, a force of twenty-four men of the 4th Illinois Cavalry were ambushed with three killed, three wounded (two seriously) and sixteen missing. He immediately sent out reinforcements that forced the enemy back across the Coldwater. This Confederate force seated west of Byhalia consisted of about five hundred men and had been harassing his trains and pickets almost every day, but was unable to launch any serious attacks because of the condition of the roads at that time of year. On January 28, a patrol of the 7th Kansas out of Germantown had to deal with a guerrilla force of 200 men operating south of Collierville.[13]

As Grant continued to reposition his troops in defense of the line from Memphis, their presence in and around Germantown shifted. Both Hurlbut's 5th Division (Laumann's), described as "near Memphis," and his Cavalry Division under A. L. Lee, headquartered at Germantown, were now defending the line. This placed 4,383 infantry with 8 guns and 1,588 cavalry along the line through Germantown.[14] With both division and 2nd Brigade headquarters at the town, it became a center of intelligence operations. Its provost marshal received all prisoners for interrogation.

The Germantown area remained densely bivouacked by a shifting array of Union troops throughout the spring. During March, troops continued to rearrange their areas of defense. On the sixth, Hurlbut ordered Denver's Division at La Grange to move down the railroad to Germantown, relieving the 4th to occupy the road from Germantown into Memphis, one brigade on the road itself and the other two on each side of the road at Memphis.[15]

These defenders faced increasing partisan pressures. Partisan warfare had reached a fever pitch. Each side's versions of the other's more desperate acts would elicit extreme accusations of criminality. Although often exaggerated or biased, there was considerable truth to the stories. Although we will never know how many Germantown men rode with Richardson's Partisan Rangers during this early phase, some did, and several would be with him later. Their wartime experience was considerably different from that of the regulars, with great long-term effect on their mentality and morality. Also the activities of Richardson's Partisans had considerable impact on life around Germantown.

As early as January 3, Hurlbut had reported to Grant that the road from Memphis to Germantown was full of guerrillas and warned that since he could not spare any guards, the road needed to "be strongly guarded down to the depot. ... I require more force than the ordinary guards, and especially cavalry, to beat up these guerrillas. Major Blyth (a Mississippi partisan leader) is within 14 miles on the Hernando road.

Richardson near Wolf River, about Germantown."[16]  He even made a dash into the Memphis suburbs as far as Chelsea and the Fair grounds.[17] Richardson did indeed get around quite freely within the territory he claimed "to hold."

By March, he was such a threat that Colonel Grierson's cavalry brigade had to launch a combined operation against him. Although his reports minimized his subsequent defeat, his forces were never so concentrated that it could be totally destroyed, and its ability to disburse into swamps and woods made him much less vulnerable to fatal damages.  His language, however, provides one clue to what was bothering his Confederate superiors. While his strength reports of 150 or 100 men in a particular engagement were probably accurate, he constantly talked about his "regimental command." He claimed that he had successfully raised ten companies, with five more in process of organization.  Although cut off from contact, "We have fought two general engagements and have had innumerable skirmishes."[18]  Given their disbursal, it is hard to tell what his total strength was at any time. This, however, was only one thing that disturbed his superiors.  He omitted any reference to activities that raised serious charges about impropriety.

As he exercised "his discretion" to confiscate and to harass and occasionally kill Unionists, but especially among the families of men serving in the Union Army, he was denounced by his erstwhile superiors. General Hurlbut announced, "I am assured by high Confederate authority that they act without and against orders, and are simply robbers, to be treated as such.  The gang must be exterminated, and the sooner the better." Given the enmity among the opposing sides within the local population and the opportunities for vindictive actions, his men inevitably deteriorated into undisciplined bands.

During a sweep against Richardson, Colonel Robert F. Looney was captured and sent back to Germantown for interrogation.  Local citizens reported that he and two other officers were there to recruit and organize a different cavalry brigade in West Tennessee.  Looney professed, however, "to have been sent there for the purpose of investigating the complaints of citizens against Richardson and his command."[19]  Both versions were true.  Richardson was under investigation.

General J. E. Johnston, Confederate Department of the West at Chattanooga directed that whatever authority Richardson had to operate should be withdrawn, because he was "accused of great oppression."[20] He had asked Pemberton, Richardson's purported commanding officer, to send Colonel Looney to arrest Richardson.  While Richardson's forces had been raiding and recruiting from Germantown up into Haywood County, Looney had been recruiting from Collierville across Fayette County before his capture.

Pemberton was then informed that Richardson's authority had expired. From the information received, Richardson had a full regiment organized, but not mustered into Confederate or state service.

> Since he has got these men together, there seems little doubt of his having exercised authority never intended to be given. ... It is thought best,... the power granted to him to raise partisan rangers be revoked; at the same time, the services of the men collected ought to be secured.[21]

Recruiting and conscripting regiments from West Tennessee was a major goal of the badly out-manned Confederacy. They needed his men, if not Richardson.

From the Union side came an equal determination to bring Richardson down. After breaking up his camp, on March 15, Hurlbut ordered Grierson to use the captured muster rolls of Richardson's force to capture or kill his men. Once identified, they would be unable to slip in and out of civilian status. Since high Confederate authority had defined Richardson' men as "simply robbers, to be treated as such," he ordered that "The gang must be exterminated.... The prisoners received are not held as prisoners of war, but as robbers and murderers, and will be so treated."[22]

After Richardson suffered a serious setback and was wounded, on April 17 the cavalry commander operating out of Jackson, reported, "I am informed by reliable citizens ... that Richardson ... crossed the Mississippi River in a canoe, with a fortune, robbed of citizens of Haywood, Tipton and the adjoining counties."[23] Although pure fiction, this was the essence of Richardson's reputation and some of the complaints being investigated by Confederate high command.

Meanwhile on April 1, Hurlbut had received reports that the partisan bands plaguing him, including Richardson had been ordered by Chalmers to report to him at Panola.[24] In fact, Chalmers was to "assume command of all the partisan corps in West Tennessee, organizing and reporting the same." He was to ascertain if Richardson's command has been mustered, and even if so to arrest him.[25]

Then between April 17 and 18, Richardson's fortunes underwent a sudden shift. On the 17th, Richardson was an illegal guerrilla, still threatened with arrest. But on the very next day, Pemberton sent a scout to Richardson to tell him to cut the rail communications from Jackson to Corinth.[26] All of a sudden, Richardson was an ostensibly legitimate commander with an official assignment. By May 1, he was operating under Pemberton's orders as a commander of a cavalry brigade harassing Federal forces in Mississippi in order to take pressure off Pemberton at Vicksburg.[27]

We may never know the details of this transition. On April 27, the *Appeal* at Grenada, Mississippi, reported an interview with Richardson, who was "at present in this city for purposes of answering some charges that have been preferred against him."[28]  For the rest of the year, the *Appeal* would lavish praise on him, indicating his popularity.  It was the threat to Vicksburg and the desperate need for cavalry against the Union Army in Mississippi that undoubtedly explains the sudden willingness to ignore doubts about Richardson.  His excuses and denials were probably accepted with some pinches of salt, and he was admonished to keep his men in line.  For the first time, at least some of Richardson's men found themselves operating as a coherent unit away from home territory.

As part of Grant's operations, on April 17, he ordered a major cavalry expedition down through Mississippi from Corinth, resulting in more changes at Germantown.  The 7th Kansas went with the expedition, to be replaced at Germantown by the 9th Illinois.[29]  By the end of the month, the reshuffling of units was complete.  Under Hurlbut, the 1st Division (Smith), headquartered at La Grange, stationed its 1st Brigade at Collierville and its 4th under Colonel William W. Sanford at Germantown.  This placed the 48th and 119th Illinois Infantry around the town and the 49th Illinois (Colonel Phineas Pease) in town, with companies scattered along the line at stations such as Ridgeway.  In addition, the 2nd Brigade (Colonel La Fayette McCrillis) of the 1st Cavalry Division was headquartered at Germantown with its 9th Illinois (Major Ira R. Gifford) also in town.[30]  The garrison around the town was reduced.

Soon, Grant's endless demands for troops against Vicksburg required yet another rearrangement.  His requests required Hurlbut to order Major General Richard J. Oglesby (headquartered at Corinth) to shift his front as far west as Germantown.  The Cavalry units remained in place.  On June 10, Oglesby reported that he had two companies at LaFayette, six companies of the 50th Indiana at Collierville with a section of artillery, and Phease's 49th Illinois Infantry still at Germantown with a section of artillery, but its companies were spread out along the State Line Road as far as White's Station.  The Cavalry Division (now Colonel John K. Mizner) was again headquartered at Germantown, also with its 1st Brigade (Colonel McCrillis) still covering LaFayette, Collierville and Germantown.[31]

Despite reductions, for the entire year, Germantown remained heavily occupied.  As regiments rotated in and out of town, they arrived more frequently by rail.  They disembarked in the middle of town at the depot with all their equipment and supplies to march off to their encampments.[32]  A steady stream of wagon trains carrying equipment and supplies also rolled through town.  With their noise and danger to pedestrians and ongoing damage to property, life in and around town would have had all the hubbub and animal waste of a busy city.

Despite such a presence, on June 12, a force of 500 men again managed to penetrate Ogelsby's defenses and tear up the rails and telegraph lines between Germantown and Collierville. They tore up the track again near Germantown on the fifteenth.[33] Hurlbut complained to Grant, "My line of railroad is not tenable. If attacked by a respectable force, it must be broken.... I will do the best I can on the line to keep it up and repel an attack, but am liable to be cut off by river or railroad, or both, at any time."[34] Although no such "respectable force" attacked, the raiders kept up the pressure.

The force that threatened the area from Mississippi was that of Chalmers. His command of the 5th Military District in Northern Mississippi headquartered at Panola included many of the West Tennessee cavalry as well as three Tennessee artillery batteries. Many components of these units traced their formation back to Shelby County.[35] Chalmers' command also sent parties into West Tennessee to recruit and conscript more. To maintain its strength, the 7th Cavalry would draw constantly on men who had not previously enlisted and served, who had left service for a variety of reasons, or even those who had been captured and paroled back home. By July, compared to the previous year when he opined that the people of Tennessee "are now much depressed," and unlikely to provide recruits, Chalmers now believed things were changing. "On the other hand, the people of those districts of which the enemy have had possession for some time, are, I am informed, now willing to enlist. West Tennessee is beginning to rally.... The number of them will be increased by the extension of the age of those liable to conscription to forty-five...."[36]

Meanwhile, Richardson had resumed operations in West Tennessee. On June 26, the *Bulletin* reported that he had returned to his haunt "in the region of the corner of the three counties of Tipton, Shelby and Fayette." Now titling himself a brigadier, he would "carry on his old trade of robber, or at least, its equivalent, since it is asserted by persons who ought to know, that Richardson has extorted from people of the three counties named upward to one hundred thousand dollars."[37] By July, refugees fleeing the area reported that he was still near Shelby Depot, with rolls estimated to contain names of 2,000 recruits and conscripts, but not yet assembled into a fighting force. There were still no more than 200 cavalry in his camp.[38]

Colonel McCrillis left Germantown on July 16 to hunt him down. Unable to catch him, he reported squads totaling about 400 men had been moving north across the Big Hatchie into Lauderdale County to join Richardson. Only about 100 were actually armed and low on ammunition.[39] Then on August 6 came the report that Richardson was back down at Okolona, Mississippi. While other partisan raiders had harassed Union forces as a distraction, the will-o'-the-wisp had gone back into Tennessee, not to raid but to recruit and conscript.

The *Bulletin* published what it alleged were conscription orders issued to "his serene demonship" Richardson by the Confederate Adjutant General. It compared Confederate policy to the Russian treatment of the Poles.

> Every white man between the ages of eighteen and forty-five in the District of West Tennessee is hereby ordered to report immediately at such places of rendezvous as may hereafter be designated. ... If a man should absent himself from his home to avoid this order, burn his house and other property, except such as may be useful to this command. If a man is found to resist the execution of this order, by refusing to report, shoot him down and leave him lying. If a man takes refuge in his house and offers resistance, set the house on fire and guard it in order the recusant may not get out."[40]

Until a copy of the actual order turns up, the accuracy of such draconian instructions cannot be tested. They, nevertheless, give a sense of the pressures under which men existed while trying to live in peace around Germantown, and of the terms under which some had to serve.

In contrast, in August after returning from his recruiting mission, Richardson reported

> I found a lively feeling of patriotism to prevail among the people, which was greatly stimulated by the knowledge of my appointment as chief for the Bureau of conscription of West Tennessee, and my proclaimed intention to put the laws in force without delay. Very soon there were not less than forty company organizations on foot throughout West Tennessee, some of these were soon formed, others dragged.[41]

The truth about responses to recruitment efforts probably lay between these extreme images. Some responded to the conscription notice dutifully. Others responded out of fear of retribution, or were even dragooned. While bringing large bands back through the lines to Mississippi to be armed, one routinely had to keep them under guard by trustworthy volunteers.[42]

On September 30, Chalmers was given command of all troops in North Mississippi, with Richardson as his cavalry commander. No independent companies or battalions were allowed to leave the state or attach themselves to any organization without permission.[43] Not only were they putting together a sizable force for Chalmers, but they sought to control their partisans for better coordinated operations. Richardson's new contingent of Tennessee partisans needed to be officially incorporated into the army in North Mississippi, and concentrated there to defend the area.

Consequently his command received official status as regular Tennessee cavalry regiments. It became the West Tennessee Cavalry Brigade and his 1st Tennessee Regiment of Partisan Ranges became the 12th Tennessee Cavalry Regiment under the command of his former Lieutenant Colonel James U. Green. The additional troops they had raised became the 13th under Colonel J. J. Neely (later renumbered the 14th Tennessee Cavalry), and the 14th under Colonel F. M. Stewart (which would become the 15th).[44] For a while, they had to cool their heels in North Mississippi.

Although we may never know which Germantown area men rode originally with Richardson's Partisan Rangers, after they became Tennessee regiments some rosters survived. In the 12th (Green's), perhaps as many as 15 area men served. Among them were apparently Joe Duke of that planter family and one of the four L. Thompsons, who served in different companies, was Louis Lycurgus Thompson, a farmer in his thirties living east of Germantown. If they had not volunteered, farmers working their fields would have been the easiest to scoop up. If a conscript did not report for duty at the specified place, the process could be more like dragooning. They, like Dr. Zivago during the Russian Civil War, might simply disappear one day to serve the cause whether they wanted to or not. Joel Harrison, Henry Massey and James Neely are also likely candidates for membership in the 12th. Even the 14th/15th may have had 4 area men. Of all the possible members identified, more than a third were in their forties and twenty percent in their teens. Such were the men, whether volunteers or conscripts, who were swept up to ride either with Richardson's Partisans or his later Tennessee cavalry regiments.

One interesting story that provides some insight into the effects of the war on both soldier and civilian relates to Joel Duke. He had enlisted at age 15 and was one of those who "rode with Forrest." Unfortunately there are no records of his service. There are clues that he was in the 12th Tennessee, but he had probably begun riding with Richardson. At one point, he was captured and not paroled, indicating he was a partisan. A friend of the family, a Mrs. Willett, visited him at the Irving Block prison in Memphis. One of those indomitable southern bells, she was on a mission to help him escape. She blackened his face and provided clothes to dress him as a "Negro waiter." In this guise, he escaped. After sneaking thorough the picket lines around Memphis, he stole a horse and rejoined his unit. Unfortunately no more of his story has been told.[45]

Throughout the summer, such men continued to harass the occupation. On July 18, Colonel Pease, in Germantown, reported that a squad of rebel raiders had captured three cavalrymen within a half mile of his picket line to the west. They had again torn up track two miles from town. Pease dispatched a squad of cavalry which overtook the rebels and rescued the captured cavalrymen and seven track repairmen. The rails were repaired in time for the morning train.[46]

Pease also reported that on August 13 a small patrol returning from White's Station was ambushed by a squad of guerrillas near Ridgeway Station. After a severely wounded captain surrendered, the guerrillas shot him. One other man was fatally wounded, while the rest escaped. Reportedly the guerrillas robbed their victims. Colonel McCrillis launched a force to intercept them. Pease reported that this was the third such incident near Ridgeway Station. He ordered all citizens along the railroad and north of Nonconnah Creek to monitor the fords and immediately report all crossings.[47] Apparently he trusted many of them to have an interest in preventing guerrilla depredations. Strangely he did not know that the Nonconnah, at that time of year, was fordable almost everywhere throughout his area.

Confederate regulars and guerrillas could still operate consistently behind Union lines, despite the seeming denseness of Union forces in the area. Although Union numbers seem impressive, there were the inevitable officer's complaints about insufficient numbers and resources.[48] In the above incident, McCrillis' troopers were so dispersed at the time of the incident that he had difficulty cobbling together enough men to mount the interception force that failed. Also, anyone old enough to remember the thick bottoms and woodlands around the area even as late as the first half of the 20th century knows how easy it would be to stay hidden or lie in ambush.

To counter the raider threat, for the duration of its stay in Germantown Colonel McCrillis' brigade, either alone or as part of larger operations, aggressively invaded north Mississippi. Germantown thus remained a seat of Union efforts to neutralize those Rebel threats. That included specifically targeting guerrilla forces in West Tennessee. On July 16, McCrillis initiated a foray north from Germantown in pursuit of Richardson's partisans. He crossed the Wolf and Loosahatchee rivers to Galloway Switch, Concordia and Covington, returning on the 19th to Collierville and then Germantown. He captured a few conscripts, but was unable to catch any of the guerrillas reported in the area.[49]

In late summer, the establishment around Germantown underwent more changes. On August 20, the cavalry of the 16th Corps was reorganized and redistributed. Colonel Edward Hatch's 3rd Cavalry Brigade, replaced McCrillis' in Germantown. The 6th Illinois and the 2nd Iowa under Colonel William P. Hepburn was specifically camped at Germantown, the latter on what is today's Festival Grounds.[50] Hatch reported his brigade as headquartered "1½ miles from Germantown, northwest, one-fourth of a mile from Wolf River, 1 mile north of the railroad, on what is known as the Nashbora [Nashoba] tract."[51] Grant again requested reinforcements, further reducing occupation forces around Germantown. Then on September 14, Hatch's brigade headquarters relocated to Memphis.[52] All infantry regiments had left by October 29.[53]

Thereafter cavalry seem to have become the primary occupiers. The 6th Illinois was the most consistent presence from August 1863 to March 30, 1864 when it was furloughed to Illinois. Nevertheless, it was away at least twice on major expeditions against Forrest, leaving only a camp detachment behind. Company K of the 1st Illinois Light Artillery, reinforced for awhile by one section of Vaughn's Independent Battery of the Springfield Light Artillery, were present in the fortifications.[54]

The constant pressure on the local population from guerrillas, Confederate partisans and raiders, Federal confiscations and retributions, and jayhawking were bad enough. To them, unfortunately during 1863 the Federals added the equivalent of their own partisans, state regiments of cavalry. The 1st and 2nd West Tennessee Cavalry quickly earned reputations as evil as those of Confederate partisans. Specifically, Colonel Fielding Hurst of the 1st became Richardson's counterpart in generating the ire of the opposite side. Likewise, he was as adored by the *Bulletin* as Richardson was by the *Appeal*.[55]

Although they had no significant activity in the Germantown area during 1863, a false report of Hurst's murder focused blame on Germantown area guerrillas.[56] Hurst, like Richardson, was becoming the object of wild rumors. The report that he had been killed originated in Collierville, claiming that he had been captured by guerrillas near Germantown, "and his cowardly captors ... shot eleven balls into his body, which they left a corpse."[57] Creative imaginations were clearly at work, and one wonders why Germantown was chosen as the location for this fiction. In fact, his short capture took place four miles south west of Somerville in Fayette County. He was rescued by his men unharmed[58]

From January to autumn, the area's population had experienced a constant shifting of occupation forces, at first in overwhelming numbers, but gradually diminishing. Always hovering around them were swarms of mounted raiders. The locals were both victims of and participants in rebel operations. Such were the problems of the Federal forces defending the line from Memphis through Germantown on the eve of the only significant battles fought near the town.

### The Battles of Collierville and Forrest's Raid into West Tennessee

In the run-up to the first battle of Collierville, both sides had their agents scouting the area. On September 1, a Confederate agent, J. A. Harrel, operating near Germantown, reported that he had just visited Memphis to gather intelligence. There were only about 3000 troops and a battalion of cavalry there – a sizable force having been sent into Arkansas. He suggested that a diversionary force be sent up between La Grange and Germantown to draw the Federals out of Memphis and engage and hold them at Germantown. Then a force of no more than 1000 cavalry could charge in State Line Road and take the city. Major General S. D. Lee, commanding cavalry in North Mississippi, rejected the idea.[59] Germantown was thus spared becoming the battlefield.

Then October 4, Chalmers launched his raid into West Tennessee to break the rail line, but primarily as a diversion for a larger raid to the east. He planned a surprise attack on Collierville. Hurlbut, tricked into sending his cavalry away for an expected attack well to the east, had nevertheless positioned a brigade at White's Station from where it could move to reinforce Collierville or La Fayette just in case.[60]

It was Richardson's Brigade combined with Chalmer's that launched the first Battle of Collierville, with Richardson commanding the entire force. During the night of October 11 two detachments, succeeded in cutting the lines and rails east of Collierville, severing communications. Two other detachments from the 12th and 14th Tennessee were sent to effect similar cuts between Germantown and Collierville. Opposing Richardson at Collierville were only 240 men. Their pickets were quickly overrun, and except for a coincidence, Collierville would have been captured.[61]

Meanwhile Sherman had returned to Memphis with orders to proceed east along the M&C to join Rosecrans at Chattanooga. Since the railroad was insufficient to move large forces, he began moving his entire force toward Corinth on the roads, but personally coming by train from Memphis ahead of them with his headquarters and a battalion of 260 men. He arrived in Collierville at noon shortly after the attack had begun.[62]

Sherman organized the defense of the depot. The firefight was brisk and lasted a couple of hours. By three in the afternoon, the Confederates withdrew in the face of major reinforcements from Germantown and LaFayette. Hurlbut had dispatched a regiment and battery from Germantown, followed by the troops from White's Station.[63] An overwhelming force pursued Chalmers back into Mississippi.[64]

Germantown's involvement in the Battle of Collierville has largely gone unreported. In fact, the little information available is both confusing and interesting. Although Chalmers reported that detachments of the 12th and 14th had failed to cut the lines between Germantown and Collierville before his raid, they apparently reached their destination in time to do damage. At least one large and two small "culverts" had been burned blocking the line between Germantown and Collierville.[65] The Nashville *Daily Union* reported "that a rebel force of some importance made an attack on Germantown at about the same time" as Collierville. Indeed, some time after the forces from Germantown had been dispatched, Hurlbut received word from Germantown. "We were attacked in camp to-day at about 12 o'clock by enemy's cavalry in overwhelming numbers, and our effective force having been ordered from camp some days hence, we were driven from the camp, which was mostly burned. Losses as yet not known, but large." This was the camp of the 6th Illinois Cavalry which had been sent east. It was located on the Nashoba Tract near the Wolf River just north of Germantown.[66] One wonders how Germantown's citizens felt as they watched Tennesseans, even local boys, riding rough-shod over the Federals around their own town.

For what it's worth, one observer accompanying the expedition reported to the *Appeal*,

> We were cordially welcomed and cheered as we passed along, and on our return their patriotism was further evinced by having large baskets of edables (sic) on the roadside for our soldiers. Their loyalty has been wrongly impugned. There may be some Union proclivities, but as far as we could observe (and we had abundant opportunities) they were a unit. These people have, by fortune of war placing them in such close proximity to the enemy's lines, probably been reduced to the alternative of having to deal with the enemy to procure the necessities of life, but their condition is more deserving of sympathy than the unjust charges against them are of credence.[67]

Although he was not specifically talking about the people of Germantown, he might well have been. Their actual experiences and the likely mix of emotions and responses they must have had as they watched the tides of war wash about them would have been the same. Strangely enough, when the Nashville paper reported on Germantown's experience, it contended that the rebel force burned some houses in the town.[68] If true, it could have been incidental to the fight or targeted reprisals against Union collaborators.

Sherman was in high dudgeon. As usual he was especially irked by what he considered the perfidy of unrepentant secesh. "Citizens who travel the road betray us; I would restrict their travel." In his determination to make Chalmers and his civilian supporters feel his wrath, he ordered Hurlbut, "Instruct your cavalry to take all horses and mules between the railroad and the Tallahatchie, burn all mills and corn fields, and let them feel that to attack our road will be surely followed by vengeance. Several of the dead at Collierville had your oath of allegiance and all sorts of passes on their persons."[69] Did this order for vengeance apply to Germantown and vicinity (south of the railroad)? Burning an occupied town would have been counterproductive.

Hurlbut actually ordered no such reprisals. In fact, when he sent reconnaissance parties south into Mississippi, he ordered them to leave receipts for any confiscated feed.[70] This was more typical of the new Union policy to reduce the hostility of the local population. Yet he was certainly set back by the raid which further shook his confidence in his ability to defend the line. He complained that he needed six more regiments to do the job.[71] The line was indeed threatened at two points, toward Middle Tennessee by Forrest and Lee. Closer to home, on October 20, he feared that Chalmers and Richardson had been sufficiently reinforced to attack again. In the event of a heavy attack, he rather timidly planned to have the troops stationed at Collierville and Germantown fall back to Memphis.[72]

Indeed, Chalmers sent a spy, Charles Pierson, to reconnoiter the entire line. He arrived in Memphis on October 14, and visited Germantown and Collierville on the 19th. He reported that the Germantown garrison consisted of the 52nd Illinois Infantry and a few cavalry totaling 500 men. He was obviously unaware that the 6th Illinois Cavalry and the artillery battery were out on patrol.[73]

Chalmers got an assignment to harass Sherman's rear as he was moving east and to cut the rail lines to disrupt his supplies. He suggested a move against either Germantown or Collierville as a distraction while Richardson could cut the lines between La Grange and Corinth. He concentrated his forces 16 miles from Germantown and 19 from Collierville to threaten both. He had scouts deployed along the rail line and the Germantown Road. The scouts reported that the Federals had evacuated the railroad and removed all infantry from the Germantown and Collierville area. Only one cavalry regiment defended each town, the 6th Illinois at Germantown. Believing his scouts, Chalmers decided to hit Collierville again on November 3, but with disastrous results.[74]

Forewarned, Colonel Hatch with the 2nd Iowa, 6th Illinois Cavalry and mountain howitzers of the 1st Illinois Light Artillery had concentrated at Germantown to best defend both villages. He took Chalmers by surprise and drove him steadily south. Since Hatch had to leave Germantown undefended, Hurlbut dispatched the 25th Indiana Infantry to garrison both Germantown and Collierville.[75] They wanted no repeat of the destruction of the cavalry camp at Nashoba. The 25th was specifically ordered to occupy the fort and area around Germantown and to guard the railroad.[76]

When Chalmers made his second attack on Collierville, Richardson was able to be of little assistance. His West Tennessee Brigade had been reduced to two regiments, the 12th and 13th of only 300 and 200 men respectively and one battery of six-pounders. The rest of his command was ostensibly a regiment and two battalions of Mississippi cavalry and some miscellaneous units The entire command had been thrown out on the east flank, headquartered at New Albany and defending as far as Tupelo.[77] This was too far from Richardson's preferred field of action.

On October 28, he wrote a long carping letter to headquarters which is worth quoting extensively for its vivid picture of the condition of his West Tennessee cavalrymen and its Germantown men.

> It is known to you that my Tennessee troops were raised for service in West Tennessee.... The design of all of which was to enable me to raise as large a mounted force as possible in West Tennessee for the defense of that region as long and when it was practical.
>
> I collected together parts of three regiments in August last, and came through the lines to this neighborhood to arm and equip my men; then to return to West Tennessee, collect the balance of my three regiments (in all about 2,000 men), and add to the forces. Through a misapprehension, I was denied equipments until everybody else called for the same things, then I was unceremoniously sat down on a back seat and made to wait until others were equipped.
>
> After a while, General Johnston, misunderstanding my powers and plans, procured ... an order assigning me to General Lee's command. Although not equipped and fully armed, I was ordered to the front, and with my men half naked and half starved, I have earnestly endeavored to serve the country in the late campaign. I was placed in command of the Northeast District of Mississippi, and under the orders of Brigadier General Chalmers, and now I am back here. My men, nearly destitute, have deserted and are deserting me to go home and get clothing and bedding.
>
> If I am to protect this district and Mobile & Ohio Railroad, you must give me more men, arms, equipments and ammunition. ...
>
> I have not a single vessel to cook one morsel of bread. My cooking has to be done as we have to beg citizens to do it. This practice is exceedingly deleterious. It leads to straggling and demoralization. For God and country's sake, make your ... quartermaster send me skillets, ovens, pots, or anything that will bake bread of fry meat. I want clothing, shoes, and blankets for my naked freezing men.[78]

Indeed, According to Chalmers, "Colonel Richardson's command had been greatly reduced by details sent after clothing and by desertion.... Colonel Richardson was unwell, and the force thus raised, which amounted to only 270 men, were placed under command of Colonel J. J.

Neely."[79]   As a distraction, they hit the railroad near Middleton, doing significant damage.[80]   Richardson managed to have his cake and eat it too, proving not only the value of his command, but also its inability to function fully under existing conditions.

On November 10, he repeated his complaints to General Johnston.[81] Again on November 13, he begged him "to permit me to move on the line of this road (M&C RR) and destroy it; at the same time execute my orders with reference to enforcing the conscription laws in West Tennessee and collect my command, the larger part of which is now in West Tennessee. ... I can destroy the road and hold West Tennessee until I can get all my command together."[82]

Several developments encouraged such dreams.   For what it's worth, the map company of James T. Lloyd produced one of its 1863 railroad maps purporting to reveal the areas actually controlled by Union forces, and those still in Rebel hands.  It contended that by October there was just a narrow band running down the Mississippi River and along the M&C and Mississippi state border.  Everything above and below that line was in Rebel hands, with Germantown and Collierville on the fringes of Union control.   The map's narrative attributed the loss of control to the Emancipation Proclamation and the dismissal of General McClellan (an obvious political opinion).[83]   Regardless of the importance of those two factors in such developments, this represented an encouraging shift in the civilian mood.

Richardson had also picked up encouraging reports that the Federals were abandoning all their defenses along the railroad, perhaps all the way from Corinth to Germantown.[84]  They soon realized, however, that what was occurring was a major relocation of troops defending the line.  As part of this redeployment, the 16th Army Corps out of Memphis had assigned Brigadier General J. M. Tuttle's 1st Division to guard the line from Memphis to Pocahontas and Chewalla.  November 12, the 72nd Ohio under Lieutenant Colonel Charles G. Eaton occupied Germantown. Hatch's 3rd Cavalry Brigade remained in place patrolling from Memphis to La Grange.[85]

On November 14, President Jefferson Davis assigned Forrest to command in West Tennessee, and Richardson was ordered to report to him.   When Forrest arrived to take command, he had brought only a small force of 271 men, 139 of whom were in McDonald's Battalion of West Tennessee men.   Included were a couple of the old companies raised in Shelby County for Forrest's original 3rd Cavalry Regiment. After campaigning in the east, these men returned to the lands they had enlisted to defend.  Forrest immediately assessed the situation, including the weakness of Richardson's available force, and decided that he should descend on the rail line.[86]

Richardson's reports to Forrest provide another picture of the state of his West Tennessee troopers as an effective fighting force, although clouded by Richardson's constant claims of a ghost-like component extant across the border. His ordinance-sergeant's report listing accoutrements indicated that none of the men were well equipped. There was 1 ambulance and 6 serviceable wagons with 22 serviceable mules. Everything else was unserviceable. To these reports Richardson attached his usual litany of complaints and boasts.

> I brought through the lines about 800 men in summer clothing, without bedding for a winter campaign, all expecting to return, as soon as armed and equipped, to West Tennessee. During the cold spells of weather many have absented themselves without furlough and gone home. I sent officers with squads into West Tennessee to collect their commands and report to me, but they have been notified of my late expected movement into West Tennessee, and will report as soon as we get there. Then I lost some by death – killed and wounded in the five battles we have fought in the last month – and some by sickness. All these causes have conspired to reduce my Tennessee command.[87]

In another ordinance report of November 20, there were only 247 serviceable horses. Armaments represented another problem. The major weapons included only 165 Enfield rifles and 65 Austrian rifles. The rest were a widely mixed component of 32 different kinds of rifles, 10 shotguns and 1 musket, and 151 Colt army and navy pistols. This mix of arms created an ammunition-supply nightmare. Apparently the Enfields and Colts were reasonably well supplied, but only 1,000 cartridges for the Austrian rifles. Richardson further clouded this picture with vague claims in an attached note.

> This report only shows the arms and equipments in the hands of my Tennesseans on this side the Memphis and Charleston Railroad. But I have issued 517 short Enfields and Austrian rifles in all to my Tennessee troops, and accouterments. This is an approximate report.[88]

In short, Richardson had a penchant for vague and ambiguous accounting. This was partially excusable by the nature of partisan organizations. There were always small, independent teams wandering the countryside, recruiting, foraging and harassing the enemy. Men who had gone home on their own initiative, who would normally be considered deserters from regular units, were given the benefit of the doubt since they did indeed need to replace clothing and attend to affairs at home. They had enlisted in the expectation of being close to home and able to do so. Consequently given their irregular nature, the commanders of regular units were not too generous in issuing supplies, as Richardson complained. But by Richardson's own accounting, some 352 Enfields were somewhere across enemy lines being put to unknown use. Whatever, Richardson's force, still little more than irregulars, would penetrate West Tennessee under Forrest's command.

General Johnston ordered Lee and Forrest to launch a joint raid "to break up as much as possible of the Memphis and Charleston Railroad." Then Lee was to return to Mississippi while Forrest moved into West Tennessee with only about 500 men. Forrest headed north with Richardson, arriving in Jackson on December third. Lee and Chalmers hovered in north Mississippi always threatening to move north on the railroad as a continued distraction for the Federals trying to catch Forrest.[89]

From the surviving military communications, the impression one gets of the entire expedition is that of a swirling dance among the armies of both sides. Federal commanders constantly exchanged intelligence and rumors of Forrest's whereabouts and his intentions. Then they dispatched units in an effort to box him in. He in turn danced around, maneuvering to cross the icy streams and avoid major Union forces, while striking where he hoped to break through.

By December 4, Union intelligence reported typical "stampedes" about Forrest ranging as far as Kentucky, threatening all the railroads.[90] On December 5, Hurlbut ordered the commanders at Germantown and Collierville to destroy the bridges over the Wolf.[91] On December 12, all reports placed Forrest at Jackson, assembling all his forces for an attack on the line. Initial estimates put his growing force at 4,000, while straggling parties of conscripts were crossing the line west of Germantown headed south. Conscripts and volunteers were drawn to Forrest, fifteen hundred of them reportedly unarmed. Federal cavalry was dispatched to come at him from all directions.[92]

By December 24, Forrest felt compelled to leave Jackson. He crossed the Hatchie and moved on Somerville, where after a skirmish, he split his forces. Colonel Champ Ferguson moved west toward Raleigh while Forrest went south to LaFayette. On the 25th Hurlbut repeated his command to destroy the bridges over the Wolf and to picket all crossings. All men at Germantown and White's Station were to be mounted on mules to ensure thorough coverage of the Wolf.[93]

On December 27, Forrest's troops took the inadequately dismantled bridge across the Wolf at Lafayette (Rossville) and drove the Union forces advancing from Collierville back into their fortifications. He rapidly reassembled the bridge and got all his unarmed men, wagons and captured cattle across and moved off south.[94] Richardson was apparently still roaming around West Tennessee at year's end.[95] Forest had so badly shaken up Federal defenders that they abandoned all efforts to operate the M&C Railroad until February of the next year.[96]

During this raid Richardson's units spread out recruiting, bringing his brigade up to about 1000. Some entire units apparently remained to operate north of the railroad, while Forrest claimed to have brought out about 3,300 men.[97]  It would seem West Tennessee would have been thoroughly drained of men suitable for service. Even from Germantown with its concentration of Federal troops, men might have been drawn off. Certainly, at least a score of area men had been along for the ride.

Once again one wonders about the mixed emotions among the civilian population when for the third time in the year, full-scale war came so close to home. Was their enthusiasm for the southern cause reignited? Or were they just experiencing more depressing disruption and uncertainty?

## *Life in Germantown during 1863*

With union occupation, county government had withered rapidly. After the Quarterly Court adjourned in May of 1862, it did not resume again until October 6, when Judge Pettit reconvened it. Its actions and authority had also been diminished by occupation authorities, for it was limited to appointing road overseers and handling estates. It ended its autumn session on December 2, and never met again.[98]  In April 1863, occupation forces established a Civil Commission for the District of Memphis to perform most duties of the former court.[99]  It is unlikely, however, that its governmental attentions ever extended as far out as Germantown.

Federally sponsored efforts to restore any form of responsible government had been frustrated by their lack of control over the area. By the beginning of 1863, the first efforts to elect a unionist government for the state under the appointed military governor Andrew Johnson had completely foundered. The House of Representatives voided the December 1862 Congressional election in Gibson County because of ongoing military operations there. Most of Dyer County "was so infested with guerrillas as to render the opening and holding of an election by the people dangerous." General Hurlbut proclaimed Shelby and surrounding counties as areas in which a fair vote could not be obtained.[100]

Throughout 1863, the county east of White's Station remained outside Federal efforts to establish and maintain any civil government and law enforcement despite heavy occupation. Since the failed December elections had produced no county officials, by June, General Veatch found it necessary to appoint a sheriff and coroner for Shelby County.[101]  Such an appointed sheriff would undoubtedly have avoided risking his neck trying to enforce the law outside the city.

By August, federal tax collectors had also arrived in Memphis to asses and collect property taxes. In 1862, Congress had applied to the

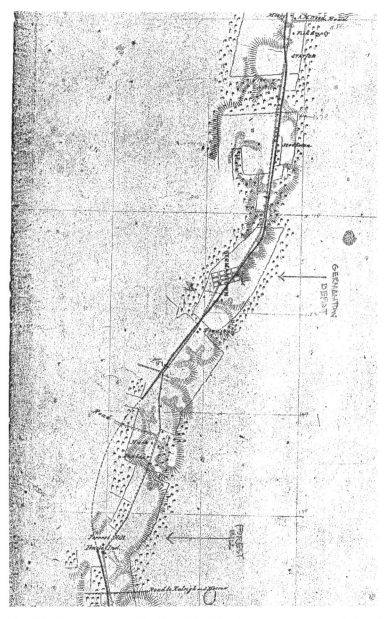

Map 10. Germantown on the State Line Road from a map commissioned by General Sherman, 1863 (SCA, original from NARA.)

"insurrectionary districts" the 1861 tax that had been levied to support the war. The tax on property was to be based on the last Tennessee assessment. However, since the collectors' reach did not extend into the county, the tax would not be collected in Germantown until after the war.[102] The citizens were temporarily spared the additional burden of taxes from which there would be no benefits. Since, however, all land owners were responsible to pay such taxes, and their property could be seized and sold to pay arrears, future loss of land threatened. That threat became especially contentious after Governor Johnson ordered that state taxes could only be paid with United States notes rather than the rapidly depreciating Tennessee State notes, much less the illegal Confederate money.[103] In districts like Germantown, beyond the currency regulation imposed on Memphis, everybody's Confederate bonds and bills might still be exchanged locally, but at considerable discount. The mixture of the other notes that were available must have been chaotic and the supply of gold and silver greatly reduced. All this added further to everyone's sense of uncertainty and foreboding.

Anyone serving as either district or town officials had to take an oath of loyalty. So both Judge Pettit and Constable Lewis would have been removed. They were fortunate not to have been expelled for having served as officials under the Confederacy. The effect of martial law was to suspend all or most town charters and their government.

At least, the establishment of brigade-level headquarters at Germantown brought the presence of a provost marshal, Captain W. P. Moore. Any locals who created serious problems would come to his attention and fall under military law. Citizens bold enough to attack or sabotage military forces would go before a courts-martial, and could be executed. Since all civilian courts were suspended, other crimes such as theft or acts of violence against fellow civilians were tried by a military commission. Locals could register complaints about the offenses of soldiers, and perhaps get some justice. The marshal also assumed responsibility for more routine civil affairs, but he might have offered the resumption of office to William Walker as JP and Job Lewis as constable, providing they took the oath. It seems they eventually did, but probably not as early as 1863. Finally most marshals concerned themselves with the wellbeing of needy women, children and the elderly. Supplies were provided for the indigent, and passes were provided for local farmers who had food to bring into town for sale at regulated markets, if any food was available.[104]

Of course, the corollary to such efforts to maintain peace and order was a determination to stamp out opposition. Marshals typically collected intelligence on the local population. The orientation of every household was of interest, and relief and just settlements could be doled out as rewards for compliance. Those identified as die-hard secesh

Illustration 17. Southern ladies coming to a Federal Commissary for provisions. One has to wonder if area ladies could actually arrive in such splendor; certainly not the more ordinary folk.

Illustration 18. Confederate prisoners being brought into town (Harper's, May 25, 1863). Such a scene must have occurred regularly in town at the Provost Marshal's headquarters. Although disheartening to locals, it may have provided some chance to offer succor to friends and relatives.

became candidates when local guerrilla activities warranted expulsions and confiscations.[105]

After the fall of Vicksburg, Grant sought to restore a greater sense of peace and order in the occupied territories. On August 1, he issued General Order No. 50 applying to Kentucky, West Tennessee and Northern Mississippi west of the Mississippi Central Railroad, all of which he proclaimed to be free of "regularly organized bodies of the enemy." Since it was "to the interest of those districts not to invite the presence of armed bodies of men among them," he announced that he would impose "the most rigorous penalties" on all irregular cavalry not mustered and paid by the Confederacy, all persons conscripting or apprehending deserters, "whether regular or irregular," all citizens encouraging or aiding them, and anyone firing on unarmed trains or boats.[106] Obviously his threat applied to any civilian playing partisan, guerrilla, scout or informant. He asserted that conscription was forbidden, enforceable or not. At least he strongly reiterated prohibitions against troops molesting peaceful civilians and restricted the confiscation of property to that approved by a corps commander and with provision for reimbursement to loyal citizens.

Whatever peace and order occupation might have provided, it was limited to within the fortress islands of heavily occupied places like Germantown. In addition to the headquarters and the regimental camp at the heart of town, a regimental camp lay tight by the eastern side, another to the north-east at Brunswick Springs, and another further east at Forest Hills. On the north, the cavalry sat in the Nashoba Tract close to the Wolf for water. South of town a camp occupied the lawns of a planter. Just to the west of town, a camp was on the Brooks plantation. Well into the twentieth century, one could see the trench-works erected around this campsite like all the others.[107]

With the ever-present threat of raiders, such light fortifications were essential for camp security. In January, Grant had ordered that at every military post or station, stockades be built. General McPherson promptly elaborated, "at all the points to be guarded, defensive stockades must be constructed to render the command safe against a sudden cavalry dash."[108] The artillery fortification that "commanded Germantown" was one such. Facing overextension along his new line, General Oglesby apparently felt the previously constructed defenses were inadequate. On June 3, he ordered, "Wherever you post detachments, you will immediately have them intrench themselves, by earthworks or stockades, in commanding positions, and so that they will cover the works they are to defend."[109] Shortly thereafter, Colonel Pease constructed an earth-work redoubt on the rail line east of Germantown that had been a frequent target.[110] Beyond these fortified perimeters, a line of pickets extended out to about two miles to provide advanced warning of attack.

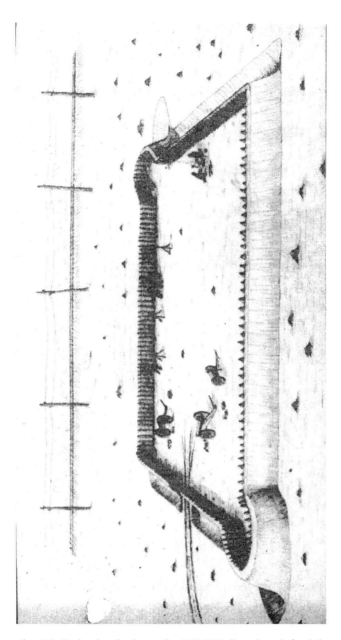

Illustration 19. Federal redoubt on the M&C Railroad to defend the great curve between the town and Forest Hill where attacks were common because the curve obstructed the engineer's view ahead. (GRH&GC)

The southern perimeter of the Germantown garrison was Nonconnah Creek.

Around these islands of security, guerrillas, partisans and raiders buzzed like angry hornets. Even the picket lines were porous, so small units could get close in. Spies wormed their way into town, and even the camps themselves. Outside town, farm families had to tread carefully to avoid acts of retaliation from both sides, and were vulnerable to each side's "confiscations." Union soldiers who sneaked out of camp to pilfer risked the vengeance of partisans. If the townsfolk experienced the mixed blessing of occupation protection, the farmers further out were still in no-man's land.

The locals actually lived in three zones with different degrees of security. Except where the Wolf River bottoms provided cover, the northern section of the district along the State Line and M&C and between the major concentrations at Germantown and Collierville was relatively secure, at least from official Federal confiscations and renegade pilfering. Farm families could reapply what resources they still had to cropping. Unfortunately the fences were gone, so fields remained unprotected from wandering livestock. South of that line down to the picket lines on Nonconnah lay a second zone of less security, though more secure than before. Confederates could not forage and Federals were restrained. South of Nonconnah was still a true no-man's-land.

In any case, already in January 1863 as full occupation had begun, Germantown was badly damaged. Eyewitness descriptions by occupiers paint different images of the degree of destruction and the attitudes of Germantown folk. The first was recorded in the diary of Fletcher Pomeroy, a trooper of the 7th Kansas Cavalry Regiment which had just taken up residence in and around the town. It was dated Monday, January 26.

> This town is fifteen miles east of Memphis on the Memphis & Charleston Railway, and but a short distance from the Mississippi and Tennessee State Line. Like most southern towns it has suffered much from the War. Some houses have been burned, and others are deserted and are used as soldiers' barracks. This country around is the best I have seen in the south.[111]

On the thirtieth, Captain Harvey Greene of the 8th Wisconsin arrived to defend the line across the area until March.[112] He described a more severe desolation.

> Germantown, Tenn., Jan. 30.
>
> We are fifteen miles from Memphis. This was once a little town, on the railroad, of a few hundred inhabitants; but it is all but depopulated, except by soldiers. The houses have been demolished, mostly, and there is not a vestige of a

fence or stake or board to be seen. One brigade only is here. We have a circular earthwork, but there is no enemy near.

NOTE. The ladies came and remained two or three weeks. … We had a boarding place at a rebel woman's house, just outside of our camp -- the men of the household all being in the rebel army.[113]

His wife wrote a letter home, detailing her experiences. Though she was prone to romanticizing, dramatic embellishing, and denigrating the locals, her observations are worth quoting. She described the train ride from Memphis as "through a suburban country" with "magnificent suburban homes," typically "of brick, large and beautiful, with a world of verandas above and below, statues scattered about the grounds, a large fountain, and the remains of trees, shrubs and banks of flowers." But we "cannot realize what war is till we see it." The homes were occupied by Union soldiers, who had put them to rough use, confiscating whatever they needed. "Can we blame them?"

Captain B. and wife, Harvey, Nelly and I are boarding in a secesh house. The hostess is a widow with a spinster sister. O, but they are rebels, they would be glad to cut our throats or poison our food if they dared; but their bread and butter depend on what they can get from Union soldiers. Such a desolate place I never dreamed of, not a tree, fence, or post -- not anything that could be utilized as firewood remains. Not a sign of anything like gardens or field of grain – nothing but ground, flowering shrubs, and a few houses remain of what was once a prosperous village. Every mill, shop or factory lies in ashes; their sites are occupied by a brigade of Union soldiers. It is a hard sight, but it is one of the curses of war.

If "every shop and factory" had not been destroyed as Mrs. Greene stated, certainly many were. The Southern Star Gin Factory was totally burned as well as the Baptist church.[114] As noted, the source of all that destruction was varied. How much resulted from acts of reprisal ordered by Union officers; how much robbing and pillaging by marauders and vandals; how much was incidental to the undisciplined stripping of buildings for fire wood and the confiscation of furniture and housing fixtures we will never know. That made little difference to the victims.

It would seem that in many cases the determined resistance of one woman could dissuade some vandals or reverse an officer's orders to burn or destroy property. Mary Thompson allegedly saved the old Webb school and family home twice. Once she simply stood in the doorway and forbade any soldiers to enter for pillaging. On another occasion, she persuaded a young Union cavalry officer, who had also been a school

Illustration 20. Gambling establishment outside the lines, near Memphis (Harper's, September 20, 1862) Occupation inevitably brought drinking, gambling and other vices to disturb local life.

teacher, to rescind an order to burn the building. He allegedly did so out of respect for her courage.[115] If her husband was the Louis Thompson who served in the 12th Tennessee Cavalry, he may have originally been riding with Richardson's Partisan Rangers and been seen as a guerrilla. That might have prompted a decision by a local officer to burn the house, one that he would have the authority to rescind.

Ladies of the upper and middle classes often had leverage against their occupiers. They discovered that most Yankee soldiers like Southerners respected white womanhood. Frequently all women had to do was to insist on being treated like ladies who had rights to certain property. Practically every area family tells stories of women almost forcefully preventing the confiscation of a horse or even retrieving it. Ladies felt free to assert themselves against the Yankees in ways their men could not dare. Women who suffered brutality at the hands of angry soldiers were almost never of respectable status. It was servants who received the unwanted attentions of occupation troops.[116]

Occupation gradually brought the abatement of the greatest fear that Southern women had felt at the approach of Federal forces. Rape by the soldiers was extremely rare, and when it occurred and was reported it produced sever punishment. Although this event did not likely occur near Germantown, a member of the 7th Illinois Cavalry reported, "Yesterday, I was out to witness a scene of seeing three men shot for committing rape on a girl 12 years old. The girl has died since I understand in hospital."[117] The execution in front of assembled troops was intended to put an end to such atrocities. Hostility toward secesh women could cause some to terrorize and humiliate them, but not rape. Women outside occupied lines, however, remained vulnerable to renegade soldiers and deserters from both armies, brutalized ex-slaves and brigands.[118]

Most sources contend that initially contempt was what women felt toward Yankee occupiers. Overt displays lessened quickly, however, at least out of necessity. To continue with Mrs. Greene's impressions of one woman

> The widow still keeps a few negroes; but the most of them had run away. All the cooking is done in the quarters, as they call them. Mrs. B. being quite ill, I have to go out there frequently for little things for her comfort. How those two old cats watch me.

She had befriended "a cute little darkey girl named Becky, about twelve years old.... She

> would follow me around and every chance she gets she will say, "Dear Missus, won't you take me with you to the Norf?" I gave her one of Nelly's picture books. ... I tried to teach her the alphabet from it, but the old cat caught me

at it and took her book away.[119] We were all standing on the front porch to-day surveying the lovely weather and enjoying the sweet fragrance of the roses and honeysuckle. The two rebel women of the house joined us. While chatting away, we heard the low rumbling of an approaching train. The railroad runs directly in front of the house a few rods distant, with quite a deep cut a short distance before reaching the house. As the train steamed by, loaded with Union troops on flat cars, the officers' wives waived their handkerchiefs. "The secesh women stood and glowered and hoped the train would go to pieces and kill them all. I wanted to wring their necks...."[120]

One more story completes a vivid picture of the hostilities generated by the war, and the inability of women on either side to empathize with the other. The officers and their wives were housed in a wing of the house, with its own exterior door opening on to a porch in the rear. One night a Confederate soldier, "dressed in butternut from head to toe," let himself in, but was driven off by her husband. Of course, they assumed the worst. "He was evidently some one sent to get what information he could of the two women of the house, and had gotten into the wrong side of the house."[121] Neither his brown homespun clothes (butternut) nor his intrusion identified him as one on a spy mission. That was her assumption. He was apparently unarmed, but probably a soldier, secretly visiting family.

Of course, perhaps she was correct. Women were key players in Confederate intelligence, and one boarding officers would have been a good source. It seems unlikely, however, that he would have bungled in unarmed and so clumsily. Just as she assumed the "glowering" face of the widow meant she was conjuring a train wreck, she assumed what she had heard about secesh women was so in this case.

Although it was easy for Mrs. Green to condone the confiscation and abuse of property by "her boys," she was totally unable to empathize with a nameless woman, widowed and without means, having to house self-righteous and privileged officers' wives. She wanted to throttle this woman because she did not rejoice at the sight of more Union troops rolling on to fight and kill her loved ones. War does more than destroy lives and property. It warps minds. The occupier can always minimize the suffering of the defeated with the idea that they brought it on themselves by supporting the war.

A third observer, a headquarters staff officer of the 52nd Illinois Infantry painted a very different picture of conditions and attitudes. Perhaps things had improved some by August when he was writing. He contradicted images of great destruction, depopulation and hostility. "There are a good many citizens here. The majority of them very well disposed. ... The ladies have arranged to board at a very fine house available by a very pleasant appearing lady whose husband is a surgeon in the rebel army. The officers here say she is now loyal and is urging her husband to come home. I think we shall find it very pleasant here." And a couple of days later, "There are a great number of citizens inside the lines and command is going to be full of perplexities. These people are living quietly at home and ought not to be molested." He went on to confirm that unauthorized confiscations by the rank and file continued to cause problems for the locals and those occupation officers who received their complaints. Also, "There is a band of cut throats hanging about our lines robbing citizens and soldiers that I am going to try to exterminate." Finally, "I think this is a very healthy place and a pretty pleasant one. Ladies are as abundant as blackberries some of them good looking and intelligent and nearly all very chatty and free."[122]    Such are the contradictions in the sources for reconstructing a picture of Germantown in 1863.

Aside from occasionally boarding Union officers, which provided some income, entire families might be forced to share or evacuate their homes for military use. For instance Woodlawn, the Joseph Brooks home well west of town near present Poplar Pike served temporarily to house sick and wounded of the regiment encamped on their land.[123]

Local historian Elisabeth Hughes remembers being told that "The real damage such as looting and burning was not primarily done by Union troops but mainly raiders called Kansas Jay Hawkers. ... In my grandmother's day to call a person a Jay Hawker was the worst insult imaginable."[124] Kansas Jayhawkers was specifically the nickname of the 7th Kansas, as opposed to simply jayhawkers. The term "jayhawker" was the Southerners' equivalent of "bushwhackers," which was the Union epithet for Confederates operating outside the conventions of war.

The 7th Kansas Volunteer Cavalry, recruited under the title of "Independent Kansas Jay-Hawkers," undoubtedly contributed to local damage. They had been involved in the early phases of the war in Missouri which descended into vicious guerrilla fighting.[125] They revealed that side of their character when they sacked Somerville. In early January, before arriving in Germantown, while the 7th was pursuing partisans it encamped at Somerville. After several hundred troopers became intoxicated, they not only plundered the town, but in the chaos that ensued, a drunken captain shot two of his own men and was shot in turn. In his later report from Germantown, Colonel Lee insisted that such behavior was not typical but resulted from an extended period of physically exhausting service followed by the unique availability of large quantities of intoxicants.[126] By their arrival in Germantown the stock of the saloons had been plundered, sparing the town from a repetition. From December 31, 1862 to April 14, 1863 Germantown hosted these 7th

Kansas Jayhawkers.[127]

The diary of Fletcher Pomeroy of the 7th Kansas Cavalry actually provides a sensitive picture of local conditions. He related the suffering of the citizens. Spring came late in 1863, and planting had not begun. The lack of available labor prevented any significant farming. The consequent lack of food and income would bring a hard year, with nothing left to fall back upon. Not only were the slaves and men folk gone, but so were the draft animals for plowing. Their cattle, hogs and poultry had been eaten, their hay and feed-corn confiscated. After less than a year of occupation, the citizens in and around town faced conditions bordering on starvation.[128]

Pomeroy also revealed the mixed nature of the occupation experience. It was not entirely one of mutual suspicion and hostility. Not only had they been able to establish rather comfortable quarters in their camp, but they had also developed pleasant acquaintances in the neighborhood. Despite the initial hostile attitudes of most southern women, extended periods of occupation led to fraternization.[129] One soldier compared their departure in April to almost like leaving home.[130] Of course, those "comfortable quarters" that occupation troops constructed were at the expense of local homes and facilities. When establishing a camp, the men immediately requisitioned "some sort of fireplace, a floor, bedsteads, writing tables, stools, carpets, etc."[131]

John Woodson lost every possession that was "movable or destructible." But at least his home survived because it was frequently occupied by Federal officers.[132] Aside from officially ordered burnings, frequently stragglers simply torched homes for the fun of it. Once, a rider tossed a burning fagot onto the porch of the Brooks home, Woodlawn. Only a prompt response saved their home. Even so, they lost most personal property. Much after the war, Joseph's widow, Agnes made a claim in vain for over $11,000 in damages. In addition to over a thousand bushels of corn, much fodder, 316 hogs, 83 cattle, 60 sheep, 46 goats, and 10 mules and horses were allegedly taken. Outhouses were destroyed and lumber and five and a half miles of fencing became fire wood.[133]

Nevertheless, there was some modicum of protection during the heavy occupation. Numerous accounts indicate that the extent of that protection may have depended on personal relations that developed between the inhabitants and the occupiers. Some fragments relating to one case survive in the Woodson family records. A Mrs. Walsh was at Germantown during the summer of 1863, when some silverware in her wagon was stolen. Two Union officers involved themselves in the effort to retrieve it. They had apparently become acquainted with Mrs. Walsh socially. William Walker became a go-between in the return of her property, since neither officer was still stationed near the town.[134] Why the records ended in the Woodson papers is unclear unless John was connected with Mrs. Walsh, William Walker and the return of her property. Since we know Woodson was a Unionist prior to the secession vote, perhaps he, Walsh and Walker all had good relations with the occupation officers housed in his home.

Having to rely on commanding officers for protection was certainly a hit-or-miss proposition. Discipline and control varied greatly among the units, such as the 7th Kansas Cavalry. Although the presence of a headquarters usually minimized the depredations, the variable character of high ranking officers offered no guarantees of peace and order. Germantown witnessed one proof of that. In November, Major Thomas Herod of the 6th Illinois Cavalry murdered his commanding officer, Lieutenant Colonel Lewis. After a dispute, he shot him four times while dining at Lucken's Inn right in the middle of town. Colonel Hatch had to draw his sword to prevent the troopers from lynching Herod.[135] Such a complete breakdown of discipline among one's protectors certainly added little to anyone's sense of security.

As the story of Mrs. Walsh's property indicates, any initial hostility toward the occupiers gradually diminished for reasons other than necessity. Some considered hatred and hostility simply unchristian. If the rowdy men of the 7th Kansas had experienced some friendly relations, when the townsfolk encountered officers of equal social and educational backgrounds, or fellow Masons, it was even easier to develop civil relations. All over the occupied South by late 1863, families began to extend to their "visitors" the sort of hospitality they would have before the war.[136]

In contrast, however, given the constant threat of guerrilla attacks and lightening cavalry raids, the occupation forces were always anxious to punish any local guerrillas who resumed civilian status by day. This put in jeopardy any adult male who had remained at home. One such was Robert F. Duke, the son who had stayed to manage the estates and protect the women while his brothers were away. These brothers reportedly had such strong family resemblances that they were easily mistaken for each other, and that almost got Robert hanged. The Duke lands adjoined Nashoba where Federal cavalry were encamped, so he was known by the soldiers. When his youngest brother Joe participated in the October raid on that camp, the troopers thought they identified Robert among the culprits. The commanding officer dispatched men to arrest him, and allegedly to "string him up immediately." He was lucky enough to stay under cover until the matter was settled somehow.[137]

The hardships of civilian life are further reflected in a letter of W. R. Hackley, Federal Treasury Agent in West Tennessee, responsible for the seven counties around Memphis.

The country has not been cultivated the past season and the

people are suffering for food. My duty will be to grant them permits to purchase from Stores in this place. Small quantities of clothing groceries provisions &c – such as will last them two month and only on application of the head of the family.[138]

This system for allowing families outside Memphis to purchase necessary foods and supplies had been established by the Treasury Department in June. The "loyal citizens of Shelby" had to apply for permits to purchase at the customhouse in Memphis.[139] This provided access to supplies greater than the meager supplies around Germantown. To qualify, however, one had to take the oath of loyalty. This was hard for wives of men in Confederate service. Widows had to apply in person, which meant traveling to Memphis. It was also presumed they had money with which to buy. Clearly men who were still at home were under increasing pressure to sign the loyalty oath for the sake of their families.

By the time occupation had begun in January, anything in the town's shops that had survived the pillaging had been consumed. Since one could bring out of Memphis only supplies limited to their own family's use, merchants had no way to restock their inventory. The other alternative available to some townsfolk was the licensed sutlers who served the Federal troops. The troops wanted items that were not supplied them, and these the sutlers provided by buying wholesale in Memphis and setting up shop at the camps. If townsfolk were not allowed to deal with them directly, they could have done so through soldiers black-marketing or just being friendly. But to do so, one had to have greenbacks. These they could earn by providing services to the soldiers, but especially providing room and board to officers, like Mrs. Green's hostess, or Herr Lucken.[140]

Unlike for the M&O RR out of Memphis, there were no advertisements for passenger service on the M&C in the Memphis papers. Some civilian traffic on the line was possible, but probably irregular. Even those who could afford and were allowed to travel ran the risk of guerrilla raid, robbery or worse. In May, Union officers' wives traveling to visit their husbands in Collierville had a fright just after leaving Germantown. The train had traveled slowly to avoid derailments, when word came that the line had been torn up just ahead. Several ladies became near hysterical, "expecting to be shot or taken prisoner." They took shelter in a nearby house, and learned that only about thirteen rebels had been in the vicinity. It seems as though this incident between Germantown and Collierville, like the first in 1862, had been the work of local partisans or totally independent guerrillas. The damage to the rails was even less severe. After less than an hour's delay, they resumed and soon crossed the picket lines two miles outside

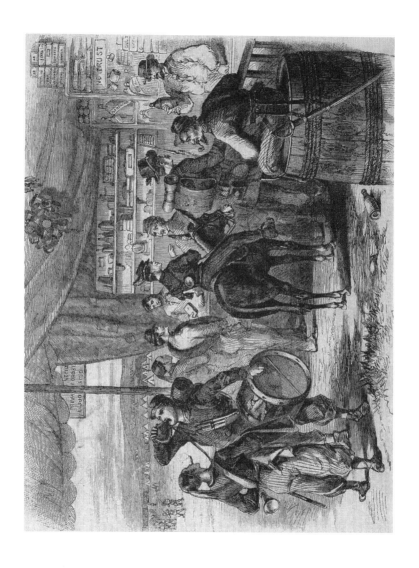

Illustration 21. Sutler's store (Leslie's Illustrated, November 29, 1862)
Such an establishment would have existed at Germantown or nearby.

Collierville, reaching safety.[141]

Diaries and letters confirm that by 1863 life in the occupied South was chaotic and ridden by anxiety. Communication among family members on opposite sides of the lines was difficult, adding greatly to tensions and feelings of loneliness, abandonment and despair by the women and children left behind. Undernourishment added to the risk of disease, always present in the best of times. Tuberculosis, malaria, and typhoid fever were common threats, and the very young and the elderly were at greatest risk. Since Federal authorities considered medicines as contraband in the countryside where Rebel troops could acquire them, women had to travel to Memphis and smuggle the medicine out, concealed in their clothing.[142]

Under such conditions, there were undoubtedly premature deaths in town. In early September, Judge Pettit died at age 65 of undisclosed causes.[143] His young widow and four minor children may have taken shelter in Memphis. During the tumultuous year of 1862, at least three women had given birth to children who survived the war: Mary McKay had Fannie; Sarah Ellis had a son; Rebecca Bradley had Miller. During the 1863 occupation, three women, probably more, gave birth to children who survived: Catherine Hurt had Robert; Mary Lucken had William; Sallie Shepherd had Thomas.[144] There are no clues to deaths in child birth and infant mortality.

Health-wise, a visit to Memphis was a risk in itself. A New York observer described the occupied city as unparalleled in its "filth, squalor, discomfort, disease, dirt and destruction." Unbelievably filthy streets and the risk of small pox greeted the woman in search of medicine.[145] Even worse, an unaccompanied woman over-nighting in the city could be subjected to the laws governing prostitutes.[146]

One consequence of the Provost Marshal's presence was a check point at the town depot. When passengers reached the town, they were subjected to search. That search was thorough enough to net women with contraband hidden in their voluminous skirts. Soldiers' wives or black women would have been employed for the searching. One victim, sixteen year-old Ginny McGhee, was headed home to Collierville with a bolt of gray cloth. Arrested and sent to Irving Block in Memphis and then a prison camp, she would die in custody. Subsequently area women would have abandoned the railroad for such purposes and resorted to carriage trips by roads where searching pickets were more easily intimidated by a disdainful woman.

Another example, Mrs. L. G. Pickett, got caught smuggling out of Memphis "one pair of citizens boots, and six or eight wool hats." For this, she was sentenced to six months in military prison at Alton, Illinois, and fined one thousand dollars. She would not be released until the fine was paid, which perhaps meant an indefinite imprisonment.[147] Because of the number of hats, she must have been supplying partisans. For the protection they provided, hats were an important item in the field year-round.

By the fall, Sherman's claims about the willingness of locals to collaborate with the occupation, resume the cotton trade and resist partisan efforts to destroy that trade seems to have been accurate. In September, the *Bulletin* reported the arrival of cotton caravans including one of up to one hundred bales. They had organized armed wagon trains, and, "We hope the time will come when trade can be freely carried on without fear of guerrillas." With income from their cotton, they could buy the essentials they needed.[148] Another encouragement was the elimination of a tax that had been levied on all merchandise sold in the city so "the country people are relieved from the 'ten percent.'"[149]

Indeed, many a planter or farmer had secreted away his bales, worth up to $500 each. Aside from the problem of avoiding the cotton-burners, one had to prove his loyalty, or hope to get through when officers were "looking the other way." Even then, he might get only a promissory note for an indefinite date, which he might sell for cash at a discount. Otherwise to sell it illegally also resulted in a great discount. In short, the desperate farmers got a small fraction of what speculators and merchants would reap on the inflated market. By October, it appears that once again only small quantities were coming into the city from the nearby districts. [150]

Whatever trade Germantown farmers may have been able to conduct with either Memphis or with military encampments was shut off almost completely in November, however, when Sherman issued more stringent orders for martial law.

> It is therefore ordered that the lines of pickets around the several military posts of this command in Tennessee and Mississippi be closed, and that no goods of any description be allowed to pass out, nor anything be brought in, except firewood and provisions, by any citizen, without the written order of some general officer,...and for the necessity of which each officer granting will be held rigidly responsible. [151]

Germantown fell within the lines of pickets of the units stationed there. Only the bare minimums of subsistence were allowed in or out, and persons so moving were subject to search. One could only take something out with a permit granted by the provost marshal. Still more important became the voluminous skirts of the ladies for smuggling.

Whenever the policies for trading in Memphis were relaxed, they fluctuated so much that their consequences became unpredictable, adding yet more uncertainty. Occupation authorities vacillated between efforts to totally cut the Confederates off from contraband sources in Memphis on the one hand and their desire to bring in local produce and cotton on the other. They became almost capricious. Some days the lines would be open, others they were closed. When closed, only persons who had taken the loyalty oath could get in and back out with a permit for specified items. When the lines were open, one could come, go, and get permits without the formal oath. Unfortunately, one could go in with the lines open, only to discover once inside that they could not get out.[152]

Nevertheless, the people of Germantown tried to maintain some modicum of normal life, but the right to pursue any activities essential to maintaining life required one to take the oath. In Germantown they were administered by the provost marshal. The oath there read,

> I do solemnly swear in the presence of Almighty God, that I will bear true allegiance to the United States of America, and will obey and Maintain the Constitution and laws of the same, and will defend and support the said United States of America against all enemies foreign and domestic, and especially against the Rebellious League Known as the Confederate States of America.[153]

The occupation made it possible for closeted unionists to enlist in the Union Army. So far, only one can be identified specifically from Germantown. On April 1, 1863, Charles Wall, listed as a resident of Germantown, joined the 7th Kansas Cavalry at Germantown. Afterward, it was involved in operations against Forrest, so Wall would have fought against some of his former neighbors. In January 1864, while camped at La Grange, the bulk of the regiment reenlisted and was shipped back to Kansas for furlough. At some point, Walls took sick and died on May 11, 1864, at Alton, Illinois.[154]

Other area men may simply have accepted the inevitable, and to prove their loyalty served in Federal forces, just as unionists and neutrals had been conscripted to serve with Richardson and Forrest. In November, General Sherman issued impressment orders.

> All persons residing under the protection of the United States, and physically capable of military service, are liable to perform the same in a country under martial law. ... (A)ll officers commanding district, division, and detached brigades of this corps, will immediately proceed to impress into the service of the United States such able-bodied persons liable to military duty as may be required to fill up the existing regiments and batteries to their maximum.[155]

Although Sherman meant this order especially to remove undesirables from the city, it clearly applied to the brigade commanders at Germantown. From this point, regardless of any sentiments, the remaining "able-bodied men" could end up in the regiments occupying Germantown. Their constantly depleted ranks must have insured that area men could have ended up in such units. A member of the $7^{th}$ Illinois, which had been recruiting up and down the M&C, reported in July 1864 that, "There had been a good many soldiers joined since we have been here."[156]

Area men now had to choose either to stay home and risk service in the Union Army, or flee south and serve there. From its base in Mississippi, the *Appeal* received reports of Shelby County men fleeing in large numbers to escape impressment. Many men who had left the Confederate cause for whatever reasons were clearly caught on the horns of a dilemma. Serve against their former friends and neighbors or return south and hope to be allowed to serve without punishment. Many joined the partisans and Forrest in the hope of serving in different units from those they had left.

From all the above, we can construct some images of daily life in Germantown. War and occupation reshaped the work life of women in direct proportion to their place on the social scale. Another factor was, of course, any continued presence of men and adolescent boys. Some slaves remained in house service or field work, depending on what they were offered to stay. If a woman of some education had connections in the city, she might find work there as nurse, clerk or teacher. Any other woman who fled to the city without family to shelter her would have been thrown into a glutted labor market that offered many less desirable opportunities. The wife of a landless laborer gone off to war had to find some sort of employ, if not in the city then at the camps.

Those who stayed in town or on the land continued to produce whatever food and goods they could. They had to fight to defend their kitchen gardens, fruit trees, milk cow and chickens. If lost, there was no replacement. They continued to make their own clothes. Like the bitter woman above, they may have taken in officers and their families as boarders. Some did sewing and cleaning for the troops. They sold things they still had, or manufactured crafts for sale. Some tutored children or even ran small schools in secret.

Life would have been hard for the children, both physically and psychologically. The skirmishes that ran through town had been dangerous but brief. Only a few saw anyone killed, but undoubtedly others saw bodies, and the wounded. They may have heard the screams of amputations in the makeshift hospitals and seen discarded limbs. They suffered hunger and cold, and their work loads were increased at every social level. While teaching in school buildings was forbidden, clandestine schools like Mary Thompson's and home schooling survived.[157]

The permanent loss of fathers, brothers or other relatives was the greatest shock a child could suffer, unless he or she actually witnessed violence against a loved-one. Even the absence of a father for the duration had its effects. The political posture of the family would have greatly determined the degree to which the child was infected with animosity toward the occupiers.

On the brighter side, just as they had when the town was occupied by the mobilizing Confederate troops, the children were drawn to the drilling and parading Union troops and their colorful bands. Soldiers are usually friendly and generous toward children, especially those who are suffering. Although I have found no records of commanders complaining of problems keeping children out of the camps, they were probably a nuisance and at risk whenever wagons and equipment was being moved. The northerners brought the game of baseball with them, and probably coached the boys in its play and in other sports as well.

The churches were shut down, occupied, damaged or destroyed. Public services were forbidden, at least for a considerable time. Ministers were closely watched, for many had been ardent supporters of secession. At least two local partisan leaders had been ministers. Nevertheless, according to local memories, the Methodist Reverend Tuggle managed to continue to serve his Hernando circuit throughout the war. Even if he could not operate from and protect his church building in Germantown, he served the Bethlehem Church at Capleville on the Mississippi border, as well as his Mississippi charges. Even missionary work to the slaves continued under Reverend Jere Williams out of Hernando or Olive Branch.[158] Tuggle's plantation was located below the Nonconnah and outside Federal picket lines, so he could have done his work while avoiding Federal patrols.

Perhaps if they took the oath, ministers or laymen were allowed to assemble small house services or out-of-doors meetings. Otherwise the people would be deprived of their customary spiritual support, and at a time when it would have been ever more important. Under these circumstances, women left alone organized house prayer groups and Sunday school classes – yet another example of the erosion of traditional ideas about woman's place and role. Sectarian differences among neighbors eroded.[159]

Although Memphis' cultural activities and entertainments resumed during occupation, with all public buildings closed or occupied in Germantown, none such were possible. Only in those homes that socialized with the occupiers could anything like the old parties and balls resume. Even then, it developed only slowly and fitfully. Perhaps on special holidays like the Fourth of July, the troops sponsored celebrations that the townsfolk could attend or at least watch.

How badly the pains of the war and the conflict of loyalties had strained personal relations inside the community is not a matter of record, and little evidence casts light on the subject. During 1862, as unionists welcomed the Federal occupiers and loyal secessionists were actively supporting Confederate raiders, each side seemed to maintain civil relationships. Or so it seems from the story of Grant's close call with Jackson's cavalry. Dr. Smith was making a friendly visit to Josiah Deloach when he was shocked to discover Grant sitting on the porch. Knowing that after Smith departed he would make a hasty trip to report to Colonel Jackson, without actually warning Grant, Deloach simply terminated the visit with a slight discourtesy. Deloach, an anti-secessionist, had a son, a son-in-law and three stepsons in the Confederate army, and it is unclear if he suffered any consequences for his continued pro-Union sentiments and contacts. He apparently relocated to Memphis where he socialized with Grant and was eventually appointed postmaster of the city. Of course, it was commonly assumed this was an award bestowed by Grant.[160] He still owned his home at Bray's Station as late as 1869 and probably used it as a summer or weekend escape from the city. Such were the differences within and among families and friends. Unlike the counties to the east and north where blood feuds erupted, perhaps personal relations in southern Shelby County survived even the terrible hardships which all shared. Since they had begun with less than enthusiastic attitudes about secession in 1861, during the course of the war, local sentiments probably vacillated widely.

By July, one Virginia newspaper was reporting sensational tales of the suffering of Germantown under occupation. For what its worth, it claimed, "There were a few Unionists about Germantown when the village was first occupied by Federal soldiers, but now all capable of bearing arms have fled. Many, even boys and very old men, have joined the guerrillas." Some, nevertheless, felt compelled to stay home for the sake of their families.[161] By December, a letter from the 72nd Ohio, camped south of town, reported that the town's former population of several hundred had shrunk to "probably not fifty." The total occupation force consisted of the 72nd, the 6th Illinois Cavalry and a light battery, all under the command of a Major Eaton.[162]

### *From Slavery to Freedom*

The war had not begun as a war for emancipation, but by 1862 Union occupation seemed to provide safe havens for escape. The result, however, was rarely like the long-awaited jubilee. There was no planning or preparation for a mass of freed slaves with no ready means for integration into the economy, no government agencies to care for the needy in such numbers. The Union field commanders would bear the initial burden, while fully preoccupied with the more pressing war. They made ad hoc policy while awaiting guidance from Washington. The guidelines that emerged were more politically motivated than by any real comprehension of the problems. As Federal agencies were created, they were staffed by well-intentioned officials whose judgment was colored by racial misperceptions. Throughout the war and into the Reconstruction era, the consequences for the liberated were disastrous. The price of freedom was far greater than usually understood.[163]

Of course, numerous slaves sought freedom, left their owners and flowed across the lines into Union camps. At first the government and commanding officers vacillated over how to deal with the overwhelming numbers. They certainly represented an impediment, and a sanitation and supply burden. Their persistence, however, resulted finally in accommodation, and many found employment among the troops. The designation applied to them was "contrabands," the same term used to describe goods that could not legally be sold to Confederates. That implied that they were still property, and they were treated as such.

Other slaves simply found themselves cut adrift as their owners fled the approaching Federal army. They had only taken with them whatever valuables they could carry and all of their most able slaves. The rest they abandoned with instructions to fend for themselves. Logically, those left behind frequently took over the fields, remaining livestock and houses for themselves. We will probably never know the extent to which this happened in the Germantown area, but the odds against former slaves trying to survive in no-man's-land would have been steep.[164]

Memphis was the most likely haven for slaves fleeing the Germantown area. As late as September 1862, however, Sherman carped, "Not one nigger in ten wants to run off." Although he estimated there were 25,000 slaves within twenty miles of Memphis, nevertheless "all could escape & would receive protection here, but we have only about 2000."[165] It would seem that local slaves were cautious about their great opportunity. For whatever reasons, they were wisely weighing their options during at least the first year of occupation. Good reasons for doing so would increase, and they were close enough to Memphis to be well informed.

Shortly after occupying the city in 1862, Sherman had decided to employ all blacks who applied as laborers on the fortifications. Although they would be fed and clothed and given a tobacco allowance, they would not be paid until their status as freed or slaves was established. Officers were forbidden to employ them as personal servants, but a regimental commander could hire them as cooks and teamsters. The post quartermaster was even allowed "when necessary, to take them by force" for labor on the fortifications. When blacks tried to flee from being pressed into labor, guards shot at them for trying to escape, often with fatal results. Out of respect for the legal rights of slave owners, Sherman ordered, "The negroes employed as laborers will be allowed to return to their masters at the close of any week, but owners are not allowed to enter the lines in search of slaves." They were, however, allowed to meet

Illustration 22. Contrabands coming into camp (Harper's, January 31, 1863)

Illustration 23, Rebel family fleeing (Harper's, September 14, 1861) Typically taking their best slaves and leaving less useful burdens behind to fend for themselves.

with their slaves and try to induce them to return.[166]

The two Confiscation Acts had merely empowered Union commanders to liberate and employ the slaves of rebels. Even after the Emancipation Proclamation, slaves were not automatically free in Tennessee. Lincoln had agreed to exclude Tennessee from his final proclamation. The presence of so many unionists slave holders militated against alienating them by abolishing their "property." Thus only when the owner was in Confederate service was his slave property forfeited under the terms of the Confiscation Acts. Consequently, a slave owner could take legal action to have a runaway returned from Memphis or any encampment.[167]

In order to hold on to their slaves, only the shortsighted resorted to the old methods of tighter supervision and harsh punishment. The wiser saw the handwriting on the wall and increased practices of leniency, freedom to hunt and fish, rights to household garden plots, and less arduous hours. Most importantly, they extended the system of share-cropping. Slaves who remained loyal might receive either cash payments, or most likely, a share of the crop. Numerous records survive indicating how prevalent this practice was in Shelby County. According to one local planter at Sulphur Wells,

> The Year before the war closed, it was almost a universal thing for all farmers, to give those negroes who still remained with them, a cotton Patch for their fidelity, in remaining with them, - Cotton, that season commanded a fabulous price, a small cotton patch made considerable money – there were other planters that gave money, which amounted to the same thing.[168]

The popular image of all slaves simply taking matters into their own hands at the coming of the Jubilee is too simplistic. According to recent studies, many if not a majority of slaves did not abandon their owners' lands, or at least stayed nearby. Others returned during or immediately after the war.[169] Some simply preferred the security or certainty of the place they knew, farms or homes where they had been treated relatively well – perhaps just the devil they knew. Some had been successfully acculturated to their lot in life. Young Ned Kearney, who reported that "Mr. Kearney was good to his slaves and wouldn't let an overseer whip us," continued to work at the "Big House" throughout the war. Whenever Union soldiers came near, his job was to help hide the valuables in the river bottom, "to keep the Yankees from stealing them." Ned did not see the Union Army as liberators but as "the enemy." Of course, Ned had yet to achieve adolescence.[170]

Most who remained, however, were hardly cowed. Everywhere owners complained of their growing insolence and laziness. They were proactive in demanding concessions, and whenever contracts were negotiated or an owner resorted to physical punishment, around occupied communities like Germantown they could turn to the Provost Marshal for enforcement and protection. On the other hand, the farther from town the more the owners had an ally in the partisans and guerrillas who loved to punish troublesome and escaped slaves.[171]

As for Germantown-area slaves who ran away, the ordeals they faced made the price of freedom high. During the fall and winter of 1862/63, Grant's Department of the Tennessee organized camps for the "contrabands." Among the places where Germantown escapees went, beyond Memphis Holly Springs and La Grange lay increasingly farther afield. The Holy Springs camp had to be relocated to Memphis and Grand Junction in December 1862 when Van Dorn raided the Union base there.[172]

Grant had no problems with using the freedmen for service and labor, but there were far too many that could not be employed or otherwise support themselves. The superintendent of contrabands was busily assigning men and women to work abandoned plantations under opportunistic entrepreneurs who contracted with the government for a sizable percentage of the profits. By the same token, former slave owners who now needed labor also contracted to hire contrabands.[173] As one scholar has put it, "The contraband camps performed a similar function to antebellum slave pens where auctioneers held people until they were sold on the market."[174]

To bring under control the large contraband population that had gathered in Memphis by the summer of 1863, occupation officials needed some system for monitoring. The Provost Marshal required the registration of all blacks, regardless of status, and their registration was the responsibility of the white person in charge of them - "his lawful property, and in his possession, or is regularly employed by him." A subsequent order clarified this decree by requiring "every free negro or mulatto, and every contraband" to enter "into the employment of some responsible white person," who would be required to get the registration. Without possession of a registration certificate, they were subject to arrest as vagrants to be sent to the Superintendent of Contrabands and removed to the contraband camp. Even the former freeman was now denied his freedom[175]

Even those who had found work in Memphis were subject to harassment and authoritarian controls, the assumption being that they were a threat and nuisance. In October 1863, the provost marshal issued Order No. 42 revoking all passes for blacks. All those caught without passes would be arrested and sent to Ft. Pickering. Those who were legitimately employed by white citizens had to give an affidavit for new passes. The theory being that if employers were held responsible for their servants' behavior, they would discipline them better.[176]

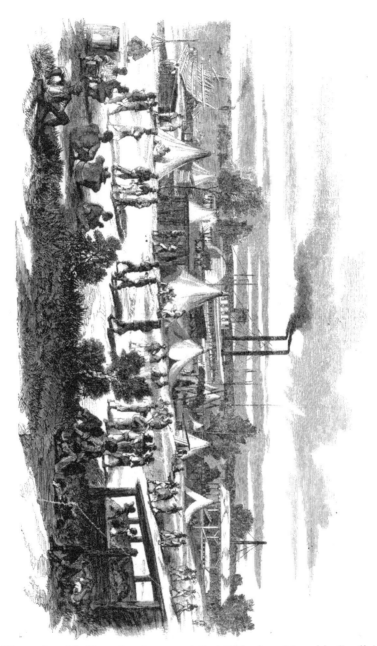

Illustration 24. Contraband camp at Fort Pickering, Memphis (Leslie's Illustrated, November 22, 1862) Of course, the journal discretely avoided depiction of more unseemly conditions.

The officers and civilians responsible for the contraband camps were confronted with confusing legalities and complicated social issues. For instance, as occupation increased problems, some masters actually evicted their slaves selectively, keeping only those they could use or control. This practice especially resulted in fracturing families.[177] Consequently, Union authorities had to deal with legal conflicts between freedmen and their former masters over family members. An owner could send troublesome parents to a freedmen's camp and keep their children. If the parents stole them away, the officer in charge of the camp would have to return them to the owner, "amid the tears and protestations of the mother."[178] The officers had to obey the laws that still prevailed.

As for their living conditions, the ex-slaves had given up what passed for security in the pursuit of freedom and self-determination. Once settled inside Union lines, it was hard to find work in such numbers. Among those who could not, at least some industrious men and women found ways to live by providing services to the troops, or setting up markets for crafts and such. Even for them, living conditions were horrendous. Housing was makeshift lean-toes, huts and shanties. Sanitation and potable water were non-existent, which of course brought the problem to the attention of military officials. Unregulated settlements clustered in Memphis, but also around many military camps. That is what led to the contraband camps where some modicum of order was maintained, and inhabitants could be assigned from there to employment for wages. Even after the establishment of the camps at Memphis, however, by April 1863, some 2500 contrabands still tried to make it on their own, neither fed nor cared for by officials.[179]

As for work from the freedmen's camps, of the 1380 men, women and children in the Memphis camps, 1236 were hired out as field hands, including all the children. Only 44 men and 70 women found work as craftsmen, teamsters or in domestic or camp service work. The system under which the laborers worked was described as

> One man regulates camp – another directs the working men, who are divided into squads of eleven; - the most intelligent selected as leader. Each three of four squads are under a white foreman, who directs and credits their work, notes and supplies their necessities.
> Erecting cabins, - preparing camp, ... sometimes most grossly abused – as, for instance, worked all day in water, drenched, nearly frozen, and then driven to tents for shelter, to sheds for sleep, without covering, and almost without fire and food, they come back to die by scores. Wages seldom paid – none in hospitals. The services of a large number have been stolen outright.[180]

At first, there was no shelter, the people were housed in tents while cabins were being built. During the first four months of the camp, 21 women had given birth, 103 men and women had died, and another 184 had taken sick. As for medical care, Chaplin Eaton reported,

> Hospital not under charge of Superintendent. Its condition wretched in the extreme. Lack of medicines, of utensils, of vaccine matter. No report of admissions, of diseases, of deaths, or discharges. No attention to sick in camp by surgeon. Sent assistants out of my own office, having no Knowledge of medicine, but surgeon refused vaccine matter & medicines. Improvement to date. *Diseases* – Pneumonia sic, fevers, small pox.[181]

In general, the white people around them, whether Northerners or Southerners, were not especially sympathetic. Blacks were the targets of contempt, violence and abuse.[182] Conditions in the camps at Memphis and of that subsequently established on Presidents Island were inadequate and only got worse. On January 12, 1864, Memphis papers reported that 356 of those settled on Presidents Island had frozen to death during a spell of unusually harsh weather.[183] It would seem that everywhere the camps deteriorated into deadly and uninhabitable compounds. Inadequate food, shelter and medical care, poor sanitation and insufficient clean water turned them into death camps.[184]

When the slaves who had stayed on around Germantown got word of these conditions, they probably preferred to negotiate for better conditions at home. Owners spread the word and offered a more paternalistic environment as preferable to the insecurity of freedom. The only other alternative for the men was enlistment.

Local African-Americans would serve in large numbers in units originally designated as "of African Descent," abbreviated A.D. to distinguish them from white regiments. Later they would be redesignated as "U.S. Colored Regiments." Among these, the 11th, 59th, 61st, and the 88th were specifically raised in Shelby County. Artillery units were also recruited there, the 3rd Heavy Artillery Regiment, and Batteries D/F and I of the 2nd Light Artillery.[185] 1863 would be the break-through year in which they would be allowed to join the Union Army in great numbers.

Whatever their attitudes about slavery, most Union officers initially had little respect for "coloreds" and certainly did not consider them suitable as soldiers.[186] At Memphis, however, General Hurlbut was desperate to man his artillery defenses. Encouraged by the report that the Navy had discovered that "blacks handle heavy guns well," he endorsed their service. On April 15, he launched recruitment for eight companies to man the heavy guns at Fort Pickering. They would be officered by whites, but NCOs would be drawn from black recruits. They would also receive the same pay and allowances as other artillerymen, in sharp

Illustration 25. Negro recruits being loaded on a train (Leslie's Illustrated, May 7, 1864)  Such a scene played out at Germantown's depot in June 1863.

contrast to the general practice of paying black troops lower wages. By May, this was to become a regiment of 1,200. By December, it had expanded into two regiments, the 1st and 2nd Tennessee Heavy Artillery (A.D.), the 1st of 1,153 men, the 2nd of 878, and the Memphis Light Battery of 99 men.[187] The Memphis Light Battery, would eventually became Company "D," 2nd U.S. Colored Light Artillery Regiment; while Battery I of the 2nd was also formed in Memphis in April 1864. The 1st Regiment of Tennessee Heavy Artillery (A.D.) was renumbered the 2nd and then 3rd Colored Heavy Artillery in the spring of 1864.[188]

At least twelve men who served in the 3rd Heavy Artillery bore the names of men who were living in the Germantown area during the 1870 census. There were three such in batteries F and I of the 2nd Light Artillery.[189] These cannot be identified precisely as former Germantown area slaves because only given names were recorded for slaves. Nevertheless, this indicates probable involvement by some in these artillery units.

In December 1863 to further augment his corps, Hurlbut decided to raise one regiment of infantry at Columbus, Kentucky, and four at Corinth, Jackson and along the railroad route to Memphis.[190] Thus began the recruitment of blacks specifically at Germantown. The 1st West Tennessee Infantry Regiment (A.D.) mustered in at La Grange in June 1863. It was first reported in the *Official Records* on October 31, 1863, as the 1st Tennessee Infantry (A.D.), with 815 men, as an unattached regiment in Hurlbut's 16th Corps, where it spent its entire term of service in West Tennessee and North Mississippi. It would ultimately become the 59th U.S. Colored Infantry Regiment.[191]

Captain Jesse H. Darnell enrolled part of Company I at Germantown, June 27, 1863. In this company, about twenty men bore surnames common among the slave owning families of the area. Among them, Henry Ellis and Henry Jones would be living in district eleven for the 1870 census.[192]

The first mention of the 2nd West Tennessee Infantry Regiment (A.D.) in the records occurred on September 16, 1863, listed as 2nd U.S. Tennessee Volunteers (A.D.). It too had mustered in La Grange during June through August 1863. Captain Malte Stuth, enrolled Co. D at Germantown in June, while Captains Henry Sturges and Charles S. Graff enrolled companies G and I at Collierville. By October 31, the regiment had 610 men. It was still at Moscow on December 4, when attacked by Lee and Chalmers. It was these men who held the bridge, ultimately repulsing of the Confederate cavalry on that day.[193]

That action first brought local black troops the recognition they deserved as soldiers. Such commendation by Union officers was progressive by the standards of the times. On December 17, General Hurlbut had his Assistant Adjutant-General issued General Orders No.

173 stating,

> The recent affair at Moscow, Tenn., has demonstrated the
> fact that colored troops, properly disciplined and
> commanded, can and will fight well, and the general
> commanding corps deems it to be due to the officers and
> men of the Second Regiment West Tennessee Infantry, of
> African descent, thus publicly to return his personal thanks
> for their gallant and successful defense of the important
> position to which they had been assigned, and for the
> manner in which they have vindicated the wisdom of the
> government in elevating the rank and file of those
> regiments to the position of freedmen and soldiers.[194]

Other commanders added their praise.[195] It would eventually become the 61st U.S. Colored Infantry Regiment.[196] At least ten area men with surnames of slave-owning families of districts ten and eleven were in Company D alone.[197]

The Union Army avidly began recruiting freedmen and contrabands. Without them, it might not have won the war for lack of manpower. Nevertheless, there was no sense that bringing them into service required any commitment to their families, who either had to be left behind in slavery or without provisions, because they had no resources to fall back upon like white soldiers' families. For commanders preoccupied with fighting the war and controlling a resistant occupied population, this was a novel and unwelcome problem. They at least displayed some sympathy in many cases and made efforts to ameliorate the problem, but assumptions about race and class prevented anyone from realizing how much family support was appropriate to compensate for the service of blacks from the occupied South.

After the formation of black military units, their families that did not remain with their owners became part of the flood of contraband refugees. By the spring of 1864, large numbers of such women and children had been concentrated at the camp at Memphis where they were getting government support. Adjutant General L. Thomas pressed for an end to this practice. He noted that some women could find work as laundresses and such with military units, but that none were entitled to government rations. The families of soldiers had to support themselves. Occupation officials at Memphis developed plans to send as many as 2000 women and children down river to Helena, Arkansas where they could be contracted out as labor on plantations. Needless to say the black artillerymen at Ft. Pickering and the men of other black regiments became "seriously alarmed."[198] This was no improvement over slave-owner indifference to family relations.

Rather than submitting to the regimentation and poor conditions in the contraband camps, the families of soldiers tried to settle close to the camps of their men for security and support. These families were frequently seen as the worse kinds of camp followers, and no efforts were made to provide for them. The complaint of the commander of one Colored Regiment stationed at Memphis was typical of such attitudes.

> There are several hundred negro women living in Temporary huts, between the camp of this regiment and the city, who have no visible means of support, and who are, for the most part, idle, lazy vagrants, committing depredations, and exercising a very pernicious influence over the colored soldiers of this Post. They are generally in a destitute condition, and their wants are partially supplied by soldiers of colored regiments who claim them as wives. The influence of these women over the members of my regiment is such, that I have great difficulty in keeping my men in camp nights, and have to be continually watchful and vigilant to enforce the severest penalties, in order to maintain any thing like satisfactory discipline, and attention to duties on the part of my men. ... I am compelled to enforce punishments continually, for offenses relating in some manner to these women. ...I earnestly request for the benefit of the service, and for the sake of humanity, that these families be removed to Presidents Island where they will be much better cared for, and where they will be no detriment to the service, and society at large.[199]

Captain T. A. Walker, the local Superintendent of Freedmen, was instructed to execute the proposal. He assigned details from the 63rd Colored Regiment to do the moving, but encountered serious resistance. The women refused to cooperate, created obstacles, and ran to their men for protection. "The husbands swear their families shall not be moved to the island and in some instances have come out under arms to prevent it."[200] Nevertheless, the order seems to have been carried out.

Germantown area blacks who had remained "at home," still legally enslaved, had to choose between the often undesirable life of a freedman and whatever inducements their "owners" offered them to stay. There they shared in the hardships of the white civilian population. Nevertheless, that was a familiar environment where they still had the networks and resources for producing food and fighting disease that the refugee had lost. They could avoid the fatal exposure to the elements and disease that killed so many within and outside refugee camps.[201]

As for the men who enlisted, service in the African-American units would be at least as dangerous as in others, or more so. Of the 20,830 men enlisted in the Mid-South during 1863, probably 5,000 had "either died of disease, been captured by the enemy, or have become lost to service by other casualties. ... The number of desertions have been few."[202] They were proving far more reliable than white soldiers on either side.

Of course, the Confederacy saw the enrollment of blacks in the Union Army as a threat. On October 30, 1863, General Johnston had ordered General Chalmers, in command of Confederate forces south of Germantown, to head off the problem. Chalmers sent detachments into the "Country adjacent to the enemies lines to arrest and remove within our lines all able bodied negroe men who are liable to be Captured by the enemy." Out of respect for the needs of the owners, only "those Capable of performing military duty will be taken." They could leave behind "Old men women & children." Thus any men immediately south of Germantown who had not already enlisted or fled were likely to be impressed into Confederate "Gov$^t$ work."[203]

Worse, the Federal recruitment of blacks to fight against Confederate troops, but especially to serve as occupation troops over the people who once held them as slaves, created both anxiety and hostility among Southerners. As the first formation of African-American troops began in the North in 1862, the *Appeal* forcefully verified the accuracy of a prediction made in the Chicago *Times*.

> ...in the event of negroes being employed as soldiers, the Confederates, "not recognizing him as a legitimate antagonist, will massacre the negroe when or where found in arms, or transport him to the cotton fields of the extreme South; they will not regard him as a prisoner of war, but subject him to all the penalties used in the case of the most uncivilized foe."[204]

Such were the brutal conclusions inherent in the racist arguments that had evolved to justify slavery. Many Southerners were locked into such logic and its conclusions. Although many would recoil from the idea that massacring blacks was justified, and it would be rejected as official policy, the prediction reflected the prevalent mood.

Thus, the presence of African American troops added to the growing hostilities between the two sides which would reach a fever pitch in the following year. One observer voiced a shrill warning to the readers of the *Appeal*.

> It is positively certain that the Federals are drilling four thousand negroes at Corinth. They are soon to be turned loose, to murder defenseless women and children in North Mississippi. The very thought of the inhumanity and cruelty which is to follow, makes the blood run cold through the veins.[205]

Many black soldiers would suffer the consequences of inadvertently becoming part of developments bringing parts of the South like West

Tennessee to the point of explosion.

## *Army Life away from Home*

1863 was also a year of attrition and hardship for the town's infantrymen fighting ever farther from home. Anderson Kirby of the 4th Infantry summarized his experience as "hard time," especially the Battle of Missionary Ridge as "devilish bad." It seems to have impressed him more than Shiloh. His wound would pain him for the rest of his life. As for food and clothing, he said, "Badly on ground Beef and Bacon Every way."[206] For the remainder of the war, he rotted away in a prisoner of war camp.

Like the 4th, the 13th participated in major battles like Chickamauga, Missionary Ridge and down through Georgia and the battles around Atlanta. No other Germantown men of the 13th fell until Joe Tuggle died at Peach Tree Creek, Georgia. A. B. Ellis had been wounded in the leg at Missionary Ridge, while the then sergeant-major Needham Harrison, severely wounded at Chickamauga, was promoted to lieutenant.

William Yates, who lived about six or seven miles north of Germantown in what is now Cordova, served in Company H along with Germantown men. He left a vivid description of what service was like in the 13th throughout the war.

> Lived very well first part of war – got pretty tough in latter part. Clothes were pretty scanty. Slept on grass or anything we could get to. Had vermin so bad at one time, although I only had one more suit of clothes, took off the one I had on and burnt it to try to get rid of some of the lice – got them so bad when we were ordered to spend the night in quarters that others had just vacated and the place seemed to be alive with them. One night it was so cold, and I had so little to keep warm with, I lay so close to the fire that when I awoke I found part of the tail of my coat (the only one I had) was burnt off. At another time, I only had one shirt and as it was so awfully dirty, decided to wash it. Had no vessel to wash it in, so went in the creek (and it was snowing too) and washed it – then took it to the fire to dry.[207]

In contrast to the images of hungry and ill-clothed troops, a description of Confederate prisoners of war coming through Memphis after Chickamauga paints a different picture.

> They were mainly large built, coarse, blousy fellows, looking very healthy and illiterate. They were dressed in the whitish gray jackets and pants, and various patterns of hats, shoes and boots. The appearance of these prisoners

indicated anything else but starvation or suffering from want of apparel.[208]

The prejudicial assumption of illiteracy was unfounded. Up to eighty percent of Confederate soldiers were literate, as were the vast majority of those from Germantown.[209]

Such a snapshot of their condition at one moment in time illustrates well the above accounts of how the quality of supplies varied greatly both at times and over the duration of the war. Like accounts of barefoot and nearly naked troops during the Revolutionary War, those for the Civil War were accurate at one moment and inaccurate at another. Innumerable variables dictated when troops got supplies and when they had only what they could forage. As late as October 1863, men in the Tennessee infantry had been reasonably well supplied. Standardization was far less possible than for the Union army, but quantity and quality was probably not much worse. As for the description of their morale included in the above account, "...they looked dispirited, and sick of the fighting business."

James McPherson's study of soldiers' letters addresses the question of what kept these men fighting with ferocious determination. Likewise he examined the issues of broken morale and desertion. He argues convincingly that what drove the initial volunteers and motivated them throughout the war were "the complex mixture of (Southern) patriotism, ideology, concepts of duty, honor, manhood, and community and peer pressure."[210] These were reinforced by the group cohesion that develops with combat among "a band of brothers." Slavery was certainly part of the ideology they fought to defend, but it was less uniformly so than liberty – the need to defend both family and hearth and Southern society from the invader who would reshape everything of value. Germantown's soldiers were among those who fought to liberate their homes from rapacious occupiers. The religious revival that swept through both armies during 1863-64 kept them going as things got ever worse.

On the other hand, relentless exposure to the horrors of combat separated the sheep from the goats. A decreasing number of men in even the best veteran regiments did the fighting, while others found safer places in which to carry on. Many ultimately broke. The growing numbers of less motivated conscripts contributed disproportionately to the numbers of shirkers and deserters. Heavy attrition undermined unit cohesion. The defeats of the year, the resultant loss of confidence in Braxton Bragg, and retreat from their home state resulted in hundreds of desertions.[211]

*****

1863 had brought developments that enmeshed soldiers and civilians of both races ever deeper into the violence and hate that any war, but

259

especially a civil war, can generate. It had seen the full birth of the irregular cavalry who plagued civilians so badly. In West Tennessee, first had come the partisans on the Confederate side. Then the Unionist government of Tennessee created its volunteer state cavalry to help combat that guerrilla threat. Many charges and counter-charges were thrown around by each side about the other's atrocities and depredations. The atmosphere of "Bloody Kansas" had migrated into the Mid-South from Missouri and Arkansas to Tennessee and North Mississippi. Each alleged that the other side's special formations had no rights as soldiers when captured, and were little more than brigands hiding behind the cause of their side. Gradually, in an effort to gain some control and discipline over these irregulars and state troops, each side upgraded them to the status of regular units in their armies, brigaded and integrated into corps with the other regulars. Nevertheless, they continued in their old ways whenever operating independently. During the next year, the mutual escalation of hostility created by their actions and the sensational charges thrown about would bring both sides to the verge of a veritable blood feud. It would leave a lasting legacy that would plague Tennessee and the Mid-South for at least a generation.

# Table 3: Civil War Incidents in and around Germantown, 1864

January 1864, *Forrest raids Middle & West Tennessee.*

March 7- April  *Forrest's major raid into West Tennessee.*

late March, 1864, **Federal occupation of Germantown temporarily broken.**

28 March, **McCulloch's sweep reaches Germantown.**

12-15 June, remnants of Sturgis' Expedition rescued at Collierville and Germantown.

24 July, skirmish with guerrillas 5 miles east of Germantown on M&C RR, near Collierville.

21 August, *Forrest's raid on Memphis.*

September-November, **sporadic Federal occupation.**

9 & 15 November, **running fights through Germantown into Collierville.**


## 1864, Germantown Returns to Anarchy:
## A Year of Blitzkrieg and Blood Lust

The new year around Germantown involved some delayed fireworks – another attempt to derail a train. On January 12, a group of "about 40 rebels" placed a shell under the rails to the east of town, but could not get it to explode until the last car of the train had passed over. Having only succeeded in breaking the rail, they fled south, soon to be pursued by 200 cavalry from Germantown.[1]

*****

The story of 1864 has to be told shifting back and forth between accounts of the area's men in arms and the effects of the war on the community. The two had become totally intertwined. Not only did the cavalry warfare occasionally impact the town, but the area's men fighting on both sides, black and white, confronted each other in increasingly bitter enmity.

During the previous year, Germantown had experienced the "protection" of a heavy Union military presence. For the next, its status would vacillate between that and the returned anarchy of being in no-man's-land. Unfortunately, no sources speak to the personal experiences of Germantown's people during this year. One can only hazard guesses as to the effect of it all on local morale and commitment to the Confederate cause. By the end of 1863, the *Appeal* had noted that there was once again "a marked feeling of depression in the popular mind in reference to our cause and its prospects." Even such an enthusiastic supporter of the effort was beginning to raise questions about the management of the war and to voice suspicions about the Confederate government asserting too much presidential authority, infringing freedom and rights. As the conscription policies expanded to boys of sixteen and men over forty-five, they were being equated to a European *levy en masse* that undermined public confidence. Matters were made worse by a loss of faith in Confederate money. Then came letters from the troops complaining how devalued currency affected them.[2] Although Germantown people were free from Confederate taxes, and temporarily from Federal taxes, the constant destruction of their property and the great difficulty of getting an income from their land was an even more severe tax. Worse, local men were subject to conscription by both sides.

From the beginning of its operations, the pro-Union *Bulletin* had painted an even more extreme picture. Wherever there was the protection of Federal troops, loyal and grateful unionists had reemerged and rallied to the national cause.[3]

A northern correspondent reported a more ambivalent picture,

> Weekly meetings are being held here relative to re-organizing the State and county governments of Tennessee; but there is yet a spirit of bitter opposition to the Federal government, and many reluctantly submit because they know there is no other way. It is very hard to give up a slave. Many who have taken the *oath* of allegiance have not changed their views....[4]

The best guess that one can make is that the pre-war mix of unionist and secessionist sentiments had resurfaced among the citizens of Germantown, while many resigned themselves to a Union victory.

Indeed by spring, there were very strange signals coming from Germantown. As part of Governor Johnson's efforts to reorganize the state's government, in March elections were held for officials in Shelby County. For Germantown's civil district eleven, the candidates of the "Unconditional Free State Union ticket" for justice of the peace were A. G. Bowen and James Hall, and for constable, W. Koch.[5] None of these men resided in the district for the censuses of either 1860 or 1870, but men of similar names did live elsewhere in the county.[6] In contrast, the appointed judges for the election were, J. M Gray, Wm. H. Walker, and L. Thompson; clerks, L. A. Rhodes and Monroe Harrison; and returning officer Job A. Lewis, all old residents.[7] These men had apparently accepted the inevitable and were working with occupation authorities to provide order.

The contest was primarily between the moderates, labeled the Lincoln Abolition candidates, and the Johnson radicals, the Unconditional Union ticket. When the results for the county were first reported, the moderates led by a margin of two hundred and fifty.

Meanwhile, however, the return of the Germantown district had been withheld for some reason. When they were brought in, the *Argus* reported, "the precinct was made to poll seven or eight times its usual vote," nearly all for the Johnson ticket. Indeed something was obviously rotten in Germantown. Although there were only 20 legal voters, Germantown fielded up to 343, all of whom voted radical. In sharp contrast, only three of these voters bothered to cast votes for the local district offices of justice of the peace and constable. The large number only voted for county offices, demonstrating no interest in local affairs. The winners for the Germantown district offices were locals, J. M. Gray and W. H. Walker for justices and J. Lewis constable,[8] moderate candidates who beat the Unconditional Unionists. All three men had held these offices before the war. One wonders why only three of the six men who qualified as election officials voted. Were the three running too modest to vote for themselves?

Even the loyal *Argus* cried foul. It published the affidavits of several officers of the 6th Tennessee Cavalry who observed that they had seen only soldiers voting at the poll site. Soldiers' votes were separate from the district's results. Other allegedly loyal papers in the state denounced "the election as a shameful jugglery." More conservative northern papers distanced themselves from the controversy, distrustful of both sides in Southern politics.[9] No records concerning this election survive in the state and county archives, but apparently another election for county officers was ordered and held.[10] All this tells us is that there was at least a small openly pro-Union but Conservative presence.

The *Bulletin* editorialized without comment on the fraud, although it had previously warned voters to beware such tricks by the opposition. It announced that the election had passed off peaceably everywhere with the Unconditional Union ticket winning the majority of the Unionist voters.[11]

Nevertheless, the *Bulletin* went on to make a more defensible argument about the long-term interests of area citizens. "Those who have stayed away through dislike to the amnesty oath will find that they have done ill for themselves." It argued that "amnesty will not continue to be offered without any limits to time – if the people ... refuse to take part in elections, they will gain nothing by their error in postponing the reorganization of the state, until harsher terms than those of the amnesty proclamation are the only ones they can get."[12] The *Bulletin* was clearly correct in its analysis of how Tennessee would fare in the future. Those who continued to hold out for the "lost cause" would suffer. Those who accepted the inevitable had a better chance to survive with something. Regardless of how the vote had been rigged, Germantown residents had begun weighing these considerations by the spring of 1864.

Occupation alone had already made the prospects clear enough to some of the wiser heads who surrendered to what seemed inevitable. Like the above-named elected district officials, one of the town's most respected citizens, the Reverend Richard Evans of the Presbyterian Church had sworn the oath of allegiance as early as June 1863 before the Provost Marshal in Germantown.[13] Coming after his negotiations saving his church building, this show of faith should have been sufficient to allow his congregation to reassemble under his tutelage in private homes. His act may have divided that congregation, but also must have had a strong effect on the less die-hard secessionists.

Whatever, a minister like Evans had to play a balancing act. For instance, the Woodson family in his congregation had originally opposed secession, but typically joined the cause when it happened, and their son was fighting for the Confederacy. When, in 1864, he wrote home in a state of despondence, Evans had to console the family and wrote Henry a letter intended to sustain him spiritually, an act that could technically have been construed as communicating with the enemy. Apparently he was not able to dispatch it.[14] Unless the records of the Provost Marshall become available, we will not know how many followed Evans and when, but the list of loyalty oaths was growing, and some were bold enough to openly participate in governance.

The general reluctance of the majority to defect from the cause, even *pro forma*, retarded Federal efforts to shift security and enforcement responsibilities to local government. The formation of a Tennessee Home Guard had been authorized by General Hurlbut in September 1863. By late January 1864, however, for the entire state, only seven companies had been fully formed. By the end of April, Memphis had enrolled some three thousand militia for defense of the city, but there were serious doubts that those pressed into service were loyal to the Union cause, and the units were if anything merely nascent formations.[15] They were to "put down and repress all robbery, violence, and irregular warfare," which meant the guerrilla and robber bands of all stripes. To protect the local population, the plan was to raise at least one company in each county "composed of loyal men alone, who are acquainted with the topography of the county, and who are familiar with the people among whom they live."[16]

In any case, not much progress was being made outside Memphis toward establishing such effective self-defense forces. In contrast, the *Bulletin* proclaimed that Tipton County had already succeeded so well in developing its home guard, "the people of Tipton have escaped comparatively unscathed the ravages of war." They had been so successful that General Hurlbut had granted them "permission to enforce law and order in their own county against all armies." They were now free from military seizure of property. It challenged the people of Shelby, outside Memphis, to take advantage of the same opportunity.[17]

They failed to do so.

Nevertheless as a result of what had seemed a stable occupation of Shelby County, in early March, Federal headquarters in Memphis initiated an open period of trade. Six main roads into the city were declared open for bringing in cotton and other produce and taking out goods and supplies. Of course, the State Line through Germantown was one such.[18] This relatively favorable situation did not last long, however. Forrest launched a disruptive campaign, raging all around Shelby County and returning the area to a state of turmoil.

What had been a stable situation turned into a roller coaster ride. On July 2, Washburn imposed martial law in Memphis and suspended the municipal government for its lack of cooperation. By August, the *Bulletin* was reporting, "The prohibition of trade has checked every avenue of business.... Regular business on cotton has been out of the question." Many people from the country could sell at 75 to 80 cents per pound, but whatever came in had to be stored with the government. Efforts to get around such controls in order to get cash could result in confiscation. Inflation was putting pressure on the currency, and gold was forbidden. Security became so tight that neither persons nor merchandise could leave the city except on the six, controlled roads. Everything was in limbo.[19]

## *Military Operations*

Paralleling these frustrated efforts at recreating orderly government and commerce, military operations once again threw the area back into chaos and threatened to unleash an even more viscous internecine warfare.

From the beginning of the year, the citizens of Germantown had watched the Federals depart on raids in all directions in their campaign to pacify the countryside. On January 11, Grierson had dispatched Fielding Hurst's 6th Tennessee Cavalry to Purdy as a base of operations. Although he had been instructed "subsist your command upon the country," his more specific orders were intended to restrain his men from further excesses.[20]

Regardless of orders, they continued to expand their evil reputation, contributing to growing tensions. Amidst all the charges and counter-charges by both sides, it is impossible to separate exaggeration from reality. The charges against the 6th can only be summarized, and usually not tested. Complaints even came from Unionists, however. "Col. Hurst burned 3 establishments belonging to 3 of the best Union men about Brownsville." Area victims had been forced to flee to Memphis and Peoria, while their personal property was being pilfered and wantonly destroyed.[21]

Much more serious charges against Hurst were leveled by Forrest.

They included the murder of six captured Confederate raiders, even torture and mutilation. On February 12, under threat of burning the city, Hurst extorted $5,139.25 from the citizens of Jackson as compensation for fines levied on his unit for damages they had done the previous summer. When the commander at Memphis was unable to respond to his satisfaction, Forrest proclaimed Hurst, his officers and men outlaws not entitled to be treated as prisoners of war.[22]

January had proven an unnerving month with the Federals chasing willow-the-wisps all over Tennessee and Kentucky. On the 14th, came an alarm that Forrest had crossed the river and was moving north with Memphis as his target, while Chalmers was going for Collierville again, and Ferguson for Pocahontas.[23] On the 17th, the command at Moscow anticipated an attack from a large force concentrated four miles to its south west.[24] On the same day, Richardson was reported at Stanton Depot with Forrest. Both Forrest and Richardson were usually reported as personally present at most encounters with raiders. Then on the 29th, Forrest was allegedly with some of his men on the Cumberland River in Kentucky. In reality, their recruitment officers and teams were simply all over the place conscripting and rounding up men away-without-leave.[25]

Before being forced back to defend Mississippi, his forces had torn up the undefended M&C RR from Corinth to La Grange, and he had planned to continue west through Germantown, if the Federal cavalry had gone down river instead of overland against him. Once again, Germantown was spared being the site of a significant confrontation. Federal control of West Tennessee and North Mississippi was so disrupted that solid Union occupation was limited to Memphis and Germantown.[26]

Sherman made a move that shifted raider activity away from West Tennessee for a couple of months. Since the pressure was off in East Tennessee, he refocused on the heart of Mississippi. His objective was the complete disruption of the Confederate supply system focused on Meridian. He launched his campaign from Vicksburg on February 3, and began the destruction of Meridian on the 14th. The immediate impact on the Germantown area would be the withdrawal of sizable forces along the rail line, followed by the relocation of some new units into the area. Germantown would again become a major center for troop concentrations. The entire campaign to pacify North Mississippi with its various side shows finally ended March 6.[27] This bold offensive put Forrest and Richardson on the defensive in Mississippi, giving West Tennessee a short respite.

In preparation, Sherman cobbled together a sizable force, removing almost all of Hurlbut's seasoned, regular regiments. Sherman ordered the significant reductions at "Memphis to two black and two white regiments."

All the Memphis and Charleston road to be abandoned save so much of it as can be safely held with the remainder of the troops herein embraced. ... Troops held too long in a city like Memphis ... become enervated. I wish, therefore,... all the men put into camp or bivouac as remote from towns as possible. The present garrison at Memphis, save the negro regiment, should form the nucleus of one of the infantry divisions named and encamp, say, at Germantown, where they can march inland or into Memphis for embarkation on one day's notice.[28]

He also gave orders for raising local self-defense by loyal citizens, but Hurlbut did nothing to execute these directives at Germantown or anywhere outside Memphis. Fortunately also Germantown did not become a base for concentrating an entire infantry division as suggested.

Nevertheless, by January 26, General Grierson began concentrating his cavalry division around Germantown and Collierville, with 2nd Brigade at Germantown, where Grierson also established his headquarters on February 6. The 2nd Brigade was an effective force of 2,900 men plus artillery. Grierson was to join Brigadier General W. M. "Sooy" Smith's cavalry expedition into Mississippi to hit the Confederates on a third front. It was to leave about February 1 and join Sherman at Meridian. From January 27, Grierson was sending out scouting units to feel out the locations of Forrest's forces with whom they were constantly skirmishing. In the orders they issued, both he and Smith sounded uncertain, slow in securing their supplies and equipment, and nervous about their opposition. Contrary to Sherman's orders, they did not leave Germantown until February 11, far too late to serve his purposes. Instead, by February 21, Forrest was free from Sherman's pressure and could concentrate on Smith's column forcing him back to Germantown by the twenty-sixth.[29]

As a result of this expedition from late January and throughout February, several thousand men and horses had concentrated in and around Germantown, and even during their temporary absence in mid-February, Germantown served as a major transit and concentration point for their supplies. All life would have been consumed by their presence, especially on the roads through town. For instance on February 7, a train of 200 pack mules arrived. As a point of interest, the bridge across the Wolf had apparently remained disassembled since Forrest's last raid. Temporary bridges were thrown across as needed, but only for military purposes.[30] Civilian traffic had to ferry.

On the return of the Federal forces, both the 2nd Brigade and the 3rd Brigade of Colonel McCrillis headquartered themselves temporarily at Germantown. Specifically encamped at the town was the 9th Illinois Cavalry Regiment from February 24 until March 17. Official reports of the 6[31] Illinois indicate it was also there until March 30.[31] The notorious Fielding Hurst's 6th Tennessee Cavalry was again at Germantown as part of McCrillis brigade. Certainly under McCrillis' nose, Hurst and his men could not have plagued the town with abuses before sent elsewhere.[32]

With Sherman still preoccupied securing Mississippi, by the end of February, Hurlbut's forces for the defense of West Tennessee were reduced to about 11,500 effectives, and Grierson's cavalry division, about 8,800 effectives.[33] The M&C Railroad, which had been abandoned for use since Sherman's expedition, was totally wrecked in the Germantown-Collierville area by raiders. It had been temporarily reopened as far as Germantown on February 26, to be abandoned again by March 26 in the face of Forrest's next raid.[34] Federal defenders were so disoriented that they were giving up the idea that they could maintain the line.

While the civilians of Germantown had been experiencing all these disruptions, their men in Forrest's cavalry participated in the continued escalation of civil war at its worst. Forrest had decided it was time to pursue his grandiose plans to liberate West Tennessee. On February 5, he had reported his ambitions directly to Jefferson Davis.

> The people of West Tennessee are generally loyal to the South, and whenever circumstances will admit of it I expect to reenter it, and am confident I shall be able to raise and organize at least four more full regiments of troops.[35]

During his previous expedition, Colonel Barteau's 2nd Tennessee Cavalry and Colonel Duckworth's 7th had played central roles. Forrest strongly commended them, "especially the new troops from West Tennessee, who considering their want of drill, discipline, and experience, behaved handsomely...." The volunteers and conscripts from the recent expeditions had been thrown into battle without benefit of training. Richardson's West Tennessee Brigade was also with Forrest, but under the command of Colonel Neely.[36]

Despite his praise of the troopers, Forrest had become thoroughly dissatisfied with the irregular nature of so many units in his command. Many problems centered on Richardson's command, made up of an excess of officers and so many men who came and went as they saw fit.[37] Forrest regularized things to his own satisfaction. He claimed that he regretted it, but he was probably not at all sad to eliminate many unit commanders from the inflated numbers he had inherited. When the dust settled, the West Tennessee formations in particular had become more standardized cavalry regiments of the Tennessee line.

Richardson was one of those who would soon disappear. For one last time, he had led his brigade against the Federal expedition against Yazoo City that had been another part of Sherman's February campaign. With him were his 12th Cavalry, now under Colonel Neely, and the 14th and 15th Tennessee Cavalry. They reportedly lost 3 killed and 27 wounded.[38]

By March 7, Forrest's command was as follows. Richardson's former command, the 1st Brigade included Duckworth's 7th, the 12th under Green, Neely's 13th and Stewart's 14th Tennessee cavalry regiments. McCulloch's 2nd multi-state Brigade contained only one Tennessee unit, McDonald's Battalion. The 4th Brigade under Bell was also a Tennessee command.[39] All these along with cavalry from Alabama, Kentucky, Mississippi and Missouri were known as Forrest's Cavalry.

He moved some of them north, east of Grierson's cavalry, and by March 24, had taken Union City, cutting all the rail lines to the south. Soon he was raiding in Kentucky.[40] While Forrest was moving north, Chalmer's division temporarily under Colonel McCulloch, was sweeping west through the North Mississippi no-man's-land arresting stragglers and deserters.[41] The land south of Germantown was reportedly heavily infested with wandering bands of brigands and deserters, robbing indiscriminately. McCulloch was to move "up as near to Germantown as possible."[42] The Federals had obviously completely abandoned the town in the face of Forrest's threat to the area. On March 28, rumors had it "Mo. McCulloch captured Germantown," and, "The rebels occupied Germantown Wednesday morning last."[43] We will probably never know what actually transpired in the town, for since whatever happened did not involve any significant combat, there are no military records of the event. We simply know that McCulloch was under orders from Forrest to "breast the country."[44] Even if it was only a conscription team, any man of conscription age, or even appearing to be, would have been "riding with Forrest" thereafter. As late as April 9, a Confederate force again drove the Federal pickets in at Germantown, to which they had apparently re-extended their outer reach.[45]

While skirmishing with Federals all over Kentucky and West Tennessee, by April 4, Forrest had set up headquarters once more at Jackson. From there he reported enough confidence to allow his troops parole to visit home. The 12th with McCulloch being especially so close to home, many of its local men must have gotten back into Germantown, which was now largely unoccupied.

By April 4, Grierson reported also encountering significant forces north-east of Memphis. In the city, Hurlbut fearfully predicted that Forrest might try to cross the Wolf at Germantown, join McCullouch and move on Memphis.[46]

## The Escalating Blood Feud

Instead on April 14, his combined force took Fort Pillow. Enough ink has been spilled on the subject of the massacre that occurred there, especially of African-American troops, and about Forrest's personal responsibility. It is not possible here to improve the picture, although its consequences must be explored. Something about moods on both sides in West Tennessee emerge from the report Forrest wrote before he became defensive about charges of war crimes. On April 15, he reported to his commanders:

> The victory was complete, and the loss of the enemy will never be known from the fact that large numbers ran into the river and were shot and drowned. The force was composed of about 500 negroes and 200 white soldiers (Tennessee Tories). The river was dyed with the blood of the slaughtered for 200 yards. There was in the fort a large number of citizens who had fled there to escape the conscript law. Most of those ran into the river and were drowned.
>
> The approximate loss was upward of 500 killed, but few of the officers escaping.
>
> It is hoped that these facts will demonstrate to the Northern people that negro soldiers cannot cope with Southerners.
>
> ...
>
> I have done but little conscripting from being so completely employed in operating against the enemy. Large numbers of the Tories have been killed and made away with, and the country is very near free of them.[47]

The bottom line is that the previous year's conflict in West Tennessee had escalated Confederate hostilities toward the "Tories" and blacks who had betrayed everything sacred and had allegedly pillaged, terrorized and murdered good Southern people. Both armies were infected with a drive to revenge insult and injury. For some Confederates it had become almost pathological. The treachery and evil acts of "Tories," but especially black Union soldiers and their white officers, demanded retribution.[48]

Forrest's defenders described the background to the massacre. He had been deluged by reports from locals "of rapine and atrocious outrage upon non-combatants of the country by the garrison at Fort Pillow." They pleaded for protection. The civilians in the fort were known to be deserters and "men of the country who entertained a malignant hatred toward Confederate soldiers, their families and friends." The troops had allegedly been scouring the country, stealing everything and insulting the women. The families of many of his officers and men had been "grievously wronged, despoiled and insulted, and in one or two cases fearfully outraged."[49] All this reportedly motivated Forrest's attack and the behavior of his men.

Witnesses on both sides were hardly dispassionate. The Federal version was replete with sensational images. Washburn asserted that "Men (white and black) were crucified and burned; others were hunted by bloodhounds, while others were made the sport of men more cruel than the dogs by which they were hunted."[50] A participant's words, though damning, probably provide a more accurate description. "Our troops, maddened by excitement, shot down the retreating Yankees, and not until they had attained the water's edge and turned to beg for mercy, did any prisoners fall into our hands. Thus the whites received quarter; but the negroes were shown no mercy."[51]

Even the death of Major Bradford, the Union commander, was allegedly an outright murder. He was "shot while trying to escape" for a second time.[52] Perhaps, given the heat that had developed on both sides, he was truly "assassinated." They were all swearing revenge on one another.

Hostility toward civilian "traitors" on the other side produced increasingly vicious retribution. When Federal troops were present, those suspected of secesh sentiments suffered, while Unionist confidence was buoyed and many men enlisted with Federal units, often hoping to defend their own towns against Confederate raiders. When Forrest experienced one of his successful liberations, he not only drew recruits, but neutrals, and even unionists were subject to Confederate conscription or worse. When possible, they fled to safety.

More emerged from Forrest's report to President Davis on April 15.

> The bands of guerrillas, horse-thieves, and robbers which infested this region have been broken up and dispersed, and many men heretofore Union in sentiment are openly expressing themselves for the South. There are as yet large numbers of men in West Tennessee who have avoided the service, and there is but little prospect of adding to our strength by volunteering. Conscription, however, would ... give us from 5,000 to 8,000 men.... I have not ... been able to do much in conscripting those subject to military duty but (intend to) send detachments in all directions to scour the country for deserters and conscripts.
>
> I am gratified in being able to say that the capture of Hawkins at Union City, and Bradford at Fort Pillow, with the recent defeat (by Richardson's brigade, of my command) of Colonel Hurst, has broken up the Tennessee Federal regiments in the country. Their acts of oppression, murder, and plunder made them a terror to the whole land.

For murders committed I demand that Fielding Hurst and such of his men as were guilty of murder should be delivered to me.... The demand has been referred to the proper Federal authorities and investigations ordered. Hurst and his command have ... been sent, in consequence of this demand, to some other locality.[53]

The pool for Confederate volunteers in West Tennessee had dried up. The ardor of many former secesh had cooled, while anti-secession sentiments had reignited. The disaffected and pro-unionists avoided conscription through flight. Having established temporary "control" over considerable territory, Forrest sent his conscription teams over the country.

Both sides felt plagued by illegal guerrilla bands and spent considerable energy trying to repress them. Previously as the seat of a major Federal camp, Germantown was protected from most such experiences. Clearly occupation was a mixed blessing, for as long as it lasted. Under pressure from Forrest, however, Federal occupation had evaporated.

Meanwhile, Forrest had received orders to return to Mississippi where another Federal offensive was expected. By this time, the mutual recriminations between commanders on both sides had reached the point of unleashing a blood feud even more terrible than what did in fact continue even after the war. A select committee of the two houses of the U.S. Congress drew up a report elaborating the atrocities at Fort Pillow, laying the blame at Forrest's feet. The whole thrust of his accusations against Hurst had been totally deflected by the massacre. The most important truth of the matter was that the blood bath there ignited even greater animosities.

Northern newspapers reported that afterwards in Memphis Union officers threatened "that unless the government take retributive steps, they will consider it their duty to shoot every man of Forrest's command they meet, and take no prisoners. Soldiers even threaten to shoot Forrest's men then in Irvin prison, if they get a chance."[54] Black troops had drawn the conclusion that in future conflict they would be butchered rather than being allowed to surrender. They took an oath among themselves that they would neither surrender nor give quarter to Confederates.[55]

Meanwhile, Forrest had thrown Hurlbut into total panic over a possible attack on Memphis. He had withdrawn all his forces and financial resources into Fort Pickering, where the paymaster with all his money and the sutlers with their supplies had joined them. The city's militia was deployed as a line of defense around the city. Except for cavalry, the rest of the county was so abandoned that Germantown could be visited by regular Confederate troops. The town was again in no-man's-land, Hurlbut was disgraced and removed. His successor would be under pressure to bring Forrest down.

Consequently Major General C. C. Washburn, Hurlbut's replacement, ordered out a large force under Brigadier General Samuel D. Sturgis to destroy the Mobile and Ohio Railroad south of Corinth and thereby draw Forrest out. Sturgis left Memphis on June first. His third brigade included the 55th and 59th Infantry (A.D.) and the 2nd Light Artillery (A.D.). The 59th and the artillery contained men from the Germantown area. They had taken the oath not to surrender, and all the troops were allegedly exhorted by their officers to remember Fort Pillow. The expedition was a disaster from beginning to end, with most of the blame lying on commanding officers.[56]

The two armies collided in the Battle of Brice's Crossroads or Tishomingo Creek on June 10. The 59th had been guarding the wagon trains in the rear, so it was last onto the field. Colonel P. Bouton, also commanding the brigade, threw his entire brigade into the line, where its "unflinching resolve" prevented immediate route. While repelling numerous assaults, it repeatedly made orderly withdrawals, constantly reforming the line, while other regiments crumbled. In Sturgis' own words, "It was now impossible to exercise any further control. The road became crowded and jammed with troops, the wagons and artillery sinking into the deep mud, inextricable.... No power could now check or control the panic-stricken mass as it swept toward the rear...." Meanwhile for the colored brigade, the fighting was often hand-to-hand, "with bayonets and clubbed muskets." At one point near the end, according to Bouton, "I was left entirely cut off and surrounded by several hundred of the enemy. My men, gathering around me, fought with terrible desperation. Some of them, having broken up their guns in hand-to-hand conflict, unyielding, died at my feet, without a thing in their hands for defense." The remainder escaped and rejoined the retreating column.[57]

Their ordeal had just begun. As the army retreated from Ripley, Mississippi, the next day, they were guarding the rear. They resupplied their ammunition by scavenging what the white troops had dropped. In the desperate, hand-to-hand fighting that ensued, they became badly dispersed, retreating back to Collierville in three separate groups along different roads. Bouton with about 170 survivors, mostly disarmed and many severely wounded, reached Collierville on June 12. They were the luckiest. The larger number, about 600 under Captain Foster of the 59th remained under attack during its retreat. Again Foster's troops formed the rear guard, and according to Wilkins, "the imperturbable coolness and steadiness of the colored troops" kept the attacking cavalry in check and prevented confusion. They reached Collierville on June 13. The last group under Captain Reeve of the 55[th,] did not reach safety before June

15.[58]

Reeve's account of their ordeal was hair-raising. At Moscow, severely harassed by cavalry and completely out of ammunition, they scattered into the woods,

> every man going in for himself. From this point until we reached Germantown the loyal citizens of Tennessee turned out and hunted us with bloodhounds as we passed along. I reached Germantown on the 15th, about 4 o'clock in the afternoon. A good many of my men got in about the same time. We there found some of our cavalry.[59]

By then, Sturgis had fled to safety in the city. Only when Reeve's group finally filtered through the area to Germantown did they encounter the safety of Grierson's patrols, sent out to round up stragglers.[60] The civilians of Shelby and Fayette counties had allegedly joined the pursuit of the fleeing black troops as though they were escaped slaves. By June 15, Germantown was only sporadically inside the patrol lines of Grierson's cavalry.

To add insult to injury, at the beginning of the expedition, Colonel McMillen had placed guards at houses along the route ahead of the 3rd Brigade to prevent the black troops from entering to get drinking water from their wells or cisterns. When Colonel Bouton complained to him, he responded that they did not need to get water from the houses, for there was standing surface water from the rains.[61] Apparently the commanders felt that the civilians needed to be protected, specifically from the black troops, for whom any puddle of water was good enough. None of the commanders of the white brigades found it necessary to record such a complaint.

Federal commanders obviously feared that their black troops might take extra revenge on Southern civilians after Fort Pillow. Although Federal records do not indicate that anything extraordinary occurred in that regard, hysterical rumors had been spreading throughout the South. The Columbia *Daily South Carolinian* reported that from the beginning at Germantown and all along the route of Strugis' march, only those who fled escaped a horrible fate. Allegedly refugees fleeing before Sturgis' army had brought tales of horror to the West Tennessee cavalrymen,

> detailing incidents which made men shudder who were accustomed to scenes of violence and bloodshed. I cannot recite the stories of these poor frightened people. Robbery, rapine and the assassination of men and women, were the least of crimes committed while the "avengers of Fort Pillow" overran and desolated the country. Rude unlettered men, who had fought at Shiloh and many subsequent battles, wept like children when they heard of the enormities to which their mothers, sisters and wives

274

had been subjected my the negro mercenaries of Sturgis. The mildest, most placeable of our soldiers became maddened when they heard how the persons of their kinswomen were violated. The negroes were regardless of the age, condition, sex or entreaties of their victims. In one instance, the grand-mother, daughter and grand daughter were each, in the same room, held by the drunken brutes and subjected to outrages by the bare recital of which humanity is appalled.[62]

The author's pornographic imagination ran wild as he detailed other alleged specifics, all of which were intended to justify his report of the fate of the black troops.

Prisoners are constantly being brought in by the country people. Very few negroes, it seems, have been captured. Perhaps not more than forty or fifty have appeared at headquarters. Most of them fled as soon as it was known that Forrest was on the battle-field. Those that were taken escaped.(?) The soldiers say they "lost them."[63]

This verifies the accounts of civilians participating in the pursuit and capture or execution of fleeing Federal troops, especially blacks. Hysterical propaganda fired fears and hates, entrenching ideas that anarchy and chaos would follow upon black emancipation, and justifying whatever force would be needed to curb it.

On June 23, the reported losses of the 3rd Brigade A.D. were 1 officer and 109 men killed 3 officers and 131 men wounded, and 8 officers and 160 men missing. Although these numbers were only about one fourth of the total infantry casualties, their killed constituted 60 percent of the total dead. In the chaos, 1,351 white troops had gone missing compared to only 168 of the 3rd Brigade.[64] The black death-toll added further to accusations that they were not allowed to surrender.

By this time, the commanders on each side were holding the others responsible and threatening escalating retributions. Forest, told that the oath had been taken in the presence of General Hurlbut, believed the black troops had been incited to take revenge. At Brice's Crossroads, their officers had supposedly called upon them to remember Fort Pillow. General Washburn insisted that Hurlbut was not present at the oath-taking, rather that it was a spontaneous act of the soldiers. Nevertheless, Forrest argued that the troops had been sent out with their commanders knowing full well what was afoot.[65]

A series of exchanges and recriminations followed between the respective commanders. Each side claimed it would follow the rules of war, but only if guaranteed that the other would treat prisoners appropriately.[66] Washburn charged that if the Confederates would not treat colored troops as prisoners of war, "then let the oath stand, and upon those who have aroused this spirit by their atrocities ... be the consequences."[67]

Forrest responded that captured blacks would receive "kind and humane treatment," but would be treated not as prisoners of war but as captured property. He then charged that Washburn was leaving "the matter entirely to the discretion of the negroes" and threatening to give orders that will "lead to consequences too fearful for contemplation." Noting that he held 2,000 prisoners as hostage, he demanded a clear response of Washburn's intentions.[68]

All involved expressed the bloody mood that possessed each side.[69] Lee had forwarded these exchanges to his commander, and fortunately indicated that he intended not to escalate things.[70] On July 3, Washburn responded to Lee in terms that were hardly conciliatory, but he too expressed a willingness to avoid further escalation. He went on, however, to refuse to excuse Forrest and Lee for the atrocities that had occurred under their commands.[71]

There the matter seems to have rested among the commanders. There are no records of what they might have tried to do to cool things among their troops. Incidents would continue as both sides suspected the worse of each other, but there was no further escalation of rhetoric by the commanders on either side. No carte blanc given for revenge. Regardless, Forrest's raid and Brice's Crossroad had created a blood-feud atmosphere among the regular troops that was approaching that already created by the Tennessee partisan and counter-partisan cavalry actions.

All total, 2,242 colored troops from West Tennessee were killed during the war, the vast majority during 1864 in confrontations with Forrest's troops. In return they had contributed to Forrest's 2,234 casualties. The casualty rate among West Tennessee's colored troops was 34 percent, almost half again as great as that for the colored troops from the entire state. In the defense of West Tennessee against Forrest, the partisans, and the guerrilla and robber bands, they played a key role in relieving regular army forces for the more decisive battles elsewhere.[72] There will probably never be an estimate of how many Germantown area blacks were among these troops and casualties. We may never know if any of them came face-to-face with their former masters. Such, however, were the seeds of an animosity that would presumably linger in the minds of black and white alike as they sought to live together around Germantown through the following years.

### Germantown Still in the Middle

Meanwhile, as soon as troops from the Brice's Crossroads disaster had returned to Memphis, significant Union advances south out of Memphis into Mississippi and Alabama were planned to put Forrest back on the defensive. In preparation to support one such expedition, the M&C was rapidly reopened, reaching Grand Junction by July 1.[73] But the contraction of Federal bases tightly around Memphis meant that the line was increasingly vulnerable. One attack occurred on June 23, at Forest Hill, "in the vicinity of the female college." To protect the next train out, a detachment was dispatched from White's Station to position itself between Bray's Station and Forest Hill.[74]

Sherman became convinced that as long as Forrest was alive, there would be no peace in the area. Consequently, on June 24 he launched an expedition to hunt him down.[75] Taking much of the cavalry with him, including that stationed at Germantown, General A. J. Smith worked his way east repairing the railroad. Ever nervous about Forrest's mobility, he asked Washburn to maintain cavalry pickets along all roads between Germantown and La Grange.[76] Then on July 5, he announced he was ready to move out toward Tupelo against Forrest, planning to send all surplus stores back at least as far as Germantown.[77] One increasingly gets the impression from their exchanges that Germantown was considered on the frontier of their securely held ground. Even so, occupation of the town seems to have been abandoned again before August.

Ironically, while this force was still out hunting Forrest, he made his famous raid into Memphis on August 21. Generals Washburn and Hurlbut narrowly escaped being captured, and were unable to wire to the force still at La Grange for help because the wires had been cut between Germantown and Collierville.[78] It seemed the Federals could hold nothing securely, while nothing could be permanently held by the rebels either. The M&C was again ordered abandoned on August 29. Much of the cavalry still at La Grange had rushed back, Hurlbut's 1st Division returning to its headquarters at White's Station with its 2nd Brigade covering the Germantown-Collierville area, and the 12th Missouri and 2nd Iowa Cavalry reseated at Germantown proper by September second.[79] Once the defenses of the railroad were abandoned east of town, the Confederates wrecked the line between Germantown and La Grange "most effectively," burning trestles and bridges.[80]

Amidst all this turmoil, Federal occupation forces underwent changes, but the records do not reveal clearly its distribution around the Germantown area. Although Grierson's Cavalry Corps was enlarged for the defense of the entire area, Hatch's 1st Division seems to have been headquartered at White's Station. As a result of this contraction of defenses around the city, Germantown and Collierville were again frequently abandoned to suffer being in no-man's-land.

In September, the railroad was only in operation to supply the base at White's Station. Even that short line was abandoned on October 15. On September 29, Forrest's scouts reported that the cavalry at White's

Station was "making raids daily to Germantown." On November 3-4, Confederate cavalry out of Oxford were again tearing up the rail lines from Germantown to LaFayette. On the evening of November 9, a sizable expedition of Union cavalry clashed with Confederate pickets inside Germantown, capturing two as they pushed through town to Collierville. From the prisoners they learned that they were from "Denis' command" which had been tearing up the railroad even farther in than Germantown. On November 15, five miles east of town a Union patrol on the State Line Road drove Confederate pickets back into Collierville.[81] On November 17, the *Bulletin* reported, "the rebel Captain Thompson is making a sweeping conscription in the neighborhood of Germantown. He has a list of nearly every resident of that section of country, and compels all he finds to go with him or pay heavily for being allowed to escape."[82] It is hard to believe any were left. Whatever life in Germantown that had survived Union occupation during 1863 was once again totally disrupted as skirmish lines repeatedly fought their way through the town. The next clear record of an occupation at Germantown was of the 99th Illinois Volunteer Regiment from late in November to the end of the year.

Nevertheless, even the road between Memphis and White's Station remained vulnerable.[83] In addition to Confederate cavalry raiders, according to his memoirs, DeWitt Clinton Fort's command ranged freely from the Mississippi border throughout south-west Shelby County during the fall and into winter. At one time, one of his companies under Lieutenant Loftin was at Germantown while he himself was at Hernando. He remembers that during October, he had orders to maintain reconnaissance across an arc running from Collierville around north-east of Memphis to Raleigh and up the river to Randolph.[84]

On December 20, the rail line had been reopened for regular traffic as far as Collierville. This was only temporary to support a raid on Confederate supply lines by General Grierson. Then December 23, Confederate scouts reported that a Federal force of 3,500 cavalry, about 5,000 infantry, nine pieces of artillery, 300 pack mules was at Germantown. After a harrowing stint back in no-man's-land, the town was once again overwhelmed by Union troops and their traffic.[85]

Heavy occupation would not last long, and a greatly reduced presence that followed confined the benefits of protection to only the immediate town. Whatever recovery and stability the area had experienced had evaporated. If they had not already given up and been forced to seek refuge in Memphis or elsewhere, the poorer yeomen and landless farmers and laborers either left or resorted to more desperate means of self-support. As elsewhere, some felt entitled to take from those who still had means. The formerly wealthy had ceased charity or sharing and there was neither government aid nor law enforcement.

Illustration 26. Leslie's Illustrated presented this propaganda piece in May 23, 1863, juxtaposing what they considered an appropriate fate for the Southern women who had so enthusiastically sent their men off to war. The bread riots in major cities were the counterpart of the rural plundering of wealthier farms. Of course, this completely overlooked the class differences involved in the defection of the women of small-holders and landless farmers.

MANUFACTURING CORN MEAL

Illustration 27. (Harper's, November 1864)  On their own, wives of
yeomen and tenant framers who remained on the land were destitute.
Without access to mills, they had to grind by hand whatever they had.

Social tensions that had smoldered below the surface before the war were fanned by Northerners who always believed the South was a decadent aristocratic atavism. The short lived Memphis *Union Appeal* advertised a rally against secession, calling on every "working men, mechanic and laborer" to turn out against the aristocrats who had disdained them. The effects of such appeals were mixed. Outbreaks of class conflict were sporadic.[86]

For the residents of the Germantown area, this was undoubtedly the nadir of the war experience, worse even than the initial shocks of pillaging in 1862. All over the occupied South, the ladies of the plantations and formerly prosperous farms recorded in their letters and diaries a mood of abject depression and near hysterical breakdown. Faced with both impossible problems of mere survival for their families and the ever present threat of worse at the hands of criminalized bands of men, some suffered stresses and trauma that produced similar effects to those their men experienced in combat. If not already dead, the condition of their men remained unknown, the future bleak and foreboding. They underwent permanent changes in their mentality, abandoning all sense of communal responsibility, focusing entirely on the needs of self and family.[87]

The desperate wives of marginal families had been encouraging their men to desert, and all the lower classes felt especially aggrieved by the unfairness of conscripting the sole breadwinners of their families. Such deserters found shelter among neighbors and conscription teams even encountered armed resistance.[88] Such tensions were also spreading through the ranks of the men away from home.

### The Men away from Home

In the midst of their relatively good year of campaigning, a considerable row had developed over Forrest's troops within the Confederate command structure. Fortunately the related correspondence and resultant report tell us a good deal about the state of affairs among the Tennessee units containing Germantown area men.

It is unclear what precipitated the investigation. It may simply have been a complaint of General Pillow's about his not having an appropriate command over some of the Tennessee troops that had ended up under Forrest.[89] It may also have been an accumulation of problems stemming from the irregular evolution of many of the Tennessee units as well as whatever had specifically resulted in Richardson's removal.

In the investigator's report, some of the murky history of the West Tennessee units emerged a little more clearly. It began, "the present organization of this command was irregular and without authority." It then listed the abuses generated by Forrest's command but was diplomatic enough not to attribute responsibility to Forrest directly. Forrest's successes and his personal charisma had apparently created problems for the rest of the army, which he had failed to alleviate. Specifically deserters from the infantry were accepted into his cavalry, seriously undermining discipline. Inspection revealed 654 deserters from the Army of Tennessee on Forrest's rolls. Two hundred of these men had formerly deserted Forrest's command. When ordered to do so, Forrest had 200 of the infantry deserters returned to their commands. "All officers who had received them knowingly were arrested and charges preferred against them."[90] In fact, on previous occasions, Forest had asked permission to retain deserters from other units, sympathetically noting that they would be humiliated to return to their former units, and proclaiming how enthusiastically they served with him. Later, Forrest would complain that the scare created by sending back the deserters led to seriously damaged moral and increased desertions in the cavalry.[91]

From all this emerges a mixed picture of the circumstances under which Germantown area men had been "riding with Forrest." Although they had eventually been officially mustered into Confederate service, their operational environment had fluctuated. Many had served only in regular military formations, most of the time, even when on raids into West Tennessee. Others had shifted back and forth between regular service to something more like privateers, especially when living off the land. Others began and ended like Robin Hood's Merry Men with a sinister edge, moving freely in and out of regular service status. Their motivations for service were equally complex. Some had been drawn by the mixed appeals of partisan service. Some had volunteered only after the units became regular cavalry. Some reported dutifully after conscription orders were posted, even while under Federal occupation. Others responded to threats of punishment if they failed to report, while some were even more forcefully conscripted.

From all indications, untold numbers had drifted in and out of this service, often more than once over the course of the war. A member of the 7th Illinois posted at White's Station in September reported, "I have not...seen a Reb since I came back, only what comes in and gives themselves up. They are a coming in every day more or less."[92] Desertion is a harsh judgment. At some point, one came to believe he had simply done all he could or should be expected to do.

A member of the 7th Tennessee Cavalry reflected on the conversations among his fellows by autumn. The handwriting seemed on the wall.

> We had little else to do than sit around and discuss such subjects as when the war would end, how it would end, and how we should be treated, if finally defeated. ... The federals had unlimited resources in men. ... Many believed

that the establishment of the independence of the Confederacy was improbable, if not impossible. ... We could only hope that something would happen that would turn the tide in our favor. It took moral courage, and plenty of it, for a man to make himself a target for bullets, when he had no very reasonable hope that, even by his death, he would save his country. While some abandoned the cause, it is to the everlasting credit of the men of the Seventh Tennessee cavalry that they stood by those who had the direction of affairs...in their hands.[93]

One must remember that for most Americans at that time, indefinite regular military service was not an obligation to which they were bound to respond. The concept of duty was more like that of the time-and-space limitations of militia service. Indefinite conscription and the indefinite extension of volunteer service violated American traditions. Defense of their homes or their region was primary. Service required to fulfill the military objectives of some national government could easily be seen as impinging on their inalienable rights and their family responsibilities. When the Confederate government failed to keep one's home and family safe and fed, one should go home to tend to it himself. Earlier ambivalences about secession resurfaced, at least until one went back home. The realities of enemy occupation might or might not have changed that.

Meanwhile for the infantrymen with the Army of Tennessee, despite all the reverses, the year began with a display of determination. In January, the men of the 13th along with the rest of the Tennessee regiments in Georgia voted to remain in service for the duration.[94]

Soon however, the war went sour. In July, Jefferson Davis had replaced the popular General Joseph Johnston with the Texan, John B. Hood. Hood had an inflated sense of southern honor and berated his men whenever they failed to live up to his romantic expectations. Before Atlanta, he had thrown them against Sherman with devastating results. He blamed them for lack of fortitude and expected them to reclaim their honor. While Sherman marched across Georgia, he embarked on a crusade to liberate Tennessee. Along the way, every frustration in his campaign led to further castigations. Then in November, at Franklin he threw them into a disastrous frontal assault that produced only massive casualties. While enduring extremely bitter winter weather without adequate shoes and clothing, the men suffered a last blow in front of Nashville. By December, his command was no longer an army in size or energy. Henry Dunavant of the 1st Tennessee Cavalry expressed the feelings of his compatriots about Hood. "All the men who Hood failed to see Slaughtered at the Battle of Atlanta on the 22nd of July 1864 he got rid of at the Battle of Franklin, Tenn. in his vain attempt to immortalize himself."[95]

Needless to say, after every major bloodletting and setback, Tennesseans suffered demoralization. Many felt betrayed, especially when they suffered from poor military decisions or policies that seemed to serve only the rest of the Confederacy. Hood's debacle was the last straw. After the winter of 1864/65, another massive drift back home ensued from the Army of Tennessee. They simply left the ranks in despair and made their way home as best they could.

The stubborn remnants were reunited under Johnston's command and in February 1865, marched into North Carolina. There along with the rest of the remnants of the Army of Tennessee, the consolidated and depleted 13th/154th ended up at Bentonville, NC, where it was further fused into the 2nd Consolidated Tennessee Infantry Regiment. It surrendered on April 26, 1865 and was paroled on May 2. Fewer then 50 officers and men remained out of the twelve-hundred plus numbers who had mustered into the 13th during the war.[96] Out of the original 1100 men of the 154th, fewer than 100 survived the war.[97]

By this time the 4th/5th had been so reduced it formed only Company D of the 3rd Consolidated Tennessee Infantry Regiment. After Bentonville, it also surrendered at Greensboro on April 26. After being paroled on May 1, the men gradually made their ways back home.[98] The remnants of the 2nd, 3rd, and 32nd with their probable contingent of Germantown men all suffered this same fate.

Meanwhile, at home the guerrilla war continued. On December 26, a company of the 29th Wisconsin, while accompanying a night train from Germantown to Memphis, "Had a slight skirmish with some guerrillas, who fired upon the train."[99] DeWitt Clinton Fort implies in his memoirs that throughout the winter up to March 1865, his command of holdouts was operating as true guerrillas, without official military commission and in defiance of orders intended to curb guerrilla depredations. "For a while we were as much afraid of our own soldiers as of the enemy. For the first time in life, I feared the gray uniform, though I wore one myself and never had dishonored it."[100]

## Prisoners of War

The fate of those who became prisoners of war rounds out the picture of the war experiences of Germantown's men. The fate of Federal soldiers in Confederate prisons, especially the infamous Andersonville, is well known. Less severe was the experience of Confederate prisoners of war, but not by much. Germantown men captured in the campaigns to the east could end up in many different camps. Those captured closer to home traveled a special route in many cases.

This was particularly true of the cavalry raiders swept up by the expeditions out of Shelby County, or those caught during Chalmers and Forrest's expeditions. Irving Block in Memphis was their first stop, for it served as a way station before transit to northern camps. Irving Block was created from "a large block of stores" – "three large brick warehouses with iron front, 120 by 75 feet, four stories high" on Irving Street off Court Square. It actually served as a general military prison for the city, housing not only Confederate prisoners, but Union soldiers and civilians under arrest. The first floor confined white male prisoners of all sorts. The second housed the kitchen, offices and short-term holding cells. The third held the hospital and cells for white female prisoners. The fourth was for "coloreds," who included soldiers as well as male and female citizens.[101] Germantown's male civilians arrested for espionage or smuggling ended in Irving as well. The internment of such females was less consistent.

Unless exchange or parole was being negotiated, Confederate prisoners were forwarded on as soon as possible. Local Federal and civilian internees could rot in cells for many months before even getting a trial. Consequently overcrowding had become serious. When he had assumed office, Captain George Williams, Provost Marshal, reported very poor conditions which he tried to correct. By June of 1864, the conditions had become scandalous, and an inspection ensued. Williams was brought up on charges, initially held responsible and narrowly escaped becoming the scape goat. The report noted that the prison was "the filthiest place the inspector ever saw occupied by human beings." As a result of subsequent improvements, by September a medical inspection gave a clean bill of health, except for the conditions of colored inmates.[102]

One of Williams' complaints had been the laxity of the guard details, which the inspection reaffirmed. Thus we get a better understanding of Henry Woodson and Joe Duke's experiences in that prison. Woodson could easily have escaped and Duke did. If Woodson had not been paroled and Duke had not escaped, they would have been shipped north to a true prisoner-of-war camp.

An early report in the *Chicago Times* described the experiences of those captured in the spring of 1862, before overcrowding and while prisoners were a novelty. Camp Douglas provided locals with something like a zoo to which they could go to observe what they expected to be something like semi-savage hicks, ... a lazy, untutored person ... exceedingly unfit for fighting." They soon learned, however, to respect the "intellectual and physical capacities of the prisoners."

> A sort of crude curiosity in this affair is being developed....
> The unfortunate captives are quite willing to answer all questions that are put to them; but it must be confessed that they are disgusted with the inquisitive glances of visitors,

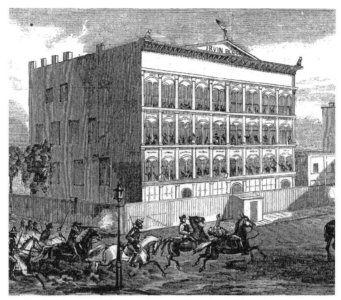

Illustration 28. Irving Block, on the occasion of Forest's raid.

CAMP OF REBEL PRISONERS AT ELMIRA, NEW YORK.—[See Page 230.]

Illustration 29. Typical Federal prisoner of war camp (Harper's, April 15, 1865)

286

and the assertions openly expressed and thrust upon them a hundred times daily, that "You are in the wrong, and I am in the right." Then there is a certain class of persons who...seek out the communicative prisoners, with whom the(y) commence to argue, just as though the settlement of this accursed rebellion depended on their own efforts.[103]

The reporter continued.

All the prisoners are receiving the best of treatment, are allowed plenty to eat, and are quartered in warm, comfortable barracks. They say they have met with extreme kindness on the part of northern people, and admit that they have uniformly fared far better than in the rebel camps of Dixie.[104]

This rosy picture of camp life coupled with negative depictions of the poor conditions in the Confederate army so early in the war was typical of prejudicial reporting in all wars. At least he went on to admit that accommodations for the sick in the camp hospital were inadequate. Soon overcrowding would change every Federal prison-of-war camp for the worse.

Union prisons were grossly inadequate, and stories of inhumane treatment abound. Inadequate food, clothing shelter and sanitation facilities prevailed. Rock Island, Illinois was a prison known to have housed Germantown men. The prison was situated on a swampy island in the Mississippi River opposite Rock Island, Illinois. The first Tennesseans to arrive tell a horror story. They were still in light-weight clothing when required to stand outside for long hours in a December blizzard with temperatures below zero, while waiting processing. Some froze to death.[105]

All year round, notoriously wet, but in winter brutally cold, icy and snowy. The fourteen-acre square was surrounded by twelve-foot wooden walls. Inside the wall, was a twenty-foot "Dead Line," marked by posts. The prisoners were warned that if they entered and ignored the single warning of a guard, they would be shot. Sometimes, however, the guards did not bother with that warning. At night, there was a curfew, and anyone outside barracks would be shot. The barracks were two-stories and wooden, so roughly put up that "the winter winds howl through the many crevices in the walls, sometimes covering the floors with a carpet of snow." With only one stove per room, "not more than a dozen, out of seventy-five inmates, can get close enough to feel its warmth." With only one blanket per prisoner, the rest had "to keep from freezing by constant exercise."[106]

Initially rations were good, and in the summer a sutler sold "luxuries" at exorbitant prices. Anonymous care packages arrived regularly, with "clothing, provisions, books, and luxuries of all kinds"

Illustration 30. This Harper's illustration of Confederate prisoners (April 15, 1862) shows crowding so early in the war, but downplays the harsh conditions that were already developing.

from the border states, Maryland, Kentucky and Tennessee, and almost every northern city. The quality of rations began to deteriorate over time, however. The sutler was forbidden. In June 1864, the government ordered rations cut further as retribution for the suffering of Union troops at Andersonville.[107] Rations were not only scanty, but quality was well below standards for human consumption. Dog and rat meat became delicacies. Most prisoners returned home skin and bones. Concerning his time in the camp at Rock Island, Anderson Kirby reported, "If not for detailed service While in prison would have starved to death." He apparently referred to opportunities to do work details to earn something to buy extra rations.[108]

Lice ridden and without proper sanitation facilities, disease was rampant, and small pox killed very high percentages. Of the 12,000 total population, almost 2,000 died. In 1864, prisoners were offered release if they volunteered for service in the Union Navy or with the Army on the frontier. By then, a thousand or more left Rock Island under those conditions. No other prison matched this defection rate, indicating the severity of its regimen.[109]

We are unlikely to know the fates of most of the other Germantown men who ended as prisoners of war. We know that a William Ellis of Company C, 13th Infantry died in Alton Prison, but he does not seem to have been one of the Germantown Ellises, though probably a relative.[110] Alton was established in an abandoned state prison also on the Mississippi River. Because Dorothea Dix had previously published an exposé of the unhealthy conditions at that prison, it had been shut down, but was recommissioned as a military prison in early 1862. It became quickly overcrowded with three men to the four foot by seven and a half foot cells. When a smallpox epidemic broke out, the sick were quarantined in an inadequate hospital on an adjacent island. There 1354 died, to be dumped in mass graves. During its three-year tenure, about 12,000 Confederates resided there.[111]

Camp Hoffman at Point Lookout, Maryland, had perhaps the worst living conditions. Established after the Battle of Gettysburg, anywhere from 12-20,000 men existed in a camp intended to house 10,000. There were no barracks, only leaky, reject tents, despite Maryland's freezing, wet winters. Drinking water became polluted, and food was so poor that here too rats became a staple supplement. 3,584 bodies have been found in a mass grave. The bitterest memory for many, however, was their treatment at the hands of the sadistic troops who guarded them.[112]

These three camps were the most frequently mentioned facilities holding men who served in the units known to have held Germantown men. As with all such stories of the abuses, we cannot distinguish the mythical and extraordinary from the true routine.

# Table 4: Civil War Incidents in and around Germantown, 1865

March, **regular, but light occupation resumed.**
28 March, **incident at Germantown.**
9 April, *Lee Surrenders.*
18 April, **ambush near Germantown**. The last combat in Tennessee.
4 May, *Lt.Gen. R. Taylor surrenders the Confederate forces in Alabama.*
**9 May, *Forrest disbands his forces at Gainesville, AL***
30 September, **occupation of Germantown ended.**

## 1865, Winding Down the War

On the first of January after Grierson's expedition, the M&C Railroad was once again completely abandoned, leaving Germantown cut off.[113] Die-hard Confederate spirits remained stubbornly resistant to the very end, and Germantown experienced its share of continued hostilities, disrupting life and commerce. One P. P. Dunbar was apparently trying to do some kind of business in Germantown under a Federal commission when Confederate raiders confiscated all his money and merchandise.[114] The area remained immersed in the total insecurity of a no-man's-land throughout January and February.

Local anarchy grew from far more than the depredations of Confederate partisans, undisciplined renegade soldiers, and the growing numbers of bandit gangs. Former slaves and poor whites showed no respect for private property as they desperately sought to survive. Unoccupied, even inadequately defended homesteads fell prey to their needs. At least the Germantown area was free from the attentions of the vengeful Unionist home guards that had emerged elsewhere. Unionists had not suffered the persecutions in relatively harmonious communities like Germantown that they had experienced elsewhere in the state.

The month of February was an especially rough transition from such anarchy back to the orderly life of an occupied town. Germantown again served as a staging point for major and minor cavalry expeditions. For instance, on February 27, William Dunaway of the 7th Illinois Cavalry wrote to his wife from Germantown, briefly recounting "a big raid" into Mississippi in which he had participated, departing the town on the eleventh and returning on the twenty-sixth. He bragged of how much damage they had done. Yet they were harassed all the way back home taking casualties. Three entire cavalry divisions had descended on the town, left on the raid and returned again for a few days. Unfortunately, he told nothing of life and the town.[115]

On March 3, the bulk of a Cavalry Division again coalesced at Germantown to mount a major expedition into northern Mississippi. 1st brigade camped on the south of town, 2nd on the north and 3rd on the west. Distrust of both the local population and his own men was apparently so high that the commander posted guards at "all the houses inhabited." Such a comment reinforces our image of how bad the state of life in Germantown had become, with some houses obviously uninhabited. The Division remained there the next day awaiting supplies by train, and finally moved on at 6 PM toward Collierville. Lieutenant Colonel Shelby of the 1st Brigade observed that there was "fine country, but no farming being done. ... Forage was scarce, but secured enough." Obviously life in the area had degenerated again. The force that had descended on and taken over Germantown for the better part of two days had consisted of 2,672 men and horses, plus officers and hundreds of pack animals. On the 11th, the expedition returned through Germantown.[116]

A reason for the commander's distrust both of the locals and the discipline of his men emerged from an event that had occurred on March 4. Three of his men had violated orders and strayed from camp to forage for corn in a barn. Despite the presence of such a large Union force, some local rebels or "bushwhackers" captured them. One managed to escape and reported that the other two had been murdered. These were the only casualties the unit suffered on the entire expedition.[117] Nothing was mentioned about retribution against local citizens.

Despite all the raids, guerrilla warfare continued to plague the area throughout February and March. Memphis newspapers ran frequent articles detailing the depredations of bandits, guerrillas or partisans. Increasingly, it was impossible to tell them apart. Even the commissioned partisan bands had degenerated into open criminality. The *Bulletin* uniformly called them guerrillas. Although they continued to burn cotton, the *Bulletin's* reports of their activities implied that their primary purpose was simple robbery. Although they certainly looked for supplies, passes and other papers they could use, they procured mostly money and other valuables. In the process, some employed torture and murder to uncover hidden treasure.[118]

One small squad of guerrillas claiming to be part of Forrest's command had been operating along the south side of Nonconnah Creek stopping all traffic and confiscating anything of value. Confederate deserters pretending to be blocking the cotton trade into the city were actually extorting the farmers, accepting payment in lieu of burning it.[119]

The growing transition of guerrilla warfare into banditry came from

Illustration 31. Guerrilla depredations (Harper's, December 24, 1864

Illustration 32. (Harper's, December 4, 1864) Among the most desperate oath takers were women in need of support for their children.

the fusion of several elements. As the partisans evolved into increasingly uncertified guerrillas, no discipline remained. They were joined by deserters from both armies. Not just outsiders, however, for most were members of the local communities cut loose as community bonds and constraints dissolved. Not just the poor, but teenagers of all classes sought to replace lost bonds with those provided by a gang. Even formerly respectable citizens had been criminalized by partisan ranging. Increasingly less concerned with punishing Yankees and Tories, they preyed upon the defenseless in pursuit of self-interest. The brutality directed at their victims exceeded that once focused on hated enemies.[120]

Finally Federal forces began to reestablish continuous occupation. To begin the process of securing the railroad, on March 19 Colonel Hasbrouk Davis of the 12th Illinois was ordered to establish himself at White's Station with detachments guarding all bridges along the line, which should have put some at the underpass in Germantown. By about March 25, he had established his headquarters at Collierville. The level of tension and efforts to defuse it becomes clear from an order he issued.

> In assuming command of the cavalry forces on the line of the Memphis and Charleston Railroad, occasion is taken to remind the troops that they are now in a country regarded by the government as conquered; that a loyal State organization exists and the inhabitants are under the protection of the Union forces. It is therefore expected that all good soldiers will conduct themselves so as to give no just cause of offense. The fact that the good name of the cavalry is at stake ought to be sufficient inducement to good behavior, but if further is needed it will be found in the fact that the commanding general has ordered all damages done to be assessed against the depredators when discovered; and in cases where no discovery is made, against the whole force. ... All stragglers will be reported at these headquarters to be placed at work upon the railroad.[121]

The military was doing its best to protect the locals, but it also had to keep its soldiers from straying into places where they could be caught by guerrillas or raiders.

At this time, the commander of the Cavalry Division headquartered at Memphis was Colonel E. D. Osband. An order he issued on March 28 tells us both about the distribution of troops in the Germantown area and how precarious Union control remained to the very end. One regiment each of the 2nd Brigade was stationed at Germantown (11th New York), Collierville (12th Illinois) and La Fayette (Rossville) respectively. They were to vary the hours of their patrols to avoid predictable patterns, and to be extremely vigilant to avoid ambush and to capture prowling bands.[122]

His regulations had been prompted by orders from General Washburn. On March 21, he had sent them to Brigadier General Shanks, commanding First Brigade Cavalry, near Germantown.

> I enjoin upon you to maintain the strictest discipline over the troops with you. Allow no straggling and no resident of the county to be disturbed. If any depredations are committed, you will ascertain at once the amount of damage done and inflict prompt and summary punishment, and stop the pay of the command by whom the depredations were committed until the loss is made good. You will press no horses or mules from any person who is behaving himself properly.[123]

With victory imminent, intelligent commanders down the line perceived the necessity of establishing some sense of normalcy and order among the civilian population. On February 10, as part of the process of creating districts for the military government of the conquered South, the Department of the Cumberland, to include Tennessee, was established under Major General George H. Thomas. On the 28th when Tennessee was divided into three districts, General Washburn was given command of the District of West Tennessee.[124]

For documentation of the public mood, one has to look outside the Germantown area. As the Confederate cause totally crumbled, Union commanders assessed that mood with an eye to restoring order. General Stanley, stationed at Huntsville, Alabama, argued for much more conciliatory practices, particularly with the civilian population. His analysis of the public mood divided the population into three groups: (1) open unionists; (2) "people who are timid about their persons and property, and might be said to be on the fence;" (3) and secessionists. "It is from this middle or kind of neutral class that we have much to expect." Local unionists had assured him that there was a good chance in the upcoming elections for the "conservative or reconstructionist" candidates to win against the secessionists. "Under this state of affairs I deem it sound policy to make as many friends as we can by a just and lenient course toward the people, and to give our enemies as few occasions as possible to bring the accusation of an unforgiving course against us."[125]

Stanley's analysis undoubtedly described Germantown during the previous two years. In his area, the harsh policies being pursued were like those experienced in Shelby County during 1862 and 1863. The provost marshal was examining persons on a list with the threat of expulsion, including many former pro-unionists who had succumbed to the pressures of public opinion and the wave of enthusiasm during the heyday of the Confederate cause.

In addition to having survived such an early wave of harassment, the citizens of Germantown had endured the depredations of almost three years of occupation and guerrilla warfare. Among the "neutral middle," there were undoubtedly many who simply wished "a plague on both your houses." They yearned only for some return to normalcy. To see the return of their neighbors – soldiers, refugees and expellees. They wanted to live together again in harmony, regardless of former differences in politics.

Stanley's description of attitudes reveals this desire to restore old community relations despite former differences, but especially in tightly knit, small communities. Unionists pleaded leniency for their secessionist neighbors who "used their utmost influence during the late Confederate occupation to protect the Unionists of this vicinity." Stanly's best argument was, "We who are engaged in this war have other homes to go to if we survive the war, but these people must live here, and it is not to be wondered at that they desire to extend kindness to their neighbors."[126]

In December 1863, President Lincoln had issued an amnesty proclamation. Together with War Department declarations about amnesty, it was printed in pamphlet form. Not only was it distributed throughout Tennessee, but cavalry forays, scouts and other agents were ordered to broadcast them in enemy territory. One object was to encourage desertion and surrender, but the other was to pave the way for reunion.[127] Unfortunately the interpretation and application of such directives were the responsibility of officers with a wide range of temperaments grown from years of war and hostility, which had reached the level of demonization of the enemy. While some prominent Tennesseans, who had vacillated back and forth during the early years of the war, found easy readmission to the rights of citizenship, the former work-a-day agents of local and state government were less likely to get the benefit of the doubt. Occupation officials, badly needing the reestablishment of local government, had to argue for the inclusion of "sheriffs, constables, magistrates, county and circuit clerks, registers, coroners, &c."[128] From all appearances, this reestablishment had already occurred at least partially around Germantown during early 1864.

By March 1865, many southerners had resigned themselves to the inevitable. Local farmers and businessmen especially wanted nothing more than to get back to business as usual. In Memphis, both the Southern merchants who had remained and a flood of Northern businessmen who had come in to take advantage of commercial opportunities were anxious to have trade barriers with the North removed and connections with the still rebellious states reestablished as soon as possible. The machinery of an interstate mercantile system had survived in Memphis veritably undisturbed. Such an opportunity for access to market would have an especially heavy influence on the agriculturalists and businessmen of the surrounding area.

At Washington, led first by Lincoln and then Andrew Johnson, farsighted officials sought a quick reunion and reconciliation to get the economy going as a bond of national unity. Needless to say, powerful business and financial interest groups supported the cause, but radical politicians and suspicious or embittered military men put vengeance first. Consequently from March through June, it remained unclear just when and how a reconstruction process would develop. Wartime laws and military ordinances had erected barriers to North-South trade and economic activities within occupied territory. Lincoln's assassination ignited more animosity and distrust while throwing his lenient amnesty plans into disarray. President Johnson, with his border-state perspective, cast about for lenient solutions while local occupation authorities interpreted the evolving guidelines inconsistently.[129] Like the rest of the South, the people around Germantown hoped for the best but continued to encounter frustrating obstacles.

Meanwhile, deserters surrendered while paroled soldiers and former refugees sought to return home, and most applied for the amnesty. The guidelines issued for screening the applicants to insure "good faith" were clearly intended to cull out those who still harbored unacceptable convictions or merely sought to escape retribution. Anyone discovered to have sworn false witness was to be subject to "trial for his former treasonable acts."[130]

In Memphis, General Washburn was ahead of the curve in efforts to find accommodation with the "neutral or middle" elements of the population. He focused especially on reestablishing production, commerce and civil government. All of which, of course, required a pacified population. He too, however, was forced to wrestle with the issue of whom to trust.

Washburn liberalized restrictions on the operation of plantations. Both outsiders who leased abandoned or confiscated plantations and owners who had remained were allowed to operate except where the local population persisted in supporting "smugglers or irregular partisans." They had to have contracts of employment with either their former slaves or freemen. Registered plantation owners would be allowed to take out the necessarily larger quantities of supplies.[131]

On March 10, a general order relaxed some of the more stringent aspects of martial law.

> The District of West Tennessee is hereby declared to be within the lines of Federal military occupation. There being no longer any organized hostile force within the district, citizens will be allowed to come freely to Memphis and dispose of their products and take back a limited amount of family supplies. All adult persons

coming to Memphis will be required to take the oath of allegiance.... Those who wish to return to their homes in West Tennessee and North Mississippi will be allowed to do so on giving satisfactory security that they will not again take up arms against the Government of the United States, or give aid and comfort to its enemies.

All products for sale had to be the results of free labor. Procedures were established to protect those bringing in products for sale from being exploited.[132]

On March 21, Thomas sent Washburn orders, some of which he had already instituted. Thomas requested that

as far as practicable ... you will endeavor to restore the confidence of the people of West Tennessee, and encourage them in any desire they may express to enforce civil laws against the outlaws and guerrillas who infest their counties. To this end you are authorized to occupy and repair the Memphis and Charleston Railroad as far as LaGrange.... This would interpose a force between the people of West Tennessee and the enemy's territory in Mississippi. Encourage all the counties in West Tennessee to organize their county courts and administer the civil laws, assuring them that they will not be interfered with by the military authorities as long as they conduct themselves in a manner loyal to the Government of the United States: encouraging them also to cultivate their farms, with the assurance that no more arbitrary seizures of private property of any kind, particularly horses, mules, and oxen, will be permitted, and that they will be permitted to carry to market and dispose of at Memphis ... whatever products of their farms they may have to dispose of without molestation. ... Say to the people of West Tennessee that it is not designed to oppress them if it can be avoided, and they may pursue their peaceful occupations without fear of being molested, but that it is expected that they will at least make an effort to redeem themselves from their present miserable condition and exhibit to the world that they are worthy of the leniency which has been shown them. It is expected that they will keep themselves well informed of all offensive movements of the enemy in their quarter of the State and inform the nearest military authority promptly of the same; and to avoid sending troops into the interior as much as possible it is expected that the people of the country will take care to preserve peace and quiet within its limits, as it will be held responsible for the same.[133]

New directives from Washburn would continue to curb financial restrictions in order to stimulate economic and agricultural activity.[134] Meanwhile on March 20, orders had already been issued to reopen the M&C Railroad. Within four days it was open to Collierville, and throughout April and May, the more extensively damaged portions were repaired to Grand Junction.[135] Perhaps this restored mail service to Germantown, although the federal army's needs would still take precedent for the duration. Perhaps the former postmaster Miller had been trusted to handle operations out of whatever might have remained of his store, or perhaps whatever federal mail came to Germantown was handled by the local commander. In any case, on October 18, Monroe P. Webb would be appointed Germantown's new postmaster, and mail service fully resumed.[136] Former school teacher for many decades and son of the Webb school founder, he must have remained a firm unionist throughout, although at one point he may have been forced to ride with Richardson. He had to have credentials that satisfied the politicians in charge of reconstruction. They, after all, had the Postmaster General's ear in making appointments.

Meanwhile, defending the rail line remained a problem. Colonel Davis at Collierville reported that on March 28 the vedettes of the 11th New York Cavalry at Germantown were attacked by "four men." Two Union men were wounded, one mortally, and one of the rebels was captured.[137] One has to wonder what prompted such futile gestures of defiance. Such a small "prowling band of soldiers" was operating independently, without support. Yet against an entrenched guard detail, they were able to inflict more damage than they suffered.

The 11th Regiment was only specifically headquartered in Germantown March 28-April 18, but obviously still in the area with elements in Germantown from February until mustered out of service on September 30. From May through June, it was the only regiment covering the entire area, with its headquarters moved to Collierville. Only companies L and M remained encamped at Germantown proper.[138]

Again, the memoirs of DeWitt Clinton Fort cast light on the mood of those Confederate die-hards during these dark moments.

> That winter was spent in making various and numerous expeditions, 'hunting a fight' as we each called it. ...many hardships undergone, many sufferings endured, many risks and perils run, and dangers defied. The winter was cold and unfavorable....
>
> But so confident were my hopes of the success of our cause that my mind could not be brought to think or dream of failure. My patriotism was too sanguine. It over did the thing. I was so infatuated by its prompting that upon all

topics connected with the success of our cause I was
mentally blinded to all but one event – Success.[139]

Undoubtedly supplemented by a bloody anger, such a mood had led him to continue guerrilla operations independently in defiance of military orders. He and others so involved would later defend their reputations against charges of being little more than bandit gangs by wrapping themselves in patriotic colors. Their "motives" or compulsions were undoubtedly more complex. They saw no future for themselves in defeat. Their lives had been no different from that of outlaw bands. They had lived and fought desperately in a style that could terminate violently at any moment. They had lived for the moment and the little material rewards that their successful adventures brought. Their desperation produced the kind of behavior that has always led occupation forces to see partisan resistance against them as banditry or terrorism. Any Germantown area men who had become involved in such die-hard resistance had crossed a line that would make reintegration into society extremely difficult.

As late as April 4, Colonel Osband from Collierville issued orders growing from an event of the previous day in which a patrol of thirty men armed with rapid-fire, breach-loading Spencer carbines had been routed by sixty Rebels armed with Enfield rifles, and the commanding lieutenant was killed. He stipulated that the light patrols scouting the railroad did not need to be enlarged, but were to focus on gathering information on when and where to send larger patrols "in expectation of finding an enemy." Those larger patrols sent out upon either flank of the railroad should consist of at least 100 men, properly officered, and even larger patrols should be mounted against reported forces like that encountered on the 3rd.[140]

Again, the Confederate side of these raids and ambushes is depicted in Fort's "memoirs." He boasted of his ability to camp right next to Union camps and spy upon them or steal their horses – particularly in 1863, it was he who had hovered around Collierville providing Chalmers with the intelligence that led to his attack. He or his men could move in and out of Germantown despite the presence of Federal occupiers. Never mentioning anything about actions that caused suffering by civilians, he bragged of being able to rob and punish Union jayhawkers who preyed upon defenseless civilians. After a period of purely unsanctioned existence during the winter of 1864/65, on March 15, his command allegedly received a commission to operate legitimately. He boasted that his small detachment struck wherever he pleased, but always avoided likely damage to itself. He claimed he had the guard detachments along the railroad terrified. Even the garrison in Memphis was uneasy.[141] If not "terrified," clearly "uneasy" describes the state of affairs up to the very end and beyond. Federal records report incidents throughout the winter and spring 1865 of his successful ambushes of patrols, even concentrating 100 to 150 men to defeat more sizable forays.

**General Lee surrendered his Army in Virginia on April 9,** and Johnston's Army of Tennessee in North Carolina surrendered April 26. Lieutenant General Taylor did not surrender the army in Alabama until May 4, and Forrest did not disband his forces until the 9th. Consequently there was time for one more skirmish at Germantown. This was the last reported incident in Tennessee and among the last east of the Mississippi, all of which were minor skirmishes.[142]

Captain George W. Smith, 11th New York Cavalry based in Germantown, reported that on April 18 a patrol moving toward Collierville was attacked about six miles out of Germantown, which would place it a little beyond Bray's Station on present Poplar Avenue. The rebel force was estimated as from 60 to 100 strong of "Ford's command" (undoubtedly Fort), while the patrol consisted of only eighteen men under Lieutenant John H. Mills, D Company. Mills was pursued to within two miles of Germantown (approximately the present Oakleigh neighborhood on Poplar Pike). The report implies that stragglers may have been unnecessarily shot. The rebels were so desperate for supplies that they took shoes and clothing from the Union casualties.[143]

In his report on the next day, Smith noted that General Washburn had ordered that no more patrols be sent out with fewer than fifty men. The captain complained that he had only 190 men at Germantown, out of which he had to maintain a picket of 32 men daily, a daily scouting party of 30 men, plus camping duties. He called for reinforcements of 50 mounted men and 100 dismounted men so he could mount operations against the guerrillas. He claimed to know their haunts and promised success.[144]

As the war wound down and Confederate units degenerated, many regular soldiers became part of this guerrilla resistance. Indeed, guerrillas like Fort kept Union forces uneasy to the very end. Until May, Smith had kept his camp widely scattered because "the garrison was continually menaced by guerrilla bands," requiring them to occupy defensible points.[145] Nevertheless, the incident of April 18 was the last recorded military incident in Tennessee.

Local tolerance for the more flagrant bandits had reached its limits. By April in response to Washburn's appeals and being free of any legitimate partisans, Germantown residents were reportedly "determined to clear out these robbers. A few days since they caught three of them, and, after a hasty trial, hung them to a limb of a tree. They were young men from Mississippi."[146]

What followed through April and May were Federal efforts to clean up the remnants of legitimate Confederate units, illegally operating partisan bands, and just plain bandits. On May 3, Washburn launched "a guerrilla hunt." One to two-hundred-man detachments went out from every base along the line to LaFayette. The detachment from Germantown left on the 4th, ordered to "beat up the country as far as the Cold Water," but to stop there and return to Germantown. This entire expedition focused on territory that remained a base for raiders and brigands despite Confederate orders. Strict orders were given to avoid offenses by stragglers and plunderers.

> People in the country will be kindly treated, but must be informed that if they are known to harbor or encourage guerrillas hereafter they shall be utterly destroyed. Should the murderers Fort and Mat Luxton be caught they will be disposed of by a drumhead court-marshal, and if rebel soldiers are captured it will be reported whether they are captured in arms or not.[147]

By this time most of the people of Germantown undoubtedly appreciated such expeditions for the relief they promised from continued insecurities.

During the months prior to surrender, Forrest, then based in Georgia and Alabama, had dispatched policing detachments throughout Mississippi and even West Tennessee to round up deserters, stragglers and roving bands of robbers and guerrillas to prevent any continuation of brigandage. In May in return for such service, Colonel J. F. Newsom operating in eastern parts of West Tennessee, when called upon to surrender, would request, "In behalf of the citizens I ask that none of the men belonging to the command of Colonels Hawkins and Hurst be sent here. The feeling that exists between soldiers of these commands and the citizens is such that private malice and private revenge might be more the result of such a policy then the restoration of order."[148]

Indeed, the two infamous commanders were no longer leading the 5th and 6th Tennessee Cavalry U.S.A. Hurst's resignation had become effective on January 8.[149] By May 13, from Eastport, Mississippi, General Hatch was reporting,

> Many bands are surrendering here under your order, among them one of the worst, Burt Hayes. I learn a Mr. Chandler, calling himself captain, a brother-in-law of Fielding Hurst, is levying contributions upon the citizens of McNairy County, Tenn., amounting to $50,000. Hurst has already taken about $100,000 out of West Tennessee in blackmail when colonel of the Sixth Cavalry (Union). What shall I do with Chandler, if he reports to me as ordered? If he does not report, shall I treat him as an outlaw?[150]

Thomas responded, "Summon Chandler to surrender, and, if he refuses,

Illustration 33. Rebel deserters coming within the Union lines (Harper's, July 16, 1864)

declare him an outlaw and treat him accordingly, and inform the people that hereafter all illegal bands will be regarded and treated as outlaws."[151]

For several months preceding formal surrender, increasingly area soldiers accepted the inevitable and came home on their own initiative. They came to Memphis as the only safe haven as long as partisan bands continued to prowl and punish. According to the *Bulletin*, "They are generally very apprehensive of harsh treatment, and are astonished when they learn the kindness extended to all who avail themselves of the amnesty proclamation." Of course, they had to swear loyalty, and to accept such changes that had occurred during the war, especially the emancipation of slaves. Interestingly, this oath included something of an escape clause to the effect that they would not have to continue to respect emancipation if Congress or the Supreme Court nullified it. As of February 28, 1,045 men from Shelby County had reportedly entered the city.[152]

The *Bulletin* also commented on the quality of this new wave of deserters. Perhaps unfairly, it dismissed former deserters as "roustabouts," as "unsteady, unreliable fellows" who had given up on the cause so easily. "The deserters who are now coming in are of a much better class...." They had fought on in a mistaken sense of honor for a bad and hopeless cause. There was nothing traitorous about their decision to give up, and they could be trusted not to perjure their oath.

As the end approached, Forrest's cavalry was assembled at Verona, Mississippi. A general and a senator addressed them in hopes of buoying morale, claiming that if Lee was forced to abandon Richmond, he would take the army west across the Mississippi to continue the war indefinitely. Such transparent nonsense backfired. It confirmed suspicions of imminent defeat, and desertions increased. When Forrest resorted to executions, that also backfired. His ranks were depleted.[153]

> *If I ever get through this war,*
> *And Lincoln's chains don't bind me,*
> *I'll make my way to Tennessee ---*
> *To the girl I left behind me.*

For the defeated Confederate soldiers of Germantown, the road home was long and difficult. For each, it was a different story, different experiences, different hardships, and different conclusions. Henry Woodson, who was in Georgia when it ended, recalled his experience.

> I left Columbus, Georgia, and started on my journey homeward, walking much of the way as there were only now and then short stretches of railroad in operation and on these stretches only one train per day of open flat cars.
>
> On leaving Columbus, there were some two or three

hundred paroled Confederates in our crowd, returning to their homes in various parts of the country. Our route was from Columbus, Georgia, via Montgomery and Selma, Alabama. At Selma I spent one night with my cousin ... and family thence to Meridian, Jackson, Grenada, Oxford and Holly Springs, Mississippi. ... When I arrived at Holly Springs. The crowd of two or three hundred ... had dwindled down to three.... Early on the morning of may 19, 1865, these three weary, dirty, hungry Confederate soldiers, having slept in a vacant outhouse by the roadside, started on our last stretch of our homeward journey. Having gone about twelve miles, two of the boys took the road leading to Mount Pleasant, I alone went on to Rossville, Tennessee, on the then Memphis and Charleston Railroad, arriving there at eleven o'clock a.m., a distance of twenty-one miles from where I started that morning. About two o'clock p.m., I boarded a west bound train. The conductor asked for the fare to Germantown, I replied, 'I have nothing but Confederate money.' The conductor saw the situation and with the remark 'I will see you later.' passed on, but the kind-hearted man made it convenient not to 'see me later.' He knew I had no money. I arrived at Germantown about 4 p.m. May 19, 1965. After a few minutes walk I reached home and loved ones.

When I left home three years previously, in the spring of 1862, my mother had given me a small pocket Testament, on the fly leaf of which she had written, 'A thousand shall fall by thy side, and ten thousand at thy right hand; but it shall not come neigh to thee.' Ps. 91:7.

It seemed almost like a prophesy and was literally fulfilled; for in all my war experience, I had never received a wound; and for this Divine protection I ascribe the praise to "Him who giveth food to the hungry' and 'marks the sparrow's fall."[154]

Most of the Tennessee Cavalrymen had been with Forrest in Southern Alabama. When the official news of Lee's surrender was broken, an officer of the 7th recalled that "many brave, strong men wept as children. Some indeed, were willing to prolong the fight, "to the death," but better councils prevailed...." They actually struck up friendly relations with their Federal counterparts, and drew plentiful rations for the ride home. They like Woodson were left to find their own way home in small mounted groups, for they were allowed to retain their horses. Some even reported that they got assistance from sympathetic Union troops along the way.[155]

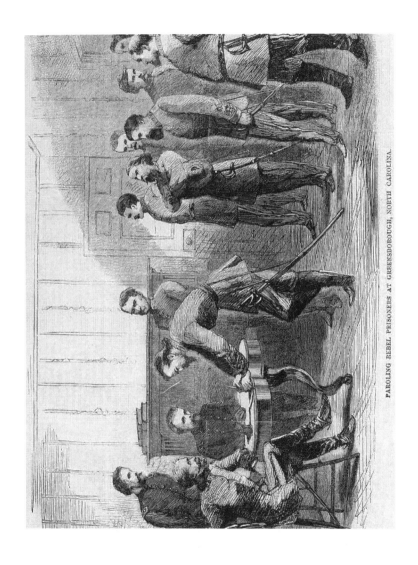

PAROLING REBEL PRISONERS AT GREENSBOROUGH, NORTH CAROLINA.

Illustration 34. Paroling Rebel prisoners (Harper's, June 3, 1865)

The general pattern was that within a week or two of surrender, the men had been issued parole passes which enabled them to return home. Ostensibly, the Federal Quartermaster's Department was supposed to provide transportation, but that failed as often as not, because the railroad network was badly disrupted. The parolee had to sign and carry an oath. "I...do solemnly swear that I will not bear arms against the United States of America, or give any information, or do any military duty whatever...." The pass specified at least the state to which he could return, and specified that he could remain there "without molestation so long as he observes the conditions of his parole, and the regulations and laws in force at his place of residence."[156] Thus, these war-weary soldiers expected to return home without anyone throwing obstacles in the way and to begin anew.

The largest contingent of Tennesseans to surrender were with Johnson in North Carolina or with Lee in Virginia. They had to make their way home across East and Middle Tennessee. Under the terms of surrender, the men were allowed to retain any weapons and horses that were their personal property, a concession essential to their livelihood on return home. This posed serious problems for the Union commanders in charge of these areas. Brigandage was already a problem, and such large mobs of armed men represented a serious threat. Consequently Federal officials appointed Confederate officers to maintain command over units which were provided with rations and baggage wagons, and were allowed to retain one-fifth of their issued rifles. They, after all, were endangered by brigands, and local unionists bent on revenge. They had to make their way on foot across the Appalachians to Greenville where most would board trains. Unfortunately in Greenville, many had confrontations with black Union troops intent on humiliating their former antagonists.[157]

The defeated soldiers trying to come east across Tennessee also had to deal with the occupation authorities, many of whom were having trouble with the concept of "amnesty" for offenders. On April 17, General Thomas began revoking some amnesties. His concern was the allegedly numerous, formerly devout rebels who had suddenly sought to escape the consequences of their behavior and save their property. They had gone to other districts to take the oath where their history was unknown.

> That all amnesty oaths administered to any person, or persons not bona fide deserters from the rank and file of the rebel army, and with the consent of the Major General Commanding, no matter where or by whom administered, since the 15th of December last, are hereby revoked and pronounced null and void, and hereafter no amnesty oath administered to persons coming to or living within this

department, will be regarded or considered valid, unless taken with the knowledge and consent of the commanding general of the same.[158]

On April 25, Thomas issued another harsh directive that further reversed any lenient policies that were ameliorating conditions in Tennessee. "No more amnesty oaths will be administered to either soldiers or citizens, and all are repudiated and annulled which have been taken since the 15th day of December last."[159]

The realities of the situation hit home, however, when on April 29 from Chattanooga, General Steedman reported,

> There are large numbers of paroled rebel soldiers from Lee's army and Forrest's here and coming into our lines at all points, who are utterly destitute, and who will inevitably be driven to stealing and robbery, if not bushwhacking, unless they can be permitted to go to their homes or be provided for in some manner. What shall I do with them?[160]

From Knoxville, General Stoneman asked for an elaboration of Thomas' directive.

> Your telegram received. Numbers of men have come into East Tennessee with authority from Gen. Grant to go to their homes, which are in East Tennessee. Do your instructions include such persons; and if so, shall they be sent without the limits of the State? There are others whose homes are in Georgia, Alabama, and the other Southern States. They are penniless and without food, and must live by begging or stealing. Can I issue such persons a limited amount of rations and send them off by rail to Dalton (the Confederate base) and get rid of them; also obnoxious and troublesome characters?[161]

To them, Thomas responded,

> By decision of the Attorney-Gen., no Confederate is entitled to come into a loyal State on his parole. He will have to take the oath of allegiance to the United States to enable him to return. You are authorized to give a limited amount of subsistence to such rebel soldiers who have to pass through East Tennessee to get to Georgia and Alabama. They must not be allowed to stop on the way.

Thomas had the appropriate first part of this directive forwarded to Washburn.[162] From all appearances, the intention was to dump most of the veterans who did not immediately take the oath on the still unoccupied states, along with the accumulated flotsam of the Federal army.

Confronted with such large numbers of Confederate soldiers, especially Tennesseans who would have been expelled south, Thomas revised his orders on May 6. "You are authorized to administer the amnesty oath to rebel soldiers, but not to officers or citizens. It is now too late for them to be reaping the benefits of the amnesty proclamation, after having maintained an attitude of hostility for four years."[163] The next day, he went further to allow all paroled prisoners who had surrendered with Lee or Johnston who lived in Tennessee to return to their homes. Others who had previously been captured in battle would continue to be processed as prisoners of war.[164] Unfortunately, Thomas and others were so vindictive and vague that they left most locals uncertain as to their own status.

One of those officers coming back from the eastern theater was Needham Harrison. The conditions under which he ended the war are obscured in the microfilmed version of his answers to the veteran's questionnaire. All that is readable says that he returned home on horse back. What's puzzling is how he evaded the restrictions imposed on officers by Thomas.[165] Apparently locals often advised the veterans how to avoid the checkpoints where guns and horses were confiscated. Avoiding local brigands was yet another problem he had to negotiate.[166]

At least, once he returned to Germantown, he found Washburn's policies slightly more tolerant.

> Citizens who left our lines and sought refuge in rebeldom, and have resisted all persuasions to return until the present moment, will not be allowed to return to Memphis at present. Confederate officers returning to this district paroled from the armies of Lee, Johnson, and Taylor will not be allowed to wear their uniform or any badge reminding of their treason. Paroled enlisted men, or those who have taken the amnesty oath, will be required to divest themselves of their rebel uniforms as soon as they can procure other clothing, and they are given thirty days from the time of their coming into the district to do this.[167]

John Kirby was discharged from Rock Island Prison on April 15, 1865, and sent home to Memphis by steam boat.[168] That seems to have been the most commodious form of transportation among all returnees, although the accommodations were certainly not first class. If they in any way resembled those of the infamous, overcrowded Sultana taking Federal soldiers North from southern prisons, they were neither comfortable nor safe, though undoubtedly a relief from confinement.

In order to get released, prisoners had to take the oath of allegiance. Those who refused remained in custody until near the end of summer. Aside from steamboats, trains brought most prisoners home.[169] The depot at Germantown must have been a welcome sight, marking the end of a long ordeal but the beginning of a new life of uncertainty.

On May 9, Washburn continued local efforts to restore peace and a working society. The large numbers who had taken refuge in Memphis for a variety of reasons were a serious problem.

> The country is now quiet, and such as are here are advised to return home and do something for themselves. Rations will no longer be issued, except to the aged and helpless and young children. There is employment for all in the country who are willing to work; it is not too late in the season to make crops; millions of acres are lying waste for lack of labor; those that can work must or starve, black or white. The Government will not encourage thriftlessness or idleness by supporting those that are able to support themselves. Transportation to the country will be furnished those who wish to go, so far as the cars run, and two day's rations to all who go.[170]

One wonders if any refugees from the Germantown area had found safe haven in Memphis. Unfortunately, putting the agricultural economy back in shape involved much more than putting pressure on the idle. Instead this effort might have merely diverted the pressure of supporting the uprooted to the countryside and towns like Germantown.

Meanwhile, Washbourn still had to arrange the surrender and security of the remaining Confederate forces inside his part of Tennessee, many of whom might join the bands of outlaws roaming the countryside. As previously related, one such was that under Colonel J. F. Newsom in the vicinity of Brownsville. Newsom was sent copies of Confederate surrender orders giving terms. Washbourn gave Major Davis at Brownsville directives for handling the surrendering troops.

> Confederate soldiers reporting to you will be paroled and allowed to go home, and such as desire to take the oath of amnesty will be allowed to do so. I send some blanks. You will keep record of all such and report to the provost marshal here. Officers and citizens will not be allowed to take the amnesty oath without first obtaining permission of the department commander. Officers reporting here will be paroled upon the terms agreed upon by the terms of the surrender of Gen. Dick Taylor.[171]

At least some officers and citizens were now being given a loophole into amnesty.

The physical condition of the soldiers who had to "bum" their way home over hundreds of miles was undoubtedly poor. They must have looked gaunt. According to the Tennessee veterans' questionnaires, most were left with a lasting sense of the futility and horror of war. They would not add their voices to those who would romanticize the war.

Undoubtedly bitterness at defeat would plague many. Initially, most were more interested in getting on with their lives and reestablishing themselves with families left behind.[172] Nevertheless, even those most focused on restoring a world of normalcy would soon encounter a long list of problems.

The Civil War equivalent of post traumatic stress disorder left many haunted and hard pressed to resume a productive life.[173] Broken spirits and shattered minds often sought recourse in drink. As always, those with shattered bodies faced a more difficult future. During the war, each southern state sought to provide the numerous amputees with artificial limbs. After the war, those who had served the Union cause, continued to have such support from the Federal government which promptly established an "Artificial Leg Office" in Memphis to serve local veterans. Confederate veterans, however, had to endure a more uncertain support. By the spring of 1866, for Tennessee veterans a Benevolent Society of Tennessee organized to provide disabled Confederate soldiers with artificial limbs. It was dependent on donations and fund-raising performances which were organized throughout the state.[174] At least one local man had lost a leg in service.[175]

Meanwhile in April and May, Federal authorities removed trade restrictions on materials that could not be used for military purposes. After Johnson and the Treasury Secretary authorized the resumption of trade with the "insurrectionary states," on May 11, General Washburn allowed stores to be reopened to sell a set amount of supplies in nine communities outside Memphis in adjacent counties. Collierville was one, but not Germantown. Presumably Germantown could be added since the Secretary provided a procedure for merchants to apply for a permit to open a store, but aside from Union veterans, only established citizens who had long been loyal were granted permits to acquire an inventory. On May 13, Washburn terminated the requirement for passes to enter and leave Memphis.[176] The city and its trade were once again open to all.

Of course, participation in such commerce still required one to take the loyalty oath.[177] No matter how badly they wanted to resume a normal economic life, some locals could not stomach the idea of a loyalty oath. Some felt it was treason to bow to the invader. Others felt insulted that they should have to swear loyalty like traitors rather than people who had stood up for their presumed constitutional rights. Increasingly, however, most bowed to the inevitable. They headed for the Provost Marshal or the U.S. Treasury offices in Memphis, took the oath and began to do business. Between May 15 and June 26, almost three thousand oaths were turned in at the Memphis office of the Bureau of Refugees, Freedmen, and Abandoned Lands that had been established on March 3 to coordinate all such affairs. Although the planters had the most money at stake, small farmers represented the largest numbers.[178]   They had mere survival for their families to worry about.  They continued to pay the highest price for a war to preserve the Southern way of life focused so heavily on the slavery from which they had not benefited.

Finally on June 14, the Cavalry Division began its staged withdrawal from the area, although elements would remain until January 1866.[179]   On July 3, martial law was lifted in West Tennessee, undoubtedly a date chosen to give locals a reason to celebrate the Fourth.[180]   Over the three years of occupation, life in the Germantown area, both town and country, had been constantly disrupted.  One had to endure not only the conscription sweeps and cotton burning by Confederates, but especially the presence of an occupation force, arresting suspected collaborators, confiscating food and property and destroying much of it.  In many respects, the position of the Union forces reminds one of the American occupation experiences in Iraq.  It was an occupation force unable to discriminate among the pacified population and those spying and supporting guerrilla and sabotage activities. Women were hardly above suspicion, for indeed some proved to be among the most successful spies and smugglers.  The people not only endured retribution at the hands of their occupiers for the guerrilla raids, but could also suffer at the hands of those very guerrillas.  There was constant skirmishing, even in the town on occasions, and several modest nearby battles that fortunately did not center on Germantown proper. However, just a troop of cavalry or an artillery team galloping through town created moments of extreme danger.   Drunken soldiers and deserters, like the guerrillas, committed rape and pillage.

Finally more death by disease accompanies any army than all its deadly weapons.  The malnourished civilian population was especially vulnerable to such diseases as cholera, dysentery, malaria, pneumonia, small pox, and typhoid fever.  Even so, during the last two years of the war, families continued to produce children in the face of such uncertainty.  Five old resident families birthed children who survived the war.  Susan Rutland lost her husband and his namesake who had been born on the eve of the war.  They had replaced him with William before her husband's death.  Elizabeth Woodson had a child, but both she and it would die in the summer of 1865.  Something wiped out the entire family of William Wilson, his wife Adeline and two of their infants.  Only little Lucy remained to be cared for by the John Callis family.[181]

For some, however, the story of Germantown and its occupiers did not end on a sour note.  The Memphis *Argus* reported that on May 15, Germantown was the site of a gala, day-long social event involving a pleasant mingling of citizens and soldiers.  "It was indeed pleasant to see the cordial and harmonious commingling of those who were so lately arrayed against each other in bitter hostilities."  When the reporter asked several of "the most prominent citizens of Germantown in regard to the conduct of the troops," they responded that the men of the 11<sup>th</sup> New York Cavalry had "deported themselves with the utmost decorum."[182]

Yet from the article emerges an incongruous set of images. First of all, although the event was held on the lawns of the home of Mr. Moliter, where "the ladies of Germantown were busy in spreading tables," it is not clear who staged the event and why. Captain Smith played the role of host, the tickets to bring the guests from Memphis were provided by the railroad, and some of the special treats for the party were provided by the Memphis company of Mepham & Bros. In addition to the reporter invited to cover this apparent PR event, the primary guest of honor was General Washburn. To start the festivities, the guests, the members of the band and all the company's officers took a horseback excursion the three and a half miles to the "shady banks of the Wolf River. ... The ladies of the company enjoyed the ride exceedingly." Among them was Mrs. Smith, the commander's wife who must surely have had residence in one of the homes of Germantown's citizens. Perhaps also Mrs. and Miss Randall were officer's family similarly situated or guests from Memphis. In any case, "We passed through a deserted lawn, in which once had stood the pleasant house of some one; the rose bushes still bloom, and the woodbines still cling to the (illegible), but the tall Lombardy poplars weep over a heap of ruins that mark the old hearthstone spot. We plucked a few of the fragrant flowers, and the ladies of the party bound up a few bouquets as memorials of the visit to a deserted home, and then passed on our way." A romantic interlude amidst the ruin brought to Germantown.[183]

Throughout the day, General Washburn's headquarters band, also brought out from Memphis, provided lively entertainment. In the evening, "All the delicacies and luxuries of the season" were placed upon the long tables set up on the lawn. "After becoming satisfied with strawberries, ice-cream, cake and confectioneries, it was soon made manifest that our entertainers had made some other provisions for our creature comfort," sparkling wine provided by Messrs. Mepham & Bros. Although the main course was described as "the plane essentials of life," one wonders how such a feast with sparkling wine and delicacies from outside went down with the locals below the level of "the most prominent citizens of Germantown" in attendance. If any remained, did they even have the plane essentials of life by this date? "One of the old citizens proposed a toast to Major General C. O. Washburn, whose actions and policy had proved so beneficial and instrumental in bringing about the present condition of affairs." After the banquet, the general was presented with "a splendid bouquet on behalf of Miss Lou Parish and Miss Nannie (Ann) Woodson, young ladies of Germantown."[184]

Why was Germantown, the town so recently "menaced by guerrilla bands," chosen for this gala event? One wonders how Sherman's "dirty hole" of guerrilla conspirators had evolved to the point that its most prominent citizens had become so thankful and convivial to their occupiers. Were they limited to the old pro-unionists, or had so many of the "middle" come to accept the new order? Certainly Mrs. Moliter had been a supporter of the Confederate cause in 1861. On the other hand, Miss Woodson's father had been an "old line Whig, a strong Union man, was opposed to secession and voted against it, but when his adopted state, Tennessee, seceded from the Union, he cast his lot with her; and all his sympathies and efforts were given to the south." Although he had not served, his son had, and he also had "given all that was in his power to aid the cause."[185] Clearly General Washburn's policies represented such a change that they had actually made "the present condition of affairs" so much better than the desolation of 1864 and the severance of all trade with the city. One has to wonder, however, were similar "PR events" held in other communities?

There is little doubt that this was a carefully staged event by occupation authorities and not some spontaneous local display of renewed harmony. The reporter's presence was arranged and the article was atypical for the *Argus*. The paper itself was an official organ of the occupation authorities, as it had been for the city government before the war. Washburn and his staff displayed considerable sagacity in their efforts to reestablish peace and order and to build on the shifting public mood.

During the relative security of the occupation of 1863, accompanied by the major defeats at Gettysburg and Vicksburg, ardor for the cause had begun to cool among old unionists and many of the "middle." As occupation authorities curbed the rapaciousness of confiscations, at least locally, familiarity also curbed hostility toward the occupiers. The returned chaos of guerrilla warfare during 1864 had reinforced the longing for order and security instead of fueling a renewed zeal for the cause, despite if not because of Forrest's successes. That year must have brought something like the highs and lows of a manic-depressive. The happy participation of the ladies in this festive event probably reflects what one student of their writings has described as "Women's growing sense of self-interest shaded into self-indulgence. ... As hardships mounted, escape seemed all the more desirable. ... (L)ong years of war had to some degree hardened southerners' feelings and had left them insensitive to others sufferings." Of course such behavior was hardly condoned universally, but especially not among the less comfortable.[186] Nevertheless the "grateful" were probably representative of the area's population, at least the majority.

On May 14, the *Bulletin*, published a report of "an intelligent gentleman, of the highest responsibility," who had toured the land south and east of Memphis to ascertain the mood. Careful to keep his disposition and intentions secret, he drew people out in casual conversation. He found only one man "who did not frankly and heartily express a desire for peace and order." They were all weary of war and anarchy, and wanted to get back to work, but greatly needed mules and farm hands. Even the great majority of those who had served as Confederate soldiers wanted to work their farms or find employment. "Those planters, who had dealt fairly with their blacks and had paid them for their work, were all doing well and satisfied with their future prospects. The railroad, now open, is doing its best to accommodate the public."[187]

The men and women who had stayed home and endured occupation had to accept the new reality. Over the years, many deserters and parolees had sought accommodation, as had perhaps also many of the refugees who were returning. Among the expellees and soldiers who had held out to the end, sentiments must have been much more complicated. Many were undoubtedly resigned and focused primarily on getting on with life – longing for home and a return to normalcy. Others retained their self-righteous indignation against Northern oppression, were bitter and humiliated in defeat, and perhaps resentful of those who too easily sought accommodation with reconstruction. Finally, as in all wars, returning veterans felt an emotional divide from the civilian population who would never understand what they had experienced.[188] As this complex mix of attitudes amalgamated, these people would also endure the continued conflict of Reconstruction.

The returning soldiers or their widows set to work promptly to restore their farms and get something in the ground for the season. Neglected fields, destroyed equipment, the loss of draft animals and disrupted labor supplies made 1865 a year of minimal recovery and production. Nevertheless, commerce and subsistence agriculture struggled back to life. The M&C Railroad had been reopened since May, with a daily train leaving Memphis for Grand Junction at 8 AM. Operations must have required considerable caution on the much damaged line, however, for it took a full eleven hours to travel the fifty odd miles. All Federal construction on the railroads had been stopped by order of April 28, but the line was not turned over to the railroad company until September 12.[189] Nevertheless, by November, one train per day was running between Memphis and Stevenson, Alabama, a twenty-four hour trip. At least, this had reestablished the old connections with major southern and north-eastern cities. Passengers and freight were again moving in and out of Germantown.[190]

As late as December, Shelby County remained the only county in the state to have established no civil government outside the city of Memphis. Civil district eleven was without any magistrate, and, without a charter Germantown had no official government of its own. The resumption of both political and economic life would become entangled in Reconstruction politics.

# Part III
## The Aftermath

For a decade after the war, the entire area struggled through a gradual recovery. It is not at all clear that the war was fully responsible for Germantown's relative decline in economic prominence and population. Collierville may already have had advantages in its commercial position that might have led to a gradual displacement without the war. The war damaged both communities severely, but Collierville's recovery was much more vigorous. Although more slowly, Germantown was recovering and by the 1870s seemed on its way to out-pace Collierville in what appeared to be an emerging suburban sprawl from Memphis, a full one hundred years before it finally happened. The lowly mosquito nipped that in the bud, and with it Germantown's recovery.

Perhaps more interesting than the story of a frustrated recovery, however, is that of the social and psychological impact of the war on what had apparently been a relatively harmonious and peaceful community. With the benefit of today's insights into the "post-traumatic stress" produced by war, we can look for predictable symptoms.

# Chapter 1
## Reconstruction

### *Reconstruction in Tennessee*

As before, the larger picture of state politics and regional economy is a prerequisite to understanding local conditions after the war. The Reconstruction experience in Tennessee was unique. The state contained the largest white, unionist presence among any of the former Confederate states. In the east, they had a strong position but were a minority elsewhere. Even in the West, what might be called the old "non-secessionist" element had reemerged to cooperate in a "reunion." In 1862, Andrew Johnson, future U. S. Vice-President and President, had been appointed Military Governor of the occupied state.[1] Thus, Reconstruction began at that point, but in Union occupied middle and western Tennessee. As the war ground down, unionists dominated the state convention and restored a civil government. Tennessee's readmission to the Union came early, July 24, 1866, so it did not fall under the post-war military controls established in 1867. Usually without Federal troops to enforce his programs, Governor William G. Brownlow had to rely on a State Guard. Tennessee was the first former Confederate state to enfranchise all African American men in 1867.[2] As a consequence of opposition generated by such Radical Unionist efforts, Tennessee remained in a state of turmoil from 1865 to 1870, after which Reconstruction wound down in the state.

When Johnson left for Washington to become Lincoln's Vice-President, a self-appointed Radical Unionist convention assembled to form a loyal government in Nashville, January 9, 1865. Its first acts nullified all acts of the secessionist state government since May 6, 1861, repudiating secession and the debts incurred, and to approve the amendment to abolish slavery. With a loyalty oath required, only ten percent of the 1860 electorate could vote. So in February, the amendment passed, and the Radical Unionist William G. Brownlow was elected governor in March.[3]

Until 1869 when the Democrats reorganized formally, there was only the Republican Party. It, however, was divided between the Radical and Conservative Unionists. The Radicals were intent on punishing the ex-Confederate majority for its treason and the havoc their war had brought. The Conservatives had opposed secession, but had also opposed emancipation, and afterward urged a conciliatory treatment of ex-Confederates. Although the Conservatives often collaborated with the ex-Confederates in anti-Radical efforts, the Radicals controlled the state government. They disfranchised all involved in the Confederate cause with franchise laws of June 1865 and May 1866. The Radicals wanted to insure that those who had just lost the war did not regain power.[4] Nevertheless and as often as not, the anti-Radical coalition managed to thwart Radical intentions, and in many parts of the state, could dominate local government and law enforcement.

On January 11, 1865, Radical Senator Almon Case was assassinated in Obion County. Predictably, the killer was a former Confederate guerrilla, and North-West Tennessee was a hot-bed of murderous anti-Radical sentiments.[5] In the countryside, guerrilla bands maintained their activity well into 1866, continuing small-scale depredations and murders. Their less-than-righteous motives were reinforced by a smoldering sense of righteous indignation at the victor and his collaborators, but they had generally lost most of the popular support they once had. Ex-Confederates were not the only source of trouble, for disbanded Federal cavalrymen from Tennessee and some ex-slaves also contributed to the lawlessness.[6]

Despite the continued threat of armed bands, in April General Thomas had disbanded the Home Guard or militia of the state and turned responsibility for combating them over to the civil authorities. Of course, he promised military support "as far as possible." He not only doubted the loyalty of some Home Guards but also feared that many were ardent unionists bent on revenge against more than just guerrillas. To pour oil on the waters of vendetta warfare, he met with Brownlow and approved the raising of state troops, which he promised to arm.[7]

The Radical legislature took up the assignment. The assembly proclaimed any armed plunderer "when in fact he or they were not at the time part of any organized army ... but who sometimes return to their homes, with the assumption of the semblance of peaceful pursuits, divesting him or themselves of the appearance and character of soldiers, are hereby declared Guerrillas and Highway Robbers and Brigands, and upon his or their conviction, shall suffer death by hanging." Also soldiers, whether in uniform or not, who took property were declared robbers and were also to suffer hanging. Former Union soldiers and all loyal citizens were allowed to wear side-arms to protect themselves. With the Sheriffs Act of 1865 allowing sheriffs to create County Guards, the state government sought to combat the brigands, but in West and Middle Tennessee, local prejudices guaranteed that the sheriffs could not or would not effectively enforce Radical policies. Likewise the Memphis race riot in May 1866 made it clear that more authority was needed in the three metropolitan centers other than Knoxville. The resultant Metropolitan Police Act gave Brownlow the power he needed to curb anti-Radical, anti-Reconstruction activities. Ultimately the Radical response was the State Guard Act of February 20, 1867. The army that the governor could raise theoretically consisted of one or more regiments for each of the eight congressional districts.[8] Nothing so great ever emerged, however.

On February 25, Brownlow proclaimed his intention to mobilize the Guard and use it forcefully to end lawlessness, but it would only be deployed in counties that failed to keep the peace and enforce the law. On the same day, he signed the act granting blacks the vote, creating yet more racial hostility and white resentment against Reconstruction. Such a law grew more from the need to create an electorate that would support Reconstruction than from commitments to legal equality.[9] Inevitably the polling station would become a point of violence and intimidation.

Raising the militia companies in West Tennessee proved difficult, although local unionists were desperate for some form of protection. Predictably most recruits were former Union soldiers and their sons, sharing a sense of dangerous isolation. By July 1867, the Western companies totaled only 175 men.[10] None were formed in Shelby County.

During the election campaign of 1867, most of the conflict involving the militia centered in Middle Tennessee, but five additional companies had to reinforce those of West Tennessee, especially to maintain order in the north-western counties, occasionally further inflaming tension. The Guards proved insufficient to prevent the disruption of polling at many rural stations. Ben Severance contends that "McNairy and Lauderdale counties were the only completely peaceful spots in the west," so Shelby must have witnessed some turmoil. There, however, the additional presence of federal troops in Memphis was sufficient to insure that 4,000 votes could be safely cast for the Radicals.[11]

This Radical victory demonstrated a strong pro-Radical presence in the county, to which local Conservatives responded by biding their time and resorting to passive resistance. Of course, the Conservatives and unrepentant Confederates blamed the victory entirely on the black vote, especially in the city, which was a well-founded argument. Despite the *Appeal's* shrill criticisms of the futility of Conservative efforts to woe the black vote, however, the Conservatives had some black support. Among the delegates the Shelby Conservatives sent to their May 8 convention were seven identified as "colored." By today's standards, the language of papers like the *Appeal* was racist and just plain "Afrophobic," especially concerning the alleged gullibility of "the sons of Ham" for Radical pie-in-the-sky promises that would never be fulfilled.[12]

During 1867 with the enfranchisement of blacks and the Republican organization of the Union League to mobilize black voters, the Ku Klux Klan evolved rapidly into a political-terrorist organization to defend against the radical erosion of the old status quo. Four companies of the State Guard had to be dispatched again to West Tennessee to supplement the two native companies. Nevertheless, in August and September, driven by financial pressures, the government reduced its militia army to eight companies. Then when things seemed quieter, it was reduced to four. Finally, the last of the militia was demobilized in February 1868.[13]

Then after the 1868 electoral victory of the Radicals, the Klan reached full force, and incidents of terrorism mounted. For the national election of November 1868, beatings, shootings and lynchings, home and church burnings were among the hundreds of incidents in West Tennessee. Local sheriffs, if not complicit, were cowed into submission. With no militia, the governor could only appeal to loyal citizens to defend themselves as best they could and to keep records about Klan offenders in the hope of future prosecution. Bellicose proclamations by Nathan Bedford Forrest, Grand Wizard, fanned the flames. In September, the Radicals in Nashville responded. An Act to Preserve the Public Peace essentially outlawed the Klan. Then the legislature passed a new militia law, which included a cumbersome procedure for imposing martial law. Fortunately to head off the possibility of a racial civil war in Tennessee, President Johnson made Federal troops available to enforce the law, and this proved more acceptable to the anti-Radicals. Democratic political clubs began to form around the Conservatives, and things looked promising for a peaceful election.[14] Unfortunately the Army proved to be over extended and indifferent to the Radical cause and the fate of black victims. In any case, the infantry units were useless against the night-riders. Thousands of terrorized blacks stayed away from the polls, and Radical returns declined, reducing their strength in the government.[15]

In January 1869, the Radicals began mobilizing for war on the Klan, by this time running rampant. In West Tennessee, Gibson was a Klan hot-bed, but initially no county qualified for the stringent requirements for martial law. Also initially, only whites were mustered into the remobilized Guards to avoid racial tensions, but the threat of black enrollments was held out in the event of Klan resistance. These threats of stern enforcement worked. Many counties promised to clean themselves up, but most importantly, Forrest, issued his disbandment order at the end of January. Forrest was dissatisfied with excesses and undisciplined behavior. Despite the decentralized nature of the Klan and much local independence, many dens complied.[16]

Meanwhile the Guard mobilized, with only one company of 40 men coming from West Tennessee – Carroll County. Then on February 20, Brownlow declared martial law in nine counties, but not Shelby. Then the tide began to turn. On February 25, 1869, DeWitt C. Senter replaced Brownlow as governor when he moved on to the U. S. Senate. A less extreme Radical, Sentner was more conciliatory in general and proceeded to limit the authority of Guard commanders under martial law. The Klan seemed to have drawn in its head in Middle Tennessee, and only minimal trouble erupted in the West. With the Klan underground and local citizens refusing to identify its members, the frustrated Guard seemed superfluous. So in March, reduction of the militia began again. The incidents of lawlessness that occurred seemed independent of the Klan, except in Gibson County. Even so, Radicals in Fayette County were fearful enough to petition the governor to extend marshal law to them.[17]

Primarily, financial and political pressures brought the second Guard mobilization to an end. The Radical party began to disintegrate and Reconstruction in Tennessee began to wind down. Their internal fighting even led Governor Senter to use his authority to nullify enforcement of the disfranchising law in order to beat his rival. Ex-Confederates regained their franchise. The Democrats would soon repeal the anti-Klan legislation and the governor's authority to raise a State Guard.[18] Reconstruction in Tennessee had ended by 1870 with the passage of a new state constitution and the election of a Democrat, John C. Brown, as governor, former Confederate general and Klan member.[19]

The elite leadership of the Klan, having achieved their political goals of reestablishing Democrat and white dominance and knowing that continued lawlessness would only undermine recovery, renounced those who continued the terrorism. Forrest increasingly denounced the acts of the rabble that remained. Although elsewhere in the South, the Klan continued its reign of terror well into the 70s, in Tennessee thereafter, its threat was usually more significant than its actions. Until its resurrection in the 20<sup>th</sup> century, the Klan was a "ghost" of its former self, a spirit around which lynch mobs and local bullies could occasionally rally.

In short, Reconstruction in Tennessee was short-lived. Radical excesses had certainly been galling, but the little they had achieved was soon reversed. Blacks had held few significant political positions and their short-lived force as voters was quickly blunted. The old racial social order had not been seriously challenged. Both the distribution of landed wealth (though seriously damaged) and political power returned to near pre-war norms. Nevertheless, the struggle at both state and local levels had been intense and generated bitter memories that compounded smoldering war-time hostilities.

## *The Status of "Persons of Color"*

The unique situations affecting the newly freed slaves in Tennessee require further elaboration before the full picture of post war life in Germantown can be painted. The Tennessee General Assembly had quickly ratified the Thirteenth Amendment to the U.S. Constitution, and then the Fourteenth Amendment, which specified that no state should "deprive any person of life, liberty, or property without due process of law." African-American men in Tennessee gained the franchise before Congress passed the Fifteenth Amendment. A few black Tennesseans were even able to take positions in local and state government.

Nevertheless, in no parts of this nation did racial discrimination and prejudices abate. In that regard, the Tennessee environment might not have been much different from national norms. The main complications affecting such attitudes were the hostilities generated by the war (and then Reconstruction) and the presence of blacks in such large numbers. The revised state constitution gave the "free-Negro" few rights, and most of the former constraints on freemen remained in place. In May 1866, while trying to legislate legal equality for African Americans, the state legislature insured the perpetuation of race consciousness and ethnic separation with the passage of the Act to define the term "Persons of Color," and to declare the rights of such persons as a separate category of human being. As a clear expression of the pervasive fears of miscegenation and the purportedly negative effects of mixed blood, persons of color were defined as "all Negroes, Mulattoes, Mestizoes, and their descendants, having any African blood in their veins" (Emphasis provided.)[20] Thus was imposed an ethnic identity that has survived to this day, and has become a badge of reversed pride for those defining themselves as African-American.

Originating as a term for young mules, Mulatto had become the designation for persons of mixed "Negro and Caucasian" parents. Mestizo had originated in Spanish settled areas to apply to any person descended from Spanish or Portuguese mixed with Native Americans.

On the plus side, this legislation provided

> That persons of color have the right to make and enforce contracts, to sue and be sued, to be parties and give evidence, to inherit, and to have full and equal benefits of all laws and proceedings for the security of person and estate, and shall not be subject to any other or different punishment, pains or penalty, for the commission of any act of offense, than such as are prescribed for white persons committing like acts or offenses. ...
>
> That all free persons of color who were living together as husband and wife in this State, while in a state of slavery, are hereby declared to be man and wife, and their children legitimately entitled to an inheritance in any property heretofore acquired by said parents, to as full an extent as the children of white citizens are now entitled, by the existing laws of this State.[21]

Thus was annulled any complications resulting for the denial of legal marriage to former slaves.

On the other hand, the act specified,

> *Provided*, That nothing in this act shall be so construed as to admit persons of color to serve on the jury: And *provided further*, That the provisions of this act shall not be so construed as to require the education of colored and white children in the same school.[22]

There would be no jury of peers for blacks, and whites would have no fear of being judged by their "inferiors." Legal segregation, and consequently social and economic inequality, began in the schools as another limitation on legal equality.

Ironically all mulattoes were living proof of the freedom with which whites had formerly used slave women for their pleasures. Miscegenation was now not only a punishable offense for both parties, but it was also considered "contrary to good morals." Like most violations of sexual mores, it was common, but white persons exposed for the crime could be arrested, tried and publicly disparaged.[23] Far worse would befall any black man even suspected of such intentions.

Segregation was proclaimed immediately for the public schools, and there were no ideas about separate-but-equal for black schools. The 1867 Act to Provide for the Re-organization, Supervision and Maintenance of Free Common Schools provided that districts were required to establish "special schools for colored children," but only when their number exceeded twenty-five. If the average of those attending fell below fifteen in any month, it became the duty of the Board of Education to discontinue such a school for a period not exceeding five

Illustration 35. Office of the Freemen's Bureau, Memphis.  Initially
blacks were assigned for gang labor to planters and bound by contract.

months at any one time. No such constraints applied to schools for white children. Thus there was a severe penalty for black families who had to hold children out of school to help with the crops or any other labor – a common requirement in most rural families of any color. Parsimonious board members could easily convince themselves that they should not squander public funds on families that did not "appreciate the advantages of a common school education." Nevertheless, such funds saved were supposed to be reserved for "the education of such colored children,"[24] presuming of course, that authorities intended to audit diligently such monies in each civil district. The language of the legislation implied that only the most elementary level of schooling was required. Local authorities had ample room for discrimination in any district.

The newly emancipated blacks were by no means merely passive recipients of this mix of paternalistic and negative attentions by the whites. Tennessee's former slaves established their own communities and institutions. They created banks, churches, cemeteries, and schools for themselves. To be sure, the local Freedmen's Bureau was there to help negotiate between black workers and white employers and provide legal advice. It was especially helpful with schools, but poor funding and local opposition limited the Bureau's effectiveness. The Bureau and its agents could also be too paternalistic, moralistic, and authoritarian with its well-intentioned efforts. The generally favorable comments in the *Appeal* about the operations and leadership of the local Bureau indicate that when it erred, it did so in favor of efforts to condition blacks to become better disciplined as an agricultural work force in a "free" plantation economy. The planters merely needed to honor their contracts, which most of them could allegedly be trusted to do.[25] In May 1866, Bureau courts for settling labor disputes in Tennessee were discontinued. Assistant Commissioner Carlin insisted that justice was nevertheless being administered by civil authorities regarding labor contracts. By 1866 in Tennessee, half the labor contracts of freemen were for a share of the crop. Those working for wages received $150-$180 a year, including clothing and housing. The transition had been disrupted in 1868 as Klan violence erupted, but by the following year most freemen were again working under contract. Existing black schools were turned over to the state in 1869, and the Bureau terminated its educational activities in 1870. Thereafter, it served only to settle claims until it was abolished in 1872.[26]

The role of blacks in the evolution of the New South plantation economy was not entirely one-sided. Although planters allegedly preferred white to black labor, the supply was never adequate. When blacks found themselves employed in the "gang" system, they resented what was tantamount to a return to slavery. It made no difference if the "driver" was white or black, he was still an overseer. Families were still concentrated in the former slave quarters. Black resistance forced many planters into the tenant system regardless of their desires. Likewise, dispersal of housing onto tenant plots was often a product of black family initiative. They erected their own shanties and benefited from both removal from owner supervision and the convenience of living on the land they worked. Planters also saw dispersal as more desirable and began erecting houses to rent to the tenant. The little worker's villages clustered around the big house disappeared.[27]

Nevertheless, some of the positive side-effects of planter paternalism survived or was forced as concessions to get a labor force. The Sabbath and holidays were observed, along with half-day Saturdays. Tenants had hunting, fishing and gathering rights in the owner's woodlands, streams and ponds. Medical care and the convenience of the owner's store were available on credit, which could be both a blessing and a debt trap. At least some planters felt obliged to provide the truly elderly with shelter and basic sustenance until death.[28]

While blacks tried to take advantage of their new civil rights, many were stripped from them before they could be fully exercised. Civil courts dispensed harsh sentences for petty offenses and prevented blacks from testifying in court, requiring the Freemen's Bureau to establish Bureau Courts to guarantee justice for blacks. When the Assembly allowed freemen testimony, the Bureau discontinued its courts in May 1866. Even so, Assistant Commissioner Carlin complained that "the enforcement of the laws in criminal cases has been very imperfect."[29] A "poll tax" appeared in Tennessee's new state constitution of 1870. Although it was repealed three years later, it would reappear in 1890. Violence could erupt between whites and blacks as they worked out their new economic relationships. In such cases, whites usually had the whip hand. The experience of acting out righteous violence fused with the injustices and counter-injustices of Reconstruction to generate an environment that would plague life in the South, including in and around Germantown.

All over America, negative stereotypes, hostility and fear were well entrenched. Conflicts between white and black soldiers had been common in the Union Army. Fears of "African savagery" evolved during the war into phobic hostility. The departure of "unfaithful servants" from their owners was one provocation. Undoubtedly nothing matched the ire raised by the sight of blacks in the uniform of the enemy. Such "treason" was exceeded only by the insolence of assuming a position of equality against their "superiors." Any incivility towards whites, but especially any abuse of power, became a provocation that far exceeded similar behavior by white Union soldiers. Offended whites vented their spleens in newspapers – even those of unionist bent were not free from expressions of concern about the "proper order" of things being upset.

In April of 1864, the *Appeal* reprinted such expressions from occupied Louisville and Nashville papers with stories of the crimes of black troops. One writer was "happy to record" an incident when "one of these uniformed sons of Ham" took a shotgun blast "that sent his adventurous spirit to mingle with the shades of Hades."

> If a few more of the arrogant scoundrels meet with the same summary disposal, it will be better for the service, and decidedly more satisfactory to all who prefer the superiority of the white race....
>
> ...I have only to say that, had I authority here, I'd end this insolence of negro soldiers, or end the existence very suddenly of enough to exert a salutary influence over the rest.[30]

Although white citizens on both sides decried the depredations of white soldiers, no one proposed mass shootings as the solution. It is not far fetched to argue that nation-wide there was a strong feeling that vigilante violence might become necessary to keep blacks in their place.

After the war, as a manifestation of the fear of blacks, newspapers always identified a criminal or disruptive person who was black as such. When the offender was white, no emphasis on color was felt necessary. The net effect of the language employed, especially of vivid descriptions and editorial comments about the criminal act, was to enhance the awareness of "African savagery" and reinforce fears. Such fears were growing by December 1865, when the Freedmen's Bureau received wide-spread rumors especially in West Tennessee about impending black insurrections. Conflicts between white employers and black laborers could erupt into violence. When the white man was killed or beaten, it was always a horrible or brutal crime. When the black man "had to be killed," it was always justified, and usually because the unreasonably belligerent villain had refused to work as he was contracted to do. There was never a question about what conditions precipitated the black man's rebellion.[31]

Few southerners actually mourned the passing of slavery. As the war had worn down and the owners foresaw slavery's inevitable doom, many began to realize that the institution was far more burdensome than it was worth. The women left at home to manage and fear slaves especially reached that conclusion.[32] Ultimately, four generals and a dozen regimental commanders of the Army of Tennessee would recommend a program of emancipation as the salvation of the Southern cause.[33] For what it is worth, the vote in Shelby County against the constitutional amendment to abolish slavery in the state was a total of 6 out of the 879 restricted voters.[34] Many, however, would constantly recite romanticized images of the loving relations that had allegedly existed between masters and slaves and bemoaned their passing.

Southerners could accept the "freedom" of the black man, but they felt that with that freedom came responsibilities that required the black man to go more than half way in solving the problems of his inclusion in a white world. A widely circulated editorial revealed an absolute certainty about the few reciprocal responsibilities needed from former masters. The "undeniable" mental and moral differences between black and white, and the superiority of the latter formed the basis of all arguments. "Uneducated, surrounded by bad advisers, and completely unsettled by their sudden changes of status, (black) ideas of the rights and privileges of freedom have assumed a wild, exaggerated form."[35]

The author then addressed the contentious issue of the imbalance of power between the white property owner and the black worker.

> Of their own accord we feel assured that most of our planters would do justice to the freedman.... But while the white man should discard all improper prejudices against the negro, the latter must be taught the difference between liberty and license. He must know that the true secret of independence is labor, and that he who obtains a living without some kind of useful toil commits a fraud upon society.
>
> If the freedman accept their new situation with the same confidence and trust that the white people of the South accept theirs, a community of interest will be established between them, and each will become necessary to the other.... In labor, there is nothing degrading; let that be the lever on which the negro depends to raise himself up from "the prison of his low estate."[36]

## *Reconstruction in and around Germantown*

With the broader picture of reconstruction politics and race relations established, we can turn to an examination of developments around Germantown. The last significant military presence in the area ended in February 1866 when the District of West Tennessee was discontinued. Only the 3rd United States Colored Heavy Artillery Regiment remained at Fort Pickering, plus a small white contingent.[37] Unfortunately the "colored" presence preserved a lingering resentment, contributing to the race riot shortly thereafter.

As an economic center tied to the national economy, Memphis accommodated itself to the new order of things better than the rural sections with less hope of a rapid recovery. So perhaps Memphis took most of Shelby and adjacent counties with it and avoided the worst extremes of anti-Reconstruction activity. Even the 1866 race riot would be more a product of socioeconomic conflict between the Irish and black

328

elements than of overt political opposition. After the dust had settled by late 1866, Shelby County avoided the imposition of martial law and more extreme Home Guard enforcement actions in western Tennessee in 1867 and 1869.[38] Consequently Germantown experienced significantly less severe conflict and external interference, although its political leadership would be heavily involved in the struggles over county government.

Well before the end of official hostilities, local government began to reemerge in Shelby County. In September, 1864, the county attempted to resume its governing court, with Memphis as the new, de facto county seat. It began with a judge pro-tem appointed by Governor Johnson, an appointed clerk and an elected sheriff. It was during this period that the previously-described vote fraud in Germantown's district eleven was rigged by the Radicals.

Amidst the continued disruptions of partisan and guerrilla operations, however, there was little hope of reestablishing stable legal and political operations. By January 1865, "the peculiar circumstances of the times" had prevented an assemblage of the magistrates to properly elect a judge-chairman, and the judge pro-tem had to continue in office. Only two justices had been elected from the districts, and, of course, Brownlow refused to allow formerly elected justices to resume office in districts that had not been able to hold a vote, even if they had not "committed any act of Treason." In April, the state legislature was forced to pass a special act to enable Shelby County to appoint its court chairman to perform constitutional duties.[39]

On the authority of the Act for the Protection of Sheriffs of 1865, Sheriff Winters had regularly employed posses of up to twenty-five men to enforce the law. Apparently in response to some mounting tensions, in December 1865, Judge Thomas Leonard relied on the emergency clause of the same act to call up and arm a County Guard of one thousand men.[40]

By the end of the year, still only two civil districts outside Memphis had magistrates to represent them in the Quarterly Court, and there was only one constable. Meanwhile bridges, roads and public buildings remained unrepaired. Governor Brownlow's appointee, Judge Leonard, forwarded recommendations to the governor, whose appointments were finally announced by the end of the month. The newly appointed magistrate for Germantown's district eleven was W. P. York.[41] As was so often the case, his name occurs in neither the 1860 nor 1870 census for the district – probably an outsider sent in to enforce Radial policies.

The county elections of 1866 certainly revealed opposition to the governor's appointments in many districts, but especially in Germantown's. Judge Leonard had exacerbated affairs by vacillating over whether or not to include his office in the election or to continue in his appointed seat. He initially announced that he would run and surrender his appointment if he lost. Then he recanted. Most papers took him to task, noting that the Code required that the elections for judges should fall in that year, and not be determined by his date of appointment. The coroner, who was responsible for holding elections, was committed to doing so, and preserving the results so that any contesting would be settled by the courts. Leonard's position was contested by four others, and he lost by 77 votes. He was even beaten in the city, and received no votes at Germantown. Nevertheless, as threatened, Leonard continued to serve until the termination of the Court's rule in 1867. Across the county, the votes in the districts outside Memphis were unanimously against the Brownlow ticket. Although Sheriff Winter won reelection, primarily on the city vote, he lost everywhere else. In Germantown, it was 74 to 3 against him.[42]

As conservative opposition to Brownlow's regime organized locally, Germantown's political leadership reemerged. By January 1866, when the county's Conservative Party appointed the standing committees for each civil district, William H. Walker, Finley Holmes and James Morgan served district eleven, and for district ten there were Thomas C. Bleckley and Benjamin Cash, both living just east of Germantown. In the spring, Conservatives formed the Johnson Club, as supporters of President Andrew Johnson's conciliatory approach to reconstruction. At the April 5th meeting of Shelby County's club, William H. Walker, Henry T. Jones and Lonallen Rhodes for district 11 were selected to canvass their district for membership.[43]

Over the next years, most of these men would serve as local leaders in the reformation of the Democratic Party and hold positions in county and district government. Thomas Bleckely, a resident since 1832 and former small slave-owning farmer of district 11, had moved after the war to his lands on the east side of town in district 10. He had served as a magistrate for many years before the war. A leading Conservative in the county, he reemerged as magistrate-justice for district ten and frequent chair of the county Circuit Court. He claimed to have been a "very strong Union man," who had changed his allegiance only after his farm had been pillaged by Federal soldiers. In his sixties, he would remain prominent in county Democratic politics. William Walker had also been a small slave-owning farmer, and remained in town to become a dry goods merchant. Despite his role in the district's 1861 secession meetings, he too seemed to have established pro-Union credentials during the occupation. He and Henry Jones, also a small farmer, served as magistrate-justices for district eleven on the county court. Lonallen Rhodes, former wagon maker turned dry goods merchant, would hold various appointed and elected district offices regularly. George W. Small was district constable, usually uncontested in elections.[44] Small had been a planter before the war. To be able to vote and hold office, although most had been ostensibly active in the secession movement, all these men must have reestablished their loyalty before 1865.

Infighting in the county among Republicans must have involved more than the division between Radicals and Conservatives, apparently limiting Brownlow's control. The two county representatives to the state assembly had resigned, requiring new elections in December 1865. S. P. Walker and W. K. Poston, emerged as the overwhelming favorites of county voters. When another election was held at the end of March, an even more overwhelming result returned these two men. The distinct loser, B. F. C. Brooks, who garnered only 101 out of 4,525 votes, actually petitioned the assembly to admit him as the recipient of "the majority of the loyal votes cast." In this convoluted process, all the voters of Germantown were disenfranchised. There was "no poll" in four of the civil districts, including eleven. Perhaps the district had been unable to get its electoral judges certified, a problem that definitely confronted other districts at times. Still dissatisfied, Brownlow ordered another election in December, which was won by W. W. Coleman and Dan Able, with a much lower turnout, apparently also because of uncertified judges of election.[45]

It quickly became obvious to radical reconstructionists that neither Memphis city nor Shelby county government officials could be relied upon to enforce the new order. The bloody race riot of May 1866, the role of some city officials in inciting the worst extremes of that event, and the failure of the entire city government to investigate and punish the culprits made this patently clear.[46]

The response was the "Act to Establish a Metropolitan Police District, and to Provide for the Government Thereof," passed on May 14. Shelby County became the prototype for a Metropolitan Police District of the State of Tennessee, constituted for the purpose of police government and police discipline. The act abolished the Memphis police and removed authority over the police from the Board of Mayor and Aldermen. It sought to create a professional police establishment for Tennessee cities, and indeed had salutary long-range effects. Its focus on the police resulted from the lawless role of police and firemen of the city in the rapes, pillaging and murders during the riot. It established Commissioners of the Metropolitan Police and a Board of Metropolitan Police with a force of up to one hundred policemen. In the event of riot, they could deputize special patrolmen from among the citizens. The police had the authority to operate in any part of the state with "all the common law and statutory powers of constables." Specifically they were

> empowered to especially preserve the public peace, prevent crime, detect and arrest offenders, suppress riots, protect the rights of persons and property, guard the public health, preserve order at elections, see that nuisances were

removed from public streets, roads, places and highways, repress and restrain disorderly houses, houses of ill fame and gambling houses, to assist, advise and protect strangers and travelers...; enforce every law relating to the suppression and punishment of crime or to the public health, or to disorderly persons, or any ordinances, or resolution of the Board of Aldermen of Memphis, or of town or village authorities in other parts of the district in relation to police, health or criminal procedure.[47]

The city and county had to bear the tax burden for this force, which was directly answerable to the governor. The new police jurisdiction extended to the entire county, and the Board had the power to appoint "Patrolmen for special service, or service in places within the Metropolitan District."[48] Nevertheless, divisions among the Board members prevented Governor Brownlow from exercising the sort of control over Memphis that he had in the other major cities.

If anything around Germantown aroused the suspicions of the Board, special patrolmen might appear on the scene to do whatever the sheriff or district constable was not doing to their satisfaction. Undoubtedly it would have required something extraordinarily disruptive to have induced them to intervene in Germantown. The mere threat, however, probably added to local tendencies to make the transition relatively peacefully.

Germantown lacked anything near the explosive combination of economic and racial tensions that had erupted in Memphis. Although the occupation forces for the entire area had been heavily manned by black troops during the last year of the war, with an entirely white unit occupying the town, the hostilities created were minimal. Or so the newspaper report of the town's 1865 picnic celebration for the occupation troops would make it seem.

The tinder for violence in the city lay in the presence of 16,000 freemen and demobilizing black soldiers in conflict with the large, laboring-class, Irish immigrant population that saw them as rivals for jobs and as depressants on wages. The Irish had dominated in the city's police and fire departments. Blacks had been part of the breakdown of law and order in the city, but the papers overemphasized their relative contribution. Increasing efforts by blacks to seek unilateral justice for abuses directed at them simply added to the general population's sense that strong measures were needed to keep them in their place. Local papers totally ignored the outright murder, rape and pillage that ensued in black neighborhoods. Instead they praised the restraint of the general citizenry that allowed the affair to subside after two days.[49]

Readers of the *Avalanche*, however, must have thought Germantown had a miniature version and that "the Radical ideas ...

(were) being attempted by negroes" there. It reported that a detail of three soldiers were escorting three black prisoners – formerly soldiers – to the prison at Nashville. "When the train reached Germantown ... an attack was made on the guard by a party of negroes, for the purpose of forcing the prisoners' release from custody." Firing ensued and one of the prisoners was killed while the other two escaped.[50]

The more detailed report in the *Argus*, mostly corroborated by a sketchy one in the *Appeal*, presented a very different version. After the train had passed the town by about one mile, the three prisoners simply jumped from the box car to escape, and one was shot.[51] There was no ambush and shootout in the town involving armed blacks. Germantown readers of the *Avalanche* must have wondered how they had been unaware of all the action. Their paper of choice was the most virulent in propagating hysteria over the black threat.

Nevertheless, the actual occurrence undoubtedly created a stir among townsfolk and may have agitated whatever fears there were about a large free black presence in their midst. Even so, Germantown's folk may have decried the excesses of Memphis' race riot. Unless some evidence to the contrary emerges, the general picture of the Germantown area seems more like that of accommodation as black and white, rebel and unionist sought to rebuild and resume their lives amid the devastation.

Nevertheless, unhappy with Judge Leonard's continued rule, the majority of county magistrates struck out against him. With Bleckely, Walker and Jones active among the leadership, in January 1867 they ordered a thorough examination of his "financial position." This was expanded to all his appointed revenue officers. All they could find as pretext for a vote of censure was his having allotted funds for emergency pauper relief without the court's formal approval. They then proceeded to draft a petition to the State Legislature to abolish the "expensive" office of County Court Judge as an unnecessary burden on the taxpayers.[52]

Not everyone in the county approved the leadership style of these magistrates, even those who opposed Leonard. A voter from another district described them as rejecting "every account, however just, if it comes from Memphis, and vote for everything that purports to come from Raleigh or Germantown. Representing one-seventh of the wealth and population of the county, these Squires control twenty-five-thirtieths of the power of the County Court. ...Instead of attending to public business, they spend nearly all their time in jowering and in badgering the judge."[53]

Brownlow struck back. In March, to replace the untrustworthy county government, the Radical legislature abolished the Shelby County Quarterly Court as its governing body and replaced it with an appointed

County Commission. Senator John Smith and the county justices questioned the constitutionality of the act in vain. Justices Bleckely, Jones and Walker were active in the protest, and most locals never accepted its legitimacy. Proponents argued that the smaller body of five commissioners and a lawyer would be less costly and more efficient. Opponents countered that the former court of magistrates, two from each civil district, consisted of men thoroughly familiar with the needs of each locality. They knew the state of their roads and bridges, who were really the local paupers in need, and the other specific issues that county government had to attend. Indeed when the commissioners met on April 1, they noted that they needed a map of the county to acquaint themselves with its specifics.[54] It would be two years before they got it - too late for them.[55]

Brownlow proceeded to appoint the Commission which consisted of a president, Barbour Lewis, and four other commissioners, J. E. Merriman, Dr. W. H. White, William Hack, and F. W. Lewis. Without directly impugning the integrity of these appointees, the *Appeal* had run an anonymous editorial ending with the cry, "let the public know the load that has been saddled upon us by the Brownlow clique."[56] It did not help matters that Barbour Lewis, former Captain of the 1st Missouri Cavalry, had headed the wartime U. S. Civil Commission governing Memphis.[57]

One of the early acts of the Commission was to repeal the censure of Judge Leonard and terminate the suits against him. Instead it commended his promptness and humanity in assisting the poor during the cholera epidemic. In their desperation to fight back, the anti-Brownlow faction had taken a petty shot out of frustration with Radical excesses. Nevertheless, to get its work done, the Commission had to rely heavily on members of the old social and political establishment of prominent planter and farmer families, including the elected magistrates like Bleckely and Walker.[58]

In the elections of 1867, the people of the county, especially the disfranchised, rallied behind the Conservative Party. Since most, however, could not vote, they could merely express that support. The Conservative platform embodied the sentiments of those citizens seeking reconciliation. It called for both loyalty to the Union and resistance to the oppression of radical politicians. The rights of disfranchised citizens were to be restored while those of "the colored race" were to be assured. "Military despotism" was to be brought to an end and President Johnson's efforts at reconciliation were endorsed. Those less reconciled, however, denounced the black vote as a tool to be exploited by hypocritical Radicals.[59]

A stumping tour of speakers arrived in Germantown on July 24, but the Radicals' speaker did not bother to visit the town, telling us something about its irrelevance to Radical power. Unfortunately the

Conservatives were not well organized with only a couple of clubs in the city. The civil districts like Germantown's had made no such moves either.[60] Nevertheless, they dominated among the 66 voters of the district. Only 10 supported the Brownlow ticket, which nevertheless won.[61]

By 1868, opposition had intensified with the Democrats reemerging in the county, titling themselves Democratic Conservative. The *Appeal* referred to the party approvingly as the "white man's" Conservative Party of Shelby County. Elections for county offices came in May, with Conservative expectations of further victories. The Conservative convention met first on February 14, with representation heavily favoring the city wards, but each civil district, such as the tenth and eleventh, had two representatives. Local voters were to choose their representatives on February 8. Germantown, however, was well ahead of the curve. On January 18, the local branch of the party met to choose its delegates. L. A. Rhodes chaired the meeting with Thomas Nelms serving as secretary. They chose Walker and Henry Jones as delegates.[62]

Several districts like the eleventh had assembled early because of Brownlow's efforts to restrict voter registration, specifically in Shelby County. They intended to make everyone aware of the need to apply for certificates of registration in time to vote. The drum beat was, of course, to get every eligible white man registered. Previously, Brownlow had replaced the Shelby County registering officer and nullified all of his registrations, because he had certified voters guilty of sympathizing with secessionists. Such an act had some justification, for there had been a flagrant marketing of illicit and defunct registrations. Now, there were allegations that the registration process was being delayed and manipulated to serve Radical ends. Indeed, on February 28, the Commissioner registering votes in the county allegedly refused to accept any more "white" and "Conservative" voters, despite their having been vouched for by federal officers. Conservative monitors claimed that not more than half the eligible citizens of the county had received certificates. To counter illicit Radical voters, the Conservatives called on their supporters who knew their neighbors to monitor the polls closely and have violators arrested.[63]

The officers appointed by the Commissioner to supervise the polls at Germantown for District Eleven were Monroe P. Webb, Wm. Hack, A .L. Thompson as Judges, and Henry Fulton as Deputy Commissioner.[64] Of these men, only two may have been residents. There was a William Hack, Massachusetts-born, elderly former merchant who had lived in the district since before 1850. If a Unionist, he might have qualified. Webb was the Federally appointed postmaster with appropriate connections and long-time residence, but the others seem to have typically been outsiders.

In June, Shelby County held a convention to appoint delegates to

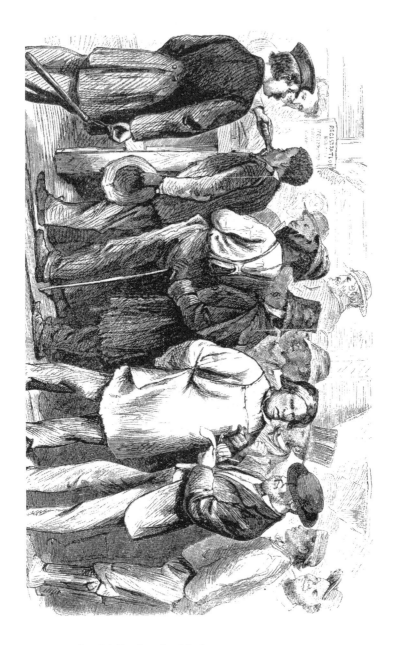

Illustration 36. Registering black voters.

the state convention in preparation for the national convention of the Democratic Party. All Conservatives and Democrats were invited to attend and a complete reorganization of the county body was called for. Among the resolutions that the county forwarded to the state convention were an acceptance of emancipation, but a denial of the freedman's right to vote and have other aspects of full citizenship. Of course, they decried the disenfranchisement of so many white citizens.[65]

The Shelby County Democrats then proceeded to reorganize themselves as the Democratic Club of Shelby County. The representatives appointed for civil district eleven to help in the formation of its club were J. B. Abbington, B. C. Bledsoe, who were not residents. Dissent erupted against party members in the city presuming to lead in organization. Specifically a citizen of White's Station bemoaned the loss of equality that had existed before the war and criticized the presumptuousness of Memphians.[66] So, Germantown's Democrats took it upon themselves to form their own club.[67]

The editor of the *Appeal,* Albert Pike, became president of the county club in 1868. Under his leadership, the emerging county Democrats refined strategies to outmaneuver the Radicals, especially their reliance on black voters. The *Appeal* proclaimed the right of former Confederates to defy the law against their carrying pistols. While carefully denying any affiliation with the Klan, it championed their right to make peaceful torchlight parades through the city at night. Presumably, similar "peaceful" demonstrations of force occurred in the countryside. Even more effective, all good men were called to deny employment to any black man who voted Radical.[68]

The official posture of the Democrats was a restoration of national harmony while denouncing Radical Reconstruction and the black vote. Implicit was a need to defend and preserve the "white race" and to undo the "disharmony" of black equality. In response to the July convention in New York, the town of Center Hill, Mississippi, converted what was to be a social and cultural celebration by its various societies into a political demonstration. They intended to "give a democratic tone to every meeting which is *white* and *decent,* and it was determined that the occasion should be seized on to ratify the doctrines of the Democracy...." People came out from Memphis on special trains to Germantown and Forrest Hill, where they joined residents for conveyance down the Center Hill Road. There they endorsed the National Democratic Platform and nominees. This was promptly followed by the band playing Dixie.[69]

From all indications, the Republican presence around Germantown was predominantly black. As the party prepared for the presidential election, a correspondent to the *Avalanche* reported that on October 1, "Beaumont, Dr. Toles and two other colored orators, of your city, came out to our quiet village to enlighten us in Radical politics, to the interest of None." They spent four hours in town, mostly "at a negro blacksmith shop," but allegedly nobody black or white came to hear them. "General W. J. Smith and about twenty of his colored friends came out from the city to speak to the darkies in Smith's interest. They had drum and fifes, with which they made much noise about the depot, drawing up about twelve or fifteen country darkies..." He disparaged the speakers and concluded, "There was no disturbance."[70]

The *Avalanche*'s partisan counterpart, the *Evening Post*, presented a different picture. Inclement weather apparently dampened attendance. The affair was chaired by Captain W. H. Wood and the first two speakers were white, one a former Confederate soldier. Both reporters, however, agreed that the thrust was to rally the blacks to register and vote, or lose their freedoms.

Predominant in the *Post*'s version was the role of white hecklers. The leader was Squire Bleckley, interrupting "in a very excitable manner." "The speaker was interrupted by Blakely (sic) and others frequently...; so much so that the chairman appealed to the crowd of white listeners to accord to the speakers common decency and courtesy.... But for the indecent interruptions of the unreconstructed, everything passed of (sic) very pleasantly."[71]

This singular picture of black and white politics in the town reveals an image darkly. Local blacks exercised their franchise with uneven openness. Some turned out boldly. The blacksmith Grant Allen and perhaps his teenage helper Arena Andrew were openly in the thick of things. Men like them had to endure quietly verbal harassment. Nevertheless, they could live and work along side the town's white folk. Other blacks would turn out publicly to receive Republican political enlightenment. One speaker alluded, however, to the behavior of many others. "He may promise to vote the Democratic ticket, yet it was not made in good faith, and he yet would vote for Grant."[72] The economic threats of landowners and employers against black Republican voters might elicit promises, but could not compel conformity. They might more likely keep a man from registering or voting. On the other side, while the town's Democrats were forming their club in July, they proclaimed their goal to be "to encourage emigration of the ... freedmen North, to reduce the numbers South."[73] On this point, the main difference between them and the racial policies of many Radicals was the latter's preference for emigration back to Africa.[74]

In the resultant presidential election, Grant took Tennessee by 71,539 over Seymour's 50,376, while in Shelby the ratio was an even higher 5 to 3.[75] This November 1868 election is the only one for which a list of area voters has survived, enabling some estimate of the relative numbers of white and black voters in the Germantown area. Although "race" was uniformly listed as "unknown," comparison with the census lists allows partial identification. Of the 56 voters, 25 cannot be found on any census. Such absences from the 1870 census make it impossible to determine which of the unidentified were black or white. No more than four can be identified as probably black. Although the high percentage of whites among those identified should not be taken as a representative ratio of the entire list, the black turnout seems to have been proportionately low, even if many of the unidentified were black. Furthermore, the almost total unanimity of votes, 52 for Etheridge and Cooper as electors to 3 for Harrison and Sentner and 53 Democratic to 3 Republican in most other cases, shows that local voters favored Conservative politics.

As for Grant's victory, one correspondent to the *Appeal* argued that Southerners in general were hopeful at the results, and that Grant was generally more popular than supposed. He was expected to act consistently with the honorable terms he had granted Confederate solders in surrender. "The people of the South are tired of political wrangling and only desire a fair and equitable Government under which they can return to their former property. ... Instead of wrangling about politics, the people want to go to work and to be allowed to enjoy the fruits of their labor."[76]

For another interesting aside, several voters were actually listed as residents of district 10 in the 1870 census. One could apparently choose to vote in a district where he owned land regardless of his main residence. As we have seen, this also applied to running for office. Such decisions may have resulted from social identities with a community like Germantown. Such a freedom must also have added greatly to opportunities for voter fraud.

The disproportionate representation of white voters in district eleven may indicate that local intimidation of black voters was effective, whether economic or terroristic. Klan terrorism was at its peak in 1868. Even the secret ballot was no ally of the black voter in tight communities. The *Appeal* had encouraged Democrats, whenever they doubted the true intentions of a voter (black tenants implied), they should accompany him to the polls, procure the right ticket, put it in his hands, and see that he deposits it in the ballot box."[77] Even Grant Allen, the blacksmith, had failed to vote. Whatever the causes, the preponderance of white over black voters apparently became a stable factor in Germantown politics.[78]

If the newspapers provide an accurate picture, the Ku Klux Klan emerged in Shelby County in the spring of 1868. While the *Bulletin* viewed it with alarm, the *Appeal* only reported occasional incidents attributed to the Klan, and by and large participated in efforts to play it down, or treat it humorously. It featured a few letters and articles that depicted it largely as a Radical myth. The *Ledger*, published occasional, boastful pronouncements, allegedly produced by the Klan, but also tended to downplay its seriousness. The *Avalanche* was even favorable in its coverage, frequently carrying cryptic advertisements for its meetings and approving its impact on Radicals and blacks. The Klan was formed by and served the interests of prominent citizens. Prominent Memphians attended its 1867 convention in Nashville where they openly proclaimed themselves a patriotic league to uphold the Constitution and restore law and order.[79]

Although no incidents in the Germantown area appear in the papers, there was such involvement. On October 24, 1868, J. W. Wells and Thomas Reasonover were tried for membership in the Klan. Although Reasonover was discharged, Wells was bound over for the Criminal Court's next term.[80] The Reasonovers had settled on a sizable farm south of Forest Hill after the war. As we shall see, Thomas was prone to violent involvements with whites as well. Wells, a Confederate veteran, was the son of the former overseer William Wells. The social structure of this Klan was not unlike that of the new Klan of the early 20th century. Quite prominent citizens were known to be in high leadership positions and frequently appeared in the ranks. They postured as above and disapproving of killings, church burnings, etc. Such "unacceptable" behavior was always attributed to an uncontrollable element whose "unfortunate excesses" were accepted as "necessary evils."

Typically the son of one of Germantown's Baptist ministers, a family opposed to guns and violence, would later comment almost dispassionately on racial violence and the Klan. "There was much excitement and bitterness, culminating in the determination of the white people to regain control of the state and county government at any cost." Immediately across the border in Mississippi where Reconstruction turmoil continued well into the 1870s, fears of the "negroes rising" led to much violence. "It was not uncommon to see negroes parading with fife and drum. At times the white people had to keep the streets patrolled at night." This mood had to have spilled over into Germantown.[81]

The conspiracy of silence about the Klan grew out of more than complicity. Even powerful people found discretion advantageous, while others feared retaliation. One former resident of the town, who after the war had moved across the Wolf to Sangin Church (Cordova), had the misfortune of being impaneled for an inquest into a lynching. For whatever personal reasons, he participated in the typical ruling "death by persons unknown."[82]

During the last of Brownlow's efforts to enforce Radical Reconstruction policies in 1869, the people of Shelby County felt threatened by martial law and militia enforcement, because local Radicals had allegedly exaggerated the Klan threat. Sheriff Curry had publicly denounced what he described as rampant Klan abuse. Both the *Appeal* and alarmed citizens countered that there had been only one such violation of the law since the previous autumn – the shooting and burning of a negro man who had run away with a white girl – and it had been freely reported and condemned in the press.[83]  Unfortunately there is no reliable information on Klan activity in Shelby County.

Meanwhile, voter registration at Germantown continued to grow.  In May, 1869, the *Appeal* announced that the Registrar had enrolled sixty voters there, 38 whites and 22 blacks.  For the election of county judicial officers for that month, the commissioner appointed for the polls at Germantown as judges William Hack, M. P. Welch, and John M. Gray, as clerks F. T. Scott and W. H. Douglas and as deputy commissioner Benjamin Cash.  Nevertheless, the *Appeal* continued to post allegations of flagrant abuses by the Radical Registrar, Williams.  Although he had promised to visit all the major communities so the planters could register without disrupting their work, he allegedly found pretexts for doing so only selectively.  He was promptly at places like Bartlett where large numbers of blacks and Radical white voters were expected, while at Whites Station and Collierville, he failed to bring enough certificates for white voters, who consequently went unregistered, but he had more than enough for blacks.  Unfortunately what happened at Germantown was obscurely passed over with the comment that he "made a very brief visit."  The result of such chicanery was that reportedly there were two black voters in the county for each white voter.   Given such an atmosphere, it was not uncommon for elections to be contested, and as a point of interest, two such hearings were held in Germantown, drawing an interested crowd out from the city.  Contested election hearings were held in a different county from that contested.[84]

Prior to the gubernatorial election of August, the *Appeal* reported that the new Registrar Mr. Boughner had dutifully visited all points of the county, including Germantown, and had described "the interest of the people in the pending election as surpassing that of any former occasion." He registered black and white alike.  Still, the *Appeal* reported gross attempts at voter fraud by the Radicals.  Efforts were allegedly directed primarily at stuffing the ballot boxes in the city by imported black voters, but were generally frustrated.  One recruiter sent out on the M&C on the morning freight going out as far as Collierville found black interests in voting in return for "a little snack and a dram" on the wane.  But most specifically, the four cars sent out to Germantown the night before to pick up about 500 "negro voters" were surreptitiously uncoupled, leaving them cussing and unable to vote because only twelve were known locally as voters and allowed to vote.  The remainders were known to be residents of Mississippi.  They allegedly assembled at flag stops along the line between Germantown and Collierville, trying in vain to flag down another train.  Since "officers of the road were not willing to assist the contemplated fraud in the election, they failed to arrest the train...."

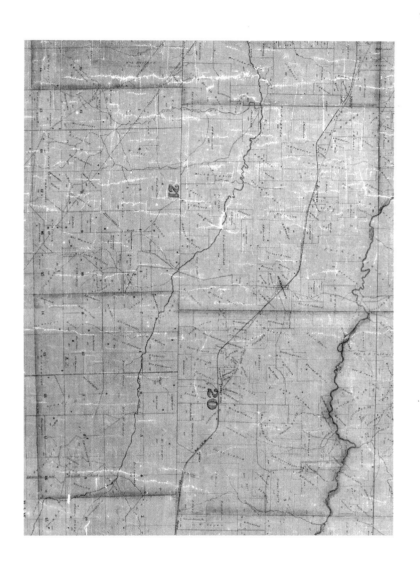

Map 11. Section of 1869 Shelby County map showing temporary redistricting creating new districts 20 and 21 (SCA)

342

John Mills and Moses Rhodes, the local conductors, and Joseph Rhodes, the depot clerk, were among those who frustrated the fraud. The subsequent vote at the town was 242 for Sentner and only 4 for Stokes, "showing a decided turning of the tables, and affording the first evidence of the full growth of the liberty of the white man."[85] Apparently, however, Germantown blacks voted overwhelmingly for Sentner as well.

Perhaps out of dissatisfaction with the trends in election politics, the Radical's County Commission completely reorganized the electoral or civil districts. It replaced the old twenty-seven districts and wards with twenty-five new districts, consolidating Memphis' ten wards into four districts. A new polling place at Forest Hill and that at Germantown served new districts 20 and 21 respectively, while Collierville, new district 12, was diminished by loss of the territory of the new Forest Hill district. The borders of Germantown's district were changed slightly.[86] Exactly what the Commission hoped to achieve is a mystery. Whatever, it did not last.

Once the tide had turned and the County Commission was replaced by the old county court system, the victors immediately proceeded to repudiate all warrants issued by the "usurped authority" of the commission.[87] Thomas C. Bleckley was unanimously elected chairman of the court in 1869, and Germantown area magistrates resumed their leading roles in county government. Redistricting was abandoned.

As the Tennessee Constitutional Convention of 1870 approached, the officials appointed to manage the polls at Germantown now had locally familiar names. Lonallen Rhodes was Deputy Commissioner, R. Weir, J. C. Callis and J. P. Winford were judges and M. P. Webb and William Carter the clerks. All were established pre-war residents. The same men would also serve for the judiciary election of 1870.[88] Since judicial candidates were non-partisan, the marked differences of opinion over local personalities between Germantown's 11th district and the 10th reemerged.[89]

By the gubernatorial and congressional election of 1870, the Democratic Party was clearly triumphant in West Tennessee, but by no means had it obliterated the Republican base. Brown ran for governor as a Democrat against Wisener, the Republican. For the congressional seat, Vaughan ran against Smith for the Republicans, and Edward Shaw for the colored Republicans. When Vaughn spoke at Germantown, the turnout appeared overwhelmingly favorable. Democrats won both races by about a 5 to 2 margin. Yet when Germantown's vote came in, the split was closer at 160 to 62. As elsewhere, Shaw failed to garner black votes, seen by most as a lost cause.[90] Such electoral results raise so many questions about the town's political atmosphere and the lines along which party affiliation were drawn.

By the elections of 1872, the relatively greater growth of

Collierville's reestablished tenth district resulted in the recreation of two polling places, giving some credence to the County Commissioner's aborted effort to divide the district. The western half of the 10th district, more oriented toward Germantown, began polling at Forrest Hill.[91] The political differences between the neighboring districts ten and eleven continued, however. For instance, they split over the effort of the more rural parts of the county to secede and form with parts of Fayette County a new county to be named Nashoba. At least according to the *Appeal*, Collierville provided strong support, but, "At Germantown the white population are in the majority, and are against the new county for various reasons." This vague reference was especially puzzling, since the rest of the article implied that the proposal originated from people interested in having more control over their blacks by separating from the city. Of course, there was no unity in either district, because one of Germantown's "more correct and upright magistrates" was "leaving no stone unturned to accomplish the success of Nashoba" and was openly intimidating the opposition.[92] One would love to uncover the real motives and interests of both sides.

Germantown's citizens continued to expand their influence in county government. Charles L. Anderson began running for county sheriff in 1872, and was ultimately elected in 1874, representing a shift in influence from the city to the country, which was, of course, appropriate since the city had its separate law enforcement. He would serve two terms until his death in 1878.[93]

In the presidential election of 1872, the town's national vote remained Republican in sharp contrast to its otherwise Democratic posture. Grant won 268 over Greeley's 175, a victory which the *Appeal* attributed to Grant's previously overwhelming victory in key northern states. Allegedly, Democrats were either too indifferent to waste their votes or voted for the winning side.[94]

By the time of the 1874 county elections, the Democrats mobilized a fiscal conservative, anti-tax campaign against the Radicals, always accused of irresponsible taxing and spending. Among the 10 candidates running for the 3 positions as delegates to the party's county convention, there were many new entries into political activity.[95] The aged Squire Bleckley had retired and other old stalwarts were perhaps grooming new blood and facing competition.

In contrast, for the state elections of November 1874, Germantown returned a Democratic majority of 76 votes out of the 345. These numbers when compared to the 1872 votes hardly support the *Appeal*'s claim that Grant won because of voter indifference. But in all these elections, the *Appeal* continued its drum beat of the threat of illegal black voting purchased by the Radicals. During the local elections of the previous summer, it warned that a large number of Mississippi blacks had once again been hired to vote in Shelby County. They were to appear at Collierville, Germantown, Whites Station and Memphis. All election officials were to be on guard against this "prospective invasion of the ballot box."[96] It's hard to take this purported threat seriously, at least in the towns where such efforts had previously been thwarted so well.

As the Democrats assembled for their county convention in 1876, Memphis still dominated the floor with each of its wards having three to four times as many delegates as the civil districts in the country. Collierville's district ten, with Forest Hill, also had five, while Germantown's district eleven had four. Nevertheless, Germantown, with its share of district ten's magistrates, managed to play a disproportionate role in the governing County Court.

The area was divided on partisan lines between Democrats and Republicans, as it had been before between Democrats and Whigs. Also as before, the Democrats had the majority. It is impossible to tell if any greater animosity among local political factions had arisen as a result of the war and Reconstruction. It also does not seem that the divide was as clearly "racial" as the *Appeal* always insisted so shrilly. At least by 1868, the blacks of Memphis had organized Conservative meetings, while blacks in the countryside were voting Conservative and then Democrat. Although the Radicals had elected Edward Shaw, the prominent black political leader, to the County Commission in 1869, dissatisfaction was growing among the blacks over the scarcity of appointments and other unfulfilled promises. Typically the *Avalanche* branded Shaw "a Northern negro, ... a representative of the ultra wing of the party." Actually he led efforts to get a better share of political power and economic opportunity for blacks, culminating in his run for governor as an independent Republican in 1876. The power of black voters had peaked in 1867, and declined thereafter, but especially after 1870. The Republicans increasingly lost interest in their cause. By the 1880s, black support for the Democrats was growing, and Shaw even campaigned briefly for Democratic candidates.[97]

Nevertheless, around Germantown, they would make a respectable showing in the district election of 1880. The baton continued to pass, for Walker had finally resigned and A. B. Ellis had moved away. C. M. Callis and James Brett won their seats. Although Callis won a clear victory, Brett beat W. F. Mitchell by only 10 votes, and a "colored" John Graham garnered 87 votes, the same as Brett.[98]

As for Germantown without a town charter, its sole source of local administration was the officials of Civil District 11. Because of the loss of local records, politics within district eleven and the town remain mostly below our radar. While Collierville recovered and reacquired its charter in 1869, Germantown apparently languished until 1880 without a town government. Although most local historians refer to a new charter granted as early as 1871, there are no such records in any of the published Acts or county court records. In 1878, the *Public* Ledger made a clear reference to the town's lack of a charter. Although it certainly could have gotten one during the 1870s, apparently the locals saw no need for anything beyond district management of its affairs. The town seems to have preferred spontaneous citizens' meetings to deal with more mundane issues as they arose. Goodspeed reported, "It was reincorporated, however, in 1880, on petition by R. T. Anderson, E. M. Cole, J. A. Thompson and seventeen others."[99]

# Chapter 2
## Social and Economic Reconstruction

### *Conditions in Tennessee*

Despite all the destruction, the economic prospects for Tennessee in general were not gloomy. Looking forward to the end of the war in February 1865, a correspondent from Nashville published an optimistic essay in the New York *Times*, "The Free State of Tennessee: Detailed Account of Its Resources, Climates, Productions, Manufactures, Railroad System, &c., &c."[100] Its purpose was to encourage investment and immigration.[101]

The author began by describing conditions and emphasizing a major shift in the population that would minimally affect Germantown.

> Since the commencement of the war, at least ten thousand citizens of the North have permanently located themselves on Tennessee soil. Nearly all the cotton baled in this State last season was raised by Northern men. Thousands of acres of land are now for sale in different sections of the State. Tennessee, for the first time during the war, is free from rebel rule, and, with the exception of small nomadic bands of guerrillas, in the extreme eastern and western portions of the State, will continue to remain so. It is the sincere desire of Gov. Johnson, and other prominent Union men, that the tide of emigration may increase in strength, and that the chances for a hundred thousand homes may all be taken, as speedily as possible.

He had less to say concerning West Tennessee than about the other two regions, limiting himself almost entirely to agriculture and the City of Memphis. Memphis proper had suffered relatively little from the war. Physical damage had been minimal, and the city's institutional structure was in tact. River and rail transportation were quickly restored, business recovered, and the population expanded rapidly, although overcrowding and inadequate housing and sanitation came with that growth. Two other major deficiencies, however, would plague the area for some time: a shortage of capital and white labor. Eastern financiers invested relatively little in the South, and local banks could do little more than meet the credit needs of the cotton planters and factors. Thus while the city's commercial and industrial ventures were credit starved, at least the farmers in areas like Germantown got the seed money they needed to begin anew. Nevertheless, the bank failures of 1868 brought a temporary setback, and banking remained unstable throughout the 1870s and 80s.[102] The entire country wallowed in a Great Depression throughout much of the 70s.

For more agrarian communities like Germantown, the economic consequences of the war were significant on several counts. A statistical study of eight counties from across the state revealed that

> The median value of real estate per white farm household fell during the 1860s by from one-half to three-fifths. In addition, slave-holding families ... suffered financial losses due to the emancipation of more than 275,000 slaves, valued by Congress at just under $100 million but easily worth three times that amount on the eve of the war.[103]

Yet the financial losses caused by emancipation had an uneven effect. If anything, it represented one of the greatest redistributions of wealth in the country's history. Of course, the former slaveholders certainly lost the value of their slaves, but they managed to adjust the new system of "free" labor to serve their needs. On the plus side, the former slaves now owned their own labor. Yet changes in the relative wealth or status of the agricultural population were hardly to their advantage.[104]

Statistics and generalizations camouflage the impact of all this on individual lives. Because of its slave-holding history, West Tennessee was the most severely affected part of the state, but the impact was unevenly spread among the land owners as a comparative analysis of the 1860 and 1870 censuses will show. Equally uneven were the capacities of the heads of household to deal with the problems and stresses they faced. Not simply a matter of the survival of the fittest; it was survival of the fortunate.

Although the wealthiest planters were severely hit, many remained socially and economically dominant. Confiscated property was returned when President Johnson offered pardons and full restoration of property to all who would swear the oath of allegiance. The distribution of land and its use was altered, but the actual distribution of land-ownership hardly changed. "The top 5 percent of agricultural households commanded from one-third to one-half of their counties' total wealth, while the bottom one-half generally controlled from 3 to 6 percent"[105]

Thus the most truly revolutionary force of change was emancipation. Far beyond its economic impact, the social-cultural shift radically affected perceptions of human relationships. Beyond being a seemingly indispensable part of the economy, slavery had been the foundation of beliefs in white supremacy and black subordination. The ideology and pseudoscience of racial differences continued to bolster such beliefs. While whites continued to demand deference from blacks, it required new forms of enforcement and readjusted expectations within black society. Ultimately, where black and white society overlapped, a pro forma deference would have to prevail. A different world evolved within black society.

For one thing, the full absorption of Christian teachings by African-Americans greatly militated against acting out. Worse, following in the footsteps of the army's management of contraband labor, the Freemen's Bureau had initially preferred organizing the men into gang labor for plantations as the best way to employ them. That coupled with organized migrations of these men had disastrous effects on the emancipated black population both physically and psychologically.[106] Some were fortunate enough either to avoid paternalistic interference or had enough ingenuity and resources to establish themselves. Across the state, the most self-reliant 10 percent of ex-slaves acquired their own farms.[107] Those who had been trained in crafts were either readily employed or established themselves independently. Most, however, had never gotten a whiff of autonomy or responsibility for themselves, and had been denied achievement of any sort. They were not prepared to operate in a world of white standards, and that reinforced the paternalistic, condescending attitudes of their white neighbors. They were also vulnerable to the predatory instincts of those hoping to create a de facto-system of slavery.

The large landowners had to solve the problem of lost labor resources. Some hoped to entice northern and foreign workers into their fields, but few came. Many planters tried to maintain the old system by using "gangs" of hired black workers under the supervision of "drivers." Between 1865 and 1880, however, the planters negotiated the transition to the New South plantation system. Although they still owned the land, much had been subdivided into smaller farms worked by families under several different arrangements.[108]

While by 1880 in the U.S. in general, about half of the landless farmers rented land from the owners, in Tennessee, over one third had to enter into a variety of tenant farming arrangements with the owners. In contrast, however, in Shelby County less than 12 percent of the farms were sharecropped. Renters had to have or borrow the means to operate a farm independently – draft animals, tools and equipment, and the costs of seeds, etc. This put them slightly below the landowning yeoman farmer. Next to the bottom of the ladder were the "sharecroppers." With little or no means of their own, they remained basically farm labor, working under the supervision of owners who provided everything and paid with a share of the crop. They lived and worked on the land they farmed. Between renter and sharecropper, was the "share tenant," owning some of his implements and draft animals. Such a tenant and the owner split the other costs of operation, such as seeds and ginning, on a set percentage basis. Consequently, the share tenant's share of the crop was proportionally greater than the sharecroppers'.[109]

Tenant farming had already been a preferred arrangement for white farm workers before the war. Although tenant farming would soon constitute one of the worst forms of exploitation, it was actually a step up for many white field hands who previously had to compete against slave labor. They had their own leased homes and lands, and a sizable percentage of what they produced. The same was even truer for black tenants, for they were now free.

Below the tenants lay the farm laborer. Somewhere between one-half and three-fifths of rural blacks experienced little advantage other than nominal freedom. In so many ways, the chains of the past remained. They could only earn wages as farm hands, the most destitute of whom had to support families.[110] The experience around Germantown involved several variations from these generalizations.

### Social and Economic "Reconstruction" of Germantown

By 1870, the official population of Germantown proper was only 162 whites and 35 blacks, down from somewhere around 400 or so whites, plus 80 odd slaves. Despite the 1850s decade of growth, during the 1860s decade of war and privation the town's population had plummeted to well below 1850 levels. Now an unincorporated village, the town was a shadow of its former self. The rest of the eleventh district held reportedly 663 whites and 1209 blacks.[111] The white population outside the town had only declined by about fifty, although most old families had been replaced. The inaccuracies of the 1860 slave schedules make a reliable comparison impossible for the blacks.

In town, only twelve of the thirty-seven white households held over from the 1860 census. With the exception of a pastor, two merchants, a mill owner and one physician, the town's elite was gone. Molitor's mills had at least been rebuilt. The Lucken establishment had been greatly reduced, while both the Southern Star and Hurt's gin factories had been totally demolished, as had the Bliss book business. There are no further references to a brick factory. Likewise all but two of the shopkeepers and craftsmen were gone, so too all the former employees and laborers.

For either the town or the district, there are no records of how many residents had left during the war, either expelled or fled. Likewise, only a few hints of who might have died from whatever causes. Many of those still present or who returned found conditions unmanageable and turned elsewhere. Young Henry Woodson described initial efforts following his return to the family farm inside town.

> As there appeared to be no opportunity for business of any kind, I went to work in the field, with a few of my father's former slaves who were still on the place, and made a little crop of corn, split rails, and rebuilt fences and outhouses, all of which had been utterly destroyed by Federal soldiers. I was married, first, on November 15, 1866, to Miss Maria

Louise Ford of Germantown, Tennessee, daughter of Lloyd
Ford and Malvina Scruggs.

By January 1867, the new couple sought greener pastures in DeValls
Bluff, Arkansas where he "engaged in the mercantile business."[112]

His father's fate was even harder. His home had been plundered,
but at least the house had been saved because it had been occupied by
Union officers.

> So the close of the war saw him stripped of all his property
> except his residence and the bare land; and with no means
> whatever of supporting his family and the few negroes
> who still remained on the place, and whom he felt as much
> bound to care for as if they had not been emancipated. In
> his dilemma he went to Memphis and secured a position, at
> a salary of $200 per month, in the shoe store of A.H.
> Borchert. This, it was hoped, would do until times got
> better. But how rapidly does one trouble follow on the
> heels of another. On June 24, 1865, his youngest child, an
> infant of sixteen months, died. Within a few days
> thereafter, his beloved wife who had been his efficient
> helpmeet in all the vicissitudes of their wedded life, was
> taken ill and died on July 4, 1865.

> Having been engaged in the manufacturing business before
> the war, he owed a great deal of money to northern and
> eastern manufacturers for cotton gin material. He refused
> to take the benefit of the bankruptcy law ... but sold his
> home in Germantown, paid off his debts and almost
> impoverished himself and family.[113]

He had been a partner in the cotton gin factory that had burned on
the eve of the war, which accounted for his debts. In 1867, he even
sought to make ends meet as an agent selling butter churn dashers in
town at $3.00 each. Remarried in 1868, he sold the home and farm in
1869, and in 1871 bought another farm near Senatobia where he lived out
the rest of his life.[114]

Stephen Truehart, Woodson's former partner and now a 40 year-old
veteran, suffered the same financial fate. He, on the other hand, had
more modern ideas about capitalism and took bankruptcy in January
1868.[115] He would hold on to remain one of the town's respected
citizens.

Colonel George W. Trueheart, his father and a lawyer, apparently
found it necessary to relocate to Memphis in his sixties. In April 1866,
the *Appeal announced* that Mr. G. W. Truehart was their authorized agent
for expanding the paper's circulation, accepting subscriptions and
advertisements in West Tennessee and North Mississippi.[116] He was one
of several professionals to depart the town and not be replaced, reflecting

its decline as a center of legal and commercial activity.

In town and country, as survivors and returnees sought about for a new life, they explored many options – different forms of livelihood. Those with land, sought to sell or rent. Renting could provide a source of income while they experimented elsewhere. The Reverend Phillip Tuggle relocated his church positions deeper into Mississippi in 1868. The Memphis papers were especially full of ads selling farm and timber land, business establishments, and homes.

### *Residents Old and New*

Among the soldiers returning, not all gave up on their prospects. Needham Harrison found himself a widower, implying that word of his wife's death had never reached him in the field. He had married Eliza Neely shortly before the war. With deep roots and a viable farm, the bereaved man immediately set to work on his 320 acres three miles south of town. Obviously able to recover, he deepened his roots, marrying his deceased wife's sister in January 1866. They eventually had seven children, five of whom would survive. Like his successful planter predecessors, he diversified, also functioning as a "merchant," and served as County Register in 1886, at which time he moved into the town proper.[117]

The former farmer, 51 years-old Nathan Booth, had apparently lost whatever property he had. By 1870, he was supporting himself and his wife as a well digger. Not only had they stayed on, but had also produced a daughter late in life. They supplemented their income with boarders, among whom were a widow, who worked as a cook, and her teenage son as a laborer, plus another laborer and a teenage girl of undefined status. As before, such mixed households were characteristic of town life.[118]

Among the town's old guard, Pastor Evans would remain for a life-long tenure and continued to teach. William Harrison's widow presided over their former plantation. Isaac Bliss, though probably never one of the town's inner circle, was all that remained of the book agent consortium, and he had lost everything. At first, he made his living as a carpenter, apparently renting a small house in which he and his wife struggled on alone. He returned to something more familiar, for by 1880 he described himself as a "huckster." Rather than being a simple peddler, he was probably more like a traveling sales representative.[119]

The remainder of the town's holdovers survived, barely clinging to respectable middle class status. On the other hand, Lonallen Rhodes, the former wagon maker who had suffered little than the loss of his slaves, now ran a dry goods store and would soon expand into hotel ownership. William Walker and Shephard's widow Sallie apparently combined their families' resources to open and run a general store. Gin manufacturer

Berry Hurt, whose factory had been destroyed, would temporarily support his family as a blacksmith before rebuilding. The merchant William Hack had given up and turned entirely to farming.

The majority of the new residents, including even many immigrants, had moved to the area after having lived somewhere else in the southern states. The community retained or even increased its immigrant mix, but they may not have added the same degree of "cosmopolitan" flavor that many of the former "foreigners" had provided. There were three new people from England, three from Ireland and two from Scotland, two Germans, two Dutch, and ten Swedes. One exotic old woman had been born in Java. Five people had moved south from northern states. Among all 23 of these immigrants, 21 had no measurable wealth. They provided various forms of skilled, semi-skilled and unskilled labor. Only one family born in Ireland possessed some means – Arthur O'Neill, one of the new blacksmiths, and his wife.

There is only one clue as to what brought immigrants to Germantown. The presence of ten Swedes and two Dutch, all living in the Greenlaw compound, was a benefit to Germantown from Memphis' concerted effort to recruit immigrants from among arrivals in New York City. Late in 1865, the city's leaders had sent agents to New York to recruit. The poverty of so many and the high cost of rail fares to the more-appealing West enabled Memphis to attract immigrants, especially Germans and Swedes. The agents simply paid their fare, and by January 1866, they were arriving in Memphis by the scores.[120] As a member of the Committee on Immigration and major employer in the city, William Greenlaw had undoubtedly employed many, and brought these twelve to service his operation in Germantown.[121]

Financially all old residents in town and country were eclipsed by the newcomers William Greenlaw and his son Eugene. They like other newcomers affected the town's social structure and milieu. In the 1870 census, the senior Greenlaw had listed $550,000 in properties, more than quadruple that of just one other local land-owner, also new. His son, also well endowed, was described as an "insurance clerk."[122] These Greenlaws were among the more prominent and wealthy families of Memphis, active in real estate development and investment in railroads and insurance, and major owners of property in the city and of plantations in Mississippi.[123] William himself had been an active secessionist and official of the Memphis Committee of Safety. He fled or was expelled from the city after its occupation, but by 1863 had returned and taken the oath. This act was typical of many under the economic threat of losing their property. Greenlaw needed to collect rents on his property in the city and to bring his cotton to market.[124] Seemingly a defector and profiteer, he may have had mixed motives. He may have collaborated with the Confederate spy, Belle Edmondson, facilitating movement through the lines between Memphis and his lands around Senatobia. His older brother had died in the service, while his two sons, one riding with Forrest, served to the end of the war.[125]

Having a home around Germantown was part of the growing trend to flee the city's filthy and unhealthy environment. The political climate under the Brownlow faction was also probably a source of irritation. The heads of the 1861 Committee of Safety, including Greenlaw, were sued for $100,000 in damages for false imprisonment and seizure of gold that the plaintiff was trying to take North in 1862.[126]

For relocation, Germantown was especially favored for its convenient rail connection. The men could commute daily, or stay in their city houses over the work-week, joining their families on weekends and holidays. Greenlaw was so prominent as a passenger that a new flag stop, Greenlaw's Station, was opened a couple of miles west of the depot to serve his people.[127] Such families could still benefit from the city's social and cultural life by rail.

The home, built in 1870 off the State Line Road was a substantial Victorian neo-Gothic of the sort favored in the city.[128] It served to house employees. Among the non-family residents were another insurance agent, two laborers and two Dutch carpenters. An adjacent house held the Johnson family of eight and one boarder – the Swedes. All the adults worked in service as gardener, cook and house servants. Two other adjacent buildings housed two black households with female heads. Among them were a cook, laborer, nurse (for children), and wash woman. This family empire had a significant social, economic and political impact on the town and surrounding area. His local estate operated as something of a model farm compared to the agricultural deterioration around them, for there were no limits to what he could invest. Greenlaw was highly influential in county government which relied on him for advice and services relating to finance.[129]

An even greater intrusion into the land-ownership pattern was James H. Anderson, who had bought up 100,000 acres. He was apparently a land speculator, who had consolidated such massive holdings around 1869, and was gone by the 1880 census. Perhaps he benefited from the urban flight before the bubble burst.[130]

A semi-newcomer was Dr. John Thompson. Illinois born, he had married Florida Pettit, the former teacher and daughter of Judge Pettit. They had been married in 1860 by Reverend Evans, and settled initially in Mississippi where she had her first son in 1861. They subsequently returned to Tennessee by at least 1864, where she had her next child.[131] Their return may have been prompted by her father's death in 1863. That was certainly a tumultuous time to be moving a family.

Among the new residents of professional status was Dr. Richard Martin who arrived in 1868 with his family from Mississippi. He was

Photo 15. Greenlaw House, later Mesick home (courtesy Walter Wills)

typical of the highly mobile Americans of the 1840s and 50s. Born in North Carolina in 1816 and trained in Philadelphia, he had joined a mass migration of neighbors in 1847, settled temporarily at Somerville, Tennessee, then Red Banks, Mississippi, before Germantown, always practicing medicine and acquiring considerable means.[132]

Robert Scruggs was a new dry goods merchant with a general store, but given the name one wonders if he did not have family connections to build on in town. Nelms Madison was a new grocer who had also moved around quite a bit in his time. He was born in Ohio around 1823. Julia, his much younger wife was born in North Carolina in 1845. His oldest son had appeared in Mississippi in 1854, by an earlier wife. He may have settled in Germantown by 1867. Railroad contractor William Gilmer and his family of five had come from Mississippi, and had also produced a new son at the same time as the Madisons, 1870. Edward Gorman, another grocer and his family of four had also resettled from elsewhere in Tennessee, as had Pennsylvania-born Samuel Gardner and his wife. To supplement his income as a plasterer, Gardner ran a profitable little farm. Then there was Mary Rhoads, a widow of some means in both land and other resources, who had moved to town from Texas sometime after 1866. Perhaps Mrs. Rhoads had inherited her estate from one of the prewar families. Two of her sons were employed by the railroad as a conductor and an office clerk, while the oldest clerked for a riverboat.

Previously the dividing line between the respectable middle class, and those below them had been their ability to have either white domestic servants or slaves as such. Even under reduced economic conditions, the presence of a pool of cheap black labor enabled many to maintain that status image. On a few occasions, a young white woman or girl was available in a household to play such roles.

Further down the economic scale respectively, but still middle status, were Thomas Chambers, an attorney who had brought his family from Mississippi between 1866 and 1869. Then there were John Mills a railroad conductor, William Miller and Thomas Webb who partnered as druggists, William Mitchell a wagon maker, and Susan Burnley another widow who must have relied on leasing her farm lands to tenants. In the 1870 census, Robert McKay, physician, had apparently arrived with limited resources to support his family of six, but by 1876 the *Tennessee State Gazetteer* listed him as one of the town's prominent physicians. Finally Thomas Sanders, who had brought his family from Louisiana after 1868, described himself simply as saloon keeper. Among the non-property-owning middle class, who are harder to assess for social status was Charles Anderson, described as a "self-made man." He was a superintendent with the M&C.[133] Clearly, the railroad was now one of Germantown's significant sources of income and employment. These persons in the 1870 census, many of whom would have occupied positions in the old town's elite were apparently just recovering from wartime losses or just getting themselves established professionally. As in the cases of Dr. McKay and Anderson, they would soon rise to local prominence, but overall, the townsfolk, new and old, suffered relative loss of economic standing compared to the rural landowners.

The remaining white households were those of skilled, semi-skilled and unskilled laborers who earned enough to rent at least a house for their families. As before, below them were the single workers, male and female who boarded.

Among the town's black households in 1870, only two were headed by men with resources to be self employed. On the edge of town was James Scott, a carpenter of reasonably good financial resources who apparently owned his house and shop. Sixty-five year-old Grant Allen, a blacksmith, at least owned his own tools, but apparently rented a modest shop. The remaining black households were occupied by families whose members worked as servants in the white houses among which they nestled or as employees for the various businesses or mills. Five such families were headed by women.

By 1880, among these blacks there would be two blacksmiths, a carpenter and a shoemaker. All were new names, although one may have been Allen's heir. Unfortunately, since the 1880 census does not list indicators of wealth, we cannot tell how well they were doing. In neither of the two households with children of school age were any attending, and the older teenage sons of one were supplementing family funds as farm laborers.[134] It is hard to tell how blacks in the town had fared over the decade of the 70s.

Outside town, according to the 1870 census, 471 whites still lived and worked side-by-side with 1109 blacks. Although the census distinguished between blacks and mulattoes, counting 34 of the latter, there are no discernible differences in their living and working conditions.

Only about twenty-six of the former white farm households tried to reestablish themselves. The rural population was even less persistent than the townsfolk. Those who stayed sought to resume life as quickly as possible, rebuilding with the same self-reliance that the original settlers had displayed. Among them, seven widows and a couple of widowers struggled on alone, the more fortunate with older children to help. A few others quickly found new mates. The regular appearance of new children testified to the drive to resume life as before. The greatly reduced number of physicians since 1860 may or may not have affected the quality of obstetrical care. With only one black woman as midwife, neighboring and family women still facilitated most birthing.

The continuation of the family names of many of the more

prominent planters guaranteed some persistence of the old social and economic order – the Bradleys, Brooks, Carters, widow Cogbill, the Dukes, Ellises, both Harrisons, the Hacks, Kimbroughs, Neelys, Rutlands, and Mrs. Walker – although several had declined significantly in wealth, if not social status. The strange omissions in the census of the Kimbroughs and Brooks can be filled in thanks to family records. Below them, the old respectable farmer families were still represented by the Callises, Featherstons, Myricks, Rodgers, Shephards, Thompsons, and Winfords. This economic group was joined by numerous new-comers, including several black households. They replaced almost all the former yeomen families of lesser means who had left. That element had been more thoroughly decimated. Below them, absolutely none of the landless poor persisted, unless one counts the former slave families that remained.

In the countryside, the property damage to outbuildings and fences, and the confiscation of livestock, especially draft animals, had completed the destitution of the farmers. For several years, those who held on survived on the margin. Those who managed to retain the most were reduced temporarily to the standards of living of the former middling yeoman; the yeoman to that of the poorest landholder. Wives and children worked the fields alongside their men, if they still had them.

By 1870, things had begun to stabilize. Most surviving families had retained their acreage, but its value had usually declined. Yet in a few cases, the value of their real estate had increased, in some cases significantly, undoubtedly by expansion of holdings bought from former neighbors. Otherwise, most families' productive land had been reduced in several ways. As late as 1870, their cleared acreage had dropped by 33-50%, reverting to scrub. The loss of slaves and livestock had significantly reduced everyone's non-land wealth. Even by 1870, the surviving agricultural households from before the war were still perhaps more than a half million dollars below their 1860 holdings.[135] Their horses and mules were fewer, there were hardly any oxen, and the sheep flocks were so badly thinned there was no wool produced for market, just homespun. Even the pig herds had not recovered.

Among the legal and financial problems faced by returnees were reestablishing ownership of property forfeited for back taxes, or held by the Freemen's Bureau as abandoned lands.[136] New taxes piled on top of old, with cash income often insufficient to pay. During 1866, the federal direct tax levied during the war on "insurrectionary districts" came due in Germantown. One hundred fifteen citizens of district eleven paid the tax plus 50% penalty for late payment. With the largest plantation, the Kimbroughs paid over $60 plus over $31 in penalties. The Nashoba Tract cost Sylvia d'Arusmont $95.50 plus $47.25 in penalties. Most of the debt was paid between March and May, but $213.73 remained unpaid.[137]

When state taxation resumed, initially things seem to have been disorganized enough that land owners had a short reprieve, but a new tax law had teeth. In 1868, the tax collector arrived in Germantown on September 18 for state and county taxes. If not paid by November, there was a two and one half percent penalty. In December, it went up to five percent, and in January ten percent. If the tax collector had to seize and/or sell the property, there was an additional fifty percent fee. To redeem one's property, one had to pay all taxes and fees, and if not done before a year had lapsed, another fifty percent penalty was added.[138] Once sucked into such a maw, one could quickly become hopeless. For all the signs of progress in the papers, announcements of bankruptcies and foreclosed sales painted a contrary picture. The names of Germantown citizens in such proceedings were not uncommon.[139] Hard luck would also strike continuously. In December 1866, James Armstrong's woolen mill burned. In 1872, Molitor's mill burned. Even after insurance, he lost $4,000. The Featherston home burned, uninsured in 1875. Ben Owen's grocery store in Forrest Hill with all his stock was lost without insurance in 1879.[140]

Even the formerly most prosperous plantation family, the Kimbroughs, had been significantly reduced. They had apparently sold several hundred acres. The entire family and its plantation inexplicably escaped the attention of the census takers in 1870. Nevertheless, we know that James passed in 1867, but his wife Mary continued to preside as matriarch until 1882. The fates of the oldest son, Syrus, and his younger brother Buck are obscure. William eventually returned to farm some of the family's lands, but had business ventures around Memphis. Albert G. Kimbrough continued to live at Cotton Plant, and served as a prominent citizen of the county and town until his death in 1934. The other brother, John, also eventually returned to live in the family home, but made his way operating one of the town's stores.[141]

The former Duke compound had declined considerably, not only due to the loss of its slaves, but also the value of its land holdings. Robert, the son who had stayed home from the war to manage the estate and family now presided over more than half of the lands, while Britton's widow Mary ruled over her share. With her lived the youngest son, Joe.

Thomas Moore was an elderly newcomer who joined the old guard by marrying the widow Caroline Gorman and acquiring the estate she inherited from her father, the Baptist minister Jeremiah Burns.[142] It is difficult to tell, without family histories just how many other apparent newcomers were tied into old families either by marriage or inheritance.

Several newcomers intruded significantly into the upper crust. Of course, James H. Anderson's 10,000 acres well out-paced the old guard. After the Greenlaws, he represented the most significant intrusion into the former social order. Also another new touch of class was provided by a wealthy settler from the West Indies, Charles Patton and his French-born wife, Adriana. John Hunt, John Quenichet and George Bennett also joined the old elite. Among the many other new names that acquired farm holdings ranging from comfortable to modest, were a number of widows. The stories of these people, what brought them here with the means to buy the farm lands would add much color to this account if they were only available. Even without the details, one is greatly impressed by the spunk of those widows who pulled up roots and came to a new community. Perhaps some already had family ties here, inheriting their property.

Among the northerners whom the state had induced to settle, only two or three had the means to set up as land-owning farmer. Widower Theodore Thompson from Ohio either rented land or was a tenant farmer, supporting his two teenage children. Another from Ohio, thirty-four year-old Joseph Thompson, who must have arrived after 1868 without resources, had to give up and sought a position as superintendent or overseer, for which he claimed to have sixteen years experience. He was ready to pack up and move again with his wife and two young children.[143] All the foreign-born immigrants came without resources and worked for others.

One of the more radical changes around Germantown resulting from the war was the new socioeconomic hierarchy with a more skewed distribution of wealth. Of the 33,553 acres of agricultural land, 15,749 was cleared for farming or grazing. 10,904 of that was owned and operated by 69 resident families, two of which were black. The remaining 4,845 was rented or cropped by 196 families, of whom 174 were black. The acreage they farmed was owned either by the other land-owning residents or absentee landlords. No longer was there a relatively smooth transition down from the elite through a large middle of yeomen farmers to a poor minority. Landed wealth now concentrated in the hands of the top five percent of families while the bottom thirty-six percent were landless laborers.

One man, James Anderson owned and operated land valued at $105,000. It took another six families including the Greenlaws to match that figure. The next 15 families owned and operated $103,195 worth. It took 18 more families to exceed $100,000, among whom the amount of acreage fell off rapidly. It took another 32 families, both owning and renting complete farms to exceed $100,000 of property. Six of them were black and eleven white women. Eleven such families lived off of agricultural income of less than $1000 per year. The remaining $84,000 plus of land was operated by 195 families with agricultural incomes ranging from $2000 to as little as $100 per year.

When other forms of wealth are factored in, the result is a much more skewed distribution of wealth than before the war. Together the

Greenlaw and Anderson "magnates," possessed more wealth than the rest of the wealthier families combined. Some twenty odd families constituted the remainder of the propertied elite, who probably treated as their social compatriots several of the surviving old professional and merchant families struggling to recoup their resources. Another 20 families might have been "comfortable" farmers. Some 40 remaining families in town and country struggled as "dirt farmers," shop keepers, white-collar workers and mechanics, a few working their way up to "comfortable."

Among the nearly 200 leasing farm families, it is impossible to distinguish with certainty between renters and croppers. None operated complete farms, only cleared acreage. The 11 families working more than 50 acres were possibly renters, 7 of whom were black. Another 9, 6 of whom were black, worked 40 acres. 25 families operated 30 to 36 acres, 54 operated 20 to 28 acres, and 95 operated 18 or fewer. The value of the leasees' livestock ranged widely, determining how well they ate beyond what they could produce for the market. Few operating below the 30 acre level had any other non-real property such as furnishings or equipment. Seven black women were among those trying to support a family on 20 acres or less. Among those scrambling to live off 15 acres or less, 15 had to do so without any draft animals to pull the plow. These black and white families lived and farmed side by side and shared all the same hardships.

Another 93 householders, men and women, most supporting families, survived as landless farm labor, while an additional 62 farm laborers, men and women, boys and girls, boarded. The census records that only $9,233 was paid out in 1870 as agricultural wages to these 155 families and individuals, an average of $60 to feed and clothe several mouths. The families, at least, usually had kitchen gardens to supplement their diets, while some of the boarders got meals in the owners' homes for whom they worked. Many people obviously had to find other sources of income in addition to their farm labor. Of these 155, 3 were white householders and 15 white boarders. Absolutely none of these people possessed any non-real property. A few may have lived as well as those with land to farm, but here was a sizable and a truly poor population.

Reported agricultural production and income were only slightly proportional to the cleared acreage in operation. Many elements other than the quality of the land accounted for this, but rarely did one generate more than $1000 with less than 50 cleared acres. Livestock owned probably made a significant difference. Unfortunately self-reported figures make the data unevenly reliable. Among the top agriculturalists, annual incomes over several thousand dollars were restoring some positions despite hard times. Below that level income dwindled down to less that $100 worth of corn and cotton going to market for the year. Two to three bales were scraped out by hard scrabble labor, sometimes without benefit of horse or mule. A decent horse or mule was valued at about $100 or more, but many had to do with animals of much less quality. It is impossible to know how many were self-sufficient enough to eat and clothe themselves adequately, but it was probably a fairly high percentage. Some consequences of all this will be explored in the next chapter.

The most telling decline for agriculturalists at all levels was greatly reduced diversity – they concentrated exclusively on corn and cotton as the only cash crops. Greenlaw was the only man with resources to afford a model, diversified farm.[144] Only one other farmer brought any wheat to market in 1870. Such a risky concentration was undoubtedly forced by their creditors focused on the cotton market. Unfortunately cotton would never provide the financial rewards of the antebellum era, and across the South, cotton production did not return to its pre-war levels until 1879.[145] Of course, they continued subsistence production of meat, grains, fruits and vegetables, but their total reliance on the city's cotton merchants and bankers for credit between crops kept many on the brink of bankruptcy. Such reliance on two crops, especially cotton for cash, greatly enhanced the danger from crop failures.

The problem of credit-and-lender-influenced cropping raises the question of the town's reestablished merchants and their place in the area's economy. Country merchants played vital roles as owners of gins and mills, as middle men in local produce trade, and controllers of local credit. Much local produce may have changed hands under the radar of the agricultural census in something of a reciprocal market. The numerous small holders, renters and croppers were more likely tied to local rather than to larger Memphis firms. Germantown certainly had no Will Varner, providing his debtors' every need and dictating agricultural practices. Its merchants were merely part of the overall, ineffective and often malfunctioning system of credit. Other market forces undoubtedly affected the farmers' cropping decisions, not to mention their agrarian acumen or lack thereof.[146]

Wide variations in the relative productivity of their market crop, cotton, indicated some reluctance to succumb to monocropping pressures. Productive energies must have gone elsewhere. This would have been especially true of blacks who eschewed that crop so associated with their enslavement. Acreage and investment in livestock devoted to subsistence production provided them a more satisfactory sense of their well being, perhaps even a better standard of living and greater independence.[147] As before, poverty was a relative state of being.

The large, new free-black element is of special interest. Among them, many had clearly remained in place or returned to the area, for they bore the family names of former local slave-owners. There were only two black land-owning farmers, but at least 7 others were renting complete farms of widely varying acreage. Fifteen were farming more than the proverbial 40 acres as owners or leasers.

Isaac Harrison leased 80 acres, producing 36 bales of cotton and generating $4,000 income. He also paid $40 in wages. William Carter's 175 acres, 75 of which were cleared, generated only $1,700 income, from which he paid $60 in wages. Lewis Jones got 9 cotton bales and generated $1,150 from his 35 cleared acres, but had to pay $650 in wages to do it. According to the agricultural census, John Bufford was something of a magician, producing 21 bales of cotton and generating $2,710 out of only 15 cleared acres of his 100 total, while Erasmus Freeman only got 15 cotton and $450 out of his 50 cleared acres. Such incongruous statistics do not generate a lot of confidence in the census, but they clearly show the success of some of the local black farmers. Their acreage was more than they and their families could handle, so they employed hands like comparable white farmers. Most had several horses or mules, plus cows, and pigs and even a few sheep.

Erasmus Freeman was one of the few blacks about whom we have more than census records. Before the war, he had lived in Mississippi where he and his wife had three children, and a fourth born immediately after the war. He served three years in the 55th USCI Regiment, receiving a wound in the shoulder, which always troubled him. In 1866, he and his wife Matilda resettled near Germantown, buying seventy-five acres. Shortly thereafter they had another girl. In addition to his land, he had about $280 in livestock. After his wife died, he married Lou, who brought three children born in slavery. He and Lou had two more children, and everybody worked the land from early age. By 1880, the value of his land had dropped considerably, but his livestock and agricultural production had increased. Nevertheless, neighbors later described the quality of his land as too wet and poor to support the family, and he suffered too greatly from his old wound to continue working. By his death in 1905, they had lost most everything of value except the land, and lived pretty much on his pension.[148]

Initially the local blacks did not come off as well as the states' average of 15 percent who owned their own lands. Nevertheless, 174 former slave families now rented or cropped several thousand acres of land, so they fared better than the average elsewhere. Living as renters, tenants, and field hands, all at least had their freedom, legal rights (with growing limitations to be sure), reasonable degrees of autonomy in their family affairs, some possible educational opportunities for their children, and, therefore, a chance for advancement. In the face of what was often a conspiracy against it, they would work hard to take advantage of whatever opportunities.

There is no way to tell what percentage of the area's black residents might have arrived as part of the massive relocation after the war. The adults' places of birth are of no use because slaves were sold around so frequently. The state of birth of the younger children provides a hint of a family's previous locations. A good number were apparently indigenous. Many had clearly migrated in.

A typical black farm family would have two to five children, depending on the parents' ages. Some had children present who had been born in slavery. Such lucky ones had been allowed to keep intact families or had been reunited, often with the help of the Freemen's Bureaus. One tenant household clearly testified to permanent loss of family connections. Eighteen year-old George Jenkins was listed as head of household, with seventeen and twelve year-old boys as residents working as farm laborers – all with different family names. These were teenagers cut adrift from families by the backwash of slavery. Other families had started or resumed their child bearing with emancipation. In almost every household, husband and wife bore the same family name, indicating the high degree to which they had sought legitimate and Christian family status as quickly as it had become available.

Occasionally a family got some extra income from boarding farm laborers, or perhaps they simply sheltered an extended family member. Some like 75 year-old Frank Piggie and his wife Rhoda (age 65) were still trying to survive under the new system, with only the assistance of a teenage daughter. The Piggies were a good example of the relative lack of social support for the under-classes. There was no such thing as retirement unless the occasional landowner had felt the obligation to provide old, faithful hands with a cottage, garden plot and light labor for some income.

It was not unusual for a man in his sixties to attempt a solution by marrying a much younger woman and beginning a family late in life. With luck he could produce some sons in time, but if his strength failed, his wife and young children were in trouble. When both partners were advanced in age and childless, they had to rely on boarders who were willing to share in the field labor. Such problems faced the elderly tenant farmers, white as well as black. They worked until they fell. Older women without families had to find a family, white or black, to take them on as cook or house keeper.[149]

Certainly this picture of black industry belies the wide-spread complaints about their unwillingness to earn their positions by hard labor. Theirs was a life of hard scrabble and depredation, but it was pursued determinedly. They may have shunned wage slavery and gang labor, but they were willing to pay the price in self-employed hardship, if they had any means of obtaining it.

Returning to the overall population, as before, family homes of both colors provided what passed for social services in the community – nursing, asylum or orphanage. Harriet Winn, a widow resident of the town before the war, supported by a daughter who had married a William Douglas and assumed the family farm, maintained in her home a former slave, Ruben Winn, classed as an "idiot." In addition, ten-year old Frank Winn was there as well, perhaps an orphaned former slave, or a child separated from its parents. One of the black land-owners, William Carter and his wife with an ample family of nine, ages twenty-four through two, had an eight-year old son, also classed as an "idiot."[150]   Long-time resident, William Hack and his wife Caroline housed two other white families, Lucy Daily and her two small children, and sixty-seven year-old Sophia Harris, now classed as "Deaf and dumb." Mrs. Harris had a teenage daughter. Perhaps they were relatives. Next door in a cabin, resided Asthen Hack and her teenage son. She was apparently a blind former slave of the family.[151] Undoubtedly the local churches, both black and white, aided the "deserving" unfortunates as far as their meager mission resources allowed, but more about problems with charity in the next chapter.

### *The Problem of Labor – Black and White*

Since most of this picture relies on the 1870 census for data and color, we may never have a clear picture of what transpired locally during the transition to the new agricultural labor system during the crucial period 1865-1870. As elsewhere, these were a troubled and rocky few years during which many land owners gave up and left. From the point of view of southern newspapers, and many northern commentaries, this resulted from the unwillingness of blacks to work the fields as before. This was, of course, considered unreasonable, since that was the obvious role through which they could find their "proper place" in society and the economy. Little or no sympathy was felt for the frustrated aspirations of the former slaves to have a place that corresponded to the contributions they had previously made in creating this economy. As though they had not worked hard and earned anything, they were now called upon to prove that they deserved the place and income of landless farm laborer.[152] Unfortunately there are no local versions of the stories from elsewhere of former slaves vainly asserting a share in a former owner's lands and buildings.

Although the belief that blacks would not work was clearly wrong, for the first two years after the war there was considerable dislocation and uncertainty among the blacks. The efforts, first by the military and then the Freemen's Bureau, often forcefully, to contract them into plantation labor were too obviously like a return to the old ways. Many of the newly emancipated were indeed "wandering the country side," looking for all the world like a vagrant threat. Many, however, were searching for wives and children, trying desperately to reestablish families torn apart. Some searched for more suitable opportunities than gang labor. Ex-soldiers hoped for pension lands. Some vainly awaited the promised forty acres and a mule.[153] With the Klan compounding uncertainties, it took more than two years for the dust to settle.

From late 1865 through 1867, there appeared numerous complaints about lack of labor to get the plantations back in production. In response, there was a swell of enthusiasm for bringing in labor from elsewhere. Agencies sprung up to serve as middlemen promising to bring workers.[154] Few foreigners joined the ranks of area farm laborers. Instead poor native whites and many more blacks became the area's tenant farmers and workers.

For instance, the 1870 census reveals a large cluster of black families who had clearly moved together from South Carolina to settle in block as renters or croppers on one planter's lands. Other smaller clusters of families seem also to have arrived together from Mississippi, while many apparently did so individually.[155] Such mass migrations may also imply that even among blacks West Tennessee had a better reputation than the coastal and deep South plantation regions.

As part of its efforts to help freemen find their "proper place" in the economy, as well as finding support for black orphans, from 1865 into the summer of 1866, the Freemen's Bureau arranged apprenticeships for the large number of orphaned black children, predominantly for farm work. Since this included taking children too young to be meaningfully productive, there was some element of charity involved. For instance, John Stout got five orphans in August 1866, four boys, ages 4-14, for farm work, and one girl, age 4, for house work. This significantly augmented his labor force of the one large black family of Isham and Harriet Stout living with the elderly John and Rhoda. They had 12 children aged from 1 to 24.[156]

For some farmers, this was simply a good way to replace their lost slave labor. Thomas Bleckley got back into the apprentice business in January 1866, taking on three older children for farm work. They were Calvin, Malvina and James "Blakely" (sic?), undoubtedly orphans of his former slaves. By January 1869, Calvin was dead.[157]

By the end of the 70s decade with all its financial ups and downs, agricultural labor and land ownership issues had worked themselves out. The 1880 agricultural census provides much more clear pictures of the farming population, breaking the acreage down among owners, renters and tenants. Unfortunately it did not identify the households by "race." 23 households owned over 100 cleared acres of land. 47 owned over 40 acres, while 57 held less than 40. 72 rented lands ranging from 125 to about 25 cleared acres. 55 share cropped anywhere from 65 to 20 acres.[158] Thus 21% involved in sharecropping locally represented a

Illustration 37. Colored Orphan Asylum, Memphis (Harper's, May 5, 1866) The source of indentured children for Germantown area farms.

considerably higher percentage than the less than 12% for Shelby county in that census.[159]

In the population schedules, which did identify "race," a person listed as "farmer" was "in the vast proportion of instances, the owner of the land he cultivated." 95 white heads of household listed themselves as farmers, only 10 described themselves as farm laborers and another 10 farm laborers were boarding in such households. About 100 black heads of household called themselves farmers, while about 260 were farm laborers. An additional 64 black farm laborers boarded in farming households. The latter included both males and females often of adolescent ages.

The difference in how black versus white framers' wives perceived themselves reveals a different self-perception. In white households, the wife was listed as "house keeper" in all except 3 cases. In contrast in black households, about 240 wives (of the 260) were listed as "farm laborers," usually along with all children, male and female, of at least 8 years of age, even younger. Although white sons, 16 or older, usually worked alongside their fathers, only 3 daughters reportedly did so. Of course, many white "house keepers" had to take to the fields with their families on occasion. It was a matter of both social self-perception and reality that accounts for the different self-labeling. White yeomen families preserved their former sense of dignity in describing the status of the wife. Although reportedly blacks had initially sought such an image of self-esteem upon emancipation, by 1880, at least locally, it had succumbed to reality.[160]

Although white households were occasionally headed by widows, women as heads was much more common among blacks, and sometimes adolescents of either sex had that responsibility. In one extreme case, twenty-four year-old widow, Martha McLemon, worked as farm laborer and servant of a white farm family. Her ten year-old son and seven year-old daughter worked as field hands beside her, all together trying to support her other 6 under-age children, the youngest of whom was 4 months. In contrast, more frequently extended families of three, even four generations cohabited, with everyone of any reasonable age contributing to the field work.[161]

Clearly some white families lived and worked in poverty. It is more obvious that at least three quarters of the blacks lived under the tightest circumstances, many simply living hand to mouth. Nevertheless, land ownership among blacks had grown considerably during the 1870s. This may have now exceeded the average for the state, but unfortunately the comparative data are vague.[162]

As for relations among blacks and whites, some unexpected points of very close contact appear in the 1870 census. Of course, some white land-owners' lands were occupied by their mostly black tenant families and workers, living as close neighbors. A few still had live-in black servants, but mostly they relied on the wives and daughters of tenants for domestic labor. The more unconventional living arrangements tended to occur within the tenant and farmhand households. Several single white farm hands boarded in black households. One of them, eighteen year-old Franklin Harrison may have been the survivor of an old area family. One white tenant in his twenties had a young black woman living with him as cook, and a young black farm hand as boarder. Two white children, ages one and two, were being raised in the home of a mulatto tenant farmer and his black wife along with their infant daughter. The white children had the same family name as a white couple living nearby, but perhaps the black family had assumed the care of orphaned children of their former owners. As late as 1880, the eleven year-old "mulatto," Mary Owens was living in the home of a white widower farmer, not as a servant, but listed as adopted daughter.[163]

Such were the complexities of racial relations. People had grown up, lived, worked and played together, so they knew each other as people. Such understandings existed side-by-side with racial prejudices and widely-held stereotypes to produce a more complex set of interracial relations. Even so, the war and emancipation had upset all former norms producing an explosive relationship.

One surprising occurrence is that black men who had served in the Union Army came back and settled after the war. Of the 225 men in the 1870 census of an age to have served, 93 have names that match men who served in black units. Unfortunately the National Park Services registry gives only names and no other information with which to verify identity. Given that there were several hundred matches for those names, it seems highly likely that many had served. Furthermore, at least 21 names belonged to companies or batteries that enlisted in Germantown or Memphis, where locals were most likely to have gone.[164] Considering the hostility directed at these "traitors," their presence seems most surprising. As Federal veterans, they were allowed to carry sidearms for protection, if they could acquire them. Yet, their presence locally, even their willingness to return, speaks to a triumph over racial hostilities by the immediate desire to get on with life, to forgive and forget among neighbors. Their return also speaks to the power of the familiar in determining where some chose to live.

Platus Lipsey's recorded memories speak clearly of typically mixed white attitudes. There were blacks of whom he had fond and warm memories of close relations. In contrast, he revealed intense fears of blacks he did not know.[165] Every day, blacks and whites lived and worked side-by-side. Both sides usually sought convivial relations. Exploitation, fear and resentment, warm feelings and charity coexisted. One incident at Germantown captures these juxtapositions. On March

21, 1871, Nathan Bedford Forrest arrived in town with a team of speakers courting subscriptions for the construction of one of the many inter-city railroads being proposed at the time. One can only imagine the enthusiasm with which the town's veterans turned out to welcome him. On the team with him was former governor Isham Harris, but also Robert Gleed "(colored) State Senator from Lowndes county Miss."[166]

### *Rebuilding the Infrastructure*

This proposed economic venture was a small part of the dreams and schemes that were fueling an economic recovery that might bring the town back to its former life. The town's place in the transportation network was its primary hope. The first step was to expand that network. The second was to capitalize on how it tied the town to Memphis and the world.

During the war, the infrastructure of roads and bridges had deteriorated. Although the Quarterly Sessions Court had resumed its old task of assigning overseers to maintain area roads, they had a lot of deterioration to catch up with. Again overseers were appointed for all the roads. Without slaves for "hands," all land owners, black and white, were legally obligated to the corvée. Surviving photographs of the crews indicate, however, that they were heavily black. Many of the bridges had been destroyed to deter Forrest's raids, requiring complete reconstruction. This included Germantown's Wolf River bridge. Throughout 1865, a ferry had to suffice. Most of the bridges over the Wolf and Nonconnah were rebuilt during the summer of 1866. Unfortunately the bridge over the Wolf must not have been very substantial. It washed out in an 1871 flood. As late as 1870, the county was still rebuilding bridges destroyed by Federal forces.[167]

Once again, in 1869 the responsibility for the State Line Road was turned over to private management, the Shelby County Turnpike Company. According to its president, once the roads left the city, "there is not a road or a drive that three miles an hour can be made on, in ordinary weather." His company competed for investments with the many railroads.[168] Both the State Line and the M&C were the town's main arteries, struggling through the first years of reconstruction.

After the Federal forces turned the M&C back over to its former management, it was able to find sufficient funding and equipment to resume reasonable operations by 1866. For passenger service, it announced that effective April 1 there would be three trains leaving Memphis eastbound, the early morning mail train and two passenger trains. Likewise, three trains would arrive from the east daily on which passengers from Germantown could come to Memphis. The eastbound trains again made connections with practically every major city in the eastern United States, and were served with "Elegant Sleeping Cars on all night trains." For freight, Germantown was the closest depot for consignments between half way to Memphis to the west and half way to Collierville to the east. To the north, it served from half way to the Memphis and Ohio Railroad. To the south, it had increasing competition for serving the area north of the Coldwater. The State Line Road into Mississippi from Collierville provided better access for much of North Mississippi than the lower quality Center Hill and Capleville roads. The latter actually funneled some traffic into the Pidgen Roost Road, which also offered a more direct route into Memphis. Such road patterns help account for Collierville's displacement of Germantown as the major commerce center for south-east Shelby County and North Mississippi. Another advantage Collierville had was less competition from depots on the Memphis & Ohio which ran farther north of Collierville than from Germantown. In any case, to induce consignment of freight through both towns, the railroad paid steamboat charges and drayage on such freight.[169] Even if Germantown was losing out to Collierville as a cotton depot, the railroad offered it another advantage.

To rebut the constant complaints, including many from vocal Germantown citizens, about the taxes involved in building railroad infrastructure, the *Appeal* showed its progressive face. It painted a picture that would eventually come true, but only after another century.

> The city of Memphis, within ten years, will overspread the whole elevated broad plateau between Wolf and Nonconnah, and Memphis and Germantown. This broad district will be converted into a vast productive garden, the cost of living will be reduced to a minimum, and then Memphis must become a great manufacturing city. Cheap food, a genial climate, cheap, healthful homes, away from the dust and crowds and vices of the city.[170]
> Such are the facts affecting property along railway lines in the city's vicinity. We propose to extend the city far into the country. Nature defines its northern and southern boundaries – Wolf and Nonconnah – and Memphis is destined to overspread the elevated plateau between those until Germantown becomes a delightful, gas-lighted, manufacturing suburb. The whole country will share advantages with Memphis and Germantown, the home of our (complaining) correspondent. His farm will have its insatiable market for all that it produces, even at its doorway.[171]

## The Benefit of Suburban Expansion

Many area citizens took advantage of their location on the rail line. Well located property offered an opportunity to get ahead or solve financial problems. In 1867, part of the Forest Hill Seminary tract on the rail line went on sale in forty-one, two to three acre lots.[172] These were clearly offered as residential and commercial lots in the little hamlet. Along the line, the desperate could sell their land at prices that covered their debts and funded new opportunities.[173]

By the spring of 1868, a developer named Almond had purchased "Forest Hill" (undoubtedly the troubled school) with plans to open it "as a place of resort." Other Memphians purchased nearby lands, putting in orchards and other amenities. The *Avalanche* touted the project.

> The community is noted for its refined society, quiet, law-abiding citizens and social amenities. Being only eighteen miles from town, it is a convenient place for business men to make their summer quarters. Many families have already prepared to go there and to other points on the railroad accessible to the city when the hot summer months set in.[174]

Within a month, a William Ammons had settled at Forest Hill as proprietor with a scheme to use the hall and dining facilities of the ladies institute to host dinner dances that would attract Memphians out to a planned summer resort. With the help of some Forrest Hill and Germantown families, he inaugurated his program with two May Balls. The evenings of dining and dancing ended at dawn, when the special train took participants back to the city. Although Germantown notables also attended, there were only about one hundred participants, because entertainments in the city provided too much competition.[175] That seems to have been the last of Ammons' promotional ventures, and he filed for bankruptcy in early 1869. Although not everybody's development schemes took off, the land from west of Germantown through Forest Hill was being settled by both seasonal residents and market gardens, providing an economic boost.

During the sixties and seventies, the city's unhealthy environment deteriorated further due to political inattention, graft and insufficient funds.[176] To accommodate a growing commuter population, the M&C increased its attention to passenger service as far east as Moscow and Somerville. By 1868, the commuter service provided by the railroad had settled into a convenient routine that presaged modern-day commuter lifestyles. The Somerville Accommodation delivered passengers to Memphis in the morning in time to begin a work day, and brought them back to town at a late afternoon hour. Going east, the Accommodation to connections at Corinth and Grand Junction could be caught at Germantown at mid-morning. The less conveniently timed express mail train stopped at stations like Germantown, but normally skipped the way-stations unless flagged. The evening (6:35 PM) freight hauled a passenger coach to accommodate specifically Germantown area commuters who needed a full day in the city. The car was left at the town, and picked up and returned by the morning freight that reached Memphis at 7:50 AM. By 1871, there was a dedicated Germantown Accommodation train.[177]

As before, train service also greatly facilitated social ties between Germantown and Memphis. Ladies coming out could catch the noon train for a weekend stay with friends or relatives, while Germantown ladies who had been visiting in Memphis would return on the same accommodation.[178] Both the Germantown and Somerville Accommodations paused at every little flag stop in the style of a true commuter train. The latter picked up its regular commuters from the southern parts of Shelby and Fayette counties. These rides provided ample opportunity for making suitable business and social contacts.

In 1872, the *Appeal* ran an editorial that described the impact of all this on the Germantown area.

> The prettiest farms in Shelby county, with few exceptions, lie along the line of the Memphis and Charleston road, between Memphis and Germantown. Annual railway tickets and the reduction of charges on local travel to a minimum have made the country densely populated. Messers. Sam Mosby, Greenlaw, Davy, Townsend, Goodyn, the stock farmer, and many others, have most attractive country homes and conduct most profitable farming and gardening operations along our great eastern road. Two lawyers of the city, like Cicero, find a Tusculum in Germantown.
>
> Esquires Bleckley and Jones report that Germantown and the surrounding country are flourishing in a remarkable manner, and this, notwithstanding the deleterious efforts of the caterpillar, the locust, the backward season and the reform movement. The people out there are bound to prosper no matter what the other parts of the country do.[179]

This leaves one wishing for more information on the insect plagues that had apparently been hitting the area recently plus the allegedly negative effects of the "reform movement."

If the Yellow Fever epidemic of 1868 in Memphis had encouraged the flight to the suburbs around Germantown, events of 1873 fueled it further. It was especially bad with a winter bout of small pox, followed in the summer by a "malignant type of Asiatic cholera" and then the devastating yellow fever epidemic.[180] By then, enterprising people were offering houses in the town to rent for the summer, "for one to six months, if desired." If one preferred to own such property, entire plantations were being subdivided.[181]

*Economic Revival*

As for the town's industry, as early as 1867, the *Avalanche* reported that, "a company is soon likely to be formed, of planters and others, in the vicinity of Germantown, to establish a cotton factory." What was meant by a cotton factory is unclear, but the paper asserted, "We...know that from the advantages afforded by water facilities in that neighborhood, it cannot fail of being a success."[182] This sounds more like the cotton mills for making yarn and cloth. If so, nothing came of that scheme, but the spirit of local enterprise was obviously reviving.

In 1873, the town became one of the post office sites along the M&C that would post the Signal Services weather reports and forecasts. These daily updates with twenty-four-hour forecasts were intended for "the benefit of agriculture."[183] Freeze and storm warnings could help save crops.

At some point the Southern Star Cotton Gin factory did get back in operation. It maintained the Neely family connection, for its main sales agent was the firm of Brooks, Neely & Co., the eldest Neely son's booming Memphis mercantile venture. By at least 1876, Barry Hurt and his sons returned to gin manufacturing. The sons would continue when he died in 1878. They had taken over the production of the Star Cotton Gin. The industrial inventiveness of the town's citizens continued also. In 1875, Fred W. Flynn's cotton-gin feeder was being marketed in the city at Payne's Gin Factory. It had the advantage of being operable by "any man, boy or girl ... a person of the most ordinary intelligence." A gin owner could greatly reduce his labor costs. Such industry, however, would soon succumb to a shift in the planter's preference away for maintaining his own mill as opposed to using the more efficient commercial operations. The market for the Star Gin would dry up. In September 1881, Hurt's gin factory "burned to the ground" at a loss of $12,000 to $15,000 against only $2000 of insurance. No further mention of gin factories appear in the *Tennessee Gazette* thereafter. Instead Kimbrough & Bradley would be operating a commercial cotton gin representative of the transition.[184]

Along with the appearance of sewing machines and the employment of a couple of residents in their sales, other aspects of the modern home were developing. In 1868, William S. Morrison patented a washing machine, but who knows how well it fared in the slowly growing but crowded market for such home appliances.[185] Certainly any who could afford them would have been anxious to do so and reduce his wife's drudgery, replacing the lost services of slaves.

In 1878, the offices of the Bluff City Insurance Company and the Hernando Insurance Company relocated to Germantown[186] New elements of commercial life arrived to serve a reviving area.

Despite the influx from the city of a consumer base for the local economy and new life in the town's industry, agriculture remained the primary resource for most area residents. After 1870, a decline in the market for agriculture, especially cotton, became an increasing deficit.[187] A goodly number of farm and town families sought to overcome such obstacles by turning to scientific farming and rational management. The institution for their support was the Grange Movement. Between 1872 and 1874, the movement exploded with the formation of 1,041 Granges in Tennessee. General Vaughan organized the town's Grange No. 19 on May 26, 1873, which held meetings in the hall over Owen's store in Forrest Hill. Membership grew rapidly from twenty-five to "about sixty – twenty ladies and forty men." Both farmers, businessmen, professionals, and their wives became active. A major goal was becoming "a cash paying people" by stopping their store credit accounts, retrenching expenditures, and intensifying their agriculture. Fewer but more productive acres, better cultivated and manured, would increase productivity and replenish the land. Several young ladies invested in one hundred chickens for the next year's market. Others already raising poultry expanded to turkeys and goose eggs. Grape vineyards and additional acres of wheat for both consumption and the market could reduce cash outflow. Meat was a problem, however, for some infection had apparently hit the hogs for several years, so the Grange planned to collectively import enough sheep to build flocks. The ladies intended to recycle hats and bonnets and to "limit their extravagance to calico dresses" with reduced yardage.[188] A combination of industry and economy boded well for the future, if good fortune prevailed.

The Grange and other encouragements for improving agriculture had clearly had their effect by 1880. Local farmers had liberated themselves from total dependence on corn and cotton for market crops. Their livestock produced butter, eggs, beef, various fowl, mutton and pork. Wool production had resumed. New specialties like broom corn had appeared along with considerable tobacco. Peas, beans, potatoes and many fruits had returned to most farms' market production. Some oats as well as wheat were back to the market, and even a little rice, while sorghum was supplementing honey as sweetener. Only one family profited from the experiment with vineyards, marketing 15 gallons of wine. Forest products augmented almost everyone's income. Unfortunately, smaller farmers could not diversify, and tenants were largely restricted to the cotton seeds the owner preferred to provide.

## Cultural Recovery

The rebuilding of the churches and the town's other cultural institutions were integral parts of recovery. The process took a good six years. From all indications, not only the Presbyterian Church and Masonic Hall, but

Photo 16. Germantown Baptist Church as rebuilt.

most of the houses and some of the shops had survived. Some public buildings like the Methodist church had been so badly damaged by the soldiers that they had to be torn down and replaced. Until then, the Presbyterians shared their facilities. The destruction of many buildings suitable for public affairs left the Masonic Hall to serve such purposes. Its use "exclusively for Charitable and Literary purposes" led the Quarterly Court to exempt it from taxes.[189] The Methodists apparently rebuilt their church by 1871 or 1872.

The Baptist began fund raising in 1869, but sufficient cash was still hard to come by. The contractor's bill was $800 plus materials. In January 1872, Miss Kate Rhodes set about soliciting more funds. By April, Monroe Webb, the postmaster, offered a major contribution for a double-barreled project. He would donate an eleven acre lot "on the condition that provision is made for the erection of ... a school house and church." What he had in mind was a ladies academy. Since the Baptists already had a lot, the acreage was for the school, "on condition that other persons furnish fifteen hundred dollars to be used in erecting a proper building on the property." Unfortunately by combining efforts to raise stock for both projects, he aroused sectarian concerns. He then tried to separate the two projects, asking interested parties to form a Germantown Female School Company and contribute $500 for the church fund, and he would give title to the land for the school. "Let those who imagine sectarian bugaboos, come down with the *cash*, so that the aggregate of public spirit shall harmonize to consummate our project."[190] Nothing further was heard of the female school.

The Baptists continued without Webb. Whatever, his enthusiasm for "mak(ing) fame for the village and render(ing) it attractive and prosperous" ran aground and he separated himself from both projects. On July 15, 1872, William Miller, pre-war postmaster and now Germantown druggist, replaced Webb and resumed duties in his store as postmaster.[191] Webb, about 70 years old, may have passed away.

Strangely, Germantown's post office had reopened well before Collierville's, while a new one at Forest Hill followed shortly. Its formal opening, however, may have come as late as December 1874, when William M. Perkins became its official postmaster.[192] Perkins was a well established local farmer who had settled there from elsewhere in Tennessee after the war.

The creation of this Forest Hill post office deflected district ten's residents from one of their former ties to Germantown. Nevertheless, although they no longer had to go to Germantown regularly for mail, their ties to the town's churches, schools and fraternal societies remained. Their village offered little to compete with the town's stores, especially after its one store burned in 1879. The focus of so many of district ten's citizens away from Collierville, as well as the growth of the district's population was reflected in the creation of both the post office and the separate polling place at Forest Hill. Although most of their political affairs and all legal actions were still seated at Collierville, they remained part of the "larger Germantown" community.

As for the town's efforts to return to its former position as an educational center, the ups and downs of that story are best told in the next chapter.

# Chapter 3
## The Troubled Rebirth of a Community

### *Changes in Social and Cultural Life*

The spirit of recovery seemed strong among the town's citizens who remained. Yet although the Memphis flight to the suburbs and efforts to reignite the agricultural and mercantile economy brought sustenance, the scars left by the war remained painful. As a result, social and cultural relations in the community became more complex – certainly worse than a return to normal.

Although the *Tennessee State Gazetteer* reported that the population had exploded from 245 in 1870 to 700 by 1876, that figure was much exaggerated for the town proper. Nevertheless, there was significant growth and once again industry in the forms of a new gin factory, smithies and wagon making, plus the usual mills and artisans, numerous stores and perhaps two operating "hotels."[1] The town continued to benefit from the nearby mineral-springs. This "healthful environment" and convenience to the city explain the growth. An accelerated "health flight" was moving those who could afford it "to the suburbs."

Perhaps the best indication of how quickly post-war life had settled into a seeming normality was the arrival of the new, great American pastime – baseball. During the occupation, to entertain themselves Union soldiers had inevitably played the game, newly popular in the north, and probably instructed the town's boys who would have gathered to watch. The American soldiers' habit of teaching baseball to the boys of occupied countries apparently dates back to the origins of the sport. As early as 1866, the fad of organized ball clubs in New York had sparked the formation of clubs in Memphis. By June of 1868, the *Appeal* announced that a Germantown Club was challenging the reigning champions, "Bluff City."[2] The sport thrived with a ball field lying between the Presbyterian Church and the Masonic Hall.[3]

But the town was never able to field anything that could compete with Memphis' premier team. In 1876, they challenged the Memphis Reds, and were trounced 38 to nothing. Among the competition, Germantown, one of many "village clubs," was classed among the "rustic nines" in the tri-state area. This implied something like a rural league, but they had all been thoroughly beaten by the Reds.[4] One has to wonder, was there a massive commute by the town's supporters to such a game in Memphis? What sort of festivities accompanied home games? What did the uniforms look like?

Despite this and other signs of positive social and cultural renewal, the wounds of war remained deep and poisonous. Although the war had little lasting effect on the work-a-day lives of each of the respective social classes, there were sinister changes in the underlying mood among them. Some of the social analysis previously explored suggests that class consciousness of the "poor" and animosity toward the privileged increased. Likewise, the propertied had become more defensive. Some evidence supports these arguments. Certainly the trauma of the war and the depressive nature of the immediate post-war environment had significantly negative psychological impact. Elsewhere, memoirs indicate that for the veterans there were post-traumatic consequences: frightful dreams, the hollow stare, uncommunicative depressive withdrawal, and bouts of uncontrollable rage. They manifested unhealthy, dysfunctional behavior, including alcoholism, family abuse and increased violence.[5]

The presence in town of four outright saloons, as opposed to the former store/saloon combination, may indicate a behavioral shift. Inebriation would be less inhibited, given the absence of women and children in an environment devoted totally to drink. Old time residents remember being told by their parents that in post-war Germantown and Mid-South towns in general, women had to stay off the streets on Saturday nights because the town's saloon scene had become so wild.[6]

According to their letters and diaries, women all over the South suffered their own versions of post-traumatic stress which were compounded by the need to succor their damaged men folk and compensate for their frequently inadequate ability to cope with the new economic environment. During the early years they described feeling drowsy, lethargic, and benumbed. Many underwent a crisis of faith which usually redounded in intensified spiritual reliance. They certainly did not seek liberation from their former status and roles. If anything they sought the return of a romanticized version. Yet at the same time, they were more ambivalent about being so reliant on men who had failed to preserve their security or to restore their means after the war. The public burdens they had assumed were freely shed. Self-interest eroded their former ideal of selfless service. They were more focused on self and family than ever before.[7] Unfortunately, we have only faint hints of how much such mental conditions actually emerged among Germantown's women.

There is also evidence that the pre-war, peaceful and law-abiding atmosphere that had prevailed locally had changed. Although there are no newspaper reports of abuse against women in the area, except one case in Collierville, after the war it had increasingly become a problem in Shelby County in general and Memphis in particular.[8] The abuse of children, spouses and lovers is frequently the result of defeat in life and the related degradation of their men. Its correlation with drink was refueling the fires of the temperance movement.

Germantown proponents participated in one temperance event held in Collierville in 1876. It was a debate on the subject "Is it expedient for congress to legislate upon the manufacture and sale of intoxicating liquors as a beverage?" An unnamed reverend from Germantown was one of the two-man jury or umpires. Perhaps this was Reverend Evans, so prominent in the movement before, or perhaps the Baptist minister. Of the two-man debate teams, Mr. Perkins of Germantown argued for the affirmative, while Dr. M'Kay was for the negative. One has to doubt the doctor's sincerity, however, for the reporter commented that King Alcohol did not get a fair and impartial trial. "The jury was not composed of his peers." The two gentlemen were probably Wilson Perkins, a sixty-six year-old farmer and Dr. Robert McKay. Miss Fannie Burnley, the daughter of the widowed farm owner Susan Burnley, was also involved, as Germantown women continued to insert themselves more publicly in their causes.[9] Theirs was a voice of concern over growing social problems.

There may indeed have been an effort by local officials to crack down on drunkenness. A Collierville wit, an "occasional correspondent" of the *Appeal,* warned travelers to stay away from Germantown. "They fine a man twenty-five dollars and cost in Germantown for a single drunk, when it only costs five dollars and cost at Collierville."[10] Unfortunately this correspondent had a penchant for humor at the expense of accuracy, something newspapers encouraged, for readers apparently enjoyed it. This was about the same time that another wit reported that the town was <u>once</u> full of drunken brawls, whiskey-shops, and roaring old debauchees, before remedial measures had been taken.[11]

The battle over "demon rum" added to the town's social tensions, although it was probably the least serious political and social conflict. By 1878, one observer described the opposite sides as "golden rule fellows, Mamma Pets and temperance lecturers" versus the "b'hoy's, Gander Pullers, and the Kangaroo Court." B'hoys and Gander Pullers were simply good-'ol-boys, but the latter term seems to have referred to a specific drinking cohort in town. His references to members of the Kangaroo Court implies they had been prominent and respected community leaders, some of whom gave their lives in service during the epidemic of 1878. The temperance lecturers allegedly had little real support or effect except in so far as some of the Kangarooians "resigned on account of their 'girls'."[12]

Eventually more than a few would be "resigning." Ministers like the Baptist J. W. Lipsey ardently preached temperance, preferably total abstinence, and ultimately prohibition. The crusaders of Germantown would finally have a triumph in 1890, cowing their husbands into submission and temporarily shutting down the town's four saloons.[13]

There were worse problems. Before the war, never a day had passed that Memphis papers failed to report crimes like theft, burglary,

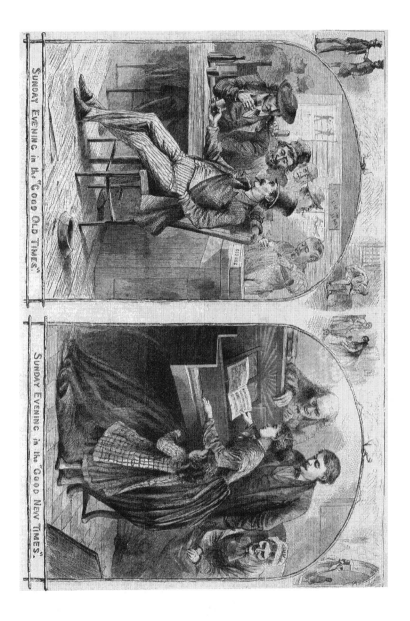

Illustration 38. Temperance Ideals  Harper's (April 13, 1867) contrasting of saloon life with that of the ideal sober home life.

violent beatings and murder in the city. Impressionistically, it appears that after the war there was a significant increase in reports of all such crimes. Reports of crime outside the city had been rare before the war, while after there was a definite increase, particularly around Germantown.[14] At first they were war related. The crimes committed by the regulars and partisans on both sides, ranging from plundering to murder, had helped to establish an environment. As the war wore on, the criminal activities of guerrillas and robber bands had increased.

The end of hostilities only brought a shift from groups disguised as guerrillas to outright robber bands. Although nothing as infamous as the James-Younger gang appeared in Shelby County, the atmosphere that produced them west of the Mississippi also prevailed locally. Indeed during the 1870s, "Mr. Howard" and brother hid in Nashville for several years and allegedly had "safe houses" in rural Tennessee counties. Locally, the threat varied widely from robber gangs operating with seeming impunity, through small teams of highwaymen, to groups of livestock rustlers.

In May 1866, a band of thieves had taken up residence in some woodland off the Germantown road a few miles from Memphis. Men or women traveling to and from Germantown were regularly robbed. Farmers desperately trying "to make up a little of what they lost while the 'cruel war' was raging" were robbed of what they had earned after delivering their produce to the city.[15]

Throughout 1866 and 1867, "cattle thieves" were stealing so many cows, pigs and chickens from local farmers that the costs of such foods in the city were high and the farmers were "impoverished." One Councilman argued that outside the city, "murder, robbery, burglary, arson, and crimes of every character have become so prevalent as to render both life and property notoriously insecure...." The Metropolitan Police got requests daily for patrolmen to come out to places as far afield as Germantown. Citizens' pleaded for an extra mounted sheriff's patrol to cover the fifteen mile radius around the city (that included Germantown). Unfortunately when both the sheriff and the Superintendent of Metropolitan Police applied to the County Commission for such a force, it was denied for lack of a petition "from the citizens wishing such a force with a full knowledge of the cost." Since the appeal for law enforcement failed, a suspect would occasionally be found hanging from a tree.[16] Despite the potential punishment, horse thieves continued to plague Germantown area farmers throughout the 70s, even brazenly selling their stolen animals in the town itself.[17] For a while in 1876, the town also suffered an infestation of burglars.[18]

In 1867, a true outlaw gang was operating from the Loosahatchie bottoms like their partisan predecessors. By 1868, a well-organized gang of horse and cattle thieves were sweeping the river-tier counties of

Tennessee and Mississippi, with bases in Cairo, Illinois, Jackson and Lafayette, Tennessee and Grenada, Mississippi. Their rustling operations had exceeded all previous depredations. This was a mixed gang of blacks and whites, with the whites generally fencing the stolen animals. One prominent operator, however, was black. Governor Brownlow took the blame for recently pardoning this John Niles in a reversal of the County Circuit Court. They had sent Niles to the penitentiary in 1866 for robbery near Germantown.[19]

In 1869, a threatening group seems to have been afoot around Collierville. What they were doing remains unclear because the one report in the *Appeal* was cryptic. In a notice dated September 6, the citizens of Collierville and vicinity responded "to certain incendiary threats" with a published resolution:

> That, whereas, this community has been thrown into a state of alarm by the threats of some evil designed person or persons to burn the town, in case a certain events took place, which are unavoidable to the citizens of the place and entirely beyond their control, and in consideration of said threats, we, the citizens assembled, do deprecate the spirit and motives which acuates and prompts such incendiary threats; therefore
>
> *Resolved*, that we...will do whatever is in out power to detect and bring to punishment any and every person who may be found guilty of circulating such incendiary threats....[20]

Whatever threat provoked this public warning, obviously the citizens along the ridge were ready to take matters into their own hands.

By 1870, country folk were so dissatisfied with efforts to curb crime that they petitioned the state constitutional convention to divide Shelby County, creating a separate Memphis County to consist of the city and its immediate suburbs. They contended that city-oriented courts were so indifferent to their needs that it was not worth the time and expense for country residents to prosecute a case. Consequently, "when things get too bad Judge Lynch steps in and gives a lesson or two."[21]

The same was true when it came to the threat of highwaymen. They were operating along every major road out of Memphis, but also along the lesser byways, and the network running out of Germantown was no exception. On September 9, 1867, the district's Constable Rhodes delivered to the Memphis jail one T. L. Hill, "a white lad, seemingly not more than eighteen years of age, but possessing a most sinister cast of countenance, charged with the double crime of attempted robbery and murder, on the highway." This "foot-pad," apparently a drifter, had been skulking around Germantown for several days, scouting out the area roads for suitable places of ambush. In need of an accomplice, he had approached a black laborer from a nearby farm. While pretending to cooperate, he immediately reported the case to his employer, who instructed him to go along and to keep him informed of the plans. The farmer proceeded to assemble a party to apprehend the criminal in the act. Somehow, the pretended accomplice was clever enough to "secretly withdraw the charges from a formidable revolver, and thus render harmless the intended instrument of the murder." Indeed when two suitable looking victims approached and Hill sprang out to "demand his money or his life" from the white man who seemed to resist, Hill tried three times in vain to shoot his victim. He was then seized by the party of vigilantes and turned over to the constable.[22]

Shortly thereafter, Sheriff Winter's deputy arrested a black man named John Ethling, also hiding on a plantation near Germantown. He had murdered Dr. M. R. Ramsey on the Raleigh Road, and was planning highway robberies in the neighborhood when a would-be accomplice reported him.[23] In the previous year, a squad of Pinkerton detectives showed up near the town to arrest one of the men involved in the robbery of a Southern Express messenger in Memphis. He too had been hiding in a black man's cabin. This band of robbers had also included both white and black men. The description of the Pinkerton's overwhelming display of firepower was like a comic scene from an old movie when the wide-eyed villain suddenly found himself surrounded by dozens of cocked pistols.[24]

In short, in contrast to the peaceful pre-war atmosphere, the citizens of the town had reason to fear the presence of organized criminals, often transients. The war had left so many men rootless and criminalized. In March 1875, one man walking along the tracks from Collierville toward Memphis fell in with two others, and they were observed by some citizens of Germantown camping by the tracks that evening. The next morning he was found dead, robbed of all valuable property. Also unlike before the war, the county no longer provided for pauper burial, for the townsmen simply buried his body where they had found it.[25]

Despite the *Appeal* and *Avalanche*'s constant, shrill efforts to propagate hysterical fear of black criminality, the involvement of Germantown's black citizens in crime seems hardly proportional to their numbers. Among them, during 1870 and 1871, there were three black on black crimes. Maryland Johnson had abandoned his wife and children to settle in Memphis where he killed another man. Steve Perkins had murdered an unnamed man in Germantown. Joseph Phillips had broken into the house of Henry Lewis to steal his gun and kill him, but was caught in time. One incident of a black attempt on a white man was a non-fatal shooting in 1870.[26]

Nevertheless, the fear of black crime resulted in false accusations. In December 1878, D. C. Rhodes (sic, Rhoads) was "assassinated" one night while sitting in a storehouse. He was described conventionally as "a quiet, orderly man, highly esteemed by all who knew him." In this case also, the unknown assailants escaped. J. H. Alsup, who was probably the constable, reported to the sheriff that it was done by "negroes," but the newspaper report implied that was not certain. A group had "stealthily approached the house and one of them fired at Mr. Rhodes." He was hit in the face and killed instantly. No motives were proposed, but he was obviously involved in business and may have held debts.[27]

James Fountain, Monroe Hunt and James Hunt, all "colored," were arrested and indicted, while two other suspected black men were released. Both Fountain and Monroe Hunt were found innocent at trail, while James Hunt was held in durance "to answer for deviltry in Mississippi."[28] If not a murderer, he was certainly some kind of "black devil." The case remained unsolved as late as 1880.

As before the war, violent acts relating to family honor, often a young lady's reputation, remained a part of life. Jack Johnson of Olive Branch wounded J. W. Cooney in such a confrontation just south of the town in 1874. In 1876, Thomas Reasonover killed Samuel H. Ellis on his way to the Masonic Hall in town. These were not duels, but nevertheless confrontations over family honor. Reasonover actually published a letter claiming self-defense. He contested the newspaper reports that he shot Ellis in the back, and described him as a threatening, foul-tempered slanderer. Ellis had spread rumors defaming their young niece. As in the Joyce incident before the war, the case became the source of great interest and contention. Reasonover and his brother38 were initially found guilty by a close margin, and then ruled innocent in a retrial.[29] The appropriateness of such violence remained a question in local minds, extending even to many accepting it as justified homicide. Another incident in 1876 had similar overtones. When "a man named Sweeney was killed by a man named Hamilton," and Hamilton's friends demanded justice, both Justice Walker and the Circuit Court seemed to treat the entire affair lightly.[30]

In Shelby County, outright murder became almost common. One man living just north of town murdered another in Bartlett. In addition to the black-on-black murder and attempted murder, more killings and murders were committed by whites around Germantown proper. In 1866, Christian Berger murdered Miss Mary Watt at Germantown. While awaiting execution, Berger died of "congestion of the brain," – a hint at a possible source of his aberrant behavior.[31]

In May of 1867, while sitting in his parlor with wife and family, Smith Wilson was shot through a window by an unknown assassin. His farm had been subjected to pilfering for some time, and he had suspects. They apparently struck first. It soon became certain that the killer was a

W. T. Knowlton, "who under the name of Peebles, was formerly a United States military detective." Knowlton and his brother were post-war settlers, and his undercover role was certain to cast him in a dark light. Wilson, from Ohio, had also settled between Forest Hill and Germantown in the previous December. His neighbors petitioned the county court and the governor to post generous rewards, but Knowlton had immediately fled the area. Their references to Wilson as an "esteemed" citizen, and "a very quiet and worthy man," who "has never before had any difficulty with any person," implies that the locals had no problems accepting "Yankee" settlers into their community.[32] Unlike those who spoke for the community, the culprit and whatever accomplices apparently resented his economic success.

In 1880, W. F. Kimbrough was tried for the murder of an unnamed black woman, an incident which seems to have drawn little attention.[33] Unlike the pre-war violence, these were outright murders, some conducted stealthily. Compared to the one case of spontaneous homicide uncovered during the entire pre-war history of the town, there were four premeditated murders, not the semi-acceptable honor killings or duels, and two other killings of a more undefined nature, and at least two honor killings. For such a small community, these add to other signals of a definite change of atmosphere.

The economic hardships of the post-war recovery had brought other signs of social conflict. In 1868, Reverend J. Dix Mills published a voluble appeal in the *Avalanche* describing the hardships suffered by the "destitute" in and around the town.

> Indeed, I know of but few families that are not more or less destitute. I know of nothing that exceeds our poverty, but our pride – and dignity of Germantown. ...
>
> When from the wars the planter returned to the charred remains of his once handsome home, began to fence the waste places, and by acts evinced a determination to bring from the earth the bread by the sweat of his brow, the merchant of Memphis ... extended to him the hand of help; placed within his reach the means to purchase the implements of husbandry, the means to purchase mules and horses, and provisions on which to live till time and labor could mature the crops. The crops failed in part, the products declined in price, and at the end of the first year ... the planter found himself in worse condition than at its commencement – in debt to the merchant, without the means to advance a single step in the direction of release.

The merchants came to their aid again, but the process repeated itself.[34]

Mills' description of the hardships in the area was accurate, and such cycles of debt and failure plagued many locals. His published appeal was, however, a vain effort to defend himself against charges that he exaggerated both the number of impoverished farmers and claimed falsely that there was insufficient local charitable assistance. Instead he was allegedly profiting from his campaign to raise funds. One anonymous "citizen" had published a warning to the people of Collierville that the shady "originator of this pauper excitement" had precipitated a meeting in their town that would bring the same "disgrace" to them that he had brought on Germantown – now to be called "Paupertown."[35]

Since January, Mills had been drumming up support for his efforts to raise funds in Kentucky. On April 18, his campaign against local poverty had resulted in a meeting at the Presbyterian Church. In addition to Reverend Evans, T. Scott, William Mitchell and Dr. John Stout had been mobilized by concern over what they determined to be twelve families in need of help. A motion was passed by a slim majority (15 to 13) to send an agent north "to solicit aid for the disabled." The dissenting minority promptly left the church. When the remainder selected "a proper person to go north," the choice fell on Reverend Mills.[36]

Members of the concerned minority called a more general meeting on April 25, to which 50 came. Led by Harmand Furstenheim, William Walker and Henry Massey, they adopted a resolution to be published in Memphis and Louisville newspapers. They denied that the community was destitute and unable to relieve the "few people unable to work." No "contributions of neighboring states" were needed. They formed a committee "to inquire into the destitution of this community" and to solicit from the community whatever aid was needed.[37]

Mills retaliated with words that inflamed the controversy. He claimed "the best men in our country" backed his project, dropping a few names, and then proceeded to castigate his opposition. Among those who had thrived after the war, two "little fellows ... to-day ... are in a position to speculate upon the pressing needs of our suffering countrymen." The destitute around Germantown had the misfortune "to be so near a town holding within her limits two or three stupid men, determined to rule or ruin every move of which they themselves are not the head and front – men noted neither for benevolence of character nor for courteous treatment of their fellow-men." He attacked an unnamed but indirectly identified Memphis merchant as "one of the leaders in opposition to this enterprise." He had "repeatedly refused to accommodate good men, only on such terms as may possibly involve them in hopeless ruin." Then he focused specifically on the author of the word "Paupertown" whose supposed wit was designed to create a true "pauper excitement" that would discredit the good cause. To make this villain's identity known, without naming names, he associated him with a well-known, failed, local political maneuver.[38]   This must have been William Walker, local merchant and magistrate.

A storm broke about Mills. Anonymous comments appeared in the *Avalanche* criticizing him for referring to a firm of merchants "who are too well known for highest business capacity and integrity.... Perhaps Mr. Mills cannot even appreciate the worth of honesty or good breeding, and had better devote himself to the study of theology."[39]

His former backers began to disassociate themselves.   William Walker proceeded to thoroughly blacken Mills' name. He "is a minister of the Gospel, of small usefulness in his clerical calling." He had been a rabid secessionist who not only failed to bear arms, but proceeded to speculate and profit in food and materials, even selling at high prices to a lone widow "on the Sabbath day."

> He goes privately to a few gentlemen with his insinuations
> and deceptions; got them to certificate him for Kentucky.
> After an absence of six weeks he returns, with (an
> abundance of supplies), the bulk of which went to his
> home. Besides this, he sent home some money by express,
> and informed a party in this vicinity that he made $2,000
> by the trip. Not a dollar had been given to the destitute ...
> for whom he went out to beg."

Noting that Mills had charged him with "a want of politeness to gentlemen," Walker responded, "I regret his reverence is not in a position to receive those little attentions due a gentleman." In other words, a duel. "With Rev. J. Dix Mills I have no further communication. If I have done him an injustice, his appeal is to the courts of the country."[40]

At this point, the editors of the *Avalanche* announced that they had washed their hands of the affair and urged the *Ledger* to do so also. The proclaimed intention of the people of Germantown to take care of their own should settle the matter. The press could not judge the merits of the case but respected the "old, influential citizens" of Germantown who had pronounced Mill's cause unfounded. "Mr. Mills' course, both in and out of print, has not been calculated to strengthen his position."[41]

In June, Mills turned to the *Appeal*, publishing a rambling "advertisement" in his defense. Since Reverend Evans had waffled on his endorsement of Mills as early as March 5, Mills castigated him for yielding as soon as opposition developed. He blamed Evans for opening the floodgates of opposition, causing others to withdraw, such as Dr. McKay. In May, Evans had demanded that Mills return his letter of endorsement, but Mills refused to surrender such evidence.[42]

Reverend Mills was reportedly a Methodist minister, but no one by that name held an appointment anywhere in the entire Memphis Conference in that or the previous year.[43]   No one challenged his credentials, especially the conference's Methodist ministers, while at the same time his opponents drummed up so many other charges against him.

The picture that emerges from all this is certainly unpleasant. By his actions, Mills clearly made major enemies, and we will never know if he had the support of the others he claimed. His enemies destroyed whatever reputation he had. Although the good people of the town now assumed some responsibilities for their unfortunate neighbors, before Mills had created an embarrassing sensation they had been too distracted by their own problems to do so. Although the responsible committees had identified a dozen destitute families around each of Germantown and Collierville, all rhetoric about them referred to farmers and former planters. Considering the previous chapter's picture of local poverty, one wonders what contemporaries considered both destitution and worthiness in order to come up with only twelve such families. Black poverty apparently lay entirely beyond the pale.

The three or four "villains" Mills identified may have been as hard-hearted or indifferent as he claimed – country and city merchants who controlled local credit. Whatever his merits or demerits, by embarrassing the town in such a public manner and attacking a few of its leaders he insured his demise. Memphis' newspaper editors rallied behind their cause, not his. Polite society demanded discretion and indirect language. Identified as a Methodist, he would also have run afoul of the emerging sectarian divisions.[44]

The town witnessed many other disturbing incidents including suicides that speak to the pressures everyone suffered. In 1869, a derelict woman was found dying by the tracks, a consequence of escape into "the excessive use of opium or morphine." Shortly thereafter, a black man was found dead on the tracks. Samuel Meachum was ruled insane, supposedly resulting from "pecuniary affairs." Three months after he disappeared from his home, N. M. Young's body was found at the Seventeen-Mile Creek one mile from his home. Coroner Jones suspected suicide. The elderly Mrs. Roberts, living with the Isaiah Stout family, had been run over by the train while walking home from town. Recently widowed and losing property, "she had been heard to say that she was completely discouraged and was weary of life." The *Appeal*'s description was unusually graphic and gory. Two days later, a Mrs. Robinson, "a milliner from New York," threw herself under the train shortly after losing her husband. The last four of these incidents coming within a three month period must have cast a pall. Adding to these shocks, two citizens suffered fiery deaths. One man was killed by the explosion of a kerosene lamp, and 81 year-old Mrs. Mary Hoff died when her clothing caught fire.[45]

More mundane tragedies added to the hardships of local families. Both were wagon accidents. Eighteen year-old Frank Kelly was crushed after falling off a cotton wagon. He was the primary supporter of his widowed mother and two sisters. J. W. Wells at least managed to save his small son who was riding with him when their wagon overturned. Wells however was crushed.[46] There was nothing new about such events in local life, just compounded tragedy.

Not all normal deaths had a routine impact however. The short-lived Greenlaw compound ceased to exist after the death of its head. William's extensive fortune, heavily in insurance and railroad investments, foundered on problems with the Memphis & Little Rock RR in 1875, followed by his death on August 23. He passed at age 61 in the Peabody Hotel, cause listed as heart disease. Then his eldest son Alonzo died of unstated causes at their home by Germantown on September 25.[47] What had promised to be a claim to prominence and a source of powerful influence for the town had evaporated with his fortune.

Having to rely on newspaper coverage as a barometer of the town's experiences is unsatisfactory. They generally covered the town's news when locals reported it, making coverage uneven. Also the papers seem to have shifted more toward sensational coverage than before, making it difficult to determine how much life had changed as opposed to the news coverage – a problem that repeats itself today. Clearly the *Appeal* and *Avalanche*'s emphasis on black crime had exploded.

Given the times, the almost complete absence of reports of acts of terror directed at blacks in the immediate area is surprising. 1869 brought the only published event involving the town, and that only peripherally. Sensationally, the *Appeal* initially reported that a teenage white girl from Bartlett had run off with a black man. Alert citizens in Germantown apprehended her, and returned her to her father. The man escaped only as far as Collierville where some horsemen caught up with him. Approvingly, the paper reported that "the darkey ... was made to 'dance on nothing,' suspended on the limb of a tree." More accurately, the Nashville *Union and American* reported that after his captors had crossed the Wolf returning him to Bartlett, an armed group of Klansmen intervened, seized and shot the man. Also, the girl had merely paid him to help her escape her father. Nevertheless, it was always a death sentence for a black man to have any dealings with a white woman. A few days later, the girl's father killed a relative of the black man "in self-defense."[48]

Even religious differences inserted themselves. Initially the post-war community maintained, even intensified, its relative ecumenical harmony. The Presbyterian Church had made its facilities available for the other congregations until they could reconstruct. They shared meetings on alternate Sundays. The pastors still served their other congregations and only conducted services in Germantown once or twice a month. Frequently members simply attended the services of another congregation where they had friends  They maintained regular Sunday schools for the edification of the children, and during this interim with its lower enrollments, they even conducted a "union Sunday School."[49]

Despite this initial harmony, sectarian conflict emerged after war-time accommodations lapsed.  Vituperative exchanges between Baptists and Methodists unleashed by the publications of Reverend J. R. Graves in Memphis were read by townsfolk, and they may have enjoyed some of the more decorous public disputations in the city.  Finally, Germantown's Reverend Lipsey invited Graves to "deliver a series of doctrinal sermons."  Attendance was high, despite the fact that Graves "hardly ever preached less than two hours."  Some were apparently put off by his attacks, but the hall remained packed.  Others were offended by any examples of "sectarian hate."[50]

Lipsey was emboldened to take on a Campbellite preacher named Lauderdale in the Methodist Church.  A moderator insured "the orderly manner of debate."  According to Lipsey's son, Platus, "The differences between Campbellites and Baptists were thoroughly aired, attention was attracted and large crowds drawn from far and near.  The people liked that sort of thing and I think got good out of it. ... At Germantown and probably most other places at that time there was a good deal of strong denominational sentiment and quite a bit of prejudice or bitterness.  The lines were clearly drawn and feeling was strong."  Platus noted that his father's outspoken manner "provoked controversy and antagonism."[51]

Young Platus freely expressed such religious convictions, but probably like most fellow citizens, managed personal friendships across such barriers.  He sought in vain to convert Dr. McKay's son, a Presbyterian.  "I asked him if he didn't want to be a Christian and go to heaven.  He tried to be funny by asking me if I had the key."[52]

If witnesses to pre-war conditions had denied significant social differences and tensions among whites, a post-war witness and other evidence says otherwise.  Perhaps this supports the theory that the war had brought previously latent conditions to the fore.  Young Lipsey put it bluntly.  "Farming was an honorable occupation, but almost any other occupation which required manual labor put a person below par.  Marriages between families of what was considered more honorable occupation and those less esteemed were not encouraged nor seemed desirable.  The difference between a 'good family' and humbler people was more accentuated than now.  The lines of demarcation were more distinct and harder to cross."[53]

As the son of a Baptist minister, he contended that he was more aware of the life of the diverse population to whom his father ministered.  He expressed a mix of his own social and sectarian sentiments when he noted, "The Presbyterians had been the leading people here for a long time and it seemed to me rather resented the progress being made by

Baptists." The alleged leveling influence of the churches was also insufficient even within denominations. When the Brooks family attended a special service north of the Wolf, after arriving in their elegant carriage, no one invited them to dinner. When Mr. Brooks explained to his indignant wife that the simple folk considered them as "quality" and were too embarrassed to take care of them, she remained scornful.[54]

Many of the pre-war symptoms of a relatively harmonious community had been displaced by those of social tension, both within and among classes. Drunkenness, violence, and crime seem to have increased. Every fire provoked rumors of arson, symptomatic of the fear of the "barn burner" – that vindictively resentful member of the underclass. The propertied were increasingly defensive and more parsimonious with their charity, which was probably more hurtfully just that.

If the small farmer and the landless had grown increasingly resentful of the slave-owning class during the war, unequally shared post-war hardships and the previously described increase in the gaps between the rich and the rest of society further increased social tensions. Although some 40 families still represented a relatively smooth spread from wealthy to "comfortable," another 50 or so occupied a more marginal place, while the rest of the population ranged down from "respectably poor" to "dirt poor." The bottom half of agricultural families did not control or even rent any property, much less the 3 to 6 percent attributed to them elsewhere. Many lived in poverty, black and white alike, although the numbers were heavily skewed against the blacks.

Racial tensions worsened such developments. White rage focused on blacks who could vote when one could not. Irresponsible journalists like those of the *Appeal* and *Avalanche* fueled racist phobias. Although it may have been less severe in the Germantown area, as one historian has put it, the Klan terror "lacks a counterpart either in the American experience or in that of the other Western Hemisphere societies that abolished slavery in the nineteenth century. It is a measure of how far change had progressed that the reactions against Reconstruction proved so extreme."[55]

Whether they liked it or not, blacks and whites were integrated in a socioeconomic structure that was badly skewed in the distribution of wealth, with a very large percentage of truly poor. Many whites were worse off than before. The previous chapter discussed the complexities of racial relations in general within the community. Perhaps more complex were those among the underclass. Seventeen white families lived among the poorer black families who at least rented or cropped. Most survived on a few hundred dollars income per year, one a little as $100. Twenty whites were among the landless laborers. An additional three white widows had no apparent means of support. All these whites lived close by their black neighbors. Their reactions to such shared conditions were by no means simple or uniform. One can speculate based on known examples throughout Southern history. Many were hostile about competition for labor with blacks and about how they threatened a fictitious racial superiority. Others, however, adjusted. They worked together harmoniously and occasionally even mixed socially, with music as a common denominator. Finally, some of the above accounts of local crime reveal a common participation in the under-class's disregard for law and property. Criminal teams, gangs and organizations were frequently integrated. White outlaws found black safe houses.

Even so, there were indeed positive contrasts to a stark picture of "reconstructed" Germantown. Parts of the previous chapter revealed a much more cheery picture. Despite all the disruptions and apprehensions about real and imagined threats and all the turnover of population, the community retained some of its former cohesiveness. When the recently arrived Dr. McKay's house burned down destroying all their possessions in 1870, Mrs. Moliter and other ladies came to the rescue. They advertised in the papers to raise donations. Despite indications in the Reverend Mills affair that citizens of means had become less sensitive to the needs of the poor before he embarrassed them, there was still a dedication to Christian charity at a more generic level. When yellow fever struck Memphis in 1873, townsfolk sent contributions to the city's relief fund.[56]

### *Social and Cultural Enrichment*

In many ways, the recovery of community life presents a mixed picture. Among the elite, their high life style and cosmopolitan contacts resumed quickly. Many young men returned to their college educations to pursue professional careers, and were joined by an increasing number from the lower classes seeking greater opportunities than those offered by small scale agriculture. Young ladies still remained mostly confined to the level of the finishing school colleges and academies.

The world of the elite Victorian lady would change little before the next century, though it would be rocked by the suffragette movement, and more women would find activist roles in the prohibition movement. The issue of women's suffrage hit Tennessee and local politics first in 1869. In sharp contrast to its hostility to African-American suffrage, the *Appeal* came out in support when Senator Nelson submitted to the Assembly a bill to enfranchise women.

In every part of the civilized world women are successfully advancing their claims to intellectual culture and freedom from the political restraints with which they have heretofore been surrounded. We hear of them now as successful medical practitioners, as teachers in all the branches of collegiate and academical institutions, as artists, preachers of the gospel, lawyers and writers for the press ... and as occupying a number of useful positions in life that twenty years ago they were debarred for entering. ... They demand as reasoning human beings – certainly the superiors of the negroes who have been forced into political equality with the white race – they shall be hereafter admitted to vote, to say who shall govern States where their children are to be raised....[57]

The paper seemed disappointed that the women of Tennessee and Memphis had yet to come out in support of Nelson's motion. In fact, women's letters and diaries indicated a withdrawal of interest in politics, even a sense of its futility. The politics of Reconstruction were off putting and distasteful.[58] They allegedly even withdrew from political discussions around the dinner table. One must wonder how men responded to the prospect in their saloons and other masculine gathering places. Though legislators voted 12 to 9 in favor, it failed to pass with the two-thirds majority required to amend the constitution. If this vote is any indication, the idea must not have been too unpopular among men, especially since enfranchising their women could help the Democrats gain political control and end their own disenfranchisement.[59] The female experiences during the war were unleashing a mix of responses. Some undoubtedly yearned for a complete return to pre-war gender roles and relations. Others realized some relations had fundamentally changed.[60]

The diary of Martha Titus, a middle-aged spinster of a prominent Memphis family describes the more conventional daily life. She occasionally came out to Germantown to stay with relatives, while they and friends came in to Memphis to visit frequently, including Reverend Evans. This enabled Germantown's elite to attend evening social and cultural events without the problems of hotel accommodations. The festivities and balls of the annual Mardi Gras was one such event, facilitated by reduced rates on the M&C. The ladies' daily life was much quieter, however. They spent their time sewing, including making their own dresses, visiting, attending church, some charity work, reading the latest novels, and corresponding with family and friends. Letter writing was almost a daily activity.[61] If only the finer homes possessed sewing machines before the war, over the next two decades they began to facilitate the labors of other ladies, responding to the numerous ads in the papers and catalogs. By 1880, the town even supported two sewing machine agents.[62]

Nevertheless, even the privileged ladies were leading an ever more public life than before the war. As the following accounts reveal, Mrs. Miller's name would appear prominently along side her husband's as managers of the girls school in Forest Hill, while the Baptist church's fund raiser was totally run and organized by the ladies of the church, whose names were proudly published in the papers. The respectable young ladies provided the singing and performed "on-stage" in the tableaux, with their names also published. Though still decorous and refined, they were public displays compared to their former performances limited to their finishing school events.

The recovery of local education also reflects the gap that had developed between the relatively privileged and others. White private educational institutions recovered at varied rates – private schools coming first. The Webb school house had been saved by the daughter's diligence, but the Thompsons lived in town in a family town house. It is not clear whether Mary still taught at their old school house. Something of the other private school buildings must have survived as well. The "Germantown Male and Female English & Classical School," with boarders, advertised intentions to "reopen" in January 1866, with A. N. Plunkett as Principal.[63] Also a "Shelby Male High School" was soon back in operation, which was definitely a continuation of the Shelby Military and Classical Institute.[64] The location of the Classical School may have been the Webb building, while presumably the Male High School was in its old facilities.

The Young Ladies' Collegiate Institute of Forest Hill was quick to get itself back in operation, announcing its first culminating "exercises" on January 2, 1866. As before, most of its students came from Memphis. Its facilities had survived unscathed. It proclaimed its advantages in exactly the same language as before, a healthy and beautiful environment removed "from distracting city influences," and "noted for the many *thoroughly educated* women it has sent forth." Room, board and fuel were $22.10 per month with tuition $5-6.00. French language and music lessons were extra. Mrs. C. F. W. Miller was Principal and Reverend H. Miller still Proprietor.[65]

Unfortunately, surviving the conflagrations of the war provided the school with no insurance against more routine calamities. On December 19, 1867, fire struck.[66] The school could not reopen promptly. By the next year, developers had purchased the property with an eye toward creating a suburban resort and seasonal residence complex. "Mr. Almond," who bought the land for speculation wanted to have the school reopened "as soon as the necessary arrangements can be perfected." Unfortunately "Mr. Ammon's" previously described promotional efforts had led to naught, and he did not demonstrate any dedication to the institute, for by November of 1868 he was trying to sell the desks and forms to cover his losses. Meanwhile, Reverend J. W. Rogers of Memphis announced that he would take over the ladies institute, with an eye to its maintenance.[67] The rest of the institution's history remains to be told, but the absence of further advertising leads one to suspect it never recovered.

An early effort to raise funds for rebuilding the Baptist Church gives us a vivid picture of the area's social life. For June 24, 1869, a gala fund-raising event was advertised extensively in the papers. It took place in the remaining Young Ladies Academy facilities at Forest Hill. As usual for such an occasion, a special train left Memphis at 6 PM. For one dollar, participants got a round trip, entertainment and supper. The train carried a sizable crowd from the city, picking up additional passengers at all the stops along the way. Others came by buggy. The entertainment lasted until 11 PM, consisting of "tableaux, singing, comic tragedy and burlesque.... The tableaux were very pretty indeed...." A tableau was an elaborately costumed scene with backdrop, with young ladies posing silently. It usually depicted a well-known literary or historical moment or a well-known painting. After the crowd applauded, the curtain would go down to prepare for the next tableau. "Afterward, a sumptuous supper – barbecued pig, mutton, turkeys, chickens, and other substantials ... besides all kinds of confectionary." The organizers were Miss Lou Parrish and Mr. Nasal Rhodes, while the meal was arranged by Mrs. Dr. Gray and Mrs. Vernon Rhodes. Other local young ladies featured in the papers were Kate Rhodes, Fannie Burnley, Susie Gray, plus Lizzie Perkins, Aggie Cash and Sallie Reasonover of Forrest Hill. When the affair ended, participants boarded the special train for home.[68]

Of course, Germantown was a satellite socially and culturally of Memphis, at least for those who could afford participation. For instance, as early as 1868, The New Memphis Theater sought to extend its audience, relying on the restored M&C service. In conjunction with the railroad, they put together a package for the premier of their "spectacular and thrilling drama," The White Fawn. The special train came in from Somerville, picking up passengers at Germantown at 6:50 PM, delivering all to Memphis for the show. The grand cost for the complete package of train and theater tickets for Germantown folks was $1.75 per head. Likewise, when the county's Old Folks at Home society held its annual meeting and ceremonies in 1870 at the Fair Grounds just outside Memphis, the M&C provided a special train, with tickets from Germantown costing fifty cents. There was dancing. Non-members were invited, but a gentleman had to pay a dollar for admission, "with or without a lady."[69]

The folk of the countryside were hardly dependent on the city, however, for their social and cultural life. Suburban and rural entertainments were not necessarily of "common culture" either. The commencement or examination ceremonies, concerts and recitals of the Forrest Hill ladies or Germantown academies provided the same level of cultural sophistication as before. Germantown purportedly had a debating society and perhaps a literary society, for there was ample academic support for both. Such societies sponsored cultural and social events that combined refined speeches and readings, with political orations, dances and barbecues. For one such in Center Hill, special trains carried passengers out from the city to Forest Hill and Germantown, from where locals joined in wagon cavalcades down Center Hill Road. Social gatherings for dancing, music and food assembled at natural arbors and idyllic spots along the Wolf from Germantown to Collierville, to which folk would travel from as far afield as Fishersville and Centerville. The Nashoba Springs remained one such spot.[70]

The town's Masonic Lodge was apparently reinstalled in 1873 with a grand affair drawing "five or six hundred of the best people of that well-to-do part of the county" and guests from the city. The ceremonies were held out at Brunswick Springs, followed by a barbecue and dancing until midnight.[71]

Black social life was undoubtedly equally rich. Much of it centered on the churches, with suppers, barbecues, fairs and excursions. The railroad made it possible for the congregations to join one another at distances for such events. Local businessmen also organized picnics at places along the line, chartered five to ten cars, sold reduced-fare tickets, and "flooded the country with handbills," to draw in the crowds. Of course, such affairs could be less than decorous. Fraternal organizations based in the city provided insurance against death and illness as well as social contacts for at least those achieving some economic independence.[72] Blacks were sometimes present at white-sponsored events, sometimes segregated, sometimes not. Unfortunately insight into Germantown's black social life escapes specific documentation except when the local papers found them occasions for denigrating humor.[73]

Local and family traditions are problematic for historians. For instance, The New Bethel Missionary Baptist Church traces its roots to a brush arbor that a white resident allegedly allowed slaves to have on her property to serve as a church in which they could also learn to read and write. It appears, however, that the white family in question, Dr. Thompson and his wife Florida were not residing anywhere in Germantown before 1863 at the earliest. So her offer probably benefited local blacks during their transition to freedom.[74] Whatever, this is when blacks especially sought to separate themselves from the authority of white ministers and needed land for an arbor.[75]

From this brush arbor base, the self-reliant members of the African-American community commenced efforts to build what would eventually become the New Bethel Baptist Missionary Church. In December 1869, community leaders acquired two acres for both a church and school for two hundred dollars. This relatively sizable building was erected east of town on a lane that ran north of the tracks (present Southern) and just east of the Germantown-Macon Road. It was high-ceilinged and competently constructed with proper plank siding. Reverend Isaac Cotten became the first pastor, while the initial leadership for the new congregation was provided by James Scott, Germantown carpenter, James Cornelius, a farmer living east of town in district ten, and Godfrey Goode, another farmer.[76]

Obviously the Freedmen's Bureau had done nothing to help develop a black school in district eleven. By the same token, area planters had not responded to the Bureau's plea to make efforts to provide schooling.[77] In 1866, the Bureau had created Fisk University to train black teachers in Tennessee, turning out over 800 per year. There is no record of who did the earliest teaching at the little black school. Malida Featherston, who worked as a cook, had somehow been able to get her son Daniel some schooling during the 1870s after which he was able to take over the teaching. Since Daniel Featherston, age 24, was listed as both teacher and farmer in 1880,[78] his salary probably was not sufficient to support his wife and small daughter.

Then in 1886, under the leadership of Phillip Cornelius, Ed Finch and Alf Hall, the church donated one of its acres to the Eleventh School District for the erection of the Germantown School building, providing the black community with its first official public elementary school. In 1897, the church would acquire more land and expand the school buildings, eventually adding a public junior high and finally a high school. To distinguish it from the white Germantown School, it was renamed the Nashoba School.[79] The self-sufficiency of the black community in building its own public school seems to have exceeded similar white efforts.

Meanwhile, Tennessee had sought to revise its public school system in 1867. The system of school districts based on the civil districts resumed with local school boards as before. Now enumeration of both white and colored youth between the ages of six and twenty determined the relative funding. The civil district's Board of Education was responsible for maintaining both elementary and high schools, employing, paying and dismissing teachers, building, repairing and maintaining the necessary school-houses or renting suitable rooms. Although they had some leeway, they were apparently required to maintain district schools of appropriate grades for at least every fifty students. There had to be at least one free common school operating each year for a period of five months of twenty school days per month. If state funds were insufficient for such a common school, the Board was

Photo 17. New Bethel Missionary Baptist Church and school. (GH&GC)

to submit a proposed tax to the district for approval. Teachers had to be examined and have certificates of qualification, while the Boards determined what studies would be taught.[80] That, of course, allowed for considerable differences among districts and Germantown's was very slow getting on board.

The 1870 census indicates that there were 230 white and 420 black "scholars" in district eleven between the ages of six and twenty. So there should have been at least four to five white and eight colored common schools or classrooms. That census, however, makes it clear that a large number of young people of both ethnicities were working in the fields and at jobs often as major or sole bread winners for their families. Although their presence in the statistics generated state funding, their unavailability for education greatly reduced the pressures on the district to supply classrooms and buildings. So did the white preference for private schools.

In 1870, outside town nestled among the tenant farmers and land owners, resided Ms. Elizabeth Rosco, a thirty-three year-old widow and her 12 year-old daughter. Since she, a white woman, was listed as school teacher,[81] this might give the impression that, in addition to what should have been a school in town, there was at least a second common school serving the more removed rural white population. Yet, what is puzzling is the presence of only two such people listing themselves as school teachers in that 1870 census, the other whom we know (Plunkett) presided over a private school. Since there were seemingly at least two private schools, clearly the district had not actually gotten around to complying with the 1867 education act, reestablishing any common schools. Also according to town tradition, a "Miss Thompson" taught a school in the east wing of the Whitlow home at present 7642 Poplar Pike.[82] Mrs. Mary C. L. Thompson, who may have been the Mary Thompson of the former Webb School, may have been this same woman, but she never listed herself as a teacher in any of the censuses, perhaps for reasons of convention. Unfortunately, when Miss Thompson's school opened is not a matter of record, but it too was a private school referred to commonly as the "Thompson Place." Over the decade of the 1870s, at least one man and five unmarried women would add to the roster of teachers. Two were the spinster daughters of ministers.[83] The appearance of some of them finally heralded the arrival of the first new public school.

There was certainly a crying need for public education, not only among the educationally deprived black population, but among the whites as well. In addition to playing catch-up for the older children, deprived during most of the war and immediately after, it was needed to serve the new generation of "scholars" that both black and white families were producing. In the 1870 census for the entire district, 25 whites over age 10 were illiterate or partially so, while 787 blacks were so classed.

Illiteracy among adult whites was most prevalent among laboring classes and older farmers kept out of school as children. Disruption by the war was apparently the most common cause for young white people to be illiterate, yet many families had worked hard to home-school or otherwise to educate their children under war-time conditions.[84] The high rate of illiteracy among blacks was to be expected, but a smattering of teenagers and young adults who had acquired literacy speaks to individual determination to overcome the lack of public education since emancipation.[85]

When in 1870 the Legislature had ordered a scholastic census, only six districts complied, including neither the 10th nor 11th. In January 1871, the County Court chided the district commissioners for failing to make their annual report, noting that twelve of the districts still had no commissioners. Without the enumeration, the county could not get the funds allocated for public education. The commissioners then reported that they were unable to carry out the education laws recently enacted. As problems, they cited the general apathy of parents and guardians and the lack of suitable buildings for schoolhouses. Finally the 11th Civil District elected its commissioners on March 25. The district was just getting around to organizing itself.[86] By October, the Court charged the commissioners with failure to comply with the state laws, having appointed no County Board of Education which had to certify all teachers.[87] In 1873, Governor John C. Brown had signed a bill that provided for a statewide system of public schools, and the legislature levied taxes to pay for new schools and teachers' salaries.[88]

In town, it was not until 1878 that the Masonic Hall finally became the site of the free common school for whites, taught by the Baptist minister, Lipsey, and Reverend A. G. Parrott's twenty-nine year-old daughter.[89] This was apparently the first public facility for whites. Until 1911, it was still the site of the white public school, when its first dedicated building was completed.[90] One young student remembers that there were many larger boys, "some were practically grown men." The community was playing catch-up with its neglected educational program. Nevertheless, the new school provided more than the old basic 3Rs. There was algebra, geometry and even Latin and Greek for advanced students with college and professions in mind.[91]

Nevertheless, real progress in public education would apparently not begin until 1882. By 1886, for the entire county, the scholastic population was 14,378 white children and 19,590 black children. For these students there were 69 white schools and 79 for blacks. One was of brick, the rest of wood, seven of which had been built that year. There were 17 white male teachers and 58 women; 59 black men and 20 women. There were 3,607 white pupils enrolled and 6,949 blacks, and the average daily attendance was high. The average teacher's compensation was $35 per month.[92] By this time, for Germantown students who could not afford to attend better schools in Memphis, the county public school system was their only recourse with the apparent exception of one private grade school.

# Conclusion

In 1860, Germantown and its environs were in many ways typical of southern agrarian communities. In some ways, however, they differed. The town had become something of a cultural gem. Its elite and middle class families had full access to the cultural and social life of Memphis, which was in no way backward in its offerings. The entire population benefited from opportunities generated by their town's churches, fraternal orders, communal celebrations, and the rallies that combined political involvement with festive social mixing. Every home, even some of the poorer, constituted the center of a network of family and friends that reached well beyond the local community. The summer attractions of the local watering holes made a Germantown-area home even more attractive to visitors. Although the presence of private academies and collegiate institutions were not unique to such communities, Germantown's stood out, drawing numerous would-be educational entrepreneurs and book vendors and hosting regular cultural events. For all classes, the level of education exceeded that normally associated with the South. Literacy was high. There were the usual problems of secularism and excessive alcohol consumption. The level of crime and violence seems limited to the petty pilfering that never reached the newspapers, with two exceptions over two decades. The town was vibrant but peaceful. On the one hand, economically it was a typical center for an extensive agricultural community, but on the other it had some nascent industry.

The area did not conform to the model of a community ruled by a plantation owning aristocracy, locked in a reactionary resistance to modernizing processes. Although Shelby County and, therefore, Germantown were part of the plantation South, Germantown clearly had more in common with the modernizing border states, especially because of proximity to Memphis. Yet its citizens certainty subscribed to the conventional attitudes and values identified with the southern culture, and would defend them against the perceived, corrosive trends at work in the North. This conservative reaction to the less pleasant aspects of modernization was not sufficient to stifle progress, however.

The seemingly self-righteous radicalism of the abolitionists was certainly one such intolerable threat. Despite the ever-present brutality of slavery, local slave owners vacillated along a spectrum of romantic denials of reality, guilt-driven rationalizations, and an unquestioning acceptance of what seemed to be the natural order of things. Some hoped for a day when slavery would dissolve somehow, but were unwilling to cut the Gordian knot. Theirs was not a unique historical conundrum. Societies have often been unable to correct their dysfunctional, even inhumane, socioeconomic or political institutions. But as long as universally American racial phobias prevailed, southerners could dismiss contemptuously northern hypocrisy and calls for abolition, the consequences of which Northerners would not have to suffer. Likewise, slave owners failed to devise any effective evolutionary end to the problem and find a compromise with the abolitionist strategy. Immediate economic needs and interests were simply too powerful.

Among the romantics were those who believed most owners truly cared for their slaves, who were basically happy with their lot and loyal to their owners. They blithely built their own separate white world, supported heavily by black labor. With the little free time left them, the blacks developed a separate world of their own – built personal and family lives and evolved an African-American cultural life. Even so, the runaway rate in the Germantown area was high. Then when the opportunity for slaves to "abandon" their owners came with the war, owners would react with anger and a sense of betrayal. Meanwhile, positive emotions about one's own slaves stood in stark juxtaposition to a general fear of black savagery. It took only one slave-revolt scare to bring out all the usual responses.

The white family values and the gender roles they entailed were typically southern. They were seen as biologically determined and properly protective of women and children. One threat was the enslavement of women and children in the industrializing North totally undermining all family values. None of this led locals to shun inventiveness and the industrial establishments that grew from it, however. Nevertheless, the only place for the employment of poorer white women and children remained in occupations directly supportive of household economies. In the area of teaching, on the other hand, as a logical extension of child care, Germantown women were already more heavily involved than in most of the South.

Another threat to traditional family values was feminist ideas infecting northeastern bourgeois family life. If women stepped outside their natural roles, they would not only disrupt the order but become vulnerable to exploitation. Nevertheless, Germantown area women were not as excluded from public involvements as were their sisters of the low country and deep South. In such a "suburban community," easy and close social contact with Memphis introduced many Germantown women to modernizing trends. Some of the less appealing aspects undoubtedly reinforced their determination to preserve traditional family values. However, there and in their town churches, they became involved in organized groups working on charitable and moral causes such as the temperance movement. Although they may not have been involved yet in leadership, the activity was so familiar that when war erupted, it took little encouragement from the city's papers for them to take the next step and enter the public arena without male guidance.

If the plantation aristocracy ruled society elsewhere in the South, generating class hostilities, that was far too simple a picture for socioeconomic relations in and around Germantown. The smooth continuity from wealthiest planter down through a majority middle to the poorer yet self-sufficient farmer contained no gaps that separated an elite from "the masses." Many young laborers had every expectation of moving up. They all belonged to a large majority that had far more interests in common than not. Even many of those below got helping hands from above. Undoubtedly the soft glove on the neighborly helping-hand occasionally slipped off to reveal condescension. More often than not, however, help did not appear as demeaning charity. The older citizens remembered the frontier environment, while most of the younger still worked hard to earn their modest comforts. Certainly any who had to compete against slave labor resented the system and those who benefited from it. The relatively few such "malcontents" hardly constituted a social problem, for they lay below the radar. Although hardly an egalitarian community that could weather severe economic crisis, it was far more meritocracy than aristocracy.

The same applies to the idea that the planters controlled politics. The early Whig planters like the Kimbroughs and Dukes lost whatever control they might have had over county and state politics to the allegedly broader based Democrats if they did not change allegiances. But party differences were not drawn along any clear class lines. The frequent differences in voting patterns between Collierville and Germantown's districts, despite identical socioeconomic populations, belie such arguments. As elsewhere, planters rarely ran for political office, leaving that to professionals, businessmen and ambitious slaveholding farmers. Although they undoubtedly had the ears of those office holders, they did not need to "control or manipulate" them. In most cases, shared interests guaranteed all that was needed.

As almost all students of the Old South have observed, slavery provided the tie that bound, even for those who did not share its alleged benefits. It had created a widely shared "consensus reality" or paradigm. Emancipation threatened far more than economic loss and the end of a more privileged life for the owners. If the slaves were ever freed, they would have to return to Africa, for they could not share or even coexist in the white American society. Any equality in citizenship was out of the question. Indeed, such ideas were beyond the pale for almost all Americans, even most abolitionists. The poor farmer and laborer saw an even greater threat. In 1863, one West Tennessee diarist mournfully looked forward to the state of affairs when free blacks in large numbers would not only bring each others' wages down, but would compete with whites of jobs.

> In this land a poor white man would have no chance to
> live. They are not willing to put themselves on an equality

with the negro as a slave. Where can be the difference? When they are in competition in labor, both of them working for the most they can get, possibly at a less rate than if one was in the usual servitude.[1]

As the Civil War erupted around them, the people of Germantown abandoned their original good judgment in opposing secession. They were swept up by the collective jubilation of a newly proclaimed crusade against invaders bent on oppression. If they had been manipulated into secession, it was made possible by their harmonious sense of community. Once the radical course of war had become the new norm, to deviate from it would have been an act of heresy.

Regardless of historical debates over the inevitability of the war, the evil institution of slavery ultimately demanded its own destruction. The price for the sins of the fathers would be inflicted upon many succeeding generations, North and South, black and white. The furor of a civil war, not just between North and South, but within the South, created an uncompromising environment after the final defeat. Fearfully the Radical minority poisoned the well and refused compromise. Ultimately the majority would respond and impose a reactionary order as northern interference tired of the fight for abstract principals it did not fully embrace for itself. Whites had the political and economic power to push the pendulum back against what they feared was a biologically inappropriate human equality. Even so, the restoration of white hegemony did involve some compromise. It left cracks in the socioeconomic structure in which blacks could exist, and even find opportunities. Their perseverance, like the pressure of ice in the cracks of a granite face, would eventually lead to the current, improved state of racial relations for all they are worth.

Detailed studies of the writings left by southern white women present a complex and contradictory picture of the effects of the war and Reconstruction on them and their attitudes about their proper place in the world.[2] They were as determined as ever to preserve proper family and racial relationships. They would gratefully accept a restoration of security and order. Yet at the same time, they became acutely aware of the inability of their men always to provide the shelter, protection and sustenance once expected. Their experience with forced self-reliance had brought a contradictory mix of an awareness of their abilities with their inability to go it alone. Male management could not be left free of female input, yet it could not be too overtly challenged without rending the proper order. When the *Appeal* seemed disappointed that local ladies had not embraced the idea of suffrage, they failed to perceive female disillusionment with all current political possibilities. If political activity lay beyond their present conceptions of proper action, organizing for moral, spiritual, charitable, and cultural causes did not. Women had learned to organize themselves effectively and to enter the public forum.[3] There is no more obvious transition in the surviving records than this regarding Germantown area women.

If gender relations evolved more subtly, the war had a most marked impact on the area's socioeconomic structure. Most of the town's middle-class economic base had been destroyed. Limited local resources for recovery required supplementation by that of newcomers. The same was true for the former planters, while the yeoman class was decimated in indirect proportion to its former wealth. Wealthy newcomers exaggerated the former concentration of wealth at the top. The middle had shrunk and the poor had become the majority. The transition to a much larger proportion of renting farmers complicated such evaluations of the life of landless farmers, for many belonged to the economic lower-middle. Most of all, social relations were complicated by the new presence of the large, free black population. They increased in numbers the farther down the economic scale one looked.

Such changes compounded war experiences that seriously undermined the relatively peaceful harmony of the Germantown community. Despite the mutual support among the congregations immediately after the war, whatever sectarianism had existed before erupted in conflict. How seriously it affected interpersonal relations is unclear, but it certainly generated interest and paralleled expressions of social resentments. Although there were still bursts of Christian charity, people had become more focused on the needs of their families than those of the community. Charity began at home. Some were seen as worthy of the sacrifices involved in giving, but many others lay beyond the pale. Alcoholism, depression and suicide became visible phenomena. Worse, lawlessness, robbery and murder now supplemented the even more frequent honor-related violence and killings. Racially directed terrorism was the order of the day, if economic pressures failed to suffice. The ravages of war left scars that gradual economic recovery would take a long time to ameliorate.

The already complex relationship that had existed between blacks and whites underwent severe stress from the experiences of both groups during the war and Reconstruction. Clearly fears and animosities grew. The Radical's overturning of racial relations was more embittering because it appeared to be directed at punishing and destroying the South. It seemed less a product of well-intentioned reforms than of the pursuit of nefarious vested interests. To do so, Radicals had not just enfranchised black men, but had incited them with promises of reward and even revenge. Few on any side in this story seriously intended for the blacks to get any proper reimbursement for their years of slave labor. Economic justice was out of the question. Radical legislation would only go beyond granting the right of freedom to the point of enfranchisement, and even that for some Radicals was driven by ulterior motives. The spectrum of the general population that ranged from conservative to unregenerate Rebel was mostly unwilling to concede even the franchise. Almost all, driven by old fears, felt the need to keep the blacks "in their place." Such sentiments did not divide the white classes.

Blacks had gained little more than emancipation from the war. The American ideal of "a society of justice for all" would have to continue its head-on battle against deeply rooted social and cultural conventions which the decade of the 1860s entrenched further. Nevertheless in communities like Germantown, blacks and whites continued to live and work in close proximity. There were no real minorities or majorities. Familiarity can breed the opposite of contempt. While negative stereotypes clouded the minds of both blacks and whites, abstractions crumble wherever real individuals encounter each other. Neither property, influence nor respect was entirely denied the blacks. There were constrained opportunities that truly benefited some, both within their own economic subset and in dealings with fair whites. Most could persevere and hope for better. Although an underclass, most blacks were not excluded from all the benefits of the society in which they had to function. Perhaps no greater percentage of them than of the white population chose to function outside society where the risks of criminal activity were no more costly than those of ordinary life. In such ventures, black and white could find themselves collaborating.

The African-American subculture of the South generated its inevitable counter-racism and maintained or even entrenched a conflicted black preference for segregation. Even if allowed to compete in a white-run educational system, they would have usually "failed." They had to struggle to overcome centuries of denied education with the illiteracy and all the lack-of-understanding that entailed. They had to build from scratch a qualified teaching profession with the limited resources of the new black universities. They expanded their own church congregations and denominations to provide strong spiritual and social systems of support. Unable to rely on a sufficient number of "fair" white business and professional men, they created their own business and professional community. They evolved their own middle class and their own "mechanics" to serve them locally, who in turn could reach out for support to an even stronger black establishment in Memphis. Most of all, they generated a rich and vibrant African-American culture, especially music, that became a major conduit for the future integration of American society.

Young, other-minded whites intruded into this black world to share in the exuberant music and spirituality. Black nannies continued to have their impact on young white minds – sometimes a lasting impact. Black and white children continued to play together, often in defiance of both sets of parents. Although adolescence inevitably drove wedges between them, continued familiarity also eroded the prejudices that drove those wedges. Yet more cracks worked away at the granite face of racism.

Everywhere in the South, the war had both divisive and cohesive effects on the population, but the latter effects were unique. If the scars of a fratricidal war fought at your door and the destruction of so much of your means had not been enough reason, the humiliation of Reconstruction with its allegations of treason guaranteed that Southerners would never forget the Civil War. Anyone who feels his acts were justified, feels unjustly punished, even abused, when he suffers the negative consequences of those acts. Already in 1869, letters to the editor in the newspapers reflected the range of feelings among whites. All expressed a sense of injustice. The Confederate soldiers who had expected to return home to peace and the lawful pursuit of their lives saw themselves as in the hands of a vengeful and rapacious faction, who controlled the state, flaunted the Federal and state constitutions, oppressed the defeated, abused authority and took advantage of every opportunity for corruption.

Indeed the Radicals had inadvertently obstructed a reconciliation of the unionist and secessionist factions of society. The harsh punishment they imposed was for what they saw as "treason," but such a charge simply defied every other southerner's sense of what had happened. Worse, as an insecure minority, the Radicals resorted to flagrant abuses of power to stay in control. They had to wink at the economic corruption of the "Scalawags and Carpetbaggers" who constituted important supporting interests. Both the harshness of Radical Reconstruction policies and the overturning of what was seen almost unanimously as "proper racial relationships" embittered.

No matter how many soldiers had come home resigned to their defeat and determined to get on peacefully in the new order, no matter how many civilians felt the same, Reconstruction soured such hopes. The loss and damage of property and the other economic obstacles to recovery were bad enough. They could not understand being treated as traitors, losing their franchise and any voice in local, state and national politics. They could not stomach being lorded over by those they had considered traitors and by outsiders who had all the rights they had lost. Perhaps worst of all, the former slaves now purportedly had all the rights one had lost. The need to "set things right" overpowered all other considerations.

As a backlash, the old "Southern patriotism" renewed itself with a vengeance. If the disillusionments of the war and defeat had originally cooled the ardor of former secessionists and intensified the sentiments of pro-unionists, the Reconstruction experience undid most of that. Even ardent unionists who had joined the Federal army, fought against secession, and had been post-war Republicans became as embittered as the Confederate hard-liner.[4]  So too did the former unionist who had reluctantly supported secession.  Likewise the war-time defector from the cause.  As early as 1866, the commander of the garrison at Memphis, Major General George Stoneman, noted that locals had become "less loyal than they had been six months before."[5]

The injustices of Reconstruction became as powerful a myth as the Lost Cause.  In Tennessee, Reconstruction only lasted four to five years, was never fully effective, and quickly gave way to something that too closely resembled the old order of things.  Nevertheless, exaggerated by tradition, it was enough to compound the sense of defeat into one of victimization.

Behind this powerful sense of injustice lurked the psychological scars, not just of defeat, but of the horrors of combat and of living with the threats to unprotected loved ones about which one could do nothing.  The guerrilla war theater had intensified all that.  On top of all the hardships they were facing, southern women had to resume old relationships with a manhood that was greatly damaged.  Students of southern women attribute the generation of the Lost Cause movement to local women's organizations that memorialized the fallen, lionized the military leadership and the heroic and honorable service of every Confederate soldier.  They campaigned for memorial services, monuments and cemeteries.  They launched a cultural and literary movement to write history as it needed to be seen for the self-respect of a defeated people.[6]

Nostalgia over the "Lost Cause" grew as Southerners memorialized their dead.  Soon, only heroes had served – no deserters or slackers.  All memories of the bitter civil war within the South among Southerners faded.  Eventually all who had vacillated in the cause remembered only their moments of support.  Any who had deserted remembered and glorified only their service.  Veterans remembered their hardships but not their loss of morale.  The real combat veterans eschewed the popular romanticizing of the war, but even most of them cherished the camaraderie of the experience.  The cultural and literary movement actually enabled the losers to write history for a change.  Such was the Southern cultural unity that was reemerging by the 1870s.  All were bonded by it.  Unregenerate Southern patriotism helped to plaster over previous cracks and provided some crutches for the more severely scarred.

# Postscript
## *Yellow Jack – the Death Knell*

The town was clearly on the road to recovery and a bright future as the decade of the 70s wound down. Recovery evaporated, however, in 1878. The fatal blow came with the great Yellow Fever epidemic, the worst in American history – the only one to reach Germantown. Because it totally terminated the urban flight that was fueling the town's recovery, its impact on the community was unique.

Although Memphians knew their filthy city was dangerous, they did nothing significant to address the problems. Every summer they feared the return of yellow fever, and warmer El Nino years had been encouraging the responsible mosquito population.[7] The disease had struck hard in 1867 and again in 1873. As the season of 1878 approached, Memphis papers expressed a mix of apprehension and complacency. For those who could afford it, the typical response remained weekend or seasonal family retreats to resorts like Germantown, encouraged by the M&C with reduced fares.[8]

In July, word came that the disease was in New Orleans and bound to come up river. That prompted the Memphis Board of Health to impose a quarantine. Posts were established on President's Island south of the city for river traffic, at Whitehaven Station south on the Mississippi and Tennessee, and at Germantown on the M&C. There, the metropolitan police with shotguns stopped anyone coming to Memphis with symptoms of fever, plus all shipments of products suspected of carrying the disease. On the M&C, an agent went out as far as Grand Junction to warn passengers that they might not be admitted through to Memphis. Germantown might be their last stop. Quarantined cargo would be stopped at Germantown also.[9] At this time, the embargo was on traffic entering the city, and no Memphians seemed concerned about the fate of such communities as Germantown serving as quarantine holding places.

Nevertheless, numerous cases had developed in Memphis by late July, and it was officially recognized on August 13. As panic ensued, 25,000 citizens fled, many to the seemingly healthier climate of Germantown and Collierville. Refugee camps were established along the rail lines within ten miles of the city, but many did not stop there. They sought shelter in accommodations in the country, if they had them, otherwise they erected temporary shelters. The devastation soon followed.[10]

Reverend Evan's day-book tells of the growing fear as the fever spread from the city. The first case to break out in the town was James Roper, a refugee from Memphis, fueling the fear that the disease was

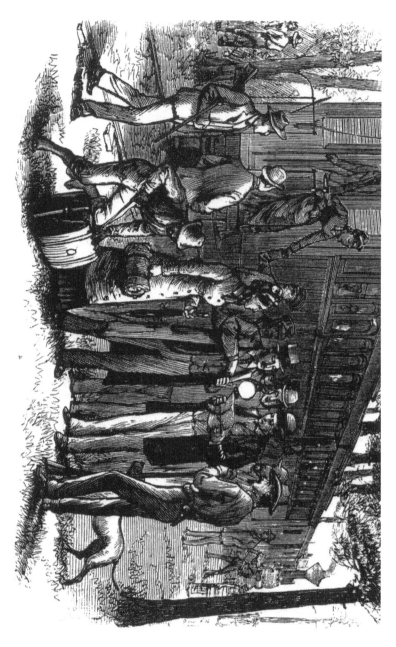

Illustration 39. Quarantine station like the one at Germantown (Harper's)

contagious. After mid-September, it was rampant in Germantown and Collierville, with people dying daily. Before it was over, 81 people in Germantown fell ill. Of them, 45 would die.[11]

As early as September 15, Collierville and Germantown appealed for assistance from the Howard Association, a relief organization. By September 29, it had set up bases, a Dr. Bryan and four nuns at Germantown. They nursed the sick and brought supplies regularly from the city. Doctors from unaffected areas, including north Mississippi, rode in regularly to help. On October 12, the Association sent out a train along the M&C to visit every affected community, bringing Germantown money, medicine and other supplies.[12]

Flight from both towns began as soon as citizens realized that theirs was no safe haven. Most settled with friends and family in the country several miles from town. The reaction of those remaining was mixed. Some expressed open hostility at their desertion, while others accepted it as understandable. One especially hostile Germantown wit disparaged those who fled as being predominantly the self-righteous "golden rule fellows, Mamma Pets, and temperance lecturers" who left behind the targets of their former criticism. It was the hale fellows who stayed and served the afflicted, often at the cost of their own lives.[13] This was yet another addition to existing social tensions.

Needless to say, newspaper reports enumerated primarily the deaths of white citizens. In Germantown, only one black man, Jack Spivey, was specifically listed as such, although one or two others may have been black. It does seem at least that blacks benefited from greater immunity, but also better dispersal through the countryside.[14]

Among the prominent dead were Joseph Molitor and his wife Mary. Typically, their younger children were then sent to Arkansas to live with relatives, and some of the older children apparently followed later. The only survivor of this once prominent family to stay was a daughter, Della, who married a Mr. Strickland.[15] William Miller, the druggist, passed in November after the worse was over, but was preceded by his wife in October. They too left orphans. The Berry Hurt family left none except for two or three older children who were apparently living out of town, for the other five or six family members also died. Long-time political leader Lonallen Rhodes passed, while his cohort William Walker recovered from the fever, but not his wife. Several families lost their mother and/or one or more children. The family of Dr. Richmond, well south of town, went unscathed. He came in to attend the sick, quarantining himself from the rest of the family. Dr. Robert McKay was not so lucky, falling early. A Dr. St. Clair, a new resident, also died. Revered R. S. Simmons, another new resident was the first town citizen to go, followed by his wife and daughter.[16]

In addition to the doctors who died fighting the fever, Lonallen

Illustration 40. Safety patrol catches refugees (Leslie's Illustrated, August 23, 1879)

Rhodes and L. B. Rainey gave their lives attending to the sick and their families. The town also honored J. H. Clark, Reverend Evans, D. C. Rhodes, and a Mr. Ware for steadfast service.[17] Whether it was brave or foolhardy to stay as the fever broke out, it was heroic to serve others as well as tending one's own family.

It is frequently told that the dead were buried at night to avoid hysteria. Reverend Evans reportedly made the rounds with a lantern in hand. He and a black helper who drove the wagon, dug the grave while Evans performed the last rites. According to tradition, the town cemetery contains unmarked mass graves where bodies were quickly interred to avoid contagion.[18] It is unlikely there were any truly "mass graves," since there were rarely more than one death per day. But there may have been some multiple family burials. Others also resorted to night burials, but it is doubtful that anyone thought they could avoid contributing to the town's panic. That was impossible. Mixed emotions were at work. The blacksmith, Arthur O'Neill, with the help of an elderly black man quietly buried his daughter Mary in the cemetery without ceremony or a marker. When rebuked by another daughter, his expressed sentiment was disapproval of ostentatious display.[19] What many may well have experienced was a depressive abandonment of the comforting communal ceremonies of tribute and mourning in the face of so much death. Who could attend to console the bereaved? Church services had been suspended, and it was October 29 before the Presbyterians gathered to memorialize their four lost members.[20]

Given the operation of occasional criminals out from Memphis, this was not the first time that Germantown residents felt that undesirable elements from the city represented a threat. As soon as the plague broke out, the town set up a vigilance committee to post quarantine guards at the depot, reversing the barrier. One wit reported that the cures to which refugees were subject upon arrival encouraged them to move on.[21] The flood of refugees seeking shelter, camping on their lands and looking for water became alarming. Those who had been hospitable became infected. Doors and gates were closed. One resident of the town observed, "The country people stood off at a great distance, with mouths and ears wide open, eager to hear news of the epidemic. Everyone is wearing sulfur bags and camphor in their boots, or bags of asafetida around their neck to ward off the fever." When papers arrived from Memphis, they were exposed to the sun before being read. Although country stores would sell to refugees, they went to ludicrous extremes to avoid any direct contact with them. Locals even tore up the bridge over the Wolf between Collierville and Fisherville to stop traffic.[22] Safety patrols scoured the countryside to arrest refugees camping in the area and to prevent anyone from stopping.

Since isolation was not the solution, luck must have been what saved families like the Dukes. They were well removed from the roads, so they barricaded themselves in and avoided expeditions to stores or anywhere else. "They couldn't get out to buy flour – wouldn't buy flour. They thought, sometimes, yellow fever was spread through flour, or salt meat. They had a mill on the place,...so they ground their own meal. ... But they all said they were so tired of eating cornbread, they didn't want to see another piece as long as they lived."[23] None of this explains their good fortune, but for some reason, infected mosquitoes rarely ventured far from populated areas or the rail lines that carried them in cargo. Up to fifty percent of the town either died or moved away.[24] By the 1880 census, the town had recovered to only 223 people, while the district had 2,917 total.[25]

When the disease hit Memphis again the next year, Germantown people were terrified. Platus Lipsey recalled, "I cannot forget the look on peoples' faces in the afternoon when the train came bearing the afternoon papers with the big headlines: 'THE SCOURGE AGAIN.'" Everybody talked of the horrors of the previous year.[26] Fortunately the town was spared a repeat.

Meanwhile the devastated and frightened community sought solace in religion. The new Baptist minister, John Lipsey, previously residing in Coldwater until 1879, had been "cut off from his appointments" in Germantown, Collierville and Whites Station during the '78 plague until early fall. When he resumed his ministry there, people were still dying. After moving his family to town in '79, he held four weeks of revival meetings and brought his membership up to 96 souls with baptisms at the Wolf. Cynics commented on "yellow fever converts." Although the young Presbyterian minister, Johnson, rejoiced in the meetings, Reverend Evans kept his distance. The Presbyterians and Methodists combined their thinned ranks and held joint meetings.[27]

The town had lost its reputation as a healthy retreat. Meanwhile, Memphis eventually got its health and sanitation act together. It cleaned up sources of contagion and employed effective quarantine procedures. After stringent measures, the city solved its financial problems and improved other aspects of its infrastructure.[28] There were no longer so many reasons to eschew city life for bucolic Germantown. Most of the city's elite and seasonal settlers departed the town.

Although the recovery of its population is usually given as the reason for the town's reincorporation in 1880, it never achieved anything near its pre-plague levels. Even a decade after the plague, Goodspeed gave it as only about 200. In any case, an 1880 petition was signed by "R. T. Anderson, E. M. Cole, J. A. Thompson and seventeen others." Anderson was a grocer, Cole, a carpenter apparently involved in a variety of ventures, and Thompson a doctor.[29] Perhaps their petition was a reassertion of life, an expressed determination to prevail.

Goodspeed's 1887 history of Shelby County documented the complete reversal of fortunes between Germantown and Collierville. He described Collierville as

> The second town or city in Shelby County.... It now boasts of 1,200 inhabitants, good brick business houses, nine dry goods stores, eight grocery stores, two drug stores, two hardware stores, two furniture stores, three livery stables, two hotels and shops, grist-mill, saw-mill, etc. ... There are two colleges, Bellevue and Miss Holdens' school. The two have an enrollment of over 300. The churches are the Methodist Episcopal South, Christian, Missionary Baptist and Presbyterian. ... The town is located near the southeast corner of Shelby County, within four miles of the Mississippi line, from which State it receives a large trade.[30]

Although his picture of Germantown was far less impressive, its many details are worth quoting to round out the story of our town.

> Germantown, comprising about 200 inhabitants, is situated about fifteen miles southeast of Memphis on the Memphis & Charleston Railroad. ... The place was incorporated about 1854 but the charter was allowed to lapse during the war. It was reincorporated, however, in 1880.... The principal business firms of the present time are C. M. Callis, G. W. Thomas, W. E. Miller, E. W. Gorman, Hatcher & King and Tuggle & Kimbrough. ... Germantown is well supplied with churches, Methodist Episcopal Church South, Presbyterian and Baptist. Each of these denominations have good houses of worship. The Presbyterian Church alone escaped the ravages of the war. The membership of these churches is about 50, 75 and 125 respectively. The most distinguished divine in this vicinity is Rev. **Evans**, of Germantown, who has been administering to the spiritual interests of his flock for more than a quarter of a century. ... Present physicians are Drs. Williams and Yancy. ... Germantown Lodge, No. 95, was instituted by dispensation in April, 1841, and was regularly chartered October 7, 1841. ... Present membership, 34. ... Caro Lodge No. 1664, Knights of Honor, was organized June 28, 1879, with thirteen members. ... The present membership is forty-seven. This lodge also meets in the Masonic Hall. ... The public schools of Germantown are taught in the Masonic Hall, first floor. The enrollment of pupils amounts to about 100. The school term lasts about five months. They are under control of Prof. B. J. T. Moss,

with Mrs. Moss as assistant, and Miss Jessie Williams primary. Other stations or villages are Buntyn, White, Ridgeway, Forrest Hill, Bailey, Ray's Station and Holly's Crossing.[31]

Perhaps because of better road connections into North Mississippi, specifically the State Line Road, Collierville was drawing off the bulk of the cotton coming for shipment on the railroad. Cutting off traffic south of Germantown, the Pidgen Roost Road led directly to Memphis or connections with the Mississippi & Tennessee RR, further narrowing Germantown's base in North Mississippi. In the crop cycle for 1872 for instance, Germantown drew just under 2,000 bales while Collierville exceeded 7,000. Fewer people were arriving and departing through Germantown's depot. In that same fiscal year, only 5,535 came through Germantown compared to 8,608 through Collierville.[32]

Another factor in the decline of the town was the inability of the local mineral springs to compete. None of them matched their rival at Raleigh, and there seems to have been no effort devoted to their marketing. Nashoba continued to draw locals into the twentieth century, but offered in facilities only a picnic ground. The Brunswick Springs had become a relatively private preserve of Dr. Richard Martin's family.[33] In contrast, the Raleigh Springs were extensively commercialized and promoted in local papers. The mineral content of each of its springs was analyzed and published in 1866, and a light rail line from the city was chartered in 1885. Railroad advertisements hawked the more distant and prestigious springs such a Hot Springs, Arkansas, and White Sulfur in West Virginia.[34] The fact that the Yellow Fever epidemic reached and devastated the town undermined its myth as a healthier retreat. There were fewer and fewer reasons for anyone outside the civil district to come to town, much less to stay overnight.

The little town would slumber peacefully for almost a century. A few stores and mills clustered around the center of town. For some time, there was a coffin factory. The number of church denominations increased, but not their sizes. It became most famous for its horse show, and was consequently misperceived as a town of rich "horsey people." That aura helped it attract a post-1960s urban flight. Building on that initial stimulus, it rapidly became again a cosmopolitan and cultured community.

# Appendix A
## Reconstructing Civil War Era Road Patterns

The old roads and how they ran are one of the more debated topics among the town's older residents. Except for one 1869 print, old maps showing the town and its immediate surroundings are of a scale and quality that obscure detail. As a permanent base of reference, the tracks of the former M&C RR, now the Burlington Northern and Santa Fe, have only changed with the elimination of occasional sidings. Even the grade levels have changed only for the addition of ballast, guaranteeing that grade level crossings and underpasses are mostly the same. The channels of the Wolf River and Nonconnah Creek changed constantly in their natural state, and have subsequently been extensively engineered. They cannot be used as points of reference for comparing old maps with new.

Even the old names of only a few local roads have survived in popular memory. Some others can be identified from old records. Even then, one can only guess about which of these old names in the documents applied to which present-day roads. Roads that led off to many different communities consequently went by more than one name adding to the confusion.

Only three surviving Civil War military maps cover the relevant parts of Shelby County. These were done by Sherman's engineers in 1862 and 1863. One covered Memphis in great detail, but only extended into the county as far toward Germantown as White's Station. Another was a reconnaissance map of the roads from Memphis to Bolivar. The third map covers from Memphis to Moscow, but is a strip map focused only on the State Line Road. Even the railroad appears only where it is adjacent to that road. Crossroads are not consistently included.

The oldest map showing any greater detail for road patterns around the town is an 1869 county map (Map 11).[1] One other is an 1880 plot map, but only irregularly showing roads other than the main roads. At least it provides the most accurate depiction of the streets within the town itself. The late 19th century maps of the Official Records of the Civil War are of such a large scale they only reveal where the major roads led. These are the problems then that plague the descriptions in this book.

*****

The center of the town was an irregular trapezoid formed by three north-south oriented streets, two blocks long and crossed by three roughly east-west streets. The limits of the incorporated town ran for a mile along the State Line Road, which zigzagged through the trapezoid. The railroad cut directly through the top of the trapezoid, running roughly east-west

(Map 3).

The town proper was defined essentially by the State Line Road. The town center was the trapezoidal grid from which radiated roads connecting with practically every community in the adjacent counties of Tennessee and Mississippi. When the town was formally chartered in 1850, it began "on that road (the State Line Road) so as to embrace Dr. J. W. W. Cornelius' dwelling house." This put the eastern side of town in the vicinity of the present high school. "Thence Westward one mile on said State line road towards Memphis," which put the western limit near where present Riverdale meets Poplar Pike. "So as to embrace all of those now living in Two hundred Yards from the center of the road North, and all those South of the road one half of a mile distant."[2] Thus the town encompassed less than a square mile straddling the State Line Road, and running predominantly west toward Memphis.

The Germantown Plank or State Line Road originated in Memphis as Poplar Avenue, and followed roughly the route of modern Poplar out as far as present Ridgeway. There it crossed under the tracks to take up a route approximating present Poplar Pike. It crossed the tracks inside the town at where present North Street ends, coming into town on that street. Whether North had a different name then is unknown. It formed the north side of the trapezoid ending at Bridge Street (present Germantown Road) which formed the east side. After recrossing the tracks and going south for about two blocks on Bridge Street, the State Line Road resumed, heading east (again present Poplar Pike). In less than a mile, it again crossed the tracks (where it does today) to run along its north side. Before reaching Collierville, it forked to continue along the ridge south to the state line into Mississippi (present US 72), while the Memphis-LaGrange Road continued east through Fayette County (present TN 57).[3] After crossing into Mississippi, the State Line or Alabama Road continued roughly the route of present US 72 toward Tupelo, and then into Alabama.

Bridge Street ran north to the Wolf River, but did not follow the route of present Germantown Road for very far before veering west to follow the route of today's Cordova Road. Out of town, it became the Raleigh-Germantown (sometimes Germantown-Bartlett and Morning Sun) Road, increasingly referred to simply as Germantown Road. It forked north of the bridge with the eastern branch going eventually to Morning Sun and the Memphis to Somerville Road. It eventually reached the Brownsville Roads (modern US 64) which connected the area to Nashville. The other branch ran north connecting with the Raleigh-La Grange Road. From that crossroads it made connections through Bartlett and Covington at least as far as Randolph.[4]

One block to the west of Bridge laid present West Street (possibly called Rose Street at the time) which ran south apparently from just below the railroad, and became variously Germantown-Capleville and Germantown-Olive Branch Road south of town. In those days, it wound westerly over to the present Cotton Plant Road, which then crossed Nonconnah Creek. Shortly after that, it forked south-west and then due west to Pidgen Roost Road (present Lamar, Highway 78) at Capleville. The eastern fork ran south to Holy Springs. It was previously referred to as the Germantown-Hernando Road, because it had originally been designated a federal post road in 1845 when it connected Macon and Hernando through Germantown.[5]

In town, one more block to the west of West/Rose Street laid Church Street (present McVay where it runs north-south). It formed the west side of the town center. Finally, a road (present McVay running east-west) connected Church and Rose Streets, and cut across to Bridge Street (a connection that has since been severed) to form the south side of the trapezoid and to connect with the east-bound State Line Road. There are no memories of the original name of this road or how far west it ran. There was a Germantown-Mount Mariah Church Road that connected with the Germantown-Olive Branch Road well south of town.

That old post road running south out of town also left Germantown running roughly north west as the Germantown-Fisherville Road, eventually connecting with roads to Macon. It branched off State Line Road at present 7642 Poplar Pike. It went under the railroad, which was on a high fill crossing two deep ravines. A sunken-road remnant survives at 7642 Poplar Pike, running between Holland Photography and Brice's Antiques. It passed through the area of the present animal shelter and ran north-east through the present Radford Estates until it picked up the route roughly of modern Dogwood (somewhere near where it crosses Poplar), and then headed east. This second-class road, eventually reached the north end of the Road to Macon (present Forest Hill Irene) which turned north-east, crossing the Wolf. Originally the 1845 post road running from Somerville through Macon and Germantown to Hernando, Mississippi,[6] it probably went into decline after the railroad connection reached Collierville, from which a better coach service was available to Macon.[7]

About a mile east of town on the State Line Road, Holyford Road (present Hack's Cross) ran south to Mississippi. By 1869, a Mrs. C. Hack owned 41 acres at the intersection, which undoubtedly gave birth to the present name of the road. Center Hill Road (present Forrest Hill-Irene), crossed the State Line Road at Forrest Hill. Two east-west roads formed a grid pattern connecting these two roads and the Germantown-Capleville Road. One, approximating part of present Winchester Road, turned north-east to connect with State Line at Bray's Station. The other

Photo 18. Sunken road remnant of old road to Macon.

may have been a predecessor of Shelby Drive. A third, even father south may have been a predecessor of Holmes. None of them ran the entire east-west distance of their present-day counterparts, merely forming connectors between the north-south roads.[8]

# Appendix B
## Identifying Men Who Served in the War

Of 237 white men of military age in the Germantown area, perhaps 153 served in Tennessee's Confederate units. Many others joined the regiments of other states, especially, Mississippi, but also Arkansas and Alabama. A few served in the Federal forces. Although this estimate is based on a problematic process, it clearly shows that more than half of the area's eligible white men served, perhaps as many as two-thirds.

Using the 1860 census as a base, and defining future military age as between 40 and 11 in that census, a total population sample was established. An 11 year-old would have reached 16 before the end of the war, and many under-aged boys served. A few men are known to have served above the age of 45, but adding older and younger to the search would have taken it beyond a point of diminishing returns. The men for this sample were drawn from all of District 11 and those from District 10, known to have lived in the Germantown postal area. The digitized Family Tree compilations of Civil War soldiers' service records and *Tennesseans in the Civil War* were searched for the names of these men.[9] Some other sources identified a few that were either not in the compilations or the census.

The problems that plague this process are several. The compilations of service records are not complete and neither are the census records. Names in both the census and in the Civil War records are not always accurate, spellings varied and frequently only initials or just first and last names are given. Furthermore only units of the state of Tennessee were researched. Including the units of other states would have made the search process impossibly arduous. The results are, therefore, inexact, but in a few cases the identities were almost certain.

In other less certain cases, many combinations of names and initials created multiple hits that increased the chances that the individual in question served, but making it impossible to identify any specific service. The search on a common name was terminated as soon as a long enough list of hits had occurred to indicate that the man in question had probably served. These are counted as "may have served." Whenever the results turned up units that recruited in Shelby County, or the Germantown area specifically, these were counted as "probably served."

Counting the men who might have served in a particular unit is, therefore, problematic. There are cases where one man's name produced multiple hits in units known to have recruited in the Germantown area. This inflates the numbers who might have served in some of those units. By the same token, however, the number of hits for a particular unit might have been even higher if the records of men with very common names had been completely pursued.

Only a broader search could produce records of service in the Federal cause. A few men born in the North were absent from the 1870 census, which may tell us that they returned home in 1861, perhaps joining units there. However, a goodly number of northern-born men clearly served in Confederate units. Some men who initially served in the Confederate army and were captured agreed to serve in the Federal Navy or units in the Indian territories for the duration of the war, so they served both sides.

Nevertheless, all this gives us some picture of how, where and when the men of the area served.

235 of military age:
41 may have served in Tennessee units;
69 probably served;
38 definitely served;
1 probably served with the Union;
1 definitely served with the Union;

The service of African-Americans is even more difficult to establish, since no names are given in the slave schedules of the 1860 census. The names of men in the 1870 census can be correlated with the sketchy military records, but that involves even more problems than with white men.

# APPENDIX C
## Assessing Population, Wealth and Property

The census data for 1850 through 1880 are the primary sources for many of the social and economic aspects of this study. Generalizations about comparative wealth and social structure have been derived from the population and agricultural schedules. Also, occasional insights into the more intimate details of a family's life and even community relations can occasionally be deduced. To avoid excessive and repetitive footnoting, one reference to this appendix has been made at the beginning of long passages dealing with social and economic generalizations. Where more specific insights have been deduced, references to the specific schedule sheets have been given.

The 1850 census gives only names, ages, gender, occupation, place of birth and value of real property. That of 1860 adds other personal wealth and school attendance. 1870's census adds race and literacy, omitting school attendance. In 1880, it dropped any information on education and property, adding marital status and parents' place of birth. Agricultural censuses become increasingly detailed in the nature and value of acreage, values of different aspects of agricultural property, ownership or lease status, types of production and its value. Nevertheless, one is frequently left guessing about the consistency among the takers in their definitions of the terms employed. Of course, a major problem is that most data is self-reported, and also depends on the interviewees' understanding of the same terms.

There are other significant problems. Although it is generally accepted that there is a 10% error in all censuses, those for Shelby County, Civil District 11 have proven to be more problematic. For the slave schedules for 1860, far more than 10% were missed. The agricultural census for 1860 is even more incomplete. In the 1870 population census, the huge estates of some of the most prominent planters were completely overlooked. Although it is understandable that census takers could overlook farms well off the beaten path, these were located on major thoroughfares.

The more routine errors to be expected are misspelled names, incorrect first names, missing middle initials, ages and place of birth. In such questions as literacy or school attendance, the attention of the takers to such issues was obviously perfunctory. It also seems that they were less attentive about accuracy when dealing with black families, and perhaps also poorer white families. Estimates of the value of property and productivity varied greatly in their apparent accuracy, and raise serious doubts about the consistency of the takers definitions of such things as real versus other property. They apparently relied on the owners' own assessments, and were cavalier about entering data about relatively insignificant property holdings, perhaps even failing to ask in such cases.

# Bibliography

## Abbreviations

CA Memphis, *Commercial Appeal*.

GBS Google Book Search

GM Germantown Museum, The. (Virtual Museum)

GPC Germantown Presbyterian Church, Historical Display

GRH&GC Germantown Regional History and Genealogy Center

GUMCA Germantown United Methodist Church Archive

M&SC Memphis and Shelby County Room, Benjamin L. Hooks Central Library, Memphis

MCA Memphis Conference Archives, United Methodist Church

MVC Mississippi Valley Collection, Special Collections, Ned R. McWherter Library, University of Memphis

NPS *National Park Service Website, Civil War Soldiers and Sailors System*

OR *War of the Rebellion: Official Record of the Union and Confederate Armies*

PS Memphis, *Press Semitar*

SCA Shelby County Archives

SOR *Supplement to the War of the Rebellion*

TCWSB Tennessee Civil War Source Book

TSL&A Tennessee State Library and Archives

# Primary Sources:

## Archives and Private Collections:

Germantown Presbyterian Church, historical display. Referred to as GPC.

> Rev. R.R. Evans, Letter to Henry Woodson, November 28, 1864.
> Rev. R.R. Evans, Notebook, Records of the Memphis Presbytery, 1855-1860.
> Rev. R.R. Evans, Notebook, Record of Tuition Paid, 1870s
> Phillips, Tom. "History prepared and read by Squire Tom Phillips," transcribed by Margaret Harrison Owen, March 27, 1938.

Germantown Regional History and Genealogy Center. Referred to as GRH&GC.

> Map and Historical Files
> Harry Cloyes scrap books. Referred to as HC/GRH&GC
> Germantown History Collection. Referred to as folder name/GRH&GC
> Germantown History Commission Interviews.
> Dean, Adelaide Sullivan, interview, 7.24.2007.
> G. Andrew Pouncy Collection. Referred to as APC/GRH&GC
> Elizabeth Hughes Collection. Referred to as EHC/GRH&GC.

Germantown United Methodist Church, Archive. Referred to as GUMCA.

> History of Germantown United Methodist Church File.
> Historical File of Elizabeth West.
> Warranty Deeds File.
> West, Betsy. "A Short History of the Germantown United Methodist Church." typescript, revised 1982.
> Wilson, Karen, "The History of the Germantown Methodist Church." typescript, May 3, 1979.

Memphis Conference Archives, United Methodist Church, Jackson, TN
> Minutes of the Annual Conferences, 1773-1958
> Journals of the Memphis Annual Conference, 1862 to current.
> Estes, Lud H. and Earl G. Hamlett, *A Short History of the Memphis Annual Conference of the Methodist Church*, n.d., n.p.

Memphis and Shelby County Room, Benjamin L. Hooks Central Library, Memphis, TN. Referred to as M&SC.

Britton Duke Papers
Civil War Letters and Diaries
M.T. Williamson, Historical Map Collection

Mississippi Valley Collection, Special Collections, Ned R. McWherter
Library, University of Memphis. Referred to as MVC.
Ayers, George B. *Descriptive Railroad Handbook of Great
Southern Route between New Orleans and Washington.*
Memphis: 1858.
Dunaway. Civil War Letters Written by William Dunaway, 7th
Illinois Cavalry. MVC- 3540.
Freemen's Bureau Papers, MVC-107
*Martha Titus Diary, 1873*, Shelby County, TN., MSS 54-84
Map Collection
Montague, A.W., papers, Acc#89-52, MS 54-127.
MS, "My Experience as a Confederate Soldier," by A.W.
Montague
Nashoba Research Files, MVC-388.
Howse (Howze), Isham R. *Isham R. Howse's Journal,* Book 8,
June 1852- September 1853. M 5388, Box 1, Folder 10.
Neely, Mrs. R.P., Memoirs, MVC-240, Box, 1, Folder 1.
Woodson Family papers, MS 114.

National Archives and Records Administration, Washington, D.C.
Referred to as NARA.
M 1911, Records of the Field Offices of the State of Tennessee,
Bureau of Refugees, Freedmen, and Abandoned Lands,
1865-1872.
M 598, Selected Records of the War Department Relating to
Confederate Prisoners of War, 1861-65, Roll 98,
Memphis, Tennessee, Provost Marshall
RG 77, Civil War Map Files.
T-227, Assessment Lists of United States Direct Tax
Commission for District of Tennessee
T-410, Records of the United States Civil Commission at
Memphis, 1863-64.
Microfilm, 1860 Census of the United States, Shelby County,
Tennessee,
Free Persons Forms, roll 278.
Slave Schedules, roll 279

Shelby County Archives.  Referred to as SCA.
Cemetery Inscriptions

Death Records, 1848-1958

Election Voter Lists, 1868

Map Collection

Marriage Records, 1820-1929

Memphis City Directories, 1859-1901

Naturalization Records, 1856-1906

Shelby County Circuit Court Minutes

Shelby County Court of Quarterly Pleas and Common Sessions
      Minutes

Records – referred to as Loose Papers

Shelby County Probate Records

Map of Shelby County, Tennessee. Compiled by J.B.
      Humphreys, Civil Engineer, Sears & Seoth of the
      Memphis Abstract Co., 1869.

Topographical Map of Road from Moscow to Memphis Tenn,
      by order of Maj. Gen. W.T. Sherman, n.d. (1863)

Topographical Map of the Environs of Moscow, La Grange &
      Grand Junction, Tenn. By order of Maj. Gen. W.T.
      Sherman, n.d. (1863)

Tennessee State Library and Archives. Referred to as TSLA.

    Lipsey, Platus Iberus. "Memories of His Early Life, (1865-
      1888)," typed MS reproduced by Julia F. and John J.
      Lipsey, Colorado Springs, CO, 1949. Robert Boyte
      Crawford Howell Papers, Mf.1270, roll 3.

    Tennessee Election Returns, State, County and Local Elections
      RG 87.


_____, and Duke University. *Tennessee Agricultural and
Manufacturing Census Records for the years 1850, 1860, 1870
and 1880*. Nashville: Tennessee State Library and Archives,
1990.

Agricultural Schedules, 1860, Roll 10, Shelby County

Agricultural Schedules, 1870, Roll 84, Shelby County

Agricultural Schedules, 1880, Roll 95, Shelby County


Wills Family papers/Kirby Farms collection, Germantown, Tennessee.

    Hopkins, John L. "The Kirby Farm House: A Brief History."
      Typescript, April 1, 1987.

    Hord, Rachel Brooks, composed and compiled by. *A Little
      History of the Brooks' Family of Pitt North Carolina
      and includes some descendants in Tennessee, Arkansas,
      Louisiana, Texas.* Crescent City, FL, 1990.

## On-Line Collections:

GenealogyBank.com.
> Google Book Search, providing an extensive on-line library of publications now in the public domain and dating to the period under study. Referred to as GBS.

Germantown Museum, The. (Virtual Museum), germantownmuseum.tngs.org/past.php. Referred to as GM.

Library of Congress, Chronicling America, historical newspapers: in addition to the *Daily Appeal*, the *Memphis Public Ledger*, plus several other period Tennessee papers and innumerable papers of other states.

National Park Service, Soldiers and Sailors System.
> www.itd.nps.gov/cwss.
> Search engine for regimental histories and personnel lists.
> www.itd.nps.gov/cwss/regiments.cfm.

Shelby County, Tennessee Genealogy and History, www.wdbj.net, referred to as TNGenWeb.

*Tennessee Blue Book.* https://www.tn.gov/sos/bluebook/.

Tennessee Civil War Source Book, (tennessee.civilwarsourcebook,com).
> A digitized collection of primary sources. Referred to as TCWSB. Includes selected excerpts from the following, plus numerous period newspapers.
> *Papers of Andrew Johnson*, Vols. 4—6, Knoxville: University of Tennessee Press.
> Pomeroy, Fletcher. *The 7th Kansas Cavalry in the Civil War: The Diary of Fletcher Pomeroy.* Topeka, Kansas: Kansas Historical Society, 1997.
> Sanderson, Jr., William F. *The Civil War Letters of Colonel William Lawrence Sanderson.* Np: 1997.

U.S. Census, Shelby County TN, Dists. 10, 11, and Germantown, raw data transcribed by volunteers, available at http://tnroots.com/tnshelby/census/index.htm:
> District 11, 1850: Germantown's rural environs.
> Germantown, 1850.
> District 11, 1860: Germantown and rural environs.
> District 10, 1860: Collierville, Forrest Hill and part of

Germantown Post Office
District 11, 1870.
District 10, 1870.
District 11, 1880.
District 10, 1880.
Cited as Census/year/district number.

*The United States Postal Service: An American History, 1775-2006.* Publication of the U.S. Post Office. https://www.usps.com/cpim/ftp/pubs/pub100.pdf.

U.S. Postal Service, Postal History Website, Postmaster Finder, Germantown Post Office, Shelby County, Tennessee at http://webpmt.usps.gov/pmt003.cfm.

University of Mississippi, Civil War Collection, Digital Archive. clio.lib.olemiss.edu/cdm4. Referred to as UMiss, CWC.

## Published Documents:

*Acts of the State of Tennessee.* 1839, 1841-42, 1851, 1854, 1855-57, 1859-60, 1861, 1862, 1865, 1868, 1869, 1871 and 1880 Referred to as Acts, year, page(s).

Bear, Henry C. *The Civil War Letters of Henry C. Bear: A Soldier of the 116th Illinois Volunteer Infantry.* Harrogate, TN: Lincoln University Memorial Press, 1961.

Berlin, Ira and Leslie S. Rowland, eds. *Families & Freedom: A Documentary History of Afro-American Kinship in the Civil War Era.* New York: The New Press, 1997.

Berlin, Ira, et. al., eds. *Freedom: A Documentary History of Emancipation, 1861-1867.* Cambridge: Cambridge University Press, Series I – II, 1986-2012.

Dyer, Fred Arthur and John Trotwood Moore. *Tennessee Civil War Veteran Questionnaires.* 5 vols. Easley, SC: Southern Historical Press, Inc., 1985.

Green, J. Harvey and Rachel. *Letters to My Wife: A Civil War Diary from the Western Front.* Complied by Sharon L. D. Kraynak, Comp. Apollo, PA: Closson Press, 1995.

Horn, Stanley F., Ed. *Tennessee's War, 1861-1865: Described by Participants.* Nashville: Tennessee Civil War Centennial Commission, 1965.

Hubbard, John Milton. *Notes of a Private.* (Company E, 7th Tennessee Regiment) St. Louis: Nixon-Jones Printing Co., 1911.

Hicks, Mildred, ed. *Yellow Fever and the Board of Health: Memphis, 1878.* Memphis: The Memphis and Shelby County Heath Department, 1964.

Lacy, Eric Russell, ed. *Antebellum Tennessee: A Documentary History.* Berkeley, CA: McCutchan Publishing Corporation, 1969.

Simon, John Y., ed. *The Papers of Ulysses S. Grant.* Vols. 5-6. Carbondale, IL: Southern Illinois University Press, 1973, 1977. Referred to as *Grant Papers*.

*Supplement to the War of the Rebellion.* Wilmington, NC: Bradford Publishing Company, 1994-2000. Supplemental reports to OR Series I, and records of events by unit. Referred to as SOR.

Sutcliff, Andrea, ed. *Mighty Rough Times, I Tell You: Personal Accounts of Slavery in Tennessee.* Winston-Salem, NC: John F. Blair Publisher, 2000.

U.S. Censuses

    *Statistics of the Population of the United States at the Tenth Census (June 1, 1880).* Washington: Government Printing Office, 1883. Cited as Census 1880.

    *The Statistics of the Population of the United States Compiled from the Original Returns of the Ninth Census (June 1, 1870).* Washington: Government Printing Office, 1872. Cited as Census 1870.

    *Population of the United States in 1860: Compiled from the Original Returns of the Eighth Census.* Washington: Government Printing Office, 1864. Cited as Census 1860.

    *Statistics of the United States, (including mortality, property, & c.) in 1860; comp. from the original returns and being the final exhibit of the Eighth Census.* Washington: Government Printing Office, 1866. Cited as Census Statistics, 1860.

    *The Seventh Census of the United States: 1850.* Washington: Robert Armstrong, Public Printer, 1853. Cited as

Census 1850.

*War of the Rebellion: Official Record of the Union and Confederate Armies.* Washington: The Government Printing Office, 1881-1898. A compilation of military reports and correspondence on both sides.

> Series I, vols. 3, 4, 7, 10, 17, 24, 30, 31, 38, 39, 45, and 49 covered reports and correspondence of both sides in West Tennessee about troop dispositions, operations and combat, and many general aspects such as dealing with the people of the occupied territories. Referred too as OR, vol. #, part #, page(s).

> Series II includes correspondence and reports concerning prisoners of war, suspect civilians and violations of the conventions of warfare. Referred to as ORII, vol.#, page(s).

> Series III includes Federal correspondence and reports concerning personnel and recruitment, including "colored troops," railroads, telegraphs, hospitals, etc. Referred to as ORIII, vol.#, page(s).

> Series IV includes Confederate reports and correspondence concerning defenses, ordinance and transportation. Referred to as ORIV, vol.#, page(s).

## Contemporary Publications:

Ayers George B. *Descriptive Railroad Handbook of great Southern Route between New Orleans and Washington.* Memphis: 1858.

Goodspeed's *History of Tennessee: From the Earliest Time to the Present.* Nashville: The Goodspeed Publishing Company, 1887.

*Goodspeed's History of Hamilton, Knox and Shelby Counties of Tennessee.* Reprinted from Goodspeed's *History*, 1887. Nashville: Charles and Randy Elder Booksellers, 1974.

Memphis Newspapers:
> *Memphis Daily Appeal* 2.27.1847-11.8.1890
> *Memphis Tri-Weekly Appeal* 4.1845-5.1862
> *Memphis Weekly Appeal* 4.21.1841-11.8.1890
> *Memphis Union Appeal* 7.-8.1862
> *Memphis Daily Avalanche* 1.12.1858-3.4.1866 [continued as *Memphis Avalanche* 1866-1890]

*Memphis Weekly Avalanche* 1.19.1858-11.6.1890
*Memphis Daily Argus* 5.1859-12.1866
*Memphis Bulletin* 9.1.1855-12.31.1868 [7.3.62-6.65 replaced
    suspended *Avalanche*]
*Weekly Memphis Eagle* 1.1848-12.9.1851
*Daily Memphis Enquirer* 1847-12.1.51 [merged with *Daily*
    *Eagle.*]
*Tri-Weekly Memphis Enquirer* 1841-12.9.1851
*Memphis Daily Eagle and Enquirer* 12.10.1851-6.30.1858
*Memphis Weekly Eagle and Enquirer* 12.16.1851-1861
*Memphis Evening Ledger.* 10.3.1857 - 1859?
*Public Ledger.* 7.18.1865 – 8.31.1893.
*Weekly Public Ledger.* 3.8.1870 – 8.26.1890.
*Memphis Evening Post.* 4.1868 – 9.1869.
*Memphis Morning Post.* 1.15.1866 – 4.27.1868.
*Daily Memphis Whig* 4.1852-7.1856

## Memoirs and Autobiographies:

Cumming, Kate. *A Journal of Hospital Life in the Confederate Army of Tennessee from the*

*Battle of Shiloh to the End of the War: With Sketches of Life and Character, and Brief Notices of Current Events during that Period.* Louisville, KY: John P. Morton & Co., 1866.

Grant, Ulysses S. *Personal Memoirs of U. S. Grant.* The Project Gutenberg EBook, 2004. <www.gutenberg.org/files/4367/4367-pdf/4367-pdf.pdf>

Nelson, Stith. "Excerpts from the Diary of Stith Nelson, University of Memphis Special Collections." *West Tennessee Historical Society Papers.* Vol 64. (2010): 119-133.

Sherman, William T. *Memoirs of General William T. Sherman.* Vol. I. New York: D. Appleton and Company, 1875.

Wallace, Lew. *Smoke, Sound & Fury: The Civil War Memoirs of Major-General Lew Wallace, U.S. Volunteers.* Jim Leeke, ed. Portland, OR: Strawberry Hill Press, 1998.

# Reference Materials:

Albertson, Eric, C. Andrew Buckner, Michael C. Tuttle, and Michael C. Krivor, *Terrestrial and Submerged Cultural Resources Survey along Approximately 6 KM of the Wolf River, Shelby County, Tennessee.* Report for Corps of Engineers, Memphis District. Memphis: Panamerican Consultants, Inc., 2001.

Allison, John, ed. *Notable Men of Tennessee; Personal and Genealogical with Portraits.* Atlanta: Southern Historical Association, 1905.

Cargill, Bernice Taylor and Brenda Bethea Connelly, eds. *Settlers of Shelby County, Tennessee and Adjoining Counties.* Memphis: The Descendants of Early Settlers of Shelby County, Tennessee, 1989.

Civil War Centennial Commission. *Guide to the Civil War in Tennessee.* Nashville: Civil War Centennial Commission, 1960.

Garrison, Webb with Cheryl Garrison. *The Encyclopedia of the Civil War.* Nashville: Cumberland House, 2001.

McKenzie, Robert Tracy. "Reconstruction." *Tennessee Encyclopedia of History and Culture.* tennesseeencyclopedia.net/imagegallery.php?EntryID=R017

McKibben, Joyce. *Index to Early Memphis Newspapers.* umdrive.memphis.edu/mckibben/www /index.html.

Miller, Alan N. *West Tennessee's Forgotten Children: Apprentices from 1821 to 1889.* Baltimore: Clearfield Company for Genealogical Publishing, 2006.

*Tennesseans in the Civil War: A Military History of Confederate and Union Units with Available Rosters of Personnel.* 2 vols. Nashville: Civil War Centennial Commission of Tennessee, 1964.

# Interviews:

Harry Cloyes, Germantown, Tennessee, July 7, 2010.

Adelaide Dean, Germantown, Tennessee, May 14, 2010.

Elizabeth Hughes, Germantown, Tennessee, June 30, July 1, 2010, September 20, 2011.

Jennifer Lynch, telephone, Washington, D.C., December 7, 2010.

Dan Rambo, Germantown, August 2, 2012.

Jane Sanderson, Memphis, February 11, March 4, 2012.

Frank Stewart, Memphis, Tennessee, August 5, 2010.

Susan Thompson, Germantown, Tennessee, June 2012, August 2, 2012

Walter D. Wills III, Germantown, Tennessee, September 31, 2011; March 29, 2013.

## Secondary Sources:

Abernethy, Thomas Perkins. *From Frontier to Plantation in Tennessee: A Study in Frontier Democracy*. Memphis: Memphis State College Press, 1955.

Aiken, Charles S. *The Cotton Plantation South since the Civil War.* Baltimore: The Johns Hopkins University Press, 1998.

Ash, Stephen V. *When the Yankees Came: Conflict and Chaos in the Occupied South, 1861-1865.* Chapel Hill: University of North Carolina Press, 1995.

Atkins, Jonathan M. *Parties, Politics, and the Sectional Conflict in Tennessee, 1832-1861.* Knoxville: The University of Tennessee Press, 1997.

Bailey, Fred Arthur. *Class and Tennessee's Confederate Generation.* Chapel Hill: The University of North Carolina Press, 1987.

Bergeron, Paul H. *Paths of the Past: Tennessee, 1770-1970.* Knoxville: The University of Tennessee Press, 1979.

Brown, Myers E., II, with the Tennessee State Museum. *Images of America: Tennessee's Union Cavalrymen.* Charleston: Arcadia Publishing, 2008.

Cappock, Helen M. and Charles W. Crawford, eds. *Paul R. Cappock's Midsouth.* Vols. II & III. Memphis: The Paul R Cappock Publication Trust, 1992 & 1993.

Clark, Blanche Henry . *The Tennessee Yeomen, 1840-1860.* Nashville: Vanderbilt University Press, 1932.

*Commercial Appeal*, Memphis. Numerous articles by local historians and references to historical articles in the Memphis *Appeal.* Cited as *CA.*

Cooper, William J. and Thomas E. Terrill. *The American South: A History.* New York: Alfred A. Knopf, 1991.

Coulter, Frederick Lee. *Memphis, 1800-1900.* Vol II. *Years of Crisis, 1860-1870.* New York: Nancy Powers & Company Publishers, 1982.

Crosby, Molly Caldwell. *The American Plague: The Untold Story of Yellow Fever, the Epidemic that Shaped Our History.* New York: Berkley Books, 2006.

Crouse, Maurice A. "A Sketch of Early Germantown History," *Germantown News, Germantown Festival Annual-1973,* September 15 and 16, 1973.

Cunningham, H.H. *Doctors in Gray: The Confederate Medical Service.* Baton Rouge: Louisiana State University Press, 1958.

Currotto, William F. *Tracking the Wolf: One Hundred and Seventeen Miles Mostly from an Armchair, 1828-1997.* Memphis: self published, n.d.

Daniel, Jack. *Southern Railway from Stevenson to Memphis: A History of the Memphis Division Southern Railway System.* Germantown: Grandmother Earth Creations, 1996.

Darnell, Dr. J. Millen, "A brief Chronological History of Germantown until the Civil War," compiled for the *Germantown News*, 1990.

Davis, Burke. *The Southern Railway: Road of the Innovators.* Chapel Hill: University of North Carolina Press, 1985.

Downs, Jim. *Sick from Freedom: African-American Illness and Suffering during the Civil War and Reconstruction.* New York: Oxford University Press, 2012.

Durham, Walter T. *The State of History in Tennessee in 2008: The Underground Railroad to 1865.* Nashville: Tennessee State Library and Archives, 2008.

Dye, Robert W. *Images of America: Shelby County.* Charleston, SC: Arcadia Publishing, 2005.

Eckhardt, Celia Morris. *Fanny Wright: Rebel in America.* Cambridge: Harvard University Press, 1984.

Faust, Drew Gilpin. *Mothers of Invention: Women of the Slaveholding South and the American Civil War.* Chapel Hill: University of North Carolina Press, 1996.

Foner, Eric. *Reconstruction: America's Unfinished Revolution.* New York: Harper and Row, 1988.

Fox-Genovese, Elizabeth. *Within the Plantation Household: Black and White Women of the Old South.* Chapel Hill: University of North Carolina Press, 1988.

Genovese, Eugene D. *The Political Economy of Slavery: Studies on the Economy and Society of the Slave South.* New York: Random House, 1967.

_____. *Roll, Jordan, Roll: The World the Slaves Made.* New York: Pantheon Books, 1974.

*Germantown News.* Numerous articles by local historians, especially Beverly Booth's Germantown Pioneers series based on interviews with old town residents.

Gibson, Christine. "Who Gets to Let States Back into the Union?" American Heritage.com.

Graebner, William. *A History of Retirement: The Meaning and Function of an American Institution, 1885-1978.* New Haven: Yale University Press, 1980.

Hall, Russell S. *Images of America: Germantown.* Charleston, SC: Arcadia Publishing, 2003.

Harkins, John E., Dr. *Historic Shelby County: An Illustrated History.* San Antonio: Historical Publishing Network,

_____. *Memphis Chronicles: Bits of History from the <u>Best Times</u>.* Charleston: The History Press, 2009.

_____. *Metropolis on the American Nile: Memphis & Shelby County.* Memphis: The Guild Bindery Press,

Harncourt, Paul. *Biography of the Memphis and Charleston Railroad.* San Jose: Writer's Club Press, 2000.

Hopkins, John L. "The Kirby Farm House: A Brief History." Typescript, April 1, 1987. Wills Family papers/Kirby Farms collection, Germantown, Tennessee.

Jemison, Peggy Boyce. *Greenlaw Rediscovered: A History.* Memphis: Metropolitan Inter-Faith Association, 1979.

Jenkins, Marie Goodman. *Church of Six Generations: A History of the Red Banks Presbyterian Church.* Holy Springs, MS: The South Reporter Printing Co., 1955.

Jordan, General Thomas and J.P. Pryor. *The Campaigns of Lieut.-Gen. N.B. Forrest, and of Forrest's Cavalry, with Portraits, Maps, and Illustrations.* Reprint. Dayton, OH: Press of the Morningside Bookshop, 1973.

Lamon, Lester C. *Blacks in Tennessee, 1791-1970.* Knoxville: The University of Tennessee Press, 1981.

Ledsinger, Anita. "Talk Offers Look into City's Past." Report on lecture by Betty Hughes. *Germantown News*, October 29, 1981. Referred to as Hughes Lecture.

Lindsley, John Berrien, ed. *Military Annals of Tennessee: Confederate.* Nashville: J.M. Lindsley & Co., 1886.

Mackey, Robert R. *The Uncivil War: Irregular Warfare in the Upper South, 1861-1865.* Oklahoma City: Oklahoma University Press, 2004.

Magness, Perre. *Past Times: Stories of Early Memphis.* Memphis: Parkway Press, 1994.

_____. *Good Abode: Nineteenth Century Architecture in Memphis and Shelby County.* Memphis: Junior League of Memphis, 1983.

McFarland, Patricia LaPonte and Mary Ellen Pitts. *Memphis Medicine: A History of Science and Service.* Birmingham, AL: Legacy Publishing, 2011.

McLeary, A.C. *Humorous Incidents of the Civil War.* Chapel Hill: University of North Carolina Press, 1997.

McPherson, James M. *For Cause & Comrades: Why Men Fought in the Civil War.* New York: Oxford University Press, 1997.

*New Bethel Missionary Baptist Church: 135 Years, 1869-2004.* Germantown: New Bethel MBC, 2004.

Norton, Herman A. *Religion in Tennessee, 1777-1945.* Knoxville: University of Tennessee Press, 1981.

Oaks, James. *Freedom National: The Destruction of Slavery in the United States, 1861-1865.* New York: W.W. Norton & Co., 2013.

*Press Semitar*, Memphis, Numerous articles by local historians. Cited as PS.

Rable, George C. *Civil Wars: Women and Crisis of Southern Nationalism.* Urbana and Chicago: University of Chicago Press, 1989.

Rich, Dorothy. *Fayette County.* Memphis: University of Memphis Press, 1989.

Russel, Clarene Pinkston. *Collierville Tennessee: Her People and Neighbors.* Collierville: Town of Collierville, the Collierville Chamber of Commerce, 1994.

Scott, Linda McGregor. *History of Germantown.* MS, n.d. Copy available at GRH&GS

Severance, Ben H. *Tennessee's Radical Army: The State Guard and Its Role in Reconstruction, 1867-1869.* Knoxville: The University of Tennessee Press, 2005.

Sigafoos, Robert A. *Cotton Row to Beale Street: A Business History of Memphis.* Memphis: Memphis University Press, 1979.

Schroeder-Lein, Glenna R. *Confederate Hospitals on the Move: Samuel H. Stout and the Army of Tennessee.* Columbia: University of South Carolina Press, 1994.

Smith, Eugenia H. *History of Germantown Baptist Church.* Germantown: Germantown Baptist Church, 1981. Copy available at GRH&GS.

Smith, Gerald. *Fort Germantown Historical Park.* Germantown: City of Germantown, 1985. Copy available at GRH&GS.

Stephens, Gail. *Shadow of Shiloh: Major General Lew Wallace in the Civil War.* Indianapolis: Indiana Historical Society Press, 2010.

*Tennessee Historical Quarterly* Referred to as *THQ.*
> Binning, F. Wayne. "The Tennessee Republicans in Decline, 1869-1876." 39 (Winter 1980), 4:471-84.
> Boone, Jennifer K. "'Mingling Freely': Tennessee Society on the Eve of the Civil War." 51 (Fall 1992), 3: 137-146.
> Cimprich, John. "Military Governor Johnson and Tennessee Blacks, 1862-65." 39 (Winter 1980), 4: 457-70.
> Lash, Jeffrey N. Lash. "'The Federal Tyrant at Memphis:' General Stephen A. Hurlbut and the Union Occupation of West Tennessee." 48 (Spring 1989), 1: 15-28.
> Luflin, Charles L. "Secession and Coercion in Tennessee, the Spring of 1861." 50 (1991), 2: 98-109.
> Zornow, William Frank, "State Aid for Indigent Soldiers and Their Families in Tennessee, 1861-1865," 13 (1954): 297-300.
> Vedder, O.F. *History of the City of Memphis and Shelby County, Tennessee.* 2 vols. Syracuse: D. Mason & Co., 1888.
> Warner, Ezra J. *Generals in Gray: Lives of the Confederate Commanders.* New Orleans: Louisiana University Press, 1959.
> Weeks, Linton. *Memphis: A Folk History.* Little Rock: Parkhurst, 1982.

West, James Durham, "The Thirteenth Tennessee Regiment – Confederate States of America," *Tennessee Historical Magazine*, 7 (October 1921): 180-89.

*Western Tennessee Historical Society Papers.* Referred to as *WTHS.*
> Aden, Mrs. R.F. (Capt. F.F. Aden), "In Memoriam, Seventh Tennessee Cavalry, C.S.A." 17 (1963): 108-117.
> Arnold, Mark L. "Baptism of Fire, Forging of Veterans: The Thirteenth Tennessee Infantry and the Battle of Belmont." 52 (1998): 95-104.
> Bailey, Robert. "The 'Bogus' Memphis Union *Appeal*: A Union Newspaper in Occupied Confederate Territory." 32

(1978): 32-47.

Baker, Steve. "Agriculture, Race, and Free Blacks in West Tennessee." 48 (1994): 107-117.

Bejack Lois D., "The Journal of Civil War 'Commando' DeWitt Clinton Fort," in WTHS, 2 (1948): 5-32,

Blankinship, Gary. "Colonel Fielding Hurst and the Hurst Nation." 34 (1980): 71-87.

Browder, George C. "Robert V. Richardson and the First Tennessee Partisan Rangers." 66 (2012): 65-97.

Coleman, L.H., "The Baptists in Shelby County." 15 (1961): 8-39.

Donhardt, Gary L. "On the Road to Memphis with General Ulysses S. Grant." 53 (1999): 1-15.

Dougan, John. "Why They Chose to Stay: The Petitions of Free Persons of Color to Remain in Shelby County, Tennessee, 1843-1853." 48 (1994): 118-125.

Dunn, Durwood, "Apprenticeship and Indentured Servitude in Tennessee before the Civil War." 36 (1982): 25-40.

Gunderson, Lawrence G., "West Tennessee and the Cotton Frontier, 1818-1849," 52 (1998): 25- 43.

Harrison, Holly Reed. "Our Relation to Persons of African Descent Has Been less than Ideal...'": The Southern Baptist Convention, the Christian life Commission, and Race Relations." 53 (1999): 118-134.

Jones, James B., Jr. "'The Reign of Terror of the Safety Committee Has Passed Away Forever': A History of Committees of Safety and Vigilance in West and Middle Tennessee, 1860-1862." 63 (2009): 1-28.

Lovett, Bobby L. "The West Tennessee Colored Troops in Civil War Combat." 34 (1980): 53-70.

Lufkin, Charles L. "A Forgotten Controversy: The Assassination of Senator Almon Case of Tennessee." 39 (1985): 37-50.

_____. "The Northern Exodus from Memphis during the Secession Crisis." 42 (1988): 6-29.

_____. "Not Heard from since April 12, 1864:? The Thirteenth Tennessee Cavalry, U.S.A." 45 (1986): 133-51.

Maness, Lonnie E., "Forrest's New Command and the Failure of William Sooy Smith's Invasion of Mississippi." 40 (1986): 55-72.

McKinney, John B. "Ned and Rose Kearney: My Dear Friends."

64 (2010): 134-142.

Mehrling, John C. "The Memphis and Charleston Railroad," 19 (1965): 21-35.

Nelson, Stith. "Excerpts from the Diary of Stith Nelson, University of Memphis Special Collections." 64 (2010): 119-133.

O'Daniel, Patrick W., "Loyalty a Requisite: Trade and the Oath of Allegiance in the mid-South in 1865," 60 (2006): 35-47.

Scarbrough, L. Alex, Jr., Vincent L. Clark, ed. "Camp Journal of Corporal Lemuel A. Scarbrough, Sr. Company E 'Dixie Rifles.'" 66 (2012): 123-47.

Waschka, Ronald W., "River Transportation at Memphis before the Civil War," 45 (1991): 1-18.

_____, "Road Building in and near Memphis," 47 (1993): 50-64.

Watlington, Elton. "Glimpses of Methodist History in the Mid-South." 56 (2002): 128-134.

Witherington, Albert Sydney, III. *History of Germantown: Utopia on the Ridge.* Germantown: self-published, 1997. Copy available at GRH&GS.

_____. *The History of the Wolf River: Diamond in the Rough.* Germantown: self published, 1997. Copy available at GRH&GS.

Wooster, Ralph A. *Politicians, Planters and Plain Folk: Courthouse and Statehouse in the Upper South, 1850-1860.* Knoxville: The University of Tennessee Press, 1975.

Wyatt-Brown, Bertram. "Community, Class, and Snopesian Crime: Local Justice in the Old South." In Orville Vernon Burton and Robert C. McMath, Jr., eds. *Class, Conflict and Consensus: Antebellum Southern Community Studies.* Westport, CN: Greenwood Press, 1982.

_____. *Southern Honor: Ethics and Behavior in the Old South.* New York: Oxford University Press, 1982.

Wyeth, John Allen, *That Devil Forrest: Life of General Nathan Bedford Forrest.* Baton Rouge: Louisiana State University Press, 1959.

Young, *Standard History of the City of Memphis: From a Study of the Original Sources.* Knoxville: H.W. Crowe and Co., 1912

# NOTES

¹ Census of 1850, p. 574.
² Thomas Baldwin, *New and Complete Gazetteer of the United States* (Philadelphia: Lippincott, Grambo & Co., 1854, pp. 261, 426 and 576.
  ³ Census of 1870, pp., 265 and 268.
⁴ Acts, 1869, pp. 376ff.; and *First and Second Reports of the Bureau of Agriculture...,* 1874, p. 1178, GBS.
⁵ Dye, pp. 115, 121 and 123; Magness, "Collierville," p. 113; Russell, ch. 9; and cf. Hall's pictures of Germantown.
⁶ John M. Keating, *History of the City of Memphis Tennessee....,* 1888, p. 133, GBS.

## Part I, Chapter 1

1 Acts, 1841, ch. XXX, sec. 12, p. 29, for the first charter issued by the State Assembly; County Court Minutes Book 6, 1850, No. 788, pp. 436-38, SCA, contains the town's petition for a charter in conformance with the act of the Assembly, January 7, 1850 (Acts, 1849-50, Ch. XVII), which was approved by the county's Quarterly Sessions Court; I have been unable to find any further records pertaining to incorporation in either the Acts or the county archives. Shelby County Map, 1839, TNGenWeb; and John M. Keating, *History of the City of Memphis Tennessee*, 1888, p. 133, GBS.

2 County Court, Minute Book 9, No. 788, July 1, 1850, pp. 437f., SCA.

3 Census, 1860, pp. xxxiii-xxxiv; and "Germantown Pioneers," *Germantown News*, July 28, 1977, p. 4B.

4 Steve Black, "Agriculture, Race, and Free Blacks in West Tennessee," WTHS, 48 (1994): 107-117.

5 *Tri-Weekly Appeal*, June 26, 1846, p. 2, col. 2.

6 Howse journal, July 23, 1852; and July 25, 1853.

7 Howse journal.

8 Census 1860, Agriculture, p 136; Agricultural Schedules, 1860, Roll 10, Shelby County, CD 11; and 1860 census, slave schedule, CD 11.

9 Abernethy, *Frontier to Plantation*, p. 289.

10 Hord, *Brooks Family*, correspondence, p. 48, Wills/Kirby collection..

11 Abernethy, *Frontier to Plantation*, pp. 289f.; and Cooper and Terrill, *South*, pp. 197-99.

12 E.g., credit problems between John Grey and James C. Anderson, 1848, loose papers 1849/20/4658, SCA.

13 Hord, *Brooks Family*, correspondence, p. 48, Wills/Kirby collection..

14 See Appendix C.

15 E.g., Loose Papers, 1844, box 9, #90, indenture, SCA.

16 Miller, *Apprentices*, p. 134; loose papers, 1841, box 7, 80 & 82; and Durwood Dunn, "Apprenticeship and Indentured Servitude in Tennessee before the Civil War," *WTHS*, 36 (1982): 29-31, 36f., and 40.

17 Ibid., p. 32.

18 Miller, *Apprentices*, pp. 134-37.

19 Fox-Genovese, *Plantation Household*, pp. 63f.

20 Faust, *Mothers*, pp. 4, 10, 20-22, 27, 31f., 56, and 78; and Rable, *Civil Wars*, pp. 1-30.

21 *Appeal*, July 27, 1852, p. 3, col. 1.

22 *Appeal*, April 17, 1861, p. 2, col. 2.

23 *Appeal,* November 8, 1856, p. 2, col. 4.

24 John to Sottie, Head Quarters 52 nd Ill. Infty., Germantown, Tenn, August 22ⁿᵈ 1863, Historic Sites folder/Civil War/GRH&GC

25 Fox-Genovese, *Plantation Household*, p.

26 Dyer and Moore, pp. 1032 and 1300.

27 Howse journal, May 7, 1853.

28  Loose Papers, 1857, box 35, #2087, Road Order – James Kimbrough (overseer) Germantown-Hernando Road,; and 1849, box 17, #000, Tuition Payment, 11th CD, SCA

29  Faust, *Mothers*, pp. 53-56 and 63f.

30  Rable, *Civil Wars*, pp. 22-24; and description of 1877 deed left to Laura F. Brett by her parents in St. John Waddel to John A. Kirby, July 14, 1898, Wills/Kirby collection.

31  Although literacy is not recorded in the 1860 census, that of 1870 indicates female literacy was still high among a property holders despite wartime disruptions; cf. Rable, *Civil Wars*, p. 18.

32  Census Statistics, 1860, pp. xiv and xliv.

33  Graebner, *Retirement*, pp. 10-14.

34  Census Statistics, 1860, p. xiv.

35  Lipsey, "Memories," pp. 13f., 18f., and 22.

36  Lipsey, pp. 11f., 23

37  Wyett-Brown, *Honor*, pp. 231-35.

38  Lipsey, p. 21, and 31f.; and Wyett-Brown, *Honor*, pp. 164f.

39  Ayers, pp. 22f.; *Weekly Appeal*, October 2, 1846, p. 3, col. 4; February 9, 1858, p. 3, col. 1; and April 15, 1872, p. 4, col. 6.

40  Howse journal, April 5, 1853; and May 9.

41  Hord, *Brooks Family*, correspondence, p. 49, Books/Kirby collection.

42  History of Education in Tennessee, Tennessee Department of Education web page: state.tn.us.education/edhist.htm; and "History of Education in Washington County," *Oak Hill School Teachers Resource and Curriculum Guide*.

43  *Acts*, 1851, Ch. 133; and 1856, Ch. 114, p. 127.

44  Bailey, *Class*,, pp. 43-49, and Appendix 2, tables 8 and 12, pp. 151, n., and 154.

45  Dyer and Moore, *Veterans Questionnaires*, vol. 3, p. 1032.

46  Loose Papers, Tuition Payments - 11th CD, 1845, box 10, #000; 1846, box 11, #000; 1848, box 14, #000; 1849, box 17, #000, SCA.

47  Loose Papers, 1855, box 30, #000, School Fund Payment - 11th CD – Mary Emma Pettit (Germantown), SCA.

48  Howse journal, April 10, 1853; May 11; July 8; and 10; and August 20.

49  Loose Papers, 1854, box 28, #92, Scholastic Population - 11th CD, SCA.

50  John Preston Young, *Standard History of Memphis, Tennessee*, 1912, p. 401, GBS; and Goodspeed, "Shelby," p. 840; Loose Papers, 1854, box 28, file 77, 1855, box 30, file 99, and 1856, box 32, file #000.

51  Loose Papers, teacher payments, 1855, box 30, #000; 1860, box 42, teacher and tuition payment files #2, 3, 4, and 5, SCA; and see Appendix C.

52  Loose Papers, 1861, box 46, teacher payment, files #1 and #3, and passim, SCA.

53  Faust, *Mothers*, pp. 82-84.

54  Loose papers, 1849, box17, #000, teacher payment to Geo. C. Furber, SCA.

55  Loose Papers, 1848, box 15, #20; 1854, box 28, #92; and 1856, box 32, #117, Scholastic Population, 11th CD; 1860, box 43, #156, School Fund Distribution – CD 1-11; and 1860, box 42, #s 1 and 5, tuition, SCA.

56  Census Statistics, 1860, p. 506.

57  Crouse; Anita Ledsinger, "The Nurenberger's – city's oldest house," reprinted in Historic Germantown 2010 supplement, *Germantown News*, p. 3.

58  "Germantown Pioneers," *Germantown News*, August 18, 1977, p. 2; and 1850 census, District 10, p. 184A.

59  Scott, ch. 3, p. 10; Ayers, *Handbook*, p. 23; and 1860 census, Dist. 10, p. 361A.

60  *Enquirer,* January 20, 1838, p. 3, col. 5, and July, 21, p.3, col. 4.

61  *Tri-Weekly Appeal*, October 3, 1846, p. 2, col. 7; and census 1850, CD 10, p. 183B.

62  *Appeal*, June 6, 1855, p. 3, col. 2; and Ayers, *Handbook*, p. 23.

63  *Appeal*, July 18, 1854, p. 2, col. 5.

64 Woodson family papers, MVC, MS 114, box 1, folder 5.
65 Census 1850, District 10; and "History of Germantown Presbyterian Church," Church Archive.
66 *Appeal*, June 6, 1855, p. 3, col. 2.
67 Ibid.
68 *Appeal*, March 8, 1855, p. 3, col. 1; July 14, p. 2, col. 6; and *Manual of Public Libraries, Institutions and Societies in the United States*, 1859, GBS.
69 *Appeal*, July 23, 1857, p. 3, col. 1.
70 *Appeal*, April 11, 1857, p. 3, col. 1; and Ayers, *Handbook*, p. 23.
71 Acts, 1857-58, Ch. 59, p. 124.
72 Ibid., pp.125f.
73 Census Statistics, 1860, pp. 509f.
74 1860 census, Searcy, White County, Arkansas, p. 4.
75 *Appeal*, August 23, 1856, p. 2, col. 7; Ayers, *Handbook*, p. 23; Acts, 1857-58, p. 262; Scott, ch. 3, p. 10; and James X. Corgan, "Towards a History of Higher Education in Antebellum West Tennessee," 39 (1985), WTHS: 65.
76 *Appeal*, January 15, 1857, p. 4, col. 3.
77 *Appeal,* July 15, 1859, p. 1, col. 4.
78 Woodson, *Genealogy*, p. 471.
79 Dyer and Moore, vol. 3, pp. 1032 and 1300; but cf. Loose Papers, 1847, box 13, #000, tuition payment to Benj. C. Harrison, showing extremely erratic attendance during a 60-day session, SCA
80 Woodson family papers, WVC, MS 114, Box 1, folder 5.
81 "125 Years Ago," *Commercial Appeal,* June 14, 1976; original article not found on microfilm or in any indexes.
82 *Appeal*, August 26, 1873, p. 1, col. 3; November 9, 1854, p. 3, col. 1; and November 10, p. 3, col. 2.
83 *Appeal,* April 15,1872, p.4, col. 6..
84 An act to abolish and discontinue Spring Musters..., January 25, 1842, Acts 1861, pp. 96f.
85 *Appeal*, September 6, 1852, p. 3, col. 1.
86 Appeal, September 24, 1852, p. 2, col. 1.
87 E. Smith, p. 7; and on the yard, Walter Chandler, "The Memphis Navy Yard, an Adventure in Internal Improvement," *WTHS*, 1 (1947): 68-72.
88 See Appendix C; Hall, pp. 12 and 14; E. Smith, p. 7; Hughes lecture; and *Appeal*, September 10, 1861, p. 3, col. 2.
89 Howse journal, May 14 and 15, 1853; August 17 and 18, and 28.
90 Pictures of typical local Methodist churches of the period, West historical file, GUMCA; Dye, p. 106.
91 Crouse, np.
92 Lipsey, "Memories," pp. 9f., and 34.
93 Faust, *Mothers*, p. 186; and Rable, *Civil Wars*, pp. 13-15.
94 Howse journal, July 22 and 25, 1853.
95 Ibid., July 18, 1852.
96 Ibid., July 10, 1853; and e.g., July 4, 185 2; November 28; January 16, 1853; and March 20.
97 Ibid., July 9, 1852; July 29; November 3; December 19; January 16, 1853; July 22; August 1; and September 25
98 Ibid., September 21, 1853.
99 Ibid., February 1 and 4, 1853; and August 25; Methodist circuit riders could change appointments annually.
100 Ibid., June 30, 1852.
101 Lipsey, "Memories," pp. 23-25.

102 Cargill and Connally, p. 24.

103 Census Statistics, 1860, p. 470; Capleville Methodist Church, May 27, 1951, pp. 8f., West History File, GUMCA.

104 Cooper and Terrill, *South*, pp. 263f.; and "Jeremiah Burns," typescript by Wm. M. Burns, EH/GRH&GC.

105 Richard Nolan, "Troublous Times: The Civil War Letters of William J. Armstrong, M.D., March 1863-September 1865, WTHS, 60 (2006): 26.

106 Cunningham, *Doctors*, p. 15.

107 Census 1860, CD 11, p. 165.

108 Hall, p. 96.

109 Bill to Britten Duke from Dr. Thos. M. Dupree, November 1854, Britten Duke Papers, M&SC.

110 Howse journal, June 30, 1852; and January 17, 1853.

111 R.L. Scruggs, M.D., "Medical and Obstetrical Cases," *The Western Journal of Medicine and Surgery*, March 1847, pp. 196f., GBS.

112 Ibid., pp. 197f.

113 Ibid., pp. 198-200.

114 R.L. Scruggs, M.D., "Typhoid Fever, as it prevailed in Germantown, Tennessee, during the fall of 1847," *The Medical Examiner: A Monthly Record of Medical Science,* vol. 4, 1848, pp. 79-83, GBS.

115 Census Statistics, 1860, pp. 29, 213, 239-44, 247, 250, 252 and 258.

116 Faust, *Mothers*, pp. 124-29; and cf. Rable, *Civil Wars,* pp. 9, and 55f.

117 Ibid., pp. 240, 258-59.

118 Kimbrough family cemetery.

119 Howse journal, June 30, 1852; March 24, 1853; and passim.

120 Terry Isbell, "The Victorian Way of Death: How Our Ancestors Buried their Dead," *Old Shelby County*, 44 (July 2002): 2-9.

121 *Appeal*, October 25, 1863, p. 3, col. 6.

122 Isbell, 3f.; Harrison account for Britton Duke, n.d., MVC 388, box 1, folder 13; and Hughes interviews.

123 Isbell., 4f.

124 Ibid., 7f.

125 Typical, surviving Germantown area homes, Hall, pp. 88, 93, 95, 96, 114, 127; and Dye, p. 118.

126 Scott, ch. 3, p. 7; and E. Smith, p. 6 (e.g., Thomas Rutherford Baptist deacon until 1856).

127 "Cotton Plant," typed notes with attached photograph, dated June 1, 1982; and typed copy of title records, January 30, 1845; private collection of Carolyn Gates.

128 Hord, *Brooks Family*, correspondence, pp. 47 and 50, Wills/Kirby collection; and Wills interview, October 29, 2011.

129 Wills interview, March 29, 2013.

130 *Avalanche*, March 10, 1862, p. 4, col. 7.

131 Aiken, pp. 12f.; Wills interview, October 29, 2011; and plan of Kirby Farm, Wills/Kirby collection.

132 Dyer and Moore, pp. 1032 and 1300.

133 Agricultural Schedules, 1860, Roll 10, Shelby County, CD 11.

134 Howse journal, January 9, 1853; January 18; February 1; February 15; March 24; and May 16.

135 1850 Census District 11, p. 193a; Old Circuit Court Minutes, book 12, reel 29, pp. 120f., SCA; *Eagle & Enquirer*, January 27, 1855, p. 2, col. 2; *Appeal*, January 28, 1852, p. 3, col. 1; July 13, p. 3, col. 1; July 16, p. 3, col. 2; July 17, p. 3, col. 1; July 19, p. 3, col. 1; and October 8, p. 3, col. 1; and cf. Howse journal, July 14,1852.

136 Old Circuit Court Minutes, book 12, reel 30, pp. 261-64, SCA.

137 Cf. Wyatt-Brown, *Honor*, pp. 364-66.

138 Old Circuit Court Minutes, book 12, reel 30, pp. 291, 295-97, 380-83, and 401f., SCA.

139 Index to Inmates of the Tennessee State Penitentiary, 1851-1870, tn.gov/tsla/history/state/inmate4.htm.

140 Howse journal, July 14, 1852; and June 2, 1853 on another duel elsewhere.

141 For a thorough analysis, Wyatt-Brown, *Honor*, pp. 350-61.

142 McKibben, Indexes.

143 Wyatt-Brown. *Honor*, pp. 368-71.

144 "125 Years Ago," *Commercial Appeal*, January 11, 1977.

145 Loose Papers, Box 45, 1860, Merchant Bond, William Essmann, #5531; and Tippling Bond, #5552, SCA.

146 *Appeal*, March 30, 1852, p. 3, col. 2.

147 *Eagle & Enquirer,* March 5, 1852, p.3, col. 1; and *Appeal*, March 5, 1852, p. 3, col. 1.

148 *Appeal*, July 12, 1860, p. 3, col. 2; and Nashville, *Union and American*, July 15, p. 3, col. 1.

149 Loose papers, Box 42, 1860, file #000, Pauper Burials, Unknown, by C.K. Holst, SCA.

150 Lipsey, "Memories," p. 32.

## Part I, Chapter 2

1 *Appeal,* May 9, 1861, p. 4, col. 4.

2 Ibid.

3 *Union and American,* July 15, 1860, p. 3, col. 1.

4 Bailey, pp. 3-19 for a historiographic summary; subsequently, Fox-Geneovese, *Plantation Household*, and Faust, *Mothers*, come down on the side of stronger social elitism, while Cooper and Terrill, *American South,* favor social harmony.

5 Subsequently published by Fred Arthur Dyer and John Trotwood Moore. *Tennessee Civil War Veteran Questionnaires,* 5 vols., 1985.

6 Bailey, pp. 18f.

7 Ibid., p. 19.

8 "October 25, 1861 – Captain A.O. Edwards, in Germantown, too his sister in Tullahoma," TCWSB.

9 Bailey, appendix Tables 4 and 5, pp. 148f.

10 Census, 1860, Agriculture, p. 239.

11 Goodspeed, Shelby, p. 916; property maps locate Twyford's lands among the present Ag Center fields near Wright's Nashoba Tract.

12 The story of Wright's failed, utopian project to prepare salves for emancipation precedes this period under study. Interested readers may consult Celia Morris Eckhardt, *Fanny Wright: Rebel in America* (Cambridge: Harvard University Press, 1984).

13 Census 1860, CD 10, p. 361A.

14 Genovese, *Political Economy*, pp. 13, 23-26, 28-31, 180-201, 206-8; and Wyatt-Brown, *Honor*, pp. 176f., and 189.

15 The 1860 census gives both occupation, landed wealth, non-real property, and place of birth.

16 Blanche Henry Clark. *The Tennessee Yeomen, 1840-1860.* Nashville: Vanderbilt University Press, 1932.

17 Ibid., p. 8, and appendices I, IV, and V, pp. 173 and 176f.

18 Ibid., p. 13.

19 Bailey, p. 26; and appendix Tables 12, 13 and 19, pp. 154f. and 158

20 Clark, pp. 16f.

21 Howse journal, June 30, 1852; August 12; November 2; November 26; May 11, 1853; June 29; and September 12.

22 Bailey, pp. 26-29; Howse's journal confirms this seasonal pattern.

23 The Howse journal extensively documents this social and cultural lifestyle.

24 These and subsequent such analyses are based on comparisons of the population

censuses for district 11 in 1860 and 1870, and the slave schedules for 1860.

25 Thomas Perkins Abernethy, *From Frontier to Plantation in Tennessee*, pp. 285f.

26 Cooper and Terrill, *South*, pp. 211-14.

27 Ibid.

28 See Appendix C; and Bailey, p. 25; and appendix Table 19, p. 158.

29 Ibid., p. 26.

30 Fox-Genovese, *Plantation Household*, pp. 224 and 235.

31 Dyer and Moore, p. xvi.

32 Ibid, vol. 3, pp. 1032 and 1300.

33 Ibid.

34 Bailey, p. 160, Appendix Table 23, tabulates ranks achieved by respondents to the Tennessee veterans questionnaire. In the volunteer regiments, officers and NCOs were elected, and there was a surprising degree of opportunity for the poor and small-holder to achieve company grade sergeant and officer's ranks. Not unexpectedly for any society, field officer and general's ranks fell to those who already had proven managerial or military command experience. Also table 20, p. 159 on political advantages.

35 Howse journal, e.g., July 20, 1852; July 23; and August 8, 1853.

36 Ibid., July 21, 1853

37 Bailey, appendix, Tables 17 and 19, pp. 157f.

38 Cf. Rable, *Civil Wars*, p. 21.

39 Bailey, appendix, Table 12, pp. 153f.

40 Bailey, appendix, Table 11, p. 152.

41 Bailey, appendix, Table 13, p. 155.

42 Bailey, appendix, Table 17, p. 157.

43 Jennifer K. Boone, "'Mingling Freely': Tennessee Society on the Eve of the Civil War," *THQ*, 51 (fall 1992), 3: 137-146.

44 Ibid, p. 142; and Wyett-Brown, *Honor*, pp. 67f.

45 Boone, p. 143.

46 Ibid, pp. 144f.; and Fox-Genovese, *Plantation Household*, pp.233-35.

47 Clark, p. 11.

48 Ibid., pp. 11f.

49 Boone, p. 142, Table 2.

50 Wyatt-Brown, *Honor*, pp. 63f., 66-69.

51 Wyatt-Brown, *Honor*, p. xii.

52 Census 1860, p.467, see Appendix C.

53 U.S. Census, 1850, pp. 574f., and 1860, p. 467.

54 Steve Baker, "Agriculture, Race, and Free Blacks in West Tennessee," *WTHS*, 48 (1954): 107-117.

55 *Tennessee Blue Book*, p. 414; Harkins, *Metropolis,* pp. 43-45; Lamon, Blacks, p. 22; and Young, pp. 25f.

56 John Dougan, "Why They Chose to Stay: The Petitions of Free Persons of Color to Remain in Shelby County, Tennessee, 1843-1853, *WTHS*, 48 (1994): 118-25; Loose Papers and Minutes if the County Court, passim, SCA; and e.g., *Appeal,* September 19, 1860, p.2, col. 2.

57 Minutes of the County Court of Shelby County, book 10, p 35, SCA.

58 Sutcliffe, e.g., pp. 77-20; and Fox-Genovese, *Plantation Household,* pp. 287-89.

59 Lane sisters interview, "Germantown," *Press-Scimitar*, August 27, 1981. The Callis' were among those missed in the slave schedule of the 1860 census, but brought at least two with them from Virginia, "Tracing the Roots of Black Germantown," *Tri-State Defender*, April 23, 1977.

60 Lamon, *Blacks*, p. 28.

61 Fox-Genovese, *Plantation Household*, pp. 151, 154-56.

62 "The Nurenberger's - city's oldest house," *Germantown News,* February 24, 2010, p. 3, reprint of original Anita Ledsinger, article.

63 Fox-Genovese, *Plantation Household,* pp. 153, 163f.; and Cooper and Terrill, pp. 214f., and 224f.

64 Faust, *Mothers,* p. 73.

65 *Appeal,* November 8, 1860, p. 2, col. 3; and Census 1860, pp. x and 467.

66 The Dred Scott Case; in the United States Supreme Court, December Term, 1856, p. 9, memory.loc.gov/cgi-bin/query/r?ammem/llst:@field(DOCID+@lit(llst020div1)).

67 Wyatt-Brown, *Honor,* pp. 3f.

68 Estes and Hamlett, *Short History of Memphis Annual Conference,* p. 13, MCA; L.H. Coleman, "The Baptists in Shelby County to 1900," *WTHS,* 15 (19612: 12f.; Holly Reed Harrison, "'Our Relation to persons of African Descent Has Been Less than Ideal...': The Southern Baptist Convention, the Christian Life Commission, and Race Relations," *WTHS,* 53 (1999): 119f.; Elton Watlington, "Glimpses of Methodist History in the Mid-South," *WTHS,* 56 (2002): 129; and *Appeal,* February 13, 1861, p. 2 col. 3; and June 15, p. 4, col. 1. For a more thorough discussion of the complexities of each denomination's positions on slavery, Herman A. Norton, *Religion in Tennessee, 1777-1945* (Knoxville, University of Tennessee Press, 1981), pp. 57-61.

69 Minutes of Annual Conferences, 1854-1867, MCA; 1860 Census, district 11, p. 179; and slave schedules 1860.

70 Howse journal, May 12, 1853; and June 26.

71 Evan's Presbytery notebook, GPC; Minutes of the Annual Conferences, MEP, 1854, p. 526, MCA.

72 Genovese, *Jordon,* pp. 186-91.

73 Coleman, "Baptists," *WTHS,* 15 (1961): 16; and cf. Harrison, "Relation," *WTHS,* 53 (1999): 22.

74 Minutes of the Annual Conferences, MEP, 1844-1860; Estes & Hamlet, *Short History,* p. 13; and Lamon, *Blacks,* p. 17.

75 Lamon, *Blacks,* pp. 17f.

76 Genovese, *Jordon,* pp. 215-84, for an extensive analysis, including African elements of beliefs and practice; and Cooper and Terrill, pp. 236-38.

77 Cooper and Terrill, pp. 234f.

78 Chaplain John Eaton, Jr., to Lieutenant Colonel Jno. A. Rawlins, 29 April, 1863, cited in Berlin, *Families,* p. 157.

79 Berlin, *Freedom,* Ser. I, Vol. III, p. 686.

80 Wills interview, October 29, 2011.

81 Hord, *Brooks Family,* correspondence, pp. 46, and 48, Wills/Kirby records .

82 Sutcliff, pp. 9, 75f., 156, and 182.

83 Excerpts from Howse diary, APC/GRH&GC.

84 "Germantown Pioneers," Germantown *News,* June 23, 1977, p. 4B.

85 Lamon, *Blacks,* p. 17.

86 A.W. Montague, "My Experiences as a Confederate Soldier," MVC, Acc#89-52, MS 54-127, p. 17.

87 *The Western Journal of Medicine and Surgery,* March 1847, p. 198f., GBS.

88 Ibid., p. 200.

89 Bill to Briton Duke from Dr. Thos. M. Dupree, November 1854, The Britton Duke Papers, M&SC.

90 Scruggs, *The Medical Examiner,* vol. 4, 1848, pp. 79-83, GBS.

91 Lamon, *Blacks,* p. 18.

92 Census, 1860, pp. xlv; and Statistics, pp. 281-83.

93 Census Statistics, 1860, pp. 281-83 and 519.

94 Census Statistics, 1860, p. 286.

95 Genovese, *Jordon,* pp. 603f.

96 Aiken, pp. 15f.; Cooper and Terrill, pp. 229-32; and Fox-Genovese, *Plantation Household*, pp. 149-51.

97 Bergeron, p. 42.

98 1836 Bill of Sale; and 1856 Estate Settlement, The Britton Duke Papers, M&SC.

99 "The Slave Laws of Tennessee," esp. Jones v. Allen, 38 Tenn., 627, 1858, genealogytrails.com/tenn/slavelaws.html

100 E.g., loose papers, 1850, box 20, #933, Inquest for Negro "Frank," JT Mason owner, Ledbetter, Sept 1849, SCA.

101 Ibid.

102 Ibid,; and Cooper and Terrill, pp. 224f., 233f.,

103 Durham, *Railway* pp. 58f., and n. 29, p. 102.

104 *Appeal,* August 4, 1843, p. 3, col. 2.

105 Census 1860, pp. xv-xvi and 337f.

106 1860 Census, pp. xv-xvi.

107 *Appeal*, September 25, 1856, p. 2, col. 6; February 5, 1857, p. 2, col. 7; and November 15, 1860, p. 1, col. 6.

108 *Appeal,* November 15, 1860.

109 Nashville *Union and American*, April 17, 1860, p. 3, col. 2, citing Brownsville *Atlas*.

110 Durham, *Underground*, pp. 51f.

111 *Appeal*, October 20, 1858, p. 3, col. 1.

112 *Appeal*, November 5, 1856, p. 3, col. 1.

113 The Slave Laws of Tennessee,.

114 Lamon, pp. 20, 22-24.

115 "The Slave Laws of Tennessee;" and Cooper and Terrill, pp. 209f.

116 Fox-Genovese, *Plantation Household*, pp. 165-68, 172-74, 176-81, 183-86.

117 Ibid., plus pp. 143f., 148f., 151f., 156, 191.

118 "Tracing the 'roots' of Black Germantown," *Tri-State Defender*, April 23, 1977.

## Part I, Chapter 3

1 Albertson, et al, pp. 18, 20f., and 23; William F. Currotto, *Tracking the Wolf* (Memphis: self published, n.d.) p. 10 , quoting anonymous ms, M&SC; Ronald W. Waschka, "River Transportation at Memphis before the Civil War," *WTHS*, 45 (1991): 1-18; Lawrence G. Gunderson, Jr., "West Tennessee and the Cotton Frontier, 1818-1840," *WTHS*, 52 (1998): 25-43; and Dorothy Rich, *Fayette County* (Memphis: The University of Memphis Press, 1989), pp. 28f.

2 Joe Curtis, "Wolf River Carried Own Steamers Once," *Commercial Appeal*, January 28, 1954, p. 36 quoting memories of John Johnson; and Nelson Diary, *WTHS*, 64 (2010): 131.

3 *The Public Statutes of the United States from 1789 to March 3, 1845*, Sess. V, Ch. 172, p. 276, GBS.

4 Wills/Kirby collection; and Wills Interview, October 2, 2011.

5 Acts, 1847-48, pp. 401, and 403f.

6 Acts, 1859-60, Ch. 72, Sec. 1, p. 55.

7 Loose Papers, 1844, box 10, #417; 1845, box 11, # 482 & 483, bridge construction payments, SCA; and Howse journal, e.g., December 23, 1852; and February 4, 1853.

8 Ronald W. Waschka, "Road Building in and near Memphis," *WTHS*, 43 (1997): 52-5, and 60; and cf. J.M. Stafford, "The Cretaceous and Superior Formations of West Tennessee," *The American Journal of Science and Arts,* 2nd Series, vol. 37, May 1865, pp. 360f., GBS.

9 Acts, 1849-50, Ch. CXLIV, Sec. 6, p. 473.

10 *Appeal*, August 6, 1848, p. 3, col. 1; and Booth , "Germantown Pioneers."

11 John M. Keating, *History of Memphis Tennessee*, 1888, p. 281, GBS; County Court, Minute Book 9, 1858, p. 1; Loose Papers, Box 47, 1861, J.M. King, Stray Mule, #906, SCA; Hughes Interview, June 30, 2010; and Acts, 1847-48, p. 402.

12  *Tri-Weekly Appeal*, January 30, 1849, p. 2, col. 5.

13  Acts, 1847-48, p. 402.

14  Acts, 1859-60, Ch. 159, Sec. 1, p. 500; and *Appeal*, June 16, 1860. p. 3, col. 2.

15  Cloyes Interview; and Hughes interview.

16  *Daily Globe*, January 7, 1854, p. 8.

17  1860 Census, District 11.

18  Lipsey, "Memories," p. 29.

19  Loose Papers, Box 47, 1861, #2446, SCA; and 1860 census, Dist. 11, p. 164.

20  Loose Papers, 1860, box 42, # 9, Petition to County Court for new road from
    Germantown Plank Road to Raleigh Road; and 1860, box 41, #000, Jury of View – W.
    Moore (juror), SCA

21  Loose papers, Box 42, 1860, file # 9, SCA.

22  *Tri-Weekly Appeal*, May 19, 1849, p.2, col. 7.  No Furber appears in any of the 1850 or
    1860 censuses, but other sources attribute to his presence during the 1850s.

23  Ibid.

24  For a general history of the early M&C RR, John C. Mehrling, "The Memphis and
    Charleston Railroad," *WTHS,* 19 (1965): 21-35; and, Paul Harncourt, *A Biography of
    the Memphis and Charleston Railroad* (San Jose: Writer's Club Press, 2000).  *Appeal,*
    July 24, 1852, p. 2, col. 6; and September 17, p. 3, col. 1.

25  Howse journal, August 2, 1852; and August 6.

26  Harcourt, pp. 93 and 237, Appendix B.  This contradicts all previous depictions of the
    first engine into Germantown, usually described as an antiquated 0-4-0 with a vertical
    boiler on the back and the engineer siting up front like a wagon driver.  This
    misunderstanding resulted from confusion with the "Best Friend of Charleston" which
    had been brought to Memphis to run out to Germantown for an historic celebration.  It
    was a replica of the engine run on the first railroad out of Memphis in the 1830s, not
    the later M&C RR.

27  *Appeal*, August 10, 1852, p. 3, col. 2.

28  *Appeal*, July 27, 1852, p.  3, col. 1; and August 4, 1852, p. 3, col. 1.

29  *Appeal*, August 10, 1852, p. 3, col. 2.

30  *Appeal*, September 9, 1852, p. 2, col. 2.

31  *Appeal*, September 18, 1852, p. 2, col. 5.

32  *Appeal*, March 5, 1852, p. 3, col. 1.

33  Harcourt, pp. 105f., citing *Appeal,* September 16, 1852 and *Huntsville Southern
    Advocate,* 10 November and 15 December.

34  Howse journal, July 2, 1852.

35  Harncourt, *Biography*, p. 251, Appendix F.

36  Daniel, pp. 24, 33, and 320; and  Stewart Interview.

37  Howse journal, April 5, 1853; April 15; June 10.

38  *Appeal*, August 4, 1852, p. 3, col. 1.

39  *Appeal*, September 24, 1952, p. 2, col. 1.

40  1860 census, District 11; in 1859, the agent was J.T. Tenbrooke, gone by 1860, *The
    Shopper's Guide: Containing a Complete List of all Railroad Stations...*, 1859, p. 122,
    GBS.

41  Mehrling, p. 31; and *Appeal*, February 6, 1855, p. 3, col. 1.

42  The relevant records are probably held by the Southern Museum, Archives and Library,
    Kennesaw, Ga., but have yet to be processed; correspondence from Dick Hillman,
    October 5, 2011.

43  *Appeal*, September 23, 1855, p. 2, col. 1; and October 4, 1855, p. 2, col. 7.

44  Mehrling, pp. 31f.; and *Appeal*, July `14, 1861, p. 3, col. 1.

45  *Appeal*, September 23, 1855, p. 3, col. 7; and April 16, 1861, p.4, col. 5.

46  Annual Report of the Memphis & Charleston RR, July 1, 1861, csa-
    railroads.com/Essays/Original Docs/AR/Ar,_M_a_C_7-1-61_S.htm;; and Headquarters

Third Division, Huntsville, April 11, 1862 (Captured M&C RR Locomotives) NA/RG94/159.

47  *Appeal*, October 15, 1852, page 3, col. 1; January 25, 1853, page 3, col. 1; September 26, 1854, page 3, col. 1; and January 9, 1857, page 3, col. 1.

48  Nashville *Union and American*, November 11, 1860, p. 3, col. 1.

49  M&C, Chief Engineer's Report, July 1, 1860, Daniel, pp. 27, and 29; and p.35.

50  Annual Report, July 1, 1861.

51  Daniel, p. 69.

52  Mehrling, pp. 33-35; and Ayer's *Handbook*, pp. 22f.

53  Daniel, p.55.

54  Interview with Jennifer Lynch, Senior Research Analyst, Postal History.

55  Ibid.; and Postmaster Finder.

56  *The United States Postal Service*, pp. 11-15.

57  Ayers, *Descriptive Handbook*, pp. 22f.; *Weekly Appeal*, August 8, 1845, p. 1, col. 5; and *.Appeal*, April 15, 1872, p. 4, col. 6.

58  1860 Census, District 11, p. 165.

59  *Tri-Weekly Appeal*, May 19, 1849, p. 2, col. 7.

60  Dye, p. 61.

61  *Appeal*, December 12, 1845, p. 2, col. 2; and p. 3, col. 7; and *Tri-Weekly Appeal*, January 22, 1846, p. 3, col. 2.

62  *Tri-Weekly Enquirer*, August 20, 1846, p. 2, col. 3; and *Enquirer*, April 7, 1847, p. 2, col. 3; May 14, p. 2, col. 5, and June 3, p. 2, col. 3.

63  J. Curtis, "Wolf's Little Flood Recalls Bigger Ones," *Appeal*, January 22, 1947, p. 18.

64  Scott, ch. 2, p. 14; Hughes interview, June 30, 2010; Howse journal, July 9, 1853; July 13; July 16; July 30; August 2; and *Appeal*, November 5, 1856, p. 3, col. 8.

65  Hord, Brooks Family, correspondence, p. 50, Wills/Kirby collection.

66  Schroeder-Lein, *Hospitals*, pp. 37f.; and Goodspeed, "Shelby," p. 915f.

67  "Germantown Pioneers," *Germantown News*, July 21, 1977, p. 16B.

68  *Appeal*, March 5, 1852, p. 3, col. 1.

69  Loose papers, 1860/42/0, jury of view, J.J. Todd; 1861/47/2462, and 1862/48/2534, road overseer, SCA

70  1860 Census, CD 11, p. 171.

71  Census 1860, p. 471.

72  Beverly Booth, "Germantown Pioneers: Traces of Germantown Settlers Obscured by Time," *Germantown News*, July 14, 1977, interview with Molly Molitor Nowlin; and cf. 1860 Census, Germantown, p. 170. It is not entirely clear that all the children listed in the household in this census and born in Mississippi and Tennessee at various dates were Francis'. Family traditions related by Mrs. Nowlin do not speak of a Charles or Martha.

73  *Appeal*, January 21, 1858, p. 3, col. 3.

74  1860 census, District 11.

75  "History prepared and read by Squire Tom Phillips," transcribed by Margaret Harrison Owen, March 27, 1938, p. 2.

76  *Appeal*, July 21, 1852, p. 2, col. 6 and July 18, 1854, p. 2, col. 5.

77  *Appeal*, May 19, 1855, p. 3, col. 5; and July 18, 1854, p. 3, col. 1.

78  *Appeal*, June 4, 1857, p. 6, col. 3.

79  Allison, *Notable Men of Tennessee*, p. 36.

80  U.S. Census, 1860, Agriculture, p. xi.

81  *Appeal*, October 31, 1855, p. 3, col. 1.

82  Hughes interview, June 30, 2010; *Journal of the Franklin Institute*, vol. 37, 1859, p. 372, GBS; Scott, ch. 3, pp. 9f.; Ayers, *Handbook*, p. 23; on occupations, see Appendix C; and Harrison's mill, *Appeal*, November 14, 1868, p. 1, col. 1.

83  Howse journal, January 11, 1853; and August 20.

## Part I, Chapter 4

1   See Oaks, *Freedom*, for an analysis of the abolitionist strategy as a real and growing threat to the long-range survival of slavery.
2   Wooster, *Politicians*, p. 45.
3   Jonathan M. Atkins, *Parties, Politics, and the Sectional Conflict in Tennessee, 1832-1861*. (Knoxville: The University of Tennessee Press, 1997), pp. 81f.
4   Atkins, p. 83, quoting period newspapers.
5   Atkins, pp. 82-88; and Wooster, *Politicians*, pp. 48f. on economic and demographic differences between the parties.
6   *Enquirer*, May 8, 1840, p. 1, col. 1, June 27, 1848 ,p. 2, col. 2, June 29, p. 2, col. 2, and May 30, 1849, p. 2, col. 3.
7   *Appeal*, August 4, 1843, p. 2, col. 1; and *Tri-Weekly Appeal*, August 9, 1845, p. 2, cols. 1 and 3.
8   *Appeal*, August 4, 1844, p. 2, col. 2.
9   *Appeal*, November 4, 1852, p. 2, col. 1.
10  *Appeal*, July 17, 1852, p. 2, col. 2.
11  *Appeal*, June 15, 1853, p. 2, col. 1.
12  *Appeal*, August 9, 1844, p. 2, cols. 1 and 3; August 16, p.2, col. 2; and June 15, 1853, p. 2.
13  *Appeal*, September 24, 1852, p. 2, col. 1.
14  *Appeal*, April 15, 1872, p. 4, col. 6.
15  *Tri-Weekly Appeal*, December 1, 1849, p. 2, col. 3.
16  TSLA website www.tn.gov/tsla/history/newspapers/tn-paper.htm; and Thomas H. Baker, "The Early Newspapers of Memphis, Tennessee, 1827-1860," *WTHS*, 17 (1963): 20-46.
17  Howse journal, December 21, 1852; February 3, 1853; and May 11.
18  Ibid., May 11, and August 18, 1853.
19  *Appeal*, August 9, 1844. p. 3, col. 2.
20  Sterling Tracy, "The Immigrant Population of Memphis," *WTHA*, 4 (1950): 72f.; and Harcourt, *Biography*, pp. 95 and 101f.
21  Keating, *History of the City of Memphis Tennessee....*, p. 245, GBS.
22  E.g., *Semi-Weekly Appeal*, August 16, 1844, p.2; *Weekly Appeal*, August 1, 1845, p. 2;
23  *Semi-Weekly Appeal*, August 16, 1844, p. 2, col. 3.
24  Faust, *Mothers*, pp. 10f.
25  *Weekly Appeal*, August 1, 1845, p.3, col. 6; *Tri-Weekly Appeal*, August 2, and August 5;
26  *Appeal*, December 5, 1855, p. 2, col. 4
27  Crouse.
28  This includes not only District 11, but those portions of District 10 that can be identified as part of Germantown.
29  Howse journal, July 6, 1852; December 2; September 8, 1853.
30  Census Statistics, 1860, pp. lvi and lviii.
31  Cooper & Terrill, *South*, pp. 316f.
32  *Appeal*, August 7, 1855, p. 3, col. 2.
33  *Whig*, August 6, 1855, p. 1, col. 3; and *Appeal*, February 10, 1855, p. 2, col. 1; and December 5, p.2, col. 4.
34  *Appeal*, February 10, 1855, p. 2, cols. 1 and 5; September 29, p.2, cols. 1-4; and November 5, 1856, p.3 col. 1.
35  *Appeal*, March 5, 1856, p. 3, col. 3.
36  *Boston Investigator*, October 4, 1848, Issue 22, col. D, citing the *Chicago Tribune*.
37  Scott, ch. 3, p. 3.
38  "Memories of the City's Settlers," *Germantown News*, June 16, 1977.
39  Howse journal, May 7, 1853.
40  Eckhardt, p. 273.

41  Nelson Diary, *WTHS*, 64 (2010): 125f.
42  *Appeal*, June 25, 1852, p.2, col. 5; July 9, p. 2, col. 2; and July 20, p. 2, col. 1.
43  *Appeal*, July 20, 1852, p. 2, col. 1.
44  *Appeal*, September 6, 1854, p. 2, col. 3; 1850 census, Germantown, Districts 10 and 11.
45  Smith, p. 7; and *Appeal*, June 30, 1853, pp. 2, col. 2, and 3, col. 1.
46  *Appeal*, July 6, 1853, p. 2, col. 2; and July 19, p. 3, col. 2.
47  Norton, *Religion*, pp. 56f.
48  *Appeal*, February 10, 1855, p. 2, col. 5.
49  Howse journal, July 30. 1853.
50  *Appeal*, June 14, 1860, p. 3, col. 2.
51  Wooster, *Politicians*, pp. 85, 99-102; and Quarterly Court Minutes, SCA.
52  Loose Papers, 1849, box 19, #473, County Court Chairman Payment, Ledbetter, Samuel W.; 1850, box 21, #552, Coroner Bond, Ledbetter, S.W.; 1854, box 29, #797, Justice of the Peace Bond, Pettit, J.W.A.; 1855, box 31, #4231; 1856, box 32, # 130; 1856, box 34, # 4552; 1858, box 36, # 689; 1858, box 37, # 869, County Court Payment, Pettit, J.W.A.; 1860, box 41, #000, Justice of the Peace - Resignation, and Judge – John W.A. Pettit, Oath of office, SCA
53  *Appeal*, November 17, 1859, p. 3, col. 3.
54  Wooster, *Politicians*, p. 99.
55  Acts, 1836, Ch. 1.
56  Sheriff's declaration, May 13, 1837, Wills/Kirby Farm collection.
57  Minutes, Quarterly Sessions Court, book 4, pp. 560 and 576, SCA.
58  Report of returns, March 15/60, RG-87B/1860-61, TSA&L.
59  See Wooster, *Politicians*, Tables 6e, 7e, ad 8e, for state legislators.
60  Minutes, Quarterly Sessions Court, book 4, p. 616; and Loose Papers, 1842, box 8, #368, constable bond, SCA.
61  Loose Papers, 1845, box 11, #444, constable bond, SCA; and 1850 census, District 11, p. 198B.
62  Loose Papers, 1844, box 10, #418, Job Lewis, deputy sheriff bond, SCA.
63  Loose Papers, 1848, box 16, #516; 1854, box 29, # 762; 1856, box 32, # 892; 1858, box 37, # 1001, Constable Bond; and County Court, Minutes Book 9, 1860, p. 506, SCA.
64  Loose papers, 1848, box 15, #000; and 1856, box 32, #000, Electors Common School Commission, SCA.
65  Fleming, "Education;" Loose Papers, passim; 1846, box 11, #000, School Payment (misc.) 11th CD, Thomas Moore; and 1838, box 14, #000, School Payment, Eugene Magevney, SCA
66  Loose papers, 1849, box 18, #26, SCA.
67  Loose papers, 1848, box 15, #000, election report; and passim, 1849-53, SCA.
68  Loose papers, 1854, box 28, #77, commission report, July 21, 1854; and census, box 28, #92, SCA.
69  In reporting these appointments, Pettit felt compelled to assert their legality, report, August? 28, 1854, loose papers 1854, box 30, #98, SCA.
70  Loose Papers, 1856, box 32, #000, Common School Commission Election, SCA.
71  *Appeal*, March 20, 1861, p. 3, col. 1.
72  County Court, Minutes Book 9, 1860, p. 526, and 1861, p. 704, SCA.
73  Howse journal, February 28, 1853.
74  Acts, 1841-42, ch. XXX, pp. 26-29.
75  E.g., Acts, 1859-60, Ch. 72, p. 55.
76  Acts, 1849-50, Ch. XVII, Sec. 2, pp. 37f.
77  Acts, 1841-42, Ch. XXX, Sec. 2, p. 27.
78  Acts, 1849-50, p. 38.
79  Genovese, *Political Economy*, pp. 13, 23f., 28; and Wyatt-Brown, *Honor*, pp. 70-87.

80  Wooster, *Politicians*, pp. 126-29, and Tables 6e, 7e, and 8e.
81  Cooper & Terrill, *South*, pp. 323f., 330.
82  Cooper & Terrill, *South*, pp. 313-15.
83  Atkins, pp. 206-212.
84  Atkins, pp. 216f.
85  *Appeal*, October 20, 1859, p. 2, col. 1, October 21, p. 2, col. 1, October 25, p. 2, col. 1, October 26, p.2, col. 1, November 5, p. 2, cols. 1-5, and November 16, p. 2, cols. 4-5.
86  Atkins, pp. 218-21.
87  Atkins, pp. 224-28.
88  *Appeal*, November 8, 1860, p. 2, col. 1.
89  Howse journal, November 30, 1852.

**Part I, Summary**

1   See Cooper and Terrill, pp. 323-33 on regional differences in southern industrialization as well as evidence against the argument that the slave economy and culture so stifled modernization that it was self-destructive.
2   Ash, *Occupied South*, pp. 4-5.
3   Wyatt-Brown, "Snopesian Crime."
4   Cooper & Terrill, *South*, pp. 333f.

**Part II, 1861**

1   *Appeal,* February 10, 1861, p.2, col. 1; and February 21, p. 2, col. 7.
2   *Appeal,* February 8,1861, p. 2; March 8, p. 2, col. 1; and Baker, "Early Newspapers," WTHS, 17 (1963): 44.
3   Charles L. Lufkin, "Secession and Coercion in Tennessee, the Spring of 1861," THQ, 50 (Summer 1991), 2: 98-109.
4   *Appeal*, April 19, 1861, p. 2, c. 3.
5   *Appeal*, April 19, 1861, p. 2, c. 3.
6   *Appeal*, April 14, 1861, p. 3, c. 2.
7   *Appeal*, April 21, 1861, p. 3, c. 5.
8   *Appeal*, April 14, 1861, p. 2, col. 1.
9   *Appeal*, April 17, 1861, p. 2, cols. 3-4 for Collierville; April 24, p. 2, col. 4 for Germantown.
10  *Appeal,* April 17, 1861, p. 2, col. 3; and April 21, p. 2, col. 2.
11  Acts, 1861, Extra Session, Ch. 1, pp. 13-18, Chs. 3 & 4, pp. 21ff.; *Appeal*, May 11, 1861, p. 1, col. 1; ORIV, 1:296-98; and Acts, 1861, Extra Session, Ch. 2, pp. 19-21.
12  *Appeal,* May 21, 1861, p. 2, col. 3. "T.W. Truceeart" was undoubtedly G.W. Trueheart.
13  *Appeal*, April 17, 1861, p. 3, col. 2; April 19, 1861, p. 3, cols. 2, and 3; *Avalanche*, April 17, p. 2, col. 2; and OR, vol. 52, pt. II, pp. 67, 134f., and 154.
14  *Avalanche,* April 16, p. 3, cols. 2 and 3; and April 27, p. 2, col. 5
15  *Appeal*, April 19, 1861, p. 3, col. 3.
16  *Appeal,* April 16, 1861, p. 2, col. 1; and *Avalanche*, April 26, p. 2, col. 1.
17  Charles L. Lufkin, "The Northern Exodus from Memphis during the Secession Crisis." *THQ*, 42 (1988): 6, and 9.
18  ORII, vol. 2: 1368-70.
19 Grievances and Memorial of the Greenville Convention," quoted in Oliver P. Temple, *East Tennessee and the Civil War* (Cincinnati: Robert Clarke Co., 1899), p. 565.
20  "Vote for Separation from the Union," June 8, 1861, p. 2, and for Report for Shelby County, RG 87/roll 1861-2, TSL&A.
21  OR, vol. 51, pt. I, p. 383.
22  OR, III, vol. 1, pp. 299f.
23  Severance, pp. 3f.
24  *Appeal*, e.g., December 8, 1860, p. 3, col. 3; April 10, 1861, p. 2, col. 2; April 16, p. 2, col. 2; April 17, p. 3, col. 3; April 18, p. 3, cols. 2 and 3; April 23, p. 3, col. 2; April 28,

p. 3, col. 4; April 30, p. 3, col. 3; May 4, p. 3, col. 2; May 14, p. 3, col. 2; and June 18, p. 2, col. 2.

25 *Appeal*, April 23, 1861, p. 1, cols. 2-3; strangely, neither Alsup, Coles, Cross, Rogers or Shepherd show up in the 1860 census for either District 11 or 10; but Cross was present in 1850, Dist. 11. The absence of some of these men appears to be a product of the inaccuracies of the 1860 census.

26 E.g., *Appeal*, December 12, 1861, p. 2, col. 6.

27 *Appeal*, April 23, 1861, p. 2, col. 2.

28 Ibid., p. 1, cols. 2-3.

29 Mark J. Arnold, "Baptism of Fire, Forging of Veterans: The Thirteenth Tennessee Infantry and the Battle of Belmont," *WTHS*, 52 (1998): 96; and Wigfall Grays historical marker, Collierville.

30 *Appeal*, April 23,1861, p. 1, cols. 2-3.

31 Ibid.

32 *Appeal*, April 28, p.3, col. 4, for the Shelby Grays.

33 *Appeal*, April 26, 1861, p. 2, col. 3.

34 Faust, *Mothers*, pp. 17-27.

35 Rable, *Civil Wars*, pp. 138-40; and Faust, *Mothers*, pp. 24f.

36 Rable, *Civil Wars*, pp. 141f.; and Faust, *Mothers*, pp. 27f.

37 Derek W. Frisbee, "'Remember Me to Everybody': The Civil War Letters of Samuel Henry Eells, Twelfth Michigan Infantry," *WTHS*, 55 (2001): 41.

38 *Appeal*, May 9, 1861, p. 2, col. 9 and p. 3, col. 3; and May 15, p. 3, col. 1 and 2.

39 Arnold, "Thirteenth," *WTHS*, 52 (1998): 96.

40 *Appeal*, August 17, 1861, p.3, col. 2.

41 A.J. Vaughan, *Personal Record of the Thirteenth Regiment Tennessee Infantry*, 1897, pp. 9, and 49-52, GBS; and James Durham West, "The Thirteenth Tennessee Regiment – Confederate States of America," *Tennessee Historical Magazine*, 7 (October 1921): 180-89.

42 Vaughn, p. 49; and Lindsley, p. 320.

43 Ibid., pp. 9, 48f., 66f., 69, and 75.

44 Acts, 1861, Ch. 17, January 31, 1861, p. 37, and Militia Laws, Ch. 30, March 22, 1860, pp. 115f.

45 *Appeal*, December 8, 1860, p. 3, col. 3; April 16, 1861, p. 2, col. 2; April 23, p. 2, col. 2.

46 Advertisement, *Appeal*, April 1, 1862, p.3, col. 3, and *Tennesseans in the Civil War*, vol. 1, pp. 27f.

47 Mrs. R.F. Aden, "In Memoriam, Seventh Tennessee Cavalry, C.S.A.," *WTHS*, 17 (1963): 109.

48 Hunt, p. 96; and Scott, ch. 4, p. 2.

49 *Sanderson Letters*; and Cunnigham, *Doctors*, p. 111.

50 Scarbrough, "Camp Journal, *WTHS*, 66: 126.

51 Goodspeed, "Shelby," pp. 826, 830f., and 835.

52 *Appeal*, April 23, 1861, p. 2, col. 2;

53 *Appeal*, May 4, 1861, p. 3, col. 2; May 7, p. 3, col. 3; and July 7, p. 2, col. 7; and cf. Acts, 1861, p. 98.

54 Letter December 6, 1861, Frederick Bradford Papers, TSLA, p. 1, TCWS.

55 Woodson, *Genealogy*, p. 471.

56 Acts, 1861, Ch. 3, pp. 25 and 30; Minutes of the County Court of Shelby County, book 10, pp. 41f.; and Loose Papers, 1861, Box 48, #0, Home Guard Regulations, n.d., SCA.

57 Acts, 1861, Ch. 3, p. 25.

58 Loose Papers, Box 48; and County Court, Minutes Book 10, 1861, p. 80, SCA.

59 Minutes Quarterly Sessions Court, book 10, pp. 41f., 46, and 59; and Loose Papers, Box 48, SCA.

60 Loose Papers, 1861, box 48, #000, Home Guard, Tuggle, J.J, 11th CD; Minutes of the County Court of
   Shelby County, book 10, p. 43, SCA; and 1860 Census, District 11.
61 Minutes, book 10, p. 43; and 1870 census, District 11, household 382.
62 *Appeal*, August 13, 1861, p. 2, col. 7.
63 County Court, Minute Book 10, 1861, p. 81, SCA.
64 *Appeal,* August 13, 1861, p. 4, col 7.
65 *Appeal*, August 17, 1861, p. 3, col. 2.
66 Vaughn, *Personal Record*, pp. 9-11, and 52; Arnold, "Thirteenth," *WTHS*, 52 (1998): 95-98; Scarbrough, "Camp Journal," WTHS, 66: 128-38; and OR, vol. 7, p. 691f.
67 *Appeal*, October 18, 1861, p. 2, col. 5.
68 Vaughn, pp. 12f. and 51; Arnold, 98-100; Lindsley, pp. 315 and 320f.; and *Appeal,* November 13, 1861, p. 2, col. 5.
69 Rable, *Civil Wars*, p. 64.
70 McPherson, *Cause & Comrades*, pp. 33-36.
71 OR, vol. 4, pp. 449f., 560f., and 564;
72 Nashville *Daily Gazette*, December 4, 1861, citing Memphis *Argus*; and *Daily Appeal,* December 18, 1861, p. 2, col. 1.
73 Bailey, appendix, Table 23, p. 160.
74 Ibid.
75 William C. Nelson to Maria C. Nelson, 23 June 1861, UMiss,CWC.
76 William C. Nelson to Maria C. Nelson, 14 June 1861, UMiss,CWC.
77 William C. Nelson to Maria C. Nelson, 21 May 1861, UMiss,CWC.
78 William C. Nelson to Maria C. Nelson, 23 June 1861, UMiss,CWC.
79 A.J. Vaughn, *Personal Record of the Thirteenth Regiment,* 1897, pp. 80f., GBS
80 Bailey, p. 104.
81 OR I, vol. 52, Pt. II, pp. 127f.
82 *The United States Postal Service*, p. 14; and interview with Jennifer Lynch.
83 Clarksville, *Chronicle*, January 10, 1862, TCWS
84 Minutes, book 10, p. 41, SCA.
85 *Appeal*, May 30, 1861, p. 3, c. 1.
86 *Appeal*, July 19, 1861, p. 3, c. 2.
87 *Appeal*, June 15, 1861, p. 4, col. 1.
88 County Court, Minute Book, 10, 1861, p. 82, SCA.
89 County Court, Minute Book 10, 1862, pp. 162 and 182, SCA.
90 *Appeal,* May 9, 1861, p. 2, col. 9; May 16, p. 3, col. 2; and late reference, December 9, 1861, OR, vol, 7, p. 749.
91 OR, vol. 51, pt. I, p. 383.
92 *Appeal,* September 26, 1861, p. 4, col. 2.
93 *Appeal*, October 31, 1861, p. 2, col. 8.
94 Nashville, *Union and* American, October 19, 1861, p. 3, col. 2.
95 *Tennesseans in the Civil War*, Vol. 1, p. 252; and SOR, Ser. 79, pp. 238-51.
96 *Tennesseans in the Civil War*, Vol. 1, p. 258.
97 *Appeal*, January 5, 1862, p. 3, col. 6.
98 Allison, *Notable Men of Tennessee*, p. 36.
99 Joe Barbiere, *Scraps from the Prison Table at Camp Chase and Johnson's Island,* 1868, p. 219, GBS.
100 Faust, *Mothers*, pp. 126f., and 146-48; and Rable, *Civil Wars*, pp. 193f.
101 "October 25, 1861 – Captain A.O. Edwards, in Germantown, to his sister in Tullahoma," TCWSB.
102 McFarland, *Medicine*, pp. 23f.; and Cunningham, *Doctors*, pp. 165f, and 188-90.
103 Schroeder-Lein, *Hospitals*, p. 43.

## Part II, 1862

104 *Appeal*, January 1, 1861, p. 2, col. 1.
105 *Appeal*, March 4, 1862, p. 2, col. 7, and p. 3, col. 4; *Avalanche*, March 10, 1862, p. 2, cols. 5 and 8, and p. 4, col. 4.
106 *Appeal*, March 25, 1862, p. 2, col. 8.
107 OR, vol. 10, pp. 297f; *Appeal*, March 7, 1862, p. 1, col. 7; March 9, p. 1, col. 3; *Avalanche*, March 10, p. 2, cols. 1 and 5.
108 Harncourt, *Biography*, p. 139; and OR, vol. 10, pt. II, p. 304.
109 OR, vol. 10, p. 298.
110 William Frank Zornow, "State Aid for Indigent Soldiers and Their Families in Tennessee, 1861-1865," *THQ*, 13 (1954): 298f.
111 *Appeal*, March 20, 1862, p. 1, cols 1-2.
112 OR, Vol. 10, pt. I, p. 409.
113 OR, vol. 10, pt. II, p. 425.
114 SOR, Ser. 78, p. 645.
115 1860 census, CD 11, p. 169.
116 McPherson, *Causes & Comrades*, p. 6.
117 SOR, Ser. 78, p. 645.
118 *Appeal*, April 20, 1863, p. 1, col. 2; April 24, p. 1, col. 5, and p. 2, col. 4; and Faust, *Mothers*, p. 116.
119 McPherson, *Cause & Comrades*, pp. 133f., 139; and Faust, *Mothers*, pp. 118, 243f.
120  Vaughn, pp. 15-19; but cf. Arnold, p. 101, whose casualty figures for Shiloh differ.
121 Horn, p. 98.
122 *Appeal*, April 27, 1862, p. 2, col. 5.
123 Harncourt, *Biography*, p. 181, citing M&C Asst. Superintendent's report, 19 June 1862.
124 ORIV, vol. 1: 1061f; and vol. 2: 727f.
125 McPherson, *Cause & Comrades*, p. 9.
126 Albert Burton Moore, *Conscription and Conflict in the Confederacy*, New York: MacMillan, 1924; reprint 1963, University of South Carolina, for the classic study; and Faust, *Mothers*, pp. 54f.
127 ORIV, vol. 1: 1062.
128 ORIV, vol. 2: 728f.
129 OR, vol. 24, pt. III, p.1024.
130  OR, vol. 29, pt. II, p. 601.
131 *Appeal*, May 11, 1862, p. 1, col. 6.
132 Sherman, *Memoirs*, p. 257.
133 Montague, "Experience," MVC, Acc# 89-52, MS 54-127, pp. 9f.
134 Aden, pp. 110f.
135 Aden, p. 111; and Nathan K. Moran, "'No Alternative Left': State and County Government in Northwest Tennessee during the Union Invasion, January-June 1862," *WTHS*, 46 (1992), pp. 24 and 31.
136 OR, vol. 10, pt. I, pp. 650f.
137 Hubbard, p. 32; OR, vol. 10, pt. II, pp. 382, 465f, and 516; and Aden, pp.109, and 111.
138 Ash, *Yankees*, pp. 16-22.
139 Ash, *Yankees*, pp. 10, 14, 19f., 31-33, 157, 223; and Rable, *Civil Wars*, pp. 156-58.
140 Ibid.; and OR, vol. 17, pt. II, p. 10f.
141 *Appeal*, 13 June 1862, p. 2, col. 2.
142 *Argus*, June 21, 1862, p. 2, col. 8; *Appeal*, July 11, 1862, p. 2, col. 1.
143 E.g., *Appeal*, March 30, 1864, p. 1, col. 1.
144  Map, "Memphis and Vicinity, surveyed and drawn by order of Major General W.T. Sherman," circa 1862/63, MVC; General Topographical Map, plate CLIV, *OR Atlas*; Shelby Co. map, 1888, M&SC; and  Hall, pp. 19 and 21.  To the north, of course, the Old and New Raleigh Roads were employed for operations.
145 *Appeal*, June 23, 1862, p. 2, col. 7; Wallace, pp. 145f.; and Stephens, pp. 113f.

146 OR, vol. 17, pt. II, p. 14.

147 OR, vol. 17, pt. II, p. 15.

148 OR, vol. 17, pt. II, p. 46.

149 Grant, *Memoirs*, vol. I, pp. 171f.; Sherman, *Memoirs*, p. 258; and Gary L. Donhardt, "On the Road to Memphis with General Ulysses S. Grant," *WTHS*, 53 (1999): 1-15.

150 OR, vol.17, pt. I, pp. 10-12; pt. II, pp. 638f.; and *Appeal*, July 2, 1862, p. 2, cols. 1 and 4.

151 OR, vol. 17, pt. II, p. 47.

152 OR, vol. 17, pt. I, p. 12.

153 SOR, Ser. 65, p. 65;ORII, vol. 5: 323; *Grant Papers*, pp. 158f, n.; and *Appeal*, July 2, 1862, p. 2, col. 1.

154 OR, vol. 17, pt. I, p. 11.

155 *Ledger*, April 16, 1869, p. 2, col. 2.

156 Ash, *Yankees,* pp. 46-48.

157 SOR, Ser. 65, p. 74.

158 Grant, *Documents*, p. 179, n. 1.

159 OR, vol. 17, pt. II, p. 44.

160 OR, vol. 17, pt. II, pp. 36f.

161 Grant, *Documents*, p. 188.

162 OR, vol. 17, pt. II, pp. 33, 40f., 44, 55f., and 60; SOR, Ser. 19, p. 599; Ser. 29, p. 46; and Ser. 53, pp. 140-43.

163 SOR, Ser. 19, p. 600.

164 OR, vol. 17, pt. II, p. 78.

165 OR, vol. 17, pt. II, p. 55.

166 *Appeal*, July 7, 1862, p. 2, col. 1.

167 OR, Ser. I, vol. 17, pt. I, pp. 10-72, and pt. II, to p. 142; for the Confederate side, e.g. pp. 692f., 696-98,

168 OR, vol. 17, pt. II, pp. 45, 49 and 79; and *Appeal*, July 4, 1862, p. 2, col. 1.

169 *Appeal*, July 7, 1862, p. 2, col. 1.

170 SOR, Ser. 44, p. 283; and *Appeal*, June 10, 1862, p. 2, col. 1.

171 Ibid.

172 *Appeal*, April 22, 1866, p. 2, col. 7.

173 *Appeal*, April 29, 1862, p. 2, col. 6; April 30, p. 2, col. 6;

174 SOR, Ser. 44, p. 282.

175 OR, vol. 10, pt. I, p. 591; and *Appeal*, July 4, 1862, p. 2, col. 1.

176 Ibid; and OR, vol. 10, pt. II, p. 592.

177 *ppeal,* July 4, 1866, p. 2, col. 1, quoting the *Avalanche.*

178 *Appeal*, July 25, 1862, p. 2, col. 7.

179 *Appeal*, November 4, 1866, p. 2, col. 1 quoting the *Bulletin* of October 31.

180 OR, vol. 47, pt. II, p. 69.

181 Wills interview.

182 *Appeal,* June 23, 1862, p. 2, col. 1.

183 Lipsey, "Memoirs," p. 34.

184 OR, vol. 17, pt. II, pp. 16, 81 and 87f.; and Special Correspondence of the Chicago *Times*, from Shiloh, May 23, 1862, p. 3, TCWS.

185 OR, vol. 17, pt. II, pp.9f., and 237; and Sherman, *Memoirs*, pp. 256-59.

186 OR, vol. 17, pt. II, p. 22.

187 Sherman, *Memoirs*, p. 258; and OR, vol. 17, pt. II, p.79.

188 OR, vol. 17, pt. II, p. 121.

189 *Appeal*, July 25, 1862, p. 2, col. 6; and July 26, p. 2, col. 3.

190 Dean interview, 7.24.2007, GHC

191 *The Ottawa Free Trader* (Illinois), August 16, 1862, p. 2, col. 4.

192 *The Athens Post* (Tennessee), August 1, 1862, p. 1, col. 2..

193 OR, vol. 17, pt. II, pp. 99f., p. 106, 109, 118f., 121-23, 128, 142, 149f., and 171; and Sherman, *Memoirs*, p. 259.

194 OR, vol. 17, pt. II, pp. 143-46; and vol. 24, pt. I, p. 4. Periodically Sherman's forces were greatly reduced when he had to dispatch significant forces, for instance Hurlbut's entire division, to deal with major Confederate threats to the east and south.

195 OR. Vol. 17, pt. II, pp. 311, 337 and 341.

196 OR, vol. 17, pt. II, p. 182.

197 McLeary, *Humorous Incident of the Civil War*, p. 9.

198 OR, vol. 17, pt. II, pp. 681 and 701 for Van Dorn's negative opinion of partisans and especially those operating as small independent commands.

199 OR, vol. 52, pt. II, p. 391; and *Appeal*, July 18, 1862, p.2, col. 8; July 22, p. 1, col. 2; and August 7, 1862, p. 2, col. 2.

200 OR, vol. 17, pt. II, p. 681.

201 *Appeal*, November 20, 1862, p. 2, col. 8.

202 As quoted in *Appeal*, August 23, 1862, p. 2, col. 6.

203 OR, vol. 17, pt. II, pp. 605, 611, 616f., 621f., and 743; emphasis added.

204 OR, vol. 52, pt. II, p. 391; vol. 17, pt. I, p. 797; pt. II, 743; and *Tennesseans in the Civil War*, Vol. 1, pp. 38, 80.

205 OR, vol. 52, pt. II, p. 391.

206 OR, vol. 17, pt. I, p. 485.

207 *Bulletin*, October 25, 1863, p. 2, col. 2; and October 11, p. 2, col. 3.

208 ORII, vol. 3: 664.

209 Specifically on July 6, General Bragg wrote Halleck complaining of Federal soldiers wantonly destroying the property of secessionists and threatening to have them shot. ORII, vol. 5: 136.

210 OR, vol. 17, pt. I, p. 23; and ORII, vol. 4: 211f.

211 ORIII, vol. 2: 402.

212 ORII, vol. 5: 948.

213 OR, vol. 17, pt. I, p. 55.

214 *Sun*, October 14, 1862, p. 2, genealogybank.co/gbnk/newspapers/doc/v2:1134300.

215 OR, vol. 17, pt. I, pp. 461f.

216 OR, vol. 17 pt. I, pp. 144f., 235f., and p. 240.

217 SOR, Ser. 3, pp. 315-18.

218 *Fremont Journal* (Ohio), November 28, 1862, p. 1, cpl. 3.

219 SOR, Ser. 33, p. 316.

220 OR, vol. 17, pt. II, p. 855.

221 *Appeal*, 20 November 1862, p. 1, cols. 1f.

222 *Appeal*, October 23, 1862, p. 2, col. 3.

223 *Appeal,* October 27, 1862, p. 2, col. 4, citing the *Bulletin* of October 24.

224 SOR, Ser. 44, p. 286.

225 *Appeal*, October 27, 1862, p. 2, col. 4.

226 Sigafoos, p. 44.

227 Sherman, *Memoir*, pp. 266-68, Sherman to Secretary of Treasury Chase, August 11, 1862.

228 *Appeal*, July 16, 1862, p. 2, col. 2.

229 OR, vol. 17, pt. II, pp. 261 and 272f.

230 *Appeal,* November 4, 1862, p. 2, col. 1, quoting Memphis *Bulletin*.

231 OR, vol. 17, pt. II, p. 351.

232 *Appeal*, November 10 ,1862, p. 2, col. 6, quoting *Bulletin*.

233 OR, vol. 7, p. 654f; and *Memphis Union Appeal*, July 6, 1862, TCWSB.

234 *Daily Union*, October 29, 1862, p. 3, col. 2.

235 *Rebel Picket --- Extra!*, 1864 broadside, Duke family papers, M&SC.

236 Woodson, *Genealogy*, p. 471f.

237 Ibid., pp. 472 and 475.
238 Dyer and Moore, vol. 5, p. 2255.
239 "Soldier's Furlough" form, 1865, Woodson papers, MVC, MS 114, box 1, folder 5.
240 Vaughn, pp. 20-23.
241 SOR, Ser. 78, p. 646; and West, "Thirteenth," p. 187.
242 Vaughn, pp. 23-28 and 49; and *Daily Appeal*, 24 January 1863, p. 1, col. 2.
243 Sanderson interviews.
244 For the different Methodist traditions, West, p.1.
245 From notebook of A.H. Holden, Germantown, 1942, Cloyes files, GRH&GC; and E. Smith, p.8.
246 Scott, ch. 4, p. 4, citing *Appeal*, July 23, 1862 seems to have been the original source.
247 *Appeal*, July 25, 1862, p. 1, col. 4, citing *Bulletin*, July 23.
248 Bear, pp. 11 and 14, n. 11, citing *Chicago Daily Tribune*, Dec. 2, 1862.
249 OR, vol. 17, pt. II, pp. 145f.; and Bear, p. 5.
250 OR, vol. 17, pt. II, p 361.
251 Although all muster reports for this period in the *OR* place the $8^{th}$ and the $116^{th}$ in different brigades, both Scott, ch. 4, p. 4 and the editor of Bear (p. 14, n. 11) assert without any source, that they were in the same brigade for this expedition. They made this assertion to explain the accusation against the $116^{th}$ versus the report blaming the $8^{th}$ for the burnings in Germantown (see n. 47). It is possible they simply assumed the common brigading.
252 *Philadelphia* Inquirer, December 5, 1862, p. 1; and Bear, p. 14, n. 11, citing *Chicago Daily Tribune*, Dec. 2, 1862.
253 NPS regimental histories; OR, vol. 17, pt. I, 603, 614, and 617; and Bear, p. 5.
254 Bear, p. 11.
255 OR, vol. 17, pt. I, pp. 10 & 72, pt. II, pp. 13, 39, 64, 144.
256 *Sanderson Letters*, extracts in TCWS.
257 Hughes lecture.
258 OR, vol. 17, pt. II, pp. 513, and 516; and SOR, Ser. 33, p. 316.
259 Hughes lecture; and West.
260 "History prepared and read by Squire Tom Phillips," transcribed by Margaret Harrison Owen, March 27, 1938.

## Part II, 1863

1   OR, vol. 17, pt. II, p. 510.
2   OR, vol. 17, II, p. 522f.
3   OR, vol. 17, pt. II, pp. 499, 504, 513 and 524. Quinby's official orders to relocate to Memphis were dated December 25 (OR, vol. 17, pt. II, p. 486), so he was already in Memphis on December 30 (Ibid., p. 506).
4   SOR, Ser. 31, p.606.
5   NPS regimental histories; and *Annual Report of the Adjutant General of Missouri*, 1866, p. 138, GBS.
6   OR, vol. 17, pt. II, pp. 513, and 516; *Annual Report of the Adjutant General of Missouri*, p. 146; *Report of the Adjutant General of the State of Illinois*, vol. 3, 1900, p. 209, GBS; and *Report of the Adjutant General and acting Quartermaster General of the State of Iowa*, p. 1047, GBS; SOR, Ser. 31, p. 451; Ser. 33, p. 317; and Ser. 66, pp. 124 and 130.
7   OR, vol. 17, pt II, pp. 524f.
8   E.g., OR, vol. 17, pt. II, pp. 870-73.
9   OR, vol. 24, pt. III, pp. 74 and 179.
10  OR, vol. 24, pt. III, pp. 35, 50, 92 and 140; and Jeffrey N. Lash, "'The Federal Tyrant at Memphis:' General Stephen A. Hurlbut and the Union Occupation of West Tennessee, 1862-64," *THQ*, 48 (Spring 1989), 1: 15-28.
11  OR, vol. 17, pt. II, pp. 565, and 576-78; and vol. 24, pt. III, pp. 20-29.

12  *Appeal*, January 12, 1863, p. 2, col. 2.

13  OR, vol. 24, pt. I, pp. 332-34.

14  OR, vol. 24, Pt. III, pp. 40 and 75.

15  Ibid, p. 88-92, 673.

16  OR, vol. 17, pt. II, p. 526.

17  *Times-Picayune*, January 15, 1863, p. 1.

18  OR, vol. 17, pt. I, pp. 797f.

19  OR, vol. 24, pt. I. p. 428; and Pomeroy Diaries, March 10, 1863.

20  OR, vol. 24, pt. III, p. 654.

21  OR, vol. 24, pt. III, pp. 696f.

22  OR, vol. 24, pt. III, p. 111.

23  OR, vol. 24, pt. I, p. 498.

24  OR, vol. 24, pt. III, p. 27.

25  OR, vol. 24, pt. III, p. 746.

26  OR, vol. 24, pt. III, p. 764f.

27  OR, vol. 24, pt. III, pp. 814-.

28  *Appeal*, April 27, 1863, p. 2, col. 2.

29  OR, vol. 24, pt. III, pp. 185 and 189.

30  OR, vol. 24, pt. III, pp. 253-57; and SOR, Ser. 19, p. 669; and Ser. 21, pp. 629, 660, and 678f.

31  OR, vol. 24, pt. III, pp. 381f., 398f., and 452-56; and vol. 30., pt. III, p. 27.

32  E.g., SOR, Sers. 19-21, and 28-29 contain frequent references to such arrivals.

33  OR, vol. 24, pt. III, pp. 406 and 965; and *Bulletin*, June 16, 1863, p. 1, col. 6.

34  June 24, 1863, OR, vol. 24, pt. II, p. 487.

35  OR, vol. 24, pt. III, pp. 702-5; and T*ennesseans in the Civil War*, Vol. 1, pp. 118-21, and 133.

36  OR, vol. 24, pt. III, p.1024.

37  *Bulletin*, June 26, 1863, p. 3, col. 2.

38  OR, vol. 24, pt. III, p. 512.

39  OR, vol. 24, pt. II, p. 683.

40  *Bulletin*, July 30, 1863, p. 2, col. 3.

41  OR, vol. 52, pt. I, p. 72.

42  Wyeth, p. 254.

43  OR, vol. 30. pt. IV, p. 718.

44  OR, vol. 30, pt. II, p. 759; and *Tennesseans in the Civil War*, Vol. I, pp. 80-90

45  Memories of the City's Settlers," *Germantown News*, June 16, 1977.

46  OR, vol. 24, pt. II, p. 684.

47  OR. Vol. 30, pt. III, pp. 26f.

48  E.g., OR, vol. 30, pt. III, p. 83, Colonel Mersy to General Hurlbut, from Corinth, 20 August, 1863; and vol. 31, pt. I, p. 244.

49  OR, vol. 24, pt. II, 487f., 492-96, and pt. III, pp. 682f.

50  OR, vol. 30, pt. III, pp. 82f, and vol. 31. pt. I, p. 822.

51  OR, vol. 30, pt. III, p. 161.

52  OR, vol. 30, pt. III, pp. 170, 622f.

53  NPS regimental histories.

54  *Report of the Adjutant General of the State of Illinois*, vol. 3, 1900, pp. 65 and 96, GBS; and SOR, Ser. 20, pp. 303 and 477.

55  E.g., *Bulletin*, July 31, 1863, p. 2, col. 2.

56  *Bulletin*, July 31, 1863, p. 3, col. 1.

57  *Bulletin,* July 30, 1863, p. 3, col. 1.

58  *Bulletin*, August 5, 1863, p.2, col. 4.

59  OR, vol. 30, pt. IV, pp. 581f.; Harrel described his location as 12 miles south-east of Memphis which would put him within the present borders of the city of Germantown,

probably within a mile or two of the old town proper. Nevertheless, no Harrel is reported on the 1860 census.

60  OR, vol. 30, pt. II, pp. 733 and 757.

61  OR, vol. 30, pt. II, pp. 731, and 759f.

62  OR, vol. 31, pt. II, pp. 569-70.

63  OR, vol. 30, pt. II, pp. 732 and 760f., and pt. IV, p. 279.

64  OR, vol. 30, pt. II, p. 762 and 781-3.

65  SOR, Ser. 5, pp. 707, and 710; and *Appeal,* quoting unidentified source from Memphis, October 24, 1863, p. 2, col. 3.

66  OR, vol. 30, pt. IV, pp. 278f.; and Nashville *Daily Union*, October 17, 1863, p. 2, Colonel 4.

67  *Appeal,* December 8, 1863, p. 2, col. 6.

68  *Daily Union,* October 27, 1863, p. 2, col. 4.

69  OR, vol. 30, pt. IV, pp. 304f.

70  OR, vol. 31, pt. I, 690.

71  OR, vol. 30, pt. II, p. 734, and pt. IV, pp. 305, and 407.

72  OR, vol. 31, pt. I, pp. 33, 673, 677, and 690.

73  OR, vol. 31, pt. III, p. 592.

74  OR, vol. 31, pt. I, 247, and pt. III, pp. 597.

75  OR, vol. 31, pt. I, pp. 242-49, and Pt. III, p. 31.

76  OR, vol. 31, pt. III, p. 33.

77  OR, vol. 31, pt. III, p. 580.

78  OR, vol. 30, pt. II, pp. 787-89.

79  OR, vol. 31, pt. I, pp. 248f.

80  OR, vol. 31, pt. I, p. 253.

81  OR, vol. 31, pt. III, p. 679.

82  OR, vol. 31, pt. III, p. 689.

83  Lloyd's New Map of the United States, the Canadas and New Brunswick, from the last surveys, showing every Railroad & Station finished to June 1863, LC, www.loc.gov/item/98688332.

84  OR, vol. 31, pt. I, p. 253; and pt. III, pp. 678f., and 684f.

85  OR, vol. 31, pt. III, pp. 132f., 544f., and 566f.

86  OR, vol. 31, pt. III, p. 641; and pp. 694, and 730.

87  OR, vol. 31, pt. III, pp. 730f.

88  OR, vol. 31, pt. III, p. 731.

89  OR, vol. 31, pt. III, p. 469.

90  OR, vol. 31, pt. III, p. 336.

91  OR, vol. 32, pt. III, pp. 366 and 386.

92  OR, vol. 31, pt. III, pp. 395; and Pt. I, p. 607.

93  OR, vol. 31, pt. III, pp. 494 and 517.

94  OR, vol. 31, pt. I, p. 620; and John Johnson, "Forrest's March out of West Tennessee, December 1863, Recollections of a Private," WTHS, 12 (1958): 146.

95  OR, vol. 31, pt. I, pp. 620f.

96  ORIII, 5: 63 and 586.

97  OR, vol. 31, pt. I, p. 620f.

98  County Court, Minute Book 10, 1862,; and Minute Book 10 ½, pp. 1 and 50; and Minute Book 11, 1864, p. 256, SCA.

99  Records of the U.S. Civil Commission at Memphis, 1863-1864, NARA #410/reel 78/p.1.

100 *Papers of Andrew Johnson,* Vol. 6, pp. 112f., and nn. 1 & 7, TCWS; *Bulletin,* December 27, 1862; and on the disrupted election, Nathan K. Moran, "Bullets and Ballots: Nathan Bedford Forrest and the Congressional Election of 1862," *WTHS,* 58 (2004): 2-31.

101 *Bulletin*, June 19,1863, p. 2, col. 8.
102 *Bulletin,* September 1, 1863, p. 3, col. 6; and October 12, p. 2, col. 1; and "Regulations for the Collection of Direct Taxes..., Instant Archive: archive.org/details/regulationsforcounit.
103 *Bulletin,* October 25, 1863, p. 1, col. 6.
104 General Orders No. 100, April 24, 1863, Instructions for the Government of Armies of the United States in the Field, Sec. I, Martial Law; OR, III, vol. 3, pp. 148-51; and Ash, *Yankees*, pp. 82-84, 87f.
105 Ash, *Yankees*, p. 59.
106 *Bulletin*, September 1, 1863, p. 4, col. 3.
107 Wills interview.
108 OR, vol. 24, pt. III, p. 162.
109 OR, vol. 24, pt. III, p. 382.
110 Fortress Germantown file, GRH&GC.
111 Diary of Fletcher Pomeroy, January 26, 1863, TCWSB.
112 NPS Regimental histories.
113 Green, *Letters,* p. 49. The date in the published version of February 20 seems strangely inconsistent with her descriptions of the weather and types of trees and flowers in bloom. Indeed, given her ending of the letter, it would have had to have been early March. Even then blooming roses and honeysuckle are premature.
114 *Notable Men of Tennessee*, p. 36
115 "Germantown Pioneers," *Germantown News*, August 25, 1977, p. 3B.
116 Faust, *Mothers*, pp. 198-201, and 205; Ash, *Yankees*, pp. 61f.; and *Appeal*, 27 June 1863, p. 2, col. 3.
117 Dunaway, June 11, 1864.
118 Ash, *Yankees*, pp. 197f., 200-202.
119 Green, p. 53.
120 Ibid., p. 54.
121 Ibid., p. 55.
122 John to Sotie, August 20 and 22, 1863, Historic Sites folder, Civil War, GRH&GC.
123 Wills interview.
124 Hughes lecture.
125 Pomeroy diary, TCWSB.
126 OR, vol. 24, pt. III, pp. 68, 141-43.
127 NPS regimental histories.
128 Witherington, p. 62, citing Fletcher Pomeroy's War Diary.
129 Frisbee, "'Remember Me to Everybody'," WTHS, 55 (2001): 41.
130 Witherington,  p. 63, citing Webster Moses.
131 Green, *Letters*, p. 41.
132 Woodson, *Genealogy,* p. 306.
133 Claim of Agnes Brooks, April 1, 1901, Wills/Kirby collection; and Cargill and Connelly, *Settlers*, p. 22.
134 Woodson papers, MVC, MS-114, box 1, folder 9.
135 *The United States Army and Navy Journal and Gazette of the Regular and Volunteer Forces*, vol. III, 1865-'66, p. 7, GBS; and *Daily National Intelligencer*, November 11, 1863, p. 3; *Bulletin*, November 7, p. 2, col. 1
136 Faust, *Mothers*, pp. 205-207.
137 "Memoirs of the City's Settlers," *Germantown News*, June 16, 1977.
138 Walter F. Fraser, Jr and Mrs. Pat C. Clark, "The Letters of William Beverly Randolph Hackley: Treasury Agent in West Tennessee, 1863-1866, in *WTHS*, 25 (1971): 25-106, p. 96.
139 *Bulletin*, June 19, 1863, p. 2, col. 8.
140 Ash, *Yankees*, pp. 78-80; and *Bulletin*, November 7, 1863, p. 2, col. 1.

141 *Bulletin*, June 14, 1863, p. 2, col. 1.

142 Nolan, "Troublous Times," WTHS, 60 (2006): 25-28, and 32.

143 *Columbus* (Georgia) *Daily Enquirer*, September 30, 1863, p. 2.

144 Based on a comparison of 1860 and 1870 censuses.

145 James B. Jones, Jr., "The Struggle for Public Health in Civil War Tennessee Cities," WTHS, 66 (2007): 69-85.

146 United States Surgeon General's Office, *The Medical and Surgical History of the War of the Rebellion*, vol. 1, pt. 3, (Washington, DC: GPO, 1888), p. 895, TCWSB.

147 *Bulletin*, August 9, 1864, p. 4, col. 3.

148 *Bulletin*, September 1, 1863, p. 3, cols. 1 and 4.

149 Ibid., p. 3, col. 3.

150 *Bulletin*, September 1, 1863, p. 4, col. 3; September 17, p. 1, cols. 4-5.; and October 30, p. 3, cols. 2 and 5.

151 OR, vol. 31, pt. III, p. 160.

152 S.A. Steele, *The Sunny Road: Home Life in Dixie during the War*.

153 Loose Papers, Box 48, W.P. Moore, Oath of Allegiance, Provost Marshal Germantown, 1863, # 71, SCA.

154 American Civil War Soldiers and Regimental History, Ancestry.com; Walls did not appear in the 1860 censuses for districts 10 or 11.

155 OR, vol. 31, pt. III, pp. 160f.

156 Dunaway, August 4, 1863, and July 20, 1864.

157 Thompson to Smith, April 17, 1861, EH/GRH&GC.

158 Capleville Methodist Church Bulletin, May 27, 1851, "History," pp. 2-3, GUMCA, West File.

159 Faust, *Mothers*, pp. 184-86.

160 Donhardt, "Grant," WTHS, 53 (1999): pp. 5f.; and Hubbard, p. 32.

161 *The Abingdon Virginian*, July 31. 1863, p. 1, col. 2.

162 *Fremont Journal* (Ohio), December 25, 1863, p. 1, col. 5.

163 Thoroughly exposed in the most recent literature, e.g., Oaks, *Freedom;* and Downs, *Sick from Freedom*.

164 Berlin, *Freedom*, Ser. I, Vol. III. pp. 622f., and 692.

165 Oaks, *Freedom*, p. 415.

166 *Appeal*, 19 August 1862, p. 2, col. 1; 10 April, p. 2, col. 7; and Sherman, *Memoirs*, pp. 265f.

167 E.g., *Daily Appeal*, 19 August 1862, p. 2, col. 1, for a summary of one of Sherman's early orders for employing "negroes" and the rights of their owners; and John Cimprich, "Military Governor Johnson and Tennessee Blacks, 1862-65," *THQ*, 39 (Winter 1980), 4: 462.

168 Berlin, *Freedom*, pp. 623, and 890-899.

169 Foner, *Reconstruction*, p. 81, and n. 9.

170 McKinney, "Ned and Rose Kearney," *WTHS*, 64 (2010): 135.

171 Ash, *Yankees*, pp. 154f., 165-68.

172 Berlin, *Families*, pp. 156f.

173 Berlin, *Freedom*, Ser. I, Vol. III, pp. 621f.

174 Downs, *Sick from Freedom*, p. 47.

175 *Bulletin*, July 30, 1863, p. 3, col. 4.

176 *Bulletin*, October 30, 1863, p. 3, col. 2; and Berlin, *Freedom*, pp. 709f., and 714f.

177 Berlin, *Families*, p. 35.

178 E.g., Brigadier General [Augustus L. Chetlain] to Lieutenant Colonel T.H. Harris, 12 Apr. 1864, cited in Berlin, *Families*, pp.35f.

179 Ibid., p. 686.

180 Ibid., pp. 686 and 689-91.

181 Ibid., pp, 686 and 689.

182 Ibid., p. 690.

183 *Appeal,* 20 January 1864, p. 2, col. 3f.

184 Lieutenant Col Jos R. Putnam to Brigadier General W.D. Whipple, 30 Jan. 1865, in Berlin, p. 78.

185 Bobby L. Lovett, "The West Tennessee Colored Troops in Civil War Combat," *WTHS,* 34 (1980): n.1, p. 53; and cf. *Tennesseans in the Civil War,* vol. 1, pp. 366f., 396, 407-9, and 436.

186 E.g., OR, vol. 24, pt. III, p. 406,

187 ORIII, 3:117, 122, and 1190.

188 ORIII, 4:164; and *Tennesseans in the Civil War*, Vol. 1, pp. 366f., 369f.

189 NPS, Soldiers and Sailors System.

190 ORIII, 3: 212.

191 *Tennesseans in the Civil War*, Vol. 1, p. 407; and ORIII, 4:165.

192 NPS, Soldiers and Sailors and System.

193 http://www.tngenweb.org/civilwar/usainf/usa61c.html.; and Tennesseans in the Civil War, vol. 1, p. 408.

194 OR, vol. 31, pt. I, p. 577.

195 OR, vol. 31, pt. I, p. 578.

196 ORRIII, 4:165.

197 NPS, Soldiers and Sailors System.

198 Ibid., pp. 820f.

199 Lieutenant Col John Foley to Lieutenant Colonel T. Harris, 11 Jan. 1865 in Berlin, *Families,* pp. 75f.

200 Captain T.A. Walker to Captain J.S. Lord, 34 Jan. 1865 in Berlin, *Families,* pp. 76f.

201 Downs, *Sick from Freedom*, pp. 21-26.

202 ORIII, 3:1190.

203 Berlin, *Freedom*, Series I, Vol. I. pp. 776f.

204 *Appeal,* 19 August 1862, p. 2, col. 3.

205 *Appeal,* March 17, 1863, p. 1, col. 5.

206 Hunt, p. 20; and Dyer and Moore, vol. 3, p. 1300.

207 Dyer and Moore, vol. 5, p. 2255.

208 *Bulletin,* October 11, 1863, p.4, col. 1.

209 McPherson, *Cause & Comrades*, p. 11.

210 Ibid., p. 13, chapter 2, and pp. 94-97.

211 Ibid., pp. 9, 35, 88f., 97, and 102f.

## Part II, 1864

1   OR, vol. 32, pt. II, p. 77.

2   *Appeal,* 8 December 1863, p. 2, col. 1; 4 January 1864, p. 2, cols. 1f.; 20 January, p. 1, col. 3; 2 March, p. 2, col. 2; and 6 May, p. 2, cols. 3f.

3   E.g., *Bulletin,* March 22, 1864, p. 2, col. 2; and New York *Times,* June 16, 1862, TCWSB

4   *Daily Illinois State Journal*, February 22, 1864, p. 4.

5   *Appeal,* March 30, 1864, p. 1 col. 3.

6   *1860 Census – Tennessee*, 5 vols., Nashville: Byron Sistler & Associates, 1981; and *1870 Census -Tennessee*, Nashville: Byron Sistler & Associates, 2 vols., 1985.

7   *Bulletin,* March 4, 1864, p. 3, col. 2.

8   *Appeal,* March 9, 1864, p. 3, col. 3, citing *Argus,* and *Bulletin*; and *Ledger*, January 23, 1868, p. 3, col. 3.

9   *Wisconsin Daily Patriot*, March 28, p. 1, quoting *Argus,* March 19, 1864, and *Chicago Times.*

10  *Ledger*, January 23, 1868, p. 3, col. 3.

11  *Bulletin,* March 4, 1864, p. 2, col. 1, and March 9, p. 2, col. 1, and p. 3, col. 3.

12  *Bulletin,* loc cit.

13  Loose Papers, 1863, box 49, #71, SCA.
14  Evans to Woodson, November 28, 1864, GPC.
15  *Appeal*, 29 April 1864, p. 1, cols. 2f.
16  *Appeal*, 27 January 1864, p. 1, col. 5; and *Tennesseans in the Civil War*, Vol. 1, pp. 410f., including General Order Number 29, September 14, 1863.
17  *Bulletin*, March 22, 1864, p. 2, col. 2.
18  *Bulletin*, March 22, 1863, p. 2, col. 7.
19  *ulletin*, August 9, 1864, p. 3, cols. 3 and 6, p. 4, col. 3.
20  OR, vol. 32, pt. II, pp. 67f.
21  *Papers of Andrew Johnson*, vol. 6, pp. 648-50, TCWSB.
22  OR, vol. 32, pt. III, pp. 117-19; and for a clarification of the extortion of Jackson indicating that the regimental fine may not have been justified, Blankinship, "Hurst," *WTHS*, 34 (1980): 79f.
23  OR, vol. 32, pt. II, pp. 86 and 97.
24  OR, vol. 32, pt. II, p. 119.
25  OR, vol. 32, pt. I, p. 152; and pt. II., p. 119.
26  *Appeal*, February 5, 1864, p. 1, col. 7.
27  OR, vol.,32, pt. I, pp. 173-79; and pt. II, p. 493.
28  OR, vol. 32, pt. I, pp. 179f.
29  OR, vol. 32, pt. I, pp. 171f., and 174f.; and pt. II, pp. 229, 240, 242, 258, 297, 302, and 493.
30  OR, vol. 32, pt. I, p. 348; and pt. II, p. 485.
31  OR, vol. 32, pt. II, pp. 493f.; and *Report of the Adjutant General of the State of Illinois*, vol. 3, pp. 65 and 96, GBS.
32  OR, vol. 32, pt. III, p. 116.
33  OR, vol. 32, pt. II, p. 505.
34  OR, vil. 32, pt. I, p. 269; and ORIII, vol. 5: 63, and 586.
35  OR, vol. 32, pt. I, pp. 346f.
36  OR, vol. 32, pt. I, pp. 351f., and 355.
37  OR, vol. 39, pt. II, pp. 640-44.
38  OR, vol. 32, pt. I, p. 208, 382-87; and Warner, p. 256.
39  OR, vol. 32, pt. III, pp. 593f.
40  OR, vol. 32, pt. I, p. 208.
41  OR vol. 32, pt. III, pp. 609 and 635f..
42  OR, vol. 32, pt. III, p. 665.
43  Galbraith, p. 103, Edmondson diary entry Monday, March 28; and *Appeal*, April 28, 1864, p. 2, col. 2, quoting Cairo *News*, of April 10.
44  OR vol. 32, pt. III, p. 609.
45  Nashville *Daily Union*, April 10, 1864, p. 3, col. 6.
46  OR, vol. 32, pt. III, p. 253.
47  OR, vol. 32, pt. I, p. 610.
48  McPherson, *Cause & Comrades*, pp. 148-53, based on soldiers' letters.
49  Horn, p. 257; and Hubbard, pp 101f.; and cf. Lufkin, "Thirteenth," 136-39.
50  OR, vol. 32, pt. I, pp. 602f.
51  *Appeal*, April 28, 1864, p. 2, col. 5.
52  OR, vol. 32, pt. I, pp. 589, and 592.
53  OR, vol. 32, pt. I, p. 611.
54  *Appeal*, April 26, 1864, p. 2, col. 6, citing unidentified Northern papers.
55  OR, vol. 32, pt. I. p. 588.
56  OR, vol. 39, pt. I, pp. 85f.
57  OR, vol. 39, pt. I, pp. 94 and 125f.
58  OR, vol. 39, pt. I, pp. 109 and 127.
59  OR, vol. 39, pt. I. p. 183.

60  OR, vol. 39, pt. I, p. 129; and pt. II, p. 119.
61  OR, vol. 39, pt. I, p. 215.
62  *Daily South Carolinian* (Columbia), June 29, 1864, issue 154, col. A.
63  Ibid.
64  OR, vol. 39, pt. I, p. 95.
65  OR, vol. 32, pt. I, p. 586, 589, 592f., 600; and cf. Lovett, "Colored Troops," *WTHS*, 34 (1980): 59f.
66  OR, vol. 32, pt. I, p. 587.
67  OR, vol. 32, pt. I, pp. 588f.
68  OR, vol. 32, pt. I, pp. 591, and 593, for two different versions of their exchange.
69  OR, vol. 32, pt. I, pp. 599-601.
70  OR, vol. 32, pt. I, p. 606.
71  OR, vol. 32, pt. I, pp. 603f.
72  Lovett, "Colored Troops," *WTHS*, 34 (1980): 70.
73  ORIII, vol. 5: 63 and 586; and OR, vol. 39, pt. II, p. 208.
74  OR, vol. 39, pt. II, p. 142.
75  OR, vol. 39, pt. II, p. 142.
76  OR, vol. 39, pt. II, pp. 149f.
77  OR, vol. 39, pt. II, p. 165.
78  OR, vol. 39, pt. I, p. 469.
79  OR, vol. 39, pt. II, pp. 318, 333 and 368.
80  OR, vol. 39, pt. I, p. 368.
81  OR, vol. 39, pt. I, p. 901, and 919; pt. II, p. 885; pt. III, p. 912; vol. 45, pt. I, p. 919 and 1228; and ORIII, vol. 5: 63 and 586.
82  *Bulletin,* November 17, 1864, p. 2, col. 1.
83  OR, vol. 42, pt. I, pp. 790, 843, and 857.
84  Lois D. Bejack, "The Journal of a Civil War 'Commando' DeWitt Clinton Fort," WTHS, 2 (1948): 24-29.
85  ORIII, vol. 5: 63 and 9909; and OR, vol. 42, pt. I, p. 866.
86  Ash, *Yankees*, pp. 177-84, 204.
87  Ash, *Yankees*, pp. 112f.; Faust, *Mothers*, pp. 235-38, 242; and Rable, *Civil Wars*, pp. 222-24.
88  McPherson, *Cause and Comrades*, pp. 9, 101f., 138, 168; and Faust, *Mothers,* p. 243.
89  OR, vol. 39, pt. II, p. 645f.
90  OR, vol. 39, pt. II, pp. 640-44.
91  OR, vol. 39, pt. II, p. 683.
92  Dunaway, September 18, 1864.
93  Hubbard, pp. 80-82.
94  *Appeal*, 20 January 1864, p. 2, cols. 2-5.
95  Bailey, pp. 92f.; and Dyer and Moore, vol. 2, p. 734.
96  Vaughn, pp. 29-34; but cf. Goodspeed , "Shelby," p. 829, who contradicts Vaughn about the end of the regiment's campaigning, which Vaughn did not witness having been invalided out of service; and *Appeal*, 12 September 1863 p. 2, col. 5. Cf. *Tennesseans in the Civil War,* pp. 202f.
97  Goodspeed, "Shelby," p. 829; and Harkins, pp. 75f.
98  Goodspeed, "Shelby," p. 831.
99  SOR, Ser. 88, p. 627.
100 Bejack, pp. 30f.
101 OR, Ser. II, vol. 7, pp. 404-408, and 920-22.
102 Ibid.
103 *Appeal*, March 9, 1862, p. 1, col. 3, quoting *Chicago Times*.
104 Ibid.
105 Dyer and Moore, vol. 3, p. 1300.

106 *Appeal*, April 29, 1864, p. 1, cols. 4-6, reprinting "Prison Life on Johnson's Island. By an Exchanged Prisoner Returned to Mobile," from the *Advertiser and Register*.

107 Ibid.

108 Dyer and Moore, vol. 3, p. 1300.

109 Bailey, pp. 95-97; Garrison, p. 214; and CensusDiggins.com,/prison, "Rock Island Civil War Prison."

110 Vaughn, *Personal Record.*, p. 49.

111 Garrison, p. 9; and CensusDiggins.com/prison, "Alton Civil War Prison."

112 Charles T. Loehr, "Point Lookout," *Southern Historical Society Papers*, vol. 18 (Jan.-Dec. 1890): 114-20; Rev. J.B. Traywick, "Prison Life at Point Lookout," *Southern Historical Society Papers*, vol. 19 (January 1891): 432-35; Garrison, p. 193; and CensusDiggins.com/prison, "Point Lookout Civil War Prison."

## Part II, 1865

114 *Argus,* September 3, 1865, p. 3, col. 1.

115 Dunaway, February 27, 1864.

116 OR, vol. 49, pt. I, pp. 76-78, 80f.

117 OR, vol. 49, pt. I, pp. 82f.

118 E.g., *Bulletin*, February 28, 1865, p. 3, col. 2; and March 1, p. 3, cols. 1 and 2.

119 *Appeal*, March 1, 1864, p. 1, col. 8, citing Chicago *Times*; December 21, 1865, p. 3, col. 1; February 9, 1866, p. 3, col. 2; *Argus*, April 3, 1865, p. 3, col. 1; May 2, p. 2, col. 4; *Bulletin*, February 28, 1865, p. 3, col. 2; and March 1, p. 3, cols. 1-2;

120 Ash, *Yankees*, pp. 204-208.

121 OR, vol. 49, pt. II, pp. 31 and 83.

122 Ser. I, vol. 49, pt. II, p. 120.

123 OR, vol. 49, pt. II, p. 52.

124 OR, vol. 49, pt. I, pp. 2f.

125 OR, vol. 49, pt. I, pp. 718f.

126 Ibid.

127 OR, vol. 32, pt. II, p. 178.

128 OR, vol. 39, pt. II, pp. 133f.

129 Patrick W. O'Daniel, "Loyalty a Requisite: Trade and the Oath of Allegiance in the Mid-South in 1865," *WTHS*, 60 (2006): 35-47.

130 OR, vol. 49, pt. I, pp. 865f.

131 *Bulletin,* February 28, 1865, p. 3, col. 5; and March 1, p. 2, col. 5.

132 OR, vol. 49, pt. I, pp. 890f.

133 OR, vol. 49, pt. II, p. 169.

134 E.g., OR, vol. 49, pt. II, p. 356.

135 ORIII. Vol. 5: 63 and 586.

136 Postmaster Finder.

137 OR, vol. 49, pt. I, p. 507.

138 NPS regimental histories; and SOR, Ser. 53, pp. 491, and 507f.

139 Bejach, p. 31.

140 OR, vol. 49, pt. II, 236.

141 Bejack, p. 32.

142 OR, vol. 49, pt. I, p. 4.

143 OR, vol. 49, pt. I, pp. 512f.

144 Ibid.

145 *Argus,* May 16, 1865, "Visit to Germantown," p.4, col. 2.

146 *Daily Illinois State Journal*, April 22, 1865, p. 4.

147 OR, vol. 49, pt. II, p. 557.

148 OR, vol. 49, pt. I, pp. 1057f.; and pt. II, pp. 711f.

149 Blankinship, "Hurst," *WTHS*, 34 (1980): 85.

150 OR, vol. 49, pt. II, pp. 750, and 800.

151 OR, vol. 49, pt. II, p. 791.

152 *Bulletin*, February 28, 1865, p. 3, cols. 3-4.

153 Montague, "Experiences," MVC, Acc# 89-52, MS 54-127, p15.

154 Woodson, *Genealogy,* p. 475.

155 Aden, p. 116; Montague, "Experience," MVC, Acc# 89-52, MS 54-127, pp. 17f.; and Hubbard, pp. 194f.

156 Woodson papers, MVC, MS 114, box 1, folder 5.

157 Bailey, pp. 107f.

158 *Argus*, May 2, 1865, p.2, cols. 1 and 4.

159 OR vol. 49, pt. II, p. 905.

160 OR, vol.49, pt. II, p. 518.

161 Ibid.

162 Ibid., pp. 518f.

163 OR, vol. 49, pt. II, p. 671.

164 *Bulletin,* May 14, 1865, p. 3, col. 3.

165 Dyer and Moore, vol. 3, p. 1032.

166 Bayley, pp. 109f.

167 OR, vol. 49, pt. II, p. 671.

168 Dyer and Moore, p. 1300.

169 Bailey, pp. 111f.

170 OR, vol .49, pt. II, pp. 692f.

171 OR, vol. 49, pt. II, p. 770.

172 Bailey, pp. 104, 113f., and 116.

173 McPherson, *Cause & Comrades*, pp. 43f.

174 *Appeal*, 6 May 1864, p.2, col. 2; 8 November 1865, p. 2, col. 9; and 30 March 1866, p. 1, col. 4.

175 *Ledger*, August 9, 1870, p. 3, col. 2.

176 *Bulletin*, May 14, 1865, p. 3, col. 7; and *Argus,* May 16, p. 1, cols. 6-7.

177 *Argus*, May 16, 1865, p. 1, col. 7.

178 O'Daniel, pp. 35f., 42f., and 46.

179 OR, vol. 49, pt. II, p. 996; and NPS, regimental histories.

180 James D. Davis, *History of the City of Memphis, Being a Compilation of the Most Important Historical Documents of the City and Early Settlement* (Memphis: 1873), pp. 43f., TCWSB.

181 Based on comparison of the 1860 and 1870 censuses.

182 Weeks, p. 76; and *Argus*, May 16, 1865, p. 4, col. 2.

183 Ibid.

184 Ibid; no Parish family or woman by that last name appear in the 1860 or 1870 censuses, but Miss Lou pops up in later newspaper reports about the town.

185 Woodson, *Genealogy*, p. 306.

186 Faust, *Mothers*, pp. 244f.

187 *Bulletin*, May 14, 1865, p. 3, col. 2.

188 McPherson, *Cause & Comrades*, p. 141.

189 *Argus,* May 2, 1865, p. 1, col. 8; and ORIII, 5: 990.

190 *Argus,* May 20, 1865, p. 4, col. 3; *Daily Appeal*, November 10, 1865, p. 3, col. 10; and freight receipt, M&C RR, December 9, 1865, Woodson papers, MVC, MS 114, box 1, folder 6.

## Part III, Chapter 1

1    Acts, 1865, pp. i-ii.

2    Acts, 1865, p. iii; and McKenzie; Gibson; Severance, p. xiii; and Foner, pp. 43-45.

3    Acts, 1865, pp. iv-vii and x-xiii; and McKenzie, Gibson and Foner, pp. 44f.

4    Acts, 1865, Ch. XVI, pp. 32-36; and Severance, pp. xii-xiii., and 5f.

5    Severance, p. 1; and Charles L. Lufkin, "A Forgotten Controversy: The Assassination

of Senator Almon Case of Tennessee," WTHS, 39 (1985): 37-50.

6   E.g., *Appeal,* February 9, 1866, p. 3, col. 2; and May 25, 1869, p. 2, col. 2.
7   *Argus,* May 2, 1865, p. 2, col. 4
8   Acts, 1865, Ch. IV, p. 19; Ch. XXIV, pp. 43f.; Ch. XXI, pp. 41f.; Acts 1865-66, Ch. XXXV, pp. 52-62; Acts 1866-67, Ch. XXIV, pp. 24f.; Acts, 1868, p. 8; and Severance, pp. 15f., and 20
9   Acts 1866-67, Ch. XXVI, pp. 26-33; and Severance, pp. 23f.
10  Severance, pp. 36-38, 52, and 55.
11  Severance, pp. 89-112, 135
12  E.g., *Appeal,* May 2, 1867, p. 3, col. 4; and August 3, p. 2, col. 3.
13  Severance, pp. 147-49, 155, 157f.. 168-72, and 175.
14  Acts, 1868, Ch. II, pp. 18-23 and Ch. III, pp. 23-25; and Severance, pp. 175f., 178f.. 183f., and 186-88.
15  Correspondence between Gov. Brownlow and Gen. H. Thomas, Acts, 1868, pp. 5-8; and Severance, pp. 188f.
16  Severance, pp. 193-98.
17  Severance, pp. 202, 206, 208f., 216, and 218-23.
18  McKenzie; and Severance, pp. 226f., and F. Wayne Binning, "The Tennessee Republicans in Decline, 1869-1876," *THQ* (Winter 1980),4: 471-84.
19  Bergeron, p. 68.
20  Acts, 1865-66, Ch. XL, p. 65.
21  Ibid.
22  Ibid.
23  E.g., *Appeal,* January 16, 1868, p. 3, col. 2.
24  Acts 1866-67, Ch. XXVII, Sec. 17, pp. 39; emphasis added.
25  E.g., *Appeal,* 8 November 1865, p. 2, col. 1; 25 November, p. 2, col. 2; and 26 December, p. 3, col. 4.
26  Field Offices, Tennessee, Bureau of Refugees, Freedmen, and Abandoned Lands, 1865-1872, NARA, M 1911,/reel 77/pp. 3-5.
27  Aiken, pp. 17-21
28  Aiken, p. 27.
29  Field Offices, Tennessee, Bureau of Refugees, Freedmen, and Abandoned Lands, 1865-1872, NARA, M 1911,/reel 77/p. 4.
30  *Appeal,* April 3, 1864, p.1, col. 6
31  E.g., *Appeal,* November 25, 1865, p. 2, cols. 1 and 4; December 5, p. 3, col. 2; December 21, p. 3, col. 1;   December 28, p. 2, col. 2; January 7, 1866, p. 3, cols. 1f. and 3; February 25, p. 3, col. 1; April 3, p. 3, col. 1; April 5, p. 1, col. 2; May 3,  p. 3, col. 2;
32  Fause, *Mothers,* pp. 60, 62, 70-74.
33  *Appeal,* 3 April 1864, p. 1, col. 3; and January 10, 1866, p. 2, col. 4; and OR vol. 52, pt. II, pp. 586-92.
34  TSL&A, RG-87, Statewide Referendum on Amendment to the State Constitution Abolishing Slavery, Feb. 22, 1865, folder 43.
35  *Appeal,* January 18, 1866, p. 1, col. 4.
36  Ibid.
37  *Appeal,* February 9, 1866, p. 3, col. 1,
38  Severance, pp. 117 and 207.
39  TSL&A, RG-87, Special Elections and County and Local Elections, 1865, folder, 80; and County Court, Minute Book 11, 1865, p. 88, SCA; and Acts, 1865, Ch. 1.
40  *Appeal,* December 21, 1865, p. 3, col. 1.
41  *Appeal,* 9 December 1865, p. 2, col. 2; 10 December, p. 3, col. 1; and 26 December, p. 3, col. 1.
42  Minutes County Court, March 12, 1866, p. 280, SCA; *Appeal,* March 1, 1866, p. 3, col.

3; March 3, p. 3, col. 1; and March 6, p. 3, col. 2.

43   *Avalanche*, April 6, 1866, p. 3, col. 2.

44   *Avalanche,* January 1, 1866, p. 3; April 6, p. 3; July 21, p. 3, col. 1; January 8, 1867, p. 3, col. 1; *Evening Post*, September 14,1868, p. 3, col. 1; and *Ledger*, October 11, 1871, p. 3, col. 2;  Bleckley's name was rarely spelled the same; Jones seems to have been missed in both the 1850 and 1860 censuses; Rhodes' name would come up as Jonathon L. Rhodes in the 1870 census.

45   TSL&A, RG-87, Special Elections & County and Local Elections, 1866, folders 29, 56 and 67.

46   "Report of an investigation of the cause, origin, and results of the late riots in the city of Memphis made by Col. Charles F. Johnson, Inspector General States of Ky. and Tennessee and Major T. W. Gilbreth, A. D. C. to Maj. Genl. Howard, Commissioner Bureau R. F. & A. Lands," Records of the Assistant Commissioner for the State of Tennessee Bureau of Refugees, Freedmen, and Abandoned Lands, 1865-1869, NARA, Microfilm M999, roll 34.

47   Acts, 1865-66, Ch. XXV, Secs. 1-40, pp. 52-62.

48   Ibid., Sec. 9, p. 55.

49   Dowdy, pp. 39-42; *Appeal*, February 25, 1866, p. 3, col. 1; May 1, p. 3, col. 1, May 2, p. 3, col. 1; and May 3, p. 2 col. 1, and p. 3 col. 2.

50   *Avalanche*, May 3, 1866, p. 3, col. 1.

51   *Argus,* May 5, 1866, p. 3, col. 4; and *Appeal*, May 3, 1866, p. 3, col. 2.

52   Minutes County Court, Book B-13, 1867, pp. 231f., and 303f.

53   *Ledger*, January 26, 1867, p. 3, col. 2.

54   *Avalanche*, March 22, 1867, p. 3, col. 2; *Appeal,* March 22, 1867, p. 3, col. 5; March 28, p. 3, col. 3; and  April 2, p. 3, col. 3; and Minutes County Court, Book B-13, 1867, p. 384, SCA

55   See Appendix A.

56   Ibid., pp. 384-88, and 448; and *Appeal*, April 2, 1867, p. 3, col. 3.

57   Records of the U.S. Civil Commission, NARA, T-410/reel 78/p. 1.

58   Minutes County Court, Book B-13, 1867, p. 502, and e.g., pp. 455f. and 535, SCA

59   *Appeal*, April 27, 1867, p. 2, cols. 1 and 3; May 1, p. 1, col. 4; May 3, p. 2, col. 3; May 11, p. 2, col. 2; August 1, p. 1, col. 4, and p. 3, cols. 3-4.

60   *Appeal,* July 7, 1867, p. 3, cols. 2 and 3.

61   *Ledger*, August 2, 1867, p. 3, col. 5.

62   *Appeal*, January 15, 1868, p. 3, col. 3; and January 16, p. 3, cols. 2 and 3; and January 18, p. 3, col. 4; and *Ledger*, January 21, p.3, col. 2.

63   *Appeal*, January 25, 1868, p. 2, cols. 2 and 3; January 26, p. 3, col. 5; February 14, p. 2, col. 1; February 21, p. 3, col. 3; and February 29, p. 3, col. 3.

64   *Appeal,* March 6, 1868, p. 2, col. 5.

65   *Appeal*, June 1, 1868, p. 2, col. 1; June 2, p. 3, col. 3; and June 3, p. 3, col. 5.

66   *Appeal,* July 2, 1868, p. 3, col. 3; July 6, 1868, p. 3, cols. 4 and 5; July 7, p. 1, col. 2; and July 11, p. 1. col. 2.

67   *Avalanche*, July 19, 1868, p. 2.

68   *Appeal*, July 7, 1868, p. 1, col. 3; July 21, 1868, p. 2, col. 1, and August 8, p. 2, cols. 1-2.

69   *Appeal*, July 23, 1868, p. 4, cols. 4-6.

70   *Avalanche,* October 4, 1868, p. 3.

71   *Evening Post*, September 14,1868, p. 3, col. 1.

72   Ibid.

73   *Avalanche*, July 19, 1868, p. 2.

74   Lamon, *Blacks*, p. 35.

75   *Appeal*, November 14, 1868, p.1, col. 4.

76   *Appeal*, November 18, 1868, p. 3, col. 3.

77 *Appeal*, November 1, 1868, p. 2, col. 2.

78 *Appeal*, January 21, 1872, p. 4, col. 3.

79 *Appeal*, July 14, 1868, p. 3, col. 6; August 29, p. 3, col. 3; 9.30.68, p. 3, col. 3; October 15, p. 3, col. 1; and October 9, p. 2, col. 2; *Ledger*, April 24, p. 1, col. 3; and Young, p. 150-52.

80 *Appeal*, October 25, 1868, p. 3, col. 1.

81 Lipsey, "Memories," p. 17.

82 *Appeal*, February 8, 1871, p. 3, cols. 3-4.

83 *Appeal*, January 28, 1869, p. 2, col. 1; and January 29, p. 2, cols. 1-3.

84 *Appeal*, May 2, 1869, p. 3, col. 2; May 5, p. 2, cols 1-2; May 27, p. 4, col. 4; May 31, p. 4, col. 2; and July 20, p. 4, col. 4.

85 *Appeal*, July 25, 1869, p. 4, col. 5; August 6, p. 4, cols. 4-5; and August 7, p. 2, cols. 1 and 3.

86 Commissioner's Minute Book, E, pp. 223f.; and Map of Shelby County, Tennessee, Compiled and Published by J.H. Humphreys, Civil Engineer. Sears & Smith of the Memphis Abstract Co., 1869 (courtesy of Walter Wills III), SCA.

87 County Court Minutes, Book, G, October Term 1871, pp. 3 and 50.

88 *Appeal*, November 20, 1869, p. 3, col. 3; and December 30. p. 3, col. 5.

89 *Ledger*, January 10, 1870, p. 3, col. 4.

90 *The Morning Republican* (Little Rock), November 9, 1870, issue 158, col. B; but cf. Nashville *Union and American*, November 9, 8170, p. 1, col. 2; and *Ledger*, October 7, p.2, col. 1.

91 *Appeal*, July 30, 1872, p. 3, col. 6.

92 *Appeal*, January 21, 1872, p. 4, col. 3.

93 *Appeal*, October 8, 1874, p. 4, col. 5; and June 24, p. 1, col. 2; and *Ledger, August 8, 1878.*

94 *Appeal*, November 6, 1872, p. 1, col. 1, and p. 4, col. 2; November 7, p. 2, col. 1.

95 *Ledger*, June 1, 1874, p. 2, cols. 2-4.

96 *Appeal*, November 4, 1874, p. 1, col. 2; and July 31, p. 1, col. 1.

97 *Avalanche,* February 24, 1868, p. 3; February 25, p. 2, col. 1; March 12, p. 3; and Lamon, *Blacks*, pp. 46-52.

98 *Ledger*, April 14, 1880, p. 4, col. 4.

99 Coppock, II: 382; Crouse; Darnell, *Germantown News,* July 3, 1986; and cf. Goodspeed, "Shelby," p. 915.

## Part III, Chapter 2

100 New York *Times*, February 16, 1865, TCWSB.

101 Acts, 1867-68, Ch. XV, pp.11-13.

102 Sigafoos, p. 49; and Dowdy, ch. 3.

103 McKenzie, "Reconstruction."

104 Ibid.

105 Ibid.

106 Downs, *Sick from Freedom*, pp. 57-60, 63f., 123f., 133f.

107 McKenzie, "Reconstruction."

108 E.g., *Avalanche*, April 15, 1872, p. 1, col. 2-3; and Aiken, pp. 16-22.

109 Ibid, pp. 29-35; McKenzie, "Reconstruction;" and Cooper and Terrill, *South* map, p. 428.

110 McKenzie, "Reconstruction."

111 U.S. Census, 1870, p. 268.

112 Woodson, *Genealogy*, p. 475.

113 Woodson, *Genealogy*, pp. 306f.

114 Ibid.; *Appeal*, December 20, 1867,p.4, col. 2; and December 14, 1869, p. 1, col. 6.

115 *Appeal*, January 22, 1868, p. 3, col. 9.

116 *Appeal,* 3 April 1866, p. 3, col. 1.

117 Dyer and Moore, vol. 3, p. 1033.

118 1870 census, district 11, p. 304A.

119 Census 1870, CD 11, p. 311A; and 1880, CD 11, p. 230B.

120 *Appeal*, January 21, 1866, p. 3, col. 2.

121 Sigafoos, p. 50.

122 1870 census, district 11, p. 313A.

123 Jemison, *Greenlaw Rediscovered*, pp. 4f.

124 E.g., Records of the U.S. Civil Commission at Memphis, 1863-64, NARA T-410/roll 1/ 27, & 83.

125 OR, vol. 32, pt. III, p. 634; Galbraith, pp. 182 and 201; and Jemison, pp. 4f.

126 Young, p. 144f.; and *Appeal,* February 27, 1869, p.3, col. 2.

127 *Appeal,* June 26, 1870, p. 4, col. 1, rental advertisement.

128 Wills Interview, October 1, 2011.

129 E.g., County Courts Minutes, April Term, 1871, pp. 414-17.

130 Cf. 1870 and 1880 censuses and 1869 Shelby County property map which was complied from records preceding his intrusion.

131 Ibid., p. 312A; and Shelby County Marriages, 1860, book 2, p. 70.

132 Jenkins, pp. 12f.

133 *Ledger*, July 3, 1874, p. 2, col. 1; and *Gazetteer*, 1876, reprinted in *Germantown News*, February 23, 2011, p. 16.

134 Census 1880, CD 11, pp. 234A, 235A, 242A, and 250 A.

135 ased on comparative 1860 and 1870 census data on non-real property, including approximation tor Kimbrough and Brook's holdings.

136 Woodson papers, MVC, MS 114, box 1, folder 6, Redemption Certificate No. 347.

137 Assessment List of the United States Direct Tax..., pp. 37-40.

138 *Appeal*, August 6, 1868, p. 1, col. 5.

139 E.g., *Appeal*, July 12, 1868, p. 3, col. 5; March 2, 1869, p. 3, col. 6; September 23, 1871, p. 1, col. 7; and October 25, 1874, p. 3, col. 8.

140 *Appeal*, p. 1, col. 6; and *Ledger*, January 10, 1867, p. 1, col. 4, July 12, 1875, p. 3, col. 2, and February 3, 1879, p. 4, col. 5.

141 Comparison of 1860 agricultural census with 1869 property map; Hall, pp. 10f. and 88; Hunt, p. 15; Kimbrough family cemetery survey, GRH&GC; and census 1880, CD 11, pp. 241 A&B.

142 Beverly Booth, "Germantown Pioneers: Memories of the City's Settlers," *Germantown News*, June 23, 1977, citing interview with Carrie Callis Sullivan.

143 *Appeal*, January 2, 1874, p. 4, col. 1; and Census, 1870, CD 11, p. 308B.

144 The absence of the Kimbroughs and Brooks from the agricultural census obscures the possibility that they were also free from the pressure to monocrop.

145 Cooper and Terrill, *South*, pp. 385, 436-39.

146 Cooper and Terrill, *South*, pp. 429-34; and Foner, *Reconstruction*, pp. 406-8.

147 Foner, *Reconstruction*, p. 108, and cf. pp. 408-9.

148 Civil War Pension Records, Lou Freeman pensioner, Cert. No. 598229, NARA

149 E.g., 1870 census, district 11, pp. 290A-293A, 296Af., 300A, 302A, and 303Af.

150 1870 census, district 11, p. 294B, and 304 B.

151 Ibid., p. 307A.

152 *Appeal*, 7 January 1866, p. 3, col. 4; and 18 January, p. 1, col. 4.

153 Fromer, *Reconstruction*, pp. 81-84.

154 *Appeal*, 9 December 1865, p. 2, cols. 1f.; 23 January 1866, p. 1, col. 7; and 3 April, p.3 , col. 9.

155 1870 census, district 11, pp. 305a-b.

156 Miller, *Apprentices*, pp. 138-44; and census 1870, CD 10, p. 255A.

157 Miller, p. 145; and census 1870, CD 10, p. 274A.

158 U.S. Census, 1880, Population, p. 708; and see Appendix C.

159 Cooper and Terrill, *South*, p. 428.

160 Foner, *Reconstruction*, pp. 85-87.

161 1880 census, district 11, p. 252A.

162 Lamon, *Blacks*, p. 37.

163 1870 census, district 11, pp. 295b, 300a, and 303a; 1880 census. district 11, p. 251B.

164 NPS, Soldiers and Sailors System.

165 Lipsey, "Memories," pp. 11, 17, 33, and passim.

166 *Appeal*, March 10, 1871, p. 4, col. 6.

167 County Court, Minutes Book 11,1865, p. 364; Book A-12, 1866, pp. 324f., 507, 509,512, SCA; Book K, 1870, p.562; and April Term, 1871, p. 429.

168 *Appeal*, June 7, 1870, p. 4, col. 6.

169 *Appeal*, 5 April 1866, p. 1, col. 6.

170 *Appeal*, June 5, 1870, p. 2, col. 2.

171 *Appeal*, December 20, 1871, p. 2, cols. 1-2.

172 *Appeal*, April 14, 1867, p. 2, col. 5.

173 *Appeal*, December 14, 1869, p. 1, col. 6; and June 26, 1870, p. 4, col. 1.

174 *Avalanche*, March 27, 1868, p. 3, col. 2.

175 *Avalanche*, May 6, 1868, p. 3, col. 5; and *Ledger*, May 4, p. 3, col. 3.

176 Dowdy, pp. 43-52.

177 *Appeal*, February 21, 1868, p. 3, cols. 2, and 8; November 22, p. 3, col. 8; and January 31, 1871, p. 4, col. 9.

178 Martha Titus Diary, March 8-18, 1873, MCV.

179 *Appeal*, May 24, 1872, p. 4, col. 2.

180 Young, p. 157.

181 E.g., *Appeal*, May 29, 1873, p. 4, col. 1; and August 4, p. 4, col. 7.

182 *Avalanche*, March 2, 1867, p. 3, col. 1.

183 *Ledger*, September 10, 1873, p. 2, col. 3.

184 *Appeal*, August 27, 1879, p. 2, col. 5; September 13. 1881, p. 2, col. 4; and excerpts of Gazette, 1887 and 1890, *Germantown News*, February 23, 2011, p. 16.

185 Census 1880, CD 11, p. 233A.Census 1880, CD 11, p. 233A.

186 *Ledger*, September 11, 1878, p. 1, col. 4.

187 Bergeron, p. 69.

188 Nashville *Union and American*, December 30, 1874, p. 4, col. 4; *Appeal*, May 26, 1873, p. 8, col. 2; and *Ledger*, February 3, 1879, p. 4, col. 5.

189 Quarterly Court Minutes, April Term, 1871, p. 346; and Assessment Lists of the United States Direct Tax..., p. 38.

190 Smith, p. 8; *Appeal*, January 31, 1872, p. 4, col. 3; April 17, p. 4, col. 3; April 20, p. 4, col. 2; April 30, p. 3, col. 3; and May 29, p. 4, col.

191 Postmaster Finder.

192 *Appeal*, 23 January 1866, p. 1, col. 3; and December 25, 1874, p. 4, col. 1.

## Part III, Chapter 3

1   *Gazetteer* entries for 1876, 1887 and 1890, *Germantown News*, February 23, 2011, p. 16; and Census 1870.

2   First notice, *Appeal*, January 4, 1867, p. 3, col. 3; and June 26, 1868, p. 3, col. 3.

3   Lipsey, "Memories," p. 29.

4   *Appeal*, August 15, 1876, p. 4, col. 2; and September 5, p. 1, col. 4; and Lipsey, "Memories," p. 26.

5   Faust, *Mothers*, p. 252.

6   Interview with Nancy Thompson, *Germantown News*, March 3, 1977, p. 7.; and Lipsey, "Memories," p. 26.

7   Faust, *Mothers*, pp. 195, 238, 242f., 256f.; and Rable, *Civil Wars*, pp. 222-26, 230.

8   Index to *The Memphis Appeal*, 1843-1869, compiled by Joyce McKibben, Reference Librarian, The University of Memphis at tn-roots.com/tnshelby/newspapers/index.htm.

9   *Appeal*, June 2, 1876, p. 4, col. 5.

10  *Appeal*, August 26, 1873, p. 1, col. 3.

11  *Appeal*, April 15, 1872, p. 4, col. 6.

12  *Avalanche*, October 21, 1878, p. 2, col. 3.

13  Lipsey, "Memories," pp. 22, and 34; and *St. Louis Republic*, December 10, 1890, p.3.

14  McKibben, *Index to Appeal*.

15  *Appeal*, May 31, 1866, p. 2, col. 2.

16  *Appeal*, January 17, 1866, p. 3, col. 2; November 30, 1867, p. 3, col. 3; December 7, p. 3, col. 4; and December 12, p. 3, col. 2; and *Bulletin*, November 3, 1867, p. 4, col. 1.

17  *Appeal*, June 26, 1868, p. 4, col. 4.; January 6, 1870, p. 1, col. 6; and August 29, 1873, p. 4, col. 2; and *Ledger*, March 1, 1871, p. 3, col. 5, and December 20, 1879, p. 4, col. 6.

18  *Ledger*, May 11, 1876, p. 3, col. 4.

19  *Avalanche*, April 18, 1868, p.3, col. 2.

20  *Appeal*, September 10, 1869, p. 4, col. 4.

21  *Appeal*, January 12, 1870, p. 4, col. 4.

22  *Appeal*, September 10, 1867, p. 3, col. 5.

23  *Appeal*, September 20, `867,p. 3, col. 3.

24  *Appeal*, February 11, 1875, p. 4, col. 4.

25  *Appeal*, March 20, 1875, p. 4, cols. 2-3; and March 21, p. 1, col. 5.

26  *Appeal*, June 27, 1870, p. 4, col. 2; June 11, 1871, p. 4, col. 3; and September 9, p. 4, col. 2; and *Ledger*, May 10, 1870, p. 3, col. 4.

27  *Memphis Public Ledger*, December 9, 1878, p. 4, col. 4; and 1870 census, CD 11, p. 310B.

28  *Ledger*, December 24, 1878, p. 1, col. 1, and February 5, 1879, p. 4, col. 3, and February 13, p. 4, col. 5.

29  *Appeal*, March 13, 1874, p. 2, col. 4; May 25, 1876, p. 4, col. 2-3; and May 28, p. 4, col. 8; *Boston Journal*, May 27, 1876, p. 1; and *Ledger*, June 22, 1877, p. 3, col. 5, July 30, 1878, p. 1, col. 7, and July 31, p. 3, col. 7.

30  *Ledger*, July 9, 1876, p. 3, col. 3.

31  *Ledger*, January 10, 1867, p. 1, cols. 2-3.

32  *Avalanche*, May 3, 1867, p. 3, col. 2; May 5, p. 1; and p.3, col. 2.

33  *Ledger*, December 6, 1880, p. 4, col. 5.

34  *Avalanche*, April 29, 1868, p. 1, cols. 2-3.

35  *Avalanche*, April 21, 1868, p. 3, col. 1.

36  *Avalanche*, April 22, 1868, p. 3, col. 4.

37  *Avalanche*, April 29, 1868, p. 1, col. 3.

38  *Avalanche*, April 29, 1868, p. 1, cols. 2-3.

39  *Avalanche*, May 2, 1868, p.2, col. 2.

40  *Avalanche*, May 2, 1868, p. 3, col. 3.

41  *Avalanche*, May 13, 1868, p. 3, col. 1.

42  *Appeal*, June 29, 1868, p. 3, cols. 5-6.

43  Appointments, 1868-69, Senior Ministers File, GUMA.

44  Norton, *Religion*, p. 76.

45  *Appeal*, February 21, 1871, p. 4, col. 2; March 28, 1875, p. 4, col. 3; June 8, p. 1, col. 4; June 9, p. 4, cols. 2-3; and June 11, p. 1, col. 3; and *Ledger*, April 3, 1869, p. 3, col. 3; December 14, p. 3, col. 3; June 10, 1871, p. 3, col. 3; June 9, 1875, p. 3, col. 2;

46  *Ledger*, April 13, 1875, p. 3, col. 3; April 11, 1878, p. 3, col. 4.

47  Sigafoos, p. 30; Jemison, p.4; and Register of Death in the City of Memphis, 1875, file # 17131, SCA; *Appeal*, September 26, 1875, p. 1, col. 3.

48  *Appeal*, January 16, 1869, p. 3, col. 2; *Nashville Union and American*, January 21, p. 1.

49  *Martha Titus Diary*, March 9 and 16, 1873; and "Germantown Methodist Church," anonymous, p. 1, GRH&GC, Germantown History Collection, Churches.

50  Norton, *Religion,* p. 76; on Graves, *Appeal,* May 12, 1875, p. 1, cols. 1-3; August 17, 1873, p. 4, col. 3; for a disputation, May 4, 1871, p. 4, col. 3-7; and Lipsey, "Memories," p. 35.

51  Lipsey, loc cit.

52  Lipsey, pp. 31 and 35.

53  Lipsey, "Memories," p. 22.

54  Lipsey, pp. 22, 29, 34,

55  Foner, *Reconstruction,* p. 425.

56  *Appeal,* May 3, 1870, p. 4, col. 4; and October 21, 1873, p. 4, col. 4.

57  *Appeal,* January 14, 1869, p. 2, col. 1.

58  Rable, *Civil Wars,* p. 230.

59  *Appeal,* February 8, 1869, p. 3, col. 5.

60  Faust, *Mothers,* pp. 256f.

61  *Martha Titus Diary,* March 8-18, 1873, MVC; and *Ledger,* February 23, 1878, p. 3, col. 7.

62  Census 1880, CD 11, p. 233A.

63  *Appeal,* January 10, 1866, p. 2, col. 7.

64  Smithsonian Institution, *List of the Institutions, Libraries, Colleges, and Other Establishments in the United States,* 1872, p. 214, GBS.

65  *Appeal,* 18 January 1866, p. 1, col. 7; and December 21, 1867, p. 3, col. 4.

66  *Appeal,* December 21, 1867, p. 3, col. 4; and December 22, p. 3, col. 4.

67  *Avalanche,* March 27, 1868, p. 3, col. 2; November 18, p. 3; and September 13, p. 3, col. 1.

68  *Appeal,* June 22, 1869, p. 1, col. 6; and June 26, p. 4, col. 3; and *Ledger,* June 25, p. 3, col. 4.

69  *Appeal,* December 3, 1869, p. 2, col. 5; and September 22, 1870, p. 4, col. 5.

70  *Appeal,* August 12, 1869, p. 1, col. 4; December 22, 1872, p. 2, col. 4; and *Ledger,* July 27, 1874, p. 3, col. 4.

71  *Ledger,* June 2, 1873, p. 3, col. 3.

72  Lamon, *Blacks,* p. 45; and *Ledger,* June 14, 1880. p. 1, col. 1.

73  *Ledger,* June 21, 1869, p. 3, col. 4.

74  Census 1860, p. 166, and 1870, District 11, p. 312; and Shelby County Marriages, 1860, book 2, p. 70.

75  Foner, *Reconstruction,* pp. 89-95, for a summary of the post-war black religious experiences and relevant literature.

76  Katharine Bennett, "New Bethel Has Rich History," *Commercial Appeal,* October 25, 2009, B7; and *New Bethel Missionary Baptist Church,* n.p.

77  *Appeal,* December 5, 1865, p. 3, col. 2.

78  Field Offices, Tennessee, Bureau of Refugees, Freedmen, and Abandoned Lands, 1865-72, NARA, M 1911/reel 77/p. 5; Census 1870, CD 11, p. 297B; and Census, 1880, CD 11, p. 255A.

79  Ibid.; and 1860 & 1870 censuses, District 11

80  Acts, 1866-67, Ch. XXVII, pp. 33-42.

81  1870 census, District 11, p. 300A.

82  Crouse.

83  Booth, "Germantown Pioneers: Memories"; Census 1880, CD ll, pp. 230A, 234A, 235A, 246B, and 247B.

84  1870 census, district 11, pp. 290A, 293B, 294B, 297A, 299Af., 301B,

85  Ibid., p. 290A-291A, 292B, 293A, 295B, 297B, 301A, 304A, 306B, 312A, and 313A.

86  County Court Minutes, January Term, 1871, pp. 324f.; and Goodspeed, p. 838.

87  Ibid., October Term, pp. 47f.

88  Goodspeed, pp. 839f.

89  Lipsey, "Memories,", p. 28; Census, 1880, CD 11, p. 230A; Goodspeed, p. 839; and

Crouse,

90 Magness, *Past Times*, p. 124,
91 Lipsey, "Memories," p. 28.
92 Goodspeed, pp. 839f.

# Conclusion

1   Spence, *Diary*, November 10, 1863, TCWSB.

2   Rable, *Civil Wars,* chapter 13.
3   Faust, *Mothers*, p. 253; Rable, *Civil Wars*, pp. 230-38.
4   E.g., *Appeal*, May 27, 1874, p. 2, col. 2.
5   Young, p. 146.
6   Faust, *Mothers*, pp. 252-f.; Rable, *Civil Wars*, pp. 236-39; and Cooper and Terrill, *South*, pp. 454-58.
7   Crosby, *The American Plague*, pp.14f.; and 42-45.
8   *Ledger*, August 9, 1878, p. 3, col. 6.
9   Hicks, pp. 6, and 10f.; and Crosby, pp. 47-50.
10  *Avalanche*, September 15, 1878, p. 1, cols. 4-5; September 21, p. 1, col. 3; J.W. Keating, *A History of the Yellow Fever: The Yellow Fever Epidemic of 1878 in Memphis*, 1879, p. 94; and *Condensed History of the Great Yellow Fever Epidemic of 1878*, 1879, GBS.
11  Notes on Evans' day-book, May 3, 1973, EHC/GRH&GC; *Appeal*, September 28, 1878 p. 1, cols. 4-5; Hicks, p. 20; and Crosby, pp. 51-55.
12  *Avalanche*, September 28, 1878, p. 1, col. 5; and October 16, p.1, col. 3; Notes on Evans' day-book, May 3, 1973, EHC/GRH&GC;
13  *Avalanche*, October 6, 1878, p. 2, col. 1; October 8, p. 1, col. 2; October 9, p. 2, col. 1; October 10, p. 1, col. 4; October 11, p. 2, col. 2; and October 21, p. 2, col. 3.
14  *Avalanche*, October 16, 1878, p. 1, col. 2; and October 29, p. 1, col. 4.
15  Beverly Booth, "Germantown Pioneers: Memories of the City's Settlers Obscured By Time," *Germantown News*, July 14, 1977, interview with Molly Molitor Nowlin.
16  *Avalanche*, October 4, 1878, p.2, col. 1; October 16, p. 1, col. 2; October 18, p. 1, cols. 4-5; and Scott, ch. 5, pp. 8 and 11
17  *Avalanche*, October 18 1878, p. 1, col 5.
18  Witherington, p. 82, citing "How It Began;" and Hughes interviews.
19  Scott, Ch. 5, p. 9
20  Notes on Evans' day-book, May 3, 1973, EHC/GRH&GC.
21  *Avalanche,* October 10, 1878, p. 2, col. 1.
22  Lipsey, "Memories," p. 27; *Avalanche*, September 28 1878; and October 10, 1878, p. 2, cols. 1-2.
23  Interview with Louise Duke Bedford, "Memories of the City's Settlers," *Germantown News*, June 16, 1877.
24  Goodspeed, "Shelby", p. 915; Cf. Magness, "Germantown," p. 124.
25  Census 1880, p. 338.
26  Lipsey, "Memories," p. 30.
27  Lipsey, "Memories," p. 30; and Smith, p. 9.
28  Dowdy, pp. 55-63.
29  *Tennessee State Gazetteer*, 1887, reprinted n *Germantown News*, February 23, 2011, p.16; Goodspeed, "Shelby," p. 915; and Census 1880, CD 11.
30  Goodspeed, "Shelby," pp. 913f.
31  Ibid., pp. 915f.
32  M&R RR, Superintendent's Report for year ending June 1872, Statement 7, Passengers, and Statement 9, Bales of Cotton, Ilks/Kirby collection.
33  Interview with Mary Martin, "Victorian Romance: A Germantown Love Story," *Germantown News*, July 21, 1977, p. 16B; and Hughes and Kirby interviews.

34 *Appeal*, July 25, 1867, p. 1, cols. 4 -5; February 14, 1868, p. 2, col. 5; and Goodspeed, Shelby, pp. 797 and 911f.

# Appendices

1 Map of Shelby County, Tennessee, Compiled and Published by J.H. Humphreys, Civil Engineer. Sears & Smith of the Memphis Abstract Co., 1869 (courtesy of Walter Wills), SCA.

2 County Court, Minute Book 9, No. 788, July 1, 1850, pp. 437f., SCA.

3 Ibid.; Map, "Memphis and Vicinity, surveyed and drawn by order of Maj. Gen. W.T. Sherman," circa 1862/63, MVC; General Topographical Map, plate CLIV, *OR Atlas*; map, Shelby Co. TN, 1888, M.T. Williamson, Historical Map Collection, M&SC.

4 U.S. Army Map, May 1862, NARA, RG 77, CWMF T43; map, Shelby Co. TN, 1888, M.T. Williamson, Historical Map Collection, M&SC; and General Topographical Map, plate CLIV, *OR Atlas*.

5 Post road, *The Public Statutes of the United States from 1789 to March 3, 1845*, Sess. V, Ch. 172, p. 276, GBS.

6 Hughes Interview, June 30, 2010; Cloyes Interview, July 7; Stewart Observations, August 5; and bridge depicted on the 1850 Wherry Map, Platt Book 2, No. 6, SCA; and Loose Papers, 1850/22/613, Macon Road Bridge over a creek, SCA; and *Public Statutes,* p. 276, GBS.

7 Ayers, p. 23.

8 Shelby Co. map, 1869, SCA.

9 Family Tree, ancestry.com, U.S. Civil War Records and Profiles.; and *Tennesseans in the Civil War,* Pt. II.

# Index

All topics, and institutions directly in the area of Germantown as defined are listed alphabetically under **Germantown**. Other major topics that fit the story of Germantown into a broader perspective are indexed in ***bold italics*** with subtopics.

All the names of persons identified in this book and known to have resided in the Germantown area are indexed. Names given in parentheses are those of slaves identified only by their given name. The family name is that of the owner, and may or may not have been taken subsequently by the person identified.

The names of national and state political figures and their movements and parties are not indexed except if and when they had a significant or unique presence or role in the Germantown area. Likewise individuals mentioned incidentally but not residents of the Germantown area are not indexed.

Military men and units are only listed if they had direct and significant involvement with Germantown other than simple occupation.

Events of the war outside the area are also not listed..

Berger, Christian 386.
Blair, William 34.
Blackley, Calvin 366.
Blackley, James 366.
Blackley, Malvina 366.
Bleckley, Thomas C. 10, 127, 330, 333, 338, 343-44, 366, 373.
Bliss, Hosea 106, 120, 144.
Bliss, Isaac.W. 106, 120, 143, 152, 154-55, 352.
Boardman, H. 154.
Boardman, Mrs. 146.
Boone, Jennifer social analysis 65-67.
Booth, Nathan 352.
Boren, James 113.
Bowen, A.G. 262.
Bradley, Miller 240, 358.
Bradley, Rebecca 240, 358.
Brett, James 345.
Brewster, Richard 145.
Brooks, Agnes 27.
Brooks, Ann Elizabeth 27, 185.
Brooks, Elijah 129.
Brooks family (see Woodlawn) 55, 185, 393.
Brooks, Joseph 27, 40, 85, 141, 145, 185, 228, 235-36, 358, 393.
Brooks, Neely & Co. 374.
Brooks, Wilks 18, 33, 40, 43-44, 55, 76, 105.
Brooks, William 8.
Brooks, Elizabeth 8.
Brown, Hartson R. 19.
Brown, Matthew 130.
Bufford, John 363.
Burnley, Fannie 397.
Burnley, Susan 146, 356, 381.
Burns, Rev. Jeremiah 30, 34, 188, 359.
Buster, John 149.
Callis, Cleon M. 150, 345, 419.
Callis, Eliza 120.
Callis family and store 57, 70, 358.
Callis, John C 311, 343.
Callis, Joseph 120.
**Capleville**: 33,
  Bethlehem Methodist Church 33, 244.
Carnel, Arthur 120.
Carter, William (Billy) 154, 343, 358.
Carter, William 363, 365.
Cash, Aggie 397.
Cash, Benjamin 330, 340
Census, U.S. 426-27.
Chambers, Thomas 356
Christian, Dr. J.R. 119.

*Civil Districts*: xiv-xv, 127-28, 155, 335, 337, 342.
  Eleven 1, 4, 127, 113, 119, 145, 153, 155, 314, 329, 330, 345, 399, 425, 427.
  Common School Commission 128-30, 402
  election fraud 262-63, 328.
  militia (Home Guard) 29, 145, 152-54, 167.
    Minute Men 153-55.
  politics 132-33.
  secession 140-41, 143.
  political differences among residents of 11 and 10 121-22, 128, 155, 344, 407.
  reorganization of 342-43.
  Ten xv, 3, 113, 127-28, 141, 145, 153, 163, 330, 339, 343, 345, 377, 425.
Clark, Blanche social analysis 57-58, 67.
Clark, Joseph, 49.
Clark, L.B. 416.
Clark, William 49.
Cole & Co. 140.
Cole, E.M. 346.
Cole, J. 129.
Cole, Samuel 141.
Cole, Wesley, 108.
Coles, Thomas 145.
Cogbill, Lucinda B. 358.
*Constitutional Party* 136.
*Contrabands* 247.
Cooney, J.W. 386.
Cornelius, A.T. 24.
Cornelius, Edward 10.
Cornelius, Eliza 10, 146, 164.
(Cornelius), Henry 82.
Cornelius, Dr. James M.M. 10, 40, 47, 56, 82, 84, 101, 106, 119, 129, 141, 145, 422.
Cornelius, James 399.
Cornelius, Phillip 399.
(Cornelius), Taylor 82.
Cotton, Rev. Isaac 399.
Crenshaw, F.B. 141.
Cross, Rev. Joshua L. 30, 145.
d'Arusmont, Frances (see Frances Wright).
d'Arusmont, Sylvia 105, 109, 358.
Daily, Lucy 365.
Davis, Charles 178.
Deadrick, M.G. 113.
DeLagutery, Eugene 105.
Deloach, Jonah 106, 178, 245.
Dennis, John 130.
Douglas, H.F. 150.
Douglas (Duglas), William.H. 340, 365.
*duels* 47-48.

497

498

Roberts, Mrs. 390.
Robinson, Mrs. 390.
Rochelle, Feraby 38.
Rochelle, Wiley 38, 150.
Rochelle, William 150.
Rodgers, James 150, 157, 358.
Rogers, M. 145.
Rosco, Elizabeth 401.
Rutland, Susan 311, 358.
Rutland, William 311, 358.
Sanderson, Col. William L. 200-202.
Scales, Margaret 85.
Semple Broaddus College, 17.
Scott, James M. 150.
Scott, James 357. 399.
Scott, Richard 150.
Scott, T.F. 340, 388.
Scruggs, Phineas 119.
Scruggs, Dr. R.L. 35-37, 77.
Scruggs, Robert 356.
Scruggs, Malvina 350.
Scruggs, Maria 13.
Secession Guards 145, 148-49, 169.
**Shelby County** xii-xiv.
    Board of Education 399-400, 402.
    Quarterly Sessions Court 1, 126-27, 224,
        328-29, 333, 370, 377, 402.
    Turnpike Company 370.
Sheppard (Shepherd), George 57, 145, 358.
Shepherd, Sallie 240, 352
Shepherd, Thomas 240.
Sherman, William T. 166, 179-80, 187-88,
    200.
Sherwin's Independent Scouts 183.
Shetter, Jeremaih 128.
Shide, Anton 26, 153.
Shute, Jos. 113.
Sims, James 154.
Simmons, Rev. R.S. 415.
**Slavery:**
    abolition, attitudes about 111-12, 405.
    financial losses from emancipation 348,
    justifications and rationalizations for 71-
        73, 405.
    maintenance 76-80.
    methods of control 76.
    overseers 60.
    ownership 55-58, 66, 68, 84-85, 107,
        155.
    post-war attitudes about 303, 327.
    punishment 76, 78, 80.
    rape and breeding programs 71.
    sales and value 69, 80.
    vigilance patrols 84, 154.

*slaves:*
    community 79, 85.
    Confederate use of 160, 257.
    Confiscation Acts 247.
    contrabands 246-52.
    escapes 70, 81-83, 406.
    Federal recruitment 252-55, 257.
    Federal use of 180, 246-52.
    labor 85.
    literacy 76.
    marriage 74-75.
    population 68, 71.
    privileges and rights 76, 80-81.
    rebellion and revolt 83-84, 174, 406.
    religiosity 73-74, 244.
    slave quarters 44.
    war-time behavior 174, 243, 246-4, 252,
        406.
Slough, James 150.
Slough, John 92.
Small, George 149.
Small, Mary 149.
Small, Richard 149, 157.
Small. William 150.
Smith, Capt. George W. 11th New York
    Cavalry 300, 311-13.
Solomon, M. 27.
Spivey, Jack 415.
St. Clair, Dr. 415.
Stanton, F.P. 117,
*State Line Road* 1, 87-91, 176, 180, 225,
    265, 370-71, 420-23.
    tolls and toll gates 90.
Stevenson, Elizabeth 37.
Stevenson, Josephine 37.
Stevenson, William 37.
Stewart, A.C. 154.
Stokes, William 170.
Stout, Harriet 366.
Stout, Isaiah 10.
Stout Isham 366.
Stout, Dr. John. 141, 366, 388.
Stout, Rhoda 366.
Stratton, T.J. 154.
Strickland, Della Molitor 415.
Tate, William 8, 106.
Tate, Mary 8.
Thomas, G.W. 419.
Thompson, A.L. 335.
Thompson, Florida Pettit 20, 56, 354, 398.
Thompson, Dr. John A. 346, 354, 398, 418.
Thomson, Joseph 360.
Thomson, Louis Lycurgus 214, 232, 262.
Thompson, Mary 23, 153, 231, 243, 396,

Made in the USA
Charleston, SC
10 June 2015